*Twenty Centuries*
*of Christian Worship*

# THE COMPLETE LIBRARY
## OF
## CHRISTIAN WORSHIP

# THE COMPLETE LIBRARY
# OF
# CHRISTIAN WORSHIP

## Volume 2, Twenty Centuries of Christian Worship

ROBERT E. WEBBER, EDITOR

The Complete Library of Christian Worship, Vol. 2, Twenty Centuries of Christian Worship.

Hendrickson Publishers, Inc.
P. O. Box 3473
Peabody, Massachusetts 01961-3473

Printed in the United States of America

Hendrickson Publishers edition
ISBN 1-56563-186-2
Hendrickson edition published by arrangement with Star Song Publishing Group, a division of
Jubilee Communications, Inc.
2325 Crestmoor, Nashville, Tennessee 37215

Unless otherwise indicated, all Scripture quotations taken from the HOLY BIBLE, NEW INTERNATIONAL VERSION. Copyright
© 1973, 1978, 1984 by International Bible Society. Used by permission of Zondervan Publishing House.

Scripture quotations marked (KJV) are from the HOLY BIBLE, KING JAMES VERSION.

Scripture quotations marked (NASB) are taken from the NEW AMERICAN STANDARD BIBLE. Copyright © 1960, 1962, 1963,
1968, 1971, 1972, 1973, 1975, 1977, the Lockman Foundation. Used by permission.

Scripture quotations marked (RSV) are taken from the REVISED STANDARD VERSION of the Bible. Copyright © 1946, 1952,
1971, 1973 by the Division of Christian Education of the National Council of Churches of Christ in the U.S.A. Used by permission.

Scripture quotations marked (NRSV) are taken from THE HOLY BIBLE: NEW REVISED STANDARD VERSION. Copyright © 1989
by the Division of Christian Education of the National Council of Churches of Christ in the U.S.A. Used by permission.

Scripture quotations marked (TEV) are taken from TODAY'S ENGLISH VERSION of the Bible, Third Edition. Copyright © 1966,
1971 American Bible Society. Used by permission.

# CONTENTS

List of Illustrations and Tables . . . . . . . . . . . . . . . . . . . . . . . . . . . . . . . . . . . . . . . . . . . . . . . . xiii
Board of Editorial Consultants . . . . . . . . . . . . . . . . . . . . . . . . . . . . . . . . . . . . . . . . . . . . . . . xv
List of Cooperating Publishers . . . . . . . . . . . . . . . . . . . . . . . . . . . . . . . . . . . . . . . . . . . . . . . xxxi
Preface to Volume 2 . . . . . . . . . . . . . . . . . . . . . . . . . . . . . . . . . . . . . . . . . . . . . . . . . . . . . . . xxxvii
**Introduction** . . . . . . . . . . . . . . . . . . . . . . . . . . . . . . . . . . . . . . . . . . . . . . . . . . . . . . . . . . . xxxix
    **101** Introduction to *The Complete Library of Christian Worship* . . . . . . . . . . . . . . . . . . xxxix
    **102** How to Use *The Complete Library of Christian Worship* . . . . . . . . . . . . . . . . . . . . . xl
    **103** Introduction to Volume 2, *Twenty Centuries of Christian Worship* . . . . . . . . . . . . . xli

## Part 1: EARLY CHRISTIAN WORSHIP

**CHAPTER 1. Links Between New Testament and Early Christian Worship** . . . . . . . . . . . . . . . 3
    **104** The Search for the Origins of Christian Worship . . . . . . . . . . . . . . . . . . . . . . . . . . . 3
    **105** An Introduction to Daily Prayer . . . . . . . . . . . . . . . . . . . . . . . . . . . . . . . . . . . . . . . 5
    **106** The Influence of the Synagogue on Early Christian Worship . . . . . . . . . . . . . . . . . . 11
    **107** The Tripartite Structure of Prayer and the Trinitarian Formulary . . . . . . . . . . . . . . 14
    **108** Ordination and Worship Leadership in the Early Church . . . . . . . . . . . . . . . . . . . . 16
    **109** Charismatic Gifts in Early Christian Worship . . . . . . . . . . . . . . . . . . . . . . . . . . . . . 19
    **110** Worship in the Book of Revelation and the Eastern Orthodox Liturgy . . . . . . . . . . 21
    **111** Bibliography on Issues in Early Christian Worship . . . . . . . . . . . . . . . . . . . . . . . . . 26

## Part 2: A HISTORY OF CHRISTIAN WORSHIP

**CHAPTER 2. The Worship of the Early Church (to A.D. 500)** . . . . . . . . . . . . . . . . . . . . . . . 31
    **112** Worship in the New Testament Era . . . . . . . . . . . . . . . . . . . . . . . . . . . . . . . . . . . . . 31
    **113** Worship in the Second and Third Centuries . . . . . . . . . . . . . . . . . . . . . . . . . . . . . . 33
    **114** Worship During the Fourth and Fifth Centuries . . . . . . . . . . . . . . . . . . . . . . . . . . . 38
    **115** Bibliography on the History of Early Christian Worship . . . . . . . . . . . . . . . . . . . . . 42

**CHAPTER 3. Worship in the Eastern Orthodox Tradition** . . . . . . . . . . . . . . . . . . . . . . . . . 44
    **116** Introduction to the Eastern Orthodox Churches . . . . . . . . . . . . . . . . . . . . . . . . . . . 44
    **117** Worship in the East Syrian Churches: Nestorian, Chaldean, and Malabar . . . . . . . . 45
    **118** Worship in the West Syrian Churches: Syrian, Maronite, and Syro-Indian . . . . . . . . 48
    **119** Worship in the Byzantine Churches . . . . . . . . . . . . . . . . . . . . . . . . . . . . . . . . . . . . 51
    **120** Worship in the Armenian Church . . . . . . . . . . . . . . . . . . . . . . . . . . . . . . . . . . . . . . 54
    **121** Worship in the Alexandrian Churches: Coptic and Ethiopian . . . . . . . . . . . . . . . . . 57
    **122** Bibliography on the History of Eastern Worship . . . . . . . . . . . . . . . . . . . . . . . . . . . 59

**CHAPTER 4. Historic Worship in the Western (Catholic) Church** . . . . . . . . . . . . . . . . . . . . 61
    **123** Liturgical Diversity and Roman Influence . . . . . . . . . . . . . . . . . . . . . . . . . . . . . . . . 61
    **124** The North African Liturgy . . . . . . . . . . . . . . . . . . . . . . . . . . . . . . . . . . . . . . . . . . . 62

**125** The Gallican Liturgy . . . . . . . . . . . . . . . . . . . . . . . . . . . . . . . . . . . . . . . . . . . . 63

**126** The Spanish Liturgy . . . . . . . . . . . . . . . . . . . . . . . . . . . . . . . . . . . . . . . . . . . . 65

**127** The Ambrosian Liturgy . . . . . . . . . . . . . . . . . . . . . . . . . . . . . . . . . . . . . . . . . 67

**128** The Celtic Liturgy . . . . . . . . . . . . . . . . . . . . . . . . . . . . . . . . . . . . . . . . . . . . . . 68

**129** The Roman Liturgy . . . . . . . . . . . . . . . . . . . . . . . . . . . . . . . . . . . . . . . . . . . . . 70

**130** Roman Catholic Worship from the Council of Trent to Vatican II . . . . . . . . 72

**131** Bibliography on the History of Western Catholic Worship . . . . . . . . . . . . . . 73

**CHAPTER 5. Protestant Worship of the Reformation Era** . . . . . . . . . . . . . . . . . . . . 75

**132** Lutheran Worship . . . . . . . . . . . . . . . . . . . . . . . . . . . . . . . . . . . . . . . . . . . . . . 75

**133** Reformed Worship . . . . . . . . . . . . . . . . . . . . . . . . . . . . . . . . . . . . . . . . . . . . . 76

**134** Anglican Worship . . . . . . . . . . . . . . . . . . . . . . . . . . . . . . . . . . . . . . . . . . . . . . 77

**135** Anabaptist Worship . . . . . . . . . . . . . . . . . . . . . . . . . . . . . . . . . . . . . . . . . . . . 77

**136** Bibliography on Reformation Worship . . . . . . . . . . . . . . . . . . . . . . . . . . . . . . 78

**CHAPTER 6. Protestant Post-Reformation Worship** . . . . . . . . . . . . . . . . . . . . . . . . 80

**137** Puritan Worship . . . . . . . . . . . . . . . . . . . . . . . . . . . . . . . . . . . . . . . . . . . . . . . 80

**138** Baptist Worship . . . . . . . . . . . . . . . . . . . . . . . . . . . . . . . . . . . . . . . . . . . . . . . 82

**139** Congregational Worship . . . . . . . . . . . . . . . . . . . . . . . . . . . . . . . . . . . . . . . . 83

**140** Quaker Worship . . . . . . . . . . . . . . . . . . . . . . . . . . . . . . . . . . . . . . . . . . . . . . . 85

**141** Methodist Worship . . . . . . . . . . . . . . . . . . . . . . . . . . . . . . . . . . . . . . . . . . . . . 86

**142** Salvation Army Worship . . . . . . . . . . . . . . . . . . . . . . . . . . . . . . . . . . . . . . . . 87

**143** American Revival Worship . . . . . . . . . . . . . . . . . . . . . . . . . . . . . . . . . . . . . . . 88

**144** African-American Worship . . . . . . . . . . . . . . . . . . . . . . . . . . . . . . . . . . . . . . . 89

**145** Restoration Worship . . . . . . . . . . . . . . . . . . . . . . . . . . . . . . . . . . . . . . . . . . . . 95

**146** Holiness Worship . . . . . . . . . . . . . . . . . . . . . . . . . . . . . . . . . . . . . . . . . . . . . . 97

**147** Adventist Worship . . . . . . . . . . . . . . . . . . . . . . . . . . . . . . . . . . . . . . . . . . . . . 98

**148** Bibliography on Post-Reformation Worship (1600–1900) . . . . . . . . . . . . . . . 100

**CHAPTER 7. Movements of Worship Renewal in the Twentieth Century** . . . . . . . . 105

**149** The Holiness-Pentecostal Movement . . . . . . . . . . . . . . . . . . . . . . . . . . . . . . 105

**150** The Impact of the *Constitution on the Sacred Liturgy* . . . . . . . . . . . . . . . . . 108

**151** Renewal in the Eastern Rite Catholic Churches . . . . . . . . . . . . . . . . . . . . . . 111

**152** The Antiochian Evangelical Orthodox Mission . . . . . . . . . . . . . . . . . . . . . . . 115

**153** The Protestant Liturgical Renewal . . . . . . . . . . . . . . . . . . . . . . . . . . . . . . . . 116

**154** The Renaissance of the Arts . . . . . . . . . . . . . . . . . . . . . . . . . . . . . . . . . . . . . 119

**155** The Charismatic Renewal . . . . . . . . . . . . . . . . . . . . . . . . . . . . . . . . . . . . . . . 121

**156** The Liturgical-Charismatic Movement . . . . . . . . . . . . . . . . . . . . . . . . . . . . . 125

**157** The Praise-and-Worship Renewal . . . . . . . . . . . . . . . . . . . . . . . . . . . . . . . . . 131

**158** The Convergence Movement . . . . . . . . . . . . . . . . . . . . . . . . . . . . . . . . . . . . . 134

**159** The Seekers' Service/Believers' Worship Movement . . . . . . . . . . . . . . . . . . 140

**160** Bibliography on Worship Renewal in the Twentieth Century . . . . . . . . . . . . 141

*Part 3:* HISTORIC MODELS OF WORSHIP

**CHAPTER 8. Pre-Reformation Liturgies** . . . . . . . . . . . . . . . . . . . . . . . . . . . . . . . . . 145

**161** The Didache (A.D. 100) . . . . . . . . . . . . . . . . . . . . . . . . . . . . . . . . . . . . . . . . . . 145

**162** Justin Martyr: The *First Apology* . . . . . . . . . . . . . . . . . . . . . . . . . . . . . . . . . 148

**163** The *Apostolic Tradition* of Hippolytus (A.D. 215) . . . . . . . . . . . . . . . . . . . . . 151

**164** The Byzantine Liturgy (Ninth Century) . . . . . . . . . . . . . . . . . . . . . . . . . . . . 152

**165** The Roman Catholic Mass (1570) . . . . . . . . . . . . . . . . . . . . . . . . . . .171
**166** Bibliography on Pre-Reformation Liturgies . . . . . . . . . . . . . . . . . . .186

**CHAPTER 9. Reformation Models of Worship** . . . . . . . . . . . . . . . . . . . . . . . .188
  **167** Luther: *Formula Missae:* Order of Mass and Communion
     for the Church at Wittenberg (1523) . . . . . . . . . . . . . . . . . . . . . . . .188
  **168** Calvin: *The Form of Church Prayers,* Strassburg Liturgy (1545) . . . .195
  **169** The Traditional Anglican Liturgy (1662) . . . . . . . . . . . . . . . . . . . . .204
  **170** Anabaptist: Hubmaier's "A Form for Christ's Supper" (1527) . . . . .216
  **171** Bibliography on Reformation Models of Worship . . . . . . . . . . . . . .225

**CHAPTER 10. Post-Reformation Models of Worship** . . . . . . . . . . . . . . . . . .227
  **172** An American Puritan Model of Worship . . . . . . . . . . . . . . . . . . . . .227
  **173** John Cotton's New England Congregational Model of Worship . . . .228
  **174** The Westminster Directory . . . . . . . . . . . . . . . . . . . . . . . . . . . . . . .230
  **175** A Baptist Model of Worship . . . . . . . . . . . . . . . . . . . . . . . . . . . . . .231
  **176** A Quaker Model of Worship . . . . . . . . . . . . . . . . . . . . . . . . . . . . . .235
  **177** A Methodist Model of Worship: John Wesley's *Sunday Service* . . . .236
  **178** A Salvation Army Model of Worship . . . . . . . . . . . . . . . . . . . . . . . .245
  **179** A Revival Model of Worship: Charles G. Finney . . . . . . . . . . . . . . .247
  **180** An Adventist Model of Worship . . . . . . . . . . . . . . . . . . . . . . . . . . .248
  **181** An African-American Model of Worship . . . . . . . . . . . . . . . . . . . . .249
  **182** A Restoration Model of Worship . . . . . . . . . . . . . . . . . . . . . . . . . . .251
  **183** A Holiness Model of Worship . . . . . . . . . . . . . . . . . . . . . . . . . . . . .252
  **184** Bibliography on Post-Reformation Worship . . . . . . . . . . . . . . . . . .256

## Part 4: THEOLOGIES OF WORSHIP

**CHAPTER 11. Approaches to the Theology of Worship** . . . . . . . . . . . . . . . .261
  **185** Defining the Task of a Theology of Worship . . . . . . . . . . . . . . . . . .261
  **186** Models of Liturgical Theology . . . . . . . . . . . . . . . . . . . . . . . . . . . .263
  **187** Liturgical Worship: Enactment of Salvation History . . . . . . . . . . . .266
  **188** Free-Church Worship: Ascribing Worth to God . . . . . . . . . . . . . . .272
  **189** Charismatic Worship: Responding to the Spirit . . . . . . . . . . . . . . . .275

**CHAPTER 12. Theologies of Worship Among the Churches** . . . . . . . . . . . .282
  **190** A Roman Catholic Theology of Worship . . . . . . . . . . . . . . . . . . . .282
  **191** An Orthodox Theology of Worship . . . . . . . . . . . . . . . . . . . . . . . .284
  **192** A Lutheran Theology of Worship . . . . . . . . . . . . . . . . . . . . . . . . . .286
  **193** A Reformed Theology of Worship . . . . . . . . . . . . . . . . . . . . . . . . .288
  **194** An Anglican/Episcopal Theology of Worship . . . . . . . . . . . . . . . . .291
  **195** A Baptist Theology of Worship . . . . . . . . . . . . . . . . . . . . . . . . . . .292
  **196** An Anabaptist Theology of Worship . . . . . . . . . . . . . . . . . . . . . . . .293
  **197** A Quaker Theology of Worship . . . . . . . . . . . . . . . . . . . . . . . . . . .295
  **198** A Wesleyan Theology of Worship . . . . . . . . . . . . . . . . . . . . . . . . .297
  **199** An African-American Theology of Worship . . . . . . . . . . . . . . . . . . .298
  **200** A Restoration Theology of Worship . . . . . . . . . . . . . . . . . . . . . . . .304
  **201** A Holiness-Pentecostal Theology of Worship . . . . . . . . . . . . . . . . .307
  **202** A Charismatic Theology of Worship . . . . . . . . . . . . . . . . . . . . . . . .309
  **203** Bibliography on the Theology of Worship . . . . . . . . . . . . . . . . . . . .312

*Part 5:* NEW DIRECTIONS IN WORSHIP

**CHAPTER 13. Contemporary Documents on Worship Renewal** . . . . . . . . . . . . . . . . . . . 317
  **204** A Catholic Statement: The *Constitution on the Sacred Liturgy* . . . . . . . . . . . . . 317
  **205** A Protestant Worship Manifesto . . . . . . . . . . . . . . . . . . . . . . . . . . . . . . . . . . . . . 332
  **206** A Pentecostal/Charismatic Manifesto . . . . . . . . . . . . . . . . . . . . . . . . . . . . . . . . 337
  **207** Bibliography on Contemporary Worship Documents . . . . . . . . . . . . . . . . . . . 340

**CHAPTER 14. Concerns for the Future of Worship** . . . . . . . . . . . . . . . . . . . . . . . . . . . 341
  **208** An Orthodox Concern . . . . . . . . . . . . . . . . . . . . . . . . . . . . . . . . . . . . . . . . . . . . . 341
  **209** A Catholic Concern . . . . . . . . . . . . . . . . . . . . . . . . . . . . . . . . . . . . . . . . . . . . . . . 341
  **210** A Mainline Protestant Concern . . . . . . . . . . . . . . . . . . . . . . . . . . . . . . . . . . . . . 343
  **211** An Evangelical Concern . . . . . . . . . . . . . . . . . . . . . . . . . . . . . . . . . . . . . . . . . . . 343
  **212** A Charismatic Concern . . . . . . . . . . . . . . . . . . . . . . . . . . . . . . . . . . . . . . . . . . . . 349
  **213** A Praise-and-Worship Concern . . . . . . . . . . . . . . . . . . . . . . . . . . . . . . . . . . . . . 350
  **214** Bibliography on New Directions in Worship . . . . . . . . . . . . . . . . . . . . . . . . . . 353

*Part 6:* PREPARING FOR WORSHIP RENEWAL

**CHAPTER 15. Preconditions and Stages of Worship Renewal** . . . . . . . . . . . . . . . . . . 357
  **215** The Restoration of *Christus Victor* . . . . . . . . . . . . . . . . . . . . . . . . . . . . . . . . . . 357
  **216** The Church as Community . . . . . . . . . . . . . . . . . . . . . . . . . . . . . . . . . . . . . . . . . 360
  **217** Unity Through Worship . . . . . . . . . . . . . . . . . . . . . . . . . . . . . . . . . . . . . . . . . . . 361
  **218** Community through Small Groups . . . . . . . . . . . . . . . . . . . . . . . . . . . . . . . . . . 362
  **219** Recovering the Gifts of the Laity . . . . . . . . . . . . . . . . . . . . . . . . . . . . . . . . . . . 364
  **220** Stages of Worship Renewal . . . . . . . . . . . . . . . . . . . . . . . . . . . . . . . . . . . . . . . . 366

**CHAPTER 16. Understanding the Principles of Worship** . . . . . . . . . . . . . . . . . . . . . 370
  **221** Principle One: Worship Celebrates Christ . . . . . . . . . . . . . . . . . . . . . . . . . . . . 370
  **222** Principle Two: Worship Tells and Acts Out the Christ Event . . . . . . . . . . . . . 370
  **223** Principle Three: In Worship God Speaks and Acts . . . . . . . . . . . . . . . . . . . . . 371
  **224** Principle Four: Worship is an Act of Communication . . . . . . . . . . . . . . . . . . . 372
  **225** Principle Five: In Worship We Respond to God and to Each Other . . . . . . . . 373
  **226** Principle Six: Worship is an Act of the People . . . . . . . . . . . . . . . . . . . . . . . . 374
  **227** Principle Seven: Worship Makes Effective Use of God's Creative Gifts . . . . . 374
  **228** Principle Eight: Worship is a Way of Life . . . . . . . . . . . . . . . . . . . . . . . . . . . . 376
  **229** Bibliography on Principles of Worship . . . . . . . . . . . . . . . . . . . . . . . . . . . . . . 377

**CHAPTER 17. Exploring the Psychology of Worship** . . . . . . . . . . . . . . . . . . . . . . . . 381
  **230** Wounds that Hinder Worship . . . . . . . . . . . . . . . . . . . . . . . . . . . . . . . . . . . . . . 381
  **231** Ten Basic Needs Met by Worship . . . . . . . . . . . . . . . . . . . . . . . . . . . . . . . . . . 386
  **232** Toward a Biblical Psychology of Worship . . . . . . . . . . . . . . . . . . . . . . . . . . . 388

**CHAPTER 18. Challenges Facing Worship Renewalists** . . . . . . . . . . . . . . . . . . . . . . 394
  **233** Lack of Concern for Worship Renewal . . . . . . . . . . . . . . . . . . . . . . . . . . . . . . 394
  **234** Contempt for Praise of God . . . . . . . . . . . . . . . . . . . . . . . . . . . . . . . . . . . . . . . 394
  **235** Substitutes for Worship . . . . . . . . . . . . . . . . . . . . . . . . . . . . . . . . . . . . . . . . . . 395
  **236** Misplaced Priority in Worship . . . . . . . . . . . . . . . . . . . . . . . . . . . . . . . . . . . . 396
  **237** The Corruption of Worship by Manipulation and Utilitarianism . . . . . . . . . . 398
  **238** McEucharist: The Allure of "Fast-Food" Worship . . . . . . . . . . . . . . . . . . . . . 399
  **239** The Corruption of Worship by Aestheticism . . . . . . . . . . . . . . . . . . . . . . . . . 402
  **240** The Problem of Form and Language . . . . . . . . . . . . . . . . . . . . . . . . . . . . . . . . 404

**241** Areas of Challenge in Free-Church Worship . . . . . . . . . . . . . . . . . . . . . . . . . . . . 404

**242** Areas of Challenge in Liturgical Worship . . . . . . . . . . . . . . . . . . . . . . . . . . . . . . 406

**243** The Need for Redefinition of Worship in Charismatic Churches . . . . . . . . . . . . . . 406

**244** The Need to Recover Celebration . . . . . . . . . . . . . . . . . . . . . . . . . . . . . . . . . . . . 407

Works Cited . . . . . . . . . . . . . . . . . . . . . . . . . . . . . . . . . . . . . . . . . . . . . . . . . . . . . . . . . 409

Alphabetical Index . . . . . . . . . . . . . . . . . . . . . . . . . . . . . . . . . . . . . . . . . . . . . . . . . . . 411

# List of Illustrations and Tables

*Illustrations*

1. Fish Lantern . . . . . . . . . . . . . . . . . . . . . . . . . . . . . . . . . . 5
2. Orders in the Early Church . . . . . . . . . . . . . . . . . . . . . . . . 16
3. Bread and Chalice . . . . . . . . . . . . . . . . . . . . . . . . . . . . . . 22
4. The Good Shepherd . . . . . . . . . . . . . . . . . . . . . . . . . . . . . 34
5. Loaves and Fishes . . . . . . . . . . . . . . . . . . . . . . . . . . . . . . 38
6. Third-Century House Church . . . . . . . . . . . . . . . . . . . . . . 43
7. Orthodox Mosaic . . . . . . . . . . . . . . . . . . . . . . . . . . . . . . . 46
8. An Armenian Church . . . . . . . . . . . . . . . . . . . . . . . . . . . . 48
9. Hagia Sophia . . . . . . . . . . . . . . . . . . . . . . . . . . . . . . . . . . 52
10. Russian Church Architecture . . . . . . . . . . . . . . . . . . . . . . 54
11. Icon of the Trinity . . . . . . . . . . . . . . . . . . . . . . . . . . . . . . 57
12. St. Peter's Basilica at Rome . . . . . . . . . . . . . . . . . . . . . . . 62
13. St. Ambrose . . . . . . . . . . . . . . . . . . . . . . . . . . . . . . . . . . . 63
14. Scripture Copier . . . . . . . . . . . . . . . . . . . . . . . . . . . . . . . 65
15. The Suffering Jesus . . . . . . . . . . . . . . . . . . . . . . . . . . . . . 67
16. Medieval Preaching . . . . . . . . . . . . . . . . . . . . . . . . . . . . . 68
17. The Loving Christ . . . . . . . . . . . . . . . . . . . . . . . . . . . . . . 70
18. Anabaptist Persecution . . . . . . . . . . . . . . . . . . . . . . . . . . 78
19. New England Church—Exterior View . . . . . . . . . . . . . . . 83
20. New England Church—Interior View . . . . . . . . . . . . . . . . 85
21. The Listening Angel . . . . . . . . . . . . . . . . . . . . . . . . . . . . . 86
22. John Wesley at Gwennap Pit . . . . . . . . . . . . . . . . . . . . . . 87
23. Camp Meeting . . . . . . . . . . . . . . . . . . . . . . . . . . . . . . . . . 90
24. Martin Luther . . . . . . . . . . . . . . . . . . . . . . . . . . . . . . . . .195
25. John Calvin . . . . . . . . . . . . . . . . . . . . . . . . . . . . . . . . . . .204
26. Balthasar Hubmaier . . . . . . . . . . . . . . . . . . . . . . . . . . . .216
27. John Cotton . . . . . . . . . . . . . . . . . . . . . . . . . . . . . . . . . . .228
28. George Fox . . . . . . . . . . . . . . . . . . . . . . . . . . . . . . . . . . .235
29. John Wesley . . . . . . . . . . . . . . . . . . . . . . . . . . . . . . . . . .236
30. William Booth . . . . . . . . . . . . . . . . . . . . . . . . . . . . . . . . .245
31. Jesus the Conqueror . . . . . . . . . . . . . . . . . . . . . . . . . . . .266
32. The Chi Rho Symbol . . . . . . . . . . . . . . . . . . . . . . . . . . . .291
33. The Nine-Pointed Star and Nine Fruits of the Spirit . . . . .332
34. Greek Cross and the Letter X . . . . . . . . . . . . . . . . . . . . . .344
35. Canterbury Cross . . . . . . . . . . . . . . . . . . . . . . . . . . . . . .361
36. The Church as Ark . . . . . . . . . . . . . . . . . . . . . . . . . . . . .373
37. The Alpha and Omega . . . . . . . . . . . . . . . . . . . . . . . . . . .396

*Tables*

Key Events in the History of Christian Worship . . . . . . . . . . . . . . . . . . . .40–41

# Board of Editorial Consultants

The Board of Editorial Consultants is made up of leaders in worship renewal from major Christian denominations. They have functioned as advisors, often through letter and telephone. Every attempt has been made to include material on worship representing the whole church. For this reason, different viewpoints are presented without any attempt to express a particular point of view or bias. A special word of thanks is due to the executive and consulting editors for their helpful input. Their ideas, suggestions and contributions have strengthened the *Complete Library of Christian Worship.* Omissions and weaknesses in all seven volumes are the sole responsibility of the compiler and editor.

Paul Bassett
*Nazarene Theological Seminary, Kansas City, Missouri*

Robert J. Batastini
*GIA Publications, Chicago, Illinois*

Kevin G. Bausman
*First Presbyterian Church of Southport, Indianapolis, Indiana*

Patricia Beal
*South Park Community, Surrey, Australia*

Christopher Beatty
*The Upright Foundation, Lindale, Texas*

John Bell
*Iona Community, Scotland*

W. Wilson Benton, Jr.
*Kirk of the Hills Presbyterian, St. Louis, Missouri*

Philip Berggrov-Peter
*Associate Professor Emeritus, University of Michigan, Dearborn, Michigan*

Jerome W. Berryman
*Christ Church Cathedral, Houston, Texas*

Harold M. Best
*Wheaton College Conservatory of Music, Wheaton, Illinois*

Perry H. Biddle, Jr.
*First Presbyterian Church, Old Hickory, Tennessee*

Warren Bird
*Charles E. Fuller Institute, Suffern, New York*

Richard Bishop
*Evangel College, Springfield, Missouri*

Robert Black
*Central Wesleyan College, Central, South Carolina*

Donald Bloesch
*University of Dubuque Theological Seminary, Dubuque, Iowa.*

Edith Blumhoffer
*Wheaton College, Wheaton, Illinois*

Markus Bockmuehl
*Cambridge University, Cambridge, England*

Richard Allen Bodey
*Trinity Evangelical Divinity School*

Nick Boone
*Madison Church of Christ, Madison, Tennessee*

Harry Boonstra
*Calvin Theological Seminary, Grand Rapids, Michigan*

P. Wayne Boosahda
*St. Barnabas the Encourager, Tulsa, Oklahoma*

Deena Borchers
*Overland Park, Kansas*

Gordon Borrow
*Western Theological Seminary, Portland, Oregon*

Lamar Boschman
*Lamar Boschman Ministries, Bedford, Texas*

Walter Bouman
*Trinity Lutheran Seminary, Columbus, Ohio*

Paul Bradshaw
*University of Notre Dame, Notre Dame, Indiana*

Vincent Branick
*University of Dayton, Dayton, Ohio*

James Brauer
*Concordia Theological Seminary, St. Louis, Missouri*

Emily Brink
***Reformed Worship**, Grand Rapids, Michigan*

John Brooks-Leonard
*Center for Pastoral Liturgy, Univeristy of Notre Dame, Notre Dame, Indiana*

Geoffrey Bromily
*Fuller Theological Seminary, Pasadena, California*

Wayne Brouwer
*First Christian Reformed Church, London, Ontario, Canada*

Donald Bruggink
*Western Theological Seminary, Holland, Michigan*

Steve Burdan
*Willow Creek Community Church, Palatine, Illinois*

Eileen C. Burke-Sullivan
*All Saints Parish, Dallas, Texas*

John E. Burkhart
*McCormick Theological Seminary, Chicago, Illinois*

David Buttrick
*Vanderbilt Divinity School, Nashville, Tennessee*

William Caldaroni
*Holy Transfiguration Orthodox Mission, Carol Stream, Illinois*

Gerald Calhoun
*Jesuit Novitiate, Jamica Plains, Massachusetts*

Alkiviadis C. Calivas
*Holy Cross Greek Orthodox School of Theology, Brookline, Massachusetts*

Melvin Campbell
*LaSierra University, La Sierra, California*

Lorene Carlson
*Womens Aglow International, Seattle, Washington*

Richard Carlson
*North Park Theological Seminary, Chicago, Illinois*

James A. Carr
*San Antonio, Texas*

David J. Diephouse
*Calvin College, Grand Rapids, Michigan*

John Dillenberger
*Graduate Theological Union, Berkeley, California*

Thomas Dipko
*Board of Homeland Ministries, Cleveland, Ohio*

Carmine Di Sante
*Service International de Documentation Judeo-Chretienne, Rome, Italy*

Brian Doerkson
*Langley Vineyard, Langley, British Columbia, Canada*

Kate Dooley
*Catholic University of America, Washington, D.C.*

Carol Doran
*Colgate Rochester Divinity School/Bexley Hall/ Crozer Theological Seminary, Rochester, New York*

Mary Doyle
*Holy Spirit Parish, Berkeley, California*

Dan Dozier
*Madison Church of Christ, Madison, Tennessee*

Arlo D. Duba
*University of Dubuque Theological Seminary, Dubuque, Iowa*

Jerry DuCharme
*Ducharme Consultant, Clearwater, Florida*

Ruth C. Duck
*Garrett Theological Seminary, Evanston, Illinois*

Mary Francis Duffy
*Good Samaritan Hospital, Baltimore, Maryland*

Regis A. Duffy
*Theological Union, Washington, D.C.*

Rodney Dugan
*Believers Grace Church, Cedar Rapids, Iowa*

Robert D. Duggan
*St. Rose of Lima Parish, Gaithersburg, Maryland*

Michael Driscoll
*Carroll College, Helena, Montana*

Warren Ediger
*La Habra, California.*

Larry D. Ellis
*Corona Presbyterian Church, Denver, Colorado*

Walter Elwell
*Wheaton College, Wheaton, Illinois*

James Empereur
*Jesuit School of Theology, Berkeley, California*

Paul E. Engle
*Biblical Discovery Seminars, Grand Rapids, Michigan*

Randall Engle
*Calvary Christian Reformed Church, Bloomington, Minnesota*

Eddie Ensley
*Contemplative Brothers, Columbus, Georgia*

Craig Douglas Erickson
*Tokyo Union Church, Tokyo, Japan*

Howard M. Ervin
*Oral Roberts University, Tulsa, Oklahoma*

Eddie Espinosa
*Vineyard Fellowship, Anaheim, California*

Brad Estep
*Union Theological Seminary, Richmond, Virginia.*

Charles Evanson
*Redeemer Lutheran Church, Ft. Wayne, Indiana*

Richard Fabian
*St. Gregory Nyssen Episcopal Church, San Francisco, California*

Johanna B. Fabke
*St. Luke's Episcopal Church, Madison, Wisconsin*

Michael J. Fahey
*The Liturgical Press, Collegeville, Minnesota*

Todd Farley
***Mimestry***, St. Louis, Missouri

Mimi Farra
*Celebration, Aliquippa, Pennsylvania*

Nancy Faus
*Bethany Theological Seminary, Lombard, Illinois*

Paul Feela
*University of St. Thomas School of Divinity, St. Paul, Minnesota*

John Ferguson
*St. Olaf College, Northfield, Minnesota*

Charles Fienberg
*Talbot Theological Seminary, La Mirada, California*

Earle Fike, Jr.
*Stone Church of the Brethren, Huntingdon, Pennsylvania*

Peter E. Fink
*Weston School of Theology, Cambridge, Massachusetts*

Thomas Finger
*Eastern Mennonite Seminary, Harrisburg, Pennsylvania*

John David Finley
*St. Athanasius Academy of Orthodox Theology, Goleta, California*

Dennis Fleisher
*Kirkegaard and Associates Architects, Chicago, Illinois*

David Fleming
 _Review for Religions, St. Louis, Missouri_

Andrew Foster
 _African Methodist Episcopal Zion Church, Red Bank, New Jersey_

Mark R. Francis
 _Catholic Theological Union, Chicago, Illinois_

John Frame
 _Westminster Theological Seminary West, Escondido, California_

Peter Frascr
 _Wisconsin Lutheran College, Milwaukee, Wisconsin_

Dennis Fredrickson
 _First United Church, Elynia, Ohio_

Debra Freeberg
 _Calvin College, Grand Rapids, Michigan_

Eileen E. Freeman
 _Archdiocese of Denver, Denver, Colorado_

Robert A. Freeman
 _Gordon Conwell Theological Seminary, Massachusetts_

Inga Freyer-Nicholas
 _The First Baptist Church of Ottumwa, Ottumwa, Iowa_

Ron Freyer
 _The First Baptist Church of Ottumwa, Ottumwa, Iowa_

Guy B. Funderburk
 _Salem College, Salem, West Virginia_

Virgil Funk
 _National Association of Parish Musicians, Washington, D.C._

Robert Gagne
 _Clinician in Music and Liturgy, Hartford, Connecticut_

John Gallen
 _Editor, **Modern Liturgy**, San Jose, California_

Michael Galvan
 _Roman Catholic Diocese of Oakland, California_

Bryan Gerlach
 _St. Mark's Lutheran Church, Citrus Heights, California_

June Adams Gibble
 _Church of the Brethren, Elgin, Illinois_

Keith Graber-Miller
 _Candler School of Theology, Atlanta, Georgia_

John Grabner
 _First United Methodist Church, Moscow, Idaho_

P. Preston Graham
 _Southern Baptist Church, Mabank, Texas_

George S. Gray
 _St. Nicholas Orthodox Church, Portland, Oregon_

Henry David Gray
 _**The Congregational Journal**, Ventura, California_

Ronald Graybill
 _La Sierra University, Riverside, California_

Philip C. Griffith II
 _Christians in the Arts Networking, Cambridge, Massachusetts_

Thomas H. Groome
 _Boston College, Boston, Massachusetts_

Kenneth Guentert
 _**Modern Liturgy**, San Jose, California_

Thomas Gulbronson
 _First Assembly of God, Alexandria, Virginia_

Gerrit Gustafson
 _Kingdom of Priests Ministries, Mobile, Alabama_

Kevin Hackett
 _Community of Celebration, Aliquippa, Pennsylvania_

Tom Halbrooks
 _Baptist Theological Seminary, Richmond, Virginia_

David Hall
 _Cogi Publishing, Memphis, Tennessee_

Stanley R. Hall
 _Austin Theological Seminary, Austin, Texas_

Donald Hallmark
 _Greenville College, Greenville, Illinois_

John Hamersma
 _Calvin College, Grand Rapids, Michigan_

Susan E. Hames
 _Graduate Theological Union, Berkeley, California._

Jerry Handspicker
 _Andover Newton Theological School, Newton Center, Massachusetts_

Daniel W. Hardy
 _Princeton Theological Seminary, Princeton, New Jersey_

Daniel J. Harrington
 _Weston School of Theology, Cambridge, Massachusetts_

Dirk Hart
 _Christian Reformed Board of Home Missions, Grand Rapids, Michigan_

James Hart
 _St. David's Center for Arts, Jacksonville, Florida_

Darrell A. Harris
 _Star Song, Nashville, Tennessee_

Louis-Charles Harvey
 _Payne Theological Seminary, Wilberforce, Ohio_

John W. Morris
  *St. George Antiochian Orthodox Church, Cedar Rapids, Iowa*

John P. Mossi
  *North American Academy of Liturgists*

Richard J. Mouw
  *Fuller Theological Seminary, Pasadena, California*

William Mugford
  *University of Chicago, Chicago, Illinois*

May Murakami
  *Christ United Presbyterian Church, San Francisco, California*

Carol Myers
  *Hope College, Holland, Michigan*

Loni McCalister
  *Lee College, Cleveland, Tennessee*

William B. McClain
  *Wesley Theological Seminary, Washington, D.C.*

Richard McDaniel
  *Steward of the Word Ministries, Chapel Hill, North Carolina*

Killian McDonnell
  *Order of St. Benedict, Collegeville, Minnesota*

William K. McElvaney
  *Perkins School of Theology, Dallas, Texas*

Gary B. McGee
  *Assemblies of God Theological Seminary, Springfield, Missouri*

Martha McIntosh
  *St. Patrick's Church, Tampa, Florida*

Elsie McKee
  *Princeton Theological Seminary, Princeton, New Jersey.*

Jean McLaughlin
  *St. Joan of Arc Parish, Toledo, Ohio*

Francis McNutt
  *Christian Healing Ministries, Inc., Jacksonville, Florida*

Philip D. Needhan
  *The Salvation Army, Atlanta, Georgia*

David R. Newman
  *Emmanuel College, Toronto, Ontario, Canada*

Kathryn L. Nichols
  *Paxton Presbyterian Church, Harrisburg, Pennsylvania*

Stanley E. Niebruegge
  *Presbyterian Church USA, Franconia, New Hampshire*

Charles Nienkirchen
  *Rocky Mountain College, Calgary, Alberta, Canada*

James Notebaart
  *Our Lady of Mt. Carmel Parish, Minneapolis, Minnesota*

David Noy
  *Austin Presbyterian Theological Seminary, Austin, Texas*

Celeste Marie Nuttman
  *Worship, Art, and Music Commission of the Archdiocese of San Francisco, California*

Carol Nyberg
  *Episcopal Diocese of Chicago, Chicago, Illinois*

Larry Nyberg
  *Episcopal Diocese of Chicago, Chicago, Illinois*

Mark Olson
  *The Other Side, Philadelphia, Pennsylvania*

Dennis Okholm
  *Wheaton College, Wheaton, Illinois*

Hughes Oliphant Old
  *Princeton Theological Seminary, Princeton, New Jersey*

Gilbert Ostdiek
  *Catholic Theological Union, Chicago, Illinois*

Richard N. Ostling
  *Time, New York, New York*

Jerome T. Overbeck
  *Loyola University, Chicago, Illinois.*

Chris Stoffel Overvoorde
  *Calvin College, Grand Rapids, Michigan*

Dean Palermo
  *Bethlehem Baptist Church, Minneapolis, Minnesota*

Lloyd Patterson
  *Episcopal Divinity School, Cambridge, Massachusetts*

Robert W. Pazmiño
  *Andover Newton Theological Schoool, Newton Center, Massachusetts*

Jim Peck
  *Wheaton College, Wheaton, Illinois*

Steve Pederson
  *Willowcreek Community Church, South Barrington, Illinois*

Hayim Perelmuter
  *Catholic Theological Union, Chicago, Illinois*

Edward Phillips
  *Union College, Barbourville, Kentucky*

Tim Phillips
  *Wheaton College, Wheaton, Illinois*

Mary Alice Piil
  *Seminary of the Immaculate Conception, Huntington, New York*

# List of Cooperating Publishers

## BOOK PUBLISHERS

**Abbott-Martyn Press**
2325 Crestmoor Road
Nashville, TN 37215

**Abingdon Press**
201 8th Avenue South
Nashville, TN 37202

**Agape**
Hope Publishing
Carol Stream, IL 60187

**Alba House**
2187 Victory Boulevard
Staten Island, NY 10314

**American Choral
Directors Association**
502 Southwest 38th
Lawton, Oklahoma 73505

**Asian Institute for
Liturgy & Music**
P.O. Box 3167
Manila 1099 Philippines

**Augsburg/Fortress Press**
426 S. Fifth Street
Box 1209
Minneapolis, MN 55440

**Ave Maria Press**
Notre Dame, IN 46556

**Baker Book House**
P.O. Box 6287
Grand Rapids, MI 49516-6287

**Beacon Hill Press**
Box 419527
Kansas City, MO 64141

**Bethany House Publishers**
6820 Auto Club Road
Minneapolis, MN 55438

**The Brethren Press**
1451 Dundee Avenue
Elgin, IL 60120

**Bridge Publishing, Inc.**
200 Hamilton Blvd.
South Plainfield, NJ 07080

**Broadman Press**
127 Ninth Avenue, North
Nashville, TN 37234

**C.S.S. Publishing Company**
628 South Main Street
Lima, OH 45804

**Cathedral Music Press**
P.O. Box 66
Pacific, MO 63069

**Catholic Book
Publishing Company**
257 W. 17th Street
New York, NY 10011

**CBP Press**
Box 179
St. Louis, MO 63166

**Celebration**
P.O. Box 309
Aliquippa, PA 15001

**Channing L. Bete Company**
South Deerfield, MA 01373

**Choristers Guild**
2834 W. Kingsley Road
Garland, TX 75041

**Christian Literature Crusade**
701 Pennsylvania Avenue
Box 1449
Ft. Washington, PA 19034

**Christian Publications**
3825 Hartzdale Drive
Camp Hill, PA 17011

**The Church
Hymnal Corporation**
800 Second Avenue
New York, NY 10017

**The Columba Press**
93 Merise
Mount Merrion
Blackrock, Dublin

**Concordia Publishing House**
3558 S. Jefferson Avenue
St. Louis, MO 63118

**Covenant Publications**
3200 West Foster Avenue
Chicago, IL 60625

**Cowley Publications**
980 Memorial Drive
Cambridge, MA 02138

**CRC Publications**
2850 Kalamazoo SE
Grand Rapids, MI 49560

**Creative Communications
for The Parish**
10300 Watson Road
St. Louis, MO 63127

**Crossroad Publishing
Company**
575 Lexington Avenue
New York, NY 10022

**Crossroad/Continuum**
370 Lexington Avenue
New York, NY 10017

**Dominion Press**
7112 Burns Street
Ft. Worth, TX 76118

**Duke Univesity Press**
Box 6697 College Station
Durham, NC 27708

**Faith and Life Press**
724 Main Street
Box 347
Newton, KS 67114

**The Faith Press, Ltd.**
7 Tufton Street
Westminster, S.W. 1
England

**Fleming H. Revell Company**
184 Central Avenue
Old Tappen, N.J. 07675

**Folk Music Ministry**
P.O. Box 3443
Annapolis, MD 21403

**Franciscan Communications**
1229 South Santee Street
Los Angeles, CA 90015

**Georgetown University Press**
111 Intercultural Center
Washington, D.C. 20057

**GIA Publications**
7404 S. Mason Avenue
Chicago, IL 60638

**Great Commission Publications**
7401 Old York Road
Philadelphia, PA 19126

**Grove Books**
Bramcote Notts
England

**Harper & Row Publishers**
Icehouse One-401
151 Union Street
San Francisco, CA 94111-1299

**Harvard University Press**
79 Garden Street
Cambridge, MA 02138

**Harvest Publications**
Baptist General Conference
2002 S. Arlington Heights Road
Arlington Heights, IL 60005

**Hendrickson Publishers, Inc.**
P.O. Box 3473
Peabody, MA 01961-3473

**Herald Press**
616 Walnut Avenue
Scottdale, PA 15683

**Hinshaw Music Incorporated**
P.O. Box 470
Chapel Hill, NC 27514

**Holt, Rinehart & Winston**
111 5th Avenue
New York, NY 10175

**Hope Publishing Company**
Carol Stream, IL 60188

**Hymn Society of America**
Texas Christian University
P.O. Box 30854
Ft. Worth, TX 76129

**Indiana University Press**
10th & Morton
Bloomington, IN 47405

**Integrity Music**
P.O. Box 16813
Mobile, AL 36616

**J.S. Paluch Company, Inc.**
3825 Willow Road
P.O. Box 2703
Schiller Park, IL 60176

**The Jewish Publication
Society of America**
1930 Chestnut Street
Philadelphia, PA 19103

**Judson Press**
P.O. Box 851
Valley Forge, PA 19482-0851

**Light and Life Publishing
Company**
P.O. Box 26421
Minneapolis, MN 55426

**Liguori Publications**
One Liguori Drive
Liguori, MO 63057

**Lillenas Publishing Company**
Box 419527
Kansas City, MO 64141

**The Liturgical Conference**
1017 Twelfth Street, N.W.
Washington, D.C. 20005-4091

**The Liturgical Press**
St. John's Abbey
Collegeville, MN 56321

**Liturgy Training Publications**
1800 North Heritage Avenue
Chicago, IL 60622-1101

**Macmillan Publishing
Company**
866 Third Avenue
New York, NY 10022

**Maranatha! Music**
25411 Cabot Road
Suite 203
Laguna Hills, CA 92653

**Mel Bay Publications**
Pacific, MO 63969-0066

**Meriwether Publishing, Ltd.**
885 Elkton Drive
Colorado Springs, CO 80907

**Michael Glazier, Inc.**
1723 Delaware Avenue
Wilmington, Delaware 19806

**Morehouse-Barlow**
78 Danbury Road
Wilton, CT 06897

**Multnomah Press**
10209 SE Division Street
Portland, OR 97266

**National Association
of Pastoral Musicians**
25 Sheridan Street, NW
Washington, DC 20011

**NavPress**
P.O. Box 6000
Colorado Springs, CO 80934

**New Skete**
Cambridge, NY 12816

**North American
Liturgical Resources**
1802 N. 23rd Avenue
Phoenix, AZ 85029

**Oxford University Press**
16-00 Pollitt Drive
Fair Lawn, NJ 07410

**The Pastoral Press**
225 Sheridan Street, NW
Washington, D.C. 20011

**Paulist Press**
997 McArthur Boulevard
Mahwah, NJ 07430

**The Pilgrim Press**
132 West 31st Street
New York, NY 10001

**Psalmist Resources**
9820 E. Watson Road
St. Louis, MO 63126

**Pueblo Publishing Company**
100 West 32nd Street
New York, NY 1001-3210

**Regal Books**
A Division of Gospel Light
    Publications
Ventura, CA 93006

**Resource Publications, Inc.**
160 E. Virginia Street #290
San Jose, CA 95112

**The Scarecrow Press**
52 Liberty Street
Box 416
Metuchen, NJ 08840

**Schocken Books**
62 Cooper Square
New York, NY 10003

**Schuyler Institute for
Worship & The Arts**
2757 Melandy Drive, Suite 15
San Carlos, CA 94070

**SCM Press Ltd.**
c/o Trinity Press International
3725 Chestnut Street
Philadelphia, PA 19104

**Servant Publications**
P.O. Box 8617
Petersham, MA 01366-0545

**The Sharing Company**
P.O. Box 2224
Austin, TX 78768-2224

**Sheed & Ward**
115 E. Armour Boulevard
P.O. Box 414292
Kansas City, MO 64141-0281

**Shofar Publications, Inc**
P.O. Box 88711
Carol Stream, IL 60188

**SPCK**
Holy Trinity Church
Marylebone Road
London, N.W. 4D4

**St. Anthony Messenger Press**
1615 Republic Street
Cincinnati, OH 45210

**St. Bede's Publications**
P.O. Box 545
Petersham, MA 01366-0545

**St. Mary's Press**
Terrace Heights
Winona, MN 55987

**St. Vladimir Seminary Press**
575 Scarsdale Road
Crestwood, NY 10707-1699

**Thomas Nelson Publishers**
P.O. Box 141000
Nashville, TN 37214

**Twenty Third Publications**
P.O. Box 180
Mystic, CT 06355

**Tyndale House Publishers**
351 Executive Drive
Carol Stream, IL 60188

**United Church of Christ**
Office of Church Life and
    Leadership
700 Prospect
Cleveland, OH 44115

**United Church Press**
132 West 31st Street
New York, NY 10001

**The United Methodist
Publishing House**
P.O. Box 801
Nashville, TN 37202

**United States
Catholic Conference**
Office of Publishing and
    Promotion Services
1312 Massachusetts Avenue, NW
Washington, DC 20005-4105

**University of California Press**
1010 Westward Blvd.
Los Angeles, CA 90024

**University of Notre
Dame Press**
Notre Dame, IN 46556

**The Upper Room**
1908 Grand Avenue
P.O. Box 189
Nashville, TN 37202

**Victory House Publishers**
P.O. Box 700238
Tulsa, OK 74170

**Westminster John Knox Press**
100 Witherspoon Street
Louisville, KY 40202-1396

**William B. Eerdmans
Publishing Company**
255 Jefferson S.E.
Grand Rapids, MI 49503

**William C. Brown
Publishing Company**
2460 Kerper Boulevard
P.O. Box 539
Dubuque, IA 52001

**William H. Sadlier, Inc.**
11 Park Place
New York, NY 10007

**Winston Press**
P.O. Box 1630
Hagerstown, MD 21741

**Word Books**
Tower-Williams Square
5221 N. O'Conner Blvd. Suite
    1000
Irving, TX 75039

**World Council of
Churches Publications**
P.O. Box 66
150 Route de Ferney
1211 Geneva 20, Switzerland

**World Library
Publications, Inc.**
3815 N. Willow Road
P.O. Box 2701
Schiller Park, IL 60176

**The World
Publishing Company**
Meridian Books
110 E. 59th Street
New York, NY 10022

**Yale University Press**
302 Temple Street
New Haven, CN 06510

**Zion Fellowship**
236 Gorham Street
Canadagina, NY 14424

**Zondervan Publishing
Company**
1415 Lake Drive S.E.
Grand Rapids, MI 49506

# PERIODICAL PUBLISHERS

**The American Center for Church Music Newsletter**
3339 Burbank Drive
Ann Arbor, MI 48105

**American Organist**
475 Riverside Drive, Suite 1260
New York, NY 10115

**ARTS: The Arts in Religious and Theological Studies**
United Theological Seminary of the Twin Cities
3000 5th Street, NW
New Brighton, MN 55112

**Arts Advocate**
The United Church of Christ Fellowship in the Arts
73 S. Palvuse
Walla Walla, WA 99362

**The Choral Journal**
American Choral Directors Association
P.O. Box 6310
Lawton, OK 73506

**Choristers Guild Letters**
2834 W. Kingsley Road
Garland, TX 75041

**Christians in the Visual Arts**
(newsletter)
P.O. Box 10247
Arlington, VA 22210

**Church Music Quarterly**
Royal School of Church Music
Addington Palace
Croyden, England CR9 5AD

**The Church Musician**
Southern Baptist Convention
127 9th Avenue N.
Nashville, TN 37234

**Contemporary Christian Music**
CCM Publications
P.O. Box 6300
Laguna Hills, CA 92654

**Diapason**
380 E. Northwest Highway
Des Plaines, IL 60016

**Doxology**
Journal of the Order of St. Luke in the United Methodist Church

1872 Sweet Home Road
Buffalo, NY 14221

**Environment and Art Letter**
Liturgy Training Publications
1800 N. Hermitage Avenue
Chicago, IL 60622

**GIA Quarterly**
7404 S. Mason Avenue
Chicago, IL 60638

**Grace Notes**
Association of Lutheran Church Musicians
4807 Idaho Circle
Ames, IA 50010

**The Hymn**
Hymn Society of the United States and Canada
P.O. Box 30854
Fort Worth, TX 76129

**Journal**
Sacred Dance Guild
Joyce Smillie, Resource Director
10 Edge Court
Woodbury, CT 06798

**Journal of Ritual Studies**
Department of Religious Studies
University of Pittsburgh
Pittsburgh, PA 15260

**Let the People Worship**
Schuyler Institute for Worship and the Arts
2757 Melendy Drive, Suite 15
San Carlos, CA 94070

**Liturgy**
The Liturgical Conference
8750 Georgia Avenue, S., Suite 123
Silver Spring, MD 20910

**Liturgy 90**
Liturgy Training Publications
1800 N. Hermitage Avenue
Chicago, IL 60622

**Modern Liturgy**
Resource Publications
160 E. Virginia Street, Suite 290
San Jose, CA 95112

**Music in Worship**
Selah Publishing Company
P.O. Box 103
Accord, NY 12404

**Newsnotes**
The Fellowship of United Methodists in Worship, Music, and Other Arts
P.O. Box 54367
Atlanta, GA 30308

**Pastoral Music**
225 Sheridian Street, NW
Washington, D.C. 20011

**PRISM**
Yale Institute of Sacred Music
409 Prospect Street
New Haven, CT 06510

**The Psalmist**
9820 E. Watson Road
St. Louis, MO 63124

**Reformed Liturgy and Music**
Worship and Ministry Unit
100 Witherspoon Street
Louisville, KY 40202

**Reformed Music Journal**
Brookside Publishing
3911 Mt. Lehman Road
Abbotsford, BC V2S 6A9

**Reformed Worship**
CRC Publications
2850 Kalamazoo Avenue, SE
Grand Rapids, MI 49560

**Rite Reasons**
Biblical Horizons
P.O. Box 1096
Niceville, FL 32588

**St. Vladimirs Theological Quarterly**
757 Scarsdale Road
Crestwood, NY 10707

**Studia Liturgica**
Department of Theology
University of Notre Dame
Notre Dame, IN 46556

**Today's Liturgy**
Oregon Catholic Press
5536 NE Hassalo
Portland, OR 97213

**Worship**
The Liturgical Press
St. John's Abbey
Collegeville, MN 56321

**Worship Leader**
CCM Communications, Inc.
107 Kenner Avenue
Nashville, TN 37205

**Worship Today**
600 Rinehard Road
Lake Mary, FL 32746

# Preface to Volume 2

The objective of *The Complete Library of Christian Worship* is not only to provide information about the worship of the Christian faith, but also to stimulate the renewal of Christian worship today.

*Twenty Centuries of Christian Worship* addresses three concerns of those who are committed to worship reform in the local church. It provides a glimpse of the way Christians have worshiped in the past, it addresses the way Christians are thinking about worship today, and it looks toward the future as it addresses the task of worship renewal. For those who desire a deep and lasting renewal of worship, three topics—history, theology, and renewal—cannot be neglected.

A special feature of this volume is that it does not look at one tradition, one theology, and one approach to the renewal of worship. *Twenty Centuries of Christian Worship* asks the reader to respect all the traditions of worship and to mine each tradition for all it is worth.

Today many Christians are altogether too isolated in their own worship tradition. Liturgical worshipers know very little about free worship or charismatic worship, and people in the free worship or charismatic traditions know very little about each other, let alone liturgical worship.

I hope *Twenty Centuries of Christian Worship* will provide worshipers with a sense of what Christians have done in the past, what Christian communities are doing now, and what worshiping communities may do in the future.

The twentieth century has already enjoyed a convergence of worship traditions, but it has been somewhat limited to the convergence of liturgical and traditional Protestant churches. Other communities of worship—the restoration movements, evangelicals, Holiness, Pentecostal, and charismatic groups—have succeeded in recapturing valid biblical and historical insights and practices of worship.

*Twenty Centuries of Christian Worship* provides an entrance into all these traditions as well as the liturgical and traditional Protestant communities of worship. And it calls on the whole church to respect and to learn from all the traditions as the twentieth century of renewal in worship forges ahead into a continually evolving convergence worship.

Robert E. Webber, Editor

# Introduction

The *Complete Library of Christian Worship* has been designed to meet a need in the church. Christian leaders and congregations are becoming increasingly interested in the subjects of worship and worship renewal in the local church. Often, however, they lack adequate biblical and historical perspective or the necessary materials and resources to engage in the renewal process.

To fulfill the demand for worship resources, publishing houses, particularly those of specific denominations, have been producing materials for the local church. While these materials may find use within the constituency of a particular denomination, only a few break across denominational barriers and become known throughout the church at large.

*The Complete Library of Christian Worship* draws from more than one hundred publishing houses and the major Christian denominations of the world in order to bring those resources together in a seven-volume work, making them readily available to all.

The purpose of this introductory material is to acquaint the reader with *The Complete Library of Christian Worship* and to help him or her to use its information and resources in the local church.

First, the reader needs to have some sense of the scope of worship studies and renewal that are addressed by *The Complete Library of Christian Worship* (see section 101 below). Second, it is important to learn how to use the *Library* (see section 102). Finally, there is a need to understand the precise content of Volume 2, *Twenty Centuries of Christian Worship*.

These three introductory entries are a key to the whole concept of the *Library*, a concept that brings together instruction in worship and vital resources for use in worship. The *Library* also directs the reader to a vast array of books, audio tapes, videotapes, model services, and resources in music and the arts. It seeks to provide direction and inspiration for everything the church does in worship.

## 101 ✦ INTRODUCTION TO *THE COMPLETE LIBRARY OF CHRISTIAN WORSHIP*

The word *library* implies a collection of resources, together with a system of organization that makes them accessible to the user. Specifically, *The Complete Library of Christian Worship* is a comprehensive compilation of information pertaining to the worship of the Christian church. It draws from a large pool of scholars and practitioners in the field, and from more than two thousand books and media resources in print.

The purpose of *The Complete Library of Christian Worship* is to make biblical, historical, and contemporary resources on worship available to pastors, music ministers, worship committees, and the motivated individual worshiper. The *Library* contains biblical and historical information on all aspects of worship and numerous resource materials, as well as suggested resource books, audio tapes, and video instructional material for every worship act in the local church.

The twentieth century, more than any century in the history of Christianity, has been the century for research and study in the origins, history, theology, and practice of Christian worship. Consequently there are seven broad areas in which worship studies are taking place. These are:

1. the biblical foundations of worship;
2. historical and theological development of worship;
3. resources for worship and preaching;
4. resources for music and the arts in worship;
5. resources for the services of the Christian year;
6. resources for sacraments, ordinances, and other sacred acts; and
7. resources for worship and related ministries.

*The Complete Library of Christian Worship* is organized around these seven areas of worship renewal. In these seven volumes one will find a wide variety of resources for every worship act in the church, and a select but broad bibliography for additional resources.

## 102 • How to Use *The Complete Library of Christian Worship*

*The Complete Library of Christian Worship* differs from an encyclopedia, which is often organized alphabetically, with information about a particular subject scattered throughout the book. The *Library* does not follow this pattern because it is a work designed to educate as well as to provide resources. Consequently, all the material in the *Library* is organized under a particular theme or issue of worship.

The difference between the *Library* and an encyclopedia may be illustrated, for example, by examining the topic of environmental art in worship. Some of the themes essential to environmental art are banners, candles, stained glass windows, lighting, pulpit hangings, table coverings, and Communion ware. In a typical encyclopedia these entries would be scattered in the B, C, S, L, P, and T sections. Although this is not a problem for people who know what environmental art is and what needs to be addressed in environmental art, it is a problem for the person whose knowledge about the subject is limited. For this reason *The Complete Library of Christian Worship* has been organized—like a textbook—into chapters dealing with particular issues. Therefore, all the matters dealing with environmental art can be found in the chapter on environmental art (see Volume 4, *Music and the Arts in Christian Worship*). In this way a reader becomes educated on environmental art while at the same time having the advantage of in-depth information on the various matters pertaining to this aspect of worship.

Therefore, the first unique feature of *The Complete Library of Christian Worship* is that each volume can be read and studied like a book.

The second unique feature of the *Library* is that the materials have been organized to follow the actual *sequence in which worship happens*.

For example, Volume 1, *The Biblical Foundations of Christian Worship*, looks at the roots of Christian worship in the biblical tradition, while Volume 2, *Twenty Centuries of Christian Worship*, presents the development of various historical models of worship along with an examination of the theology of worship. Next, Volumes 3 through 7 provide re-

sources for the various acts of worship: Volume 3, *The Renewal of Sunday Worship*, provides resources for the various parts of worship; Volume 4, *Music and the Arts in Christian Worship*, presents resources from music and the arts for the different aspects of worship. Volume 5, *The Services of the Christian Year*, branches out to the services of Advent, Christmas, Epiphany, Lent, Holy Week, Easter, and Pentecost, providing resources for those special services that celebrate the saving acts of God in Jesus Christ. Volume 6, *The Sacred Actions of Christian Worship*, deals with Communion, baptism, funerals, weddings, and other special or occasional acts of worship. Finally, Volume 7, *The Ministries of Christian Worship*, deals with evangelism, spirituality, education, social action, children's worship, and other matters impacted by Christian celebration.

Each volume contains an alphabetical index to the material in the book. This index makes desired information readily available for the reader.

The resources in these volumes are intended for use in every denomination and among all groups of Christians: liturgical, traditional Protestant, those using creative styles, and those in the praise-and-worship tradition. Resources from each of these communities may be found in the various volumes.

It is difficult to find material from the free churches (those not following a historic order of worship) and from the charismatic traditions. These communities function with an oral tradition of worship and therefore do not preserve their material through written texts. Nevertheless, a considerable amount of information has been gathered from these oral traditions. Recently, leaders in these communities have been teaching their worship practices through audio tapes and videotapes. Information on the availability of these materials has been included in the appropriate volumes.

The written texts have been the easiest to obtain. Because of this, *The Complete Library of Christian Worship* may give the appearance of favoring liturgical worship. Due to the very nature of written texts, the appearance of a strong liturgical bent is unavoidable. Nevertheless, the goal of the *Library* is not to make free churches liturgical. Rather, it is to expand the perspective of Christians across a wide range of worship traditions. In this way, liturgical resources may serve as guides and sources of inspiration and creativity for free churches, while insights from free traditions may also enrich the practices and understanding of the more liturgical communities.

In sum, the way to use *The Complete Library of Christian Worship* is as follows:

1. *Read each volume as you would read a book.* Each volume is full of biblical, historical, and theological information—a veritable feast for the curious, and for all worshipers motivated to expand their horizons.
2. *Use the alphabetical index for quick and easy access to a particular aspect of worship.* The index for each volume is as thorough as the listings for an encyclopedia.
3. *For further information and resources, order books and materials listed in the bibliography of resources.* Addresses of publishers may be found in your library's copy of *Books in Print.*
4. *Adapt the liturgical materials to the setting and worship style of your congregation.* Many of the worship materials in *The Complete Library of Christian Worship* have been intentionally published without adaptation. Most pastors, worship ministers, and worship committee members are capable of adapting the material to a style suitable to their congregations with effective results.

## 103 • INTRODUCTION TO VOLUME 2: *TWENTY CENTURIES OF CHRISTIAN WORSHIP*

This volume is presented to the reader as an invitation to dialogue with other worshiping traditions, both in the way in which they have worshiped and in the understanding that they have of worship. We hope that as you, the reader, encounter other traditions of Christian worship, your own practice and understanding of worship will be both challenged and enriched.

This volume contains six parts, each of which is designed to enrich the worship of all traditions.

Part 1, Early Christian Worship, develops the links between New Testament worship and the worship of the early centuries of the Christian church. For many, this is a period of history that is unknown. The articles in this section will demonstrate how the worship seeds laid in the New Testament era flowered in the golden age of the early church mar-

tyrs and progenitors of orthodoxy (literally, "right praise").

Part 2, A History of Christian Worship, develops the history of Christian worship from the New Testament era through the early church, the history of Eastern Orthodox worship, and the history of Catholic worship. It then pays special attention to Reformation worship and to the post-Reformation era from 1600–1900. A special feature of the post-Reformation section is its emphasis on traditions that are frequently overlooked—namely, the Holiness tradition, restoration worship, and black worship. This section concludes with a comprehensive presentation of the twentieth-century movements that have reshaped our approach to worship.

Part 3, Historic Models of Worship, does something that is available nowhere else. It presents the text of historic models of worship in every major tradition and provides along with the text a commentary describing the intent of the liturgy and the experience of the worshiping community.

Part 4 is called Theologies of Worship. It begins with an introduction to the concept of models in theology, then gives an overview of liturgical, free church, and charismatic theologies of worship, since these theologies are converging in the modern worship renewal. It then presents the theologies of worship expressed in various communities of faith. While these theologies demonstrate the variety of approaches taken toward worship, they do more. They demonstrate the incredible unity toward worship found among the churches.

Part 5 explores New Directions in Worship. It looks at contemporary statements on worship from Christian groups and concludes with the hopes and concerns of a wide array of spokespersons representing many traditions.

Part 6, Preparing for Worship Renewal, answers a fundamental question: How does one go about thinking and putting into practice the renewal of worship in the local church?

This volume invites students, pastors, music ministers, members of worship ministry teams, and all worshipers to enter into dialogue with the whole church. It speaks to the reader out of the conviction that worship and the renewal of worship must be firmly grounded in biblical tradition and intensely aware of the way biblical worship has found expression in different cultures and in a variety of settings.

# PART ONE

# Early Christian Worship

# Links Between New Testament and Early Christian Worship

*Twentieth-century scholars of the history and theology of worship have searched for links between the worship of the New Testament and the liturgies that begin to emerge around the fourth century. Resources from the first several centuries are meager, and scholars have differed as to how the continuity of liturgy evolved through this period. Evidence does suggest certain lines of development between the worship of the New Testament church and that which emerged during succeeding centuries. The entries in Part 1 explore these connections.*

*This chapter probes the relationship between New Testament and early Christian worship. Contemporary scholars have disputed the exact shape of early Christian worship and of its development from apostolic worship. However, enough evidence exists to grasp basic connections between the New Testament worshiping communities and those of the early churches.*

## 104 • THE SEARCH FOR THE ORIGINS OF CHRISTIAN WORSHIP

*It is tempting to assume that the worship practices of the earliest churches are reflected in the more developed liturgical traditions that emerged in the fourth century. A resulting view has been that Christian celebration has exhibited essentially the same shape since the apostolic period. This entry challenges that assumption and suggests that the most ancient forms of Christian worship were not uniform but quite diverse.*

The basic problem we encounter in the search for the origins of Christian worship is that evidence for liturgical practices during the first three centuries of the church's history is simply too meager, and fragmentary to enable us to paint a clear picture of it.

Liturgical historians, however, have not been content with this limitation, but have attempted to bridge the chasm of ignorance that stretches between the beginnings of Christianity and the fourth-century church. In order to do this, they have had to make a number of assumptions: (a) that we in fact know what Jewish worship in the first century was like, and therefore have a good idea of the starting point of the worship of the first Christians; (b) that early Christian communities would

have wanted to remain faithful in their liturgical customs to the traditions laid down by Jesus and the apostles, and thus would not have differed much in their ways of worship from one another or changed those practices very substantially in the course of time; (c) that the remarkable similarity that we can observe in many fourth-century Christian worship practices in widely different geographical regions is a sign that these practices go back to the very beginning of the church's history; and (d) that the pieces of evidence that we do have from the second and third centuries will all fit into the line of development that we can thereby trace from the Jewish roots to the fourth-century church. Today, however, in the light of modern scholarship, those assumptions are all open to question.

First, it is not at all clear that we *do* know what Jewish worship was like in the first century. Although there are some contemporary sources, they do not tell us all that we would like to know. Therefore Jewish scholars, like their Christian counterparts, have attempted to reconstruct first-century worship on the basis of much later sources, assuming that Judaism did not change much and that most of what they found there would faithfully reflect what Jews of earlier times had done in their worship. More recently, however, Jewish scholars have challenged this method of reconstruction in two ways. Joseph Heinemann, in the 1960s, argued that Jewish liturgy was not standardized from the first, that there was no such thing as a single original form of worship. On the contrary, a large number of different forms of prayer and ways of worshiping were practiced, and only later, beginning in the second and third centuries of the Christian era, did the rabbis gradually attempt to reduce this variety and impose an increasing uniformity on it. Furthermore, Jacob Neusner has subsequently brought into existence a new school of scholarship that views rabbinical literature in a way quite different from that of earlier generations. Formerly, scholars had regarded this later literature as an accurate record of the sayings of individual rabbis that had been carefully handed down over the centuries. Neusner, however, has argued that those who compiled the literature were not simply trying to chronicle the past but also to promote and justify their own worldview, and for that reason were inevitably selective in their approach and exercised a high measure of editorial freedom in their work. Treating this later rabbinical literature, therefore, as though it were a completely reliable guide to Jewish thought and practice in the first century is rather like attempting to reconstruct the life of the historical Jesus from the statements made in fourth-century Christian homilies. The material may certainly contain some valuable evidence for the events of Jesus' life, but it is extremely difficult to distinguish such evidence from the speculations, interpretations, and accretions that surround it.

Secondly, the supposition that early Christian communities would not have differed much in their ways of worship from one another or changed those practices very substantially in the course of time is challenged by recent New Testament scholarship. This scholarship has demonstrated that primitive Christianity was not a single uniform entity nor a single theology, but was essentially pluriform from as far back as we can trace it. Since the idea of one single apostolic faith is not confirmed by the sources, except in the broadest terms, it seems extremely unlikely that the worship of the earliest Christian communities—with all their geographic, linguistic, cultural, and theological differences—would have been essentially the same everywhere. Descriptions of worship practices in one New Testament book or in some other early Christian writing, therefore, cannot automatically be assumed to hold

true for other Christian communities of the same period, or for earlier or later generations of believers.

Thirdly, what of the remarkable similarity that we can observe in many fourth-century Christian worship practices in different parts of the world? Is that not a sign that they go back to the very beginning of the church's history? Two responses may be made to this. First, the overall similarity is by no means as great as scholars have tended to suppose. By concentrating on aspects and details that do resemble one another and by ignoring or glossing over differences, it is certainly possible to paint a harmonized picture. However, if one notes more carefully the differences that exist between practices that superficially appear to be similar, a somewhat different picture emerges. Second, there is another possible explanation for the similarities than the claim that they are proof of the great antiquity of the practices in question. While it is probable that some of the likenesses we can observe are certainly the result of continuity of practice from very early times, in other cases the standardization may well be a new development, a consequence of the changed situation of the church in the fourth century. As the church expanded, as communication—and hence awareness of differences—between different regional centers increased, and above all as orthodox Christianity tried to define itself over against what were perceived as heretical movements, any tendency to persist in what appeared to be idiosyncratic liturgical observances was likely to have been interpreted as a mark of heterodoxy, and hence would have caused local churches to scramble to bring their customs into line with others.

Recent scholarship indeed has begun to point to instances where it appears that this is exactly what happened, among them the emergence of the season of Lent, the spread of the custom of pre-baptismal exorcism and post-baptismal anointing, and the universal choice of Easter as the preferred season for baptism.

Even the classical shape of the eucharistic prayer appears to be more a fourth-century creation than the result of the preservation of a primitive pattern. We need to be more cautious, therefore, in assuming that uniformity is always a sign of antiquity and diversity a sign of later evolution; the exact opposite may frequently be the case.

Finally, there is the claim that the pieces of evidence we do have from the second and third centuries will all fit into a single line of development. This scholarly position has always had to struggle to argue its case and has often been able to do so only by conveniently ignoring, or attempting to explain away, pieces of evidence that cannot be forced to fit. For example, the prayers that occur in chapters 9 and 10 of the early church order known as the *Didachē* are very similar to Jewish meal prayers but very different from all other known eucharistic prayers of later centuries. While some scholars have ingeniously tried to explain how it was possible for later prayers to have evolved out of this very different pattern, others have rejected them from consideration altogether on the grounds that they are not eucharistic prayers at all—this conclusion being defended by the circular argument that they cannot possibly be eucharistic prayers because they do not resemble other known eucharistic prayers! Similarly, eucharistic prayers found in the apocryphal literature of the period have generally been eliminated from any serious attempts at reconstruction of the line of development because they too fail to conform to expectations of what a eucharistic prayer should look like. In other words, the theory has been give priority over the evidence itself and allowed to determine what should and should not be regarded as legitimate material for inclusion. We know that one can prove almost any hypothesis as long as one disregards anything that might constitute evidence to the contrary. When, however, the evidence is viewed more dispassionately, what is revealed suggests the evidence of quite varied forms of worship in the early church rather than one homogenous line of development.

The conclusion to be drawn from this more recent scholarship, therefore, is that we simply do not know anywhere near as much about early Christian worship as we once thought we did, nor are we ever likely to know as much as we would wish. We must learn to remain content with a measure of "liturgical agnosticism." Moreover, we must learn to allow our conclusions to be shaped by the evidence itself, rather than by some predetermined theory of how it "must have happened." We should neither give undue weight to the limited and scattered sources that we do possess, nor eliminate or play down pieces of evidence that prove inconvenient to our favorite hypothesis. Above all, we must be open to the possibility of a much wider diversity of primitive Christian liturgical practice than we have tended to recognize hitherto, and be willing to admit that the single normative pattern that some liturgical enthusiasts of today often imagine does not seem to have existed in early Christian worship.

Paul F. Bradshaw

## 105 • AN INTRODUCTION TO DAILY PRAYER

*Ancient sources reveal that a tradition of daily prayer at stated hours developed quite early in the history of the church. The practice of assembling for these times of daily prayer was derived in part from Jewish custom and is mentioned in the New Testament. Christian daily prayer evolved into two forms: monastic prayer, practiced by members of separated communities (originally of lay people), and cathedral prayer, for which members of the local congregations would assemble with their bishop and other leaders. Daily prayer included the recitation of psalms and hymns, with congregational responses. Some elements in historic Christian liturgies seem to have originated in the practice of daily prayer.*

### ——— The Tradition of Daily Prayer ———

Prayer has always belonged to all Christians, but has been perceived in some historical periods as the possession of the clergy. In the last decade, rising interest in such prayer forms as meditation and chanting has been paralleled by a growing interest in "historical" Christian prayer forms. Christian spirituality, spiritual direction, contemplative prayer, and prayer groups are no longer the domain of only religious and clergy, but of all the people of God.

In no case is this more true than that of the Liturgy of the Hours (Daily Prayer or the Daily Office), the name given to the communal celebration of particu-

*Fish Lantern. Depicted here is an ancient lantern made in the form of a fish. In the early church, the letters that spelled "fish" (ΙΧΘΥΣ—ichthus) formed an acrostic that read* Jesus Christ, God's Son our Savior. *For Christians, the fish was an emblem of profound significance, expressing salvation through Jesus Christ.*

lar times of the day in order to mark them with a Christian meaning by prayer. Its complicated history was misunderstood at some key points in liturgical renovation, resulting in prayer books better suited for private prayer than liturgy, which is always the corporate prayer of the people of God.

The liturgical tradition upon which the restored books drew was a mixture of two different types of liturgy: one monastic and one popular (known as the "cathedral" form). In order to begin the restoration of the Daily Prayer in parishes it may be helpful to understand these two different traditions of prayer services and separate them from each other.

The primary hours of Daily Prayer are morning prayer and evening prayer. Morning prayer is a prayer of thanks and praise for the new day and for salvation in Jesus, symbolized by the rising sun. Evening prayer is the Christian way of closing the day, a reflection on the good of the day and reconciliation for the wrongs done. The symbol of Jesus at evening prayer is again light, here the light of the candle that symbolizes the light of Christ dispelling all darkness.

Morning and evening prayer (also known as matins and vespers, or evensong) were part of the prayer environment of early Christians. The charge to "pray without ceasing" in the New Testament was observed in different ways among early Christians. First, and foremost, was the weekly celebration of the Eucharist on the Lord's Day, Sunday. Second was the prayer of the "domestic church," the family gathered to pray at meals and at sunset and sunrise.

The early Christians inherited this tradition of praying at the turn of the day from Judaism, adding their own Christological meanings to it. By the second century, Christians were gathering together to observe morning and evening prayer in some form. The form was elaborated in the third century and written down in great detail for us by the fourth.

What we can see is a liturgy intended in every way to be "popular"—in other words, to be celebrated by the whole church on a daily basis. The key to the celebration was to make it relevant to the time of the day (morning prayer should celebrate morning, evening prayer, evening) and to the season (Easter morning prayer should be somewhat different than Advent).

One major witness to much of the prayer detail is a woman named Egeria, a pilgrim in the late fourth century to Jerusalem and the Holy Land. She wrote back to her friends (believed to be in northern Spain or southern France):

> What I found most impressive about all this was that the psalms and antiphons they use are always appropriate, whether at night, in the early morning, at the day prayers at midday or three o'clock, or at Lucernare (evening prayer). Everything is suitable, appropriate, and relevant to what is being done (*Egeria's Travels,* ed. John Wilkinson, [Jerusalem: Ariel Publishing House, 1981], ch. 25).

The other important part of these popular prayer services was the use of standard hymns and psalms. These were repeatable components of the liturgy designed to enable all lay people to participate in them. This, along with the use of incense, candles, and processions made for a colorful, celebrative event in which anyone could participate.

Developing in the same historical period (fourth century) was another kind of daily prayer, monastic prayer. In the deserts of Egypt, Syria, and Palestine, the growing monastic movement gave rise to another type of morning and evening celebration. Monastic prayer can be more properly thought of as a service of prayer and meditation on Scripture than as liturgy. The primary reason is that liturgy implies the whole church of God gathered together to pray (including clergy), and the monastic movement in its beginnings was a lay movement.

The monastic service was designed for a stable community in which there were fewer distinct roles, and in which silence played a major part. The use of the Psalms was not so much a means to praise God (as in the popular office) but a way of listening to the voice of God. The Psalms were therefore recited by one person while everyone listened in silence. There was no concern for specific times of day. The Psalter was simply read from beginning to end in the course of a week. There was also little regard for the liturgical year; this was not the focus of the monastic course of prayer.

Eventually it was the general history of the church that determined how these two types of prayer evolved. The monastic movement became urban when many monks moved into the cities from the desert. Many city churches became monastic centers where the cathedral or popular office became a combination of monastic and popular elements. The outcome of this merging of ideas was the dominance of the monastic style. Along with this, the rise of clergy in the monastic movement made this dominant style the domain primarily of clergy and monks. The final step in this de-evolution of popular daily prayer was the trend toward private recitation, originally a spoken or non-choral celebration of morning and evening prayer that became solo— truly private.

Lizette Larson-Miller[1]

## Evidence for the Origin of Daily Prayer

**Jewish Hours of Prayer.** In the Temple at Jerusalem sacrifices were normally offered only twice each day, in the morning and in the evening, with additional offerings being made on Sabbaths and festivals. In the case of ordinary Jews not connected with the temple cult, however, there is evidence of some variety in prayer times. While all Jews would have offered prayer at mealtimes, some also recited the Sh<sup>e</sup>ma‘ (Deut. 6:4-9; 11:13-21; Num. 15:37-41) twice a day, and others apparently followed a custom of praying three times a day (cf. Dan. 6:10). By the first century the middle of these times, probably originally observed at noon, had become associated—at least by some—with the hour of the evening sacrifice in the temple, the ninth hour of the day, which is around 3 P.M. in our reckoning (Acts 3:1). These prayers would have been said both by individuals on their own and by groups gathering together at home or in the synagogue. In the Jewish community at Qumran, more time seems to have been devoted to prayer, with sections of the community taking turns to maintain a vigil of meditation on God's law throughout each night.

The Jewish tradition of prayer centers around the temple, the synagogue, and the home. The following texts evidence the practice of prayer throughout the day and confirm the continued involvement of Jesus and the early Christians in the Jewish practice of daily prayer.

**Jesus.** "Very early in the morning, while it was still dark, Jesus got up, left the house and went off to a solitary place, where he prayed" (Mark 1:35). "After he had dismissed them, he went up on a mountainside by himself to pray. When evening came, he was there alone" (Matt. 14:23; see also Mark 6:46; John 6:15; Luke 6:12).

**The Disciples.** The third hour: "These men are not drunk, as you suppose. It is only nine in the morn-

ing!" (Acts 2:15). The sixth hour: "About noon the following day as they . . . were approaching the city, Peter went up on the roof to pray" (Acts 10:9). The ninth hour: "Cornelius answered: 'Four days ago I was in my house praying at this hour, at three in the afternoon'" (Acts 10:30, see also Acts 10:3; 3:1). Evening prayer: "About midnight Paul and Silas were praying and singing hymns to God, and the other prisoners were listening to them" (Acts 16:25).

**Early Christians.** "Every day they continued to meet together in the temple courts. They broke bread in their homes and ate together with glad and sincere hearts" (Acts 2:46). "When he had led them out to the vicinity of Bethany, he lifted up his hands and blessed them. While he was blessing them, he left them and was taken up into heaven. Then they worshiped him and returned to Jerusalem with great joy. And they stayed continually at the temple, praising God" (Luke 24:50-53).

**Daily Prayer in the First Three Centuries.** The early Christians continued the Jewish practice of praying at mealtimes and at set hours of the day. The _Didachē,_ a primitive Christian manual of instruction, prescribes prayer three times a day; Clement of Alexandria and Origen in the third century refer to a similar custom in Egypt, as well as to prayer in the night. At the same period in North Africa, however, Tertullian and Cyprian describe a more extensive pattern of daily prayer. They believe that the only absolute apostolic injunction is to "pray without ceasing" (1 Thess. 5:17, NRSV), but they both recommend that, in order to fulfill this, Christians should pray no less than five times a day—in the morning, at the third, sixth, and ninth hours (about 9 A.M., noon, and 3 P.M.), and in the evening—and should also pray again in the middle of the night. Their evidence is largely supported by the ancient church order known as the _Apostolic Tradition,_ although it is difficult to know how much of this part of the document really does go back to the third century.

Psalms were apparently not commonly used at these times of prayer; Tertullian says that the more assiduous included those psalms featuring the "Alleluia" response—thereby implying that the rest did not. Instead they were generally sung at meals, and especially at the _agapē,_ where various individuals sang either a hymn they had composed or one of the canonical psalms to the others, who responded to each verse with an 'Alleluia' refrain (see also 1 Cor.

14:26; Eph. 5:18-20; Col. 3:16). Bible reading would have been a part of the daily devotions of those few Christians wealthy enough to own copies of the Scriptures, but for the majority this activity would have been restricted to catechetical classes and occasional services of the Word during the week. Below is an example from the early third century written by Hippolytus in *The Apostolic Tradition*:

Let every faithful man and woman, when they have risen from sleep in the morning, before they touch any work at all, wash their hands and pray to God, and so go to their work. But if instruction in the word of God is given, each one should choose to go to that place, reckoning in his heart that it is God whom he hears in the instructor.

For he who prays in the church will be able to pass by the wickedness of the day. He who is pious should think it is a great evil if he does not go to the place where instruction is given, and especially if he can read, or if a teacher comes. Let none of you be late in the church, the place where teaching is given. Then it shall be given to the speaker to say what is useful to each one; you will hear things which you do not think of, and profit from things which the Holy Spirit will give you through the instructor. In this way your faith will be strengthened about the things you will have heard. You will also be told in that place what you ought to do at home. Therefore let each one be diligent in coming to the church, the place where the Holy Spirit flourishes. If there is a day when there is no instruction, let each one, when he is at home, take up a holy book and read in it sufficiently what seemest to him to bring profit.

And if you are at home, pray at the third hour and bless God. But if you are somewhere else at that moment, pray to God in your heart. For at that hour Christ was nailed to the tree. For this reason also in the Old (Testament) the Law prescribed that the shewbread should be offered continually as a type of the body and blood of Christ; and the slaughter of the lamb without reason is this type of the perfect lamb. For Christ is the shepherd, and also the bread which came down from heaven.

Pray likewise at the time of the sixth hour. For when Christ was nailed to the wood of the cross, the day was divided, and darkness fell. And so at that hour let them pray a powerful prayer, imitating the voice of him who prayed and made all creation dark for the unbelieving Jews.

And at the ninth hour let them pray also a great prayer and a great blessing, to know the way in which the soul of the righteous blesses God who does not lie, who remembered his saints and sent the word to give them light. For at that hour Christ was pierced in his side and poured out water and blood; giving light to the rest of the time of the day, he brought it to evening. Then, in beginning to sleep and making the beginning of another day, he fulfilled the type of the resurrection.

Pray before your body rests on the bed. Rise about midnight, wash your hands with water, and pray. If your wife is present also, pray both together; if she is not yet among the faithful, go apart into another room and pray, and go back to bed again. Do not be lazy about praying. He who is bound in the marriage-bond is not defiled.

Those who have washed have no need to wash again, for they are clean. By signing yourself with moist breath and catching your spittle in your hand, your body is sanctified down to your feet. For when (prayer) is offered with a believing heart as though from the font, the gift of the Spirit and the sprinkling of baptism sanctify him who believes. Therefore it is necessary to pray at this hour.

For the elders who gave us the tradition taught us that at that hour all creation is still for a moment, to praise the Lord; stars, trees, waters stop for an instant, and all the host of angels (which) ministers to him praises God with the souls of the righteous in this hour. That is why believers should take good care to pray at this hour.

Bearing witness to this, the Lord says thus, "Lo, about midnight a shout was made of men saying, Lo, the bridegroom comes; rise to meet him." And he goes on saying, "Watch, therefore, for you know not at what hour he comes."

And likewise rise about cockcrow, and pray. For at that hour, as the cock crew, the children of Israel denied Christ, whom we know by faith, our eyes looking towards that day in the hope of eternal light at the resurrection of the dead.

And if you act so, all you faithful, and remember these things, and teach them in your turn, and encourage the catechumens, you will not be able to be tempted or to perish, since you have Christ always in memory.

(Geoffrey J. Cuming, ed., *Hippolytus: A Text for Students* [Bramcote, Notts., U.K.: Grove Books, 1976], 29–31.)

## Cathedral Prayer East and West

After the conversion of Constantine in the early fourth century, the daily public celebration of morning and evening prayer became a regular practice in major towns and cities. A few places, including

Jerusalem, which had become a great pilgrimage center, had more frequent services each day, and it was hoped everywhere that individuals and families might still continue to pray at the other hours of the day that had been observed by Christians in the third century, but only the exceptionally pious appear to have done so.

Because the clergy and people would generally gather under the presidency of their bishop for these daily liturgies, they are usually referred to by scholars as "cathedral" offices. They consisted principally of praise and intercession. The praise was expressed in selected psalms and canticles—noncanonical compositions as well as biblical songs—usually unchanging from day to day, except for Sundays and festivals. Thus, for example, Psalms 148–150 became established as the universal morning song of praise, while the hymn "Hail, Gladdening Light" was a common evening canticle, generally accompanying a ritual lighting of the lamp (Lucernarium).

Scripture reading was not a part of these daily offices, but was still generally restricted to catechetical classes and occasional services of the Word during the week, as it had been in the third century, and to vigil services, which seem to be a new development. We have descriptions of an early morning vigil service on Sundays, which seems to have originated in Jerusalem as a weekly commemoration of the Resurrection and included the gospel account of the death and resurrection of Jesus, and also of an all-night vigil on Fridays composed of psalms and Bible readings. The latter, however, may be a result of monastic influence.

An excellent description of these services is found in the writings of Egeria, who in a visit to Jerusalem, reported them thus:

Loving sisters, I am sure it will interest you to know about the daily services they have in the holy places, and I must tell you about them. All the doors of the Anastasis are opened before cock-crow each day, and the "monazontes and parthenae," as they call them here, come in, and also some laymen and women, at least those who are willing to wake at such an early hour. From then until daybreak they join in singing the refrains to the hymns, psalms, and antiphons. There is a prayer between each of the hymns, since there are two or three presbyters and deacons each day by rota, who are there with the monazontes and say the prayers between all the hymns and antiphons.

As soon as dawn comes, they start the morning hymns, and the bishop with his clergy comes and joins them. He goes straight into the cave, and inside the screen he first says the Prayer for All (mentioning any names he wishes) and blesses the catechumens, and then another prayer and blesses the faithful. Then he comes outside the screen, and everyone comes up to kiss his hand. He blesses them one by one, and goes out, and by the time the dismissal takes place it is already day.

Again at mid-day everyone comes into the Anastasis and says psalms and antiphons until a message is sent to the bishop. Again he enters, and, without taking his seat, goes straight inside the screen in the Anastasis (which is to say into the cave where he went in the early morning), and again, after a prayer, he blesses the faithful and comes outside the screen, and again they come to kiss his hand.

At three o'clock they do once more what they did at mid-day, but at four o'clock they have Lychnion, as they call it, or in our language, Lucernare. All the people congregate once more in the Anastasis, and the lamps and candles are all lit, which makes it very bright. The fire is brought not from outside, but from the cave—inside the screen—where a lamp is always burning night and day. For some time they have the Lucernare psalms and antiphons; then they send for the bishop, who enters and sits in the chief seat. The presbyters also come and sit in their places, and the hymns and antiphons go on. Then, when they have finished singing everything which is appointed, the bishop rises and goes in front of the screen (i.e., the cave). One of the deacons makes the normal commemoration of individuals, and each time he mentions a name a large group of boys responds _Kyrie eleison_ (in our language, "Lord, have mercy"). Their voices are very loud. As soon as the deacon has done his part, the bishop says a prayer and prays the Prayer for All. Up to this point the faithful and the catechumens are praying together, but now the deacon calls every catechumen to stand where he is and bow his head, and the bishop says the blessing over the catechumens from his place. There is another prayer, after which the deacon calls for all the faithful to bow their heads, and the bishop says the blessing over the faithful from his place. Thus the dismissal takes place at the Anastasis, and they all come up one by one to kiss the bishop's hand.

Then, singing hymns, they take the bishop from the Anastasis to the Cross, and everyone goes with him. On arrival he says one prayer and blesses the catechumens, then another and blesses the faithful. Then again the bishop and all the people go behind the cross, and do there what they did before the cross, and in both places they come to kiss the bishop's hand, as they did in many candles in front of the Anastasis, and also before and behind the cross. By the end of all this it is dusk. So there are the services held every weekday at the cross and at the Anastasis.

(J. Wilkerson, *Egeria's Travels* [London: SPCK, 1971], ch. 24)

## ———— Monastic Prayers East and West

There had always been some Christians whose spirituality was not satisfied with frequent times of prayer during the day but who wished to fulfill more literally the injunction to "pray without ceasing." This attitude was inherited by the Egyptian desert fathers of the fourth century, whose aim was to maintain as near as possible a ceaseless vigil of meditation, punctuated only by the minimal interruption for food and sleep. As monastic communities proper emerged in Egypt, however, more formalized rules of prayer established, which, while expecting the monk to persevere in praying throughout his waking hours, prescribed two particular occasions of prayer each day, on rising in the morning and before retiring to bed at night. John Cassian's description captures the spirit of these daily devotions, even if he appears to have mingled together the practices of Upper Egypt with the somewhat different customs of Lower Egypt. As can be seen, their basic purpose was not praise and intercession, but silent meditation on the Word of God heard in the Psalms and/or Scripture readings.

Monastic communities in other parts of the East and West followed rather different customs. They tended to preserve the times of prayer formerly observed by all Christians in the third century—morning, third, sixth, and ninth hours, evening, and during the night—and sometimes added further hours to these, often including a weekly all-night vigil. But, influenced by the Egyptian desert fathers, the content of all these services was generally meditation on psalms and Bible readings.

Below is an example of monastic prayer as seen in the writings of John Cassian:

One rose up in the midst to chant the Psalms to the Lord. And while they were all sitting (as is still the custom in Egypt), with their minds intently fixed on the words of the chanter, when he had sung eleven Psalms, separated by prayers introduced between them, verse after verse being evenly enunciated, he

finished the twelfth with a response of Alleluia, and then, by his sudden disappearance from the eyes of all, put an end at once to their discussion and their service.

Whereupon the venerable assembly of the Fathers understood that by divine providence a general rule had been fixed for the congregations of the brethren through the angel's direction, and so decreed that this number should be preserved both in their evening and in their nocturnal services; and when they added to these two lessons, one from the Old and one from the New Testament, they added them simply as extras and of their own appointment, only for those who liked, and who were eager to gain by constant study a mind well stored with Holy Scripture. But on Saturday and Sunday they read them both from the New Testament; viz., one from the Epistles or the Acts of the Apostles, and one from the Gospel. And this also those do whose concern is the reading and the recollection of the Scriptures, from Easter to Whitsuntide [Pentecost].

These aforesaid prayers, then, they begin and finish in such a way that when the psalm is ended they do not hurry at once to kneel down, as some of us do in this country. . . . Among them, therefore it is not so, but before they bend their knees they pray for a few moments and while they are standing up spend the greater part of the time in prayer. And so after this, for the briefest space of time, they prostrate themselves to the ground, as if but adoring the divine mercy, and as soon as possible rise up, and again standing erect with outspread hands—just as they had been standing to pray before—remain with thoughts intent upon their prayers. . . . But when he who is to "collect" the prayer rises from the ground they all start up at once, so that no one would venture to bend the knee before he bows down, nor to delay when he has risen from the ground, lest it should be thought that he has offered his own prayer independently instead of following the leader to the close.

That practice too which we have observed in this country—viz., that while one sings to the end of the psalm, all standing up sing together with a loud voice, "Glory be to the Father and to the Son and to the Holy Ghost"—we have never heard anywhere throughout the East, but there, while all keep silence when the psalm is finished, the prayer that follows is offered up by the singer. But with this hymn in honor of the Trinity only the whole psalmody is usually ended . . .

When, then, they meet together to celebrate the aforementioned rites, which they term synaxes, they are all so perfectly silent that, though so large a number of the brethren is assembled together, you would not think a single person was present except the one who stands up and chants the psalm in the midst; and especially is this the case when the prayer is completed, for then there is no spitting, no clearing of the throat, or noise of coughing, no sleepy yawning with open mouths, and gasping, and no groans or sighs are uttered, likely to distract those standing near. No voice is heard save that of the priest concluding the prayer. . . . They think it best for the prayers to be short and offered up very frequently . . .

And, therefore, they do not even attempt to finish the psalms, which they sing in the service, by an unbroken and continuous recitation. But they repeat them separately and bit by bit, divided into two or three sections, according to the number of verses, with prayers in between. For they do not care about the quantity of verses, but about the intelligence of the mind, aiming with all their might at this: "I will sing with the spirit: I will sing also with the understanding." And so they consider it better for ten verses to be sung with understanding and thought than for a whole psalm to be poured forth with a bewildered mind . . .

. . . except Vespers and Nocturns, there are no public services among them during the day except on Saturday and Sunday, when they meet together at the third hour for the purpose of holy communion.

(E. C. S. Gibson, ed., "The Twelve Books of John Cassian on the Institutes of the Coenobia," in *The Nicene and Post-Nicene Fathers*, series 2, vol. 11 [Grand Rapids: Eerdmans, 1964], 207–213.)

Paul Bradshaw

## 106 ✦ THE INFLUENCE OF THE SYNAGOGUE ON EARLY CHRISTIAN WORSHIP

*The New Testament records that Jesus and his disciples, as well as early Christian preachers such as Paul and Barnabas, attended the synagogue assemblies. The true influence of the synagogue on early Christian worship, however, is difficult to assess. Contacts between Christians and Jews continued up to the fourth century; thus, in the post–New Testament period Jewish influence can be seen in the development of Christian prayer and the Christian calendar.*

That Jewish worship influenced ancient Christian liturgy is widely assumed in contemporary liturgical studies. However, the scholarly landscape has shifted enormously in the years since the publication of W. O. E. Oesterley's *The Jewish Background of the Christian Liturgy* (Oxford: Clarendon Press, 1925) and C. W. Dugmore's *The Influence of the Synagogue Upon the Divine Office* (London: Humphrey Milford, 1944). Biblical and historical studies since the Second World War have demonstrated the diversity and complexity of first-century Judaism. Therefore, contemporary scholars are hesitant to speak with Dugmore and Oesterley's certainty about the structure and content of Jewish worship in the first century, when the Jewish influence upon the liturgical life of the nascent Christian movement would have been most direct. We can no longer say that there was in first-century Judaism a standard synagogue that influenced Christian worship; rather, Christian worship emerged within the context of a variety of Judaisms, each with its own developing liturgical traditions.

Even after the separation of the Christian movement from Judaism, the relationship between Christian communities and their Jewish neighbors was complex and varied greatly according to geographical locale. Some fourth-century Christians borrowed prayers that appear to be Jewish in origin, perhaps as a result of the ongoing contact between Christians and Jews in some areas.

### — First Century Synagogue Influence —

**The New Testament Period.** The New Testament records the traditions of Jesus' attendance at synagogue services, and the disciples' frequenting the temple after the Resurrection (cf. Mark 1:21, 6:2, and parallels; Matt. 4:23 and parallels; Matt. 9:35; Luke 4:15-16; 6:6, and parallels; Luke 13:10-27; John 6:59; 18:20; Acts 2:42, 46-47). We know little, however, about the content of these liturgical services in which Jesus and his disciples participated, because the evidence for the content of Jewish worship before 70 C.E. is scant. The most that we can say is that synagogue worship in the first century contained readings from the Torah and prophets, the *Shēmaʿ*; and a form (varying from synagogue to synagogue) of the *Tᵉfillah,* or "prayer," containing a variable number of sections. It is difficult, therefore, to determine the extent to which Jewish liturgical traditions influenced the development of Christian worship. How the liturgical practices of the earliest Jewish disciples carried over into the liturgical life of the earliest Christian communities is largely unknown.

**The Eucharist and Its Roots in Jewish Prayer.** The primitive Christian Eucharist provides a good example of the ambiguity involved in determining the Jewish roots of Christian worship. While the Gospels and Paul clearly place the Last Supper in the context of the Passover (whether or not the Last Supper actually was the Passover meal), it is impossible to know the extent to which first-century Jewish Passover rituals contributed to the structure of the first-century Eucharist. The prayers of *Didachē* 9 and 10 (see below) resemble most closely Jewish table prayers (which were also used at the Passover meal). In the next glimpse we get of Christian weekly worship (in the *First Apology* of Justin Martyr, mid-second century), the Eucharist had acquired a "shape" that was to become standard: a service of readings, preaching, and prayer followed by a ritual meal (Justin, *Apology I* 67). While most scholars today recognize the Jewish roots of these two parts of the Sunday service, no evidence exists that links the readings and meal of the Eucharist to specific Jewish liturgical texts. The most that we can say is that both Jews and Christians read Scripture at their services, and that both Jews and Christians had traditions of prayer at their sacred meals.

**The *Didachē*.** The *Didachē*, or *Teaching of the Twelve Apostles,* reached its final form by the end of the first century, although portions of this church order may be as old as the 50s or 60s of the first century C.E. Of all first-century sources, the *Didachē* contains the clearest example of some early Christian liturgical practice related to Jewish worship. Chapters 9 and 10 describe a ritual meal that consists of: (a) a prayer over cup and bread (chapter 9); (b) a meal; and (c) a thanksgiving after the meal (chapter 10). The thanksgiving after the meal of *Didachē 10* is very similar in content and structure to the Jewish blessing after the meal, or *Birkat hammazon,* and appears to be a Christian version of that prayer, a form of which appears as early as *Jubilees* 22 (second century B.C.E.).

**Thanksgiving or Blessing?** *Didachē 10* points to the predilection of Christian prayer for thanksgiving (*todah*) rather than blessing (*bērakah*), which by the second century became the usual form of Jewish prayer. The extent to which the Christian thanksgiving form of prayer is rooted in other first-century Jewish forms of prayer (such as those attested at Qumran) continues to be debated. However, it would be wrong to press too far this distinction

between the Christian "thanksgiving" and the Jewish "blessing": prayers found in the second and third century apocryphal "acts" (i.e., the *Acts of John, Acts of Paul, Acts of Peter,* and *Acts of Thomas*) are often couched in both terms.

Reproduced below are two "trajectories" of the Jewish blessing after meals: a Christian text (*Didachē 10*) dating anywhere from 50 to 100 C.E.; and a version of the prayer from a very early Jewish prayer book, the tenth-century *Siddur Rav Saadya.* Although these two texts are separated by nine centuries, they show a striking similarity in themes. Note that the prayer for Jerusalem in *Rav Saadya* dates from after 70 C.E.

The New Testament records that Jesus said a blessing before he miraculously fed multitudes of people (Mark 6:41; Matt. 14:18; Luke 9:16; Mark 8:6-7; Matt. 15:36; John 6:11). The narratives of the Last Supper (Mark 14:22-25; Matt. 26:26-29; Luke 22:15-20; 1 Cor. 11:23-26) also record that Jesus said a blessing at the breaking of bread, and the story of the post-resurrection appearance to the disciples at Emmaus mentions Jesus' saying the blessing at the beginning of the meal (Luke 24:30, 35). Given this wide attestation in the tradition to Jesus' use of the Jewish liturgical practice of blessing God at meals, it is not unlikely that the great prayer of thanksgiving at the Eucharist derives to some extent from forms of the Jewish blessing before and after meals familiar to Jesus and his disciples.

***Didachē 10.*** And after you have had your fill, give thanks thus:

> We give thanks to you, holy Father, for your holy name which you have enshrined in our hearts, and for the knowledge and faith and immortality which you made known to us through your child Jesus; glory to you for evermore.

> You, Lord Almighty, created all things for the sake of your name and gave food and drink to men for their enjoyment, that they might give you thanks; but to us you have granted spiritual food and drink for eternal life through your child Jesus.

> Above all we give you thanks because you are mighty; glory to you for evermore. *Amen.*

> Remember, Lord, your church, to deliver it from all evil and to perfect it in your love, and bring it together from the four winds, now sanctified, into your kingdom which you have prepared for

it; for yours are the power and the glory for ever-more. *Amen.*

**Rav Saadya.** *Blessing of him who nourishes*

Blessed are you, Lord our God, King of the universe, for you nourish us and the whole world with goodness, grace, kindness and mercy. Blessed are you, Lord, for you nourish the universe.

*Blessing for the earth*

Blessed are you, Lord our God, King of the universe, for you nourish us and the whole world with goodness, grace, kindness and mercy. Blessed are you, Lord, for you nourish the universe.

*Blessing for the earth*

We will give thanks to you, Lord our God, because you have given us for your inheritance a desirable land, good and wide, the covenant and law, life and food. And for all these things we give you thanks and bless your name for ever and beyond. Blessed are you, Lord our God, for the earth and for food.

*Blessing for Jerusalem*

Have mercy, Lord our God, on us your people Israel, and your city Jerusalem, on your sanctuary and your dwelling-place, on Zion, the habitation of your glory, and the great and holy house over which your name is invoked. Restore the kingdom of the house of David to its place in our days, and speedily build Jerusalem.

On the feast of Passover, this embolism follows in the Jewish prayers:

Our God and God of our fathers, may three arise in your sight, and come, and be present, and be regarded, and be pleasing, and be heard, and be visited, and be remembered our remembrance and our visitation, and the remembrance of our fathers, and the remembrance of the Messiah, the son of your servant David, and the remembrance of Jerusalem, the city of your holiness, and the remembrance of all your people, the house of Israel; for escape, for prosperity, for grace, and for loving kindness and mercy, for life and for peace, on this day of the Feast of Unleavened Bread. Remember us on this day, Lord our God, for prosperity, and visit us on it for blessing, and save us on it for life. And by the word of salvation and mercy spare us, and grant us grace, and have mercy on us, and save us: for our eyes look to you, for you, O God, are a gracious and merciful king.
Blessed are you, Lord, for you build Jerusalem. Amen.

*Blessing of the good and beneficent*

Blessed are you, Lord our God, King of the universe, God, our father, our king, our creator, our redeemer, good and beneficent king, who day by day is concerned to benefit us in many ways, and himself will increase for us for ever in grace and kindness and spirit and mercy and every good thing.

## Continuing Influence of the Synagogue on Christian Worship

After the first century, Christian liturgy continued to develop in a variety of trajectories largely independent of those followed by post–first century Jewish worship. With the destruction of the Jerusalem temple in 70 C.E. and the formal separation, toward the end of the first century, of the Christian movement from Judaism, the links between the two were never again as close as they were formerly. Yet contact between Christians and Jews continued, as evidenced by the fourth-century church councils that legislated against Christian attendance at Jewish worship (cf. Council of Laodicea, canons 29, 37, 38; *Apostolic Canons* 70–71: see *Apostolic Constitutions* VIII.47.7–71). In addition, the eight homilies against the Jews preached by John Chrysostom in Antioch in 386 and 387 also suggest that Christians and Jews were worshiping together in that city.

**The Christian Calendar.** The Quartodeciman controversy of the second century, so-called for the observance of Passover on the Jewish date 14 Nisan (described by Eusebius, *Ecclesiastical History* V. 23–24), indirectly attests to Jewish influence upon the Christian calendar. The issue at stake in Quartodeciman practice (reflected, for example, in the second-century *Epistula Apostolorum*) was whether or not Easter should be celebrated at the same time as the Jewish Passover (which may very well have been the more ancient practice). Some have also suggested that the Christian appropriation of Wednesday and Friday as special liturgical days (cf. *Didachē* 8) may be related to an Essene solar calendar that highlighted those particular days of the week.

**Christian Borrowing of Jewish Prayers.** The *Apostolic Constitutions,* a church order compiled in the environs of Antioch around the year 380, contains a collection of prayers of Hellenistic Jewish origin on a variety of topics (VII, 33–38). The existence of these prayers in the *Apostolic Constitutions* points to the ongoing appropriation of Jewish liturgical forms by at least one Christian community after the first century.

## Conclusions

The decades before the fall of Jerusalem in 70 C.E. saw the greatest influence of Jewish worship upon Christian liturgy. After the destruction of the temple and the emergence of rabbinic Judaism at the end of the first century, Christian and Jewish worship continued to develop independently. Contact between Christians and Jews continued in subsequent centuries, but there is little evidence for any ongoing Jewish influences upon Christian worship after the formative period of the first century.

We should not expect direct verbal or structural parallels between first-century Jewish and Christian worship. In the first century, both liturgical traditions were diverse, not yet committed to writing, and in flux. To be sure, first-century Christians and Jews drew from a fund of liturgical structures, terminology, and imagery that each group used in increasingly divergent ways in subsequent centuries. Therefore, the Christian and Jewish liturgical traditions that emerged after the first century were more nearly cousins than siblings, descendants of liturgical ancestors that in the first century may have been closer relatives.

Grant Sperry-White

## 107 • THE TRIPARTITE STRUCTURE OF PRAYER AND THE TRINITARIAN FORMULARY

*Jewish table prayer, thought by some historians of liturgy to be the antecedent of the early Christian eucharistic prayer, evidences a threefold pattern of praise, remembrance, and petition. In a general way this sequence corresponds to the formula "Father, Son, and Holy Spirit" in Christian worship. Thus, liturgical practice may have helped to shape classical Christian Trinitarianism.*

In recent years, more and more attention has been given to three issues that bear upon the understanding of the classic eucharistic prayers. First, there has

been a developing concern to discover the possible relationships, both of continuity and change, between Jewish worship practices and prayers and the worship and prayers of early Christianity. Second, there has been a growing interest in the way in which prayers are structured. Thus, it has been observed by many scholars, both Jewish and Christian, that traditional prayers usually embody a pattern or sequence of themes and emphases. Third, throughout these studies there has been an acknowledgment that praying shapes believing. An example of this dynamic is the way in which the classical doctrine of the Trinity evolved gradually as Christians began to pray *to* the Father, *through* the Son, and *in* the Spirit.

## Parallel Prayers in Jewish and Early Christian Tradition

It is clear from the New Testament that Jesus and all of his disciples were Jews accustomed to the beliefs and practices of their time. Luke 2:41 tells that Jesus and his parents went to Jerusalem for the feast of Passover "according to custom." And at Nazareth, according to Luke 4:16, "on the Sabbath day [Jesus] went into the synagogue, as was his custom."

Throughout the New Testament there are numerous and quite significant evidences of the dependence of early Christianity upon its religious background in Judaism. An outstanding example is the Lord's Prayer, as it appears in Matthew 6:9-15 and Luke 11:2-4. The themes of "hallowing" God's name and asking for the coming of God's kingdom appear to be important in the Jewish piety of New Testament times. Although the text we now have of the Jewish *Kaddish* comes from much later compilations, it begins with words which are remarkably similar to those of the Lord's Prayer:

> Exalted and hallowed be His great Name
> in the world which He created
> according to His will.
> May He establish His kingdom. . . .

Here and elsewhere the parallels between the prayers of Jews and Christians are striking.

Furthermore, the language and contents of the *Didachē,* which is perhaps the earliest manual of Christian guidance for living and church order, indicate that early Christianity was developing in paths that may have been somewhat similar to those suggested in the *Mishnah* as characteristic of the Judaism of the first century. Surely this is true insofar as both of these religious guidebooks emphasize the importance of meals as occasions for the blessing or thanking of God. Meals, for Christians and Jews, are religious events, with solemn meaning.

## The Structure of Jewish and Christian Prayers

More recently, however, the discussion has shifted. There is a growing recognition that, while questions of style and content remain important, there is much to be learned from the *structures* of prayers. Several scholars are now fruitfully studying the patterns of the prayers found in the Bible, the synagogue, and the church. A splendid example of this approach is Moshe Greenberg's recent study of *Biblical Prose Prayer* (Berkeley: University of California Press, 1983), which recognizes that such ordinary human acts as petitioning, confessing, and expressing gratitude have their own patterns. These "patterns remain constant throughout the Scriptures, regardless of source, because they arise immediately and naturally from life." Among others who have done significant structural studies of Jewish and Christian prayer are Joseph Heinemann, Louis Ligier, and Thomas Talley.

One of the significant results of these structural studies is the discovery of a classic example of a Jewish table prayer in the Book of Jubilees 22:6-9. Jubilees was written sometime before 100 B.C., and it gives evidence of what may have been a typical table blessing from the time of the Maccabees. It attributes the prayer to Abraham, and its structure is formed by the acts of praising, remembering, and asking.

[praising]
And he ate and drank, and he blessed the Most High God, who created heaven and earth, who made all the good things on the earth, and gave them to the sons of men so that they might eat and drink and bless their creator.

[remembering]
And now, *he said,* I give thee thanks, my God, because thou hast let me see this day: behold, I am a hundred and seventy-five years old, an old man with a long life-span, and I have prospered all my days. The enemy's sword has never at any time prevailed against me, nor against my children.

[asking]
My God, may thy mercy and thy peace be upon thy servant, and upon his descendants, that they may be thee a chosen nation and a possession out of all the nations of the earth, now and in every generation on the earth for evermore.

## The Tripartite Pattern of Prayer

This fundamental structure continues in the traditional Jewish table blessings, the date of whose origin remains unknown, but which remain in use (with only minor alterations) until this day. The three earlier benedictions (and responses) of the *birkat hammazon* may be reconstructed as follows:

[praising]
*Blessed are you,* Lord our God, King of the universe, for you nourish us and the whole world with goodness, grace, kindness and mercy. *Blessed are you,* Lord, for you nourish the universe.

[remembering]
*We will give thanks to you,* Lord our God, because you have given us for our inheritance a desirable land, good and wide, the covenant and the law, life and food. And for all these things we give you thanks and bless your name for ever and beyond. *Blessed are you,* Lord our God, for the earth and for food.

[asking]
*Have mercy, Lord* our God, on us your people Israel, and your city Jerusalem, on your sanctuary and your dwelling-place, on Zion, the habitation of your glory, and the great and holy house over which your name is invoked. Restore the kingdom of the house of David to its place in our days, and speedily build Jerusalem. *Blessed are you,* Lord, for you build Jerusalem. *Amen.*

The tripartite structure is clear. And, as Joseph Heinemann comments, here, and elsewhere in Judaism, we find juxtaposed the three basic motifs of creation, revelation, and redemption, with emphasis upon the beginning of history, the giving of the Torah as the turning point, and the move towards the goal of history (cf. Joseph Heinemann, ed. *Literature of the Synagogue* [New York: Behrman House, 1975] and his *Prayer in the Talmud: Forms and Patterns* [Hawthorne, N.Y.: Walter de Gruyter, 1977]).

It is this tripartite structure that appears with vigor and clarity in the classic eucharistic prayer which may have been composed in the third century in the *Apostolic Tradition* of Hippolytus. In that prayer the structure begins, analogously, with thanks to the God who made all things, then recounts the story of Jesus, and finally asks for the sending of the Holy Spirit. As a result, one can see a liturgical impulse at work in the shaping of the classical Trinitarian formulary. The sequence "Father, Son, Holy Spirit," although found in Matthew 28:19, is not that of some other "Trinitarian" passages such as 1 Corinthians 12:4-6, 2 Corinthians 13:14, or Ephesians 4:4-6. The tripartite structure of prayer may have contributed to the establishment of the classical Trinitarian sequence.

John E. Burkhart

## 108 • Ordination and Worship Leadership in the Early Church

*Ordination is rooted in the need for order within the Christian community. It tends both to reflect and to shape the church's life and witness amid changing historical circumstances. An important development in the post–New Testament period was the emergence of a three-office structure for ordained ministry (bishop, presbyter, deacon) and the subsequent transformation of that structure into a more authoritarian one as the church came to assume a public role in a wider cultural context.*

### Emergence of a Threefold Office Structure in the Early Church

The earliest Christian communities had no common, universal structure for leadership. Though most, if not all, had been formed in response to the preaching of itinerant apostles and prophets, the cultural contexts in which those churches were planted helped produce a variety of patterns for local leadership, some informed by Jewish models, others by models derived from Greco-Roman society. Immersed as these early churches were in the apocalyptic worldview of early apostolic preaching, such communities assumed that Jesus' return was imminent. As a result, there was little, if any, urgency to develop norms for office and ordination that would assure continuity in the church's organizational leadership.

Concern for developing reproducible leadership models—less particular, more universal models—could not emerge until the church as seen in the

*Orders in the Early Church. An adaptation of a miniature from the ninth century that portrays the developed orders of the church. At the top oval in the center is the bishop flanked on his left by a priest and on his right by a deacon. On the bottom from left to right is the beadle with his keys, the reader with his book, a subdeacon with the chalice and a flask for pouring wine or water, the exorcist with a book and ball, and the acolyte with a candle. Adapted from an illustration in a sacramentary of the ninth century, preserved in the town library of Autun.*

later Gospels and Epistles began to realize the need for securing a historical future. By the end of the New Testament era, a number of factors including the death of the original apostolic witnesses, the demise of the church in Jerusalem, and the delay of the Parousia, forced the church to adopt forms of church order in which the authenticity of apostolic teaching could be maintained.

### Emergence of a Threefold Office Structure

Earlier patterns of ministry had relied upon both the teaching authority of itinerant apostles, charismatic prophets and evangelists, and the organizational and the leadership authority of diverse forms of collegial local church leaders. The pattern that emerged toward the end of the first century, however, consolidated the functions exercised by both local and itinerant leaders and vested them in three congregational offices of leadership: (1) single pastor-bishops, elected by each community, who presided over all aspects of the congregation's life and worship; (2) groups of collegial community-elected leaders known as presbyters, who oversaw the life of the community under the leadership of the bishop; and (3) service-oriented ministers called deacons, who assisted the bishop in both ministry and worship. Though some forms of itinerant charismatic ministry (e.g., the prophets) continued to function alongside this new order for ministry for a while, their authority increasingly was subordinated to that of the local leaders, particularly the pastor-bishop.

This form of church order is known as "monepiscopacy." Its defining characteristic is the emergence of a single bishop, elected by each congregation, who is charged with presiding over the community's life and worship in a shared and mutually cooperative way with others. The classic apology for this model is found in the letters of Ignatius of Antioch early in the second century. The bishop, says Ignatius, represents God the Father within the community, presiding over the council of elders (presbyters) and assisted by deacons. The bishop—as a representative leader—functions as a "type" for God within the community, just as the deacons become a "type" for Christ and presbyters become a "type" for the apostles. The bishop is not merely "first among equals" for Ignatius, but the one whose office preserves the unity of the church's life and worship (cf. _Epistle to the Magnesians_). Though the roots of all three offices may be traced back to the New Testament, the particular configuration of the three offices and their interpretation by the early church fathers are both innovations arising from the church's second-century concern for preserving its unity and perpetuating its historic mission.

The sources for tracing just how these leaders were chosen and ordained for these tasks are practically nonexistent until the beginning of the third century. We know from the writings of Irenaeus and Hegesippus that "succession" (_didadochē_) had become an important norm governing the election and ordination of bishops in order to counter Gnostic claims of revelation. The issue, however, was not framed in terms of a linear succession of persons, but in terms of fidelity to and continuity with apostolic teaching. In order to assure that fidelity and continuity (and as a sign of communion between churches) all new bishops were ordained by the bishops of neighboring congregations. During the sometimes bitter struggle to preserve orthodox teaching in the face of numerous heterodox challenges during the fourth and fifth centuries, this provision became a significant means of providing accountability in teaching.

Though some questions remain regarding its normative status for churches in other parts of the empire, the third-century church order known as the _Apostolic Tradition_ (c. 215) provides the first substantive evidence of the rites by which persons were admitted to office in the Western church. Because Hippolytus, the author to whom the _Apostolic Tradition_ is attributed, is believed to have been an arch-conservative, anxious to challenge the legitimacy of new thinking and practices within the church, this document is thought to reflect church practice at Rome as far back as the mid-second century.

In any case, Hippolytus provides descriptions and prayers for the ordination of bishops, presbyters, and deacons, as well as descriptions and rites for appointment of persons to other, non-ordained offices as well. The following elements formed the matrix within which ordination took place:

First, fidelity to apostolic teaching is explicitly noted as a characteristic needed in those ordained as bishops: ". . . in order that those who have been well taught by our exposition may guard that tradition" (_Apostolic Tradition_ 1).

Second, ordination takes place on the Lord's Day in the midst of the assembly, which must give its explicit approval to the choice of the candidate. Bishops are ordained by the laying on of hands of neighboring bishops, together with a prayer which seeks the graces needed to carry out their ministry (_Apostolic Tradition_ 2). Presbyters are ordained by the laying on of hands of both the bishop and the congregational presbytery, together with a prayer that seeks the "Spirit of grace and counsel of the presbyterate" (_Apostolic Tradition_ 7). Deacons are ordained by the laying on of hands by the congregation's bishop, together with a prayer that seeks the spirit of "grace and caring and diligence" (_Apostolic_

*Tradition* 8). In all cases, the prayer of the presiding minister is preceded by a period of silent prayer by the whole community for the descent of the Holy Spirit, thus underscoring that ordination is an action of the whole community and not merely of its representative leaders.

Third, those ordained as bishops receive the kiss of peace as a sign that they have been made worthy, and then immediately preside at a celebration of the Eucharist, using a prayer which thanks God for holding "us worthy to stand before you and minister to you" (*Apostolic Tradition* 4). This prayer is now officially approved for use at the Eucharist in nearly all mainline Protestant churches as well as the Roman Catholic church.

Later patristic era church orders in both the East and the West preserve these basic elements of the rite. Some of them also add other elements such as the bestowal of symbols of office and a formal declaration of ordination.

## Transformation in Understanding of the Threefold Office Structure

Though the substance of the ordination rites for bishops, presbyters, and deacons remained fairly constant throughout the patristic era, the church's understanding of both the offices themselves and the meaning of ordination began to change as the church began to assume a more public role in society. Three such changes were to prove particularly important.

The first such change was a gradual reappropriation of Old Testament priestly typology for interpreting the functions of ordained ministers. The earliest strata of Christian teaching had eschewed the language of priesthood in describing church leaders, insisting that priesthood belonged only to Jesus Christ (Heb. 4:14ff). Other New Testament witnesses extended that language by analogy to the whole body of Christ, the church (1 Pet. 2:9). Beginning toward the end of the first century (*Clement* and the *Didachē*) and with increasing frequency during the second century (Justin Martyr, Polycarp and Tertullian), the language of priesthood began to be used to describe the office of bishop (and later, the office of presbyter). This usage was increasingly linked to presidency at the Eucharist.

The second change arose as a by-product of the legitimation of Christianity, which occurred by fits and starts during the second and third centuries and obtained critical mass by imperial fiat during the fourth century. The structure of ordained ministry attested to in the *Apostolic Tradition* included a local bishop or pastor who taught and preached and presided at worship, a collegial council of advisors and overseers known as presbyters, and deacons who carried out the church's ministries of benevolence. The increasing legitimation of the church, however, eventually led to rapid growth in church membership and strained the capacity of that model to meet the needs of a growing, and increasingly urban, church. Moreover, the church's increasingly public status provided sanction for appropriating and adapting the political models of the Roman Empire for its own use.

Little by little, the assumption that every congregation would have its own bishop-pastor to preside at the Eucharist and its own council of presbyters to share with the bishop in overseeing its common life gave way to a more prelatical model in which a single bishop would oversee multiple congregations within a particular region. In turn, the council of presbyters became less a collegial body of locally elected persons chosen to lead the congregation together with its local bishop-pastor, and more a group of episcopal assistants dispersed by him to preside at the Eucharist in the smaller or less important congregations under his care. The functions of deacons, who had been representative leaders not only in each congregation's worship, but in those congregations' care of their own members and outreach to others, came to be understood primarily in terms of their liturgical roles.

The third change involved a gradual redefinition of the relationship between ordained office-bearers and the rest of the church. Though there is, particularly within the Catholic Epistles, some movement in the direction of "character tests" for those who would lead the community of faith, for most of the New Testament the most theologically and ritually significant boundary is not between leaders and members, but the boundary between those who are "in Christ" (the priesthood of all believers celebrated in baptism) and those who are not.

By the end of the patristic period, however, the focus on eucharistic presidency as the radical principle undergirding the office of bishop or pastor, the appropriation of priestly typology and imagery for understanding ministry, and the appropriation of imperial models for organizing and overseeing the church's life and mission led, at least implicitly, to the drawing of a new line between clergy and laity. The sign and seal of this new boundary was celibacy, a discipline that arose first as an expectation for those ordained as bishops, but which became _de rigeur_ for the other major offices as their responsibilities were redefined in increasingly liturgical terms. In its most developed form during the Middle Ages, the order of clergy included a series of minor offices to which persons were ordained to exercise functions that, during the early years (cf. _Apostolic Tradition_ 9–14), had been exercised by nonordained members of the congregation (e.g., exorcist, acolyte, porter, lector).

During the Middle Ages, these transformed understandings of ministry were wedded to juridical understandings of authority, ultimately laying a foundation for the crisis and critique of the Reformation.

J. Frederick Holper

## 109 • CHARISMATIC GIFTS IN EARLY CHRISTIAN WORSHIP

_The New Testament spiritual gifts—especially prophecy, tongues, and interpretation, along with healing—continued to manifest themselves in the life of the church up to and beyond the fourth century. Evidence in the literature from this period indicates that these gifts were respected among the "established" church leadership, referred to by important theologians, and practiced especially throughout the "underground" church._

The question of spiritual gifts in worship has become a crucial issue as a result of the rise of the twentieth-century Pentecostal and charismatic movements. Prior to the twentieth century, most scholars and pastors relegated the spiritual gifts to the first century and explained them as witnesses to the supernatural character of Jesus' ministry. It was argued that the gifts ceased to be available to the church at the close of the apostolic age.

Research into the writings of the first three centuries of the church demonstrate that this presupposition regarding the gifts of the spirit to be inaccurate. This chapter presents material from church Fathers representing different ecclesiastical centers, all of whom refer both directly and indirectly to the experience of charismatic gifts.

## Gifts of the Spirit in the Earliest Church

The New Testament Christian community was keenly attuned to the Holy Spirit. Jerusalem, Caesarea, Antioch, Ephesus, Thessalonica, Corinth, and Rome all had seen dramatic spiritual power demonstrated among Christians. In addition, the Petrine community and that behind the letter to the Hebrews were familiar with experiences of the Spirit. In New Testament Christianity, the spiritually extraordinary was commonplace.

The central passages of Scripture on the spiritual gifts are Romans 12 and 1 Corinthians 12–14. One can define a gift of the Spirit as an occasional, unusual ability, given by God, which enables a person to minister effectively and directly in a particular situation. It is a moment when God's presence and compassion are manifested by God's responding to human need through another human being.

In exploring the life of the church between approximately A.D. 90 and 320, one dominant observation regarding the gifts of the Spirit emerges: evidence of the ongoing presence of spiritual gifts among Christians appears at least until the middle of the third century

The life of the church up to A.D. 150 was in a state of creative flux. In the midst of dispersion and growth, Christians grappled with issues of social status, community structure, doctrine, and worship. Throughout it all, the gifts of the Spirit continued as a feature of corporate experience.

The general tone of Christianity in Syria is expressed in the _Odes of Solomon_. This second century document is a creation of rich poetic expression. More importantly, the _Odes_ have a decidedly prophetic tenor. There is an intense feeling of rapture about the _Odes_. The author had experienced ineffable encounters with God, but felt constrained to share the impressions gained through those experiences. The author was conscious of having received a "word" from God that she or he must relate to others.

A similar spiritual climate is to be found in the _Didachē_, which arose from approximately the same time and place as the _Odes_. However, the _Didachē_ does not enshrine the exuberance of an enraptured soul the way the _Odes_ do. The _Odes_ are an individual expression, whereas the _Didachē_ is an ecclesiastical manual. There is a concreteness about the _Didachē_, a narrowing of focus, and the appearance of structure within the Christianity of a particular area.

There were itinerants who were identified as prophets, and their ministry was valued highly. In the context of the Eucharist, prophets were to be permitted to ". . . give thanks as much as they wish" (*Didachē 10.7*), and when they were ". . . speaking in the Spirit" (11:7), they were not to be judged. However, beside them existed locally chosen bishops and deacons (15:1-2), and the prophets were already encountering suspicion (1-2, 8).

At Antioch in Syria, the impulse of structure and the impulse of the Spirit were wedded in the person of Ignatius. As bishop of the church in that city, Ignatius argued for recognition of the episcopal office and also spoke prophetically (Philadelphians 7.1-2). The church in Syria was working through a structural metamorphosis while at the same time being prodded and stirred by spiritual gifts.

Conditions in the West were comparable. From Rome, Clement strongly advised the church in Corinth to respect its leaders. In the same letter, he urged it to recognize what God might do through people by means of the gifts of the Spirit (*I Clement* 38.2). The enigmatic *Shepherd of Hermas* contributes to the pictures by showing that distinguishing among prophets was a major issue among second century Roman Christians (43.1-21).

These admittedly sparse sources from the church of the first half of the second century do give glimpses of Christian experience. They show that worship and ministry under the direction of the Spirit were well known by many Christians.

### Gifts of the Spirit and the Church "Establishment"

The term *established* is hackneyed, but it arouses the correct images: the official world of power, decisions, and patriarchal control. The issues that concerned the establishment centered around identifying truth and then guarding it. This was precisely the world we today regard as inimical to extraordinary spiritual phenomena and behavior. In the second and third centuries, it was not.

The list of people relevant here includes Irenaeus, who defended the faith against second-century Gnosticism in what is now France; Hippolytus and Novatia, third-century conservatives who both led factions that split from the "progressive" Roman church; Cyprian, the Carthaginian martyr and ecclesiologist; Dionysius, irenic late third-century bishop

of Alexandria; and Firmilian, third-century bishop of Cappadocian Caesarea.

The information they provide is fascinating. Irenaeus knew of healings, prophecy, tongues, exorcisms, and even resurrections from the dead (*Against Heresies,* II, 49:3 and V, 6:1). He thought one could not begin to count the number of spiritual manifestations that occurred among Christians. Both Hippolytus (*Apostolic Tradition* 15.1 and 35.3) and Novatia (*Concerning the Trinity* 29) were familiar with spiritual gifts. They talk about tongues, healing, and prophecy.

The mid-third century Carthaginian church was charismatically alive. Its bishop, Cyprian, was known as a prophet (*Letter* 78, 2), and he valued dreams, visions, and prophecy (*Letters* 16, 4, and 66, 10 and *Concerning Mortality* 19). Dionysius and Firmilian do not bear conclusive witness to ministry through spiritual gifts, but they demonstrate that an open climate persisted in their parts of the church. Down to the middle of the third century, the ecclesiastical establishment showed a remarkable degree of comfort with the gifts of the Spirit.

### Gifts of the Spirit in the "Underground" Church

Beneath the official world of the ante-Nicene church was a vibrant but (to us) invisible Christianity. These people have been banished to the shadows by history for many reasons: the fact that their ideas were, in varying degree, unusual and different from those of other Christians; a perceived threat to the developing authority structures; and the greater role given female leadership.

The first part of this underground Christianity to note is a movement known as Montanism. This movement alarmed the second-century church in what is now central Turkey. The sources show that it had extreme views on certain issues, but it is difficult to find any real heresy.

Montanism was a prophetic movement led by Montanus, Maximila, and Priscilla whose view of prophecy was, in fact, not greatly different from what was common in the church at large. The Montanists also spoke in tongues.

Flourishing at the same time as Montanism were the people who produced what we know as the apocryphal *Acts of the Apostles*. A strong case is currently being made by several authors for the female authorship of these documents. Whichever the gender of their authors, these rough echoes of the canonical Acts lift the lid off the "shadow" church.

There is little that is truly historical in these moralistic novels, but they open windows into the vivid religious imagination of the ordinary Christian of the era. What one sees is a mind completely comfortable with the unapologetically fabulous. Here are wonder-working apostles, magnificent female heroes, and particularly germane to this study, prophecy, tongues, and healings.

The last person to be considered here is Theodotus. He illustrates just how marginalized nonconforming Christians became. Belonging to a syncretistic, exotic Gnostic group known as the Valentinians, he wrote in the second century. His work has largely vanished; scraps of his thinking are preserved only in the notes someone made while studying him. What is of importance is his clear statement that prophecy and healing were common within the group of which he was a member (Clement of Alexandria, *Excerpts of Theodotus,* 24, 1).

The picture that emerges from the "shadow church" is intriguing. Theodotus was active in the second century; the Montanists and the apocryphal Acts appeared then, then continued into the third. They, and others, constituted a heterogeneous but vibrant strain of Christianity that was gradually forced to the periphery. However, these Christians were most comfortable with spiritual gifts and extraordinary acts of God.

### The Theologians and the Gifts of the Spirit

The last stream of early Christianity to be tapped is composed of the theologians who were unconsciously forging that ambiguous relationship with the church in which theologians have found themselves ever since. The church has never stigmatized the following three theologians as heretics, but it has accepted them only with reservations. Their restless minds led them into strange places. Justin wanted to baptize Socrates; Tertullian embraced a wild-eyed rigorism and "the new prophecy" (Montanism), and Origen speculated about the preexistence of souls. All three knew the gifts of the Spirit.

Justin's work clearly records the gifts as parts of his second-century church. He even tendered some theological reflection upon them. The gifts of the Spirit had been gathered from the Jews, localized in

Christ, then distributed among Christians (*Dialogue with Trypho,* 87 and 88).

Tertullian provided solid evidence for the widespread practice of the gifts among Carthaginian Christians in the early third century. Evidence for the gifts of the Spirit come from all parts of his literary career, early and late. If there was a "conversion" to Montanism for Tertullian somewhere in mid-life, it did not change his thinking or his observations about the place of spiritual gifts.

Finally, Origen provides considerable information about Christian religious experience in a work known as *Against Celsus.* Celsus, a pagan philosopher of the mid-second century, had met Christians who spoke in tongues and prophesied (*Against Celsus* 7, 9). He worked his experience with these people into a scathing attack on Christianity.

Around A.D. 248, Origen responded to Celsus' comments about these Christians. As he did so, he demonstrated that the gifts of the Spirit were known in the third century over the wide geographical area with which he was familiar. Origen talked about "traces" of spiritual gifts, but occasionally, he indicates that, these traces were substantial in reference to miracles, prophecy, and exorcism. (*Against Celsus* 1, 2; 2, 8; and 7, 8).

Like the "shadow Christians" and those who bore the burden of leadership, theologians among the early Christians were touched to varying degrees by the charismatic phenomena. The cumulative weight of the evidence available from the late first century to the early fourth century would suggest that throughout this period the gifts of the Spirit played a significant role in Christian experience.

Ronald Kydd

## 110 • WORSHIP IN THE BOOK OF REVELATION AND THE EASTERN ORTHODOX LITURGY

*The Revelation to John makes dramatic use of the rich symbolism of the sacrificial ritual of the Jewish temple. A comparison of the language and imagery of the book of Revelation with the Divine Liturgy of the Orthodox churches suggests that in the Revelation we see an early stage in the development of Christian liturgy, especially that of the Eastern churches.*

Recent studies on the worship described in the book of Revelation indicate its vision of worship made a significant impact on that of the early church, particularly Eastern Christian worship. This article points to images within this ancient vision of worship that correspond to images in the worship of the Orthodox churches.

## Introduction

The Revelation of St. John the Theologian is a verbal icon of liturgy. The Revelation presents at once an almost kaleidoscopic image of the past, the present and the future, the earthly and the heavenly. Through our worship the same phenomenon occurs. In liturgy we thank God for and make "remembrance" of "all those things which have come to pass for us; the Cross, the tomb, the resurrection on the third day, the ascension into Heaven, the sitting at the right hand, and the glorious second coming."

In the Eastern Christian worship, God's saving events of the future are "remembered" in anticipation.

The text states that the revelation itself was received on the Lord's Day (i.e., Sunday—Revelation 1:10). The vision begins by setting the scene for the celestial liturgy. In fact, the whole of the Revelation was recorded in the context of the celestial liturgy. Tradition holds that it records the ecstasy that St. John experienced during the Sunday celebration of the eucharistic liturgy among the colony of persecuted Christians on the island of Patmos. While worshiping, St. John (called the Theologian in Orthodox Christianity) entered into the presence of the Holy One.

The Apocalypse, in its familiarity with Jewish sacrificial ritual, show evidence of having been written by one intimately acquainted with the liturgy of the Jerusalem temple—a member of the priesthood, perhaps, or at least a member of a priestly family living in the vicinity. If the traditional identification

***Bread and Chalice.*** *This eucharistic symbol of baskets of bread and a chalice with a fish is from the catacomb of Callixtus, second or third century.*

of the apostle John with the anonymous "other disciple" in the fourth Gospel is well founded, then the New Testament attests that John was well known to the Jewish high priest (John 18:15-16). Perhaps the Gospel intends to identify him as one of the two disciples (the other being Andrew) who left the circle of John the Baptizer to follow Jesus (John 1:37); John the Baptizer himself was from a priestly family (Luke 1:5-25). If John the Theologian was indeed from priestly circles, he was not unusual in this respect among Christians; the Acts of the Apostles records that many priests were converted to the Christian movement in the earliest days of the Jerusalem church (Acts 6:7).

In order to better understand worship in the Revelation, it is helpful to review certain elements in the worship of the Old Covenant.

The temple in Jerusalem had (by the time of the Savior) become the focal point of Israel's whole life: everything was oriented and organized around it. The temple was the earthly dwelling of the Holy One, the place of theophany. In temple liturgy Israel encountered the Almighty. By the first century, this temple liturgy had developed into an exacting and precise ritual. It basically consisted of the Tamid: the elaborate daily sacrificial offering of lambs (one in the morning and one in the evening) to pay the penalty of sin, and thus cleanse and purify the people of Israel. Other offerings and oblations were made in the temple throughout each day by various individuals and for various reasons. These were the private sacrifices (see Luke 2:2-28).

In brief, the twice-daily temple oblation ritual consisted of the following: the vesting of the priests; the casting of lots for the tasks involved in the ritual; the preparation of the victim; the slaughter and butchering of the sacrificial lamb; the lighting of the seven-branched candlestick; a service of prayer; the opening of the gates of the temple; silence followed by the thundering of percussion instruments; the billowing of smoke caused by casting incense upon the altar of incense and casting portions of the lamb on the altar of holocaust; a full prostration toward the Holy of Holies by all present; the priestly blessing upon the assembled faithful; psalms and canticles sung to the accompaniment of trumpets, stringed instruments, and percussion that were played by the temple priests; and the final "Amen!"

Temple sacrifices were intended to establish a point of meeting between Israel and God: they were a means of communion, or, for those who had fallen away through sin, a restoration of that communion. The Hebrew word for "sacrifice" is *qorban,* the root meaning of which is "coming near."

Next, some background into the worship of the Christians of the first century is necessary in order to understand the liturgical background of the Revelation. From the New Testament we know that Paul, James, and other Christians continued to worship in the temple in Jerusalem. When the temple was destroyed in A.D. 70, it was the synagogue (which had its own services) through which early Christians continued to participate in formal worship.

Eventually, however, as the first century drew to a close, it became increasingly impossible to be a Christian and worship with one's fellow Jews. Nonetheless, early Christians preserved a continuity of worship from the Old Covenant to the New. They did not invent a new manner of worship. They employed elements from the Jewish temple liturgy, the synagogue liturgy, and the rituals of the Jewish home.

The New Testament bears witness to the fact that the liturgy of early church included psalms, doctrinal hymns, spiritual songs, doxologies, confessions and creeds, readings, proclamations and acclamations, homilies, thanksgivings, prayers, the Sanctus ("holy, holy, holy"), supplications, the holy kiss, memorial meals, blessings, daily prayer. These liturgical elements were carried out in a consistent manner under the oversight of an ordained ministry.

The Scriptures, together with the witness of the *Didachē,* Ignatius of Antioch, and Justin and Clement of Rome all help to create a picture of the liturgical environment of the Revelation and its Christian community. These all bear witness to this one fact: The liturgy of the Old Covenant has become fulfilled and completed in the liturgy of the New Covenant.

These Old and New Testament liturgies are reflected in the liturgy of the book of Revelation, which in turn is reflected in the liturgy developed by Eastern Christian churches.

## Worship Symbolism in Revelation and in Eastern Liturgy

**The Throne.** One of the most important liturgical images in the book of Revelation is the throne of the Holy One (4:2). This image appears frequently throughout the Old and New Testament and indicates the presence of God. This image is used over forty times in the Apocalypse itself. It is interesting to note that in Church Slavonic vocabulary, the word that refers to the altar is *prestol,* meaning literally, "throne." Thus, the holy table in an Orthodox church is considered to be the throne of the Most High.

**Pantocrator.** We read in Revelation 1:8, "'I am the Alpha and the Omega' says the Lord God, who is, and who was, and who is to come, the Almighty." This same text appears around the fresco of Christ in majesty, located in the central dome of a properly appointed Orthodox church. The name for this icon is "Pantocrator," meaning "The Almighty."

**Lamb of God.** Revelation 1:13 records that John saw "Someone 'like a son of man,' dressed in a robe reaching down to his feet and with a golden sash around his chest." The vesture is that of the high priest of the temple. John later notes (5:6) that he "saw a Lamb, looking as if it had been slain." This Lamb bears the marks of temple sacrifice, yet it is triumphant, standing in readiness for action. In both these instances, the reference is being made to the crucified victim who is also the victorious, risen Lord. As the Orthodox liturgy declares, the Savior is "the offerer and the offered; the receiver and the received." He is the Lamb of God who takes away the sin of the world, *and* he is the heavenly High Priest.

**Twenty Four Elders.** Around the throne of the Almighty there were "twenty-four other thrones, and seated on them were twenty-four elders. They were dressed in white and had crowns of gold on their heads" (4:4). They "fall down before him who sits on the throne, and worship him who lives forever and ever" (4:10). This "synthronos" of the twenty-four elders is the basis of the "synthronos" of the apse in an Orthodox church—the semicircle of presbyters that surrounds the holy Table during the celebration of the Divine Liturgy. The celestial presbyters in Revelation wear the vesture of the Old Testament priesthood.

**The White Robe.** The alb, or white robe, serves today as the basic priestly garment. It is an image of the baptismal garment given to all who have been clothed in Christ, the garment of salvation, the robe of light. It symbolizes blessedness, good deeds, purity and innocence, triumphal joy, eternal life, the resurrected and glorified body. It recalls the wedding banquet of Matthew 22:1-4, which is intended for all who are called to the wedding supper of the Lamb of God (Rev. 19:1-8).

**The Celestial Court Liturgy.** The *synthronos* of elders provides a concrete image of the celestial court liturgy. Vested in priestly attire, they fall down in worship. They sing hymns, they offer incense, they present the prayers of the saints, they play their instruments. They proclaim the mighty acts of salvation—as did the priests of the Old Covenant.

**The Martyrs.** Under the altar were "the souls of those who had been slain because of the word of God and the testimony they had maintained" (6:9). The words *witness* and *testimony* come from the Greek word *marturia*. The sacrifice of the martyrs was associated with the sacrifice of Christ. The imagery of the righteous dead dwelling under the altar comes from ancient Judaism (cf. J. Massyngberde Ford, *Revelation,* The Anchor Bible [Garden City, NY: Doubleday, 1975], 110). The early church continued to use this imagery. From the second century, memorials and eucharistic liturgies were celebrated on or near the tombs of the martyrs and other saints. When a bishop today consecrates an Orthodox church, he solemnly deposits the relics of the saints (ideally martyrs) under the top of the altar table. This practice is reflected in the petition of the Augmented Litany: "Furthermore, we pray for the blessed . . . believers, [who have] departed this life before us, who here and in all the world lie asleep in the Lord."

## Worship Components in Revelation and Eastern Liturgy

Hymns, doxologies, acclamations, the Wedding Supper of the Lamb of God, and Communion are five major components of the celestial liturgy as recorded in the Apocalypse. The Old Covenant liturgy contained these elements (either in fact or in "type"). We find them in the liturgy of the New Covenant as well.

**Hymns and Doxologies.** The hymns and doxologies of the Revelation are addressed to the Father, to the Lamb, or to both. At one time or another during the celestial liturgy, they are sung by the four living creatures, the twenty-four elders, the hosts of angels, the sealed ones, and finally by every creature in the universe. Much of what we find in the text of the Eastern liturgy reflects the very words of these hymns and doxologies.

We may compare a portion of the hymn of 11:17-18 to the dialogue between the celebrant and the faithful at the anaphora [Great Thanksgiving] of the divine liturgy: "We give thanks, O Lord God Almighty. . . ." A segment of the hymn of 15:3-4 is quoted during the prayer blessing the water for baptism and for the Feast of the Theophany: "Great and marvelous are Your works, O Lord God Almighty!" "The Lord God Almighty . . ." of 4:8a (inspired by Isaiah 6:3) was probably used in the synagogue liturgy of the first century and has continued in use in Christian liturgies since at least the fourth century. A slightly varied form, known as the *trisagion* ("Holy God, Holy Mighty, Holy Immortal . . .") has been a part of the Orthodox liturgy since the fifth century.

To God and to the Lamb are ascribed glory, dominion, blessing, honor, power, riches, and wisdom for ever and ever. The various doxologies found in 1:6; 4:11; 5:12; 5:13; etc., reflect the liturgical practice of first century Christianity. This can also be seen in the conclusion of the Lord's Prayer as found in Matthew 6:13. The First Epistle of Clement, as well as *Didachē* bear witness to early Christian doxologies. It is important to note that exactly the same glory is given to the Lamb as to the Holy One. The Father and the Son are accorded the same divinity, equal in majesty and glory.

**Amen.** The doxology of 7:12 begins and ends with an "Amen!" "Amen" is a liturgical acclamation that was common in the liturgy of the Old Covenant. It signifies "so be it!" or "I ratify!" and acknowledges as one's own whatever has been previously uttered by the liturgical celebrant. It was carried over into the Christian liturgical assembly, as we can see from the witness of 1 Corinthians, The *Didachē, 1 Clement,* and Justin's *First Apology.* In Revelation this acclamation is found in 5:14; 19:4; and 22:20. In the Eastern Orthodox liturgy it abounds. It is most solemnly proclaimed as a response to the initial "Blessed is the Kingdom of the Father, and of the Son, and of the Holy Spirit!" immediately following the words of institution; and again as a response to the prayer of the *epiklēsis,* the prayer of the anaphora that calls down the Holy Spirit upon the gifts.

**Alleluia.** Next comes the "Alleluia." The only place in the New Testament where the "alleluia" is found is in Revelation 19:1, 3-4, 6. This Hebrew liturgical word, which means "praise the LORD," is found throughout the Psalms. It was sung in synagogue and temple alike. The primitive Christians did not desire to make a translation of it, so they kept the Hebrew in Greek transliteration. The Alleluia remains in the Orthodox liturgy today as a conclusion to the singing of Psalms. It follows the reading of the Epistle; it is sung during the offices of burial and memorial; it occurs during the matins service of Great Lent; it is featured in the divine Liturgy of Holy Saturday.

## Worship in the Presence of the Holy One

Revelation 8:1-6 provides an important clue to the liturgy. "When [the Lamb] opened the seventh seal, there was silence in heaven for about half an hour. And I saw the seven angels who stand before God, and to them were given seven trumpets. Another angel, who had a golden censer, came and stood at the altar. He was given much incense to offer, with the prayers of all the saints, on the golden altar before the throne. The smoke of the incense, together with the prayers of the saints, went up before God from the angel's hand. Then the angel took the censer, filled it with fire from the altar, and hurled it on the earth; and there came peals of thunder, rumblings, flashes of lightning, and an earthquake. Then the seven angels who had the seven trumpets prepared to sound them." We find here an image of the temple ritual of Jerusalem, the liturgy of the church, and the celestial liturgy. The passage records something that has a direct correspondence with the most solemn portion of the temple liturgy; the act of worship in the presence of the Holy One. The occurrence of thunder, rumblings, lightning, and earthquake is reminiscent of the theophanies recorded in the Old and New Testaments.

At the end of the whole scene, which begins with Revelation 8, the theophany occurs in the celestial liturgy: "Then God's temple in heaven was opened, and within his temple was seen the ark of his covenant. And there came flashes of lightning, rumblings, peals of thunder, an earthquake and a great hailstorm" (11:19). We later read, "'Now, the dwelling of God is with men, and he will live with them. They will be his people, and God himself will be with them and be their God. He will wipe every tear from their eyes. There will be no more death or mourning or crying or pain, for the old order of things has passed away'" (21:3-4). This proclamation, based on Isaiah 25:8, is echoed in the funeral liturgy of the church. The reality expressed here is

this: In the final analysis, the new order of the universe will be that God's people wall partake of his divinity (2 Pet. 1:4). There will no longer be the need for anything that is merely an image of God's presence, for his presence will be complete (Rev. 21:22). God will be all in all, filling all things with himself (1 Cor. 15:28; Eph. 1:23; Col. 3:11). The new order will simply be God.

## The Wedding Supper of the Lamb

Finally we come to the Wedding Supper of the Lamb of God: Holy Communion in Jesus Christ. This communion is announced by the hymn of 19:6-8: "Hallelujah! For our Lord God Almighty reigns. Let us rejoice and be glad and give him glory! For the wedding of the Lamb has come, and his bride has made herself ready. Fine linen, bright and clean, was given her to wear."

The concept of a marriage between God and his people is deeply rooted in the Old Testament where the covenant relationship is described as a marriage. This theme was proclaimed scripturally at the Feast of the Passover. In the New Covenant, it is applied to Jesus, who is the Bridegroom. It is with this theme that we enter into the services of Holy Week.

The image of a messianic banquet is taken from both the Old and New Testaments. Eating and drinking in the kingdom of God form one of the most significant images we can find to express the concept of Communion. Since the communion in Paradise was broken by a disobedient act of eating (Gen. 3), restoration of that communion (and return to paradise) comes about in part through the obedient act of eating (1 Cor. 11:24-25).

Eating of the tree of life (Rev. 2:7) and partaking of the hidden manna (Rev. 2:17), or tasting of the bread from heaven (John 6:31; Heb. 9:4) is linked with the spiritual food (1 Cor. 10:3) of the Eucharist. Ignatius describes the Eucharist as "the medicine of immortality." The Lord declares: "Here I am! I stand at the door and knock. If anyone hears my voice and opens the door, I will come in and eat with him, and he with me" (Rev. 3:20). The mystical supper of the Lamb of God is the ultimate reality of the kingdom.

In this world, and until he comes, that reality is celebrated most profoundly at the feast of feasts, the Holy Pascha of the Lord (Easter). In the middle of the night, vested in bright and pure fine linen, the bride awaits her risen Bridegroom for the festal consummation of their love. Mystical communion with the Lord occurs by partaking of the bread that is his essence (Matt. 6:11) and by drinking of his cup of salvation (Ps. 116:13).

"The Spirit and the bride say, 'Come!' And let him who hears say, 'Come!' . . . Whoever is thirsty, let him come; and whoever wishes, let him take the free gift of the water of life" (Rev. 22:17). In the Divine Liturgy, the celebrant exhorts the communicants, "With awesome fear of God, in faith, and in love, come near to the holy gifts." The Bridegroom declares "Yes, I am coming soon!" (Rev. 22:20). His bride hears him. She recognizes the voice of her beloved and runs to meet him (Matt. 25:6). In the delight of their marriage, filled with excitement, she answers him, "Amen. Come, Lord Jesus." (Rev. 22:20). Thus the mystical supper begins.

Through these images it can be seen that those within the church "standing in the temple, stand in heaven."

Robert Gray

## III ✦ BIBLIOGRAPHY ON ISSUES IN EARLY CHRISTIAN WORSHIP

### Worship in the New Testament

Cullman, Oscar. *Early Christian Worship*. Collegeville, Minn.: Liturgical Press, 1953. A highly regarded examination of the origin and development of primitive worship. Also contains a study of the gospel of John and its relationship to early Christian worship.

Hahn, Ferdinand. *The Worship of the Early Church*. Philadelphia: Fortress Press, 1973. A critical examination of the New Testament sources of worship with particular emphasis of worship in the various communities such as the Aramaic, the Jewish, the Early Gentile, the Sub-Apostolic and the Apostolic Fathers.

Jeremias, Joachim. *The Eucharistic Words of Jesus*. New York: Scribner, 1966. A classic study of Gospel evidence.

Martin, Ralph P. *The Worship of God*. Grand Rapids: Eerdmans, 1982. Protestant. Based on contemporary scholarship. A study of worship in the New Testament touching on matters of praise, praying, singing, the offering, confession, the sermon, baptism, Table, Holy Spirit in worship, and the unity and diversity of New Testament worship.

Schweizer, Eduard. *The Lord's Supper According to the New Testament*. Philadelphia: Fortress Press, 1967.

Shepherd, Massey. *The Paschal Liturgy and the Apocalypse*. Ecumenical Studies in Worship 6. Richmond: John Knox Press, 1960. Argues that the structure of the book of Revelation is based on the liturgy of the early church.

### Early Liturgical Sources

Brightman, F. E., ed. *Liturgies Eastern and Western*, Vol. 1. Oxford: Clarendon Press, 1896; reprinted 1965.

Deiss, Lucien, ed. *Springtime of the Liturgy: Liturgical Texts of the First Four Centuries*. Collegeville, Minn.: Liturgical Press, 1979.

Hamman, Adalbert, ed. *The Mass: Ancient Liturgies and Patristic Texts*. Staten Island, N.Y.: Alba House, 1967.

*The Ante-Nicene Fathers*. Vol. 10: *Liturgies and Other Documents of the Ante-Nicene Period*. Grand Rapids: Eerdmans, 1956.

### Links Between Jewish and Christian Worship

Bradshaw, Paul F., and Lawrence A. Hoffman, eds. *The Making of Jewish and Christian Worship*. Notre Dame, Ind.: University of Notre Dame Press, 1991. Covers the birth and evolution of Jewish and Christian worship from the new perspectives afforded by recent research. The entries maintain the sense of connectedness between the reconstruction of past worship patterns and current worship practice.

Di Sante, Carmine. *Jewish Prayer: The Origins of Christian Liturgy*. New York: Paulist Press, 1985. An ecumenical exploration of both Jewish and Christian worship, with great appreciation for both traditions.

Fisher, Eugene J., ed., *The Jewish Roots of Christian Liturgy*. New York: Paulist Press, 1990. Articles from *SIDIC*, the journal of the Service International de Documentation Judeo-Chrétienne.

### Daily Prayer

Bradshaw, Paul. *Daily Prayer in the Early Church*. London: SPCK, 1981. A standard work that elucidates the origin and early history of the daily office of prayer from its Jewish background to the office of St. Benedict.

Guiver, George. *Company of Voices: Daily Prayer and the People of God*. New York: Pueblo Publishing Co., 1988. Deals with the history and content of daily prayer with an eye toward making the practice or prayer available to the common person.

Fisher, Dominic F., TOR. *The Liturgy of the Hours.* Petersham, Mass.: St. Bede's Publications, 1987. A historical overview of the liturgy of the hours with practical guidelines for implementing the liturgy of the hours in the local parish.

Taft, Robert, S. J. *The Liturgy of the Hours in East and West.* Collegeville, Minn.: Liturgical Press, 1986. A scholarly investigation of the origins of the liturgy of the hours in the cathedrals and monasteries of both the East and the West.

**Studies in Early Christian Worship**

Altaner, Berthold. *Patrology,* 3 vols. Edinburgh-London: Nelson, 1960. This standard introduction to the early church contains references to the formation of early Christian liturgies and discussions of literature and fathers of the church that relate to the development of worship.

Bouyer, Louis. *Eucharist: Theology and Spirituality of the Eucharistic Prayer.* Notre Dame, Ind.: University of Notre Dame Press, 1968. A classic book that presents the historic connection between the Jewish meal prayers, the *berakah,* and the eucharistic prayers of the early church. This work contains the meal prayers themselves with an analysis of their context.

Bradshaw, Paul. *The Search for the Origins of Christian Worship.* New York: Oxford University Press, 1992. Argues for acceptance of "liturgical agnosticism," that is, refraining from speculation in the face of fragmentary and sparse evidence we have of early Jewish and Christian worship. Rather than suggesting a common source and an original unity of early Christian worship, Bradshaw suggests that the extant materials indicate a diversity of style and content.

_____. *Ordination Rites of the Ancient Churches of East and West.* New York: Pueblo Publishing Co., 1990. This festschrift to E. C. Ratcliff probes early Christian worship as particular scholars of renown address the early history of the eucharistic liturgy, the early history of the baptismal liturgy, the liturgy of ordination, the liturgy of the Reformation era, and the liturgy of the Book of Common Prayer.

Cuming, Geoffrey J., ed. *Hippolytus: A Text For Students.* Grove Liturgy Study 8. Bramcote,

Notts., UK: Grove Books, 1976. A scholarly and widely accepted investigation of the text and meaning of *The Apostolic Tradition* of Hippolytus.

_____. *Essays on Hippolytus.* Bramcote, Notts., UK: Grove Books, 1978. A critical textual study on the liturgical material of *The Apostolic Tradition.*

Dix, Gregory. *The Shape of the Liturgy.* New York: Harper & Row, 1945. One of the early books of the liturgical movement to present the case for early Christian worship. While some of the theses set forth in this work are now in question, the book remains a valuable introduction to worship in the early church.

Gingras, George, ed. *Egeria: Diary of a Pilgrimage.* Westminster, Md.: Newman Press, 1970. Egeria, a female pilgrim to Jerusalem in the fourth century, recorded her experience of worship, especially during Holy Week. In this volume she tells of the three-day festival of Maundy Thursday, Good Friday, and of the Great Paschal Vigil, and much more. The book not only contains her account but provides a commentary as well.

Jungmann, Joseph A. *The Early Eucharist to the Time of Gregory the Great.* Notre Dame, Ind.: University of Notre Dame Press, 1959. A scholarly treatment of worship in the primitive church, in the third century, in the age of Constantine, since the fourth century, and the Roman Liturgy before Gregory the Great.

Kelly, J. N. D. *Early Christian Creeds,* 3d ed. New York: David McKay, 1972.

Kydd, Ronald A. H. *Charismatic Gifts on the Early Church: An Exploration into the Gifts of the Spirit during the First Three Centuries of the Christian Church.* Peabody, Mass.: Hendricksen Publishers, 1984. Evidence from the early church fathers suggests that the charismatic gifts did not cease at the end of the N.T. era as so many argue. Examples from the *Didachē,* Clement of Rome, Ignatius of Antioch, the Shepherd of Hermas, Justin Martyr, and many others attest to the active presence of the gifts in the worship of the early church.

Mitchell, Nathan. *Mission and Ministry: History and Theology in the Sacrament of Order.* Wilmington, Del.: Michael Glazier, 1982.

O'Meara, Thomas F. *Theology of Ministry.* New York: Paulist Press, 1983.

Rordorf, Willy, et al. *The Eucharist of the Early*

*Christians.* New York: Pueblo Publishing Co., 1978. Here is a detailed study of the major eucharistic prayers of the early church. The work is scholarly but accessible.

Schillebeeckx, Edward. *The Church With a Human Face.* New York: Crossroad, 1985.

Van der Meer, F. *Early Christian Art.* London: Faber & Faber, 1959. A presentation of the liturgical art of the first centuries of the church. Written from the conviction that art was not created for art's sake but that it was created to express a message of faith and truth.

Van Olst, E. H. *The Bible and Liturgy.* Grand Rapids: Eerdmans, 1991. The special feature of this work is its exploration into the liturgical structure of the Bible and of the use of scripture such as psalms and canticles in the liturgy of the early church.

PART TWO

# A History of
# Christian Worship

# TWO

# The Worship of the Early Church (to A.D. 500)

From the early centuries, Christian worship has seen a continuous process of development and change in response to theological and cultural factors. Although the basic elements—the service of the Word and of the Lord's table—have remained constant, their shape and setting have undergone modification from century to century, from region to region, and from Christian community to community within both the Eastern and Western branches of the church. The result of this process is the great variety of liturgical forms through which Christians worship the Lord across the world today.

Part 2 begins with a survey of the evidence for Christian worship in the earliest centuries. This is followed by a description of the liturgical traditions of the Eastern churches and a discussion of the various regional rites of the Western (Catholic) church that culminated with the establishment of liturgy uniformity at the Council of Trent. Discussion of the worship in movements of the Protestant Reformation is followed by a survey of worship in the major movements and denominations that developed in the post-Reformation era. The section concludes by considering the impact of twentieth-century renewal movements on Christian liturgy.

Our sources for the study of Christian worship in the early post-biblical period are not liturgical texts, such as missals or prayer books, or systematic treatments by theologians of the era. Instead, these sources usually make incidental references to Christian liturgy in writings devoted to other purposes, such as the defense of the Christian faith against pagan opposition, the refutation of false teachings within the Christian community, and the instruction of the faithful in scriptural exposition and sermons.

It would be a mistake, however, to infer from the nature of our sources that the church's liturgical practices during this period were informal, undeveloped, and without consistency. Even the documents of the New Testament reveal a worshiping community that practiced baptism and eucharistic celebration, and mention of these practices occur in the writings of the fathers of the church through the following centuries. The existence of the worshiping community is an underlying datum in this patristic literature, the ongoing evidence of the creation of a new covenant people through the death and resurrection of Christ, and the continued operation of the Holy Spirit to establish the kingdom of God.

## 112 • WORSHIP IN THE NEW TESTAMENT ERA

*Worship in the New Testament period was ordered around baptism and the Eucharist. Baptism marks the entrance of the believer into the worshiping community, while the Lord's Supper, together with the teaching of the Scriptures, forms the content of the worship gathering.*

——— **The Oral-Formal Tradition** ———

Early Christian liturgy, like its Jewish and pagan counterparts, was an oral-formal phenomenon. The early liturgical gatherings were not lacking in basic shape and structure, in the use of specific confessional formulas, and structures of prayer. Although what was said allowed for improvisation and adaptation, it was not by any means "extemporaneous" in our modern sense. It followed rules, essentially unwritten, but important for that very reason to be observed by those responsible for their conduct if others were to take their appropriate parts. But it was, in principle and practice, not something to be written down for reading in the manner of later times. Those familiar with the classical tradition of poetry and oratory, and of public speaking or rhetoric more generally, will at once recognize here an assumption as natural to that time as it is foreign to ours.

The oral-formal character of early Christian liturgy helps to explain the general value placed on liturgical language as a means of appropriating and transmitting the Christian proclamation (tradition, *paradosis*), as in the famous dictum of Prosper of Aquitaine that the structure of prayer underlies the structure of belief (*Lex orandi statuat legem credendi*). But it has a specific significance for the study of the sources that provide us with descriptions of liturgical gatherings. These sources were written only in particular circumstances, with the specific purposes of preservation, explanation, and—often most important—when there was dispute over what should be done and said. These sources are mishandled when studied as if they were extracts of liturgical books of the sort with which we are familiar. They need to be studied in the light of the particular purposes that impelled their writing in the time before circumstances made continuation of the oral-formal tradition difficult.

## The Physical Evidence

Early Christian liturgy, like that of any period, is physical as well as vocal. The physical evidence of places used for liturgical gatherings has at last begun to receive the attention it deserves. This evidence includes the so-called "house churches" ("Christian houses" or sometimes, by an obvious association, "temples of the Christians"), renovated domestic structures of which we have increasing evidence from the second century onward. It also includes the baptisteries and basilicas, and the complexes of buildings of which they were part, erected under the auspices of Constantine and his successors following the period of persecution. These all, whether still in use or in ruins, tell us much about the character and significance of the rites for which they made physical provision. So, too, do the pictorial evidence of the catacombs at Rome, and elsewhere, and the wall decorations of the later buildings—which show us the people who gathered for the Christian meetings and the vesture and furnishings with which they were familiar.

## The New Testament Evidence

Particular problems are posed by our earliest written sources. Many but by no means all of these

writings were later collected into the New Testament. The rest were designated "Apostolic Fathers" by the Anglican patristic scholar Archbishop James Ussher (d. A.D. 1656). For our purposes, all of these writings provide evidence of the liturgical practices of the communities of the first and early second centuries. Those later regarded as "Scriptures," however, must also be studied for their subsequent liturgical influence. A case in point is the command of Matthew 28:19-20 to baptize into the name of the Father, the Son, and the Holy Spirit, itself an interpretation of the significance of baptism rather than a liturgical formula, which had a wide influence on later catechetical and baptismal practice. Another is the Last Supper tradition of 1 Corinthians 11:23-25 (cf. Mark 14:22-24; Matt. 26:26-28; Luke 22:17-19), once again not itself a liturgical formula, which became the institution narrative incorporated into later eucharistic prayers.

**The Writings of Paul.** Among the writings that later became part of the New Testament, the Pauline letters deserve special attention. 1 Corinthians contains our earliest references to baptismal practice, at least in the negative sense of insisting that it is baptism "into the name" of Christ rather than that of the baptizer (1:15). It also contains our earliest references to eucharistic practice in the form of instructions for the observance of the blessings over the bread and wine mandated by the Last Supper tradition (11:17-34), with its own even earlier implication that the Eucharist is a "memorial" of the new paschal sacrifice of Christ (cf. 1 Cor. 5:7-8). In both cases, these rites are interpreted by Paul as entrance into and sustenance in the life of the members of the body of Christ effected by the Holy Spirit (12:12-31).

**The Gospels.** The synoptic gospels, however different in genre from the Pauline letters, must also be read as documents intended for communities constituted by baptism and Eucharist. Here baptismal allusions include reference to Jesus' death as a baptism foreshadowing the martyrdoms of principal disciples (Mark 10:38-40; Luke 12:50). Moreover, in Matthew the account of the baptism of Jesus is so treated as to anticipate the new relationship to God, in Christ, through the Spirit in which the baptized stand, and into which others are to be brought. Indeed, the command of Matthew 28:19-20 ("make disciples . . . baptizing them in the name of the Father and of the Son and of the Holy Spirit, and teaching them . . .'') may well assume a pattern of practice, conversion, baptism, and catechesis [instruction] not unlike that assumed by Paul.

Synoptic eucharistic allusions abound. The accounts of the miraculous feedings (Mark 6:41-42; 8:6-8; Matt. 14:19-20; 15:36-37; Luke 9:16-17), which employ the technical language of "taking, blessing over, breaking, and giving," almost certainly were viewed in the churches as foreshadowings of the Eucharist before their incorporation into the gospel narratives. Moreover, the passion narrative includes a form or forms of the Last Supper tradition (cf. 1 Cor. 11:23-25) placing the last meal on the day of the slaughter of the Passover lambs. This is a crucial element in the tradition's view of Jesus' death as a new Passover sacrifice. Whatever the historical accuracy of this narrative, it incorporates an already established "tradition" conveying this interpretation of the death of Jesus through the use of eucharistic terminology familiar to its readers.

Of particular interest is Luke 24:13-35, where the appearance of the risen Christ to the disciples at Emmaus is recounted in language reminiscent of a eucharistic meal, perhaps even suggesting familiarity with an introductory interpretation of the Scriptures but certainly employing the technical language of "taking, blessing over, breaking, and giving" at the supper of which the risen Christ is the host.

In the gospel of John, baptismal and eucharistic allusions are carefully disguised. However, the subject of baptism is easily recognized in the discussion between Jesus and Nicodemus over being "born again" through the Spirit (John 3:1-15), while allusion is again made to the baptism with which the disciples must be baptized (16:1). Similarly, while John replaces the Last Supper "tradition" with the account of the washing of the disciples' feet and its accompanying command (13:3-11), he gives a eucharistic interpretation with the miraculous feeding (6:25-65) and to the discussion of the vine and branches at the last meal (15:1-17). Baptism and Eucharist are doubtless to be discerned in the references to water and wine (or blood) in the account of the marriage feast at Cana (2:1-11) and in the passion narrative (19:34).

**Other New Testament Evidence.** Among the other writings now collected in the New Testament, special interest centers on the book of Hebrews, which exhorts those who have been baptized and have participated in the Eucharist to resist apostasy in the face of persecution (6:1-8), and was later appealed to (by Cyprian) as grounds for rigorous refusal to restore apostates to the communion of the church. 1 Peter, whether or not it is the baptismal instruction some have found it to be, assumes that its readers belong to the community of the baptized (1:3, 21-23; 2:2) and are eucharistic participants (2:5). Revelation, which describes its vision as received on the Lord's Day (1:9-10), has been thought to reflect a structure of scriptural interpretation and eucharistic action and certainly promises the martyrs "hidden manna" and "a new name" at the final "wedding supper of the Lamb" (2:17; 19:7-9).

More specific references to baptismal and eucharistic practice are found in the Acts of the Apostles. While something like a paradigmatic sequence of repentance, baptism "into the name of Jesus Christ," and the gift of the Spirit, seems to be assumed (2:38), the accounts of baptism (presumably drawn from diverse sources) do not exhibit this sequence in practice (8:9-16, 26-40; 10:44-48). The reference to a daily "breaking of bread" in the primitive Jerusalem community (2:46), if it is eucharistic, is unusual in view of the normal practice of meeting for the Eucharist on the Lord's Day. But clearer, even graphic, is the account of Paul's healing of Eutychus during a meeting for the "breaking of bread" at Troas (20:7-12), presumably on the evening of the end of the Sabbath and the beginning of the Lord's Day on the Jewish reckoning of days from sunset.

## 113 • WORSHIP IN THE SECOND AND THIRD CENTURIES

_Worship during the second and third centuries continued to follow the course set by New Testament liturgical traditions. Consequently, the discussion of worship during this period centered on the significance of baptism and of the Eucharist, understood in its full content of the service of Word and of the Lord's table._

### — Evidence in the "Apostolic Fathers" —

The works designated "Apostolic Fathers" also contain allusions to the significance of baptism and Eucharist in the same period as that of the New Testament.

Of these, two are Italian in provenance. "The First Letter of Clement to the Corinthians" (_1 Clement_) is a formal letter from the Roman church, to be dated after the Domitian persecution at Rome in A.D. 96,

***The Good Shepherd.*** *This reproduction of a fourth century mosaic from the Basicila of Theodoriana in Aquileia, Italy, is that of the Good Shepherd. This common and favorite depiction of Jesus is found in many catacomb paintings and sacrophagi of the same period.*

supporting the authority of the leadership of the Corinthian church against certain detractors. The letter probably has the baptized in view when it speaks of the duties of those who bear "the name" of Christ (58:1-2). But it certainly has the eucharistic community in view when it elaborates the Pauline theme of the various functions of the members of the body of Christ (1 Cor. 12:12-31) with a complicated analogy between the responsibilities of the high priest, Levites, and people in offering the sacrifices of the Old Covenant and the functions of the apostolically appointed leaders and members of the church (*1 Clement* 42–44). Moreover, the lyric blessing prayer for the unity of the church, with which the letter draws to a close (59:3–64:1), is a free adaptation of the structure of Jewish blessing prayers with which we may assume Clement was familiar from eucharistic use.

Closely related to 1 Clement, both in time and place, are the apocalyptic visions of the *Shepherd of Hermas,* which exhort the leaders of the church to oversight of the baptized (*Visions* IX, 7–10) and take baptism as the mandate for repentance and the cultivation of purity (*Mandates* III, 1–7) in seeming qualification of Hebrews 6:1-8.

Of Asian provenance are the letters of Ignatius, bishop of Antioch, written to the churches he expected to visit on his way to martyrdom at Rome in the reign of the Emperor Trajan (d. A.D. 117). In warning against "docetic" teaching of a proto-Gnostic sort, which denies the incarnation of the Word, Ignatius asserts the importance of the eucharistic gathering of the baptized with the bishop, elaborating Johannine themes (cf. 1 John 1:18-25; 5:6-12) to show its importance as exhibiting the faith that "there is only one flesh of our Lord Jesus Christ and one cup to unite us in his blood" (*Epistle to the Philadelphians* 4; cf. *Epistle to the Ephesians* 13:1; *Smyrneans* 7:1, etc.).

Also of Asian provenance is the *Martyrdom of Polycarp,* bishop of Smyrna (d. A.D. 156), himself numbered liturgically among the "Quartodecimans" who observed the Passover on the Jewish date 14 Nisan (see the discussion of Justin, below). This work, which contains evidence of later elaboration of various sorts, nonetheless preserves a blessing prayer attributed to Polycarp at the time of his death (ch. 14), which may well reflect his normal eucharistic blessing prayer but is here adapted to giving thanks for his being worthy of death and asking that he be accepted as a "pleasing sacrifice." Like the blessing prayer of 1 Clement 59:3–64:1, it is evidence of the free Christian use of the form of Jewish blessing prayers.

## The Didachē

Among other writings, "The Teaching of the Twelve Apostles" (*Didachē*) was long unrecognized in an adapted version incorporated in the late fourth-century *Apostolic Constitutions,* but is now known through the late nineteenth-century discovery of an independent manuscript. This is an unusual second-century Greek compilation and editing of early Aramaic materials from Syria-Palestine (a minority view says Egypt) perhaps as early as the late first century. In its present second-century form, *Didachē* brings together moral instruction, the "two ways" document (1–6), directions "about baptism" (7), fasting and prayer (8), and "about the Eucharist": blessings to be said over wine and bread before the meal and a connected set of blessings to be said afterwards (9–10). Directions follow covering the right of visiting prophets to give thanks and the need to appoint bishops and deacons (11–15), together with an exhortation to observe the Sunday Eucharist (14).

As a second-century document, _Didachē_ follows an outline roughly similar to that found in Justin and Hippolytus (see below), in which a pre-baptismal catechesis precedes a description of paschal baptism and Eucharist, and is followed by reference to the Sunday Eucharist and other matters. It is, for this reason, sometimes called an early "church order." The particular circumstances that impelled its effort to conform earlier materials to newly emerging norms of practice, however, are not clear.

As to these early materials, interest naturally centers on the blessings to be said before and after meals, unquestionably Christian adaptations of the Jewish Sabbath and festival meal blessings. The order of wine and bread, and the lack of reference to the Last Supper "tradition," still cause some skepticism regarding them. But plain words of the text, as well as the paschal context in which they have been set in conjunction with baptism, make it likely that they are eucharistic blessings, and even that the connected series after the meal, Christian adaptations of the Jewish blessings over the final "cup of blessing," supply us with the long-needed clue as to the structure of prayers into which the blessings over the eucharistic bread and wine were set together when it became normal to gather for the Eucharist apart from an actual meal.

## Justin Martyr

From the mid-second century to the end of the period of persecutions, we have an increasing body of liturgical evidence in the form of actual descriptions of liturgical practices, as well as of other writings with liturgical implications. The former, Justin Martyr's _First Apology_ and Hippolytus' _Apostolic Tradition,_ require special attention, though at least a selection of the latter must be noticed.

Justin's _First Apology,_ the work of a teacher of the Greek-speaking Roman church (d. A.D. 167), is easily neglected where it is assumed that liturgical writings will be of the sort with which we are familiar. As a general explanation and defense of Christianity for a pagan readership, it concludes with a description of Christian meetings for baptism and Eucharist (61–67) designed to allay suspicions of

ghastly secret ceremonies to which their private character gave rise. Consequently, the description seems incomplete from our perspective. Despite its generality, however, this description follows precisely the pattern, not of Justin's making, wherein details of paschal baptism and Eucharist ("how we dedicated ourselves to God when we were made new through Christ," 61) are followed by reference to the Sunday Eucharist ("on the day called of the sun, there is a meeting in one place," 67). Indeed, this pattern, roughly that already encountered in the present _Didachē,_ doubtless reflects the practice of the Roman church once the Passover had come to be celebrated on a Lord's Day following the Jewish feast, as was the case by the time of the visit of Polycarp of Smyrna to Pope Anicetus in A.D. 155 (Eusebius, _Ecclesiastical History_ IV, 14).

Moreover, Justin's description is by no means lacking in specific detail. The paschal description assumes pre-baptismal catechesis, fasting, and prayer before a threefold washing "in the name of the Father and of the Son and of the Holy Spirit" (cf. Matt. 28:19), after which the newly baptized join the Eucharist for common prayers and the kiss of peace (61, 65). The elaborate interpretation of this new birth and remission of sins, with the use of the term _illumination_ (cf. Heb. 6:4) and exposition of the divine triad (62–64) is likely catechetical in origin.

Justin's appended description of the Eucharist (65), repeated briefly in his treatment of its weekly use (67), exhibits the sequence of "taking, blessing over, breaking (here omitted), and distribution" as it had evolved when detached from an actual meal, with a unified oral-formal blessing prayer and assenting _Amen._ His interpretation of the rite as a "memorial" commanded by Jesus (cf. 1 Cor. 11:23-26), participation in the body and blood of Christ, and the pure sacrifice of the New Covenant (66, cf. _Dialogue with Trypho_ 41, 70, 117) likely reflects the themes expected to inform the blessing prayer. But the treatment of the Sunday Eucharist adds reference to preliminary readings from the Jewish Scriptures and the "memoirs of the apostles," followed by a homily, before the common prayers and kiss of peace, and thus provides our earliest evidence of such a Christian adaptation of the synagogue service in connection with the Sunday Eucharist.

## Irenaeus

Unavoidable among theological writers of liturgical significance is Irenaeus of Lyons (d. A.D. 190?), native of Asia Minor, correspondent of members of the Roman church, presbyter and bishop of the Greek-speaking community at Lyons. His "Detection and Refutation of Falsely So-called Knowledge" (*Adversus Haereses,* or *Against Heresies*) is at once a response to Valentinian, Marcionite, and Gnostic teachings and a compendious presentation of Christian belief of far-reaching influence. His brief *Demonstration of Apostolic Preaching* is a catechetical digest of its main themes.

Irenaeus' liturgical value is at once seen in his main contention that his opponents rely on a false interpretation (*hypothesis*) of the Scriptures different from the apostolic tradition (*paradosis*) communicated by the bishops at baptism (*Against Heresies* I.8.1, 9.1, 4, cf. III.2.2, 3.3). This tradition is "what we believe" about the one God and Father, the one Word incarnate in the flesh, and the Spirit which communicates new life in Christ to believers (I.10.1, cf. I.3.6, 22; II.28.1–3). Not only does Irenaeus refer here to the baptismal catechetical instruction with which he is familiar and which would eventually take shape in baptismal confessions of faith (creeds), but his whole work is, in *genre,* an expanded form of such instruction.

Irenaeus' treatments of baptism and Eucharist assemble and develop now traditional interpretations, particularly those of baptismal rebirth (I.21.1; II.22.4; III.17.1) for the remission of sins (III.12.7) and the gift of righteousness and incorruption (III.17.2), and of the Eucharist as the prophecies' pure sacrifice of the last days (IV.17.5), the oblation commanded by the Lord (IV.18.1), in which the bread and wine become the body and blood of Christ after "the invocation of God" (IV.18.5). In his own view, the baptismal and eucharistic use of water, bread, and wine as means of participation in Christ show the goodness and usefulness of the physical creation (III.17.2; IV.18.2, 4–6; V.2.2–3) in contrast to the views of his opponents, who theoretically equate matter and evil, yet inconsistently continue the use of water, bread, and wine. (IV.18.5).

## The *Apostolic Tradition* of Hippolytus

It is hard to overestimate the importance of the identification (by E. Schwartz [1910] and R. H. Connolly [1916]) of a Coptic document, discovered in 1848 and called "an Egyptian Church Order," as the *Apostolic Tradition* listed among the writings of Hippolytus of Rome (d. A.D. 236). Now pieced together, on this basis, from a hitherto unidentified Latin manuscript, from Greek excerpts included in the later fourth-century *Apostolic Constitutions,* and from other sources, this work is now generally regarded as that of Hippolytus, an Irenaean theologian, presbyter of the Roman church, opponent of the bishops Zephyrinus (d. 217) and Callistus (d. 233), and schismatic bishop. As such, it purports to describe the proper conduct of the rites of the Roman church in Hippolytus' time. While still not a liturgical book, it is an invaluable discussion of Roman liturgical practice.

The *Apostolic Tradition* follows the outline already familiar from Justin. Here, however, an extensive section on ordinations (2–15) precedes that on paschal baptism and Eucharist and includes a detailed description of the Eucharist of the newly ordained bishop. In consequence, the paschal section (16–23) treats baptism in detail, but adds only brief notes on the Eucharist that follows it, while the Sunday Eucharist is omitted in the interest of a scattering of directions on other matters, including the continuation of communal meals whose noneucharistic character is insisted on (25–26).

The Roman provenance of the *Apostolic Tradition* is evident from its broad structural similarities to Justin, and its use in the paschal baptism of interrogations accompanying the three washings ("Do you believe . . . ? I believe . . .") that employ much of the language of the Roman baptismal confession later attested by the letter of Marcellus of Ancyra to Pope Julius I in A.D. 340 (Epiphanius, *Panarion* 72) and by Rufinus of Aquileia's early fifth-century *Commentary on the Apostles' Creed.*

An uncertain number of features of the *Apostolic Tradition,* however, may be Hippolytus' own adaptations or proposals. His rigorist position on the restoration of apostates in persecution is evident in the care with which he insists catechumens be selected (16), in his acceptance of the "baptism of blood" as an alternative to baptism in water (19), and possibly in the dramatic positioning of the baptismal interrogations. The careful descriptions of the functions of bishop, presbyters, and deacons in the ordination prayers (3, 8, 9) may also owe something to his own views, as may the unified language of his episcopal eucharistic prayer or *anaphora* (4), the theological stress on the independent existence of the Word in its opening thanks for the work of God, and in the appearance of an oblation of the "memorial" and invocation of the Spirit following the "institution narrative." In this latter respect, its similarities with later Eastern eucharistic prayers rather than the later Roman canon have often been noticed. But there is no reason why a Roman prayer should not have had parallels with contemporary Asian types (cf. *Martyrdom of Polycarp,* 14), and we are not clear as to the limits of improvisation acceptable at the time.

## Some Other Evidence

Only a selection of other materials from the third century can be noticed here, and then only for its correspondence with the types of evidence thus far encountered.

**Didascalia.** From Syria, perhaps quite early in the third century, comes the "Catholic Teaching of the Twelve Apostles and Holy Disciples of Our Savior" (*Didascalia*), now reconstructed by conflating a Syrian translation with Greek excerpts incorporated in the later fourth-century *Apostolic Constitutions.* Though often described as a "church order," this work does not follow the structure that we have in the present *Didachē,* Justin, or *Apostolic Tradition,* but is a "disorderly" collection of material on various matters of belief and morals. Its liturgical interest lies in its provision, in connection with the comments on the pastoral responsibilities of the bishop, of prayer forms for the reconciliation of the excommunicate (6–7), its brief reference to the bishop's liturgical functions (9), and its assortment of graphic details concerning the physical arrangement and appropriate conduct of the sorts of people who might gather at the eucharistic meetings (15).

**Tertullian.** Other contemporary liturgical evidence is found in the two major Latin writers of the period. Of these, Tertullian (d. A.D. 220) is the earlier and more comprehensive, a presbyter (?) of the church of Carthage, appropriator of Irenaeus and contemporary of Hippolytus, who came to accept the claims of the Montanist martyrs to a special possession of the gifts of the Spirit. By contrast, Cyprian (d. A.D. 258), bishop of Carthage, though a devoted reader of Tertullian, supported the authority of bishops to restore apostates to communion, and opposed the claims of the "confessors," who had been

prepared to die in persecution, to special powers of forgiveness.

Tertullian's treatise *On Baptism* (*De Baptismo*), the only work on the subject in our period, might be the exception to our rule that liturgical matters are not subjects of treatment in themselves, were it not essentially an anti-Gnostic tract, concerned to defend (cf. Irenaeus) the regenerative power of water, the primordial source of life, when the Spirit is invoked upon it, the triune name employed, and the Spirit given through anointing and laying on of hands (2–8). In pursuing this subject, Tertullian provides details of baptismal practice not otherwise found in Justin or even Hippolytus (e.g., baptism at Pentecost and at the paschal feast), as well as, with the challenge of persecution in view, endorsing (16) the "baptism of blood" (see Hippolytus) and discouraging (18) the apparently hitherto common practice of baptizing infants (i.e., "households").

Tertullian's *On Prayer* (*De Oratione*) is perhaps more topical, though in arguing the superiority of Christian to Jewish prayer it provides the earliest commentary on the Lord's Prayer (2–9), incidentally taking "daily bread" to refer to the Eucharist— "daily" referring to the "perpetuity" and "indivisibility" of our membership in the body of Christ (6). Once again, the treatise supplies details otherwise lacking, in this case of practices of corporate and private prayer, such as comments on kneeling and standing with hands extended (*orans*), the exchange of the kiss of peace and the reception of the Communion, and the prohibition of kneeling at the paschal feast and Pentecost.

More at large, Tertullian develops themes of Irenaeus to the point that the body is washed and fed in baptism and Eucharist so that both body and soul may be saved (cf. *De Resurectione Carnis,* 8), and introduces his own subsequently influential interpretation of the eucharistic sacrifice as a service or duty assigned as means of rendering satisfaction to God (*On Prayer,* 19).

**Cyprian.** Cyprian's extensive debt to Tertullian includes an underlying assumption regarding the purity of the church, which leads, in his case, to insistence on the importance of eucharistic communion with the bishop rather than of such extraordinary spiritual gifts as Tertullian had come to value in the Montanist's (*On the Unity of the Church,* 5–6, 8, 23). Thus he rejected (perhaps recalling Tertullian, *On Baptism,* 15) the baptism performed by the schismatic bishops who followed Novatian in condemning, in part on the basis of Hebrews 6:4-8, his willingness to allow the restoration of apostates to Communion (*Epistles* 69–74).

In this badly so-called "rebaptism" controversy, Cyprian was opposed by the Roman bishop Stephen, who supported the reception of the schismatically baptized. Cyprian, in his stress on unity with the bishop as the guarantee of the purity of the church, inadvertently laid the foundation for the later Donatist schism, which originated in refusal of Communion with any bishops who had committed apostasy in persecution. For our purposes, this controversy is further indication, here provided in characteristically Latin form, of the significance of baptism and Eucharist as defining true Christian identity.

## 114 ✦ WORSHIP DURING THE FOURTH AND FIFTH CENTURIES

*The fundamental pattern of early Christian worship continued to develop through the fourth and fifth centuries. However, "families" of liturgical practice began to emerge, and styles of worship varied from one Christian region to the other. By this time, one can begin to speak of "Eastern" and "Western" characteristics of Christian liturgy.*

With the end of the persecutions and the beginning of the period in which Christianity became the public cultus of the Roman imperial government, the number and variety of liturgical sources multiply, though they still reflect the oral-formal tradition continued in these new circumstances.

It has been common to speak of this period as witnessing the emergency of "families of rites," results of the growing influence on local practices of the great sees [areas governed by prominent bishops] of the time. It would perhaps be truer to say that our evidence, still scattered and incomplete, suggests a more specific process of consolidation, at least in the East.

### ——— Evidence for Eastern Liturgy ———

The *Apostolic Constitutions,* coming from Antioch in the late fourth century, is the central body of evidence. Long available, it has been recognized only recently for the compilation of the diverse materials it is. It opens with directions for various aspects of Christian life (I–VI) containing excerpts of *Didascalia,* incorporates the blessing prayers of

*Didachē* partially reorganized into a contemporary eucharistic structure (VII, 25–26), and includes a version of the ordination section of the *Apostolic Tradition* (VIII, 1–5). If *Apostolic Constitutions* is still a "church order" based on the sort of structure of description found in *Didachē,* Justin, and the *Apostolic Tradition,* it has been stretched out of shape by the diverse materials accommodated within it, perhaps in an effort to organize the variety of practices in use in the region of the Syrian capital.

Central to the *Apostolic Constitutions,* however, are elaborate directions and prayers for baptism (VII, 39–45) and Eucharist (VII, 6–15), generally thought to reflect the practices of the church of Antioch itself. Distinctive features of baptism include a unified taking of the confession of faith separate from the washing itself and a subsequent episcopal anointing with invocation of the Spirit. Those of the Eucharist include the dismissal of catechumens and litanic prayers of the faithful led by deacons, and an elaborate *anaphora* similar in shape to that reflected in the *Apostolic Tradition,* but including extended Preface and Sanctus and introducing diaconal prayers for the living and dead before the concluding doxology.

Less well known from this period is the recently discovered east Syrian evidence of the use in the church of Edessa of the *Anaphora of Addai and Mari,* notable for retaining early Jewish Christian blessing forms reminiscent of the type found in *Di-*

*Loaves and Fishes. The miracle of the loaves and fishes was a favorite theme in the catacombs of the early church and presumably in early Christian worship. The above painting is taken from the Crypt of Lucina in the Roman catacomb of Callixtus.*

_dachē,_ but set within a structure roughly similar to that elaborated in _Apostolic Constitutions._ From Egypt as well, light has been shed on the background of the Alexandrian Liturgy of St. Mark by the late nineteenth-century discovery of the "prayer book" (_euchologion_) of Serapion (d. 360?), bishop of Thmuis and correspondent of Athanasius. This collection may have been preserved because of the intrinsic interest of its prayers at the Scripture readings, homily, dismissal of the catechumens, and common prayers before the Eucharist (1–12) and at the baptismal (19–25) and ordination (26–38) rites. But it also preserves an _anaphora_ different in shape from _Apostolic Constitutions_ and of undoubted Egyptian pedigree (cf. the _Der Balizeh_ and _Strasbourg_ fragments), in which Preface and Sanctus are followed by invocations over the oblation before and after the institution narrative.

For the East in general, however, similarities between the _Apostolic Constitutions_ and the later rite of Constantinople suggest that its central sections contain a version of the rites eventually adopted in the new imperial capital. With additions of its own, notably its use of the _anaphora_ attributed to John Chrysostom (d. 407) and occasionally replaced by those of Basil of Caesarea (d. 379) and the Jerusalem Liturgy of St. James, these latter rites eventually commended themselves widely where imperial influence extended in the East.

Egeria's _Diary of a Pilgrimage,_ the account of a journey of a Gallo-Hispanic religious woman through Asia Minor, Palestine, and Egypt at the turn of the fifth century, offers graphic descriptions of liturgical life, including the paschal rites at Jerusalem and its environs.

### ——— Evidence for Western Liturgy ———

Comparable Western evidence is restricted to much later books, all showing effects of the promotion of the Roman rites under the Frankish auspices of Pepin IV and Charlemagne in the eighth and ninth centuries. The peculiar features of the north Italian _Ambrosian Missal,_ the Gallo-Hispanic _Missale Gothicum_ and _Missale Bobbiense,_ and the Gallo-Irish _Stowe Missal,_ many of which may reflect the appropriation of Eastern practices throughout Italy, must be studied in the light of such writings as those of Ambrose of Milan (d. 396) and Isidore of Seville (d. 636). Evidence of the rites of Latin Africa, before the Vandal conquest of the fifth and the Justinian reconquest of the sixth century, is entirely in the form of allusions in such writings as those of Augustine (d. 421).

Of the Roman rites themselves, after the fourth century introduction of Latin as the liturgical language, such evidence as we have comes from similarly later books, though it is here possible to identify the oldest form of the Roman eucharistic prayer or canon, wrongly attributed to Gelasius I (d. 496), and early seasonal materials that may partly derive from the time of Leo I (d. 461), before encountering the work attributed to Gregory I (d. 604), whose name is traditionally attached to the rites adopted by the Frankish liturgical reformers. Apart from a certain restraint in the adoption of Eastern practices, and the formulation of a eucharistic canon different in structure from that of the _Apostolic Tradition_ but perhaps not entirely without contemporary parallels (cf. Ambrose, _De Sacramentis_), we may think of the earliest Latin rites of the Roman church as similar to those that preceded them.

### ——— Instructional and Homiletical ——— Material

Of unique significance for this period are the bodies of catechetical and homiletic material, which are themselves liturgical in character as well as in contents, which reflect the newly public position of the church, and provide a wealth of detail about liturgical practice.

While we have references to catechetical instruction before baptism in Justin and the _Apostolic Tradition,_ and in Tertullian, Origen (d. 254?), and other earlier writers, it is from the fourth century onward that we have evidence of two types of formal episcopal addresses: the first delivered at and after the formal acceptance of candidates for the paschal baptism, devoted to the exposition of the teachings of the baptismal confession of faith, and occasionally the Lord's Prayer; the second consisting of postbaptismal ("mystagogical") addresses devoted to the meaning of baptism and Eucharist for those who had now participated in them.

Of such addresses, we have a series, not always complete or given in the same years, by Cyril, Bishop of Jerusalem (d. 386), Theodore of Mopsuestia (d. 428), and John Chrysostom (d. 407), the last as presbyter of Antioch. We also have two postbaptismal catecheses of Ambrose of Milan, _De Mysteriis,_ and (now widely accepted) _De Sacramentis._

## Key Events in the History of Christian Worship

| Century | Liturgical Documents/Writers | Church Events/Persons | World Events/Persons |
|---|---|---|---|
| 1st | *Didachē* <br> *First Clement* | N.T., A.D. 50–135 <br> Neronian persecution | fall of Jerusalem, 70 |
| 2nd | *Letter of Pliny* <br> Irenaeus <br> Polycarp <br> Ignatius <br> Justin Martyr <br> Clement of Alexandria <br> *Epistle of Barnabas* | spread of church around Mediterranean <br><br> sporadic persecution | |
| 3rd | Tertullian <br> *Apostolic Tradition* <br> monastic origins <br> Origen (c. 185–c. 254) <br> Cyprian (d. 258) <br> *Didascalia* | monastic origins <br> empire-wide persecutions | |
| 4th | *Apostolic Church Order* <br> Sarapion <br> Cyril of Jerusalem (c. 315–86) <br> Egeria <br> *Apostolic Constitutions* <br> Eusebius of Caesarea <br> *Epitome* <br> Basil (c. 330–79) <br> Chrysostom (c. 347–407) <br> Theodore of Mopsuestia <br> (c. 350–428) <br> Ambrose (c. 339–97) <br> Jerome (c. 342–420) <br> Augustine (354–430) <br> *Testamentum Domini* | conversion of Constantine, 312 <br> Council of Nicaea, 325 <br> Trinitarian controversies <br> Council of Constantinople, 381 <br><br><br><br><br><br><br><br> gradual conversion of northern tribes | Christianity made legal, <br> then official <br> division of empire <br><br><br><br><br><br><br><br><br> barbarian invasions |
| 5th | *Canons of Hippolytus* <br> Cassian (c. 360–435) | Christological controversies <br> Council of Ephesus, 431 <br> Council of Chalcedon, 451 | fall of Rome, 455 |
| 6th | Benedict of Nursia <br> (c. 480–c. 550) <br> Gregory I (590–604) | organization of Western monasticism | |
| 7th | *Ordo Romanus Primus* <br> sacramentaries | | spread of Islam |
| 8th | Hadrianum sent to Charlemagne | John of Damascus (c. 675–c. 749) <br> Iconoclastic controversy <br> Council of Nicaea, 787 <br> Bede (c. 673–735) | |
| 9th | supplement added <br> Benedict of Aniane <br> (c. 750–821) <br> Ratramnus (d. 868) <br> Paschasius Radbertus <br> (c. 790–865) | | Charlemagne crowned, 800 <br> learning revived |
| 10th | | low ebb of Rome and papacy <br> Cluniac monastic reforms | |
| 11th | Berengarius (c. 999–1088) <br> Lanfranc (c. 1005–89) | schism East and West, 1054 <br> Anselm (1033–1109) <br> Gregory VII (1073–85) <br> Crusades begin | emperor intervenes in <br> Rome |

| Century | Liturgical Documents/Writers | Church Events/Persons | World Events/Persons |
|---|---|---|---|
| 12th | Suger (c. 1081–1151)<br>Hugh of St. Victor<br>  (c. 1096–1141)<br>Peter Lombard (1095–1159) | invention of gothic<br>Cistercian monastic reforms | |
| 13th | Innocent III (1198–1216)<br>Thomas Aquinas (c. 1225–74) | Francis of Assisi (1181–1126)<br>scholastic theology<br>mendicant orders<br>Fourth Lateran Council, 1215<br>Crusades end | |
| 14th | John Wycliffe (c. 1329–84) | Avignon papacy, 1309–77<br>split of papacy, 1378–1417 | |
| 15th | *Decree for Armenians,* 1438 | John Huss burned, 1415<br>Council of Basel, 1431–49 | fall of Constantinople,<br>  1453<br>invention of printing<br>Columbus reaches<br>  America, 1492 |
| 16th | Martin Luther (1483–1546)<br>Ulrich Zwingli (1484–1531)<br>Martin Bucer (1491–1551)<br>Menno Simons (1496–1561)<br>John Calvin (1509–64)<br>John Knox (1514–1572)<br>Thomas Cranmer<br>  (1489–1556)<br>revised Roman books,<br>  1568–1614<br>Thomas Cartwright<br>  (1535–1603) | Erasmus (c. 1466–1536)<br>Reformation begun, 1517<br>founding of Jesuits, 1540<br>Council of Trent (1545–63)<br>missions expand<br>Bible translations<br>*Schleitheim Confession,* 1527<br>Marburg Colloquy, 1529 | colonization of Latin<br>  America<br>defeat of Spanish Armada,<br>  1588<br>reign of Elizabeth I,<br>  1588–1603 |
| 17th | *Millenary Petition,* 1603<br>Westminster Directory, 1645<br>Robert Barclay's *Apology,*<br>  1676<br>Christopher Wren<br>  (1632–1723) | age of baroque art<br>Puritan ascendancy<br>Quakers originate<br>age of Jansenism | colonization of North<br>  America<br>Isaac Newton (1642–1727) |
| 18th | John Wesley (1703–91)<br>*Sunday Service,* 1784<br>American BCP, 1789<br>J. S. Bach (1685–1750) | latitudinarianism<br>Synod of Pistoia, 1786<br>Febronianism<br>Immanuel Kant (1724–1804) | age of enlightenment<br>American Revolution<br>French Revolution |
| 19th | Charles G. Finney (1792–1875)<br>John Nevin (1803–86)<br>Alexander Campbell<br>  (1788–1866)<br>Prosper Guéranger<br>  (1805–1875)<br>A. W. N. Pugin (1812–1852) | scientific study of the Bible<br>Christianizing of the American fron-<br>  tier<br>Oxford movement<br>worldwide missions<br>Pius IX (1846–78) | Charles Darwin (1809–82)<br>Karl Marx (1818–1883)<br>age of reform<br>abolition of slavery<br>women's rights |
| 20th | Fanny Crosby (1825–1915)<br>Pius X (1903–14)<br>Lambert Beauduin<br>  (1873–1960)<br>*Mediator Dei,* 1947<br>BEM, 1947<br>revised R.C. rites<br>LBW, 1978<br>BCP, 1979<br>ASB, 1980<br>UMH, 1989 | Pentecostal churches<br>anti-modernism<br>liturgical movement<br>Vatican II, 1962–1965<br>Karl Barth (1886–1968)<br>Karl Rahner (1904–1984)<br>Faith and Order, 1927<br>World Council of Churches, 1948 | World War I<br>World War II<br>atomic age, 1945<br>space age, 1957<br>Korean War<br>Vietnam War<br>Iraq War |

SOURCE: James F. White, *Documents of Christian Worship: Descriptive and Interpretive Sources* (Louisville: Westminster/John Knox Press, 1992), 11–13.

Among other evidence, Augustine, *De Catechizandis Rudibus,* provides advice and a model *narration* to a Carthaginian deacon charged with the initial address to those seeking admission as catechumens, while his *De Fide et Symbolo* purports to be based on his catechetical instructions as presbyter of Hippo. Maximus the Confessor's (d. 663) *Mystogogia* is a mystical interpretation of the Constantinopolitan eucharistic liturgy of his time, and an important source for its instruction.

Such earlier homilies as survive include that of Melito, bishop of Sardis (d. 190), *On the Passover,* and the great collections of the scriptural homilies of Origen. From the fourth century onward, however, comes a profusion of homilies too great to be enumerated, including series by Gregory of Nazianzus (d. 390), Gregory of Nyssa (d. 395), John Chrysostom, and Cyril of Alexandria (d. 444), as well as of Ambrose, Augustine, Leo I, and Gregory I. With respect to all of these, it can only be noticed in general that the public liturgical assemblies of this period allowed and even required new forms of homiletic address, having in view non-Christians as well as Christians, and larger physical spaces than had before been the case. Several writings of the period, most notably Chrysostom, *On Priesthood,* but also Gregory of Nazianzus, *On His Flight,* and even Ambrose, *On the Duties of Ministers,* are of interest as addressing or reflecting the challenge of preaching in these circumstances.

Such catechetical lectures and homilies were, in this period as distinct from ours, regarded as integral parts of the liturgy itself rather than as attachments or additions to it. Initially taken down in shorthand in the course of delivery, they often reflect another stage in the appropriation of classical styles of public oratory for Christian purposes.

## Later Theological Issues

Liturgical theology in this period turns on the theological significance of liturgical practice. Thus, both Athanasius (*Ad Serapion* I.14, 30) and the "homoisousian" [holding that the Son is "of like substance," rather than of "the same substance," with the Father] Basil of Ancyra (Epiphanius, *Panarion* 73.3) argue for their different ways of stating the equality of the persons of the Godhead against the Arians on the ground that Father, Son, and Spirit are together at work in baptism, while the enhanced specificity of the invocation (*epiklēsis*) of the Spirit on the oblation in the various forms of *anaphora*

in the Constantinopolitan rite emphasizes what seemed the orthodox Trinitarian implications of earlier liturgical prayers. While the Carolingian theologians Ratramnus and Radbertus developed their several views of the relation of the body and blood of Christ to the eucharistic bread and wine with references to a variety of early Christian writers, it is doubtful if the latter would have understood the terms of the debate, prone as they were to proceed by reference to the theology inherent in liturgical language rather than to raise questions on the basis of it.

## Conclusion

The erosion of the oral-formal tradition of liturgical practice is not easily traced in our sources themselves. The consolidation of rites in the East may well have impelled a new concern for precision in liturgical language, though the ninth-century Constantinopolitan *euchologion* (Barberini manuscript) is the first surviving document to appear to assume the actual use of liturgical books. For the West, it may be assumed that inroads upon the classical tradition required the use of such books at a much earlier date, perhaps particularly in Spain and Gaul; though the late date of our actual sources, which generally assume their use, makes it hard to say when this occurred. It is only in Carolingian ivory book covers that liturgical books appear on altars in tandem with books of the Gospels, though these may reflect a practice long-familiar at the time.

The issue here is not a small one. Much that is central to the character of early liturgical practice hinged on the continuation of the oral-formal tradition and was obscured when the cultural decline of the later centuries necessitated its abandonment. At that point, whenever and by what stages it occurred, different notions of the nature of Christian liturgical gatherings began to make their influence felt.

Lloyd G. Patterson[2]

## 115 ◆ Bibliography on the History of Early Christian Worship

See also Section 111, Bibliography on Issues in Early Christian Worship

Alexander, J. Neil. *Time and Community.* Washington, D.C.: Pastoral Press, 1990. This valuable work, written by a number of scholars, tackles the issues of liturgical time, liturgical history and liturgical theology. In the historical section, studies are presented on the liturgy in various geographical settings such as Antioch in the time of Severus (513–518), the early Syrian tradition, Sunday worship in fourth-century Jerusalem, and the liturgy of the hours beyond cathedral and monastery.

Jungmann, Joseph A. _The Early Eucharist to the Time of Gregory the Great._ Notre Dame, Ind.: University of Notre Dame Press, 1959. A scholarly treatment of worship in the primitive church, in the third century, in the age of Constantine, since the fourth century, and the Roman Liturgy before Gregory the Great.

Roberts, Alexander, James Donaldson, and Cleveland Coxe, eds. _The Ante-Nicene Fathers,_ 10 vols. Grand Rapids: Eerdmans, 1951–1956.

Schaff, Philip, and Henry Wace, eds. _A Select Library of Nicene and Post-Nicene Fathers,_ First and Second Series, 28 vols. Grand Rapids: Eerdmans, 1952–1956.

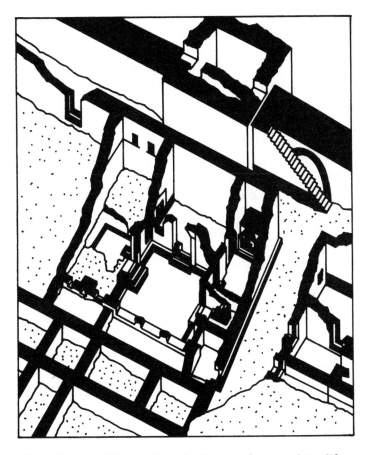

**Third-Century House Church.** _Houses for worship differed from other homes only in the baptistery (see top right), where a large baptismal tank was installed under a canopy. The walls were decorated with paintings that recalled biblical scenes. This drawing is based on a house in Dura-Europa, Syria._

# ❧ THREE ❧

# Worship in the Eastern Orthodox Tradition

*The liturgical traditions of the East (the Orthodox churches) are rich and varied. Although these traditions derived from common roots shared by several prominent ancient churches, they developed distinctive theological emphases and spirituality. God was seen as the distant and holy Other, yet also as the One "made flesh" who "dwelt among us." The liturgy reflected other contrasts. Worshipers were invited to participate in the heavenly mysteries, but they were also reminded that they were unworthy to approach them; they rejoiced in the triumph of Christ, but also expressed a patient endurance until the day when that victory would be fully revealed; they stood erect before the majesty of God, but also bowed in humility and awed adoration. The Eastern traditions emphasized the divine Mystery of God the Creator, of Christ the Redeemer, of the Spirit the sanctifier, in a colorful and many-faceted manifestation.*

## 116 ◆ INTRODUCTION TO THE EASTERN ORTHODOX CHURCHES

*The liturgical traditions of the East derive ultimately from the forms of worship used in Antioch and Alexandria. As with all ancient Christian liturgies, the Service of the Word led into the sacramental offering of the Eucharist. The Eastern traditions comprise the East and West Syrian, the Byzantine (including the Greek and Russian Orthodox), the Armenian, and the Coptic/Ethiopian.*

The distinction within the ecumenical church between the churches of the East and the churches of the West is rooted in patterns of evangelization and evolution in the first six centuries of the Christian era. As Christianity spread beyond Jerusalem to the whole Mediterranean world, four regions, in addition to Jerusalem, became major centers of Christian life: North Africa (Carthage), Rome, Antioch, and Alexandria, each developing its own distinctive forms of faith and prayer.

These initial centers had varying destinies. Jerusalem was destroyed in A.D. 70. The church of North Africa, where Latin Christianity was born and developed (Tertullian, d. *c.* A.D. 240); Cyprian, d. *c.* A.D. 258), was destroyed by the Moors in the seventh century, but not before exerting a major influence on the church of Rome. This latter (Rome) evolved

in three stages: a primitive apostolic stage (Clement of Rome (fl. *c.* A.D. 80); a developed Greek stage (Hippolytus of Rome, d. A.D. 235), and, in the fourth century, Latin Rome (usually taken to be the Roman tradition) which adopted as its own, and further evolved, the Latin Christianity of North Africa. The church of Alexandria developed for a time as the major intellectual center (Clement, d. A.D. 215; Origen, d. A.D. 253/254; Athanasius, d. A.D. 373; and Cyril (d. A.D. 444)] until the Council of Chalcedon (A.D. 451), which Alexandria rejected. Alexandria is also known for its monastic movement, which likewise had an effect on its evolving liturgical forms.

The Antiochene influence was felt throughout Asia Minor with the churches of Cappadocia (Basil of Caesarea, d. A.D. 379; Gregory of Nazianzus, d. A.D. 389; and Gregory of Nyssa, d. A.D. 394) helping further to shape both theological and liturgical evolution. Finally, from the later fourth century onward, the new imperial capital at Constantinople began to emerge as yet another major Christian center, under whose influence the later Byzantine church, still Antiochene in root, would develop its own distinctive liturgical forms.

The term *liturgical tradition,* as it is employed here, refers to these five centers (Jerusalem, Rome,

Carthage, Antioch, and Alexandria), the forms of faith and prayer characteristic of each, and the forward evolution of these forms in the many churches that constitute the one church of Jesus Christ. Though there are countless instances of mutual influence, one tradition on another, it can generally be said that the Latin tradition (Carthage and especially Latin Rome) is the root tradition of the churches of the West, while the Syriac and Greek traditions (Jerusalem, Antioch, and Alexandria) form the root traditions of the churches of the East.

Because of the early disappearance of the Jerusalem church, the extant liturgical traditions of the East are derived from either Antioch or Alexandria. The Jerusalem tradition was absorbed into certain strains of Antiochene Christianity and no longer exists as an independent living liturgical tradition. Antioch gave rise to an East Syrian strain manifest in the Nestorian and Chaldean churches of Iran and Iraq and in the Malabar church in India, and a West Syrian strain which appears in several layers of evolution. In its most primitive form it shows itself in the Syrian (monophysite [holding that Christ's nature was divine only, not divine and human] and Catholic) and Maronite churches of the Middle East, and in the Orthodox and Malankara churches of India. In more complex and developed form it appears in the Byzantine churches and also in the Armenian church, which has been significantly influenced by other traditions (e.g., Cappadocia and Rome) as well. The two primary manifestations of the Alexandrian tradition are the Coptic church in Egypt and, though again with a variety of secondary influences (especially West Syrian), the national church of Ethiopia.

The primary focus here will be on these [eucharistic] traditions as they exist in living churches today. The aim is to examine each of these ritual forms and uncover the distinctive theology and spirituality which they contain.

All of the churches follow the standard ritual pattern where proclamation of the Word precedes and leads into the sacramental offering. It is the general Eastern custom to prepare the bread and wine for offering at the beginning of the liturgy, and it is a common understanding in the East that these gifts somehow already represent Christ even before the consecratory anaphora or eucharistic prayer. In many of the churches the ancient custom of conducting the first part of the liturgy from the *bema* (raised platform for the celebration of the Word) and

away from the altar is being restored. Except in cases where Western influence imposed other practice, these churches generally use leavened bread and distribute the eucharistic wine by intinction [dipping the bread into the wine], by spoon, or directly from the chalice. Some of the liturgies, notably the Byzantine and the Armenian, and to some extent the Coptic, are space-dependent [i.e., the celebration of the liturgy depends upon certain architectural features of the place of worship]; others less so, or not at all.

## 117 ✦ Worship in the East Syrian Churches: Nestorian, Chaldean, and Malabar

*The East Syrian Christians engaged in widespread missionary activity across the Asian continent, but the rise of Islam reduced their communities to small remnants. The liturgy of these churches is doxological in character, filled with expressions of praise and emphasizing the fulfillment of Christian hope in the kingdom of heaven.*

Antioch was the original center of Syrian Christianity, with a second center developing by the end of the second century in Edessa. Edessa itself became divided by early Christological disputes between Monophysites (one person, one nature in Christ) and Nestorians (two persons, two natures in Christ), and soon political pressure drove the Nestorians further east into the Persian Empire.

### The Churches

The Nestorian church was centered at Nisibis and organized as a distinct church in the fourth century by the bishop of Seleucia-Ctesiphon. Because it developed outside of the Roman Empire, it did so with a large measure of independence from what it called "the churches of the West" (i.e., everything to the west of itself). The Nestorian church preserves a very primitive layer of liturgical evolution.

These East Syrian Christians adhered to the decrees of Nicea, but not to those of Ephesus or Chalcedon, and eventually they adopted Theodore of Mopsuestia (d. A.D. 428), who was condemned by the Chalcedonian churches, as their champion theologian. From the fourth to the seventh centuries they engaged in great missionary activity throughout the East. The rise of Islam, however, put a stop to their missionary expansion, cut the mission territories (such as the Malabar church) off from the mother church, and left the Nestorian church but a

***Orthodox Mosaic.*** *A reproduction of a twelfth-century mosaic depicting the three great fathers of the Eastern Orthodox church: St. Gregory, St. Basil, and St. John Chrysostom. From Capella Palatina, Palermo, Sicily.*

remnant community living peaceably, if under severe restrictions, among the Muslims. Since the sixteenth century some have been united to the church of Rome, these being the Catholic Chaldeans, while others remain non-Chalcedonian Nestorians.

The Malabar church, also called St. Thomas Christians because they claim Thomas the apostle as their link to the apostolic church, came under the missionary influence of the Persian Nestorians until they were cut off from them by the advance of Islam. The St. Thomas Christians were rediscovered in the sixteenth century cby Portuguese missionaries,

who tried unsuccessfully to impose the Latin liturgy upon them. These missionaries did succeed, however, in heavily Latinizing the Malabar liturgy, a deed which has only recently been undone. Liturgical revisions begun in 1962 have restored the Malabar Eucharist to its Syro-Chaldean form, and translated it from Syriac into modern Malayalam.

The liturgy of the Nestorian, Chaldean, and Malabar churches is essentially the same. The primary anaphora (eucharistic prayer) is that of Sts. Addai and Mari, which is unique in that no words of institution are to be found in it. These words are inserted in the text by the Catholic Chaldeans and Malabarese. Two other prayers are also found in the tradition, one attributed to Nestorius and one to Theodore of Mopsuestia, though these are used only occasionally by the Nestorians and Chaldeans, and not at all by the Malabar church. These prayers do contain the institution narrative in its proper place, which makes its absence from the Addai-Mari text, in spite of great efforts to prove otherwise, most probably a simple omission rather than a reasoned deletion.

The text cited to examine the East Syrian liturgical tradition as it lives today is in the revised text of the Syro-Malabar church (Biblical, Catechetical and Liturgical Centre, Bangalore, _Celebration of the Eucharist According to the Syro-Malabar Rite_ [1973]). Differences between this and the Chaldean liturgy are noted. The major differences between the Chaldean and Nestorian liturgies are the saints who are called upon in the prayers and, of course, the insertion of the institution narrative in the Addai-Mari text.

## The Liturgy

**Introductory Rites.** The introductory rites of the liturgy are remnants of a monastic office. They consist of an abbreviated _doxology_ ("Glory to God in the highest and to all on earth, peace and hope forever"), the Lord's Prayer, a variable psalm, and a prayer of incense, which concludes with the _lakhoumara,_ a fourth-century prayer of praise to Christ the Lord. The gifts are prepared in the Chaldean rite simply, and before the liturgy begins; in the Malabar rite the offerings are prepared during the pre-anaphora, after the celebrants have come to the altar. In an earlier version of both rites, the gifts were prepared more formally between the _lakhoumara_ and the _trisagion._

**Liturgy of the Word.** The liturgy of the Word begins with the _trisagion_ ("Holy God, holy strong one, holy and immortal, have mercy on us") and consists of two (Malabar) or four (Chaldean) readings. A homily, prayer of the faithful (Malabar), and creed conclude this part of the liturgy. An earlier version of both rites concluded with an imposition of hands and blessing of the people, and probably the dismissal of catechumens as well.

**Pre-anaphora.** The pre-anaphora includes the "access to the altar" by the celebrant(s), transfer of the gifts (if prepared elsewhere) or their presentation and preparation.

**Anaphora.** The anaphora or _Qurbana_ of the Apostles (Addai and Mari) follows. The anaphora includes more than the eucharistic prayer alone. It begins with a prayer of gratitude on the part of the ministers (". . . through the multitude of your mercies, you have made us worthy to be ministers of the sacred mysteries of the body and blood of your Christ . . ."), the greeting of peace, the unveiling of the gifts (the veil is folded and placed around the gifts to represent the sepulcher of Christ), and the incensing of the gifts. After the customary dialogue, the eucharistic prayer gives thanks to God for creation, leads into the "Holy, Holy, Holy," and continues in thanksgiving for the incarnation and redemption. At this point the narrative of institution is inserted.

There follows the prayer of remembrance (_anamnēsis_), prayers of intercession (it is characteristic of the East Syrian tradition to locate the intercessions here), the invocation of the Spirit (_epiklēsis_) and the concluding doxology.

**Post-anaphora.** At the conclusion of the anaphora, priest and people proclaim faith in the living and life-giving bread of heaven. The bread is broken and signed with the precious blood. The people are invited to "approach the mysteries of the precious body and blood of our Savior" with an invitation as well to "turn away from our faults." A litany prayer for forgiveness and the Lord's Prayer (a second time) lead into the distribution of Communion to all. This is followed by a brief thanksgiving prayer, blessing, and dismissal.

## Theology and Spirit

The overall tone of the Syro-Chaldean liturgy is one of glory and praise to God. This doxological note is set at the very beginning with the "Glory to God" and the Lord's Prayer. It continues in the prayer that concludes the psalm ("For all the helps and graces you have given us, for which we cannot thank you enough, we will praise and glorify you unceasingly in your triumphant church forever") and in the _lakhoumara_ ("You, Jesus Christ, we glorify; you are the one who raise our bodies, and you are the savior of our souls"). After the _trisagion,_ and before the first reading, the presiding priest prays, "that love and hope may grow in us, that we may find salvation, and praise you forever." Before the gospel: "O Christ, light of the world and life of all, glory forever to the eternal Mercy that sent you to us." In coming to the altar, the priests pray: "We give you thanks, our Father, Lord of heaven and earth, Father, Son and Holy Spirit, for though we are sinners, you have made us worthy by your grace to offer you these holy, glorious, life-giving and divine mysteries . . ." A prayer of praise introduces the greeting of peace ("We offer you praise and honor, worship and thanksgiving now and always and forever") and again the fraction rite ("Glory be to your name, O Lord Jesus Christ, and worship to your Majesty forever"). Finally, the concluding prayers and blessing continue this theme to the end: "It is our duty, O Lord, Father, Son and Holy Spirit, to offer always to your most blessed Trinity praise and honor, worship and perpetual thanksgiving . . ." and "Let us sing the praises of Christ who has nourished us with his body and blood."

The liturgy is heavily Christocentric. While many of the prayers are addressed to the triune God or simply to the Father, many more are addressed directly to Christ himself. Even within the anaphora, a prayer most often addressed exclusively to the Father, the section on redemption is addressed to Christ.

The East Syrian liturgy is a remembrance that looks forward to the eschaton rather than to the past (the Lord's Supper) or present (*this* eucharistic offering or the heavenly mysteries as they are *now* being enacted). This is captured most forcefully in the *epiklēsis* of the Addai-Mari anaphora; "let your Holy Spirit come and rest upon this oblation of your servants; may he bless it and sanctify it that it may be unto the pardon of our offenses and forgiveness of our sins, and for the hope of resurrection and for the new life with the just in the kingdom of heaven."

Finally, the East Syrian liturgy exhibits a theological note derived from Theodore of Mopsuestia who considered the bread and wine, once placed upon the altar and before the invocation of the Spirit, to represent Christ in the tomb, with the *epiklēsis* itself signifying the Resurrection. Once the gifts are prepared, the veil is folded around them "as a sepulcher" and is not removed until after the *epiklēsis*.

The Addai-Mari anaphora has several distinctive marks. In addition to being in part addressed to Christ, the intercessions are placed between the *anamnēsis* and *epiklēsis*, and therefore form part of the offering itself. The *anamnēsis* is untypical in that, while it does commemorate the "passion,

*An Armenian Church. This church of Odzoun is from the late sixth or seventh century. It shows the cupola, suggesting the Byzantine dome, but the structure rests on the Roman-type basilica. The interior of Armenian churches are dark, symbolizing the withdrawal of the church from the world.*

death, burial and resurrection" (no mention is made in the *anamnēsis* of the future coming of Christ), it does not lead into the offering of the gifts, but only to the more general offering of "praise and honor, worship and thanksgiving." Finally, the institution narrative, where it is inserted by the Catholic Chaldeans and Malabarese, is in fact a somewhat awkward fit; most probably the original text served as a perfectly adequate eucharistic prayer without it. If so, it bears witness to a primitive strain of eucharistic understanding that was lost to other liturgical traditions.

## 118 &#x2666; WORSHIP IN THE WEST SYRIAN CHURCHES: SYRIAN, MARONITE, AND SYRO-INDIAN

*The liturgy of the West Syrian churches derives from Antioch, although some elements are believed to have come from the Jerusalem church of which James, the brother of Jesus, was the head. The tone of the liturgy is optimistic, and different parts anticipate the triumphal return of Christ.*

The churches that follow the primitive West Syrian tradition are the primary heirs to the tradition of Jerusalem. Though these churches employ many anaphoral texts, the oldest and most treasured among them is that attributed to St. James, "the brother of the Lord." The three churches, Syrian, Maronite, and Syro-Indian, need to be identified separately.

In the wake of the Council of Chalcedon, the West Syrian church of Antioch was divided between those who accepted the council's decrees and those who tended toward monophysitism. The former, considered not only orthodox Catholics but also loyal subjects of the emperor, came to be called _Melchites_ (also, _Melkites,_ from Hebrew _melekh,_ "king, monarch, emperor"); the latter, organized by the monk Jacob Baradai, came to be called _Jacobites._ In the centuries that followed, the Melchites came "more and more under the ecclesiastical domination of Constantinople, and by the end of the thirteenth century they had abandoned their own liturgies to the Monophysites and adopted that of imperial Byzantium" (Donald Attwater, _The Christian Churches of the East,_ rev. ed. [Milwaukee: Bruce Publishing Co., 1947], vol. 1, 55). The Syrian church was in effect the Syro-Jacobite church. In the seventeenth century, some of these sought union with Rome, and since that time there have been Syrian Catholics as well as Syrian Jacobites. It is questionable just how strongly monophysite these Jacobites are; the preferred term for them is non-Chalcedonian Syrians.

The Syro-Jacobite tradition came to the Malabar region of India as a result of resistance to the Portuguese missionaries, who tried first to Latinize the St. Thomas Christians but succeeded only in Latinizing their East Syrian liturgy. Some who resisted sought support from the West Syrian Jacobites, and these West Syrian Orthodox Christians continue to flourish today. In 1934, some of these sought union with Rome, thus forming the Syro-Malankara Catholic church.

The history of the Maronites is transmitted more by legend than by established fact. Legend has it that a fifth-century monk, Maron, founded a monastery in Syria and supported the positions taken at Chalcedon. Threat of persecution drove these "Catholic" monks to the mountains of Lebanon where, in the seventh century, under their first patriarch John Maron, the monastery of Maron became the Maronite church. Legend further has it that these Maronites were from their beginning loyal to the see of Rome and in communion with it. Available facts paint a much less precise picture, and suggest a probable Jacobite origin to this corporate entity that emerged only in the eighth century as a distinct Maronite church (cf. Matti Moosa, _The Maronites In History_ [Syracuse, N.Y.: Syracuse University Press, 1986]).

Over the centuries, the Maronite liturgy was heavily Latinized. In a post–Vatican II revision, it has been restored to its primitive West Syrian form. The text cited to examine the West Syrian liturgical tradition as it lives today is this revised Maronite text (Diocese of St. Maron, U.S.A., _The Maronite Liturgical Year_ [1982]).

## The Liturgy

**Introductory Rites.** The liturgy begins with a hymn sung during the entrance of the ministers and the preparation of the gifts. This latter is done simply at a side table. The introductory rites and Service of the Word are conducted at the _bema._ The opening doxology and prayer are followed by a general greeting of peace ("Peace be with the church and her children"), which is followed in turn by a seasonal psalm. The rites conclude with the _hoosoyo,_ a penitential prayer of incense, which is unique to the West Syrian tradition. It consists of a _proemium_ or introduction, which invites the assembly to "praise, glorify and honor the Lord"; the _sedro,_ which is a rich, seasonal instruction as well as a prayer; a psalm to be sung or recited by the assembly; and the _etro,_ or conclusion, asking the Lord to "be pleased with our service of incense."

**Liturgy of the Word.** The Service of the Word begins with the _trisagion,_ chanted in Aramaic, and the _mazmooro,_ a psalm chanted by the assembly and priest. One or two readings precede the gospel, which is introduced by the characteristic "Let us be attentive to the gospel of life and salvation of our Lord Jesus Christ as recorded by . . ." A brief seasonal response of the assembly, the _korozooto,_ the homily, and the creed conclude the Service of the Word.

**Pre-anaphora.** The service of the Mysteries begins with the pre-anaphora, which consists of the prayer of access to the altar ("I have entered your house, O God, and I have worshiped in your temple. O King of glory forgive all my sins"), the transfer of the offerings to the altar, the prayer of offering, and an incensation of offerings, altar, cross, and assembly.

**Anaphora.** As in the East Syrian liturgy, the anaphora includes more than the eucharistic prayer itself. Strictly speaking, the term refers to the whole second part of the liturgy, right through its concluding prayer and blessing. It begins with the rite of peace, in which the "peace" is sent from the altar (which represents Christ) to the whole congregation. The eucharistic prayer follows the typical West Syrian structure: dialogue; thanksgiving narrative which includes the "Holy, Holy, Holy," and the narrative of institution; *anamnēsis; epiklēsis;* intercessions and final doxology. Even where the liturgy as a whole is celebrated in a local vernacular, it is customary, at least among the Maronites, to chant the institution words in Aramaic: not only the "words of Jesus" but the language of Jesus as well.

The bread is broken and signed with the precious blood. The Lord's prayer follows. A brief penitential rite (priest touching the consecrated offerings with one hand, extending the other over the congregation and praying for forgiveness) leads into the invitation to communion ("Holy things for the holy, with perfection, purity and sanctity"). Communion is distributed by intinction.

**Concluding Prayers.** The conclusion of the rite is simple: a prayer of thanksgiving and the final blessings. The last prayer is a "farewell" to the altar: "Remain in peace, O altar of God, and I hope to return to you in peace . . ."

## Theology and Spirit

The dominant theme running through the West Syrian liturgy is that of anticipation. The Eucharist is celebrated in expectation of the Lord's second coming. While the liturgical texts are generous in singing the glory of the Lord, it is a glory that is yearned for rather than already present in its fullness. The Eucharist is at one and the same time *rabouno,* a pledge of the glory to come, and *zou-odo,* a viaticum [provision for future needs] which transforms us into citizens of the heavenly kingdom.

The typical prayer ending is both forward-looking and optimistic. Three examples: (a) "Then we will praise you, your only Son, and your living Holy Spirit, now and forever" (rite of peace, *Anaphora of the Twelve Apostles*); (b) "Make us worthy to live by your Spirit, leading a pure life, and we shall praise you, now and forever" *(epiklēsis, Anaphora of the Twelve Apostles);* (c) "We will glorify your Father who sent you for our salvation and your Holy Spirit, now and forever" (rite of incense, First Sunday of Epiphany). This ending reveals a subtle nuance, namely, a sense of confident hope in the future that is anticipated.

The *anamnēsis* is the eucharistic prayers is also typically a prayer that "looks forward." Even where

the note of offering is included as well, it remains secondary to the expectation and anticipation. This prayer combines both the pledge of glory to come and the purification that transformation into God's kingdom requires. "We remember, O Lover of all, your plan of salvation, and we ask you to have compassion on your faithful. Save us, your inheritance, when you shall come again to reward justly everyone according to his or her deeds" (*Anaphora of the Twelve Apostles*).

The *hoosoyo,* the offering of incense for purification, always begins, in some form or other, "May we be worthy to praise, confess, and glorify the Lord who . . . ," where a seasonal reference follows the word "who." It is a prayer for purification, but it is not a self-conscious prayer that focuses on the sinfulness of those who pray. The emphasis is rather on the deeds of God recounted in narrative form and on the *confidence* with which we approach, even while the sense of unworthiness is strongly stated. Again, the conclusion anticipates the requested action of God which allows us (will allow us) to give God praise and glory.

As with the East Syrian liturgy, the West Syrian Eucharist is strongly Christocentric. Christ is addressed in prayer. After the institution narrative in the eucharistic prayers, Christ is first prayed to ("We commemorate *your* death, O Lord. We confess *your* resurrection. We await *your* coming") and then asked in turn to pray with the church to the Father ("Your people beseech you, and through you and with you, the Father saying . . ."—the prayer returns to direct address of the Father). The greeting of peace is given to all present from the altar which represents Christ. At the prayer of forgiveness before communion the priest places one hand on the consecrated bread and wine while praying blessing on the assembly: "Bestow your blessings upon your people who love you and await your mercy" (*Anaphora of St. James*); "O Lord, with the strength of your powerful right hand, come now to bless your servants who bow before you" (*Anaphora of St. John the Evangelist*).

The liturgy moves comfortably between the awesome language of mystery and the harsh realities of everyday life. This is nicely illustrated in the peace prayer of the *Anaphora of St James:* "O Lover of all people, through your redemption, free us from personal bias and hypocrisy, that we may greet each other in peace. Then, united in a unique bond of love and harmony by our Lord Jesus Christ we will glorify and praise you and your living Spirit, now and forever."

The West Syrian liturgy captures the full scope of eschatological prayer. It is optimistic, prayed in hope against the horizon of a victory already achieved. Yet it is realistic, prayed in the face of ample evidence that the victory has not yet unfolded in its fullness in human life and human history. Finally, though it is indeed forward-looking in anticipating and yearning, it is nonetheless a prayer that recognizes the importance of the present. The *eschaton* is even now unfolding in the lives of those who pray. The announcement of the victory at one and the same time (a) proclaims a victory achieved, (b) unveils the historical incompleteness of that achievement, and (c) purifies those who yearn for the victory proclaimed.

## 119 ✦ WORSHIP IN THE BYZANTINE CHURCHES

*The churches in the Byzantine tradition are those with an historic relationship to the church of Constantinople (originally Byzantium); they are familiar to North Americans as the Orthodox churches (among them the Greek and Russian). The Byzantine rite is complex and proceeds as two interwoven liturgies, one conducted with the congregation and the other performed by the celebrants behind the icon screen (iconostasis) that separates the altar from the rest of the church. The dominant theme of this liturgical tradition is the presence of Christ, both in his incarnation and in his heavenly ministry.*

The family of churches that follow the Byzantine rite is comprised of three groups: those directly linked to the see of Constantinople; those historically evangelized from the church of Constantinople, particularly Russia and the Slavic countries; and the contemporary national churches (e.g., the Orthodox Church in America, with links to the church of Moscow) which likewise claim the title Orthodox. Catholic Byzantine churches (in union with Rome) include Melkites, Ukrainians, Russian Catholics, and Ruthenians. Apart from very slight differences, both Orthodox and Catholics follow essentially the same liturgical rites. For the Eucharist three ritual forms are used: most commonly that attributed to St. John Chrysostom, occasionally that attributed to St. Basil of Caesarea (Cappadocia), and on some days during Lent a liturgy of the presanctified gifts attributed to Gregory the Great. The liturgical texts cited here are from *The Byzantine Liturgy of St. John Chrysostom* (New York: Fordham University Russian Center, 1955).

### The Liturgy

The Byzantine liturgy is a complex ritual form that evolved in several stages from the sixth to the fourteenth centuries. Structurally it has the form of two interwoven liturgies, that which is prayed in the sanctuary (holy of holies) by the bishop and priest concelebrants, with the assistance of the deacon, and that conducted by the deacon with the assembly in front of the icon screen. A third layer of prayers consists of private prayers of the priest who prays in support of the action of the deacon and the assembly. The icon screen, and indeed the iconic display throughout the church, are integral to the liturgical act. They provide a visual focus for contemplative prayer which itself is aided by the abundant mantra-style litanies which form the heart of the liturgical act of deacon and assembly. In some churches a deacon is not regularly employed, though this obscures the structure and flow of the liturgy itself. The liturgy is an evolution of the West Syrian Antiochene tradition.

**Introductory Rites.** Two elaborate rites introduce the Byzantine liturgy: the *proskomidia* (preparation of gifts) and a collection of litanies, hymns, and prayers that are remnants of a liturgical office. The *proskomidia* is conducted by the priest and his assistants at a small table in the sanctuary; the three litanies are introduced and concluded by the priest and led by the deacon, with the assembly or the choir providing the antiphons and hymns.

The primary focus of the *proskomidia* is the round loaf of leavened bread bearing the letters IC XC NIKA ("Jesus Christ conquers"). The center square is cut and placed on the paten to represent Christ. From the rest, particles are cut and arranged in rows to honor Mary, the angels, the apostles, and the saints, and to commemorate the living and the dead. A particle is added for the priest himself. This whole represents the church: Christ, the Lamb, at the center gathering the church in heaven and the church on earth into one. The gifts are covered (the bread covered with the asterisk or "star of Bethlehem"), offered, and reverenced with incense. The sanctuary, the icon screen, the church, and the assembly are honored with incense as well.

The second introductory rite begins the public prayer. It is introduced by the priest ("Blessed is the

***Hagia Sophia.*** *The greatest of all churches of the East is the Hagia Sophia, built in Constantinople by the Emperor Justinian in the sixth century. While the exterior of the building is stunning, the full conception of the church is in the interior. Here heaven is brought down to earth, and worldly thoughts are set aside in favor of the inner, the spiritual, the heavenly. The cross section of the interior above provides the student with the sense of awe and majesty of God communicated by this space.*

kingdom of the Father, and of the Son, and of the Holy Spirit, now and always and for ever and ever") and consists of a long litany, with a prayer and antiphon, and two shorter litanies, also with prayer and antiphon. The hymn of the incarnation ("O only-begotten Son and Word of God . . .") is sung after the second antiphon.

**The Liturgy of the Word.** The liturgy of the Word once began with the entrance of the bishop. This is now the "Little Entrance," with the gospel book representing Christ carried in solemn procession ("O come, let us worship and bow down to Christ. Save us, O Son of God, risen from the dead, save us

who sing to You Alleluia"). Two seasonal hymns, the *troparion* and the *kontakion,* and the *trisagion* (the thrice-holy) precede the Scripture readings. After the Epistle and Gospel, the prayer of intercession (the insistent litany) and prayer for and dismissal of the catechumens bring the liturgy of the Word to a close.

**Pre-anaphora.** The pre-anaphora begins with a prayer of access to the altar ("We thank You, O Lord, Almighty God, for having allowed us to stand here now before Your holy altar . . ."). This leads into the litany prayer of the faithful and the transfer of the gifts. Known as the "Great Entrance," the transfer of the gifts is made in solemn procession while the choir sings the Cherubic Hymn ("Let us who here mystically represent the Cherubim in singing the thrice-holy hymn to the life-giving Trinity, now lay aside every earthly care so that we may welcome the King of the universe who comes escorted by invisible armies of angels"). The hymn is stopped halfway through so that the commemorations of the day may be announced. The gifts are placed on the altar and incensed, the priest prays the offering while the deacon and assembly sing the litany of offering.

**Anaphora.** The greeting of peace and the creed precede the eucharistic prayer proper. This latter, though more elaborate, follows the standard West Syrian structure: narrative of thanksgiving, including the "Holy, Holy, Holy," and narrative of institution; *anamnēsis* ("Remembering . . . we offer"); *epiklēsis* for consecration (". . . and make this bread the precious body of your Christ, and that which is in this chalice the precious blood of your Christ, having changed them by the Holy Spirit"); the commemorations and the final doxology.

The preparation for Communion consists of a litany of supplication, the Lord's Prayer, a blessing of the assembly, the presentation of the Eucharist to the people ("Holy things for the Holy"), and a prayer of personal faith ("I believe, Lord, and profess that you are in truth the Christ . . ."). Communion is distributed with a spoon or, in some churches where wafers are used, by intinction.

**Concluding Prayers.** The liturgy concludes with a thanksgiving, dismissal, and blessing. There are additional prayers as well, and frequently the Eucharist is immediately followed by one of the liturgical hours or other prayers. The liturgy thus concludes slowly and in stages.

## Theology and Spirit

The theology and spirit of the Byzantine liturgy are as complex as its ritual form. Indeed the two evolved together, with perhaps a greater influence on each other than in any other liturgical tradition. It does have a single, strong theme: the *presence of Christ*. This presence, however, has many forms and many manifestations. It is at one and the same time the presence of Christ *in* the liturgical action and the presence of the liturgical assembly with Christ *to* the heavenly liturgy which is eternally enacted. The liturgical forms reveal this presence; so too does

the iconic design of the liturgical space in which the liturgy unfolds.

Some sense of the evolution of this liturgy is required to understand its complex theology and spirit. Hans-Joachim Schulz (*The Byzantine Liturgy* [New York: Pueblo Publishing Co., 1986]) traces its successive stages from the time of John Chrysostom (A.D. 344–407) and Theodore of Mopsuestia to its fourteenth-century codification.

Chrysostom spoke of the liturgy as mystery, whereby heavenly realities are made manifest in human form. Theodore focused on the individual rites as imaging different aspects of the saving work of Christ (e.g., gifts on altar representing Christ in the tomb; *epiklēsis* as the resurrection). Special attention was given to Christ as "high priest" understood less in terms of "interceding" and more as "seated at the right hand of the Majesty in heaven."

This theological (mystagogical) reading of the liturgical actions took a turn to the spiritual in Dionysius the Areopagite (sixth century), who "became *the* model for later Byzantine explicators" (Schulz, 25). Liturgical forms do indeed mediate salvation but they do so by unveiling a spiritual process which unfolds in a higher sphere. It is the reverse of Theodore's stress on the actual liturgical forms making "present" Christ's saving work.

Under Maximus the Confessor (d. A.D. 662) the church structure itself became "liturgical." With the Hagia Sophia [in Constantinople] set as norm, the church building was envisioned as an image of the cosmos: two spheres, the earthly (the nave) and the heavenly (the sanctuary), not separated by, but bridged by the iconostasis. After the iconoclast controversy (eighth century) and the vindication of reverence to icons (Nicea II, A.D. 787), decoration of the icon screen and the church itself became part of the liturgical act. Schulz says of this middle Byzantine development:

In this decorative use of images the Byzantine church structure shows itself to be what it had to be according to Dionysius' vision of the world and what Maximus actually saw it as being: a copy of the cosmos that comprises heaven and earth, a cosmos ordered to Christ and filled with a cosmic liturgy. By reason of the images that adorn it the church itself henceforth becomes a liturgy, as it were, because it depicts the liturgico-sacramental presence of Christ, the angels, and the saints, and by depicting it shares in bringing it about. The iconography of the church also shows it to be the place in which the mysteries of the life of Christ are made present (p. 51).

The Byzantine liturgy exhibits this dual focus. The life-of-Jesus symbolism gives shape to the *proskomidia* which is interpreted as the birth, infancy and hidden life of Christ. It shows itself as the gifts are placed on the altar ("The venerable Joseph took down from the cross your immaculate body, and wrapping it in a clean shroud with sweet spices, he carefully laid it in a new grave") and at the *epiklēsis* ("O Lord, who sent your most Holy Spirit upon your apostles at the third hour, do not, O gracious One, take him away from us, but renew us who pray to you"). The heavenly liturgy symbolism is expressed in the Great Entrance, with its Cherubic Hymn, and the prayer at the Little Entrance ("O holy God, who rests among the saints, whose praises are sung by the Seraphim with the hymn of the trisagion, who are glorified by the cherubim and adored by all the powers of heaven"). Both are integral to the iconic design of the liturgical space where, on the one hand, the *Christos Pantokrator* [visual portrayal of Christ Almighty], set majestically in the dome, looks down over all, and, on the other hand, the biblical events of Jesus' life are set out in rich, visual display.

In several places the Byzantine liturgy reveals itself as a public statement of Christian doctrine. The "Hymn of the Incarnation" ("O only-begotten Son and Word of God, though You are immortal, You condescended for our salvation to take flesh from the holy mother of God and ever-virgin Mary") was introduced in the sixth century as a proclamation of orthodox faith against the Nestorians. The wording of the *epiklēsis* (". . . having changed them by your Holy Spirit") is a clear affirmation of the role of the Spirit as consecrator of the bread and wine, in contrast to the Western belief that it is Jesus' own words, rather than the *epiklēsis,* that effect the consecration.

The liturgy conducted, mostly in silent prayer, by the bishop and priest concelebrants in the sanctuary is, by and large, the West Syrian liturgy. This liturgy is hidden from the assembly in silence, and occasionally by a drawn veil. The priest and his actions are part of the visual iconic display. The deacon is the primary link between these actions and the assembly, assisting the priest, announcing what is taking place, and leading the assembly in an appropriate litany prayer (e.g., during the offering: "For

*Russian Church Architecture. This particular church, the Church of the Intercession, was built on the river Nere in the twelfth century. It displays the onion dome so characteristic of Russian churches. The dome is the symbol of the universe. Jesus, who is depicted in the dome, is recognized as the Lord of the whole cosmos.*

the precious gifts that are offered, let us pray to the Lord"). The experience of the assembly is not shaped by the intrinsic meaning of the various liturgical actions, but rather, as an aesthetico-religious contemplative experience, by the sensual environment composed of music, iconography, incense, and the various bodily movements (bows, signing oneself with the cross, kissing of icons, etc.) that are assigned to them. By entering into the assembly, they enter into a cosmos ruled by God and filled with mystery, and are transported to that realm where the heavenly liturgy is eternally unfolding.

## 120 • WORSHIP IN THE ARMENIAN CHURCH

*The liturgy of the Armenian church reveals the influence of many sources, but is basically of Syrian origin. It expresses the theme of sacrifice more than other Eastern liturgies and has the flavor of a temple rite.*

The church of Armenia was evangelized from Edessa, and later by missionaries from Cappadocia.

Its early liturgy was thus both Syrian and Greek. Its evolution as the Armenian church, with its own distinctive liturgy, is due to Gregory the Illuminator, a late third/early fourth century aristocrat who was converted to Christianity in Caesarea (Cappadocia), and who returned to Armenia to convert the king (Tiridates II) who had been, up to then, persecuting the Christians. As a result, Christianity became the state religion in A.D. 301, and Gregory became the leader (*Catholicos*) of the Armenian church.

## The Church

Gregory is not acclaimed as the "apostle of Armenia." The legends which recount the origin of Christianity in Armenia attribute [early evangelization] to Jude, Thaddaeus, and Bartholomew. The Armenians thus claim apostolic roots. Gregory's accomplishment was the conversion of the whole country and the establishment of the Armenian church.

Under Gregory, the church was more aristocratic than popular; the people had no access to the liturgy which was in Syriac and in Greek-revisions came only in the fifth century. These involved the creation of an Armenian alphabet and the translation of both Scripture and the liturgy into Armenian. The Armenian liturgy is certainly Antiochene in its roots, but, apparently for political reasons, the Armenian church sided with Alexandria after the Council of Chalcedon. Hence it recognizes only the first three councils. Today there are Armenian Catholics in union with Rome, and Armenians who remain an independent church. The preferred title for these latter is the Armenian Apostolic Church.

The liturgy of the Armenian church, called "The Liturgy of our Blessed Father Saint Gregory the Illuminator, revised and augmented by the Holy Patriarchs and Doctors, Sahag, Mesrob, Kud, and John Mandakuni," is, as noted, rooted in the Antiochene tradition. Its evolution, however, reveals the influence of many sources: Coptic, Byzantine, and later (twelfth century) Latin. There is a substratum of the Syrian liturgy of St. James, which may have come via the liturgy of Basil (in use in Cappadocia). It was later embellished with texts from the Chrysostom (Byzantine) and Latin liturgies. It is not therefore *simply* an evolution of the Syrian/Antiochene tradition. Nonetheless it remains Syrian at its deepest level. The texts cited here are from the English translation published in *The Armenian Liturgy* (Venice: Armenian Monastery of St. Lazarus, 1862).

## The Liturgy

**Introductory Rites.** The introductory rites consist of the vesting of the ministers in the sacristy, the entrance and absolution of the officiating priest, and the preparation of the gifts. The first two are carried out in rich ceremonial; the last is done without the elaborate ritual of the Byzantine *proskomidia*. When prepared and veiled, the gifts are honored with incense. Most significant in these rites is the focus on the priest.

**Liturgy of the Word.** The liturgy of the Word originally began with the chanting of the *trisagion*. It was later embellished with texts from the Byzantine liturgy. It begins now with the blessing ("Blessed be the reign of the Father, the Son, and the Holy Ghost . . ."), the *Monogenes* of the Byzantine liturgy ("O only-begotten Son and Word of God . . ."), which may be replaced with a seasonal hymn, a blessing, and four prayers recited by the priest while the choir sings the psalm and hymn of the day. These four prayers are the three antiphon prayers from the Byzantine introductory rites and the prayer of the Byzantine "Little Entrance."

The *trisagion* is then sung, while the priest prays the Byzantine prayer of the *trisagion*. This is followed by a litany, the Epistle and Gospel reading, the creed (to which is appended an anti-Arian *anathema*), another litany and blessing, and the dismissal of the catechumens.

**Pre-anaphora.** The pre-anaphora begins with a proclamation ("The body of our Lord, and the blood of our Redeemer are about to be here present . . ."). There follows the *hagiology* of the day (a seasonal catechesis), while the celebrant, if a bishop, removes the vestments of honor, or, if a priest, removes his cap. The gifts are transferred to the altar while the choir sings the Cherubic Hymn and the priest prays the corresponding Byzantine prayer "humbled, before the altar." The gifts are incensed, the deacon exhorts the assembly ("With faith and holiness, let us pray before the holy altar of God, filled with profound dread . . ."), and the priest prays the prayer of oblation.

**Anaphora.** The anaphora proper begins with a benediction and peace greeting. The deacon kisses the altar and the arms [sic] of the priest, and then brings the greeting to the others. The eucharistic prayer, after the customary dialogue, again follows the classic West Syrian structure: thanksgiving narrative for creation and redemption, including the "Holy, holy," and leading into the institution account, *anamnēsis, epiklēsis,* intercessions and doxology. This prayer is interspersed with other prayers, blessings, greetings and gestures (incense, signing with cross, etc.), and it includes seasonal commemorations as well.

**Post-anaphora.** The Lord's Prayer and incensing of the people begins the Communion or post-anaphora. This is followed by a prayer of penitence addressed to the Holy Spirit. The gifts are presented to the people in rather elaborate fashion: a Trinitarian benediction oft repeated by deacon, choir, and people. The priest then invites all to Communion: "Let us partake holily of the holy, holy and precious body and blood of our Lord and Redeemer Jesus Christ, who, descended from heaven, is distributed among us. He is life, the hope of the resurrection, the expiation and pardon of sins. Sing to the Lord our God . . ." This last part is echoed by the deacon. Then, with curtain drawn, the priest prepares to take Communion with a series of prayers and gestures, the longest prayer being that of John Chrysostom ("I give thee thanks, I exalt thee, I glorify thee, O Lord my God, thou hast rendered me worthy on this day to partake of thy divine and fearful sacrament . . .").

After Communion of the faithful, the priest blesses all ("Lord, save thy people, and bless thine inheritance . . ."). The bishop, if presiding, puts on his episcopal robes. There are prayers of thanksgiving, a prayer for a blessing, the prologue of John read as the "last gospel," a prayer for peace, and the final blessing. As is customary among the Byzantines, the Armenians too distribute blessed bread as the people leave.

## Theology and Spirit

The tone of the Armenian liturgy is that of a "temple" liturgy, and throughout the text it stresses the notion of sacrifice more than any other Eastern liturgy. References to the temple are clear and abundant. The hymn sung during the vesting proclaims that "holiness becomes thy dwelling, since thou alone art enveloped in splendor." After the confession and absolution of the priest, he prays: "Within the precincts of this temple . . . we adore with trembling." And again: "In the tabernacle of holiness, and in the place of praise . . . we adore with trembling." During the preparation of the offerings, the priest incenses and prays: "In the Lord's temple, open to our offerings and our vows, united as we are to accomplish in obedience and in prayer the mystery of this approaching and august sacrifice, let us together march in triumph round the tribune of the holy temple . . ." And he is clearly a temple priest who prays: "Thou hast confided to us the priesthood for this holy ministry and for thine unbloody sacrifice."

References to the sacrifice are likewise clear and abundant. A prayer during the vesting reads: "Full of fear and awe we approach thee, to offer the sacrifice due to thine Omnipotence." The deacon proclaims just before the eucharistic prayer: "Christ, the immaculate Lamb of God, offers himself as victim." The intercessions of the same prayer are introduced by: "Grant by virtue of this sacrifice . . ."; and a thanksgiving prayer chanted by the deacon mentions sacrifice no less than four times.

The way the liturgy views the priest is consistent with both temple and sacrifice. In contrast to the Byzantine *proskomidia,* with its elaborate focus on the bread and wine as Christ, the Armenian introductory rites come to focus much more strongly on the priest. He confesses his sins ("I confess in the presence of God . . . all the sins I have committed") and receives absolution ("May the all-powerful God have mercy on you, and grant you the pardon of all your sins . . .") before going ahead with his service. Prayers of purification are numerous.

In addition, the texts of the liturgy put a strong accent on the majesty of God. They are more than generous in speaking of God as profound, incomprehensible, boundless, infinite, inscrutable, etc., and thus worthy of glory power, worship, honor, praise.

Finally, note should be made of the place of the Holy Spirit in the Armenian liturgy. While it is common in both East and West to address the Spirit in the mode of invocation (*epiklēsis, Veni Sancte Spiritus*), the Armenian text addresses the Spirit in other forms of prayer as well. To give but one example, the blessing after the Lord's prayer: "O Holy Spirit! Thou who are the source of life and of mercy, have pity on this people who, kneeling, adores thy Divinity . . . ," with its adjoining doxology: "Through Jesus Christ our Lord, to who, as to thee, O Holy Spirit, and to the Almighty Father, belong glory . . ."

*Icon of the Trinity. Eastern churches are filled with icons and frescos depicting the Godhead, saving events, prophets, apostles, and saints. The finest example of an icon is Andrei Rublevs fifteenth-century Old Testament Trinity, shown here. It does not directly represent the Father, Son, and Holy Spirit, but rather the three angels who appeared to Abraham at the Oak of Mamre.*

## 121 • WORSHIP IN THE ALEXANDRIAN CHURCHES: COPTIC AND ETHIOPIAN

*The Coptic and Ethiopian liturgies are textually similar but quite different in style and setting. The Coptic liturgy is sober and restrained, while the Ethiopian liturgy is full of life and exuberance.*

Legend has it that Christianity spread to Egypt at the hands of St. Mark, and to Ethiopia via the eunuch of Candace (Acts 8:26-40). The legends concerning Mark attribute to him the complete shaping of the church in Alexandria: he was bishop and first patriarch, ordained deacons, presbyters and other bishops, and in general was responsible for establishing the church order that was in fact a much later development (see Aziz S. Atiya, *A History of Eastern Christianity* [London: Methuen, 1968]). With regard to Egypt it is more likely that, because of the commerce between Jerusalem and Alexandria, the path of Christianity's spread was much less precise. As for Ethiopia, it is not until the fourth century, under Frumentius and Aedesius of Tyre, that any authentic evangelization is recorded (Donald Attwater, *The Christian Churches of the East,* rev. ed. [Milwaukee: Bruce Publishing Co., 1947] vol. 1, 138), with more serious evangelization coming still later at the hands of Monophysite monks from Syria.

In the sixth century, however, the Coptic church was given missionary responsibility for Ethiopia, and the church there came under the jurisdiction of the Coptic patriarch of Alexandria, a dependency, and although the Ethiopian church had other influences as well, and indeed does have its own particular liturgical "flavor," the two can be taken to constitute a single liturgical tradition. This tradition is Alexandrian in its theological outlook, dominantly Monophysite in its Christology, and in many ways it is the polar opposite of the traditions rooted in Antioch.

The Coptic liturgy is austere, and quite evidently the product of monastic origins. Among the Ethiopians the liturgy is far more colorful, with dance, elaborate costume and a far more vibrant musical setting. Textually, however, the two liturgies are similar. The Coptic text cited here is from *The Coptic Morning Service for the Lord's Day,* translated by John Patrick Crichton Stuart (London, 1980); the Ethiopian text, which has been modified and somewhat simplified, is taken from *The Ordinary and the Anaphora of the Apostles,* edited by T. Baraki (Washington, D.C., 1984).

### The Coptic Liturgy

The Coptic liturgy employs three readings before the gospel itself: from the letters of Paul, from the catholic epistles, and from the Acts of the Apostles. Attached to each is a lengthy prayer. Between these readings and the gospel there are a series of petitions, accompanied by additional reverences to (processions around) the altar, an offering of incense on behalf of the people and the *trisagion.* After the gospel, which is greeted in a solemn and elaborate procession, the priest prays the gospel prayer (". . . may we be made worthy to hear Thine holy gospels, and may we keep thy precepts and commandments . . ."). Catechumens may have been dismissed at this point.

**Pre-anaphora.** A prayer is prayed privately by the priest as he approaches the altar (prayer of the veil). The priest then introduces the intercessions which are each led by the deacon (response of the people: "Lord, have mercy") and augmented by the priest. The ministers, the people, and the altar are incensed and all proclaim the Nicene Creed.

**Anaphora.** As in the other Eastern liturgies, the greeting of peace precedes the eucharistic prayer. The eucharistic prayer of Basil is West Syrian in its structure: thanksgiving narrative, which includes the "Holy, Holy, Holy" and the Supper narrative, *anamnēsis, epiklēsis,* intercessions, and doxology. The institution narrative is interspersed with frequent acclamations of the people ("Amen"), as is the *epiklēsis* ("Amen" and "I believe"). The intercessions, which include a reading of the diptychs of the dead, are quite lengthy.

**Post-anaphora.** The prayer of fraction, which precedes the Lord's Prayer, includes acclamations of faith in the presence of Christ and acts of adoration. The Lord's prayer is followed by several prayers of remembrance and one of absolution (addressed to the Father). The gifts are presented ("The holy to the holy"), and after a further series of preparation prayers, including an additional proclamation of faith ("I believe, I believe, I believe and confess till the last breath that this is the life-giving flesh which thine only begotten Son, our Lord and God and Savior Jesus Christ took from our lady, the lady of us all, the holy mother of God, the holy Mary . . ."), Communion is distributed. The liturgy concludes with prayer, blessing, and dismissal.

## The Ethiopian Liturgy

The Ethiopian tradition knows of at least 22 eucharistic prayers, unique among which is one addressed in part to the Virgin Mary. The most commonly used, however, is the anaphora "of the Apostles," which is in fact an Alexandrian derivation from the prayer of Hippolytus (third-century Rome), and a variant on the Coptic anaphora of St. Cyril. The liturgical language is Ge'ez, though it is usually celebrated in the contemporary vernacular, Amharic.

**Introductory Rites.** After the opening sign of the cross (remnant of the Coptic office of incense), the priest announces: "How wondrous this day and how marvelous this hour in which the Holy Spirit will come down from the high heaven and overshadow this offering and sanctify it." This same text is employed in the West Syrian liturgy as a diaconal announcement prior to the *epiklēsis.*

Attention is then turned to the offerings with the same lengthy ritual form as in the Coptic liturgy. The bread is blessed ("Christ, our true God, sign with your right hand [sign of the cross] and bless this bread [sign of the cross], hallow it with your power and strengthen it with your Spirit"). The of-

fering is made (again, a West Syrian text), the chalice is blessed, and then the bread and wine both are given the Trinitarian blessing. A doxology introduces a prayer of thanksgiving and another of absolution, and the first anaphora (addressed to Christ) is begun. Reminiscent of Theodore of Mopsuestia, whose theology is evident in both the East Syrian and West Syrian traditions, the prayer of the veil, as the celebrant covers the bread and wine, recalls: "What we have placed upon this blessed paten is in the likeness of the sepulcher in which you stayed three days and three nights . . ." Long prayers of general intercession conclude the introductory rites.

**Liturgy of the Word.** The liturgy of the Word begins with an invitation to stand, a greeting of peace, and invitation to adore "the Father, the Son and Holy Spirit, three persons, one God," and the prayer to Mary, recited by all ("You are the golden censer, that bore the glowing charcoal . . ."). The traditional four readings are reduced to two though the "readings prayers" have been retained. Between the Epistle and the Gospel praises of Mary and the *trisagion* are prayed and the blessing of the four "cardinal points" is given.

**Pre-anaphora.** The rites before the eucharistic prayer include: a prayer of blessing and intercession, the creed, a prayer of purification (washing of hands), a doxology ("Glory to God in the heavens, and peace on earth to men of good will"), and kiss of peace.

**Anaphora.** The anaphora of the apostles is essentially the Hippolytus text, with the "Holy, Holy, Holy" and other acclamations of the people included. There are, as in the original, no intercessions within the eucharistic prayer proper.

**Post-anaphora.** A complex fraction rite follows the eucharistic prayer, and, together with a prayer of thanksgiving, introduces the Lord's Prayer. This is followed by a series of prayers (of blessing, for forgiveness, of remembrance—including the commemoration of the dead). When the gifts are presented to the people ("Holy things to the holy"), a prayer over penitents and a profession of faith in the Eucharist is made ("I believe, I believe, I believe and profess . . ."). Final prayers of preparation for Communion follow.

After Communion there are prayers of thanksgiving, an imposition of hands in blessing of the people, a final blessing and dismissal.

## —————— Theology and Spirit ——————

The Alexandrian theological tradition stands in contrast to the Antiochene on several counts. Its emphasis on the majesty and otherness of God is stronger, its ability to deal with the fullness of the incarnation weaker. In Trinitarian theology it tends towards subordinationism, of Son to Father, of Spirit to both. In Christology it tends to emphasize the divine over the human. In liturgical theology it tends to stress the spiritual meaning of the symbols and the eternal realm in which that meaning resides. The sanctuary screen in the Coptic churches separates heaven from earth rather than uniting the two and bridging the gap.

Probably the most notable piece in both the Coptic and Ethiopian liturgies is the attention given to the bread and wine in the introductory rites and the seemingly consecratory "first anaphora" to Christ. There is a parallel in the Coptic baptismal liturgy which may illuminate this prayer. Before the baptism, ordinary water is solemnly "consecrated" for the baptism; afterwards with a prayer equally as solemn, it is "returned to ordinary use." It is as though materials of the earth, in this case the bread and wine, require a preliminary "consecration" to render them fit for the subsequent consecratory actions of God.

Equally of note, at least in the Coptic version of this liturgical tradition, is the attention paid to the altar. The altar is the altar of sacrifice which the priest approaches unworthily. Many of the processions around the altar, including kissing the altar's four corners, accompany prayers of intercession offered in worship to God. The altar is likewise a symbol of the one who is offered ("We adore thee, O Christ, and thy good Father, and the Holy Ghost. Behold, thou hast come, thou hast saved us"—said while incensing the altar). Placing the gifts upon the altar places them as well on the altar above ("Receive them upon thine holy reasonable altar in heaven for a sweet savor of incense"—said while incensing the gifts placed upon the altar).

Finally, the place of Mary is unique. She is called the "censer of gold" whose "sweet cloud is our Savior" (Coptic) and the "golden censer that bore the glowing charcoal whom the blessed One . . . accepted from the sanctuary" (Ethiopian). She is also the one who makes strong supplication for us before God.

Peter E. Fink[3]

## 122 • BIBLIOGRAPHY ON THE HISTORY OF EASTERN WORSHIP

Antiochian Orthodox Christian Archdiocese of North America. _Service Book of the Holy Eastern Orthodox Catholic and Apostolic Church._ Ed. by Isabel F. Hapgood. Englewood, N.J.: Syrian Antiochian Orthodox Archdiocese of New York and of North America, 1975. The service book follows the Greek Orthodox liturgies of St. John Chrysostom and St. Basil. Also used by the Antiochian Evangelical Orthodox Mission.

_The Book of Hours of the Order of Common Prayers of the Armenian Apostolic Orthodox Church._ Evanston, Ill.: n.p., 1964. The complete prayer tradition of the Armenian church.

Butler, A. _The Ancient Coptic Churches of Egypt,_ 2 vols. Oxford: Clarendon Press, 1970. This classic work, originally published in 1884, contains a thorough excursus into the worship of the Coptic church. Its aim is to make a systematic study of the liturgical antiquities of Egypt. Volume 1 deals with various historic churches while Volume 2 deals with the liturgy in its entirety.

Cabasilas, Nicholas. _A Commentary on the Divine Liturgy._ Crestwood, N.Y.: St. Vladimir's Seminary Press, 1977. Orthodox. The commentary of a fourteenth-century mystic on the St. John Chrysostom liturgy.

Dalmais, Irenée. _Eastern Liturgies._ New York: Hawthorn Books, 1960. This work introduces all the Eastern churches of antiquity as well as those of the present day. It then presents the various liturgical families of the East and the unity and diversity of these liturgies. Special studies are also included on each of the sacraments.

Germanus of Constantinople. _On the Divine Liturgy._ Crestwood, N.Y.: St. Vladimir's Seminary Press, 1984. Presents an eighth-century commentary on the Liturgy of St. Germanus, who was the patriarch of Constantinople from 714 to 730. This liturgy exercised a tremendous influence on the Byzantine Christian world into the fourteenth century.

*The Maronite Liturgical Year,* Vols. 1–3. Detroit: Diocese of St. Maron, U.S.A., 1983.

Meletius, Michael Solovii. *The Byzantine Divine Liturgy: History and Commentary.* Cambridge, U.K.: Cambridge University Press, 1970. A thorough study on the historical origins and development of the Byzantine liturgy, plus a commentary on all the prayers and rites of the Divine Liturgy.

Mercier, S. *The Ethiopic Liturgy: Its Sources, Development and Present Form.* Milwaukee: The Young Churchman, 1915. This work situates the Ethiopic liturgy in the setting of the early church, then develops the liturgy proper by examining it in detail.

Meyendorff, John. *The Byzantine Legacy in the Orthodox Church.* Crestwood, N.Y.: St. Vladimir's Seminary Press, 1982.

Nersoyan, T., trans. *The Divine Liturgy of the Armenian Apostolic Orthodox Church.* New York: The Delphic Press. This work contains the entire Divine Liturgy of the Armenian church plus a commentary on each of the parts of the liturgy.

Paul of Finland. *The Feast of Faith.* Crestwood, N.Y.: St. Vladimir's Seminary Press, 1988. A very helpful explanation of and commentary on the St. John Chrysostom liturgy.

Schmemann, Alexander. *The Eucharist.* Crestwood, N.Y.: St. Vladimir's Seminary Press, 1988. This extraordinary work provides an interpretation of the entire celebration of Eastern worship. Perhaps Schmemann's most important and thoughtful work.

———. *For the Life of the World: Sacraments and Orthodoxy.* Crestwood, N.Y.: St. Vladimir's Seminary Press, 1988. Another marvellous work by Schmemann, this one dealing with all of the sacraments of the Eastern churches. A commentary suitable for general readership, of deep humanity and deep spirituality.

Schulz, Hans-Joachim. *The Byzantine Liturgy: Symbolic Structure and Faith Expression.* New York: Pueblo Publishing Co., 1986. A detailed examination of the origin and development of the Eastern rite, with a helpful commentary on the various parts of the Byzantine liturgy.

Taft, Robert. *The Great Entrance: A History of the Transfer of Gifts and Other Preanaphoral Rites of the Liturgy of St. John Chrysostom,* 2d ed. Rome: Pontificium Institutum Studiorum Orientalium, 1975. The most complete study of the Great Entrance of the Eastern Orthodox liturgy available.

Vasileios, Archimandrite. *Hymn of Entry.* Crestwood, N.Y.: St. Vladimir's Seminary Press, 1984. In the Eastern church, a theologian is one who does liturgy. This work is an excellent example of theology in the making.

Wybrew, Hugh. *The Orthodox Liturgy: The Development of the Eucharistic Liturgy in the Byzantine Rite.* Crestwood, N.Y.: St. Vladimir's Seminary Press, 1990.

# FOUR

# Historic Worship in the Western (Catholic) Church

---

*The Roman rite was only one of several rites that existed in the Western church prior to the time of the Reformation. As the Roman rite gained influence, the traditions of other regions became assimilated to it. Some of the regional rites, however, retained a distinctive character up to the Reformation era. In the Council of Trent, Catholic liturgy was standardized and remained largely unchanged until Vatican II.*

---

## 123 • LITURGICAL DIVERSITY AND ROMAN INFLUENCE

*While there is a common core to historic Western Christian liturgy, there is also considerable diversity. Rites differed from region to region and from place to place. Regional improvisations on the basic framework of the liturgy led eventually to a proliferation of liturgical books in the Western church, with much variation even within the same regional traditions.*

In origin, evolution, and spirit, the liturgical tradition of the Western church is complex and diverse. What is known as the Roman rite was only one of several Western rites which existed between the fourth and sixteenth centuries; the others are known as the North African, Ambrosian, Spanish, Gallican, and Celtic rites.

In matters of worship, local churches were free to develop their own forms, and often did so in conjunction with the churches of the same region under the authority of the metropolitan bishop who served as primate of the region or "diocese" as it was termed in the Roman Empire. The bishop of Rome, as primate of the part of Italy extending south of the city of Rome (i.e., *Italia suburbicaria*), had the right to insist that churches in that region conform to Roman usages (see letter of Innocent I to Decentius of Gubbio, 19 March 416). In like manner, the bishop of Milan as primate of *Italia annonaria,* the bishop of Carthage as primate of Africa, the bishop of Carthago Nova (until 531) or of Toledo (after 531) as primate of Hispania, the bishop of Arles as primate of Septimania, and the bishop of

Lyons as primate of Gaul, could convoke synods and insist upon adherence to liturgical canons.

Until 1080, the Roman see never attempted to control the liturgical observances of churches outside of *Italia suburbicaria.* Indeed, because of the Lombard invasions, its sphere of liturgical influence was limited to the narrow corridor which joined Rome and Ravenna. As a matter of fact, the bishop of Rome was well aware of the need for diversity of forms to suit the temperament of different peoples. In 597, when Augustine of Canterbury wrote to ask Gregory I why the churches of Gaul and of Rome had different usages and which rite to use for the newly converted Angles, the pope replied:

> You should carefully select for the English church whatever is most able to please almighty God, whether it come from the Roman, Gallican or whatever church you may find it. . . . Things ought not be loved because of the place from which they come, but because they are good in themselves. Therefore choose elements that are reverent (*pia*), awe-inspiring (*religiosa*), and orthodox (*recta*) from each and every church and arrange them as in a little book in accord with the mind of the English and so establish them as custom (*Monumenta Germaniae Historica, Epistolae* 2, 334).

Although most of what we know about the individual rites can be discerned only from the evidence of extant liturgical texts and artifacts, the various Latin rites emerged when improvisation was still predominant, and long before the date of the oldest surviving manuscripts. The practice of improvisation,

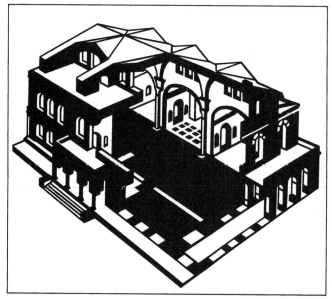

*St. Peter's Basilica at Rome. The Emperor Constantine built this basilica of wood in the fourth century. It was torn down and replaced by the present edifice in the Renaissance period.*

however, presupposed the faithful observance of certain canons, guidelines, or principles which were transmitted in the local church from one generation to the next. At the core of this liturgical patrimony was the structure of the service, the framework for improvisation. In all the traditions, the first composition of written texts was nothing more than a new type of improvisation. A set of texts was prepared for a specific celebration and afterwards placed in the local archives as a record of the celebration. Fifth-century Rome witnessed the production of a great number of variable texts for the Eucharist, the composition or editing of euchological texts for the administration of the sacraments and for use at the liturgy of the hours. By the end of the same century, samples of this written improvisation had found their way to northern Italy, southeastern Gaul, and northeastern Spain, inspiring a veritable explosion of euchological creativity throughout the West, giving additional impetus to the emergence of the local rites, and leading eventually to the compilation of the numerous liturgical books of each tradition (sixth-ninth centuries).

## 124 ✦ THE NORTH AFRICAN LITURGY

*It is thought that North Africa was the birthplace of Latin Christianity. Because of Muslim expansion, however, the church did not survive in North Africa beyond the eighth century. Since no actual texts of the ancient North African liturgy are extant, the outline of the rite can only be reconstructed from other sources.*

It is certain that North Africa, the cradle of Latin Christianity, was likewise the first place to use Latin in the liturgy. Without discouraging the ancient practice of improvisation, councils and synods (e.g., Hippo [393], canon 25) provided guidelines for formulating liturgical prayers and insisted that prayers composed elsewhere be approved by the teachers (*fratres instructiores*). The composition of prayers by heretics prompted a later synod to direct that "*preces, prefationes, commendationes* and *impositiones manuum*" be composed under supervision of the hierarchy and used by all (Carthage [407], canon 10).

African collections of *libelli missarum* and even sacramentaries are referred to in writings from the fifth century; but, apart from a few Arian fragments, no actual liturgical texts have survived. Nevertheless, details of the rite have been gleaned from nonliturgical sources, e.g., conciliar decrees like those already mentioned and especially the writings and sermons of Augustine of Hippo. The following order of the Mass is based on a reconstruction by F. Van der Meer (*Augustine the Bishop* [New York: Harper & Row, 1961], 388–402).

(In this and all subsequent outlines, the asterisk marks a chant by the people or choir; the readings are indicated by CAPITALS.)

Entrance of the Clergy
Greeting
EPISTLE
*PSALM (Augustine considered this a reading)
GOSPEL
Homily
[announcements]
Dismissal of the Catechumens
Solemn Intercessions
Offering with *Psalm singing
Preface dialogue
Improvised Preface without Sanctus
Approved Eucharistic prayer
"Amen"
Fractio
Lord's Prayer
Communion with *Psalm 33
Final prayer
Dismissal

*St. Ambrose. A representation of a fifth-century mosaic of St. Ambrose that was found in the church that bears his name in his home city of Milan. Because he lived to A.D. 397, this sketch may very well be similar to his actual appearance. However, one cannot be certain because churchmen were often portrayed by stereotypes.*

The year after Augustine's death (430) the African church saw the beginning of more than a century of bitter persecution by the Arian Vandals. In 698, Carthage was taken by the Moors and the church that had given birth to Latin Christianity ceased to exist altogether.

## 125 ✦ THE GALLICAN LITURGY

*Great diversity evidently existed in the liturgies used in southern Gaul. Lack of documentation, however, makes it difficult to reconstruct some parts of the liturgy. By the ninth century, the Gallican liturgy had become fused with the Roman rite. The spread of Roman influence is clearly shown by early Gallican sources.*

Properly speaking, the Gallican rite refers exclusively to the liturgical tradition which emerged in the southern part of Gaul at the beginning of the sixth century, and which remained in use throughout the province until it was replaced (fused) with the Roman rite under the Carolingians (late eighth-ninth centuries).

The study of the Gallican rite is hampered by the sparsity of its liturgical books, and some major

elements of the liturgy remain completely deprived of any documentation. There are euchological texts for the celebration of the Eucharist and for the administration of the sacraments (*Missale Gothicum, Missale Bobbiense, Missale Francorum,* and several Mass-fragments; benedictionals: collections of episcopal blessings given before communion; diptychs: tables of names for the commemoration of the living and dead; and *ordines scrutiniorum:* formulas for the celebration of the scrutinies). The system of readings has left fragmentary evidence in lectionaries, *capitularia* (lists of first and last words of the pericopes) and *passionaria* (lives of the saints read both at Mass and the office of their feasts). No Gallican antiphonary for the Mass or hours has been preserved, though the hymns of the Gallican hours and a few genuine Gallican chants may have survived in the Gregorian chant tradition. To complicate matters further, most of the sources already mentioned include Roman material; for example the Bobbio missal preserves the structure of the Gallican Mass only as far as the preface where it abandons the variable Gallican prayer for the Roman canon.

In contrast with the Spanish, Milanese, and Roman rites, the Gallican sources indicate an enormous diversity, even between neighboring dioceses; for example the church at Auxerre—as evidenced in the collection of Masses published by Mone in 1850—used very different formularies but followed basically the same order of service as the church of Autun where the *Missale Gothicum* was compiled. At the same time other rites were being codified and standardized to some extent, the churches of Gaul and Septimania suffered the successive invasions and ensuing political divisions of the Visigoths, Ostrogoths, and Franks—all in the first half of the sixth century. Codification was far from systematic or uniform in spite of the attempts of local councils to regulate church life and worship.

The following outline of the Gallican order of the Mass has been reconstructed from letters of Pseudo-Germanus of Paris (*Expositio antiquae liturgiae gallicanae,* ed. by E. C. Ratcliff [London: Henry Bradshaw Society, 1971]) and the sacramentaries mentioned above:

[Preparation of Offerings at side altar or in
    sacristy]
*Antiphona ad praelegendum with Psalm
Call for silence and Greeting

*Trisagion and *Kyrie
Prophetica (*Benedictus;* or a hymn in Lent)
Collectio post Prophetiam
LECTIO PROPHETICA
*Responsorium (?)
LECTIO EX APOSTOLO
*Canticle from Daniel (*Benedictiones* on feasts:
    or ?)
*Trisagion ante evangelium
EVANGELIUM
*Sanctus post evangelium
Homilia
Preces
Collectio post precem
Dismissal of catechumens
Solemn presentation of the Gifts with *Sonus
Praefatio missa and collectio
Names and collectio post nomina
Collectia ad pacem and Pax
Contestatio (Immolatio missae) and *Sanctus
*Vere sanctus*—institution narrative—*post
    mysterium*
*Confractionem
Lord's Prayer
Episcopal Benediction
Communion and *Trecanum*
Post Eucharisticam and Collectio post
    communionem
Dismissal

A distinguishing characteristic of the Gallican rite lies in its use of variable texts in the eucharistic prayer before and after the institution narrative (*post sanctus* and *post mysterium*). In this it contrasted with the fixed canon in the Roman and Milanese rites but also to some degree with the Spanish rite, which also used variable pieces in the eucharistic prayer. The Gallican provides no system but simply a repertoire of texts for the three pieces—*contestatio* (preface), *post sanctus, post mysterium*—without coordination or connection among them. This is all the more noteworthy given the fact that there was an attempt to match "proper" orations for the other parts of the Mass to the feast or season.

With regard to the euchology for other ritual and sacramental celebrations, the typically Gallican approach included an introductory invitation directed to the faithful (bidding) which anticipated and sometimes contained the blessing which followed. In the case of ordinations, the unit included three elements: the instruction of the candidates, the invi-tation to prayer, and the blessing/ordination prayer. This form was an expansion of the ancient and universal liturgical prayer unit (which is best known in the Solemn Intercessions on Good Friday in the Roman rite): invitation to prayer—silent prayer—concluding oration. The practice is so characteristic of the Gallican rite that a number of the variable texts for each Mass originally assumed this form of instructive invitation to prayer (*Praefatio missa, Post eucharisticam*). The combination of instruction, invitation, and prayer in the compilation of texts for other ritual and sacramental celebrations was amply employed by the liturgical compilers of the Carolingian period and served as one of several ways in which the ancient Roman liturgy was "Gallicanized."

Given the heterogeneity of the Gallican repertoire, it is almost impossible to make an evaluation of style and content that is universally applicable. However, those texts which actually originate with the Gallican rite betray a conservative tendency in using the traditional vocabulary, phrasing, and syntax that are found in the oldest Gallican sources. Although the same phenomenon has been noted in a few Ambrosian and Spanish prayers, it is a veritable characteristic of Gallican euchology. An important indication of the adherence to the tradition appears in the Gallican equivalent to the *anamnēsis* in the *post mysterium:* only the *death* of the Lord is recalled, as in the Pauline gloss of 1 Corinthians 11:26, and as seems to have been the case in North Africa at the time of Cyprian. In this, the Gallican rite stands alone; even the Spanish include at least the death and the resurrection in the *post pridie.*

It has often been suggested that the Gallican style is one of exuberance and prolixity, elaborate ceremonial and splendor. Such an evaluation is not justified and neither does it take into account the varied origin of the Gallican repertoire of prayers and practices. In reality, at least among the texts which are genuinely Gallican, one finds extreme conciseness and density of content, reflecting the prose style of the time and region. The fact that so much was so readily borrowed and adapted from Eastern and Spanish sources—another Gallican characteristic in itself—contributes to the impression that Gallican means long-winded.

On the other hand the later Gallican compilers did add extra prayers to the rites. The so-called *apologiae* and "accompanying prayers" first make their appearance in Gallican sources, though it is difficult

_Scripture Copier. A common occupation of monks in the middle ages was to copy Scripture and liturgical books. Here a monk is depicted at his art._

to say whether or not they were inspired by the Irish. The apologies were private prayers in which the priest acknowledged his sinfulness and unworthiness; the others include private prayers for vesting, for the offertory, and for before and after communion. Many of these made their way into the Gallicanized-Roman books of the eighth and ninth centuries, but the famous _Missa Illyrica_ (sacramentary of Sigebert of Minden [tenth century]) includes nearly 200 of them newly composed or complied from several sources.

## 126 ✦ THE SPANISH LITURGY

_Ecclesiastical leadership in the Iberian peninsula held the liturgy in high esteem as a means of communicating the truths of the Christian faith. Spanish liturgical creativity, therefore, was marked by a stress on doctrinal precision._

The Spanish liturgy, also known rather inaccurately as Mozarabic or Visigothic, is the autonomous liturgy which was in constant use in Spain from the beginning of the sixth century until it was suppressed by the Council of Braga (1080) at the insistence of Pope Gregory VII (1073–1085). At the time of its codification, when Visigothic rule reached its greatest extension (seventh century), the Spanish rite was celebrated throughout the Iberian peninsula

and in the religion of southwestern France known as _Gallia Narbonese._ After its suppression, it continued to be celebrated in a few parish churches for a time, and with intermittent periods of complete abandonment, in a single chapel at the cathedral of Toledo into the twentieth century.

Among the surviving manuscripts of the Spanish liturgy there are _dittici_ (variable texts for the Eucharist) that may have been copied from third-century sources and constitute the major evidence of a native liturgical patrimony. In the _dittici_ contained in the _missale mixtum_ of Cisneros (sixteenth century), there is resonance with both the letters of Cyprian of Carthage (d. 258) and the _Acta_ of the martyrdom of St. Fructuoso of Tarragona (d. 258) who, like Cyprian, suffered under the persecution of Valerian.

Although inspired by the Roman _libelli_ of variable texts, neither the Spanish nor the Gallican authors renounced the order of the Mass they had received as part of their ancient liturgical patrimony. The Spanish left the prayer of the faithful and the kiss of peace where they had been after the liturgy of the Word and composed a series of variable texts for them (_ad orationem; ad pacem_) in addition to the variable _inlatio, post sanctus_ and _post pridie_ which formed their eucharistic prayer. Thus, in contrast to the Roman system, which spread variable texts throughout the Mass but maintained a fixed canon, the Spanish concentrated their variable texts at the center of the celebration.

In spite of the relative independence of individual pieces, the Spanish used brief formulas (remnants of the old improvisational structure?) to make a transition from one piece to the next. With this system it was possible to achieve innumerable variations on the same theme, and at the same time give a sense of unity and cohesion to the whole euchological complex. The aim for unity and cohesion with great variety is a distinguishing trait of the Spanish authors and one that was maintained throughout the evolution of the rite.

This characteristic is apparent as well in the richness, harmony, and refinement of the chants and orations of the office books and in the _Liber Ordinum_ (ritual/pontifical for other sacramental celebrations). The coordination of the Mass and hours with the other sacramental celebrations is also worthy of note; for example, there was not only a votive Mass for marriage, for the sick, for the dead, but a votive office in each case as well. The ritual/pastoral care extended beyond the actual exchange of rings, anointing, or burial to include the entire liturgical life of the community and the role of the individual in that life. The introduction to the Lord's Prayer in the votive Mass for the sick illustrates the strong ecclesial sense in the Spanish rite; it ends: "so that when the sickness of body and soul have been driven out, these who are ill may pray *with us,* saying, 'Our Father . . .'" (Férotin, *Liber Ordinum,* col. 377).

Several historical factors contributed to the systematic codification of the Spanish rite. From the times of its invasion by the Arian Visigoths in 414 until the invitation of the Moors in 711, the Iberian peninsula was politically united. With the conversion to Catholicism of the entire kingdom in 589, the political unity was reinforced by religious unity. The resulting climate favored the collection, codification, and eventual standardization of liturgical texts and practices.

In addition, because their greatest liturgical creativity postdates that of the other Western rites, the Spanish could incorporate the "teaching" of liturgical texts from other rites, the canons of the Christological councils, and the liturgical theology in the patristic sermons of such as Augustine and Leo. As in Milan, the liturgy in Spain was considered the most efficient means for planting the truths of the faith in the minds and hearts of the Christian people and was purposely formulated with orthodox precision. In part this explains why the Spanish authors of this era applied themselves to the composition of liturgical texts instead of the production of ascetical or dogmatic treatises, exegetical commentaries on the Scriptures, or long homiletic sermons.

A clear example of their high esteem for the liturgy is the *De ecclesiasticis officiis* of Isidore of Seville (d. 636), the first treatise on the liturgy which not only describes the local rite, but contains much useful information about Milanese and African uses as well. Complementing Isidore's treatise are the invaluable liturgical canons of the synods and councils, especially the "national" Councils of Toledo IV–X (633–656). Knowing their own rite to be in a state of flux, the council fathers enumerated and illustrated the ancient liturgical uses which they felt should be maintained by all but simultaneously provided a forum for exchanging the innovations of the liturgical creativity which flourished in the various provinces. As a result, the Spanish rite represented euchological schools from several provinces: Tarragona —St. Eugenius (d. 657); Seville—Sts. Leander

(d. *c.* 600) and Isadore (d. 636); Braga-Profuturus (fl. *c.* 538) and St. Martin (d. 580); Toledo—Sts. Eugenio II (d. 657), Ildefónso (d. 667), and Juliano (d. 690). The saintly bishops of Toledo were responsible for the definitive form of the liturgical books that survived the subsequent onslaughts of the Moslem invasion, Carolingian expansion, and theological controversies that would reach a climax in the Gregorian suppression of 1080.

With regard to the office, the Spanish and Gallican churches maintained a strict distinction between "cathedral" and "monastic" hours. Iberian councils directed that monastic and ecclesiastical customs should not be mixed (Braga 563, canon 1); and that monks were not permitted to use the public churches for anything but cathedral services: matins, vespers, and Mass (II Toledo 675, canon 3). One of the earliest books produced in the Spanish rite is the *Liber psalmographus,* an office book filled with several series of psalm prayers which constituted a veritable commentary on the Psalms, most of which have been given a Christological and ecclesiological interpretation.

The Spanish order of the Mass is outlined as follows:

*Prelegendum with psalm
Trisagion
Greeting
LESSON (PROPHETIC)
*Psallendum/Psallmo (Trenos in Lent)
[*Clamor on certain days]
EPISTLE
GOSPEL
*Laudes
Dismissal of catechumens
*Sacrificium with verses for offertory
   procession
*Missa* (bidding)
Alia oratio
Nomina Offerentium
Diptychs
Post Nomina
Ad Pacem
Pax
Preface Dialogue ("Aures ad dominum" . . .
   "Sursum corda" . . . "Deo ac Domino nostro,
   Patri, et Filio, et Spiritui Sancto, dignas laudes
   et gratias referamus". . . )
*Inlatio* and *Sanctus
Post Sanctus

*Missa Secreta* (Institution Narrative)

Post Pridie

*Laudes ad Confractionem

[Creed on Sundays and Feasts]

Ad orationem Dominicam

Lord's Prayer and variable embolism

Commixtio and Trisagion

*Benedictio* (Three-fold Blessing of the people)

Invitation to communion

*Ad Accedentes* (variable, often beginning with
   Pss. 33–34)

Communion of all with both species

*Completuria* post-communion prayer (after tenth
   century)

Dismissal

## 127 • THE AMBROSIAN LITURGY

*The Ambrosian, or Milanese, liturgy shared common features with both Western and Eastern rites and served as a link between them. A central feature of the Ambrosian liturgy is its Christocentric nature, reflecting an ongoing struggle with Arian influence. Never suppressed by ecclesiastical authorities, the Ambrosian liturgy continues in use today.*

Though usually associated with the metropolitan see once occupied by Saint Ambrose (d. 397), the Ambrosian rite includes in addition to the liturgy celebrated in the city of Milan (i.e., the Milanese liturgy), the liturgy of several other dioceses of Northern Italy (Bergamo, Ticino, Novara, Vercelli, etc.), and to a certain extent, the liturgy of Aquileia.

Unlike the other non-Roman Western rites, the Ambrosian liturgy was never *officially* suppressed by emperor or pope. In spite of Carolingian and later attempts to "Romanize" everywhere, the Ambrosian liturgy survived with numerous medieval accretions (Roman and non-Roman), but underwent major restorations first under Carlo Borromeo (d. 1584) and then at the beginning of the twentieth century under Cardinals A. Ratti (later Pius XI) and I. Schuster. It was completely revised and translated into Italian in the 1970s.

The liturgical patrimony of the Ambrosian liturgy was largely the result of strong Roman and Eastern influences. After its emergence as a distinct rite it came to share many of its features with all the Western rites, often serving as the bridge between East and West. What distinguishes it from all the other liturgical traditions, however, can be understood

*The Suffering Jesus. From the eleventh century on, piety regarding Jesus focused primarily on his suffering as crucified redeemer. Paintings normally portrayed Jesus as deceased, with his head on his right shoulder, the arms drooping, the body sagging, and the legs crossed and held by one nail. The body assumes the shape of the letter S and expresses the agony at the helplessness of death. This theme is reflected in the Roman liturgies of the medieval era. The above sketch is adapted from the* Album de Villard de Honnecourt *from the second half of the thirteenth century, now in the Bibliothèque Nationale.*

only in the context of the theological and political anti-Arianism in which it arose and evolved. With the exception of the Roman liturgy, the Arian controversy had a major effect on the euchology of all the Western traditions, though in no case did this struggle perdure as at Milan. In fact in its emergence (fourth-fifth centuries), its development (sixth-seventh centuries), and in the period of its stabilization (eighth-ninth centuries) the Ambrosian liturgy had to fight constantly against this heresy in one form or another. The most obvious result is the strong Christocentricism of the Ambrosian prayers, in both original texts and in the editing of texts borrowed from Roman and Carolingian sources.

The centrality of Christ is manifest not only in the careful consideration of the Incarnation and the virginal birth but also in the veneration of the Virgin Mary. In Ambrosian iconography it is possible to trace a progression from the *Kyrios-Pantocrator* to *Deus-Homo, Homo-Deus,* and *Nobiscum-Deus,* which corresponds to the various stages in the development of Ambrosian euchology. It is here that the Ambrosian influence on the other Western liturgies was most strongly felt.

In the early Middle Ages, the Ambrosian Eucharist had the following order:

*Ingressa no psalm
*Kyrie
Oration super populum—collect
PROPHETIC LESSON
Psalmellus
EPISTLE
*Alleluia* with verse (*Cantus* during Lent)
GOSPEL
Homily
Dismissal of Catechumens
*Kyrie and *Antiphona post Evangelium
Pax
Oratio super sindonem
Offertory procession: *Offerenda* with *verses*
Proper Preface and Sanctus
Invariable Canon
Fraction and Commixtio; *Confractorium*
Lord's Prayer and embolism
Communion: *Transitorium* no psalm
Oratio post communionem
*Kyrie and Dismissal

The Ambrosian office was unique in the West in spreading the psalter over two weeks. Like the Roman and Benedictine *cursus,* however, the Ambrosian assigned Psalms 109/110–147 to vespers. As in the cathedral office of fourth-century Jerusalem and the "Chaldean" rite, the morning office at Milan consisted of three canticles, the *Laudate* psalms (148–150), gospel reading, and a procession to the cross or baptistry, while vespers began with the *lucernarium.*

The Ambrosian chant tradition is preserved in

*Medieval Preaching. In the medieval period, preaching in worship went into decline. The friars of the late Middle Ages took this task on themselves and became renowned as preachers. They preached out of doors and to vast audiences. Forbidden to preach on doctrine, they spoke mostly about morals and told legends of the saints to inspire people to live active Christian lives. The above illustration is from Caoursin,* Rhodiae Obsidio, *1496.*

some 300 north Italian manuscripts, most from the late twelfth century and later. Though sharing many features and texts with Gregorian chant, the Ambrosian has a closer affinity to the Old Roman and Beneventan traditions.

## 128 ✦ THE CELTIC LITURGY

*Celtic liturgies show the wide-ranging influence of the Irish missionary-monks, who tended to appropriate liturgical elements from all parts of the Greek and Latin churches. The Celtic liturgy emphasizes a strong personal relationship with Christ and with the Trinity.*

The term *Celtic rite* has been used for the ancient liturgy celebrated in Ireland, Scotland, Britain, Gallicia, and Brittany before these churches gradually adopted the calendar and liturgy of Rome (as early as 633 in Gallicia and as late as the eleventh century in Scotland). In a more restricted sense, the "Celtic rite" refers to the liturgy celebrated in the churches and monasteries of Ireland and regions heavily influenced by Irish missionary-monks from the late sixth to early ninth century.

With regard to the Mass, the liturgy represented by the few books and fragments that are of Irish provenance do not possess a sufficient cohesion nor do they reflect a work sufficiently autonomous and original to constitute a separate rite. While all rites borrowed elements from other traditions, the Irish seem to have done very little in the way of composing original prayers or codifying texts and arranging ceremonies. Some evidence indicates the adoption of an expanded Roman ordinary with few variable texts (exemplified in the Stowe Missal) while other sources follow a Gallican or Spanish order (as in the sacramentary fragments of Fulda and St. Gall). When the work of an Irish hand does appear, it betrays a remarkable familiarity with obscure patristic writings and liturgical formularies from all over the Christian world—Egypt, Rome, Gaul, but especially Spain and Milan—genuine "souvenirs" of the missionary activity of Irish monks.

In outline, the structure of the Mass in the Stowe Missal follows:

Confession of sins and litany of saints
  (Roman and Irish)
[preparation of gifts at the altar]
several collects
*Gloria
Collects
EPISTLE and collect
*Psalm and collect
Diaconal litany
Collects post preem
GOSPEL
*Alloir: Alleluia
Oratio super evangelium
Partial uncovering of the gifts
Creed
Full uncovering of gifts
Collect
[Names or litany]
Oratio post nomina
Additional collects
[Pax]
Preface Dialogue
Celtic preface and *Sanctus
Roman canon (with names for both *mementos*)
  or post sanctu leading to *qui pridie*
Elevation of Chalice and Host
Fractio with *Antiphon and collect
Lord's Prayer with embolism
Pax
Commixtio
Communion; *Processional hymn
Collects
Dismissal

According to the "tract" that follows the Masses in the Stowe missal, the Mass was sung in its entirety. Although no written melodies survive from the Celtic chants, the Irish are known to have taught them to the monks of Northumbria (northern England) who abandoned them when John the Archcantor from St. Peter's was "borrowed" to teach the Roman chants (*c.* 675).

Dependence on continental sources is also discernible in the Celtic celebration of the hours, though similarities to other Western rites are not as pronounced as in the Mass. What survived of the early cathedral office in Irish monastic rules relates closely to the cathedral tradition in the rest of the West; lauds in the Antiphonary of Bangor (late seventh century) is almost identical to the office at Milan. The purely monastic hours, on the other hand, show remarkable creativity. None of the Gallican monastic rules followed Cassian's description of Egyptian monastic practice as closely as the Irish who arranged the psalms for the *horae diurnae* (secunda [*sic*] prime, terce, sext, none, vespers), assigning three thematically appropriate psalms to each. For the night office, the Irish monastic rules are unique: Columba assigned twelve psalms to the first two night hours (*initium noctis:* Gallican *duodecima?, medium noctis*) but during the third hour (*matutinum* or *vigilia*) his monks prayed anywhere from 24 (summer weeknights) to 75 psalms (Saturdays and Sundays from November 1–January 31). The division of the night office into three hours is itself unique to the Irish.

Unlike the liturgists of the Mediterranean rites, the Irish authors had neither an ancient liturgical patrimony nor a tradition of Christian-Latin literature of their own as a basis for formulating Celtic euchology. The fact that they used a language that was not their own may explain, at least in part, the extent of their eclecticism. But the Irish monks were avid scholars, collectors, and copyists of everything they could obtain—Greek and Latin. Their particular choice of elements from so many liturgical traditions betrays, if anything, a fascination with the unusual and the obscure.

The Irish proved themselves most original in illumination of manuscripts and the composition of hymns and collects for the office. They used the idioms, language, ideas, and forms that had grown out of the various traditions of the church and transformed them into artistic and poetic forms that clearly reflect their native genius. The Eastern influence can be discerned in their illuminations which are nevertheless filled with Gaelic serpents and dragons. Though in Latin, many of the hymns and collects in the Antiphonary of Bangor are composed in meter that do not reflect either classical or accentual rhythmic patterns but instead follow the ancient meters of their native poetry, replete with rhyme and alliteration.

The devotional practices and original texts of the Celtic authors reflect a lifestyle that is centered more on a personal than on an ecclesial relationship with Christ and the ever-present Trinity. The most obvious and influential example is the practice of private penitence which followed the missionary monks on all their journeys. This typically Irish individualism was absorbed into the "renaissance" of the Carolingian era and reflected in its reshaping of the Western liturgy. The piety which produced long lists of *apologiae* (prayers of unworthiness) and influenced the Romano-Frankish or Romano-Germanic liturgy for the rest of the Middle Ages was manifest quite early in the liturgical texts of Ireland.

## 129 ◆ THE ROMAN LITURGY

*The Roman Rite, originally celebrated only in the city of Rome and its environs, was adopted by other Western churches in an effort to introduce a fully organized and standardized liturgy.*

The Roman rite was originally confined to the city of Rome and its suburbicarian dioceses. But even within the city itself there were differences in ceremonies, prayers, chants, and melodies for the Mass and office.

(a) *Ordo romanus I* prescribes a stational Mass when the pope presides. The stational liturgy was celebrated only on certain days and was intended as

*The Loving Christ. In the Middle Ages, Christ was often shown in a loving and tender relationship with his church and its people. Here Christ is leaning forward to receive St. Bernard of Clairvaux. This theme is also expressed in the liturgy, particularly the Eucharist. From a manuscript from the one-time Cistercian Abbey at Wettingen, founded in the fifteenth century.*

the main liturgical celebration of the day or hour. As such, it was attended by "everyone" in the city or at least by the clergy.

(b) *Ordo romanus II* prescribes a different order if one of the seven "suburban" (as opposed to nearly 100 "suburbicarian") bishops, or one of the Roman presbyters as the pope's representative, presides at the stational liturgy.

(c) A simpler order was used by the presbyters when they presided in the *titulii* on stational days (no basilica was large enough for the whole city) or on ordinary Sundays when there were no stational celebrations.

(d) The presbyters—and later the monks—who had the task of supplying the daily liturgical needs of pilgrims at the cemeterial shrines combined elements of both the stational and titular celebrations.

The differences in celebration was first recorded in different collections of *libelli missarum* and *ordines* that were later shaped into the so-called Gregorian (stational) and Gelasian (presbyterial or titular) sacramentaries and in *ordines romani* (collections of rubrics for nearly every kind of celebration). In the meantime records were being kept of the cycle of feasts, the readings, and the chants of the stational celebrations that would eventually be compiled into lectionaries and antiphonaries. Once the major basilicas were staffed with their own full-time clergy and monastic communities (fifth–tenth centuries), records were kept of particular customs, chants, and reading lists for Mass and office that differed considerably from one side of the city to the other.

The order of the Mass in all these different circumstances was eventually, if not always, identical to that described in *Ordo romanus I*:

Entrance of ministers: *\*Introit* with psalm
*Kyrie
[Gloria; at first at presbyteral masses on Easter
   only]
Collecta
APOSTOLUS
*Gradual (Alleluia in Easter)
*Alleluia (Tractus in Lent)
EVANGELIUM
OFFERTORY PROCESSION; *Offertorium* with
   psalm
Super oblata (Secreta)
Preface Dialogue
Praefatio and *Sanctus*
Canon missae
Lord's Prayer and embolism
Pax
[Announcements/Dismissals]
Fractio; *Agnus Dei*
Communion with both kinds; *Communio* with
   psalm
Ad completa (post communionem)
Dismissal

This was the Roman liturgy that impressed the Germans and Franks long before the Carolingian era. Beginning in the seventh century, bishops or monks returning from pilgrimage or diplomatic mission to Rome were anxious to adopt Roman customs—especially those of St. Peter's or the Lateran—in their churches and monasteries. They were the first to bring copies of *libelli*, sacramentaries, *ordines*, lectionaries, antiphonals, even relics of the Roman martyrs, and choir directors to teach the *cantilena romana* so they could truly replicate the "rite of the Apostolic See."

The decision by Pepin (d. 768) and Charlemagne (d. 814) to replace the chaos of the Gallican rite with what they perceived to be a fully organized and standardized liturgy from Rome simply continued the process of Romanization. It was only partially successful, however, for two reasons: (1) the reform extended only as far as real authority was able to enforce it; and (b) the papal (stational) texts sent from Rome were incomplete and had to be supplemented with additional material drawn from the local, previously Romanized sources (i.e., the Gallicanized Gelasians of the eighth century). Even where a Roman text was complete, the Frankish copyists tended to insert Gallican elements they simply refused to do without (e.g., the paschal candle and its *Exultet*). The next two centuries saw the continued creation of a hybrid, Romano-Frankish or Romano-Germanic liturgy that, under the influence of the German emperors (962–1073), became the Roman rite in the city itself.

The hybridization of the rite did not mean the deletion of Roman material; it meant the addition of new material. Both the hours and the Mass became so overburdened with accretions (such as the votive offices of the dead, of all saints, and of the Blessed Virgin and the numerous *apologiae* already mentioned) that the public worship of the church became an unbearable burden. "Medieval monastic life suffered from sheer exhaustion, from overnutrition, and consequent spiritual indigestion" (S. J. P. Van Dijk and J. H. Walker, *Origins of the Modern Roman Liturgy* [Westminster, Md.: Newman Press, 1960], 16–17). In order to get its work done, the papal court had to prune back the overgrowth and practically abandon the ancient stational system of the city, producing shorter offices and less elaborate ceremonial for celebrations *in cappella* (in the papal chapel).

There is an undeniable difference in the theology of the Eucharist, holy orders, and church between late antiquity when the Roman rite developed as a expression of the church of Rome gathered around its bishop and the Middle Ages with its piling up of Masses and its ordaining of priests to "offer the sacrifice for" a multitude of intentions. The liturgical forms and *formulae,* however, though suffocated by accretions, were maintained throughout the Middle Ages "as a treasured inheritance of the liturgy, guarded as the "tradition of the Apostles from the City of the Apostles" (Cyrille Vogel, *Medieval Liturgy: An Introduction to its Sources* [Washington, D.C.: Pastoral Press, 1986], 158).

With so many accretions to choose from, ancient local traditions to preserve, the lack of efficient means for standardization, liturgical uniformity could hardly be attempted if even conceived. For the remainder of the Middle Ages and beyond, there were enough divergences in calendars, texts, chants, and ceremonial from one diocese to the next or from one religious congregation to the next to constitute separate "rites," though technically there were countless variants or "uses" of the Roman rite; to list a few: the "Uses" of Sarum, York, Hereford, Aberdeen; the "liturgies" of Nidaros, Lyons, Rouen, Braga, Benevento, Hungary, and Jerusalem; and the "rites" of the Cluniacs, Carthusians, Cistercians, Praemonstratensians, Dominicans, and Franciscans. This last usage (Franciscan) is nearly identical to the abbreviated form used regularly in the papal chapel. Carrying this "papal" Mass and office on their journeys across the Alps, the friars couldn't have realized history was repeating itself. The liturgy in this form was the direct ancestor of the *Breviarium Romanum* (1568) and the *Missale Romanum* (1570) "restored by the sacred council of Trent; published by order of the supreme pontiff Pius V," and for the first time made binding—with some reservations—on the whole Western church.

John Brook Leonard[4]

## 130 ◈ Roman Catholic Worship from the Council of Trent to Vatican II

*The Council of Trent (1545–1563) initiated a period of liturgical standardization in the Roman Catholic church. Catholic worship remained largely uniform throughout the world until the appearance of the* Constitution on the Sacred Liturgy *of the Second Vatican Council (1963).*

The Council of Trent (1545–1563) sought to bring about a conservative reform by radical means. The fathers of Trent were concerned to end avarice, corruptions, and superstitions in worship, but their minds were directed to defending the status quo whenever possible, partly because the lack of liturgical scholarship allowed them to believe, for example, that St. Peter had composed the Roman canon and that to change existing practices was to abolish that which was apostolic. Furthermore, changes

would be seen as conceding that the Protestant Reformers were right after all.

The method of reform chosen was that of liturgical standardization, a possibility with the advent of the printed book. The revision of the liturgical books was entrusted to the curia and proceeded with the breviary (1568), the missal (1570), the martyrology (1584), pontifical (1596), bishops' ceremonies (1600), and the ritual (1614). The means of enforcing global uniformity was entrusted to the new Congregation of Rites, established in 1588. So began almost four centuries of liturgical uniformity, reaching even to China (and thus devastating evangelization of that country). The "era of rubricism" that ensued found theological safety in rigid liturgical uniformity.

At the same time, much of the worship did not change, because books and bureaucrats could control only so much. A brilliant period of baroque architecture spread around the world, inspired by the work of Gian Lorenzo Bernini (1598–1680) and the example of the Jesuit church in Rome, Il Gesu. Joseph Jungmann speaks of the baroque spirit and the traditional liturgy as "two vastly different worlds"(*The Mass of the Roman Rite* [Westminster, Md.: Christian Classics, 1986], vol. 1, 142). New devotions came to the forefront, especially benediction and exposition of the Blessed Sacrament; the cult of the saints came to focus largely on the Virgin Mary. Devotions to the Sacred Heart of Jesus and visits to the Blessed Sacrament became popular. In France, the new standardized books were resisted for three centuries, coming into consistent use only in the late nineteenth century after experimentation with much local variety and vernacular uses.

The Enlightenment of the eighteenth century failed to make much of a mark, despite the efforts of the Synod of Pistoia (1786) to make reforms that were two centuries too early. The nineteenth century saw the beginnings of the first liturgical movement, led by Prosper Guéranger (1805–1875) and a series of monastic leaders, notably Lambert Beauduin (1873–1960), Virgil Michel (1890–1938), and Odo Casel (1886–1948). This lasted until after World War II and was acknowledged in the conservative encyclical *Mediator Dei* (1947). A later liturgical movement began after the war, deriving its agenda largely from Protestant worship (vernacular, cultural pluralism, active participation, preaching at Mass, popular hymnody) and centered largely in countries with Protestant majorities.

More recently, Vatican II in its *Constitution on the Sacred Liturgy* (1963) moved Roman Catholicism to embrace these newer reforms. The result has been revision of the Tridentine liturgical books in less than 25 years and translation of them all. The introduction of the vernacular has been accompanied by much more flexibility and a variety of options in the rites. While these reforms have been widely welcomed by the laity, Rome seems presently concerned with preventing adaptation or inculturation from going too far. Even so, the distance traveled since Trent has been enormous.

James F. White[5]

## 131 ✦ BIBLIOGRAPHY: HISTORY OF WESTERN CATHOLIC WORSHIP

Braga, C., and A. Bugnini, eds. *The Commentary on the Constitution and on the Instruction on the Sacred Liturgy.* New York: Benziger, 1965. This is a helpful and thorough commentary on each part of the *Constitution on the Sacred Liturgy,* written by experts in each of the fields of liturgical study addressed by the *Constitution.*

Foley, Edward. *From Age to Age.* Chicago: Liturgy Training Publications, 1991. This volume discusses the Western Roman liturgy from New Testament times to the present. A unique feature of this work is the integration of music and the arts with the text of worship. Every attempt is made to help the reader experience the full input of the liturgy, as opposed to a mere recitation of the facts. The volume is also enhanced by numerous drawings of churches and of the use of arts in worship.

Fortescue, Adrian. *The Mass: A Study of the Roman Liturgy,* 2d ed. London: Longmans, Green, 1955. An older but helpful study of the pre-Vatican II liturgy, this work provides a history of the Mass in the first three centuries, discusses the origin of the Roman Mass, and comments on the order of the Mass and each of its parts.

Harper, John. *The Forms and Orders of Western Liturgy From the Tenth to the Eighteenth Century: A Historical Introduction and Guide for Students and Musicians.* New York: Oxford University Press, 1991. A serious and scholarly study of Western worship, especially of the Middle Ages, this work is nevertheless practical in nature. It enables the reader to have an idea of how worship was conducted in the Middle Ages and beyond the Reformation era.

Jungmann, Joseph A. *Christian Prayer Through the Centuries.* Trans. by John Coyne. New York: Paulist Press, 1978. In this concise but most helpful volume, the author reviews the way Christian habits of prayer have evolved from Apostolic times to the post-Tridentene era. This narrative links Christian faith and Christian culture in a rich and meaningful way.

———. *The Mass of the Roman Rite: Its Origin and Development,* 2 vols. Trans. by F. A. Brunner. Westminster, Md.: Christian Classics, 1986. This work is a thorough study of the form and interpretation of the Mass from the primitive church to the Mass of Pius X.

Klauser, Theodor. *A Short History of the Western Liturgy.* Trans. by John Halliburton. New York: Oxford University Press, 1979. This volume presents the most important facts and problems of the history of the Western liturgy. Sections deal with the early church, the medieval era, and the period from Trent to Vatican II. It does not contain material on the Protestant history of worship.

Pfaff, Richard W. *Medieval Latin Liturgy: A Select Bibliography.* Toronto: University of Toronto Press, 1982.

Salmon, Pierre. *The Breviary Through the Centuries.* Trans. by Sr. David Mary. Collegeville, Minn.: Liturgical Press, 1962. This book contains three articles dealing with the history of the breviary. The first addresses the delegation of reciting the office, the second provides a history of the breviary as said in urban churches from the fifth to the eighth century, and the last provides insight into the interpretation of the Psalms during the formative years of the office.

Schroeder, H. J., trans. *Canons and Decrees of the Council of Trent.* St. Louis: Herder, 1941. This work contains all the canons and decrees of the Counter-reformation movement which culminated at Trent. Of special interest to students of the liturgy are the canons and decrees on the reform of worship, reforms which remained in place until the changes instituted by the reforms of Vatican II.

Spielmann, Richard M. *History of Christian Worship.* Ann Arbor, Mich.: Servant Publications, 1966. Easy-to-read books on the history of Christian worship are difficult to find. This book, written by an Anglican, lays out the broad periods of history and provides a splendid analysis of each period.

Vogel, Cyrille. *Medieval Liturgy: An Introduction to its Sources*. Rev. and trans. by William G. Storey and Niels Krough Rasmussen. Washington, D.C.: Pastoral Press, 1986. This is a thorough listing and commentary on all medieval sources of the liturgy, organized by periods of historic development.

Wegman, Herman. *Christian Worship in East and West: A Study Guide to Liturgical History*. New York: Pueblo Publishing Co., 1985. This volume presents a thoughtful examination of the development of worship in the first three centuries, the Constantinian era, the Roman-Frankish-Germanic liturgy in the West, the Council of Trent, and the Byzantine liturgy of the East.

Willis, G. G. *Further Essays in Early Roman Liturgy*. Alcuin Club Collections 50. London: SPCK, 1968. This scholarly book treats the various kinds of liturgy found in the Roman church. It also examines the prayers for the Roman Mass, investigates the dedication masses of the various rites, and presents a study on the English liturgy.

# FIVE

# Protestant Worship of the Reformation Era

*The Reformation's break with the Roman Catholic church was expressed in the work of various synods, particularly in new documents and confessions. But nowhere was it more clearly visible to the ordinary Christian than in worship itself. Protestants conducted worship in the vernacular and in forms that were distinctly different from those of the Roman church. Perhaps the most powerful expression of this difference was in the emphasis on the Word of God read and expounded.*

## 132 • LUTHERAN WORSHIP

*Luther's liturgical reform was guided by the principle that if the Scriptures did not expressly reject a particular practice, the church was free to keep it. Consequently, Lutheran worship retained much of the ceremonial practice of Catholic worship.*

There are a number of reasons for considering the Lutheran tradition as the most conservative of the Protestant traditions of worship. Martin Luther (1483–1546) had a high respect for the existing Christian cultus; his inclination was to purge those aspects that could not be reconciled to his theology and to retain the rest. He could be quite radical on occasion (as with the canon of the Mass) but on the whole retained more than he rejected. He tended to move carefully; others anticipated him on vernacular liturgies.

After statements in *The Babylonian Captivity* (1520) that were to be determinative for almost all subsequent Protestant sacramental theology, Luther moved to liturgical reform with vernacular baptismal rites in 1523 and 1526. The same years also saw new eucharistic rites, the *Formula Missae* (in Latin) and *German Mass*. Later years saw forms for marriage, ordination, and penance. In general, existing practices endured, but rites were conducted in the vernacular, and popular participation was promoted whenever possible.

Three emphases stand out: music, preaching, and frequent communion in both kinds. Luther considered music one of God's greatest gifts, and cultivated its use in worship through service music and hymnody. He led the way in writing hymns himself, and vigorous hymn singing has always been a hallmark of this tradition. Luther's insistence that preaching be a part of all congregational worship contributed to a rebirth of preaching. He also encouraged all the laity who were properly prepared to receive the bread and wine at each Eucharist.

As for vestments, images, and much of the medieval cultus that was theologically neutral, Luther allowed their continuance; they came to be known as *adiaphora* or things indifferent. Thus much more survived in Lutheran countries, especially in Sweden and Finland, where Lutheran worship remained its most conservative, than in other Protestant countries. Yet even this is relative. Recent studies have shown just how much survived during the long period of Lutheran orthodoxy. In Bach's Leipzig there were daily public prayers, a weekly Eucharist with a great many communicants, and a rich observance of the church year. Although the services were in German, one gets the feeling that not all that much had changed from the Middle Ages in two hundred years of Lutheranism.

The real change came not with the Reformation but with the Enlightenment. Daily services in Leipzig ended in the 1790s and much of the continuing medieval cultus vanished in the face of rationalism, even in the Church of Sweden. Much of this has been blamed on the influence of the Reformed tradition, but more is probably due to the spirit of the age. The nineteenth century saw a gradual reaction to the Enlightenment with an attempt to recover early Lutheran worship. In Germany, Wilhelm Loehe (1810–1895), in Denmark, Nikolai Grundtvig (1783–1872), and various other leaders elsewhere sought a return to Lutheran orthodoxy and orthopraxis. The indication of their success is successive revisions of various service books and hymns. More recent versions, especially the American *Lutheran Book of Worship* (1978), have moved into the ecumenical mainstream while retaining a Lutheran character, especially in the emphasis on music.

James F. White[6]

## 133 • REFORMED WORSHIP

*Calvin argued that only practices explicitly taught in Scripture could be used in worship. For this reason, churches influenced by Calvin have been less inclined to restore pre-Reformation practices of worship perceived as unbiblical or "Catholic."*

The Reformed tradition has several roots: Zurich, Basel, Strassburg, and Geneva. In some ways, it preserved more than its share of the penitential strain of late medieval piety. In other respects, however, it moved beyond the forms which Lutheranism and Anglicanism were content to continue. In time it was largely seduced by the Puritan tradition (in Great Britain) and the frontier tradition (in America).

Ulrich Zwingli (1484–1531) began his reformation of Zurich heavily influenced by humanistic studies and a thorough biblicism. He was anxious to return worship to its biblical roots and eager to make it more spiritual, reflecting the gap he saw between the physical and the spiritual. Although a fine musician, he rejected music in worship as distracting one from spiritual worship. Iconoclasm in Zurich purified or devastated the churches, according to one's viewpoint. Zwingli retained the four Sundays or festivals when his people were accustomed to receive communion or the Eucharist, a preaching service being held on the other Sundays. These four occasions saw a drastically simplified rite which focused on transubstantiation of the people, not the elements.

Martin Bucer in Strassburg and John Oecolampadius (1482–1531) in Basel began experimenting with vernacular services. At Strassburg this included daily prayer services and a Sunday service derived from the Mass. Bucer's influence was spread further by a visiting preacher out of a job, John Calvin

(1509–1564). While serving temporarily a French-speaking congregation in Strassburg, Calvin adapted the German rite Bucer was using. Calvin brought this rite to Geneva, and from 1542 on it became the model for much of the Reformed tradition. Although deriving its structure from the Mass via Bucer, it had moved to highlight the penitential aspects of worship and was highly didactic and moralistic. Relief from this somber mood was wrought by encouraging the congregation to sing metrical paraphrases of the psalms, which they did with fervor. Such devotion to psalmody (and the exclusion of hymnody) marked Reformed worship for several centuries, and still does in some churches.

Calvin's low esteem for human nature was balanced by a high view of God's Word and of the sacraments. (Although almost all Protestants considered baptism and the Eucharist as sacraments, Luther was willing to include penance, Calvin possibly ordination, and Zinzendorf marriage.) Calvin's doctrine of eucharistic feeding on Christ through the operation of the Holy Spirit, although certainly not without problems, was the most sophisticated Reformation eucharistic doctrine but was largely lost by his heirs.

John Knox (c. 1505–1572) transmitted this tradition to Scotland as others brought it to France, the Netherlands, and the Germanic countries. Knox's liturgy, renamed the *Book of Common Order,* flourished in Scotland for eighty years after 1564. Only then did the Scots yield to the Puritan effort to achieve national unity in worship through the *Westminster Directory* of 1645. This moved away from set forms to more permissive patterns; yet the *Directory* remained vaguely normative in later editions in America. On the American frontier, the newly emerging frontier patterns of worship tended to engulf the Reformed tradition.

A pattern of recovery slowly eventuated in America. Charles W. Baird (1828–1887) led the way in 1855 with a title many thought oxymoronic, *Presbyterian Liturgies.* German Reformed Christians experienced a recovery of both theology and liturgy in the so-called Mercersburg movement. Eventually an American service book, the *Book of Common Worship,* followed in 1906, as did service books in the Kirk of Scotland. In recent years, Presbyterians have followed closely in the same post-Vatican II ecumenical mainstream as other traditions of the right and center, signified by publication of their *Supplemental Liturgical Resources.*

James F. White[7]

## 134 ♦ ANGLICAN WORSHIP

*Anglican worship has a variegated history, having fluctuated between worship forms similar to those of Catholicism and worship influenced by the Puritans. This accounts in part for the variations in worship within the Anglican communion of today. Nevertheless* The Book of Common Prayer *is basic to all Anglican churches.*

The Anglican tradition is ambiguous: what started off as a fairly moderate reformation, and remained so for three centuries, reversed itself in the nineteenth century and moved to reappropriate a great deal of the medieval cultus. To modern observers, Anglican worship seems more conservative than Lutheran; but the theological origins are far more liberal. Anglican liturgy began with Archbishop Thomas Cranmer's (1489–1556) two editions of *The Book of Common Prayer,* that of 1549 and the much more radical 1552 book. Using the latest technology, Cranmer sought to put all the services in the hands of everyone by translating, condensing, and revising them before publishing them in popular versions under a price ceiling.

Cranmer succeeded in recovering daily services of public prayer, which became a staple of Anglican worship. Many of the ceremonies associated with the sacraments and other rites disappeared from the 1552 edition and the theology became much more unambiguously Zwinglian. Martin Bucer (1491–1551) provided much of the structure for the ordination rite, but Cranmer was not prepared to accept as high a view of the Eucharist as Bucer and Calvin. A great ornament of the book was Cranmer's linguistic ability to cast traditional Latin prayers in the language of his contemporaries.

After the brief regression of the Marian years, Anglican worship tended to stabilize during the long reign of Elizabeth I. As a political settlement, episcopal forms of church government were retained, as well as something of the appearance of public worship, although there had been much iconoclasm even before the rise of Puritanism. Weekly communion proved to be too radical a step for most people, and canon law eventually settled for a minimum of three celebrations a year. The normal Sunday ser-

vice came to be morning prayer, litany, antecommunion, and sermon. Popular hymnody was lacking, but magnificent choral daily services characterized worship in the cathedrals. The poet-priest George Herbert (1593–1633) offered an example of Anglican parish ministry at its best.

The Puritan takeover of the Church of England from 1644 to 1660 moved things leftward in a radical direction, but only temporarily. The restoration period afterwards attempted to return to the status quo of 1604, as the prayer book of 1662 showed. Despite the survival of a high church traditions (without much ceremonial), most Anglicans were comfortable in a tradition that avoided the excesses of either Catholicism or Puritanism. In the eighteenth century, this meant worship that was edifying and moralistic but with little concern for the sacraments or anything overtly supernatural.

In the nineteenth century, reactions came in the form of a recovery of patristic theology (the Oxford Movement, Tractarianism, Puseyism) and to a fullscale recovery of late medieval ceremonial (the Cambridge Movement, Ritualism). These brought back weekly celebrations of the Eucharist at just the same time this was occurring among Disciples of Christ, Mormons, Plymouth Brethren, and the Catholic Apostolic church. A new emphasis was placed on baptism, penance, and the revival of medieval architecture, liturgical arts, and choral music. Congregational hymnody also made its advent.

The twentieth century has seen an indigenous liturgical movement in the Church of England, manifesting itself as the parish communion movement in the 1930s. Recent years have seen wholesale revision of Anglican prayer books around the world, usually either following the patters of Cranmer or trading in such later medieval forms for the thirdcentury model of Hippolytus.

James F. White[8]

## 135 ♦ ANABAPTIST WORSHIP

*Anabaptists argued for a pure church and a radical discipleship in absolute obedience to Scripture. They refused to countenance any form of worship that could not be substantiated by Scripture.*

It is not easy to generalize about the Anabaptist elements of the radical Reformation, known largely today as Mennonites, Amish, and Hutterites, but we

*Anabaptist Persecution. This drawing depicts the death of an Anabaptist leader by drowning. Many Anabaptists were put to death by drowning, burning, and hanging, and many others were tortured for their faith by both Protestants and Catholics.*

can trace some common features. Surprisingly, the more radical traditions tend also to be most conservative when it comes to stabilizing and continuing the same worship forms across the centuries.

The earliest Anabaptists, the Swiss Brethren, began in contact with Zwingli in Zurich. But they took his biblicism a step further than he was willing to and argued vehemently against the baptism of any but believers. Their basic premise came to be the need for a pure church of believers who led holy lives. This was impossible to reconcile with the magisterial reformation that relied upon state support. Both Protestants and Catholics vied with each other to persecute Anabaptists, or "rebaptizers" as they came to be known, because of their refusal to accept their own baptisms as infants. Immersion was not an issue, and most of these groups baptized by pouring or sprinkling.

A variety of leaders arose with small groups of followers. The typical congregations met in a secluded spot under a leader called and ordained by the congregation. Because persecution was so constant, martyrdom was frequent and a rich hymnody of martyrdom developed, some of it still in use. For the church to be kept pure, not only must the entrance be narrow in the form of baptism for believers only, but members not living a holy life were

expelled by the ban and shunned in accordance with biblical precept (1 Cor. 5:13).

Despite their radical origins, several Anabaptist groups have kept faithful with genuine conservatism. The Old Order (Amish) worship in private homes much as their ancestors did, the Hutterite communities even retain the use of sixteenth century sermons, and even the larger Mennonite groups resisted most nineteenth century American influences by remaining relatively isolated communities. Although their numbers continue to be small, the disciplined lifestyle of these people makes them much admired.

James F. White[9]

## 136 • BIBLIOGRAPHY ON REFORMATION WORSHIP

Brilioth, Yngve. *Eucharistic Faith and Practice: Evangelical and Catholic.* London: SPCK, 1965.

Brand, Eugene. "Luther's Liturgical Surgery," in F. Meuser and S. Schneider, eds., *Interpreting Luther's Legacy.* Minneapolis: Augsburg, 1969, 108–119.

Cuming, G. J. *A History of Anglican Liturgy,* 2d ed. London: Macmillan, 1982. This work provides a detailed history of the English Liturgy from the Middle Ages to the reshaping of the liturgy in the 1960s. Of particular interest in the study of the first stages of change and of the First and Second Prayer Books of Edward VI.

——— *The Durham Book.* New York: Oxford University Press, 1961. Being the first draft of the revision of the Book of Common Prayer in 1661, edited with an Introduction and Notes.

Horn, Edward T. *Outlines of Liturgics.* Philadelphia: Lutheran Publication Society, 1890.

Jacobs, Henry Eyster. *The Lutheran Movement in England.* Philadelphia: Frederick, 1894.

Mabry, Eddie Louis. *The Baptismal Theology of Balthasar Hubmaier.* Unpublished Ph.D. dissertation, 1982. Ann Arbor, Mich.: University Microfilm, 1985. Hubmaier's baptismal theology is set in his doctrine of the church as a visible assembly of regenerated saints.

Klaassen, Walter. *Biblical and Theological Basis for Worship in the Believer's Church.* Newton, Kans.: Faith and Life Press, 1978. A brief but helpful presentation of the main convictions of Anabaptist worship.

Pipkin, H. Wayne, and John H. Yoder, trans. and eds. _Balthasar Hubmaier: Theologian of Anabaptism_. Peabody, Mass.: Hendricksen, 1989. Contains original writings of Hubmaier, a central reformer of the sixteenth century, including his writings on worship.

Reed, Luther D. _The Lutheran Liturgy_. Philadelphia: Muhlenberg Press, 1959.

Thompson, Bard. _Liturgies of the Western Church_. Cleveland, N.Y.: World Publishing Co., 1961. Contains the liturgies of Justin Martyr, Hippolytus, the Roman Mass, Luther, Swingli, Bucer, Calvin, Anglican _Book of Common Prayer_ (1549 and 1552), John Know, English Puritans, the Westminster Directory, Richard Baxter, and John Wesley, with scholarly introductions to each. Of particular interest to students are the full texts of the Reformation liturgies.

Vajta, Vilmos. _Luther on Worship_. Philadelphia: Muhlenberg Press, 1958.

# Protestant Worship in the Post-Reformation Era

Between 1600 and 1900, Protestant movements proliferated in a continuous search for biblical Christianity or for renewal and restoration. The result was the establishment of many different worship traditions, since these Christian groups tended to express their differences in the language of worship.

## 137 • PURITAN WORSHIP

*A number of Protestant churches trace their descent from the Puritan heritage. In their worship, these groups share a commitment to a common principle: worship must be ordered according to the Word of God alone. Puritan worship is also characterized by covenant theology and an emphasis on prayer.*

The American Puritans provide a seemingly inexhaustible mine from which historians continue to quarry their writings. Any attempt, therefore, to provide an overview of Puritan thought and practice in so short a space will be found wanting. Our emphasis, then, will be to highlight a few themes which characterize the Puritan outlook, and which are played out in their corporate worship activities.

The reasons for the establishment of the Church of England under Henry VIII were more political and personal than theological. The Thirty-Nine Articles, which form the stated doctrinal confession of the Church of England, were drawn up by Thomas Cranmer, Archbishop of Canterbury from 1532–1553. Puritans affirmed the Reformed content of the Articles, but they did not tolerate the way in which the English faith was practiced in the churches.

To the Puritans, the English Reformers had not gone far enough. The Puritans sought to reform the Reformation, or, more specifically, to carry the Reformation further, to fully purify the church of what they regarded as the malignant influence of Roman Catholic tradition. The English Puritans were a varied group, rather than a well-defined religious bloc. An entire spectrum of Puritan attitudes has been noted, ranging from those with moderate reforming intentions, who desired to remain within the Church of England, to those of more radical bent who separated themselves from what they perceived to be dead orthodoxy (at best) or, in some cases, apostasy. The label "Puritan" was originally applied derisively, mocking the scrupulous attitude of these reformers. The Puritans, as the epithet implies, sought a pure church, free from either secular or "popish" influence, beholden only to the Scriptures.

Some American Puritans, known to us as the Pilgrims, are of the latter variety—the separatists. Others retained official ties to the English church, but were no less zealous in their desire for change. Sincere and pious, the American Puritans came to the colonies to worship God apart from the forced constraints of the established hierarchy. Their hardline Calvinism would not allow them to accept and work within the more broadly conceived English system. Areas of concern which directly affected liturgical practice include:

**Sola Scriptura.** Understanding this Reformation tenet in its most literal fashion, the Puritans sought to use the Bible as their only source and guide in both worship and daily life. For them, the thorough study and application of the Scriptures was the cornerstone of life. In Puritan worship we can see this belief exhibited in the extended portions of the Bible read aloud at each service, interspersed with illuminating commentary from a deacon, and in lengthy sermons which were the focus of the Puritan liturgy.

Further, the influence of Scripture on the liturgical practices of the Puritans is evident in their rejection of the "popish" and human traditions remaining in Anglican practice. The drab garb of everyday life befit the minister rather than ornate vestments; metrical psalms sung by the congregation replaced chanting. Puritan worship stressed both head and heart knowledge of the Word: truth imparted in worship was lived out in daily life. Congregants took copious notes on the sermon, and the head of the household frequently quizzed his children and servants to ascertain their attentiveness to the sermon—their spiritual well-being was his responsibility.

**Covenant Theology.** The doctrine of election, as developed by Calvin, states that God elects persons through no merit, work, or choice on their part, and covenants with them to be their God. While the Thirty-Nine Articles affirmed this understanding the English church of the seventeenth century did not uphold it in practice. Similar to the children of Israel in the Old Testament, with whom many parallels were made, the Puritans viewed themselves as a holy people, set apart by and for God: a people for his name. This covenant is evidenced in two directions: between God and man, both individually and corporately, in God's redemptive and providential action; and among the individual members of the covenant community, in their mutual commitment to one another.

**Ecclesiology.** The church is comprised of those persons who have been elected by God to the covenant community. The question then arises: How can one determine who has, and who has not, been elected? First, an individual must have had a definite conversion experience—a work of saving grace—which imparts a confirming knowledge of one's salvation. Second, the veracity of this new life in an individual is confirmed through the witness of the community through observation of an individual's life. One cannot be saved by good works or pious acts, but such evidences will surely follow in the life of one who is truly of the elect.

In worship, this aspect of covenant theology became most apparent in the administration of the sacraments, baptism and the Lord's Supper. The word "sacrament" itself, although employed by the Puritans, is problematic. No divine grace is mediated in the sacraments, but rather they are "seals" of the Lord's covenant. They are the marks whereby God identifies his covenant with his people through visible, tangible means.

**Baptism.** The Puritans practiced infant baptism. Although not believing that any grace was mediated through this activity, they recognized that baptism denotes the parents' membership in the community, and their commitment to nurture the child in the ways of God. Important as well is the trust that God has also predestined these infants to eternal election. Baptism, then, is both a sign of commitment and a step of faith on the part of the parents regarding the future of the child. In order for the child to become a fully participating member of the community in adulthood, evidence of election would have to be demonstrated as he or she matured.

**The Lord's Supper.** Limited only to members of the covenant community, the Lord's Supper provides the means of continuing identification with that community. Before the Sunday on which the sacrament was observed, members had to examine themselves, make amends for any wrongs, make apologies for offenses, and ask forgiveness for any sins. Both the bread and the cup were given to eligible communicants, served first by the minister to the deacons, then by the deacons to the members.

**Prayer.** One last aspect of worship which must be noted is that of prayer. Prayers often continued for lengthy periods of time, even hours, with the congregation standing. While spoken by the minister, the prayers should be considered an aspect of worship in which the congregation actively participated. Although we have no record of any audible response given by the congregation to the prayers, their participation came through the substance of the prayers: in them, the needs and burdens of the people were lifted to God. Prior to the service prayer requests were given to the minister who, presumably, elaborated according to his knowledge of the persons or situations involved.

We must not harbor the impression of Puritan worship as a dry, staid affair. Sober attitudes, lengthy, content-oriented sermons and extended prayers, while incongruous in our fast-paced twentieth-century world, provided a means of touching and reaching the religious needs of the people of the early seventeenth century. Indeed, the Puritan vision did sustain serious blows in the last half of the century; these developments are beyond our discussion here. Yet, for a few brief, shining decades, the Puritans began to realize their dream of establishing a truly Christian community on earth. Their legacy has left an indelible mark on American worship and religious life in the centuries since.

James R. Peck

## 138 • BAPTIST WORSHIP

*Baptists, like the Puritans, desired a pure scriptural worship. Early Baptist worship sought to maintain a radically biblical worship that the Spirit was free to direct. Later, however, in response to what they considered to be excesses in other movements, Baptists came to place more emphasis on worship according to biblical form and order.*

As Baptists developed out of the Puritan movement in seventeenth century England, they were of two types: General Baptists and Particular Baptists. The General Baptists, who arose earlier, were given their name because of their belief that Christ's atonement was "general," sufficient for all persons. The Particular Baptists espoused the view that Christ's atonement was "particular," for God's elect only. Both groups, however, exhibited some of the Puritan concerns for purifying worship. They sought to eliminate the human forms of the established church and to base worship purely on the simple patterns provided by Scripture. But they also sought to involve the congregation in worship and to provide openness for the movement of God's Spirit.

The first Baptist congregation was composed of a group of Puritans who moved to Amsterdam to escape persecution. In 1609 John Smyth, their pastor, led them to the position that the church should be composed only of regenerate persons and that to attain a regenerate church, baptism should be for believers only. Smyth, who had been schooled at Cambridge but had rejected his former Anglican views, then led the congregation in developing the earliest Baptist patterns of worship. True worship had to be scriptural and involve no books which would inhibit the movement of the Spirit. Not only did these earliest Baptists reject *The Book of Common Prayer,* even the Bible had to be laid aside after the text had been read.

The minister began the worship with an extemporaneous prayer and then preached on the text which he had already read. Then as many as three or four lay people preached or exhorted on the same text, as long as time permitted. Finally, the minister prayed, an offering was taken for the poor, and a benediction concluded the morning service. A similar service followed in the afternoon, and on occasion it was concluded with the Lord's Supper. Any singing in these services was done extemporaneously by an individual; no fixed liturgical psalms or hymns were allowed to impede the movement of the Spirit. The General Baptists, who eventually moved back to England, followed the worship practices initiated by Smyth, including the use of more than one preacher. However, they did read the Bible more freely during worship.

Later, in the 1630s, the Particular Baptist movement emerged. These Baptists followed the same principles in worship as the General Baptists. They stressed the necessity of following Scripture in worship, and they rejected all prepared elements or forms, because these tended to take the place of the Holy Spirit. Yet, many of them gave a greater role to the congregation by singing psalms in worship, and they often had only one preacher. Still, the loss of preachers did not inhibit the movement of the Spirit; anyone called forth by God and approved by the church could preach or administer the ordinances of baptism and the Lord's Supper.

Events during the mid-seventeenth century, however, caused both Baptist groups to change their emphases. During this time the Quakers and other more radical Protestant groups arose. Some of these placed greater stress on the Spirit than on Scripture. In the eyes of Baptists their worship was often chaotic, with little order or form. Not wishing to be associated with these groups, but rather desiring to align themselves more closely with the more respectable Congregationalist and Presbyterian dissenters, Baptists began to place less emphasis on the movement of the Spirit in worship and more on following Scripture. They also stressed that only those officially set apart as ministers by the church could lead in worship.

Although it varied, worship during the rest of the seventeenth century tended to follow a similar pattern among both General and Particular Baptists. The morning worship began with an appointed layman reading a psalm and leading in a time of prayer. Then he read additional Scripture until it was time for the sermon. The minister entered the elevated pulpit in the plain meeting house and preached, concluding the sermon with prayer. The service was concluded with the singing of a psalm, sometimes preceded by an offering. The afternoon service followed the same pattern; once a month, however, the Lord's Supper was observed before singing the closing psalm.

The Lord's Supper was celebrated in a manner that became quite common among Baptists. After the sermon and prayer, the minister went to the table (in front of the pulpit) where bread and wine had been placed. He spoke of the deep meaning of the supper and encouraged the members to receive it properly. Then, taking the bread in his hands, he gave thanks and broke it, repeating the words of Christ, "This is my body, which is broken for you" (1 Cor. 11:24, KJV). After partaking of the loaf, he gave it to the deacons to partake and to distribute to the seated congregation. He urged the people to receive the bread as an expression of their feeding on Christ the true bread. In the same manner he took the wine, gave thanks, and poured it into the cup, repeating the words of Christ, "This cup is the new testament in my blood" (1 Cor. 11:25, KJV). He then partook, gave it to the deacons to distribute, and invited the people to partake. Finally, after a brief meditation on the great blessing Christians have in Christ, the service was concluded with the singing of a psalm.

Baptists had begun with a desire to purify the worship of the church by basing it on what they saw as the simple patterns of Scripture. They also emphasized the role of the congregation, and the spontaneous movement of the Spirit in worship. But as Baptists moved through the seventeenth century they had to locate these liturgical emphases between the two poles of the formless worship of the radicals on the one hand and the formal worship of the established church on the other. In the process they set the course for Baptist worship for future generations.

G. Thomas Halbrooks

## 139 • CONGREGATIONAL WORSHIP

_Congregational worship was influenced by the radical wing of Puritanism, which stressed a worship shaped by biblical teaching alone. Worship was stripped to its New Testament essentials, centering on the exposition of the Word and the observance of the sacraments. Customs and features of worship not expressed in Scripture were dropped._

_New England Church—Exterior View. One purpose of both the exterior and interior architecture of Puritan meetinghouses was to depart as far as possible from the liturgical church with its altar as centerpiece. The external architecture is simple and speaks of the Puritan commitment to simplicity of worship. Pictured here is a church built in 1702 in West Springfield, Massachusetts._

The movement which came to be known as Congregationalism owes its origin in the middle of the seventeenth century to a revolt against both the "high-church" liturgy and the hierarchical government by bishops in the state-supported Church of England. These objections, which necessarily brought with them a radically different order of worship, stemmed from a Reformed or Calvinistic theological opposition to the remnants of Roman Catholic liturgy and government in the Church of England.

The objectors were themselves divided into a more moderate Puritan wing and a radical separatist wing. While the Puritans wished to remain within the Church of England and purify what they considered unbiblical ceremonialism, the separatists viewed the Puritan cause as hopeless, advocated a "reformation without tarrying for any," and called for an immediate separation. Excepting a few early Puritan bishops, the Puritan cause was further subdivided into two subgroups. One subgroup, the presbyterians, wished to replace government by bishops with government by regional presbyteries of ministers and elders. The other faction, the independents or "congregationalists," argued that since Scripture frequently mentions the pastors, elders, and deacons of the local congregation but is largely silent about any officers or bodies outside the local congregation, neither presbyteries nor bishops were permitted by Scripture to exercise authority over congregations other than their own. Under persecution by the Church of England the distinction between separatists and Puritan independents tended to disappear, both parties eventually merging into a congregationalism under Cromwell's rule, 1640–1660.

The Puritans were ridiculed by their opponents for supposedly taking this as their creed: "I believe in John Calvin, the Father of our religion, disposer of heaven and earth, and in Owen, Baxter, and Jenkins his dear sons our lords, who were conceived by the spirit of fanaticism, born of schism and faction, suffered under the act of uniformity." Both John Owen the congregationalist and Richard Baxter the presbyterian were tarred with contempt for their Calvinism, and both were persecuted further under various acts of uniformity for refusal to participate in the legally enforced worship services of *The Book of Common Prayer.*

Even the enemies of the presbyterians and congregationalists recognized the basic unity of their Reformed principles of worship. What are these Reformed principles? As specified by the congregationalist *Savoy Declaration of Faith and Order* and echoed in the presbyterian *Westminster Confession of Faith:* "The acceptable way of worshiping the true God is instituted by Himself, and so limited by His own revealed will that he may not be worshipped according to the imaginations and devices of men, or the suggestions of Satan, under any visible representations, or any other way not prescribed in the Holy Scripture" (*Savoy Declaration* 22:1, cf. *Westminster Confession* 21:1).

This principle, known as the *regulative principle,* indicates that Scripture regulates the method by which God may be worshiped. It was one of several issues that divided the Protestants at the time of the Reformation. While Lutherans and Anglicans argued that Protestant worship could retain any Roman Catholic ceremonies which were not explicitly forbidden by the Word of God, Calvinists retorted that man should not worship God in any ways he did not explicitly prescribe in his Word.

Where did this view come from? It is derived from the Reformed emphasis on the total depravity of humanity. If "there is no one righteous, not even one" (Rom. 3:10), people are certainly incapable of knowing the will of God apart from his revelation in Scripture. In fact, Scripture must clearly indicate the will of God or no one can be saved. Any addition to Scripture will serve only to suit one's sinful desires, and any subtractions will serve only to salve awareness of one's sinful disobedience. A specific example is the second commandment, in which God declares "I, the LORD your God, am a jealous God" (Exod. 20:5) and curses those who worship him in idolatrous ways. This twin emphasis on human sinfulness and Scriptural authority produced immediate consequences in congregational worship.

**Centrality of Scriptural Exposition.** First, worship services became centered on Scripture exposition, rather than on liturgical prayers and ceremonies. While some Anglican priests were content to read brief homilies prepared by others and were defended in their actions by leading bishops, Puritan preachers of all stripes insisted on preaching and expounding the Word of God. Sermons were seldom less than an hour in length and often much longer; pastoral prayers sometimes exceeded the length of the sermon. Even church architecture symbolically reflected this emphasis by placing the pulpit in the center of the meetinghouse with a communion table and baptismal font underneath. At times these were further reduced into a flip-up shelf for communion and a small bowl for baptism attached to the pulpit itself.

**Care in Administration of the Sacraments.** Second, although the sacraments were definitely secondary to the preaching of the Word, they were administered with great caution. The churches practiced either "closed" or "close" communion, restricting participants to members in good standing of the local church or to those known with certainty to be members in good standing of another solidly Reformed church. Baptism was also reserved for the children of church members. Although the "halfway covenant" ideas of Solomon Stoddard relaxed these standards for a time, the evangelistic preaching of his successor Jonathan Edwards and Edwards' followers soon placed an even higher priority on the need for a converted church membership. With this emphasis on conversion came a still stronger emphasis on preaching the Word of God.

**Scriptural Reform of Worship.** Third, all ceremonies and features not specified in Scripture were categorically eliminated. This meant a refusal to wear the medieval vestments of the Roman Catholic priesthood, which to the Puritans symbolized the Mass as a reenactment of the sacrifice of Christ. The entire Christian calendar of saints' days and holy days—including Christmas and Easter—was eliminated and replaced by a strong emphasis on the celebration of the Lord's Day. Simplicity in worship and removal of anything that might distract from the preaching of the Word were deemed essential. The order of the worship service itself was rearranged; the traditional order of the Mass was replaced with what was thought to be a copy of first-century worship. Here congregationalists and presbyterians parted company. Although the two groups cooperated in developing the _Westminster Directory for Public Worship,_ some real differences emerged which are noted in the Directory's liturgical commentary.

As a result of these factors, the worship of all Puritans, especially that of the congregationalists who saw themselves as the more rigorous and stricter party within Puritanism, was radically simplified. The Anglican priest and poet John Donne could claim that the Puritan

> But loves her only, who at Geneva is called
> Religion, plain, simple, sullen, young,
> Contemptuous, yet unhandsome; as among
> Lecherous humors, there is one that judges
> No wenches wholesome, but coarse country
>   drudges. ("Satire 3")

The congregationalists might well have agreed with Donne's criticism, but they would have taken his description of their plain and simple Genevan worship as a compliment to the ruthlessness of their biblical pruning knife.

Darrell Todd Maurina

## 140 • QUAKER WORSHIP

_Quaker worship, to varying degrees, is unstructured. It is characterized by silence and by the leading of the Spirit._

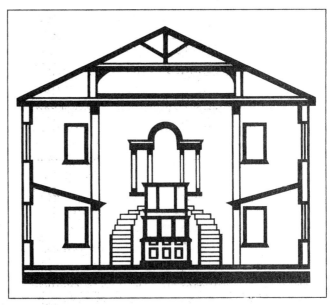

_**New England Church—Interior View.** The interior speaks to the centrality of the Word of God in worship. In the above figure, the pulpit is elevated to the central position and may be reached by stairs at either side._

It is easy to identify the Quakers or Society of Friends as the most radical tradition of all in its break from late medieval forms of worship. Other groups emerging from the Reformation have clergy, the preaching of sermons, and outward and visible sacraments. The classical forms of Quaker worship have none of these, although one may detect some indirect links with medieval mysticism. Paradoxically, most Quakers have tempered their radicalism by being the most conservative in fidelity to their original forms. Roman Catholic worship has changed far more than has Quaker worship in England or on the east coast of the United States.

The origins of Quaker worship lie in the soul-searching of George Fox (1624–1691) and his discovery of the "inner light" in every human. This inner light brought one closer to God than Scripture or sacraments, for it was direct access to the Spirit itself with no need for the mediation of clergy or set forms. Furthermore, such direct access was available to all, male or female, slave or free. Thus, any study of liturgy and justice must begin with the Quakers, for what they practiced in worship was what they felt compelled to practice in all of life. What F. D. Maurice (1805–1872), Percy Dearmer (1867–1936), Virgil Michel (1890–1938), and H. A. Reinhold (1897–1968) later advocated had been common practice among Quakers for several centuries. Since all were equal before the Spirit, women had as much right to speak in worship as men, and anyone who could see the Spirit in a black person had no right to keep him or her in slavery. Since no one was marginalized in worship, it also meant no one should be honored by clothing or title in society. Decisions were to be made by the "sense of the meeting," since a vote always means a defeat for a minority.

But though it could dispense with sermons and sacraments, the one thing Quaker worship could not surrender was the Christian community itself, the "meeting." Hence, the most important act in worship for Quakers is coming together in Christ's name. Quaker worship is a form of corporate mysticism in which the Spirit uses individuals to speak to the group. Greatly to be feared is putting oneself forward by rushing into words. Only after a time of "centering down" can one feel ready to speak under the compulsion of the Spirit. Quakers feel that Christ did not intend outward baptism and communion to continue any more than footwashing, so these sacraments occur in invisible and inward ways only.

Quaker worship always has involved a great sense of personal restraint. Even great Quaker saints such as John Woolman (1720–1772) worried after first-day meeting (Sunday) that they might have spoken from the self rather than the Spirit. A high degree of biblical literacy is also presupposed. The Spirit, after all, is the author of Scripture too and will not contradict itself whether in the Bible or in reason.

On the American frontier, like so many other traditions, some Quakers adopted frontier forms of worship, especially in Indiana. Thus, services evolved with structured worship, paid clergy, and even outward sacraments. Sometimes unstructured or unprogrammed worship could be integrated into services which were basically structured. But many East Coast and English Quakers worship still in ways that would not astonish George Fox, so stable has Quaker worship been.

James F. White[10]

## 141 • METHODIST WORSHIP

*John Wesley was an Anglican clergyman who sought to bring new life to the Church of England through conversion and*

*enthusiastic response to God in sacramental worship. In America, Wesleyan forms of worship did not survive. There Methodists tended to follow the frontier-revivalist pattern of worship.*

Methodism can be seen as a counter-cultural movement in the midst of the Enlightenment. When the sacraments were on the margin of church life, early Methodism put them at the center; when religious zeal was in disrepute, Methodism made enthusiasm essential; where religion was confined to the churches, Methodism took it to the fields and streets. John Wesley (1703–1791), the founder of Methodism, was a faithful son of the Church of England and never ceased in his love for its worship. The Methodists under Wesley functioned virtually as a religious order under a General Rule within the established church.

Distinctive features of early Methodist worship were "constant communion," i.e., frequent Eucharist, fervent preaching for salvation, vigorous hymn singing (then a novelty), care of souls in small

*The Listening Angel. Quaker worship is distinguished by its emphasis on listening for the Holy Spirit. From Southwell Cathedral.*

groups, and a mixture of extemporaneous and fixed prayers. Charles Wesley (1707–1788) wrote hymns by the thousands; he and John created a great treasury of 166 eucharistic hymns. John Wesley practiced pragmatic traditionalism, preferring ancient forms for modern needs when possible: vigils became the Methodist watch night, the _agapē_ surfaced as the love feast, and the covenant service was adapted from Presbyterianism. In 1784, John Wesley published his service book for America, the _Sunday Service,_ advocating, among other things, a weekly Eucharist.

Much of this did not survive the transit of the Atlantic, and American Methodism soon discarded Wesley's service book but not his hymn book. Much of the sacramental life was dissipated (although the texts for the rites remained largely intact). Instead, Methodism tended to adapt many of the techniques of the frontier. Camp meetings abounded for a time and eventually resulted in a distinctive revival type service. Fanny Crosby (1820–1915) wrote many hymns of personal devotion to the blessed Savior, while Charles A. Tindley (1856–1933) was a prolific black hymn writer.

Despite the prevalence of revival style worship, there persisted in America a number of areas where more formal worship was preferred, such as in Birmingham and Nashville. Thomas O. Summers (1812–1882) was the leader of a nineteenth-century liturgical movement in the South which effected the reprinting of Wesley's service book and produced a standard order of worship. Wesley's prayer book long remained in use in England, or even _The Book of Common Prayer._ In general, Methodists in the nineteenth century reacted against the new ritualism of the established church in England, only to adopt some aspects of it several generations later.

Revivalism gave way to a period of aestheticism with much discussion of "enriching worship." This, in turn, gave way to a neoorthodox period of recovering historic liturgies, especially Wesley's. Recent decades have seen more attention to assimilating the post-Vatican II Roman Catholic reforms, especially the lectionary. The new (1989) _United Methodist Hymnal_ shows how far this has gone and may mark the beginning of a neoProtestant emphasis on keeping the identity of one's own tradition.

**James F. White**[11]

_John Wesley at Gwennap Pit. Here Wesley is depicted preaching at Gwennap Pit Amphitheater, where it is said he preached to thirty thousand people._

## 142 ◆ SALVATION ARMY WORSHIP

_The Salvation Army, founded in London in 1865 by William and Catherine Booth, is an international, evangelical part of the universal Christian church. Its mission is to preach the gospel of Jesus Christ and meet human needs in his name without discrimination. Salvation Army officers (ordained leaders) and soldiers (lay members) operate corps community centers, schools, hospitals, shelters, feeding sites, and other programs in ninety-six countries around the world._

From its beginning, The Salvation Army has been thoroughly evangelical. The founder, William Booth, served as an evangelistic revivalist preacher from 1849 to 1861 with both the Wesleyans and New Connexion Methodism, and from 1861 to 1865 in independent ministry. As an evangelist, Booth preached convincingly on the themes of personal conversion and sanctification. Using almost any means available—open-air preaching, tambourines, brass instruments—to attract attention to his gospel message, Booth soon had a following of loyal supporters.

From the early open-air meetings, Salvation Army worship moved inside to disused pubs, dance halls, theaters, even a tent on a Quaker burial ground. The meetings were lively. Army musicians took secular tunes from pubs and dance halls and gave them unmistakably evangelistic words. (For instance, "Here's to good old whiskey, drink it down" became "Storm the forts of darkness, bring them down.'') Converts testified enthusiastically to the change wrought in their lives by salvation. Preaching, by men and women Salvationists alike, was fiery and always aimed at the individual's need for salvation in Christ.

In an 1889 article, "Salvation for Both Worlds," Booth expanded his message to include the social dimensions of salvation. Redemption meant not only individual, personal, and spiritual salvation, but corporate, social and physical salvation, as well. Booth and his followers believed that preaching had to be complemented by caring for the physical needs of the poor to whom they preached. Booth's book, *In Darkest England and the Way Out* (1890), became the textbook for an all-out, aggressive two-front war for the souls of people and for a rightly ordered society.

Today, Salvationists are still fighting "The Great Salvation War" on those two fronts. Salvation Army worship emphasizes spontaneity, personal experience, and congregational participation in worship. A typical worship service might include congregational singing with brass band accompaniment, spontaneous testimonies from members of the congregation, and an invitation for individuals to publicly respond to the biblical call to holy living.

In theology, The Salvation Army is Wesleyan. In philosophy, it is practical. An Army slogan, "Heart to God, Hand to Man," explains the commitment of salvation soldiers around the world to preach, teach, counsel, shelter, feed, clothe, and befriend their brothers and sisters of all races, colors, creeds, and ages.

"We are a salvation people," William Booth wrote in 1879. "This is our specialty, getting saved, and then getting somebody else saved, and then getting saved ourselves more and more, until full salvation on earth makes the heaven within, which is finally perfected by the full salvation on the other side of the river." More than one hundred years later, the heart of all Salvation Army worship and work is still preaching and personal experience of salvation for all people and sanctification from all sin.

Lesa Salyer

## 143 • AMERICAN REVIVAL WORSHIP

*A definite pattern of worship developed in the revival movements of the American frontier and in the campaigns of American evangelists. This "revivalistic" approach to worship has continued as the dominant tradition in the "free churches" of America, and is found today particularly within the fundamentalist and evangelical communities.*

Interest in religion waned in the years immediately following the American Revolution. Westward expansion certainly did not help matters. It dispersed sparse populations across vast expanses of the West, away from formal, organized communities and away from organized parish life. The revivalists of the early nineteenth century initially sought to provide this scattered population with the essentials of religion. The revival camp-meeting developed as a means to provide the most basic rudiment of all: conversion.

Charles G. Finney, the leading revivalist of the early nineteenth century, adapted the format of the backwoods revivals and brought this frontier phenomenon to the cities of the eastern seaboard. When in the mid-1830s Finney decided that, for the sake of his family, he must curtail his travels and settle down to a pastorate, the methods used in his revival campaigns became the basis for a revised approach to liturgy. Finney and his methods (called the "new measures") are cited below as archetypes of revivalist influence. Revivalist patterns, though, were as varied as were the numerous American denominations of the period.

**Conversion-centered Worship.** The rambling frontier lifestyle in the West contrasted sharply with the traditional American liturgical forms as practiced in the more cosmopolitan East. The established denominations in the East largely employed well-educated clergy who directed their attention toward a relatively educated populace (that is, when compared with the population of the West). The set, traditional liturgies and the often scholarly bent of the homilies did not touch the hearts of the rough and independent settlers in the West and were discarded by the revivalists as "dead orthodoxy." The revivalists believed that the Spirit brings life, full and vibrant, to touch the soul; they sought, therefore, to reach their listeners on a visceral level. Finney and his revivalist contemporaries aimed at producing "true heart-felt religion," implying that religion not felt by the heart was not true religion. The emotional emphasis inherent in revivalism, a type of vernacular romanticism, reflects this yearning for a heartfelt faith.

Stemming as well from the romantic ethos of the

age was the individualistic emphasis in revivalism—not only dramatic, heartfelt conversions, but dramatic heartfelt *individual decisions* for Christ. Faith must be chosen; informed mental assent must be given to the truth of Christianity. One could not become a Christian by birth, but only by a *new* birth, a birth by choice, founded on a decisive, dramatic experience. Finney, a lawyer by training, was known to plead with his audiences, as with a jury, arguing the case for repenting and coming to Christ.

Finney brought with his new measures a new ecclesiology, which, in turn, brought about a new approach to liturgy. Departing from the centuries-old model of the church as a covenant community whose primary responsibility was to worship God and to encourage individual and corporate growth in faith, Finney posited evangelism as the primary focus in church life. This focus on evangelism led to a new liturgical stance for Sunday worship, one following the camp-meeting model. Finney tried to do away with what he saw as "dead orthodoxy"—prepared and lengthy prayers, erudite written sermons, ominous psalm-singing—in favor of sprightly songs directed to the needs of the sinner, emotionally stirring sermons designed to promote repentant response on the part of the hearers, and fervent, heart-felt praying for the souls of the lost. The focus and content of sermons changed to imitate the revival pattern as well. With conversion rather than corporate worship as the focus, the sermon became the most direct means of persuading the unconverted in the congregation to give their lives to Christ. Altar calls, previously unheard of in a worship service, became frequent elements of the liturgy. The role of the pastor changed from worship leader to preacher.

It would be inaccurate to imply that all of Finney's pastoral sermons were "salvation" sermons. Indeed, Finney sought to address doctrinal and social topics as well. His passionate preaching, however, coupled with his quasi-Arminian theology which emphasized the role of the individual will in the process of salvation and spiritual growth, demonstrated his belief that constant introspection and repentance are necessary elements of the Christian life. Extant is a letter from one of Finney's parishioners which notes a sermon delivered in 1845 which, although not on an evangelistic topic, produced such a response in the congregation that a spontaneous, congregationally led altar call followed the sermon.

**Revivalism and Church Architecture.** A secondary outcome of the revivals was architectural change. Finney's designs for the two churches he pastored (Broadway Tabernacle in New York City and First Church in Oberlin, Ohio) illustrate these changes. Eighteenth-century family box pews were done away with, and slip (bench) pews took their place. This new arrangement could seat more people in a given area and focused attention on the "stage" area. Finney designed his churches with the emphasis on preaching; pews were set in a semicircular manner in order to bring the parishioners closer to the preacher. The change in seating arrangements reflects the individualistic emphasis of revivalism; whereas the box pews had accommodated family participation, the new pews allowed the attention of each congregant to be centered on the preacher. Choir and organ were moved, in the new designs, from the side of the nave or from the balcony to the stage, an arrangement reflecting their change in function from worship aids to accouterments of evangelistic performance. Rather than a large pulpit at the side of the chancel area, Finney desired a smaller, central pulpit or lectern. The communion table was moved back or to one side, deemphasizing the sacrament as a primary focus of the liturgy.

Certainly not all members of the Protestant community were enamored of the methods of Finney and the other revivalists. While some ministers eagerly employed the "new measures," others decried them as heretical or improper. Yet, despite the debates over revivalist methods, who could argue with their success, if we measure success in terms of numbers of respondents? Within a generation, religious interest had moved from the fringes of American life to a central position in society.

James R. Peck

## 144 • AFRICAN-AMERICAN WORSHIP

*Churches in the African-American community share a distinct worship culture that is the result of the integration of Christian worship forms with a worldview shaped by a traditional African ontology (understanding of being). In addition to the African heritage and religious perspective, the experience of blacks in American slavery has also helped to shape African-American worship patterns. Because most North American Christians are unfamiliar with the African heritage, this entry covers more background than the others in this chapter.*

*Camp Meeting. Camp meetings were often held in the woods, where people came and camped for days to sing, to hear evangelistic preaching, and to get their lives straight with God. Some camp meetings were conducted from the stump of a tree while others, more organized (such as the one depicted above) were held in clearings, with a platform for the preacher. The scene here is adapted from an illustration in B. W. Gorham's* Camp Meeting Manual *(1854).*

## Introduction

Any discussion of Christian liturgy, regardless of particularities, begins from one basic premise: God, in the beginning of time, initiated and set the momentum for worship. God's initiative is *a priori* to the individual or corporate response of a people. In Jesus the Christ, God entered fully into the conditions of humanity and the world. In Jesus Christ God's initiative shaped ritual action, setting the direction for praise, adoration, thanksgiving, confession, acts of prayer, proclamation, remembrance and offering. In the Holy Spirit, God takes the initiative and remains actively present, transforming, empowering and sustaining human lives.

It is in response to God's divine initiative that the people of God, enabled by the power of the Holy Spirit, acknowledge and respond to the mysterious presence of the divine in the world and in their lives.

The priority of God's initiative is the theological foundation for our discussion. Upon this foundation we will explore ways that a particular people have heard and responded to God's call to worship. The people around whom this discussion will focus have taken upon themselves the designation "African-American," affirming a uniqueness which

incorporates a plethora of converging roots and traditions. (1) One root is deeply embedded in rich African soil, with all that this implies. (2) Another root is American, a heritage which we vociferously claim. (3) Christian African-Americans also acknowledge a faith root in the Judeo-Christian religious tradition which binds the body of Christ. (4) The fourth root is a common liturgical history which has been shaped by the Graeco-Roman cultures of the West.

Out of these four major converging roots, African-Americans have been able to transform existential experiences in America into particularities: ways of praying, liturgical patterns, and ways of theologizing. Ritual action that may indeed appear to be the same as Euro-American liturgical action may be informed by a totally different worldview or theological base. On the other hand, certain liturgical assumptions common to both Euro-Americans and African-Americans will evoke totally different worship responses and patterns. Herein is one of innumerable examples of the mysterious power of God to communicate with people and to allow them to respond out of their particular cultural context. It also speaks to the helpful scholarship of cultural anthropologists, who remind us of the numerous similarities in the way that myths and rituals are shaped by humans to reflect responses to life situations.

As we provide some clarity about African-American liturgy in context, let us bear in mind that there are indeed differences in worship practices among African-American worshipers, both within and across denominational lines. Nevertheless, in spite of our differences, there is much that we share.

Traditionally, active participation in worship, rather than active discussion, has been foremost for African-Americans. Recently, however, we are attempting to hear God clearly in this age as we "discover" and "recover" liturgical options available to us from our African and slave heritages. We do not seek merely to "hear" exactly as our forebears did, for we are not at the same place and time. We can observe how they heard with such intensity that they were able to make sense out of the realities of their circumstances in worship and life. We are also able to determine what remained essentially the same in the transition from African traditional religions to African-American Christianity. In this data we are discovering avenues for liturgical and spiritual renewal not only for ourselves, but for Christian liturgy in general. We begin first with a discovery of African worship practices.

## African Liturgical Practices and World View

Over the four centuries of the Atlantic slave trade, Africans were taken from many parts of the continent. Therefore, those who would ultimately shape African-American liturgical traditions came from a variety of diverse cultures. From the seventeenth through the nineteenth centuries a majority of Africans brought to the Americas were taken from a 3,000 mile stretch along the west coast of Africa, from Senegal south to the southern part of Angola. They did not bring with them beliefs and practices which would accurately be called a unified or monolithic "African culture." Peoples of Africa south of the Sahara, like those of North Africa, created a myriad of languages, religions, customs, political systems and institutions, all of which differentiated their societies. It is more appropriate, then, to refer to traditional African religions rather than to a universal African religion.

Societal religions did not include carefully honed creeds and theological formulas which were to be recited. Nor were beliefs spread by missionary or evangelistic efforts. No doubt, some of the religious ideas may have been disseminated through migrations and inter-familial linkages. Large portions of societies or tribal groups are known to have migrated basically intact to different locations, taking their beliefs and practices with them. The new environment would create a need for alterations in ritual and possibly adjustments in belief.

African peoples did share a fundamental primal worldview, a basic system for perceiving realities and making sense out of existential situations in order to survive. This fundamental view helped to provide a common means for cultural expression and a basic sense of common identity. In order to understand religious rituals and ceremonies of Africans in diaspora, one must understand the context in which worldviews were shaped and disseminated. A search for elements of continuity through an investigation of primal worldviews will not limit us to what some researchers would refer to as "survivals" from African cultures. To do so would misinterpret the nature of culture as a fixed condition, rather than as a process. The strength and resiliency of culture is determined by its ability to react creatively and responsibly to the realities of a new situa-

tion. The evidence of the African continuum in Christian worship among the rapidly growing churches in Africa and in the diaspora attests to the resiliency and adaptability of African cultural roots.

We begin then, with common African primal worldviews as the basic context of continuity which helped Africans to adapt to new environments, and to shape unique liturgical practices.

## Interaction with the Spirit Realm

First and foremost, for Africans, the whole of existence is a religious phenomenon. The African scholar John S. Mbiti states quite succinctly, "Africans are notoriously religious. . . . Religion permeates all departments of life so fully that it is not easy or possible to isolate it"(*African Religions and Philosophy* [Garden City, N.Y.: Anchor/Doubleday, 1970], xvii). The prevailing African ontology, or understanding of being, essentially views spiritual realities as bound up with the lives of people. This anthropocentric ontology is centered in an awareness of a sovereign God who is the originator and sustainer of all there is. God the Creator is all-wise, ubiquitous, all-powerful, beyond our grasp, as well as present. To use the classical metaphysical terms, which are meaningless in African thinking, one could say that God is omniscient, omnipresent, omnipotent, transcendent and yet immanent. God is also Spirit, and yet spirits (with a small "s") permeate the cosmos. Some spirits begotten of God serve as intermediaries or divine emissaries for God.

Included in the spirit world are spirits of humans who have died and are categorized as "living dead." For Africans, the concept of the "living dead" (according to Mbiti) means the deceased are still living within the active memory of the community and interact with it. Those who have lived a full and fruitful life become ancestral spirits, and libations are poured on the ground as a sign of this interaction. Contrary to the opinion of many Euro-Americans, who say that this is merely evidence of ancestral worship or a form of spiritual necromancy, the function of the "living dead" is in some ways similar to that of saints in Christian traditions. Some scholars have proposed that the importance of the spirit of the ancestors in African traditional religions could provide a link to the Christian concept of the "communion of saints" (*communio sanctorum*). Rather than assuming that the ancestral saints are objects of worship, one must understand the interplay between the "living dead" and the temporal community.

Since all parents are respected, especially the elders of the community, the spirit of the deceased ancestral parent continually helps maintain coherence in family life for the living. Age is a symbol of impending transition into the divine state of ancestral spirit. The spirit of the deceased, who now lives closer to God, serves as a guardian of ethics, family traditions, and community custom. Ancestors are remembered and celebrated in a form of representing or reliving the life of a person who served the community well while alive. This is also a reminder that neither life nor community ends with physical death of persons.

## Wholeness of Life

The second concept in an African ontology is the perception of wholeness of life, where there is no separation into sacred and secular realms. To be fully human is to "belong," to belong to God. Thus, to be in solidarity with the whole community is to be bound up with all that comprises the cosmos: humanity and the natural environment, past, present, and future. Ritual action allows the community to reconnect with, and maintain, the reality of the "rhythm of life." Wholeness of life, epitomized in ritual action, necessarily involves the whole person, body and soul. While some verbal communication takes place, a larger proportion of communication takes place in bodily movement and in song. Dance evolves from full corporate participation in worship and is considered communal. Even when there are special performers, the community participates in some manner. Word, song, and action are often simultaneous, and the community understands what is being communicated. Just as life is viewed from a holistic perspective requiring the participation of the entire person, so involvement in life requires that the whole person participate in the process.

A consistent understanding of rites of passage in African traditional religions recognizes that in the "rhythm of life" one is born, then dies and is reborn continually from one state of existence to another. The rhythm of life begins long before a child is born, since the perpetuation of life calls for the anticipation of a continual process of birth. John S. Mbiti eloquently explains this process: "Children are the 'buds' of society, and every birth is the arrival of spring" (Mbiti, 143).

The first rite of passage for individuals and societies is the moment of one's physical birth. At this time the community claims the child as its own. It is the task of the entire community to nurture and help prepare the child to become a corporate person, one who belongs to the whole. Through appropriate rituals the community helps to mark each stage of a person's life as an experience memorable for all. Rites of adolescence or puberty, marriage, parenthood, and death abound with ample amounts of music, dancing, pouring of libations, and the reciting of appropriate words.

Since all of life is regarded as sacred, elements of nature can be used symbolically in ritual action. Water, so basic in the creation process, was and remains an important symbol in rituals. Prior to an understanding of water baptism in the Christian tradition, Africans understood water as a gift from God, and used it in most rites of passage. The word for water or rain in some African societies is the same as, or synonymous with, the name and attributes of God or "divine outpouring." For without water—without God—there is no life. For example, the name given to me in a Kikuyu naming ceremony is *nyambura,* which combines two terms, *nya,* meaning a female person, and *mbura,* meaning the pouring out of rain. *nyambura* is a female who pours out special blessings from God. *Mbura* is also the name of a clan of rainmakers in the traditional Kikuyu society who pray for rain around the sacrificial tree called *mugumo.* Following their special prayers, rain would invariably fall in a matter of a few hours or minutes. Rain, therefore, is a gift of life and a blessing from God, who often comes with the drops of rain. For this reason, water, palm wine, beer, or some other liquid is used for the pouring of libations to symbolize the continuing existence of life and the presence of God. Water is also used for rites of purification and regeneration, symbolizing cleansing and re-creation.

Sounds of nature are incorporated into the performance of ritual. The percussive rhythms of drums, rattles, bells or any improvisatory device which makes a sound of its own, as well as sounds produced by any other instrument, are for the most part imitations of the sounds of nature. In addition to melodic and percussive singing, a number of strident vocal sounds, such as squalling, twirping, and ululation (loud wailing) are imitative of sounds that are heard in the environment. All such sounds are likely to be included in traditional African as well as

Christian worship. Thus the wholeness of life is incorporated in the worship of God.

## Kinship and Community

The concept of wholeness of life leads naturally to the third aspect of African ontology, which has to do with kinship, family, and extended family relationships. In African thought, each person is an individual with unique qualities and personality, but his or her existence is intricately interrelated with others and with the natural environment. In a variety of ways, most societies would affirm the African adage: "I am because you are; and since we are, therefore, I am." One comes to traditional worship aware that he or she is part of the whole. Communication takes place not because a person has something to say or do, but because the familial community exists. A "call and response" form of communication is evident in singing, as well as in verbal communication. One does not merely deliver information nor tell a story to the community. The listeners participate with the informant, the _griot_ or storyteller, interacting with interest in what is being said as though they were part of the story. Verbal dialogue also provides a means of evoking the best efforts of the presenter. Call and response dialogue is also reflected in music and dance as the community responds and participates spontaneously and informally. One cannot help but feel and be drawn into the communal kinship which prevails in these moments.

The African concept of family—and extended family—includes those living, those yet to be born who are still in the loins of the living, and the "living dead," those up to five generations past who have died. The sense of kinship binds together the entire life of the society and is extended to cover animals, plants, and nonliving objects. I am told that the use of musical instruments made from animal skins and from resources in the natural environment is one way of incorporating the cosmos into the human community. The improvisatory gifts of the community reflect the whole of creation working together with human beings. Kinship largely governs the behavior, patterns of thinking, myths, and rituals of each society.

## Relativity of Time

The fourth concept of African ontology involves the relativity of time. In traditional African societies, time is not calculated linearly, but is conceptualized in the light of natural phenomena: the passing of day and night, lunar cycles, and the regular cycles of seasons. Time is viewed as meaningful in virtue of the content of the event, not because something will happen at a mathematically preconceived moment. Where rites and rituals are regularized, the community is notified to gather by a variety of means, particularly the talking drums. The time to start an activity arrives whenever enough people are gathered. The length of the activity, including worship, depends upon the involvement of the community. In worship one is likely hear that "God is not to be hurried; and this is God's time!"

## Sacred Space

The fifth and final concept has to do with sacred space. In traditional religions, space and time are closely linked; the same word is often used for both. Just as with time, space is defined by the content or intent of action. What matters most to the people is what is geographically near. For that reason, Africans are particularly tied to the land; it is a concrete expression of both the past and the present (_zamani_ and _sasa_). The land, like all of creation, is sacred because it provides Africans with the roots of existence, and binds them mystically to the departed who lived there before them. Certain space within the designated worship area is often set apart as special and considered "off limits" for certain people. Rites performed to sacralize space are incorporated in Christian worship ceremonies. While attending the dedication of a church building in Kenya recently, I observed that the sacralizing ritual combined traditional Kikuyu and Christian practices. The church had been carefully locked after the builders, both members and non-members of the church, had completed their task. A very lengthy worship service, which included the ordination of the pastor who had been called to the church, took place under a tent on the church lawn. Officials of the denomination then led the procession to the church door, which was blessed by the presiding minister. Only church officials were allowed in the church, and the door was securely locked behind them. A ritual of blessing required that the officiant touch every space that the congregation would use, including the center aisle, the pews and floor space between them, the chancel area, pulpit, lectern, and the area for the choir. The initial words in Kikuyu were repeated in Swahili, loud enough for the waiting congregation to hear.

While I did not understand any of the words, it was exciting to read the expressions of approval on the faces of the people and to note how eagerly they listened. The time seemed endless, but thirty minutes later the pastor (who was not allowed to enter before the blessing ceremony was over) responded to a knock on the door from the inside and announced in the languages of the people that the church had been blessed! As the community burst into song, a translation was provided in English, indicating that the ritual was a combination of African traditions and Christianity. Worshipers were rejoicing that the spirits of those who slept in the land had freed the church to worship in that space. I was also reminded that there was no electricity, and that if it were ever added, another ceremony would be required.

Once inside the building, the entire congregation took part in additional ceremonies blessing every piece of furniture that had not been blessed before. This included kneeling pads for baptism and marriage, the communion table and baptismal font, and the battery-operated clock on the wall in the room. The strangers from America were also cleansed, blessed, and welcomed to walk on the soil of the spirits of their—and perhaps our—ancestors. Needless to say the five-hour celebration, which included a meal of barbecued goat, was emotional and heartwarming.

## The African Heritage in Christian Worship

In summary, Africans did not arrive in America with a *tabula rasa,* but with a network of understandings, potentials, and liturgical practices based on African primal worldviews. These are the foundation for liturgical elements which we have discovered, recovered, and in which we freely engage as a form of renewal. All three aspects of this network converge as we equip ourselves for and open ourselves to God's enabling empowerment. Ours is a deeply religious heritage built upon a cluster of understandings and potentials which our forebears understood:

**Awareness of God.** As they were already aware of one sovereign God, omnipotent, omniscient, omnipresent, transcendent and immanent, they were able to relate this awareness to the God of Jesus Christ. Some of the slaves had been introduced to Christianity in Africa. Thus, as they were evangel-ized in America, they were able to deepen their faith in a God who is "always on time." Their African memory of God as Spirit helped them to understand the enabling power of God in Jesus Christ.

**Wholeness of Life.** The concept of the wholeness of life which is not compartmentalized into "sacred" and "secular" results in a perspective which does not confine spiritual concerns to a once-a-week event (on Sunday). "Notoriously religious" Africans continued to build upon their traditions, and in some instances substituted African concepts and terms for those of the Christian faith. For Africans who became Catholics, especially during the slave trade via the Middle Passage to the West Indies, Louisiana, and other southern states, the concept of the saints could serve as a reminder of highly respected ancestors. Wholeness of life undergirds worship, a time when the individual personhood of all gathered is affirmed and celebrated. Empowerment to participate fully in the liturgy is more accurately described as "having church." Amidst what some have described as liturgical confusion in African-American worship is the African continuum of seeking and finding God at the deepest spiritual level available to an uninhibited, whole people!

Needless to say, the various styles of preaching and praying as well as the forms and style of music and singing in the liturgy reflect this concept of wholeness. Herein is the foundation for improvisation and the use of the whole body in response to the Word of God. It is not difficult to fathom the similarities between forms and styles of music in everyday life and music "in church." The beat and improvisatory techniques of blues, ragtime, and jazz are employed in some black gospel music, and there is an "alrightness" about it.

**Family Ties.** The importance of family, extended family and familial relationships in African ontology reinforce the awareness of the beloved community, the body of Christ at worship. Worship provides an opportunity for the community to interact at a level at which knowing and praising God in Jesus Christ and believing that God cares binds individuals to one another. The family and extended family at worship may place limits on or determine parameters for what things are done and how, because people care about each other. This is one reason that early African-Americans sought private spaces for worship: common needs and bondings are necessary for viable worship, hence the emergence of separate congregations and denominations among African-American Christians.

**Rites of Passage.** The importance attached to rites of passage, rituals, and ceremonies has persisted among Africans in diaspora. Under the slave system, many rites of passage, which helped maintain the wholeness of the community, were restricted. However, remnants of African funeral and burial rites persisted. Later, Christian baptism was filled with reminders of African initiation rites which used water in symbolism of new life and re-creation, dying of the old, purification, regeneration, and cleansing. The symbolic act of going to or being carried to the water continues to be meaningful. It is not unusual in Africa for baptisms to occur where there is running water, a reminder of the living waters related to renewal and regeneration.

**The Lord's Supper.** The Lord's Supper in African-American churches is related to eating traditions among African peoples. In Christian understanding the gods and spirits are not to be fed, but humans are fed by the Son of God. The action at the Lord's table carries with it an African understanding of the significance of the offering of food. The concept of _anamnēsis_—remembering as if the community actually transcends time and space—partially coincides with the tradition of the African _griot,_ storyteller or oral historian, and thus relates the Lord's Supper to the function of the preaching of the Word.

**Worship Time.** The broad parameters governing time in African culture continue in the diaspora, and are especially prominent in worship practices. African-Americans have accepted the linear notion of time and have established beginning times for worship. Often operating underneath "established" time, however, is the worldview which regards time as strictly relative. Where this worldview is most evident, worship services may start close to the established hour, but will end when the Holy Spirit determines that worship is over; then and only then is the benediction pronounced.

**Sacred Areas.** The sacredness of space in God's creation is observed especially in the way African-Americans view the space for worship. While the nave or sanctuary is sacred, it is available to all worshipers; the area around the pulpit, the communion table and the baptistry, however, are special, sacred spaces. This sacredness is extended to include those

divinely "called" such as the preacher or deliverer of the Word and those appointed to preside at sacred rituals.

**Leadership.** African community leaders whose roles continue in some form in African-American worship include both males and females. Those in leadership functions are usually viewed with awe and surrounded with mystique, as a result of a perceived divine call to serve in such a capacity. Leadership roles in worship are the mysterious incarnations of the ancient African custodians of worship. The aura of African diviners, priests, prophets, and medicine men and women is absorbed into the roles of preachers, celebrants, and charismatic leaders. The category of mediums, those gifted with insight to discern the degree or quality of spirituality in the ritual and who serve as conduits through which the spiritual is manifested, is absorbed in the matriarchal "Aunt Jane" types and often in the preacher. The African _griot_ is the community historian and storyteller who often "sings" the story; this role is now absorbed in that of the preacher and song leader.

Melva Wilson Costen

## 145 ◆ RESTORATION WORSHIP

_The restoration movement of the early eighteenth century in Britain and the United States attempted to return to the practices of worship outlined in the New Testament. This movement has shaped the worship life of several Protestant groups that use the name "Christian Church" or "Church of Christ."_

Worship practices of the restoration movement took shape during the eighteenth century, beginning in Britain. However, the idea of restoration can best be understood as a particular expression of the Reformation. Luther, Calvin, Zwingli, and Knox sought, in various ways, to restore the faith and doctrine of the church to conformity with the Scriptures. During the 1600s, reformers shifted their attention to the issue of administration: Should the church be governed by bishops, by synods, or by independent congregations? Asking this question threatened the entrenched authority of state churches; spectacular power struggles typify Christianity during the seventeenth century. As opportunities for religious liberty opened, not only in North

America but also in Britain, Congregationalists, Independents, and Baptists found ways to survive persecution. They disagreed among themselves and wrote definitions of what set their group apart and made it more correct in its application of the Scriptures than other fellowships. The number of small sects mounted.

John Glas, a Presbyterian minister, left the Church of Scotland in 1728 because he disagreed with the method by which that church managed its affairs. In separating himself from the state church, Glas began to commemorate the Lord's Supper more frequently than the monthly observance practiced in the Church of Scotland. He read in the New Testament that the apostles came together on the first day of the week for the breaking of bread. In other ways also, Glas began to revive practices he believed accurately reflected life in the primitive or earliest church.

His son-in-law, Robert Sandeman, carried on the restoration movement. As a prolific writer and clear thinker, Sandeman influenced independent-minded Christians in Scotland and England in the second half of the eighteenth century. He promoted weekly observance of the Lord's Supper, greeted other Christians with a "holy kiss," took regular collections of alms for the poor, and held love feasts—all practices he found in the New Testament. Eventually, at least twenty small churches began ordering their practices according to Sandeman's views. In 1763, Sandeman settled in Danbury, Connecticut, where he founded a congregation that united with the Disciples of Christ in 1840.

A similar movement begin in Edinburgh and Glasgow, Scotland, led by the two Haldane brothers, James Alexander and Robert. These wealthy laymen thought the Church of Scotland was too formal and sterile, so they built an independent tabernacle in Edinburgh in 1799 and carried on an extended revival with the help of the English evangelist Rowland Hill. They also established a seminary in Glasgow, where they taught congregational independence and the weekly observance of the Lord's Supper. In 1807, the Haldanes decided that immersion was the scriptural form of baptism.

Glas, Sandeman, and the Haldane brothers influenced many churches and Christian leaders in Britain in the late 1700s and early 1800s, including several who came to North America. Their ideas shaped the kind of Christianity that spread across the frontier in groups using the names "Christian Church" or "Church of Christ." Even the Church of Jesus Christ of Latter-Day Saints (Mormons) was influenced by their thinking.

The most prominent attempt to apply the principles of the restoration movement in North America appeared in a body of believers now divided into three groups: (1) the Christian Church (Disciples of Christ), (2) the Churches of Christ, and (3) Christian Churches and Churches of Christ not related to the other two groups. Ironically, these three groups emerged from an effort distinguished by its plea for Christian unity. Modern day descendants of this American restoration movement look back to four men as founders: Thomas Campbell, his son Alexander Campbell, Barton Warren Stone, and Walter Scott.

The father of Thomas Campbell had been raised a Catholic in Ireland, but as a young adult he conformed to the state religion and became an Anglican. Despite his conversion he married a woman descended from French Huguenots. After launching his career as a school teacher, Thomas undertook five summers of theological training in order to receive ordination as a Seceder Presbyterian minister. In 1798 he became the minister of the Ahorey Church near Rich Hill in Ireland. In 1807, he left his family in Ireland and sailed for North America. He settled in Washington, Pennsylvania, and started preaching for the Presbyterians in the area. A year later, he sent for his family. Shipwrecked on the way, however, they were forced to stay in Glasgow for another year until they could try again to cross the ocean. While in Glasgow, Thomas' son Alexander, now 20 and having been tutored by his father until he could teach along with him, attended the University of Glasgow. There he was swayed by the teaching of the Haldane brothers.

While Alexander Campbell was studying at Glasgow, his father left the Seceder Presbyterians because he disagreed with their restrictive attitude concerning who should be served the Lord's Supper. In 1809, Thomas Campbell wrote a *Declaration and Address*. This important document, often considered the charter of the American restoration movement, outlines Thomas Campbell's goal of recovering the unity of the church by means of restoring New Testament patterns of "doctrine, worship, discipline, and government."

Within a year after joining his father in North America, Alexander Campbell preached 100 sermons. The next year he married Margaret Brown and was licensed to preach as a Presbyterian minister. In 1812, he and Margaret became parents and soon faced the decision of whether to baptize their infant daughter (according to Presbyterian practice) or wait until she could receive believer's baptism by immersion. After a year of study, Alexander Campbell, his wife, his parents, and his friends in the Brush Run Church were immersed, and the Brush Run Church joined the Redstone Baptist Association. Eight years later, Alexander Campbell, having established a reputation as a skilled debater, started publishing a periodical called _The Christian Baptist,_ which further enhanced his reputation. While on a trip to Kentucky the following year, he met Barton Warren Stone. For twenty years Stone had been preaching a message remarkably similar to that of the Campbells.

In 1827, Alexander Campbell persuaded the Mahoning Baptist Association to employ Walter Scott as a traveling evangelist. A few years later, when Campbell left the Baptists and took many congregations with him, he also retained the loyalty of this skilled communicator. This departure took place in 1830; Campbell ceased publishing _The Christian Baptist_ and replaced it with a new periodical, _The Millennial Harbinger._ The millennium announced in this title was the golden age dawning as Christianity spread around the world. Campbell was optimistic about the United States of America as the land that best demonstrated how God wanted people to live. Many of Alexander Campbell's views changed, and his tone certainly changed, when he started this new journal.

In 1832, "Raccoon" John Smith represented Alexander Campbell's movement, now known as the Disciples of Christ, in a monumental meeting with Barton W. Stone and his followers, who preferred to be known simply as Christians. This meeting, which took place at Hill Street Church in Lexington, Kentucky, marked a merger of the Christians and the Disciples of Christ and propelled the American restoration movement forward.

Barton W. Stone, nearly sixteen years older than Alexander Campbell, was born on a small plantation near Port Tobacco, Maryland. One of his cousins had signed the Declaration of Independence when Barton was three years old; his older brothers had fought in the Revolutionary War. In 1798, when Stone was being ordained into the Presbyterian ministry at Cane Ridge, Kentucky, he answered the question, "Do you accept the Westminster Confes-

sion of Faith as containing the system of doctrine taught in the Bible?" by saying, "I do as far as I see it consistent with the Word of God." He contended against the Calvinist doctrine of predestination. In 1804, a year after Stone and the ministers and members of fifteen churches left the Synod of Kentucky to form the Springfield Presbytery, they wrote _The Last Will and Testament of the Springfield Presbytery,_ wherein they declared their intention to seek union with the whole body of Christ. Within a few years, Stone and his friends began to practice immersion. Stone published a monthly paper called _The Christian Messenger._

After settling in Georgetown, Kentucky, in 1819, Stone met Alexander Campbell five years later. They recognized the similarity of their ideas and began discussing the possibility of union. Their discussion climaxed in the handshake of Christian fellowship and unity in Lexington in 1832. Barton Stone lived until 1844 and Alexander Campbell until 1866. The movement that grew out of the teachings they advocated is still sometimes called the Stone-Campbell Movement, even by those who no longer subscribe to all of the assumptions or goals of the restoration movement.

Philip V. Miller

## 146 • HOLINESS WORSHIP

_The holiness movement traces its origins to John Wesley. The worship of the holiness churches, however, was shaped primarily by the liturgical forms of the camp meeting movement._

In 1784 John Wesley recognized the establishment of the Methodist Episcopal Church in America and attempted to offer guidance for its worship through the publication of his revision of _The Book of Common Prayer._ Wesley's work was entitled _The Sunday Service of the Methodists in North America and Other Occasional Services._ Elements which survived Wesley's abridgment of _The Book of Common Prayer_ included morning and evening prayer, baptism, the Lord's Supper, rites of ordination (for deacons, elders and superintendents), the Psalms, the litany and collects, and Epistles and Gospels for the Lord's Supper. Worship was to be marked by weekly sacramental celebration. _The Sunday Service,_ however, was never widely accepted or used in America. Wesley had not accurately perceived the

North American situation, nor had he anticipated the influence of Francis Asbury, the General Superintendent. The "father of American Methodism" was not committed to worship in the prayer book tradition. By the general conference of the Methodist Episcopal Church in 1892, only one year after the death of Wesley, the restructuring of worship was apparent. *The Sunday Service,* a book of more than three hundred pages, had been reduced to fewer than forty pages of "Sacramental Services, &c" which were included within the church's *Discipline.* What remained of Wesley's services were the orders for baptism, the Lord's Supper, and ordination. An order of worship was also included in the 1792 *Discipline;* the standard, however, was no longer a service of Word and sacrament, but one in which evangelistic proclamation, occasionally followed by eucharistic celebration, was primary.

Within ten years of the 1792 *Discipline,* camp meeting religion was crossing the frontier. Although originally an interdenominational enterprise, camp meetings quickly became predominantly Methodist institutions. Methodism's theology, organization, and evangelistic fervor were well suited to the challenge of an isolated, often illiterate, and largely unchurched populace. Camp meetings provided fellowship with rarely seen neighbors and relief from the hardships and monotony of life on the frontier. Worship utilized simple and repetitive "gospel songs." Above all, camp meeting religion called the unchurched to a conversion experience.

By the 1820s, the simple, evangelistic worship model of the camp meeting was being appropriated by revivalists like Charles G. Finney to meet the challenge of the new frontier, the unconverted city. The rise of revivalism ran parallel to an increasing emphasis upon the doctrine of holiness as understood by John Wesley. In the same year that Finney published *Lectures on Revivals of Religion* (1835), Sarah Lankford and Phoebe Palmer began, in New York City, the "Tuesday Meetings for the Promotion of Holiness." By 1839, Timothy Merritt's *Guide to Christian Perfection* provided the holiness movement with a vehicle to promote the cause and to publish the effects of this recovered doctrine. No longer was worship intended solely to call the unconverted to conversion; it was also to call the converted Christian to a complete consecration. The holiness movement appropriated for its own purposes the prevalent revivalistic model of worship consisting of singing, praying, preaching, and the

call to response ("harvest"). The holiness movement of the nineteenth century was not a movement of liturgical reform; it was, rather, the revival of a doctrinal emphasis perceived to have been lost. The origins of the Church of the Nazarene, the Christian and Missionary Alliance, the Wesleyan church and the Pentecostal movement can be traced to the era and theological thrust of the holiness movement.

Brad Estep

## 147 • ADVENTIST WORSHIP

*Adventist worship from the beginning followed a simple format, marked in its earlier stages by enthusiastic outbursts and an emphasis on singing. Worship was not a distinctive emphasis of the Adventist tradition, and its worship patterns were adapted from other movements, with one major exception: most Adventists meet for worship on the seventh rather than the first day of the week.*

Adventists are those conservative Protestants outside the dispensationalist camp whose religion focuses on the second advent of Christ. They also have some genetic relationship to the advent awakening of the 1830s and early 1840s, led in America by William Miller. Today, the largest of these groups is the Seventh-day Adventist Church, on which this discussion is centered. Several smaller denominations, including the Advent Christian Church and the Church of God (Seventh-day), also acknowledge William Miller in their heritage.

The Millerite movement cut across denominational lines, attracting Methodists, Baptists, Presbyterians, and Congregationalists, probably in that order as far as number of adherents are concerned. When Christ failed to return to earth literally in 1844 as Miller had predicted, the movement broke up, and one faction eventually (in 1863) organized itself formally as the Seventh-day Adventist Church. Many Millerites were or had been active in the reform movements of the day, notably abolitionism, and thus tended to be found primarily where abolitionism thrived: in small towns and rural areas of the northeastern United States.

The worship practices of the Millerites who became Seventh-day Adventists were probably influenced most by Methodists, Baptists, and the Christian Church of New England, or Christian Connection as it was sometimes called. The latter was staunchly anti-creedal, anti-Trinitarian, and anti-liturgical. Two of the founders of the Seventh-day Adventists, James White and Joseph Bates, had previously belonged to the Christian Connection; the third founder, Ellen G. White, had Methodist roots. Adventists were also influenced by the "Christian anarchy" of the abolitionist movement, a view which regarded all earthly institutions, even governments and churches, as fallen and evil. Hence it was nearly twenty years after the Millerite movement ended before Seventh-day Adventists finally decided that formal church organization was both necessary and divinely sanctioned.

These influences insured that early Adventist worship would be simple, informal, and vigorously non-liturgical. When the first _Church Manual_ was adopted, reluctantly, in 1883, it made no mention how regular worship services should be conducted, although it did lay down some guidelines for the "ordinances of the Lord's house," by which Adventists meant the Lord's Supper and the accompanying footwashing service. The first description of an order of worship for Adventist churches appears to be a 1906 book by a prominent Colorado pastor, H. M. J. Richards:

> The minister enters the pulpit and kneels for a few moments in silent prayer to God. All the people bow their heads and unite with their minister in silent prayer, imploring the Divine blessing upon the services of the hour. Then the minister announces the opening hymn, then all stand and join in singing. After this the minister and all the people kneel in prayer, while he leads them in a public extemporaneous prayer of moderate length and appropriate to the needs of the people and the subject of the sermon. Usually a second hymn is then sung, and the sermon follows this. The service is concluded by another hymn sung by the entire congregation, after which the benediction is pronounced by the minister. (H. M. J. Richards, _Church Order_ [Denver: Colorado Tract Society, 1906], 64).

Even this order of service was not ironclad. Richards allowed for some variations such as "special music," including sacred solos, duets, quartets, or anthems; and also occasionally "a short Scripture reading at some time before the sermon; and at times a short prayer is introduced after the sermon, when the Spirit so directs." Richards' only concessions to liturgical propriety was his insistence that no announcements would intrude on the worship service and that the "benediction" be pronounced by an ordained minister. Ten years earlier the same reservation had been expressed, describing a benediction as "a blessing pronounced upon the congregation. In doing this the minister usually raises his hands and blesses the congregation in the name of the Lord, pronouncing grace, mercy, and peace upon them. This function . . . ought to be confined to ministers of the gospel" (G. C. Tenney, "To Correspondents, #68," _Review and Herald_ 73 [March 31, 1896], 202).

Scattered hints in earlier sources mention such elements as "prayers, singing, exhortation, and preaching,"(D. M. Canright, "A Few Thoughts About Meetings," _Review and Herald_, 28 [Oct. 30, 1866], 173) but recommend no specific order and seem to be far more concerned with the spiritual preparation of the worshiper, promptness and reverence, than with the content or order of the service.

Whatever the exact order of service might have been, Adventists during the early years of their movement, like the "shouting Methodists," often enjoyed an enthusiastic worship service. Fervent cries of "Glory!" "Hallelujah!" "Praise God," and "Blessed Jesus!" punctuated worship services. A believer from Vermont reported that "free and full 'Hallelujahs' ascended to God and He was glorified with praise, love and adoration" (Hiram Edson, "Brother Hiram Edson writes . . . ," _Review and Herald_ 1 [Feb. 1851], 48). Another tells of a meeting where "the house rang from the full shouts of praise" (James White, "Eastern Tour," _Review and Herald_ 15 [Dec. 1, 1859], 13.). Ellen White, cofounder and spiritual leader of the Seventh-day Adventists, also experienced ecstatic public visions during the early days of the movement. Occasionally a worshiper was prostrated or "slain by the Spirit" during a service, and in three or four instances, believers spoke in tongues, although the practice was never encouraged and never became widespread.

These practices died down fairly quickly after the Civil War. In part this development followed the trend of the times; Methodists were also becoming more sedate. It was also a response to fanatical abuses of "exercises." By the end of the century Ellen White, who had encouraged shouting in 1850, instructed her fellow believers that the praise of God did not lead to "wild demonstrations." No, she said, "Softly and silently the power of the divine Spirit does [his] work." (Ellen G. White, "Sermon at Ashfield, Australia," November 3, 1894 [Manuscript

49, 1894]; "My Dear Brethren," *c.* April, 1889 [Letter 85, 1889]).

Singing was a prominent part of the Adventist worship experience both early and late. During their Millerite days, Adventists imbibed the folk hymns and white spirituals of the Second Great Awakening. Their early hymnody drew on this source, but included a respectable number of hymns of Isaac Watts and Charles Wesley as well. Four hymnals and five supplements were published by Seventh-day Adventists even before the formal organization of the church. As late as 1870 it was reported that during worship services "singing makes up one half of the meeting" (D. T. Bourdeau, "Punctuality in Attending and Taking Part in Religious Meetings," *Review and Herald,* vol. 35 [March 8, 1870], 95).

An Adventist worshiper in the latter quarter of the nineteenth century still experienced a simple, non-liturgical service. When emotion did appear, it was expressed in weeping. Worshipers were said to have had a "melting time," as hearts melted and tears of repentance, gratitude, or joy filled their eyes.

[A group of Adventists near Washington, New Hampshire, began to observe the seventh day as a Sabbath in 1844. In 1846 Joseph Bates issued a pamphlet on seventh-day observance that publicized the question and created wide interest. Before long a number of Adventist leaders, including James White and Ellen Harmon (later to become Ellen White), began to advocate the seventh-day Sabbath in various publications, along with other distinctive Adventist teachings. Seventh-day Adventist doctrine stresses the Ten Commandments as a reflection of the character of God, revealed in Jesus Christ, and as a universal standard of righteousness; observance of the seventh day is based on the fourth commandment.—*ed.*]

Ronald Graybill

## 148 • BIBLIOGRAPHY ON POST-REFORMATION WORSHIP (1600–1900)

### General Works on the Origins and History of Protestant Worship from 1600–1900

Davies, Horton. *Worship and Theology in England* 5 vols. (Princeton: Princeton University Press, 1961–1970). The purpose of this five volume series is to give an account of worship and the theology that undergirds it from the Reformation to the middle of the twentieth century. This masterful and thorough work is written out of the conviction that the worship of the church rather than this or that theologian gives the deepest clue to the interior life of the church. The emphasis is not only an Anglican worship, but the worship of the Puritans and separatists. Music and architecture are treated as revelatory of worship patterns.

White, James F. *Protestant Worship: Traditions in Transition.* Louisville: Westminster/John Knox Press, 1989. A comprehensive historical treatment of the worship of nine communities of worship: Lutheran, Reformed, Anabaptist, Anglican, Separatist and Puritan, Quaker, Methodist, Frontier, and Pentecostal.

Willimon, William. *Word, Water, Wine, and Bread.* Valley Forge, Pa: Judson Press, 1980. A brief but excellent overview beginning with the Jewish heritage and following through on the early church, the medieval era, the Reformation, and modern eras.

### Puritan and Free Church Worship (Baptist; Congregationalists; Separatists)

Adams, Doug. *Meeting House to Camp Meeting: Toward a History of American Free Church Worship From 1620 to 1835.* Saratoga, N.Y.: Modern Liturgy Resource Publications, 1981. Adams amply details seventeenth-century Puritan worship, and its heir, eighteenth-century Congregational worship. Particularly interesting and useful is his reconstruction of and commentary on a seventeenth-century Puritan service, using Cotton Mather's model.

Beebe, David Lewis. "The Seals of the Covenant: The Doctrine and Peace of the Sacraments and Censures in the New England Puritan Theology Underlying the Cambridge Platform of 1648." Th.D. dissertation, Pacific School of Religion, 1966.

Cotton, John. *A Modest and Cleare Answer to Mr. Bell's Discourse of Set Forms of Prayer.* London: n.p., 1642.

———. *Singing of Psalms, A Gospel Ordinance.* London: n.p., 1650.

Davies, Horton. *The Worship of the American Puritans, 1629–1730.* New York: Peter Lang, 1990. Puritan worship has had a decided impact on the free church worship of American Christianity. This book deals with the pioneering type of worship that was biblically based, that introduced extemporaneous prayer, expressed the priesthood of all believers and encouraged lay piety. All aspects of Puritan worship is covered—praise, prayer, sacraments, marriages and funerals, ordination, architecture, and more.

Miller, Perry. *The New England Mind.* New York: Macmillan, 1939. American Puritanism is an inexhaustible mine for historians. Among the numerous volumes available, Perry Miller's account provides the foundation for further study.

Miller, Perry, ed. *The American Puritans, Their Prose and Poetry.* Garden City, N.J.: Doubleday, 1956.

Miller, Perry, and Thomas H. Johnson, eds. *The Puritans.* New York: American Book Co., 1938. A thorough collection of primary materials, edited and with an introduction. Although the volume may overwhelm those desiring only an acquaintance with the Puritans, reading even a few of these period pieces engenders a deeper appreciation of the Puritan ethos.

## Presbyterian & Reformed

Baird, Charles. *The Presbyterian Liturgies: Historical Sketches.* Grand Rapids: Baker, 1960. The work was originally written in 1866. It traces Presbyterian worship from Calvin through John Knox, the Scottish Liturgy, the early Puritans, Baxter and others. No actual liturgies are provided.

Barkley, John M. *The Worship of the Reformed Church.* Richmond: John Knox Press, 1967. This helpful work provides an exposition and critical analysis of the eucharistic, baptismal, and confirmation rites in the Scottish, English-Welsh, and Irish Liturgies.

Brillioth, Ynvge. *Eucharistic Faith and Practice, Evangelical and Catholic.* London: SPCK, 1930. Argues that the Reformation was a rediscovery of the Eucharist, but that since the time of the Reformation the story of the Eucharist has been one of decline. Sketches the history of the Eucharist and argues for its recovery.

Davies, Horton. *The Worship of the English Puritans.* London: Dacre Press, 1948. A study of the free church tradition of worship, with an attempt to show the relevance of Reformed worship for today. Addresses a wide variety of issues including the relationship of free church worship to liturgical worshipers.

DeJong, Gerald. *The Dutch Reformed Church in the American Colonies.* Grand Rapids: Eerdmans, 1978. A study of the Reformed church in America, with comments on the ministry and on the church architecture.

Donnelly, Marion C. *The New England Meeting House of the Seventeenth Century.* Middletown, Conn.: Wesleyan University, 1968. The worship of meetinghouses in various periods of English history are treated in depth.

Earle, Alice Morse. *The Sabbath in Puritan New England.* Lima, Ohio: CSS Press, 1896. This is more than a study of the Sabbath. It is a discussion of Puritan worship that deals with the New England meetinghouse, its seating, pews, length of service, the singing of psalms, and many more matters of interest in Puritan worship.

Edwards, Jonathan. *Thoughts on the Revival of Religion in New England.* New York: American Tract Society, n.d. This work argues that the revival is a work of God and should be promoted. It also addresses some errors, such as lay exhorting and the mismanagement of the singing of the praises of God.

Hollifield, Brooks E. *The Covenant Sealed: The Development in Old and New England 1570–1720.* New York: Oxford University Press, 1974. A study in the sacramenture debates in England and New England among the Puritans. These debates demonstrate how seriously the Puritans took sacramental understanding and practice.

Melton, Julius. *Presbyterian Worship in America: Changing Patterns Since 1787.* Richmond: John Knox Press, 1967. This book traces the divergent practices stemming from two very different convictions about worship. On the one hand were those convinced that worship should only follow the specific guidelines of Scripture; others argued worship could be influenced by changing cultural attitudes and needs. The history of Presbyterian worship is brought into the twentieth century.

Spinks, Bryan. *Freedom or Order: The Eucharistic Liturgy in English Congregationalism.* New York: Pilgrim Press, 1984. This work presents actual liturgies of English congregationalism between 1645 and 1980.

Nichols, James Hasting. *Corporate Worship in the Reformed Tradition.* Philadelphia: Westminster Press, 1968. A study of the intent and practice of worship among the Reformers and post-Reformation developments in the Reformed tradition. The study includes chapters on Puritanism, Pietism, and Evangelicalism.

### Quaker Worship

Barclay, Robert. *The Inner Life of the Religious Societies of the Commonwealth,* 3d ed. (London: n.p., 1879 ). An extensive examination of the origins and beliefs of the Friends.

Green, Thomas F. *Preparation For Worship.* London: George Allen & Unwin, 1952. The author argues for a preparation of worship that arises out of a willingness to wait on the Spirit.

Moon, James H. *Why Friends Do Not Baptize With Water.* Philadelphia: The Leeds and Biddle Company, n.d. Argues that the baptism taught by Jesus is only a baptism of the Spirit.

Nicholls, G. L., ed. *The Journal of George Fox.* Cambridge: Cambridge University Press, 1952. Primary source material in which George Fox, the leader of the Quakers, expresses his view of worship.

Steere, Douglas V. *Where Words Come From.* London: George Allen & Unwin, 1955. A Swarthmore College lecture in which the author argues for the ability to feel words as the ground of true conversation and of prayer and worship.

Tellack, William. *George Fox, The Friends and the Early Baptists.* London: S. W. Partridge & Co., 1868. This work presents a comprehensive description of the life of George Fox and traces the doctrines of the Friends back to the early Baptists.

Woolman, John. *Worship.* A Pendle Hill pamphlet. Pendle Hill, Wallingford, Pa., n.d. John Woolman was an eighteenth-century leader of the Quaker movement and a radical social reformer. Woolman saw worship at the center of life and society and argued for an inward stillness and humility in outward living.

### Adventist

Stevens, James L. *Worship Among the Pioneers: A Study of the Religious Meetings of the Early Seventh-Day Adventists.* Niles, Mich.: Adventist Heritage Center, 1977. A brief but very helpful exploration into the origins of Advent worship. While there are no orders of worship, there are several descriptions which are insightful.

White, Ellen G. *Testimonies to Ministers.* Omaha: Pacific Press Publishing Association, 1923. This work contains instructions to ministers including

advice on preaching and material that relates to worship.

### Camp Meeting and Revival Worship

Finney, Charles Grandison. *Lectures on Revivals of Religion.* Ed. by William G. McLaughlin. Cambridge, Mass.: Belknap Press of Harvard University Press, 1960. While this work does not address worship as such, it does speak to the shape of revival and to the place of prayer and preaching in a revival service.

Gay, Ralph Gerald. "A Study of the American Liturgical Revival, 1825–1860." Ph.D. dissertation, Emory University, 1977. Gay demonstrates that revivalists approached liturgy in a distinct and novel fashion, and argues that they established these approaches in a new cultus.

Johnson, Charles. *The Frontier Camp Meeting.* Dallas: Southern Methodist University Press, 1955. This work addresses the camp meetings of the trans-Allegheny west in the first four decades of the nineteenth century. It explains how this Kentucky revival weapon of Presbyterian origin became largely the property of the church of John Wesley, utilized by the circuit rider to extend Methodism.

Sizer, Sandra S. *Gospel Hymns and Social Religion: The Rhetoric of Nineteenth-Century Revivalism.* Philadelphia: Temple University Press, 1978. Although Sizer's work concentrates primarily on later revival hymnody—D. L. Moody and his contemporaries—it illustrates the interplay of music within the revival service and the development of distinct revival hymns.

Weiss, Ellen. *City in the Woods: The Life and Design of an American Camp Meeting on Martha's Vineyard.* New York: Oxford University Press, 1987. A detailed examination of a particular camp meeting, with discussion of the setting and the message.

### Holiness

Hunter, Harold D. *Spirit-Baptism: A Pentecostal Alternative.* Lanham, Md.: University Press of America, 1983. The purpose of this work is to explore exegetical and historical studies to determine the validity of the classical Pentecostal argument for a distinct work of the Spirit.

Synan, Vinson. *The Holiness-Pentecostal Movement in the United States.* Grand Rapids: Eerdmans, 1971. A solid study of the rise, development, and theology of the many holiness churches that have emerged in America.

## Restoration Worship

Campbell, Alexander. The Christian System in Reference to the Union of Christians and the Restoration of Primitive Christianity as Plead by the Current Reformation. St. Louis: Christian Publishing Company, 1839. Argues for a return to the first three centuries of the church, including its worship.

Gates, Erratt. *The Early Relations and Separation of Baptists and Disciples.* Chicago: Christian Century, 1904. This work explores the work of Alexander Campbell and the origins of the restoration movement.

Richesin, L. Dale, and Larry D. Bouchard. *Interpreting Disciples: Practical Theology in the Disciples of Christ.* Fort Worth: Texas Christian University Press, 1987. Addresses all the areas of the life of the church, including that of worship.

Watkins, Keith. *The Breaking of Bread: An Approach to Worship for the Christian Churches.* Nashville: Broadman Press, 1966. This work probes the origins of Discipleship worship and applies that worship to the worship of Disciples today.

## Methodist

Baker, Frank. *From Wesley to Asbury: Studies in Early American Methodism.* New York: Oxford University Press, 1976. A study in the historical development of Methodist life, thought, and worship.

Bishop, John. *Methodist Worship in Relation to Free Church Worship.* New York: Scholars Studies Press, 1975. This book contains material very difficult to find. It explores the origin of free church worship dealing with matters such as praise, prayers, the lessons, the sermon, and the sacraments. Another equally valuable section deals with the origin, development and practice of Methodist worship.

Bowmer, John C. *The Sacrament of the Lord's Supper in Early Methodism.* Fort Worth: Dominion Press, 1951. A thorough study of the origin and development of Methodism, with particular emphasis on the understanding and practice of the Lord's Supper.

Hilderbrandt, Franz, and Oliver A. Beckerlegge, eds. *The Works of John Wesley.* Vol. 7: *A Collection of Hymns for the Use of the People Called Methodist.* London: Oxford University Press, 1983. A critical edition of the 1780 Methodist hymnal.

Tripp, David. *The Renewal of the Covenant in the Methodist Tradition.* London: Epworth Press, 1969. A study of the renewal of the covenant in its historical setting and in its worship context.

White, James F. *John Wesley's Prayer Book.* Cleveland: DSL Publications, 1991. A facsimile of the 1784 *Sunday Service,* with introduction.

## African-American Worship

*Adventures of Charles Ball, a Black Man.* New York: J. S. Taylor, 1837. Reprinted as *Fifty Years in Chains.* New York: Oxford University Press, 1970. Accounts of worship rituals, including descriptions of slave funerals, with comments and thoughts from the vantage of a slave.

Allen, William F., Charles Pickard Ware, and Lucy Garrison, eds. *Slave Songs of the United States.* New York: A. Simpson and Co., 1867. A collection of 136 songs compiled by the authors in 1867. Valued historically as the first published collection of slave songs. The preface includes sketchy but helpful information on worship practices and singing styles of the nineteenth century.

Berry, Mary Frances, and John W. Blassingame. *Long Memory: The Black Experience in America.* New York: Oxford University Press, 1982. A scholarly synthesis of recent research on black history, black ritual, and its significance for family life are highlighted in Chapter 3, "Family and Church: Enduring Institutions."

Clarke, Erskine. *Wrestlin' Jacob: A Portrait of Religion in the Old South.* Richmond: John Knox Press, 1979. A recounting of the story of the quest for dignity and freedom among black slaves in the antebellum South. Excellent vignettes of slave worship.

Jones, Charles Colcock. *The Religious Instruction of the Negroes in the United States.* Savannah: Thomas Purse, 1842. Historical sketch of the religious instructions of black Americans from 1620 to1842, with catechism and other doctrinal statements that white religionists taught newly converted blacks.

Haynes, Leonard L. *The Negro Community within American Protestantism, 1619–1844.* Boston: Christopher Publishing House, 1953. A significant documentation by the grandson of slaves that highlights the evidence of community among black slaves within the Protestant tradition. Provides evidence of the overt rejection of Christianity by certain African slaves.

Herskovits, Melville. *The Myth of the Negro Past.* Boston: Beacon Press, 1958. One of the earliest scholarly documentations of evidence of the survival of African influences in worship practices of black Americans.

Higginson, Thomas Wentworth. *Army Life in a Black Regiment.* Boston: Fields, Osgood and Co., 1869. Reprint. Boston: Beacon Press, 1962. A frequently quoted source that documents the life of black servicemen in the Union Army. Examples of the "Shout," a ritual both in the content of worship and in informal gatherings of slaves and ex-slaves, are described with much detail.

Lyell, Charles. *A Second Visit to the United States of America,* 2 vols. New York: Harper and Brothers, 1849. These volumes provide rare glimpses inside black worshiping congregations in the South and support evidence that Muslim slaves from Africa continued the customs of Islam.

McClain, William B. *Black People in the Methodist Church.* Cambridge, Mass.: Schenkman Publishing Co., 1984. The history of blacks in the Methodist church from the baptism of two (nameless) converts in 1758 to the present day, with brief examples of worship practices and significant religious pioneers.

McIntyre, Paul. *Black Pentecostal Music in Windsor.* Ottawa, Ontario: National Museum of Man, 1976. A well documented history of blacks in southwestern Ontario, descendants of former slaves who went to Canada from the United States prior to the Civil War. Equally well documented are liturgical practices of the Church of God in Christ in Canada.

Rivers, Clarence Joseph. *This Far by Faith: American Worship and Its African Roots.* Washington, D.C.: National Office of Black Catholics, 1977. An anthology of major papers presented during a conference in 1977 on "Worship and Spirituality in The Black Community."

Scherer, Lester B. *Slavery and the Churches in Early America, 1619–1818.* Grand Rapids: Eerdmans Publishing Co., 1975. A scholarly account of the history of blacks during slavery, the Christianization process, and the attitudes of various Protestant church members in this process. Examples of the oppressive sermonizing and baptismal vows required provide insight into the need for separate worshiping places and different worship rituals.

Smith, Warren Thomas. *Harry Hoosier: Circuit Rider.* Nashville: Upper Room Books, 1981. A bibliography of "Black Harry," a Methodist circuit preacher par excellence in the colonial period.

Wade, Richard C. *Slavery in the Cities: The South, 1820–1860.* New York: Oxford University Press, 1964. An excellent source providing a glimpse into black worship styles in southern cities.

Weatherford, Willis D. *American Churches and the Negro.* Boston: Christopher Publishing House, 1957. Historical presentation with detailed accounts of attitudes of major Protestant denominations, Quakers, and Roman Catholics.

Wesley, Charles H. *Richard Allen: Apostle of Freedom.* Washington, D.C.: Associated Press, 1935. An autobiography of one of the leading preachers of the eighteenth and nineteenth centuries, a moving force in the establishment of the AME Church.

Turner, H. W. *History of an African Independent Church,* 2 vols. London: Oxford University Press, 1967. This work studies the phenomena of the African Independent Church of the prophet-healing type known as *aladura* (praying) churches in Western Nigeria.

Wilmore, Gayraud S. *Black Religion and Black Radicalism: An Interpretation of the Religious History of Afro-American People,* 2d ed. Maryknoll, N.Y.: Orbis Books, 1983. While providing a scholarly treatment of the history of black religion and the black church, the author highlights the inseparable bond between religious beliefs and rituals and the psychological realities of daily existence.

Wimberly, Edward P., and Anne Streaty Wimberly. *Liberation and Human Wholeness: The Conversion Experience of Black People in Slavery and Freedom.* Nashville: Abingdon Press, 1986. A meticulously documented study utilizing the voices of slaves and free Afro-Americans to examine conversion experiences vis-a-vis psychological, theological, and social cultural world from 1750 to 1930. Provides a fascinating look at religio-mystic human liberation from the perspective of a unique African-American coming to Christ.

Woodson, Carter G. *The History of the Negro Church.* Reprint. Washington, D.C.: Associated Press, 1972. One of the earliest scholarly presentations of the history of the black church in America.

# SEVEN

# Movements of Worship Renewal in the Twentieth Century

Perhaps more attention has been given in the twentieth century to the deliberate renewal and revision of Christian liturgy than in any previous century in church history. The renewal of worship that began with the neoorthodox movement in Protestantism took root in the Roman Catholic church and has extended to nearly every denomination and community of faith. The rise of the Pentecostal, charismatic, and praise traditions has changed the shape of worship throughout the world. Today the two major streams of worship renewal—the liturgical and the charismatic—are converging into new patterns that bear a strong similarity to what some believe early Christian worship was like.

## 149 • THE HOLINESS-PENTECOSTAL MOVEMENT

*The origins of the Holiness-Pentecostal movement are found in the work and teaching of John Wesley. Worship within the movement varies widely, but it seems to thrive in contexts that encourage spontaneity and freedom. Traditional Pentecostal worship is currently undergoing significant change because of the growing popularity of contemporary worship choruses.*

Throughout their history the Holiness and Pentecostal movements have been characterized by an extemporaneous vernacular style that assigns a large role to music in the expression of corporate and individual worship.

The American holiness movement traces its origins to John Wesley and his associate, John Fletcher, whose persuasion that a conversion experience should always be followed by a dynamic encounter with sanctifying grace stands at its core. In the course of the nineteenth century, some American Methodists derived from that premise the teaching that an instantaneous second definite work of grace should be part of every Christian's religious experience. They—and people from many other denominations who embraced the general teaching that practical holiness was part of the essence of Christianity—gathered in camp meetings and brush arbors around the country for simple teaching, enthusiastic singing, and agonizing prayer. Gradually, the most radical among them severed relationships to historic denominations. Over several decades,

they generated a new cluster of Holiness denominations such as the Church of the Nazarene, the Free Methodist Church, and the Wesleyan church.

Methodists were well-known for pursuing intense religious experiences and for "raising the shout" when they "broke through" and experienced grace. They sang the majestic hymns Charles Wesley had bequeathed them, the pietist hymns John Wesley translated from German, and the simple songs of exhortation and testimony that were spawned by revivals and camp meetings. Because they dealt in verities that touched the deepest human emotions, they regarded tears, groans, vocal praise and audible individual prayer as appropriate, even necessary, in corporate and individual worship. They made room in their services for personal testimonies, partly because testifying to an experience seemed to them to be part of "owning" or appropriating that experience for themselves.

Holiness emphases on grace and cleansing generated a holiness idiom which found expression in devotional literature and gospel songs. The new style used Old Testament stories of Israel's crossing the Jordan into Canaan as analogues for the "second definite work of grace" and the "baptism with the Holy Spirit." Like early Methodism, it also emphasized the blood of Jesus. It popularized the holiness experience as both an end and a beginning: it ended the first phase of the Christian life and introduced believers into a new dimension of Christian living. It made them "happy" and "free" and gave them assurance of cleansing from sin. A significant number of the gospel songs that were incorporated into the hymnals of twentieth-century evangelicals expressed the sentiments of these women and men whose deep religious experiences seemed naturally to find musical expression. Elisha Hoffman, Annie Johnson Oatman, Mrs. C. H. Morris, Fanny Crosby, Charles Price Jones, A. B. Simpson, and Phoebe Palmer Knapp are just a few of those whose names are found in many Protestant hymnals. Their songs, read through a Holiness lens, reveal much of the movement's message and power.

One wing of the Holiness movement, the Salvation Army, was often denounced for setting religious words to popular secular tunes. The Salvation Army also popularized the use of band instruments in outdoor evangelism and worship services. Parading through city streets in military-style uniform, and playing popular melodies, they regularly drew crowds that responded to their vernacular style.

Holiness people gathered in all kinds of settings, some formal and many informal: camp meetings, brush arbors, tabernacles, missions, homes, churches. They welcomed participation by everyone in attendance, often providing opportunities for both corporate and individual involvement, as well as structured and spontaneous participation. Fringe groups gained notoriety when they opted for either extreme legalism (such as reinstituting the Old Testament law and feasts) or boisterous behavior (contortions while fighting demons, or falling, shouting and jumping during services). The movement's mainstream, both African-American and white, however, made a rich contribution to American religion, not least through the thousands of songs written to express the admittedly inexpressible bliss of the sanctified soul.

While singing, testimony, shouts of praise and demonstrative prayers frequently marked Holiness worship, controversy raged in some circles over the use of musical instruments in church worship. In the 1890s, for example, Free Methodists argued heatedly about organ accompaniment. The debate seriously jeopardized the denomination's future.

When Pentecostalism, after 1901, emerged as an identifiable religious movement, it appropriated much of the idiom of the Holiness movement, reinterpreting some of it to nuance its understanding of the baptism with the Holy Spirit. Many of the songs Pentecostals have sung over the years to describe their experience were written before Pentecostalism

began, by Holiness people intent on describing sanctifying grace. The two movements shared religious language about life in the Spirit that had very different theological connotations in each context.

From the beginning worship style and musical tastes in Pentecostalism varied widely. Like the Holiness movement, Pentecostalism thrived in contexts that encouraged spontaneity and individual expression. What was perceived as corporate worship might alternatively be described as simultaneous individual worship. Pentecostals perhaps met together as much to pursue individual experiences as to express corporate solidarity as the people of God. Their corporate unity tended, then, to be more apparent than real, except during sporadic opposition. Referring to one another as "brother" and "sister" on the surface seemed to cultivate a sense of family unity, but that was not generally reflected in worship style. That family language has long since disappeared in many quarters, as has opposition, and individualism thrives.

Pentecostals sang the gospel songs of their day, some of the better-known hymns of the church, new songs written by adherents, and choruses billed as "given" by the Holy Spirit. In many places, they kept singing songs they had sung before, adding some to express new dimensions of religious experience. Southern gospel music has always been popular. Vocal and instrumental ensembles and musically talented evangelists were part of the movement from its inception. Singing was incorporated throughout the worship service. Through songs, people expressed emotions, declared doctrines, glorified God, exhorted one another, entreated sinners, responded to testimonies, invoked miracles, and yearned for God's tangible presence. Early Pentecostals were probably right in the observation that singing was an essential part of what adherents understood Pentecostalism to be.

An additional dimension in Pentecostal worship is known as "singing in the Spirit." Variously described, this involves one, several or all the gathered worshipers in singing simultaneously and harmoniously in either tongues or the vernacular. In its most elementary form, this happens as a congregation moves from singing a worship song into sung expressions of individual praise. Singing in the same key and moving among several basic chords, individuals express their feelings in words meaningful to them. The music may seem to flow from one individual to another, the voice of one occasioning another's participation until many are involved. Another form is believed by participants to involve the orchestration by the Holy Spirit of the worship of several or all of the worshipers. Sometimes individuals who are understood by those around them to be "in the Spirit" may sing solos that hearers describe as beautiful songs. This resembles the "singing exercise" described in Barton Stone's well-known account of the Cane Ridge camp meeting.

Pentecostalism's ethnic diversity was also reflected in its worship traditions, which have always ranged from Quaker-like waiting for the Spirit to camp-meeting style to dignified formality. German and Scandinavian Pentecostals have preserved some of the hymnody of the Reformation and Pietism; Hispanic Pentecostals have used their culture's musical idiom; black Pentecostals have contributed significantly to the music of the movement as a whole, especially through the songs of people like Thoro Harris, G. T. Haywood, and more recently, Andrae Crouch.

Aimee Semple McPherson, one of the most prolific Pentecostal musicians, used innovative worship techniques that extensively influenced American Pentecostalism. Reared in the Salvation Army but converted to Pentecostalism by an evangelist she later married, McPherson blended the Holiness and Pentecostal traditions with such creativity that in the 1920s, she was widely hailed as Los Angeles' premier star. Her dramatic entry down a ramp and into her pulpit at her 5,000-seat Angelus Temple was always preceded by thirty minutes of singing led by award-winning choirs and accompanied by an excellent orchestra seated in a hydraulic orchestra pit. She composed songs for her people, operas for their holiday entertainment, and graphic sermons to convey her message. She represented a style that gained increasing favor among Pentecostals, a style which featured one or more performing stars. She altered the nature of individual participation, which she professed to value but at the same time insisted on controlling. In many ways her style was the trend of the future.

In recent years, both the Holiness and Pentecostal movements have significantly modified the form and content of their worship. These innovations have moved through several generations of hymnals and have replaced many of the songs that once provided each with its distinctive idiom. Some denominations in these families have become increasingly

like other evangelicals in both their music and their worship style. On the other hand, the charismatic renewal has generated a fresh musical style that has greatly influenced Pentecostalism and, to a lesser extent, virtually every form of Christianity. Rejecting much traditional hymnody and the gospel songs of an earlier era as outdated, charismatics opted for simple choruses. They set Scripture to music or composed worship choruses that enabled people to express their feelings, their experiences, and their praise. In many Pentecostal congregations, overhead transparencies have virtually replaced hymnals which are used selectively, if at all. Almost overnight, and with no struggle, Pentecostal churches have abandoned the musical vocabulary through which they had once understood and expressed the meaning of their religious experience. Having gained a vast repertoire of praise choruses, they have lost the stirring exhortations to mission and evangelism, the declarations of doctrine, and admonitions about the second coming and the hope of heaven that had once prodded them along the "upward way."

Praise choruses, then, both symbolized and facilitated a change in Pentecostal worship style. By the 1960s, singing generally occurred only at stated times in the service, not whenever a worshiper felt inclined to introduce a song. Large Pentecostal churches had begun hiring professional musicians who not only worked with choirs and orchestras, but who also led congregational singing. The introduction of these "music pastors" significantly impacted congregational worship style in a manner which requires further study and analysis. With the acceptance of praise choruses came a turn toward other charismatic practices like standing for long periods at the beginning of services, lifting up hands, and repeating the same choruses. Choreographed dancing, favored by some charismatics, also gained acceptance in many Pentecostal congregations.

The Holiness and Pentecostal traditions historically have been hospitable to the expression of individual spiritual longings. They have been sufficiently adaptable to mirror the desires and needs of common people in different times and places. By encouraging private and public expression of profound human emotions, they have become traditions through which people enact privately and corporately the passion of personal responses to the gospel. Richly textured, relying on a familiar idiom that relates divine grace to everyday experience, and open to infinite variety, these traditions have offered ways through which people can affirm God's presence and power in their lives.

Edith Blumhofer

## 150 • THE IMPACT OF *THE CONSTITUTION ON THE SACRED LITURGY*

*The* Constitution on the Sacred Liturgy *of the Second Vatican Council is one of the most influential documents on worship renewal in the twentieth century. It has resulted in vast changes in Roman Catholic worship and has also made a noticeable impact on Protestant worship, especially in the mainline denominations. The intent of the document is to call the church back to early Christian worship and spirituality.*

The liturgical reform of the Second Vatican Council has been the single most concrete and dynamic change within modern Roman Catholicism. The *Magna Carta* of this reform is the *Constitution on the Liturgy, Sacrosanctum concilium,* issued on December 4, 1963 (referred to in this article as "*S. C.*"). This document was not only the first fruit of Vatican II, but also was one of its major contributions to the internal renewal of Christianity. Such importance, at least for the Catholic church, was stressed by Pope Paul VI when he promulgated the constitution: "Treated before others, in a sense it has priority over all others for its intrinsic dignity and importance to the life of the Church" (Address, December 4, 1963).

### Formulation of the Liturgical Constitution

This document constituted the official and universal approval of a new synthesis between the doctrinal and pastoral agenda of the liturgy. Also, it helped to develop a new ecclesial vision, founded on biblical and patristic theology. This liturgical-pastoral movement, which intensified at the beginning of the century with Pius X (especially from 1903 to 1914), gave rise to different centers of study in France, Germany, and elsewhere and became progressively a European and American movement after the encyclical *Mediator Dei* of Pius XII (1947) and the international pastoral congress of Assisi (1956). This historical movement made possible the relatively simple preparation of the conciliar schema by an international commission of bishops and liturgical consultants. Under the direction of A. Bugnini, the preparatory liturgical commission approved the schema after four drafts and presented it to the president, Cardinal Cicognani, in January of 1962. Despite the many amendments made during the first fifteen general meetings of the council (fall of 1962), the original schema was accepted without substantial change. The biblical-patristic basis and the liturgical-pastoral vision of the movement had inaugurated a new ecclesiological horizon radically different from the defensive and juridical framework of the Council of Trent. The inherent value of the liturgical reform, which provided the theological tone and the pastoral horizon of the council, was seen as a sign of God and as a movement of the Spirit in the church (*S. C.,* 43).

The goal of the constitution was the revival of Christian spirituality and pastoral life in bringing the faithful to the source of Christian life in the Christ mystery of the liturgy. The constitution was rooted in biblical theology and consequently provided the fundamental elements of a liturgical celebration in the framework of a new ecclesiology. Its development went hand in hand with the *Constitution on the Church*. This theological vision of the nature of worship was characterized by the criteria of reform and development, adaptation and creativity, with concrete directives in regard to the sacraments and all liturgical exercises. The profound and ecclesiological vision centered around the priestly ministry of Christ in the mystery of the church and opened up new perspectives particularly regarding the role of the people of God in the local church.

From this paramount ecclesial perspective important liturgical understandings evolved: the baptismal priesthood of the faithful, the full participation of the people at both tables, word and Eucharist, the importance of the sign of the assembly, the need for flexible ritual norms, relevant symbolism, and catholicity of worship rooted in tradition (unity and stability). All of these are exposed to the dialogue of inculturation in a church open to the world—to its creativity and its pluralism. In the light of the constitution this new order of worship restored a more Roman and patristic structure, and it opened the way for the transcendent universality inherent in ecumenical pastoral praxis and theological thinking.

### Implementation of the Reform

A month after the approval of the *Constitution,* Paul VI created the main organ of its implementation, the Concilium (January 25, 1964), headed by the renowned Cardinal G. Lecaro, with A. Bugnini as his secretary. The fundamental purposes of this official council, under the direct supervision of the pope, were to direct the correct and concrete application of the constitution in the reform of the liturgical books and to promote the conciliar magisterium through doctrinal and practical liturgical instructions. The international nature of the Concilium, formed by bishops and a body of internationally renowned experts with a few non-Catholic observers, made the liturgical reform a collegial enterprise. Following the spirit and directives of the council, this reform had to be rooted in tradition, and at the same time open to legitimate progress, responding pastorally to the needs of the people of our time and cultures. From 1965 on, an informative organ of the Concilium, the journal entitled *Notitiae,* was issued. A parallel Vatican office, the Congregation of Rites, officially issued the instructions of the Concilium until they both merged into the Congregation of Divine Worship (May 8, 1969). After a lengthy preparation of many interim directives and theological-pastoral instructions, the main work of the reform was promulgated, the *Roman Missal* of Paul VI (June 1970). Following not only the specific guidelines of the *Constitution,* but also the primary criteria and ecumenical scope of the whole body of conciliar doctrine, a thorough revision of all the rites and liturgical books was undertaken, and new *ordines* were issued from 1968 to 1978.

Although the liturgical restoration of the rituals was substantially accomplished by 1975, the suppression of the Congregation for Divine Worship that year and the dismissal of A. Bugnini as its secretary signalled a more direct institutionalization of the liturgical-pastoral movement by the Roman Curia.

At the level of the local church, the reform was thoroughly planned in Rome and, on the whole, enthusiastically implemented as its ancient texts were faithfully translated into more than 350 languages or dialects. However, the liturgy in general was only minimally adapted "to the genius and traditions of peoples" (*S.C.,* 37–40). If, in one instance, episcopal conferences seemed to prevail in adapting the vernacular, the attempt to make the preservation of Latin a mandate of the council, at least in regard to the divine office of the bishops, was limited, for the most part, to establishing the structures of the

new *ordines* and enforcing the liturgical norms issued by the Holy See. The trend toward uniformity and centralization now seemed apparent from the creation of the Congregation for the Sacraments and Divine Worship in 1975, and the Congregation of Divine Worship and the Discipline for the Sacraments in 1988, and in the new Code of Canon Law (canon 1257) of 1983. This was so despite the mandate of the council to enter into communion with cultures and talents of peoples (*S.C.,* 37; Gaudium et spec, 48).

The historical restoration was only partially achieved. A great challenge remained in regard to inculturation, especially in the non-Western world. Examples like the officially approved Roman rite for the church in Zaire and other experiments in the "third world" countries, were only the first attempts as symbolic and linguistic creativity, maintaining, however, the substantial unity of the Roman rites (*S.C.,* 38).

The reform certainly constituted a strong movement of pastoral awareness and missionary concern in opening the spiritual treasure of liturgy to the people and making it the center of the life of the local church. By and large, the new order of worship was well received. Two factors seemed to be underlying causes of dissatisfaction: the lack of adequate liturgical catechesis [instruction] needed to invigorate the renewal of both worship and the community, and the impoverishment of the contemplative, religious and symbolic action of worship which calls for a continuous revival. Planned from above, the reform was then handed to the people. It was not sufficiently animated from below and made relevant to the spiritual needs of the people.

In regard to the possible celebration of the old Latin Tridentine Mass under very restricted circumstances and with the permission of the ordinary, the decision in Rome (1984) was seen as a sign of compromise. The impending crisis brought about by such sweeping reform in this most sensitive area of religious life, revealed the need for a new phase of the liturgical movement of renewal from below.

## Outcome and Future Directions

For Catholics, and even for many Protestants, the liturgical constitution has remained the undisputed charter yet to be fully implemented in its broad vision and goals. Despite the remarkable progress made through a mainly historical restoration from across a thousand years of evolving Christian worship, the primary goal of the pioneers of the liturgical movement and the conciliar fathers is yet to be realized in a credible and profound way. A reform of a more flexible and essential nature has been established, not without some polarizations and even contradictions; but from now on we foresee the prospect of perennial renewal in the celebration.

The work of a generation should not be considered the point of arrival, but rather the point of departure. Much lies ahead, and this demands new attitudes and a new reception on the part of the hierarchy and of the people. In biblical terms, "new wine must be poured into new wineskins" (Luke 5:38). This means more than "mere observance of laws," a passive and rubrical reception of the changes. It means rather a creative assimilation of the fundamental dimensions of the liturgical renewal: on the one hand, biblical symbolism, ecclesiology of communion, mystagogy (interpretation of the sacraments); and, on the other hand, an understanding of the anthropological grounding and the "mental grammar" of the religious experience of today's people. If liturgy builds community, community makes liturgy.

Though an assessment of the reform is needed, it is difficult, because the reality of worship in the lives of people is a complex phenomenon which goes beyond the limits of the context of worship itself. Critics usually refer to three major areas of concern in the present crisis of worship: leadership, catechetics, and the emergence of new problems.

**Leadership.** Despite the many compromises and dilemmas of the reform (the most apparent being the rite of penance), the new rituals and the hundreds of documents issued in Rome provided both a flexible ritual which was normative and a theological-pastoral direction for the future. The constitution demanded not only a translation into the vernacular, and structural changes, but also adaptation, reception of the letter and the spirit of the reform, liturgical sensibility, and a new mind in promoting its ideals. A long-range need is the creativity of inculturation and indigenization. In this sense, the council has opened the door to new opportunities for liturgical growth, foreseeing a balance between the universal oversight by the primacy and the promotion of liturgical action by the episcopacy.

This collegial balance can foster decentralization and pluralism, safeguarding "the substantial unity of the Roman rite" (*S.C.*, 37–47). However, because of the tight control from above, some bishops have made it the practice to show more interest in juridical approval of the changes than in facing the compelling spiritual needs of the people. The problems of the promotion of renewal of liturgical praxis certainly have been compounded by profound cultural transition and the new secular trends of the post-Vatican II years. In fact, as the World Council of Churches has acknowledged, "behind the crisis of worship there is a general crisis of faith" (Uppsala, 1968).

**Catechetics.** The underestimation of long-term liturgical catechetics has been a perennial problem reflected in the poor reception of the reform. The quality of participation in engaging liturgies depended on preparation and renewal of the community. The crisis of meaning could stem not only from the irrelevant spirituality of ritual and textual mystification, and inadequate symbolic expression of the mystery, but also from the lack of an experiential initiation into that mystery. In this respect, the new Rite of Christian Initiation of Adults (1972) is a serious effort to cultivate the great potential of liturgical catechetics, but only if this most authentic and far-reaching reform is taken seriously.

**New Problems.** Finally, new problems emerge from several areas. The restoration itself seems too pragmatic, with the consequent impoverishment of contemplative and festive sense of the mystery, and the translation of the old texts seems inadequate to a renewed spirituality. In addition, the new liturgy demands a faithful expression in the role of the presider, a renewed liturgical music, and good preaching. Moreover, the new liturgical vision projects unforeseen demands, especially from the self-discovery of the local church and the priesthood. Other unexpected developments could be added, such as the crisis of the oral confession, the priestless liturgies (*Directory* of the Congregation for Divine Worship, 1988), and the emergence of non-ordained ministries, especially the ministry of women and the global phenomenon of grassroots communities.

All these point to an unfinished agenda of the liturgical renewal and the need for ecclesiastical leadership which would further the dynamic spirit of the council. In fact, after a quarter century of the promulgation of the liturgical constitution, "the work of liturgical reform and renewal remains at the heart of the Church's life and mission" (National Council of Catholic Bishops, *Promoting Liturgical Renewal: Guidelines for Diocesan Liturgical Commissions and Offices of Worship* [Washington, D.C.: Secretariat, Bishops' Committee on the Liturgy, 1988]). This renewal and reform will be chiefly along the two poles of the current liturgical dialogue: the anthropological-cultural pole, between human sciences and liturgical theology and praxis which will help us understand the concrete religious story and experience; and the ecclesiological pole, which through serious consideration of the common priesthood of the community-celebrant will renew a liturgy that builds community within and is expressed in active mission and ministry.

The liturgical reform of the council was highly positive, especially in its theological and pastoral dimensions. The ecclesiological dimension, developed in the *Dogmatic Constitution on the Church,* is still in need of theological clarification and pastoral affirmation, especially from the perspective of the local and ministerial community. The anthropological and cultural dimensions, the least explicitly developed in the Vatican documents, will be an important part of the unfinished agenda of liturgical creativity and inculturation. Pastoral liturgical studies have been ever since in search of a deeper understanding of a phenomenology of worship which embodies the essential fullness of Christian belief and the living religious traditions.

German Martinez[12]

## 151 ✦ RENEWAL IN THE EASTERN RITE CATHOLIC CHURCHES

*The Eastern Rite Catholic churches are communities that follow a form of the Eastern liturgy but which are under the jurisdiction of the Roman pontiff rather than one of the Eastern Orthodox patriarchates. Renewal in the Eastern Catholic churches has involved a slow process of the rediscovery and implementation of a variety of ancient traditions of worship.*

The Second Vatican Council in its *Decree on Eastern Catholic Churches* expressed its high esteem for the rich traditions of these churches and urged the latter to preserve and honor their liturgical rites and restore them where they had been altered or abandoned. Changes within Eastern Catholic liturgical rites since that time have come about at a slow pace

through local desire to return to authentic traditions as well as through the urging of the Oriental Congregation in Rome. Many of these changes have appeared in the form of the return to traditional vesture and the reintroduction of ancient liturgical *anaphoras* (central eucharistic rites) and prayers. Alongside these, in many places, the vernacular has replaced the ancient languages in liturgical celebrations, and many of the Latin Catholic liturgical insertions have been dropped.

Not all of these Latin influences (Latinizations), however, have been forsaken everywhere, since some of these practices (such as prayers before the statues of saints, the rosary, stations of the cross, and daily Mass) have become identified in the minds of uninformed faithful with tradition itself. Nor has the return to traditional ways been complete where it had begun. The return to ancient architectural settings and liturgical forms still remains a challenge for many Syriac churches that await the reintroduction and use of the *bema* (a central platform for the liturgy of the Word), the lack of which leaves many of the prayers and liturgical actions out of tune with their proper liturgical context. Along with these, some juridical restrictions are still in effect and are in need of reform (e.g., the married priesthood is still restricted outside the immediate jurisdiction of these churches).

The carrying forward of this process of returning to tradition has become even more of a challenge in recent times, since many of these churches have considerable immigrant populations in the West, creating new pastoral situations and the need for liturgical recontextualization and readaptation. Thus, not all practices within a church's liturgical tradition would be appropriate for modern needs, and prudent adaptations by liturgical commissions would be necessary. Many of these adaptations have taken the form of liturgical abbreviations and simplifications where the reform efforts are unorganized and without clear directions. Alongside these efforts lie the urgent need for the religious education of the faithful to enlighten them about the riches of their traditions, along with the arts and means of appropriating these traditions for modern needs. Much in this regard depends on the leadership and direction of the persons in authority in these churches—especially on their discernment of a clearer sense of future directions for their people—together with the liturgical and catechetical commissions in their diocese and the cooperation of the Latin church.

In the following paragraphs I have sketched some of the efforts in liturgical reform made by the various Eastern Catholic churches in their attempts to return to tradition and to keep in step with the times. In many cases these reforms are small and uncoordinated. They reveal the complexity of carrying forward such a challenging task and how much more effort and organization need to be undertaken.

## The Maronites

The liturgical reforms in the Maronite church worldwide began in the early 1970s and continue today. The renewal, or better said, restoration of the Maronite Sunday liturgy began in both Lebanon and the United States (which has more than 50 parishes) through the guidance of the Vatican's Sacred Congregation for Eastern Churches in Rome and the activities of the Patriarchal Synod and Liturgical Committee in Lebanon to restore the Maronite liturgy to its original framework. These reforms have led to the restoration of the cycle of prayers and hymns of the Sunday liturgy of the Word, as well as the uncovering of a very rich tradition of liturgical prayers and hymnals. While the yearly cycle for this Sunday liturgy has been recovered—replacing the single form which had become common up to the end of the 1960s—the architectural aspect, including the use of the *bema* (an enclosed platform) still remains to be restored. Many of the prayers and sacramental forms in this tradition, originally in Syriac, have been translated into Arabic and English for modern-day use.

Among the restorations of the Sunday liturgy have been the separate preparation of gifts at a side altar and the dropping of the penitential rites and offertory prayers which were Roman additions. Thus the Mass begins with the liturgy of the Word, with its own proper focus that is separate from the rites around the altar. The offertory procession has been restored with its prayers and incensing. The *bema*, however, has not been reintroduced as yet, and thus the first part of the Mass is held in front of the altar with the priest and deacon facing the people. Some of the litanies for this part have been abbreviated. The veil in front of the altar has not been restored. Among the innovations, the priest now faces the people during the liturgy of the Eucharist, and some

of the prayers from the Anaphora of Sharar and priestly prayers have been dropped or abbreviated. The traditional formula for the words of the institution has been restored with its variant forms according to the different anaphoras. The *epiklēsis* has been brought to its proper position as an integral part of the consecration. Attempts at restoring early Maronite musical and hymnal forms have been made at the Holy Cross University and Maronite Seminary in Lebanon. In the United States the office, along with texts for all the sacraments, has been translated (and also revised) into English. Some experimentation at integrating the matrimonial rite or the office with the Mass has also been attempted. With the exception of a memorial Sunday liturgy, however, only a few Maronites attend their own parishes on a regular basis.

## The Chaldeans

Among the Chaldeans since the Second Vatican Council some changes have begun to take place in Iraq and the United States, based on mostly local initiatives and without formal organization. Among these have been the use of modern Syriac as well as Arabic languages in place of the classical Syriac. This latter, however, still remains in use in some parishes. Aside from the dropping of the feasts of Western saints and the restoration of the feast days of the Syriac saints in the liturgical calendar and some abbreviations of liturgical prayers, very little has been done in terms of organized liturgical reform. In many of the parishes in Iraq the priest faces the people for the liturgy of the Word, but his back is turned on them for the eucharistic liturgy. By contrast, in the United States and in other Western countries the Chaldean priest faces the people during the whole liturgy. In this rite, too, the *bema* awaits to be restored for proper liturgical celebration in its authentic tradition.

In Iraq, in the cities, eucharistic celebrations are held mostly in Arabic with some Syriac included, while in most villages they are held in modern or in classical Syriac (still understood by some) with an Arabic Scripture sometimes included. The Sunday Mass is usually sung at least in part. Variant hymns (some ancient and some modern) are also sung in all three linguistic forms: Arabic, modern Syriac, and classical Syriac. There is generally a good level of participation in the Mass, and in some parishes, when the deacon is not present, the laity are assigned to the ministry of reading from Scripture.

The other sacraments as well, such as baptism and matrimony, are often celebrated in Arabic or in modern Syriac with responsorial participation from the laity. In some parishes these Sunday activities are supplemented with a basic local catechetical program for children. Bible prayer groups for adults are also emerging now in the cities.

### ——— The Malabar Churches of India ———

Liturgical reform in the Malabar rites in Kerala was becoming evident after the Vatican Council, as the main liturgical language was changed from Syriac to Malayalam, the native tongue. An experimental version of the Chaldeo-Malabar rite in Malayalam was implemented and approved by the Oriental Congregation in Rome in 1968. This text of the Mass—Qurbana—with some adjustments was fixed in 1981. The latter move, however, has been criticized by scholars who consider the fixing of the present text as obstructing the process of return to authentic traditions, a process which is not yet liturgically completed and which still has a good residue of the old Roman rite practices. In this rite, too, the _bema_ needs to be restored.

A similar case can be made for the Syro-Malabar churches, which have also translated their liturgical forms into the native tongue Malayalam. A few diocesan variations of the Sunday celebration have emerged. The first part of the Mass—the liturgy of the Word—is often celebrated with the priest facing the people. For the eucharistic liturgy, depending on local piety, the priest either faces the people or turns his back to face the altar. In the last few years there has been a preference in some dioceses to have the priest turn towards the altar with his back to the people. A very few churches still use the original Syriac for consecration. Participation in the liturgy is adequate due to the original participatory nature of the liturgy and because of the present use of the vernacular along with hymns and songs in Malayalam.

As with the other Eastern rites, office prayers seem to have fallen from use. In the place of the office in many homes family prayer is common where the rosary is often recited. Vocations (calls to the priesthood) are high and many priests are from the middle-class and from among those families that pray together. Parish priests often live together in basic support groups. All these elements—the use of the vernacular in liturgical prayer with participa-

tion, prayer at home, and community life for the clergy—seem to enhance the spiritual life of the community. The need to continue the process of reform and renewal, however, is evident. There are still old customs, especially towards women, that are in effect and that need to be changed (e.g., the purification of the mother before the baptism of her child). Some reforms also appear to be taking place in the Syrian Orthodox Church (rite of Malankara). A recent Synod in Kotayam has enacted reforms to enhance the role of women in the church. Among these are the following: young girls, and not just boys, are taken around the altar at their baptism; no longer does the first child to be baptized in the newly consecrated font have to be the male; and the bishops are encouraging women to read to the congregation from the Bible during the liturgy and to take part in the general meetings of local parishes.

### ——————— The Melkites ———————

The Melkites have adapted their liturgy to local languages wherever they have immigrated; thus, English was in liturgical use in the United States and Canada three decades before the Vatican II reforms. Other liturgical reforms, however, have taken place, mainly in the form of dropping some of the Roman liturgical insertions and devotions. The original Greek usage is very limited, and in the West either English or Arabic (in case of newcomers from the Mideast) dominates. Priests tend to improvise and select their own prayers based on the three anaphoras and the litanies combined. An abbreviated version of the Mass has been provided for priests where parishioners have complained about the length of the Sunday liturgy. Attendance, especially of youth, tends to be low.

The biggest immigrant Melkite population is in South America (followed by the U.S.), especially in Brazil, which also has the lowest church attendance. In the United States, where there are about 40 Melkite parishes, regular Sunday church attendance is low, and on average the American-born Melkites attend more often than the Mideastern ones. Shortages in the number of priests constitute a major problem for this immigrant community spread over vast areas. The Sunday eucharistic celebrations have been supplemented with a religious education program for youth, prepared in the early 1970s, that is common among all the Byzantine rites, with adaptations made by each.

## The Ruthenians and the Ukrainians

There has been limited change within the Catholic Byzantine rites of the Russian traditions. Liturgical reforms and renewal have taken the form of dropping many of the old Roman rite insertions along with reductions of litanies and of some priestly private prayers. In some parishes in the United States, daily Mass has become an accepted tradition. Frequent Sunday communion is now encouraged. Most Sunday liturgies among the Ruthenians are sung in English, while among the Ukrainians a few are still celebrated in the native language. New translations of liturgical prayers have appeared, depending on the efforts of each diocese, along with pastoral applications suited for local needs. Most eucharistic liturgies are conducted from behind the iconostasis (a screen, with icons, separating the altar area from the nave), including the liturgy of the Word in some dioceses. In most dioceses, however, the priest comes out to read the gospel to the people and to preach from in front of the iconostasis. Other developments within the Byzantine Catholic communities are appearing very slowly in the form of local adaptations arranged mostly by liturgical commissions in each diocese.

Differences in Sunday eucharistic celebrations between the Orthodox Byzantine churches and the Catholic ones in the United States show that the Orthodox tend to use choirs, while the Byzantine Catholics have relied mostly on cantors who lead the people in singing the liturgical prayers. The strong presence of Russian Orthodox churches in the U.S., along with a major seminary and publishing press (St. Vladimir's), as well as other Orthodox seminaries, has further helped to establish this Byzantine tradition and make it known and better understood. Some considerations towards further church renewal have been suggested by a few on both the Orthodox and the Catholic sides. Among these have been the creative use of the iconostasis in liturgical celebrations, the readmitting of children's communion after baptism for Catholic Byzantine churches, and a greater liturgical participation by all. However, no major changes are planned or expected on either side.

## The Armenian Catholics

There is a strong national and ecumenical affiliation between Catholic and Orthodox Armenians (as well as the few Protestants) with a common sense of being united as one ethnic and Christian people. The co-suffering of the Armenians under persecutions in this century has strengthened their sense of affiliation and communion. On the Catholic side this sense of unity is expressed in terms of liturgical conformity with the Orthodox. Another way in which Armenians have shown their sense of unity is through their social clubs and schools which welcome all Armenians and even share in a common religious education. Memories of persecution as well as of recent suffering and the earthquake tragedy of the Armenians in the former Soviet Union have brought the parties into even greater national and spiritual communion.

The Mass, as in the Orthodox liturgy, is still celebrated in classical Armenian. However, some adaptations and abbreviations have been made. For example, at the liturgy of the Word the Scriptures may be read in modern Armenian, and the sermons are in the vernacular to facilitate understanding. In the United States preaching is done sometimes in English along with modern Armenian. Most Roman introductory prayers and insertions were dropped after the Second Vatican Council. Thus the present form of the Catholic Armenian Sunday liturgy is in conformity with the Orthodox, the only differences being of brevity in some places.

## The Copts

The Copts of Egypt constitute a sizable majority among the Christians in the Middle East. Most of these are Orthodox, with a small minority of Catholic Copts. There is also a sizable number of immigrant Copts in the West (in the U.S. the Orthodox have 35 churches). It would be best to describe liturgical developments in this rite primarily in terms of lingual adaptations for the benefit of the new multi-lingual congregations emerging today. In Egypt the Sunday Eucharist is celebrated in Coptic and Arabic, while in the United States it is a trilingual celebration in Coptic, Arabic and English. The celebration lasts more than three hours. The Catholic Copts, fewer in number, celebrate the same liturgy but in a more abbreviated form.

## Summary Observations

It would be reasonable to conclude from the above observations that long-term planning is necessary and even essential for a worthy process of liturgical reform and renewal for the Eastern Catholic churches. When a clear outlook to the future is lacking, the liturgical process becomes lost in its direction, and many "band-aid" solutions to keep up with the times begin to emerge. These temporary solutions, often in the form of improvisations, do not draw properly on the riches of that church's tradition, nor do they adequately meet the spiritual needs of the faithful. It would be of great importance that Eastern Catholic bishops work collaboratively, with frequent consultations with the laity, to insure that this process continues to perform adequately over the years. Since many of the Eastern churches today experience themselves as overextended minority communities around the world, the interest, support, and cooperation of local Latin rite churches would be important in helping these Eastern Christian communities to value and share their heritage.

Stephen Bonian[13]

## 152 • THE ANTIOCHIAN EVANGELICAL ORTHODOX MISSION

_What has become known as the Antiochian Evangelical Orthodox Mission (AEOM) is part of a movement among Evangelicals and other Protestant Christians toward liturgical and sacramental worship, and toward the rediscovery of the faith and practice of the historic church._

During the 1960s, a group of leaders in Campus Crusade for Christ, including Peter E. Gillquist, Jon Braun, Jack Sparks, J. Richard Ballew, Gordon T. Walker, and Kenneth Berven, became increasingly dissatisfied with the disconnection between evangelism and the church. In their evangelistic efforts on the college campus, the church was virtually nonexistent as a corporate visible entity. Converts were generally left to their own individual experience of faith and not well integrated into communities of worship and faith development.

Beginning in 1968, these persons left the staff of Campus Crusade and pursued their own ministries in different parts of the United States. In 1973, they resumed their relationship with one another in an effort to improve their own individual ministries and to see how they could best do the work of evangelism in the context of the church. They formed an organization called the New Covenant Apostolic Order (NCAO), which was designed to be a voluntary community of "apostolic workers" called to mutual commitment and support in minis-

try, with the purpose of establishing and building churches.

Since they were all from different Protestant backgrounds (Lutheran, Baptist, Evangelical Covenant, Methodist), it was necessary to work toward a common understanding of church, worship, doctrine, and parish life. To that end, the NCAO met for a week each quarter to study these issues. In order to find a common ground, the participants decided to undertake a historical study of these issues, including a careful reading of the patristic sources, with the results being carefully examined in the light of the Scriptures. Further, when the study was completed and consensus reached on an issue, they committed themselves to implementing the findings in the local parish setting.

The early studies of the NCAO convinced them that the worship of the church had been liturgical and sacramental from the beginning. The outline of the eucharistic liturgy described by Justin Martyr in his _First Apology_ became the basis for the worship of this sphere of churches. Studies of the Council of Nicea and the development of the doctrine of the Trinity and of the Incarnation led to a deepened and fuller understanding of the historic Christian faith. Study of the writings of Ignatius, Cyprian, and others led to the conclusion that the church should be structured with bishops, presbyters, and deacons leading the people of God. The writings of Irenaeus, Tertullian, Hippolytus, and Vincent of Lerins contributed also to the group's growing understanding of the relationship between the church's tradition and the preservation of the truth of the gospel.

Over a period of five years during the mid-1970s, the NCAO continued to study the issues and events of the first Christian millennium. The Seven Ecumenical Councils of the church were examined in detail, and their teachings embraced by the members of the NCAO and their churches. When the issues surrounding the Great Schism of 1054 were examined, the conclusion was reached that the Eastern Orthodox church was correct on the issues of papal authority and the Filioque clause in the Nicene Creed. This led to the desire to establish some relationship and dialogue with the modern day Orthodox church.

As these findings concerning church structure and government, doctrine, and liturgy were taught and implemented in the local churches, it became clear that the NCAO was no longer a loose collection of churches, but had become, for want of a better term, a denomination. Consequently in February 1979 these churches organized the Evangelical Orthodox Church (EOC), seen as "a denomination within the One Holy Catholic and Apostolic Church." Bishops were chosen and consecrated and a denominational structure was developed. Peter E. Gillquist was chosen to be the Presiding Bishop. A publishing house, Conciliar Press, was established in Ben Lomond, California, and a quarterly magazine, *AGAIN*, was begun.

At the same time, the Holy Synod of the EOC had a conscious awareness of the need to be integrated into the historic church in some fashion. To remain independent churches was outside the conception of the patristic faith to which EOC was committed. The EOC was one of the few denominations ever formed that had as one of its stated goals at inception to lose its independent existence through union with the historic church.

Later in 1979, the EOC opened a formal dialogue with the Orthodox Churches in North America with the goal of establishing canonical unity between the EOC and the other Orthodox churches. Theologians such as John Meyendorff and Alexander Schmemann, and hierarchs such as Bishop Dmitri of Dallas and Bishop Maximos (Greek Orthodox Diocese of Pittsburgh), were the key figures in the early discussions. The theology and liturgical practice of the EOC began to reflect more and more the experience and teaching of the Orthodox church.

One of the difficulties in establishing a relationship with the Orthodox Church in North America is that there is no single jurisdictional entity with which dialogue can be conducted. The church is administrated through the various parallel ethnic jurisdictions. As a result, the EOC's progress toward unity with the Orthodox church was slow. Discussions with the Orthodox Church in America, the Greek Archdiocese of North and South America, and a pilgrimage to the Ecumenical Patriarchate in Istanbul (Constantinople) in 1985 failed to bring about the establishment of communion. In September, 1986, the Holy Synod of the EOC met with Metropolitan Philip (Saliba) of the Antiochian Orthodox Christian Archdiocese of North America, and accepted his offer to be received into the Orthodox church.

Beginning on February 9, 1987, the churches of the EOC were received into the Antiochian Archdiocese, and the clergy ordained to the diaconate and priesthood of the Orthodox church. Seventeen parishes with over 2000 members from the United States and Canada were thus canonically and sacramentally united with the Orthodox church. Metropolitan Philip (Saliba) renamed the EOC the Antiochian Evangelical Orthodox Mission (AEOM), and commissioned them to "bring Orthodoxy to America."

Since being received into the Orthodox church, the AEOM has continued to be involved in the establishment of churches and the developing movement of Christians back to the historic church with her sacraments and liturgical life. Nearly twenty new churches have been established, and many more are in various stages of preparation. Conciliar Press continues to publish books, pamphlets, and magazines promoting the Orthodox faith, church, and spiritual life. International preaching missions have been carried out in India and Romania.

The early 1990s have seen a growing number of people from various backgrounds, Episcopal, charismatic, evangelical, who are searching for a fuller experience of worship and sacrament, faithfulness to the historic Christian faith, and the development of spiritual life in the context of the local parish. The AEOM hopes to be the vanguard of a larger movement bringing Christians back to the historic church.

For further information, see Peter E. Gillquist, *Becoming Orthodox.* Ben Lomond, Calif.: Conciliar Press, 1992.

Frederick Gregory Rogers

## 153 • THE PROTESTANT LITURGICAL RENEWAL

*Liturgical renewal among the ecumenical churches of mainline Protestantism has brought about a widespread consensus in worship style. In the spirit of the Reformation, not only the Scriptures but also the sacraments are being restored to a central position in worship. Protestant congregations are coming to a new appreciation of the importance of symbol and ceremony that allows all members to participate in the act of worship.*

To describe the diverse worship practices of the many and varied Reformation churches is almost beyond possibility. Lutherans, Presbyterians, Methodists, Anglicans, Congregationalists, Pentecostals, the Society of Friends, and Baptists are only some of the multiplicity of denominations and sects that were spawned by the Reformation and by various revivals and splits since. An acknowledgment of diversity, then, is perhaps the first thing that has to be said about these churches before proceeding to talk about liturgical reform. The possibility of such diversity appears to have been a fundamental characteristic of the Reformation challenge to the authority of the Roman Catholic church in the sixteenth century.

A preliminary look at liturgical reform in the twentieth century, however, reveals a movement, not toward greater diversity, but rather toward ecumenical convergence in liturgy. This is seen in such achievements as the World Council of Churches' document on *Baptism, Eucharist and Ministry*, with its accompanying consensus eucharistic service, the Lima liturgy. The convergence extends to almost all areas of liturgy, including the Eucharist, Christian initiation, calendar and lectionary, daily prayer, and other services such as ordination, marriage, the funeral and a wide range of pastoral liturgies. A new generation of services has been emerging among the churches in the decades of the 1970s and 1980s that have in common a reform of worship in all these areas.

This convergence is far from being only a Protestant phenomenon. Much of its impetus has come from the liturgical movement in the Roman Catholic church earlier in this century that bore remarkable fruit in the Second Vatican Council. The reform also reaches out to embrace with new appreciation the worship of the Orthodox churches. And now new sources of challenge and renewal beyond the traditions of the West are emerging globally from newer churches in Asia and Africa. There is also an increasing knowledge and appreciation of worship in other religions which were at one time dismissed as heathen. Furthermore, new voices calling for reform are emerging nearer at hand from the poor, the oppressed and the generally disregarded ones in our midst, including women, native peoples, the physically challenged, and others.

The picture is exceedingly vast and difficult to comprehend. But we have still been looking only at the movement of ecumenical convergence that is happening primarily among those churches which are usually characterized as being more "liturgical" or "mainstream." Other churches, which have identified themselves as "evangelical," "fundamentalist," or "charismatic," have not participated as yet to any great extent in the ecumenical convergence. They indeed would probably regard their freedom for diversity to be truer to the Protestant ethos than is the movement of convergence.

The convergence in the mainstream churches, however, is not simply a recovery of a pre-Reformation uniformity. It is rather a movement toward unity that can embrace difference and indeed encourages new and creative responses in liturgy through the charismatic and artistic gifts of the people. This openness is clearly indicated in the rubrics of many of the new service books. They ask their users not merely to follow a prescribed liturgy, but to use the contents of the books—the prayers, responses, symbolic actions—as resources and samples to assist and guide the people's own work and initiatives in liturgy.

This recovery of the people's participation in the liturgy is profoundly in keeping with the Reformation insistence on the priesthood of all believers. The Reformers sought to render the liturgy accessible to all the people through such means as translation of the liturgical texts into the vernacular and the encouragement of congregational singing of psalms, hymns and canticles. The recovery of the notion of the whole people of God as celebrants in liturgy may indeed be one of the greatest contributions of the Reformation to the modern climate of liturgical renewal. This remains a goal even if history has also shown the Reformation to unleash factions that disrupt the unity of Christ's body.

Convergence, then, is a primary characteristic of the current movements of liturgical reform among the churches, Reformed, Orthodox, and Catholic alike. We need to consider what is at the root of this convergence and whether there is anything in the legacy of the Reformation, despite the diversity it unleashed, that has contributed to it. The modern liturgical convergence, it can be argued, has its source in a recovery of the biblical basis for Christian prayer and praise. The biblical witness to the saving acts of God in covenant with the people of Israel and culminating in the life, death and resurrection of Jesus Christ is the source without equal of the Christian enactment of faith in the liturgy. Christians see all the events of their lives in the light of God's illuminating Word, proclaimed and enacted in the liturgy. Our own stories, as is commonly said, belong in the larger context of the biblical story, and, together, these are celebrated week-by-week in the liturgy.

A unique place was given to the Scriptures as the primary authority for faith and worship in the

Reformation principle of *sola scriptura.* The Scripture principle was enunciated by the Reformers in their conflict with the teaching authority of the Roman church with its claim of equality with the authority of Scripture. Whether that is a correct reading of the Catholic understanding of authority does not need to concern us here. Of continuing importance is the Reformers' efforts to restore the Bible to the people and to reaffirm its authority for all matters of faith and life. But the Scripture principle did not ensure unity among the Reformation churches. Many of the churches differed in how they understood *sola scriptura.* Some, like the Puritans, maintained that worship ought to consist only of that which is directly authorized by the Scriptures. The consequence of the strict application of this criterion to worship was a drastic reduction of ceremonial practices and a focusing almost exclusively on the Scriptures read and preached and on prayer. Other churches of the Reformation, including those that followed Luther and Calvin most closely, regarded *sola scriptura* not as eliminating all other sources for liturgy, but rather placing Scripture in the position of being *without equal* beside all other sources. Both Luther and Calvin appealed often, for example, to the authority of the primitive churches and the church fathers. Their study of both the Scriptures and the early church led them to advocate a weekly celebration of the Eucharist with both bread and wine distributed among the people.

Whereas the Reformers are noted for their efforts to restore the Scriptures to the people, it is less known that they sought, albeit unsuccessfully, to do the same for the sacraments. Calvin's efforts to establish the Eucharist every Sunday in Geneva, for example, were stymied by a ruling of the city magistrates, who favored the practice of four times a year that was already the rule in Zwingli's church in Zurich. This rule has been, with some exceptions, the practice in most Reformation churches until the recent liturgical reform. Perhaps the failure of the Reformation to fully restore the sacraments has to be understood in relation to their application of the Scripture principle. Whether *sola scriptura* was applied strictly or more broadly, it served to cleanse the liturgy of what the Reformers regarded as human inventions and accretions. Only baptism and the Lord's Supper, for example, of the seven sacraments designated by the church of the Middle Ages, had the required dominical institution for acceptance as sacraments in the Reformation churches.

In the Eucharist Luther also almost totally eliminated the Roman canon because of its unbiblical emphasis on sacrifice. According to his understanding, to make the Mass into a sacrifice that could be repeated was a denial of what God had done once-for-all in the sacrifice of Christ. The biblical notion of justification by faith in this once-for-all sacrifice of Christ became a criterion for rejecting any worship that became a pious work rather than a response in thanksgiving to God's work of grace. The Reformers regarded much of the ceremonial practices and private acts of devotion in the Roman church as pious works designed to win God's favor rather than to express joyful thanksgiving for that favor already bestowed. This Reformation insight into the biblical doctrine of grace has had immense significance for the modern understanding of true motivation for prayer and worship.

The Reformers, however, did not recover, as have modern churches in their eucharistic renewal, the biblical understanding of *b*ᵉ*rakah,* or blessing God, as an act of praise for God's saving acts. The worship of the Reformation churches tended to retain the penitential note of medieval piety. To that they added a strong note of moral exhortation and didacticism, partly because of the emphasis on word as opposed to symbol and ritual. The Hebrew understanding of *b*ᵉ*rakah* was missed by the Reformers largely because the Scriptures were not fully accessible to them in their attempts to reform the liturgy. Greater accessibility has come only with the development of the modern discipline of historical-critical study of the Scriptures. Paradoxically, this approach arose in large measure out of the empiricism and historicity of the eighteenth-century Enlightenment period with its rejection of metaphysics and faith as giving access to truth that is beyond ordinary human sense experience. Because the churches for long regarded the atheistic tendencies of the philosophy of the Enlightenment as antagonistic to religion and worship they tended also to reject historical-critical study of the Scriptures. The acceptance of the value of this study for greater discernment of the truth of the Scriptures in many modern churches, both Reformation and Catholic, is a prime factor, I believe, in the present liturgical convergence.

Because Protestant scholars generally have been, until recently, in the vanguard of scriptural study,

Catholics have regarded their work as one of the greatest contributions of the Reformation churches to liturgical reform. At the same time the Reformation churches have been able to see more clearly the value of the great liturgical heritage of the Roman Catholic and Orthodox churches, particularly as those churches have been rediscovering through critical study their roots in the churches of the first few centuries. Inquiring behind the circumstances of the beginning of Christendom in the establishment of Christianity as the favored religion of the Roman Empire is being seen by many Christians today as an important source for renewal. The Reformation churches have been quick to appropriate such historical discoveries as the _Apostolic Tradition of Hippolytus,_ among other early sources, for the structure and content of the eucharistic prayer. Early baptismal practices that were the sole rite of membership in the church, following an extensive catechumenate, combined with ample use of water, anointing with oil, and the laying on of hands with prayer for the Holy Spirit, are seen as essential in this era of recovery of the ministry of the whole people of God. Discoveries pertaining to the liturgy of time, including the calendar and lectionary and the liturgy of the hours or daily prayer, are being acknowledged also as critical to living in a secular realm by the rhythm of the gospel.

This appropriation of liturgical practices by the Reformation churches has been made both possible and necessary because of a new appreciation of the nature and function of symbol and ritual. Modern study of language is revealing the dynamic nature of both words and symbols. Liturgy comprises both word-events and sign-acts. And both are means by which God can communicate and be present with human beings and human beings with God and one another. Liturgy that seeks to embrace the whole of reality, as revealed by a God who acts in incarnational ways, must be an embodied liturgy, appealing to all the senses of the body. Symbolic liturgy that includes sights as well as sounds, actions and gestures, the movements of procession and dance, and a renewed appreciation of the sacraments, opens up new possibilities for all to participate as they are able. For many Protestants, with their suspicion of ritual and symbol, the discovery by anthropologists that human beings are, by nature, ritual-making creatures has been an important one. It is through their rituals that human beings can come together in community around the apprehension of a deeper

reality. Symbols and rituals are means by which reality is communicated and people are enabled to participate.

Many of the earlier debates between Protestants and Roman Catholics concerning the mode of God's presence in the sacraments are being superseded by a new language that speaks of God's presence in the symbolic action of the liturgy. The discovery of the biblical notion of the eschatological nature of the gospel has provided a new understanding of God's presence both within and beyond history. The words and symbols of the liturgy express both the "now" and the "not yet" of the reign of God that was proclaimed by Jesus and inaugurated in his ministry. Liturgy can be experienced as a foretaste of the future God has in store for the world. To participate in this anticipatory event is to commit oneself to working toward the justice, peace and love to which God is beckoning the whole world.

The renewal of liturgy in the Reformation churches finds its genuine motivation, in unity with other churches, in praise of a Creator who summons all earthly creatures to respond in faith, and in commitment to the renewal of a creation that is still "groaning as in the pains of childbirth. . . ." "For in this hope we [are] saved" (Rom. 8:22, 24).

David R. Newman[14]

## 154 • THE RENAISSANCE OF THE ARTS

_The twentieth century has seen a significant recovery of the arts in both secular and religious culture. The following essay delineates some of the areas in which the arts have emerged within the church and discusses the contribution that the arts make to the worship of God._

A renaissance of art has occurred in twentieth-century worship. A wide variety of new music is being written, much of it in "contemporary" styles. Sermons are being acted out as dramas. Permanent and temporary visual art graces the worship environment. Even solo, ensemble, and congregational dancing is being used to give bodily expression to our praise. Where did all this creative activity in worship come from? Why is it now in our liturgies and services? Many congregations are asking these questions and others. In what follows, we will examine some of the impulses and influences that have helped bring about this intensified artistic expression in worship.

From the beginning of this century, many factors have been operative in the regeneration of the arts in worship, some from within the church and some from without. Several artistic revivals have taken place in the Christian community, each bringing with it some change or enhancement in worship, as well as a greater creativity and freedom of expression. Social changes affecting our culture have also affected the church and its creative response in worship. Changes and developments within the artistic community itself have made an impact on the role of art within the church.

Congregations, artists, and theologians have grappled with the issues raised when the arts are introduced more fully and more broadly into worship. Who should present it—professionals or amateurs from the congregation? Should it be a regular feature, or reserved for special events? For Catholics, Vatican II and the subsequent liturgical renewal opened up these questions, some of which have been addressed by the Bishops' Council on the Environment and Art in Worship. Christian artists, as individuals and as a group, have struggled with how best to offer their gifts to the glory of God.

As the church has responded to the culture around it, seeking to reach out in relevant ways, it has made use of the arts with increasing regularity. The emphasis on evangelism and church growth has brought about an enlarged role for drama and other arts in worship. In trying to communicate with the unchurched, many congregations have used music, mime, drama, and other art forms to attract new people into worship services. Churches have found a focus on the arts to be a helpful way to win back former members.

**Movement Arts.** Artistic trends have affected the use of dance and other movement arts in worship. In the early twentieth century, Pentecostalist worshipers would raise their hands, wave, do the "Holy Ghost jig," or run. This activity may not have seemed like refined, choreographed dance, but it was a break from the staid and static worship that preceded it.

The "Jesus people" movement and the charismatic renewal added increased momentum to the liturgical dance movement. Contemporary worship choruses often invite those who sing them to lift their hands, bow, kneel, run, and even dance before the Lord. With the establishment of the state of Israel and the rise of messianic Jewish groups,

Israeli-style folk dance began to be included as part of celebration and worship.

The development of modern dance has also influenced its use within contemporary worship. The impetus for modern dance was the desire to express the inner soul of men and women through movement. Ballet was seen as too rigid and out of touch with the ordinary person's experience to be able to communicate the emotional or spiritual side of humanity. It is interesting to note that Ted Shawn, one of the fathers of modern dance, had been a seminary student before his career shift into dance. He and Ruth St. Dennis, the founders of the Denishawn School, were very interested in religious matters and performed many works based on Bible passages. Ted Shawn also loved to turn theater audiences into a congregation, and vice versa, through the program of dance he presented. Many Denishawn students shared this interest in the spiritual, which was reflected in their work. The result of this phenomenon was that both students and audience wanted to take the spiritual side further and incorporate it into worship. This type of dance would be called creative, interpretive, or dramatic movement.

**Music.** The counter-culture movements of the 1960s and 1970s brought innovations to musical style in worship, such as the folk mass. Contemporary forms of linguistic expression, along with contemporary music and other media, began to appear in the effort to interpret the relevance of the gospel to a new generation. During the last decade or so, choruses and musical styles once thought inappropriate for worship have become dominant. This has occurred not only in newer church movements; it is evident also in the recent hymnals of historic denominations.

**Visual Arts.** The visual arts in the church have also been affected by contemporary artistic trends in society as a whole. The growing popularity of the craft industry has created an appreciation for handmade items which add a personal touch to church decor. As visual artists and sculptors have found a receptivity to their medium within the church, their creations have emerged as more than mere "decoration" in the place of worship. Such works can serve as powerful expressions of the truth and reality of the gospel, in a visual language we in the West are beginning once again to understand and appreciate.

With the demise of communism, the opening up of the "iron curtain" countries to travel and exchange has encouraged a new interest in the iconography of the Eastern Orthodox church. The whole question of the church's attitude toward art in worship, and the issues joined during the iconoclastic controversy of the eighth century, are being brought to light once again for artists and for the local congregation, not just for the theologian or seminary student. Our society is fast becoming (or already is) a visually-oriented, rather than literature-oriented, culture; this trend has profound implications for the role of visual arts in Christian worship.

Christian artists have been searching within worship for an outlet for the expression of the gifts they have to offer. Today many regional or disciplinary groups of artists around the world are meeting for discussion of issues relevant to their role in the Christian community. Challenged by thinkers like Hans Rookmaaker and Francis A. Schaeffer, such artists wrestle with the questions of art and faith. Worship-related issues can play a major part in these discussions, depending on whether the artistic discipline in question is already used in the church. Many artists wrestle with their role as Christians in the secular market place. Others are more concerned with how to find their place within the church, especially if their discipline does not yet have a recognized role in worship.

The philosopher of aesthetics, Calvin Seerveld, has said, "Art is worship." We recognize the work of art as something which goes beyond ourselves, a work which transcends us and points towards another reality. Father Alexander Schmemann spoke of sign and symbol in art as an "epiphany of reality." To be sure, not all art points towards God! But let us continue to respond to that creative expression called art as it speaks to us in our worship, and makes present the reality of our Creator and Redeemer.

Philip Griffith III

## 155 • THE CHARISMATIC RENEWAL

*The charismatic movement of the twentieth century has made an impact on nearly every denomination and has given rise to a number of new churches and fellowships. This discussion traces these developments and emphasizes the influence of the charismatic movement in contemporary worship.*

The "charismatic renewal" of the late twentieth century is one of several movements in the history of the church emphasizing the power of God and the manifestation of miraculous and revelatory gifts of the Spirit, especially tongues and prophecy. Earlier charismatic movements included Montanism in second-century Phrygia, the Irvingite movement of nineteenth-century Britain, and the worldwide Pentecostal movement in the early twentieth century.

The charismatic renewal probably received its name at the fourth international convention of the Full Gospel Businessmen's Fellowship International (FGBMFI) held in Minneapolis on June 25–29, 1956, where one or more of the invited speakers used this term to describe the movement of which they were a part. During these meetings, David J. DuPlessis advocated a decidedly ecumenical emphasis—an innovation to many of its participants (C. E. Sonmore, *Beyond Pentecost* [1992], 10–17).

Prior to this time, perhaps partly due to some of the efforts of DuPlessis, there had already been some Pentecostal activity among members of traditional churches. For example, the Christian cell movement of the late 1940s and early 1950s emphasized charismatic gifts, healing, and "body ministry" among Episcopalians, Methodists, Presbyterians, and others. "Cells" of Christians met together in many parts of the United States for fellowship, prayer, and the exercise of the gifts of the Spirit. One of the leaders of this movement, Samuel Shoemaker, Rector of Calvary House Church in New York City, published *Faith at Work,* a periodical which enjoyed a fairly wide circulation and which laid important groundwork for the later efforts of the FGBMFI and similar organizations.

In the 1960s, the charismatic movement began to find increasing acceptance within the traditional churches and sometimes came to be called "Neo-Pentecostalism." Developments in the Roman Catholic church were typical of what happened in many Protestant denominations. In 1966, several Catholic lay faculty members at Duquesne University in Pittsburgh came together for prayer and discussion about the vitality of their lives as Christians and met some friends of theirs, Steve Clark and Ralph Martin, who introduced them to *The Cross and the Switchblade* by David Wilkerson. At the same time Ralph Keifer, a theology instructor at Duquesne, happened to read *They Speak With Other Tongues* by John Sherrill. Through William Lewis, vicar of St. John's Student Parish in East Lansing, Michigan, these Duquesne professors met Betty Schomaker, an Episcopalian who brought them to a prayer meeting at the home of Florence Dodge, a Presbyterian, where, on January 13, 1967, Ralph Keifer spoke in tongues. The following week, two other Duquesne faculty members were baptized in the Holy Spirit, and by February, four of them had received the pentecostal experience. In mid-February, about thirty students and faculty spent a weekend retreat in prayer, and the Holy Spirit was poured out upon them. This "Duquesne weekend" was seminal for the subsequent spread of the charismatic gifts among Catholics. As a result of prolonged discussions between Ralph Keifer and Kevin and Dorothy Ranaghan, nine people from the University of Notre Dame came together in an apartment in South Bend on March 5, 1967, to seek the baptism in the Holy Spirit. The following week, at a subsequent meeting, many of these persons received the gift of tongues. Meetings of this kind continued to multiply, and the movement quickly spread to Catholic student groups at Iowa State, Holy Cross, and Michigan State University, where Ralph Martin and Stephen Clark started a prayer group after visiting Duquesne. In May of 1969, the first Catholic Charismatic Conference was held at Notre Dame and attended by 450 people. After six years of growth, the annual Notre Dame conference met at St. Peter's Basilica in Rome, with close to 20,000 people in attendance. Similar growth was experienced among Protestant charismatic groups during this time.

During the late 1960s and early 1970s, the charismatic movement was described by observers as a prayer movement. The central purpose of the charismatic prayer meeting was considered to be worship. One of its distinctive features was spontaneity; there was no prescribed agenda, and anyone could contribute. Kilian McDonnell provided an eyewitness account of a charismatic prayer meeting. It started with a hymn, followed by a Scripture reading; then there was silence while people meditated and prayed silently. After about five minutes someone prayed aloud, using as a basis the text which had just been read. This was followed by more silence, broken with short prayers by various members for the gift of praise, for strength, and for sensitivity to the needs of others. Someone with a guitar started singing a hymn, and the other members began to join in. A young businessman then gave a testimony of how God had enabled him to come to understand and help a difficult co-worker at his office since

the time of the previous meeting. Two others gave testimonies, then there was silence for several minutes. An older man then asked for prayers for a domestic problem. He knelt in the middle of the room and the others gathered around, laying hands upon him. One of them spoke in tongues for about half a minute, while others quietly prayed in English. After three minutes he rose, and everyone sat down again as before. A young girl read a psalm, then there was silence. Someone then suggested that they break for coffee.

After twenty minutes, the meeting resumed, and the guitar player sang a hymn that he had written. Then there was extended silence, until a man who had been there a few times previously suggested that the group pray for him that he might be baptized in the Holy Spirit. He knelt in the center, and the others gathered around, placing hands on his head and shoulders. He did not at that time speak in tongues. After three or four minutes he rose and everyone returned to his or her place. Somebody began to recite the Lord's Prayer, and everybody else joined in. Then the members of the group began to tell of special prayer concerns. One man had an appointment for a job interview, another had housing problems, and another needed guidance for his life's direction. There was a pause, then a member prophesied about God's mercy. After another silence, someone began singing in tongues, and three or four joined in. The singing was followed by silence and the recitation of a psalm by the group. The entire meeting lasted about two and a half hours, which was "very modest by classical and neo-Pentecostal standards" (Kilian McDonnell, *Catholic Pentecostalism: Problems in Evaluation* [1970], 25–27).

The Latter Rain revival of the late 1940s and early 1950s was a major source of the charismatic renewal. One of its distinctive forms of worship, the "heavenly choir," first became manifest at meetings held in Edmonton, Alberta, in October of 1948, attended by members of several Pentecostal denominations, including the Assemblies of God and the Pentecostal Assemblies of Canada. The "heavenly choir" was a spontaneous form of congregational choral worship, metaphorically described by James Watt as "a mighty organ, with great swelling chords, and solo parts weaving in and out, yet with perfect harmony." According to George Warnock, "from that day forth scriptural song became part and parcel of ministry that came when the body came together" (R. M. Riss, _A Survey of 20th-Century Revival Movements in North America_ [Peabody, Mass.: Hendrickson, 1988], 116).

Worship within the Latter Rain movement was later described by Bill Hamon as "praise flowing up and down like rhythmic waves of gentle ocean breezes and then rising to a crescendo of melodious praises. . . . In the 1950s, the praise service would flow continuously from thirty minutes to three hours. Most Charismatics of the 1960s and 1970s came into the Latter Rain type of worship" (_The Eternal Church_ [Point Washington, Fla.: Christian International, 1981], 257–258). Hamon also has observed of the Latter Rain movement that "worship in these churches would continue with uplifted hands for about twenty minutes, then subside to a melodious murmur. Several prophecies would come forth, then worship would go on for another twenty or thirty minutes. Then the cycle would continue with more prophecies and more worship" (_Prophets and the Prophetic Movement_ [1990], 116).

Many of the Scripture songs and praise choruses that later gained wide currency among charismatics were originally products of the Latter Rain movement and were written by such people as Phyllis Spiers (who was associated with Sharon Bible School in North Battleford, Saskatchewan, and later with Elim Bible Institute in upstate New York), Rita Kelligan (also of Elim), and many others. Because these people felt that their music was born of the Spirit of God, they were not particularly interested in obtaining credit for these works through copyright registration. As a result, there were several cases in which music which originated with them was attributed to others.

In 1954, praise in the dance was introduced at a Latter Rain conference at Crescent Beach, British Columbia. During a time of worship, a woman prophesied, "The King is coming, the King is coming—go ye out to meet Him with dances and rejoicing." She began taking ferns out of a flower basket, waving them in the air and laying them down as if before the Lord, praising the Lord in the dance. "Within a short time, most of the Latter Rain churches on the West Coast were praising God in the dance" (Hamon [1981], 260).

Various forms of dance have become an important part of charismatic worship, particularly in Kenya, Chile, Australia, Britain, and the United States. The liturgical dance movement was well known within Anglicanism prior to the advent of the charismatic renewal, and many charismatics have embraced it wholeheartedly. The Christian Dance Fellowship of Australia has had a tremendous worldwide influence, incorporating pageantry into worship. In an article on dance as a part of the charismatic movement, Nell Challingsworth described one occasion at which the colors for the dancers' robes were taken from the stained glass windows, using ruby, gold, purple, sapphire, and emerald (D. Martin and P. Mullen, eds., _Strange Gifts?: A Guide to Charismatic Renewal_ [Oxford: Blackwell, 1984], 126).

With respect to the worship of the charismatic movement in general, D. L. Alford has written that "freedom in worship, joyful singing, both vocal and physical expressions of praise, instrumental accompaniment of singing, and acceptance of a wide variety of music styles are all characteristic of this renewal," and that "it is not unusual to find Charismatic worshipers singing, shouting, clapping hands, leaping, and even dancing before the Lord as they offer him sincere praise and thanksgiving." He observes that charismatic worship has several important characteristics, including (1) emphasis upon the singing of psalms and Scripture songs; (2) reliance upon music for praise and worship in church, at conferences and festivals, in small groups, and in private; (3) use of musical instruments; (4) emphasis upon congregational singing with the use of praise leaders; (5) use of dance and pageantry, both spontaneous and choreographed; (6) use of drama and pantomime; and (7) emphasis upon the prophetic role of, or anointing upon, the musicians (S. M. Burgess and G. M. McGee, eds., _Dictionary of Pentecostal and Charismatic Movements_ [Grand Rapids: Regency Reference Library, 1988], 693–694). Bob Sorge observes that "to move prophetically in worship is to move with an awareness of the desire and leading of the Holy Spirit moment by moment, to discern the direction of the Spirit, and to lead God's people to a fuller participation of that" (_Exploring Worship: Practical Guide to Praise and Worship_ [Son-Rise, 1987], 125). Other characteristics of charismatic worship include the uplifting of hands, the linking of arms, the freedom for all participants to contribute, especially in the functioning of prophetic gifts and in acts of healing, and the use of music, art, and color as sacramental signs. There is a fresh emphasis upon meaning in worship and a recognition that Scripture should be read with great emphasis and care, that actions should not be perfunctory, and that words should correspond with actions (Martin and Mullen, 109).

By 1974, some liturgists began to discern an urgent need to incorporate some of the charismatic distinctives into the liturgy. Certain important characteristics of charismatic worship therefore soon came to be incorporated into the worship of both Catholics and Protestants. For example, on Pentecost Monday in 1975, the first charismatic Mass was conducted at St. Peter's Basilica in Rome with Cardinal Leon Josef Suenens as celebrant, where "young American Charismatic leaders from Ann Arbor, Michigan, delivered prophecies from the high altar of the basilica. Joyful and anointed singing filled the church" (Vinson Synan, *In the Latter Days: The Outpouring of the Holy Spirit in the Twentieth Century* [Ann Arbor, Mich.: Servant Books, 1984], 116). Prior to this time, Josephine Massyngberde Ford had written that speaking and singing in tongues were already in use at pentecostal Catholic eucharists during the synaxis, or preparatory section of the Mass, and after the reception of Holy Communion (M. P. Hamilton, ed., *The Charismatic Movement* [Grand Rapids: Eerdmans, 1975], 117).

Charismatic Anglicans have made extensive use of Rite A in the *Alternative Service Book* in order to celebrate an extended Eucharist. Within certain parts of this rite provided by the Liturgical Commission of the Church of England, it is possible to include many of the elements from charismatic prayer meetings and to create inspiring celebrations, such as that which took place at the first International Anglican Charismatic Conference in 1978 at Canterbury Cathedral, where the Archbishop of Cape Town and thirty Anglican bishops presided (Martin and Mullen, 89).

A British Anglican, John Gunstone, has written that "one place where the Charismatic Renewal is having a wide influence is in the worship of parish churches. The renewal has, through its prayer meetings, introduced Anglicans to forms of praising, praying, singing and sharing which most of them had never experienced before. . . . The popular, Scripture-based choruses, which have been the voice of the Charismatic Renewal in worship, are heard everywhere, and there is a more relaxed freedom in the conduct of worship nowadays. Evangelicals have discovered the liturgical dance and Catholic Anglicans the personal testimony" (Martin and Mullen, 87–89).

Another important element of the charismatic renewal (and those whom it has touched) has been the public praise movement, which advocates marches for Jesus. Two of the primary exponents of public praise are Graham Kendrick in Britain and John Dawson in the United States. One of the earliest expressions of this type of worship took place in 1974 in Auckland, New Zealand, where there was a "march for righteousness" under the leadership of Rob Wheeler and Peter Morrow (both of the Latter Rain tradition), Anglican bishops, and pastors of most of the churches of that city.

The "praise and worship" movement which swept through many traditional churches in the 1980s and 1990s had its roots in the charismatic movement and its antecedents. Most praise and worship songs were originally sung among charismatics. At the outset of the charismatic movement, one of the first distributors of music tapes of this genre was Maranatha! Music of Laguna Hills, California.

According to Harry Boonstra ("With Reservations: A Review of Three Influential Books on the Praise and Worship Movement," *Reformed Worship* 20 [1991], 36–37), three of the most influential books of the movement were written by Graham Kendrick (*Learning to Worship* [Minneapolis: Bethany House, 1985]), Jack W. Hayford (*Worship His Majesty* [Waco, Tex.: Word Books, 1987]), and Judson Cornwall (*Let Us Worship* [Waco, Tex.: Word Books, 1983]), who had been an almost ubiquitous guest speaker on praise and worship at charismatic conferences for several decades.

In North America, the widespread influence of the praise and worship movement among traditional churches may have been precipitated by the International Worship Symposium (IWS), founded by Barry and Steve Griffing in 1978 at Shiloh Christian Fellowship in Oakland, California, a "revival" church heavily influenced by the Latter Rain Movement of the 1940s and 1950s. In 1978, its founders invited a number of music ministers to come together on an informal basis for a mutual exchange of their knowledge and experience. About 120 came to share new music with one another, to discuss problem solving, and to trade observations. This session became a yearly event. In 1979, 90 of them met in Findlay, Ohio, at Hope Temple pastored by Moses Vegh, where, spontaneously, an entire symphony orchestra came together, playing extemporaneously under the anointing the Holy Spirit. The 1980 symposium met at George Rohrig's church in Santa Ana, California. Larry Dempsey, who grew up in this church, became an IWS director at this time. In earlier years, Dempsey had been an organist for A. A. Allen and for R. W. Schaumbach.

In 1981, about 450 people came together for the IWS at Shady Grove Church in Grand Prairie, Texas. By 1982, IWS attendance, this time at Zion Evangelistic Temple in Clawson, Michigan, had risen to 850 daytime registrants, with 2,000 attending evening meetings. The son of Zion's pastor, Leonard Gardner, was Dan Gardner, music minister of the church. He became one of the directors of the IWS from this time until 1984, and has written many of the songs of the praise and worship movement.

In 1982 and 1983, some of the important pastors of the revival fellowship of churches wanted to make the IWS a symposium for Latter Rain "restoration orthodoxy." However, the younger music leaders of these churches felt that IWS meetings should not be restricted in this way, since they were commissioned to bring the worship of that tradition to the broader church, and since their particular emphases would have an impact upon all of the church through that medium. This disagreement came to a head at the 1983 symposium at Living Waters Church in Pasadena, California, where there were over 1,000 registered delegates. The pastor, Ione Glaeser, defended the young IWS directors and withstood the pastors, some of whom objected to the use of dance in worship, instrumental song, extemporaneous song, and the idea of a corporate prophetic anointing. Opponents of the broader approach also feared that the involvement of large numbers of people would lead to compromises, opening the door to commercialization of what had been freely given by God.

The "word of faith" movement became involved in IWS after Dan Armstrutz, the worship leader of Grace Fellowship in Texas, insisted that both Bob Yandia, his pastor, and Machan Dellovan, the head of the vocal department at Oral Roberts University, accompany him to the IWS symposium in 1983. This event opened the way for meetings of the symposium at the University the following year. Here, these meetings became far more than small fellowship gatherings, and the level of scholarship in the teaching sessions increased considerably.

Members of traditional churches first came to the IWS in large numbers in 1985 at Duquesne University, then the following year in Washington, D.C., where there were 2,300 registered delegates and

4,000 attending every evening. These meetings may have helped to inspire Gerrit Gustafson and others to form Integrity Hosanna! Music, which almost immediately become one of the most important sources for praise and worship choruses.

As is often the case with folk music, it is difficult to determine the names of the original composers of the Scripture choruses and praise songs that have recently come into widespread use. Some of them were composed during previous revivals, including that of the late 1940s of which the Latter Rain was a part. Other choruses originated with people such as Beverly Glenn, but later came to be attributed to others. Some additional known composers of praise and worship songs include Donna Adkins, Bruce Ballinger, LaMar Boschman, David Butterbaugh, Shirley Carpenter, Kay Chance, Margaret Clarksen, Tommy Coombs, Andrae Crouch, Bob Cull, Kirk Dearman, Larry Dempsey, Chuck Fromm, Bill and Gloria Gaither, Dan Gardner, Less Gerrett, Bob Gillman, Debbye Graafsma, Gerrit Gustafson, Jack Hayford, Kent Henry, Naida Hern, Anne Herring, Roy Hicks, Jr., Kurt Kaiser, Graham Kendrick, Laurie Klein, Karen Lafferty, Bob McGee, Audrey Meier, Pauline Mills, Don Moen, Dave Moody, Martin Nystrom, Michael O'Shields, Twila Paris, Randy Rothwell, Pete Sanchez, Jr., John Sellers, Henry Smith, Leonard Smith, Michael W. Smith, Timothy Dudley Smith, Leona Von Brethorst, Brian Wren, and Kathy Zuziak. While this list is far from exhaustive, most, if not all praise and worship composers attribute the origin of its music not to themselves, but to the creative work of God himself.

Richard M. Riss

## 156 • THE LITURGICAL-CHARISMATIC MOVEMENT

_For decades the charismatic movement has been influencing the forms of worship practices in many of the older historic churches. Millions of Catholics, Episcopalians, Lutherans, and others worldwide have found that the informal, spontaneous, and exuberant worship style of charismatics can bring new warmth and energy to traditional services—services whose formal structures and restrained atmosphere once felt cold and routine to them._

Today, more churches than ever are likely to be bridging the gap between ancient forms and Pentecostal fervor. But surprisingly enough, many of them are now building the bridge from the other direction.

Across the country, groups of nondenomination charismatic believers seeking to deepen and enrich their worship are exploring the traditional forms of the oldest Christian communions. They're finding that what is often called "liturgical worship" has a balance, breadth, and rootedness often lacking in more spontaneous forms. They're learning that liturgy was a part of the worship of the New Testament church. And they're discovering that the Holy Spirit is not afraid of structure—that liturgical forms can be filled with Pentecostal power to provide the environment for a rich and dynamic encounter with God.

### The New Liturgical Charismatics

Some charismatic churches are merely borrowing (or as they would call it, reclaiming) an eclectic assortment of elements from the liturgies of the Anglican, Catholic, and Orthodox churches: a weekly Eucharist (the Lord's Supper), clerical vestments, litanies, incense, processions, fixed prayers, and creeds. Others, however, have decided to embrace the formal approach to services as a whole, adopting the entire order of worship practices by the Episcopal church or even joining—an entire congregation or denomination at a time—with a historic body like the worldwide Anglican communion or the Orthodox churches of the East.

Here's a sampling of the phenomenon:

- In Valdosta, Georgia, a whole Pentecostal congregation—Church of the King—has taken a journey that began with processions, vestments, creeds, and weekly communion, and led ultimately to its admittance into the Episcopal Church of America.
- St. Michael's Church in San Clemente, California—a charismatic congregation closely associated with the prophetic and pro-life movements—has adopted the Episcopal Book of Common Prayer for its worship services and joined other churches in California and Arizona to form a new denomination: The Charismatic Episcopal Church of North America.
- A handful of charismatic students at Oral Roberts University in Tulsa startled their classmates several years ago when they joined the Eastern Orthodox Church. Some of them have even become priests.

- Graham Kendrick, internationally known worship leader and songwriter from Great Britain, has incorporated in his works several traditional liturgical elements—the Apostles' Creed, responsive readings, fixed prayers, and words from the ancient *Kyrie* litany—reintroducing these forms to charismatics through Integrity's *Hosanna!* worship tapes and the international Marches For Jesus.

Meanwhile, the liturgical renaissance among charismatics is only part of a much wider phenomenon. Several evangelical Christian leaders have sounded a call to return to the church's "classical" roots, which include formal liturgical worship.

Not surprisingly, Christians who make the move to a more liturgical setting are often viewed with suspicion or confusion by their fellow believers who aren't moving in the same direction. Sometimes the apprehension is simply based on ignorance. For example, when one Pentecostal pastor in Arizona first introduced liturgical elements in his service, he got a call from a local Baptist pastor who thundered, "I hear you folks are worshiping candles!"

More common, however, are the thoughtful objections that merit a serious response. Those who were reared in an older Christian tradition yet found its forms of worship unsatisfying may wonder why charismatics in particular would want to go back to "dead forms" and "empty rituals." They question whether liturgy is biblical or merely a "tradition of men," and they fear that so much structure leaves little room for the Holy Spirit to operate.

### Why Liturgy?

**What Is Liturgy?** To understand why some charismatics are finding a new appreciation for liturgy, we need first a working definition for the term. The English word "liturgy" comes from the Greek *leitourgia,* which originally meant "work of the people." In the New Testament and other Greek literature of the same period, *liturgy* typically refers to a public function in which service is rendered—in secular settings, most often a service to the state; in the Bible, a service to God.

In this general sense, all churches have a liturgy in their worship, a particular approach to the public meetings in which they seek to serve God. Even churches that emphasize spontaneity and continual novelty in their services typically fall, sooner or later, into a more-or-less standard order of service and a distinctive way of doing things. They may not intentionally establish a liturgy, but regular forms develop all the same. As one pastor raised in a Pentecostal congregation describes it: "On any given Sunday, at any given place in the service, you know what's coming next."

For charismatics who are making use of older forms of worship, then, the issue is not whether they will have a liturgy; all churches do. The issue is: What liturgy will they use? On what pattern will they base their services?

**Charismatic Discontent.** In this light, then, to speak of charismatics rediscovering liturgy may be misleading. Perhaps we might more accurately say that some charismatic churches are realizing that the liturgy they have is lacking.

For some, the discontent with the typical charismatic service grew with the weariness of trying to make every meeting unique. Their search for freshness became in reality a worship of novelty and led only to the pursuit of one charismatic fad after another. As habits and routines developed despite their best intentions, these churches found they could slip into "empty ritual" just as easily with praise choruses as with old hymns. They could be distracted by worries about burning the oven roast back home whether they were making a joint "faith confession" for personal prosperity or reciting the Apostles' Creed.

In short, they discovered that Isaiah's words about honoring God with their lips while their hearts were far away (Isa. 29:13) weren't written just for Episcopalians.

Other charismatics came to realize that their worship services were more minister-centered than God-centered. Much of their unrecognized liturgical forms tended to focus attention on the worship leader, band, special vocalists, preacher, or healing minister. The more skilled the speakers and musicians, and the more flashy their presentation, the more "anointed" people assumed the service to be.

At the same time, charismatic worship forms often seemed to be, as some have termed it, "entertainment-driven." Emphasis was too often placed on the congregation's feelings: how much they "enjoyed" the service, how "excited" they were and how much they "got out of it." Instead of assembling in order to glorify God with their worship, people were looking to be entertained.

For still others, the primary motivation for change was a deep sense—often felt more than understood—that the Lord's Supper needed to be recognized as a source of spiritual life and health to be received every Sunday. Through study, they learned that from ancient times the Eucharist (as the oldest churches call it) has been held by the church as the climax of the worship service, when worshipers encounter Jesus in a unique way; and they experienced that reality for themselves.

## Rediscovered Elements of Liturgical Worship

What kinds of traditional liturgical elements are being adopted by charismatics in worship? Here's a partial list:

**Weekly Eucharist.** The Lord's Supper—the climax of corporate worship throughout most of church history and in most of the Christian world—assumes prominence in weekly services.

**Fixed Prayers.** These are prayers whose words are planned rather than spontaneous, just as the words of most worship songs are fixed.

**Creeds.** These confessions of faith are succinct summaries of the essential Christian doctrines as they have been held from earliest times. The two most popular are the Apostles' Creed and the Nicene Creed.

**Litanies.** These are prayers or praises consisting of a series of petitions or biddings sung or said by a leader, to which the congregation offers a fixed response.

**Traditional Hymns and Classical Church Music.** Many churches are rediscovering the theological richness of lyrics in the great hymns of the faith, as well as the beauty of classical church music.

**Processions.** These are ceremonial walks of the ministers (usually in a particular order), who wear vestments and carry items such as crosses, candles, banners, and the Scripture. Processions may, for example, bring ministers into the sanctuary to begin a service.

**Church Calendar.** Like the ancient Jewish calendar, the Christian calendar in its simplest form establishes a cycle of corporate celebrations, memorials, and seasons that focus on the most important truths of the faith within the space of a year. The major features are Advent (leading up to Christmas), Epiphany, Lent (leading up to Easter), Easter season, and Pentecost, but it also includes observances like Trinity Sunday and Ascension Day.

**Lectionaries.** These books offer systematic collections of scriptural passages, each of which is appointed to be read on a specific day of the year, coordinated with the church calendar (see above). The texts are organized so that all the major teachings of the Bible are included in the yearly reading cycle, and each Sunday provides coordinated passages from (1) the Psalms, (2) the rest of the Old Testament, (3) the Gospels and (4) the rest of the New Testament.

**Divine Office.** The practice of saying fixed prayers at certain times of the day or night, inherited from Jewish custom.

**Vestments, Paraments, and Insignia.** Vestments are the special clothing worn by those ministering. Paraments are the fabric hangings and the altar and pulpit coverings used in the sanctuary. The colors used are determined by the church calendar and have symbolic significance. The insignia include objects like the crosses carried in processions or standing on the altar.

**Sacramentals.** These are traditionally defined as objects or actions used to aid in the church's worship or in personal devotion, such as candles, incense, holy water, table blessings, and making the sign of the cross. Technically, this term also includes vestments and litanies.

## ———— Biblical Roots ————

Much charismatic teaching tends to assume that worship in the New Testament church was informal and spontaneous—that is, like today's charismatic worship. This view draws its inspiration primarily from two sorts of biblical passages. First are those that denounce Jewish or pagan legalism, ungodly traditions, and hypocrisy (Gal. 4:9-11; Matt. 6:5-18; 15:1-14). Second are those that suggest early Christian meetings were highly participatory and allowed for the spontaneous operation of spiritual gifts (e.g., 1 Cor. 12, Col. 3:15-17). From this perspective, the formal, carefully structured forms of the ancient Christian traditions are viewed as a kind of corruption or regression to Old Testament Judaism that occurred as the church lost its original purity and power.

For that reason, many nondenominational charismatics have been startled to discover the historical evidence that New Testament worship included formal liturgy. Divinely sanctioned patterns of Old Testament worship were highly structured, and we know from abundant textual sources that in Jesus' day many of these forms remained the norm among Jewish people. The liturgical services of temple, synagogue, and home had an abundance of fixed prayers, litanies, chanted psalms, and ritual actions, and Jesus and the apostles took part in them (Luke 4:16-21; 24:53; John 2:13; 18:20; Acts 2:46; 3:1; 14:1).

Jesus warned against the empty repetition of insincere prayers (Matt. 6:7-8). But in the same breath, he gave us a set form of words—what many call "the Lord's Prayer"—as a model for our conversations with God. That fixed prayer has been on the lips of the church ever since.

After Pentecost, the first Christians, who were almost all Jewish, quite naturally incorporated the liturgical structures of the synagogue and temple into their worship as well. For example, the apostles continued to observe the Jewish liturgical "hours of prayer" set for specific times (Acts 3:1). Paul also spoke of Christians singing the Psalms, a practice borrowed from the synagogue, where these texts were chanted according to a fixed traditional schedule (Col. 3:16). In addition, Paul's letters occasionally quote "sayings" that had apparently taken on fixed poetic forms and were used as Christian parallels to the Jewish liturgy (Eph. 5:14; 1 Tim. 3:16; 2 Tim. 2:11-13).

Church historians have debated whether Jesus' last supper with his disciples was actually a ritual fellowship meal common among private religious societies of the time, a Passover meal, or something else. But whatever the source of the ceremony, the New Testament descriptions of the Lord's Supper fit what we know of the general structure of domestic Jewish liturgy around the table, with its fixed prayers of blessing and ritual acts. Even today, the words of the Catholic, Anglican, and Orthodox liturgies surrounding the Eucharist still echo at points the ancient Jewish table blessings.

Other biblical passages also gave hints that the early Christians thought in liturgical categories. When Luke says the church leaders at Antioch were "worshiping the Lord" (Acts 13:2) the Greek verb is *leitourgounton* and could just as easily be translated "performing the liturgy." The apostle Paul used the ritual terminology of the Jewish temple when he said he wanted to be—literally translated—a liturgical minister serving in a priestly manner on behalf of the Gentiles, so that they might become a sacrificial oblation that has been ritually purified by the Holy Spirit (Rom. 15:16).

Most striking of all is John's description in Revelation of heaven's worship. He paints a picture of elders in special garments, chanting fixed prayers before an altar with incense and burning lamps (Rev. 4-5, 7, 15). This picture is also similar to what Isaiah described (Is. 6).

Whether the book of Revelation describes the actual worship of heaven or simply symbolizes spiritual truths with concrete images, it still presents a New Testament affirmation of formal liturgical worship. Either such worship reflects somehow the worship in heaven—and what more powerful reason could there be for practicing it?—or else it employs images drawn from the worship experience of the New Testament church.

The earliest post-biblical sources we have for learning about the nature of early Christian worship confirm that much of it was highly structured, though integrated with spontaneous singing, prayer, and the exercise of spiritual gifts. As early as the second century—when the church still had leaders who had known the first apostles personally and long before Christianity became "corrupted," as some would have it, into the state religion of Rome—the church was already developing ritual with roots in the Jewish liturgies of temple, synagogue, and home.

### Why Use Traditional Liturgy?

For those charismatics who insist that we must imitate the New Testament church as closely as possible, the knowledge that the first Christians worshiped with set rituals is sufficient motivation for adopting liturgical forms. But even those who believe Christians aren't bound to imitate the early church in all things have found that many ancient traditions of worship enrich their congregational life. Intentionally liturgical charismatics have often cited these benefits:

First, traditional liturgy can help us center our worship on God rather than the ministers. Those portions of the service that are formally structured rather than spontaneous allow less opportunity to speakers and musicians for inserting themselves into the congregation's worship or keeping attention

turned on themselves with long-winded and flashy performances.

Second, traditional liturgy teaches congregations to view worship as a discipline and privilege rather than entertainment. Though most charismatics by no means want to give up the joy of worship for a sense of grim duty, the discipline of participating in prescribed forms, whether or not we feel like it, takes the focus off what we ourselves gain from services. Instead, it emphasizes that we worship God because he is worthy of it—not because the activity excites us.

Third, traditional liturgy contributes to the maturity of our teaching and understanding of the Christian faith. The words of the ancient liturgies, carefully shaped over hundreds of years, have much to say about gospel truths that charismatics have often overlooked, forgotten, or resisted. Liturgical forms can enrich our theology and practice through several advantages:

- *theological balance*—Pastors tend to focus on their pet doctrines, spending a disproportionate amount of time on certain subjects—faith, tithing, prophecy, social action, or whatever—and consequently neglect matters of equal or greater importance. The ancient liturgical forms encourage us to keep our teaching balanced. For example, following the church calendar allows us to make sure that within the course of a year we teach the fundamentals about the nature of God, the nature of Christ, and the nature of the Spirit-filled church.
- *theological depth*—Not all pastors are equally gifted in plunging into the depths of the Scripture and conveying what they find to the congregation. But many profound insights have been stated clearly and succinctly in older liturgical forms, especially in the lyrics of the best hymns.
- *theological precision*—The words of the ancient liturgies are not only concise, but also precise. In particular, our own teaching can be corrected and sharpened by the words of the creeds—those wise and beautiful summaries of Christian doctrine carefully hammered out by some of the most brilliant minds and devoted hearts the church has ever seen.
- *devotional balance*—Measure the time spent on various activities in most charismatic services, and you'll find the great majority is spent

in praise, special music, and preaching. How often do such congregations devote time to corporate confession of sin, intercession for government officials and church leaders, praying the model prayer Jesus taught us, or just listening to the public reading of Scripture? Though we tend to neglect these activities, all of them are commanded by the Bible, and the ancient liturgies are designed to include them (cf. James 5:16; 1 Tim. 2:1-2; Matt. 6:9-13; 1 Tim. 4:13).

Fourth, traditional liturgical forms encourage the unity of faith. The same sense of agreement and solidarity that comes from singing songs as a group is also cultivated by praying and declaring the creeds in congregational unison.

Fifth, traditional liturgical forms have a carefully cultivated beauty of language, color, and movement that makes our worship more fitting for our beautiful Savior. We must be careful not to allow artistic considerations to outweigh other more important concerns; that would only lead to a different kind of "entertainment-driven" worship. But the visual and linguistic poverty—even sterility—of many charismatic services misses an opportunity to honor God by reflecting his beauty. It also inhibits us from worshiping him with all that we are because it neglects the aesthetic part of human nature.

Sixth, traditional liturgies connect us to Christians in other churches and in earlier generations. When we sing the same songs, pray the same prayers, and declare the same creeds as those used by believers around the world and across the ages, we gain a greater sense of our place in the body of Christ. We demonstrate our kinship with those who, despite wide differences in race and culture, have all worshiped the same Lord with the same faith.

Seventh, restoring the Eucharist to its ancient position of prominence in worship allows us to experience its mystery more deeply. The notion that the Lord's Supper is only a memorial ceremony has found wide acceptance among independent charismatics in this country, but that particular teaching has been rejected by most of the church for most of its history. Even Protestant reformers like Luther and Calvin, though they opposed the Catholic doctrine of transubstantiation, nevertheless maintained that Christ is truly present in the bread and cup—and that this sacrament can act as a powerful channel of God's grace.

Eighth, most importantly, ancient liturgical forms can benefit us because some aspects of life in the Spirit are best communicated and experienced through concrete, visual, and acted symbols rather than through words. This insight, assumed almost universally throughout the church until the time of the Reformation, is based on several realities.

God created human beings not just with wills and intellects, but also with emotions and bodies. Much of our experience—and many of our needs—lie outside the realm of mere rational thought and verbal expression. These experiences and needs are best expressed in symbolic, nonverbal ways.

Further, not all spiritual realities can be understood intellectually or expressed verbally. Such mysteries of our faith are best represented by symbols that point to these realities rather than try to explain them.

Although much of God's communication with the world has been verbal, his supreme self-revelation was Jesus, the Word made flesh in a living, concrete way. Through this incarnation, God reaffirmed that created matter is good and not to be disdained as "unspiritual." God also demonstrated in Jesus what might be called the *sacramental* principle: the truth that he can use what is natural, physical, and human as the vehicle for what is supernatural, spiritual, and divine. Spoken words, physical touch, even humble inanimate matter like the hem of a garment or clay mixed with spittle, can be channels of God's love, power, and grace.

Through the ages, sacramental theology and practice has reflected these truths with its insistence that worship must involve more than mere words and rational categories. The church has looked to concrete symbols—the carved wood of a cross, the light of candles, the smell of incense—to represent the mysteries of salvation, revelation, and communion with God in prayer. It has also used the material elements in the sacraments—such as the bread of the Eucharist and the water of baptism—to be channels of the grace that the sacraments point to.

Sadly enough, Western philosophy—deeply influenced by pagan Greek thought—developed a rationalist orientation over the centuries that disdained human emotion and viewed human beings as spiritual intellects trapped in unspiritual physical bodies.

For many, theology lost its mystery and became a pseudo-science that attempted to corral God in rational categories and reduce divine revelation to verbal propositions.

The eighteenth-century movement called the Enlightenment, whose leaders often attacked Christian faith, demonstrated this philosophical direction most clearly. But the seeds of the problem had already germinated in the Reformation, when the Reformers reacted to medieval excesses in the church by exalting the role of the intellect and the written Word in Christian experience.

This tendency in Christian circles reaches its climax in the so-called liberalism and fundamentalism of the twentieth century. Though these two movements appear to be in opposition, they are actually mirror images of the same rationalist system that seeks to reduce both God and humanity to manageable proportions. The result: Both liberals and fundamentalists typically disdain mystery and deny the role of the supernatural in human affairs.

In an important sense, then, the Pentecostal and charismatic movements came as a reversal of this deadly rationalizing tendency in the modern church. Holy Spirit baptism, leading to experiences of nonrational tongues and unexplainable miracles, reintroduced Christians to the mystery of God and his exaltation over our understanding. In addition, the Pentecostals and their heirs recaptured the truth that the human being is body and emotions as well as intellect. They testified that God was interested in physical and emotional healing, and that worship involved not just our minds, but also our emotions and bodies. Furthermore, charismatics found that God could work mightily through the spoken word and the laying on of hands, the anointing oil and the prayer cloth—that is, they rediscovered the sacramental nature of the Christian life.

Little wonder, then, that many nondenominational charismatics have begun putting down roots in the traditions of the church. They've been nourished by its sacramental realities all along, though few probably realized it until now.

The danger, of course, is that the new liturgical charismatics may replace the power of Pentecost with formal structures of worship, rather than synthesizing the two. But if they can succeed in combining the fertile soil with the life-giving water and sunlight of the Spirit, we may soon witness a thrilling transformation in the vineyard of the Lord.

**Paul Thigpen**[15]

## 157 ✦ THE PRAISE-AND-WORSHIP RENEWAL

*"Praise and worship" is a phrase used to designate a worship style that draws on contemporary choruses, usually in a flowing or connected sequence. The praise-and-worship style is influenced by charismatic worship and often features the lifting of hands in praise, ministry through the laying on of hands, and an inviting and informal climate in worship.*

A new style of worship has been spreading throughout North America and other parts of the world in the last several decades. While this approach to worship goes by a variety of names, the designation that seems to be gaining most acceptance is "praise and worship" (P&W). This discussion seeks to explain what this style of worship is and how it may affect traditional worship in the future.

### Where Did "Praise and Worship" Originate?

P&W emerged from several trends in the sixties and early seventies. These trends include the perception some people have that traditional worship forms are dead. Along with that conviction goes a concern for an immediacy of the Spirit, a desire for intimacy, and a persuasion that music and informality must connect with people of a post-Christian culture.

One of the earliest expressions of these trends was the rise of testimonial music through the leadership of Bill Gaither in the early 1960s. Songs such as "He Touched Me," "There's Something About That Name," "Let's Just Praise the Lord," and "Because He Lives" touched many lives and introduced people to a new genre of music. At first these were performance songs, but soon they became congregational: people sang along or at least joined in on the refrain. A second expression of these trends came in the late 1960s on the West Coast (and all over the world) in the "Jesus movement." A major emphasis of this movement was the singing of praise choruses, some of which were written and sung right on the spot.

Since those early days in the 1960s and early 1970s, this form of music and the style of worship it has engendered have developed into a new worldwide approach to worship.

## Characteristics of the Praise and Worship Movement

While the exact origins of the P&W tradition are ambiguous, the movement itself is not difficult to describe.

First, P&W moves beyond a post-Enlightenment-style expression of worship. Since the eighteenth century, Western thought has been influenced by the Enlightenment's rationalistic and scientific explanations of our existence. Worship influenced by the Enlightenment is essentially cerebral, appealing to the mind and to the intellectual side of our beings. It is "left-brained." In contrast, P&W touches the affective side of the person. It is "right-brained," reaching into the feelings and emotions of the human personality. However, it is not correct to dismiss it as merely emotional worship or as worship lacking in content or biblical foundation.

Indeed, a second characteristic of P&W is that it seeks to recapture the lost element of praise found in both Old and New Testament worship. It stands in the tradition of the Talmud, saying "Man should always utter praises, and then pray." Praise God first and foremost, *then* move on to the other elements of worship, say the proponents of P&W.

## Distinguishing Praise from Worship

A major feature of the P&W movement is its tendency to distinguish praise from worship. Judson Cornwall, a P&W leader and author of more than a half-dozen books, addresses the distinction between praise and worship in his book *Let Us Worship* (1983). Cornwall argues that the Scriptures present praise as something different than worship, and he cites Psalm 95 as a good example of this distinction. In the opening verses, the psalmist invites praise:

> Come, let us sing for joy to the LORD;
>   let us shout aloud to the Rock of our salvation.
> Let us come before him with thanksgiving
>   and extol him with music and song (vv. 1-2).

Only then, *after* praise has been offered, does the psalmist invite worship:

> Come, let us bow down in worship,
>   let us kneel before the Lord our Maker (v. 6).

So Cornwall concludes that "the order is praise first, worship second" (p. 143).

"Praise," Cornwall writes, "prepares us for worship"; it is a "prelude to worship." Praise is not an attempt to get something from God; it is a ministry that we offer to God. We offer praise for what God has done—for God's mighty deeds in history and his continued providential presence in our lives.

While we praise God for what he has done, we worship God for who he is. The one extols the acts of God, the other the person and character of God. Cornwall clarifies this distinction between praise and worship:

> Praise begins by applauding God's power, but it often brings us close enough to God that worship can respond to God's presence. While the energy of praise is toward what God does, the energy of worship is toward who God is. The first is concerned with God's performance, while the second is occupied with God's personage. The thrust of worship, therefore, is higher than the thrust of praise (p. 146).

## The Temple Sequence

The order of the service, the swing from praise to worship, is patterned after the movement in the Old Testament tabernacle and temple from the outer court to the inner court and then into the Holy of Holies. All of these steps are accomplished through song. The song leader (or the worship leader, as she or he is more often called) plays a significant role in moving the congregation through the various steps that lead to worship.

He or she begins with choruses of personal experience or testimony, such as "This is the Day the Lord Has Made" or "We Bring Sacrifices of Praise into the House of the Lord." These songs center on praise, are all upbeat in tempo, and relate to the personal experience of the believer. They are songs that often mention "I," "me," or "we." In the tabernacle typology, during this first step the people are still outside the fence that surrounds the tabernacle. They cannot worship until they come through the gates into the tabernacle court.

This movement by way of song prepares us for what takes place in the second step: the mood and the content of the music shift to express the action of entering the gates and coming into the courts. Here the song leader leads people in songs that express the transition from praise to worship. These are songs of *thanksgiving,* such as the Scripture song from Psalm 100: "I will enter his gates with thanksgiving in my heart, I will enter his courts with praise" or "Come let us worship and bow down, let us kneel before the Lord our God, our Maker."

According to Cornwall:

It is a matter of bringing them from a consciousness of what has been done in them and for them (testimony) to who did it in and for them (thanksgiving). The procession through the eastern gate into the outer court should be a joyful march, for thanks should never be expressed mournfully or negatively. While the people are singing choruses of thanksgiving, they will be thinking both of themselves and of their God, but by putting the emphasis upon the giving of thanks, the majority of the thought patterns should be on their God. Singing at this level will often be a beginning level of praise, but it will not produce worship, for the singers are not yet close enough to God's presence to express a worship response" (p. 156).

The third step, into the Holy of Holies, brings the believer away from himself or herself into a full conscious worship of God alone. No longer is the worshiper thinking about what God has done, but rather of who God is in person and character. A quiet devotion hovers over the congregation as they sing songs such as "Father, I Adore You," "I Love You, Lord" and "You Are Worthy." In these moments of worship "the emotional clapping will likely be replaced with devotional response of upturned faces, raised hands, tears, and even a subtle change in the timbre of the voices." For when there is an "awareness that we have come into the presence of God, we step out of lightness with sobriety" (p. 157).

The third phase of the sequence is often described as an experience of "the manifest presence of God." This experience does not differ greatly from the liturgical experience of the presence of Christ at the Lord's table. In this atmosphere, the *charismata,* or gifts of God, are released, and, just as men and women throughout the history of the church have experienced physical and spiritual healing while partaking of the table of Christ, so many today are tasting of special manifestations of the Holy Spirit in worship renewal as he inhabits, i.e., settles down, makes his home, and abides in the praises of his people (Ps. 22:3).

## Variations

While the tabernacle/temple order of worship is quite prominent in praise and worship churches, it is not the only order or sequence of song. For example, the Vineyard Church in Anaheim, California, is a church that fits into the broader category of the P&W tradition of worship. Worship there has a slightly different variation of the progression that brings a worshiper into God's presence.

Vineyard Church worship begins with an *invitation phase,* which is like a call to worship. Songs of invitation such as "I Just Came to Praise the Lord" may be sung with clapping, swinging the body, and looking at other worshipers, smiling and acknowledging their presence.

In the next movement, the *engagement phase,* the people are brought closer to God, and their songs are addressed to him, not to one another. A good example may be "Humble Yourself in the Sight of the Lord."

The song leader then moves the people into the *adoration phase.* In this stage of worship the broad range of pitch and melody that characterized the previous phases is exchanged for the smaller range of music and the more subdued tone of songs such as "Jesus, Jesus, There's Something About that Name" or "Father, I Adore You."

Next, the congregation is led into the *intimacy* phase, which is the quietest and most personal part of worship. Songs such as "O Lord, You're Beautiful" and "Great Are You, Lord" are personal statements of an intimate relationship directed from the believer to the Lord. As these songs are sung, people become highly intense and lose themselves in the ecstasy of the moment. During this phase of the worship service that I attended at the Vineyard Church, people stood with heads and hands turned upward and eyes closed as they sang these songs of what John Wimber calls "love-making to God." Some people, especially in the front rows, were kneeling or even prostrate on the floor during this "quiet time."

The final phase of the Vineyard worship progression is a *closeout* song, a song that helps the people move out of the experience of being transfixed on God to prepare for the next segment of the service, the time of teaching.

### Praise, Worship, Teaching, Prayer, Ministry

It is common in the P&W tradition of worship to distinguish between the various acts of a typical service. The most significant distinction is that of praise from worship, as described above. Other acts in the service include the time for teaching, the time for intercessory prayer, and the time for ministry.

Because most P&W churches are informal, the various acts of the service are done in an informal way. For example, while teaching is fairly straightforward, it may end with a time of brief feedback or discussion (depending on the size of the congregation).

Intercessory prayer may also be informal. The idea of the traditional pastoral prayer may be replaced by a prayer circle. After prayer, many churches enter a time of ministry. People are sent into various rooms where those gifted with ministry for particular needs lay hands on them and pray for hurt and broken lives as from the Master's hand. What is experienced in this setting can be very meaningful, ministering in a powerful way to the people of God.

### Response to Praise and Worship

Broadly speaking, traditional churches have responded to the spread of P&W in three ways.

First are those churches that have not responded at all—perhaps because they are not consciously aware of the P&W tradition. These congregations may have heard one or two P&W-style songs and be vaguely aware of the existence of such a style of worship in nontraditional churches, but for the most part they are impervious to P&W.

Second are those congregations who are more aware of the P&W traditions but are indifferent to it or who actively dismiss it, arguing that it is "too superficial" or "too charismatic."

The third set of traditional churches are not only aware of P&W and its relevancy to a post-Enlightenment culture but also seek to integrate this new approach to worship into the local church.

Robert E. Webber[16]

## 158 • THE CONVERGENCE MOVEMENT

*The breakdown of denominational distinctions has led to a convergence of many worship traditions. Broadly speaking, traditional and contemporary worship are blending to create a new celebrative style of worship. Advocates of liturgical renewal draw on liturgical/sacramental, charismatic, and evangelical aspects of the Christian faith to develop a style of worship that is rooted in Scripture, aware of its history, and committed to relevance.*

"Therefore every teacher of the law who has been instructed about the kingdom of heaven is like the owner of a house who brings out of his storeroom new treasures as well as old" (Matt. 13:52).

This verse of Scripture summarizes the insight and discovery which has led to a fresh stream of thought and renewal throughout the wider body of Christ. Described as the convergence movement (CM), or "convergence of the streams," this emerging trend appears to many, both observers and participants, to be another contemporary evidence of God's continuing activity in history to renew, replenish, and unify his people in one heart and purpose in Christ. Arising out of a common desire and hunger to experience the fullness of Christian worship and spirituality, CM seeks to blend or merge the essential elements in the Christian faith, represented by three major streams of thought and practice: the liturgical/sacramental, the evangelical/Reformed, and the charismatic. An increasing number of local congregations and leaders from many backgrounds are finding "treasures old and new" in the spiritual heritage of the church universal.

The table on the following page illustrates the essential elements and emphases being drawn upon by the majority of those currently participating in the movement.

The blending or converging of these traditions is seen by those involved as the work of God the Holy Spirit imparting a spiritual operation of grace best captured in the vision of Psalm 46:4: "There is a river whose streams make glad the city of God, the holy place where the Most High dwells." Thus, the "city of God" is seen as the church, the rivers as the action and flow of God's presence through his church and the many "streams" as the expressions of the one river's life that have developed or broken off from the main river through history, all of which are necessary to enrich and make glad the city with the fullness of God's life, power, purpose, and presence. These tributaries now appear to be converging into a main stream.

Anglican minister David Watson once wrote,

This break with Rome (the Reformation), although probably inevitable due to the corruption of the time, unfortunately led to split after split within the Body of Christ, with the result that the mission of the Church is today seriously handicapped by the bewildering plethora of endless denominations. . . . A torn and divided Christianity is, nevertheless, a scandal for which all Christians need deeply to repent" (*I Believe in the Church* [Grand Rapids: Eerdmans, 1979], 27).

This call to be one undergirds the desire of many in CM to see the streams of the church come together. Wayne Boosahda and Randy Sly of Hosanna Church of the King, one of the key churches in the Kansas City area reflecting the impact of the movement, have expressed the conviction that "out of the days of the Reformation, we see God's heart now moving in a kind of 'reverse reformation,' or restoration, of His One, Holy, Catholic and Apostolic Church."

## History of Emergence and Growth

The convergence movement has clear antecedents in two major movements of spiritual and worship renewal: the charismatic movement and the liturgical renewal movement in both Catholic and mainline Protestant churches. The charismatic renewal began in the early 1960s primarily within mainline denominations. Those in the renewal saw a blending of charismatic or Pentecostal elements, such as healing, prophecy, and spontaneous worship and praise, with the more traditional elements of mainline (and, eventually, Roman Catholic) liturgical practices.

What some have called the "third wave" or "signs and wonders movement" began about 1978 with the emergence of the ministry of John Wimber and the Vineyard Churches that arose through his influence. James Robison, Jim Hylton, Ras Robinson, and other Southern Baptist leaders witnessed a "third wave" explosion in the "fullness movement," which primarily impacted their denomination. Peter Wagner and others from Fuller Theological Seminary solidified the movement through their writings, which acted as a filter and focal point. The "third wave" has been described by some as an epilogue to the charismatic renewal, bringing together charismatic elements of worship, experience and practice with the evangelical tradition.

The other key influence upon CM has been the liturgical renewal movement, which arose originally in the nineteenth century in Roman Catholic circles in France and in the Oxford or Tractarian Movement in the Church of England. The liturgical renewal caused a resurgence of interest in recapturing the essence, spirit, and shape of ancient Christian worship, as practiced and understood by the church of the first eight centuries. Particular emphasis was placed upon the fathers of the ancient, undivided church until about A.D. 390. The recovery of the theology and practice of worship and ministry during that fertile era overflowed into the mainline Protestant churches and began to have major impact upon them, from the 1950s onward, when several denominations developed their own platforms for liturgical reform.

A common component in the current CM, which came from these earlier movements, is a strong sense of concern for unity in the whole of Christ's body, the church. While not associated with the official ecumenical movement, those involved in CM seem broadly gripped by the hunger and desire to learn from traditions of worship and spirituality other than their own and to integrate these discoveries into their own practice and experience in the journey of faith. Indeed, leaders in the fledgling movement often describe their experience as a compelling "journey" or "pilgrimage." Many times, in very unsought-after ways, "sovereign" events, relationships, books, or insights have given rise to an

| Liturgical/Sacramental | Charismatic | Evangelical/Reformed |
|---|---|---|
| Theology | Biblical Foundation | Fivefold Ministry and Government |
| Orthodoxy | Personal Conversion | |
| Universality | Evangelism and Mission | Power of the Spirit |
| Historic Connection | Pulpit-centered Worship | Spiritual Gifts |
| Liturgical Worship | Personal Holiness | Charismatic Worship |
| Social Action | | Kingdom |
| Incarnational Understanding of the Church (based on theology, history, and sacrament) | Biblical and Reformational Understanding of the Church (pragmatic and rational) | Spiritual, Organic, and Functional Understanding of the Church (dynamic and informal) |

understanding of the church that is quite different from previous perspectives and backgrounds. One case in point is Richard Foster, a Quaker by background, whose personal pilgrimage led him to write the classic *Celebration of Discipline,* in which he unfolds an integrated practice of spiritual disciplines drawn from five basic traditions of spirituality in the church through history. As a result of his developing interest, Foster convened a conference called "Renovare," which gathered in Wichita, Kansas in 1988. The conference was a direct precursor to the "convergence of streams" concept.

The convergence movement was not openly recognized until about 1985. Many in the movement have discovered others on the "journey" from various church backgrounds who had similar or identical experiences and insights. One by one, congregations and leaders have found one another, underlining the sense that God is doing something on a grass-roots level similar to an underground river about to break out onto the surface.

Key contemporary pioneers shaping the thought of the movement are men like Dr. Robert Webber, author and professor of theology at Wheaton College; Dr. Robert Stamps, former chaplain of Oral Roberts University; Peter Gillquist, former leader with Campus Crusade for Christ and now an Eastern Orthodox priest and evangelist; Bishop Earl Paulk, pastor of Atlanta's 12,000-member Chapel Hill Harvester Church; Howard Snyder, theologian, author, and Christian educator; Stan White, former Assembly of God pastor, now an Episcopal priest; and others, such as the late David DuPlessis, Pentecostal minister and key instigator of the charismatic ecumenical dialogue between Roman Catholics and Pentecostals; current Archbishop of Canterbury, George Carey; members of the United Methodist liturgical Order of St. Luke; and Peter Hocken, Roman Catholic theologian. Although all of these individuals from diverse backgrounds are not actively involved in CM, all have helped shape and influence the vision, thought, and developing practice of those who are.

Noted classical Pentecostal and charismatic leader Earl Paulk has boldly declared both publicly and in his books (*Spiritual Megatrends* and *The Church: Trampled or Triumphant*), that today God is calling for a merging of "form with power." He also has strongly advocated a return to understanding the supernatural power of God's presence and grace available to believers in the sacraments of the church. Paulk and his staff have implemented this convergence perspective in many creative ways through the use of the arts, clerical collars and vestments, blended musical styles, and an increased use of liturgy in Sunday morning services. An early service is now held, called "Charismatic Mass," which is basically a Rite II Eucharist service straight out of *The Book of Common Prayer.*

Robert Webber has written a number of books on the history and practice of Christian worship: *Worship Old and New, Worship Is a Verb,* and *Signs of Wonder: The Phenomenon of Convergence in the Modern Liturgical and Charismatic Churches,* all of which have been highly influential on those involved in the movement. His book *Evangelicals on the Canterbury Trail,* which describes a trend of evangelical Christians moving toward liturgical churches, and the reasons why, was one of the first discoveries for many who are now clearly operating within a convergence perspective.

Greater public awareness of the new movement came through Stan White, a young fourth-generation Assembly of God pastor from Valdosta, Georgia. White caused a major stir when he took his entire independent charismatic congregation into the Episcopal church. The story was written up in the September 24, 1990 issue of *Christianity Today* (Randall Balmer, "Why the Bishops Went to Valdosta," 19–24) and in the April 1991 issue of *Charisma,* the major magazine of the charismatic movement.

Peter Gillquist, a former Campus Crusade for Christ leader in the 1960s, left the collegiate movement with a number of other fellow leaders, searching for the real New Testament church. Gillquist's book, *Becoming Orthodox: A Journey to The Ancient Christian Faith,* chronicled their fascinating journey of over 15 years of seeking, studying, and researching the early church. Their discoveries led them to full reception into the Antiochian Orthodox Church. Two thousand evangelical/charismatic believers from various backgrounds who made up the membership of the fifteen congregations they had founded also became part of that church.

As news of these events and additional materials began to circulate, others on the "pilgrimage," as many had begun to identify it, took heart that God was indeed at work. Leaders and participants in CM were, in fact, increasingly relieved to discover they were not the only ones thinking this way or being compelled by the vision. In a quite unexpected way,

God seemed to be confirming his call and initiation towards the possibility of unity in the body of Christ, in conformity with the spirit of Jesus' prayer in John 17 and his statement in John 10:16: "I have other sheep that are not of this sheep pen; I must bring them also. They too will listen to my voice, and there shall be one flock and one shepherd." The movement seemed to promise a unity that would not only leap boundaries, but would also lead to an enlargement and enrichment of the faith, vision, worship, and practice of the fullness of Christ in his church.

Two key clusters of local congregations that represent and reflect the vision, values, and developing practices of CM are found in the metropolitan Kansas City area and in Oklahoma City. Hosanna Church of the King, founded in 1988 in the Kansas City area as an independent, "third wave" charismatic congregation, was instrumental in stirring interest and building relationship, locally and regionally, in response to the convergence of streams awakening. Planted and established by Wayne and Stephanie Boosahda, the church is now pastored by Randy and Sandy Sly, who have worked together with the Boosahdas to foster awareness of this fresh work of God's Spirit. Others in the Kansas City area being influenced in the convergence direction include Episcopal, independent charismatic, evangelical holiness, and mainline Protestant congregations and their leaders. Pastors Ron McCrary of Christ Episcopal Church and Randall Davey of Overland Park Church of the Nazarene are two others in the metropolitan area who have been impacted by convergence thought and practice.

In Oklahoma City, pastors Mike and Beth Owen of Church of the Holy Spirit, formerly a "third wave" Vineyard Christian Fellowship, and Dr. Robert Wise and wife Marguerite of Community Church of the Redeemer have, along with their congregations, made a formative impact on the area, as they have shared their journeys with other congregations and leaders, especially within liturgical and charismatic circles. They also developed strong ties with the CM groups of Kansas City, formalizing the national and transdenominational focus on the movement's essential vision and values. These churches and leaders, together with a number of others across the wider church of Jesus Christ, are convinced they are involved in something of historic significance and promise for the "one, holy, catholic and apostolic church" of Jesus Christ in our time.

## Common Elements of Convergence Churches

Those who are being drawn into this convergence of streams can be characterized by several common elements. While these are not exhaustive or in any order of importance, they form the basis for the focus and direction of the convergence movement.

**1. A Restored Commitment to the Sacraments, Especially the Lord's Table.** Those from the evangelical and charismatic streams of the church have not traditionally emphasized the sacramental dimension of the church. In fact, for some churches, Holy Baptism and Holy Communion have been seen more as ordinances than sacraments—commands by the Lord that must be undertaken by the church, but for no other purpose than that of obedience.

From a more sacramental view, these two expressions of church life are seen as holy and sacred unto the Lord, a symbol with true spiritual meaning used as a point of contact between man and God. The Lord's presence and power are released in these acts as the worshiper encounters God through the elements.

**2. An Increased Motivation to Know More about the Early Church.** For many Christians a vacuum exists between the New Testament era and the contemporary church, resulting in a disconnected body with no historic heritage. Like a boat adrift, the church can no longer explain who she is, where she came from, or why she exists. A recent shift in perspective has sent Christians searching for their roots, in order to find a common connection to the greater whole in God's kingdom.

Studying the early church has given many an opportunity to see New Testament principles being applied by those who were discipled by the Twelve and those who followed them. These writings provide a window into an earlier time, explaining how the early church approached faith and practice, how it worshiped, and how it established leadership for a growing movement. It is believed that the bloodline of the body of Christ can be traced through succeeding generations, revealing both the successes and failures in faith.

**3. A Love for the Whole Church and a Desire to See the Church as One.** The various expressions of Christianity have remained distinct for years because of sectarianism and denominational separatism. Convergence churches are looking beyond these artificial barriers to learn more about the uniqueness of the many bodies of faith. Jesus' prayer in John 17 was that the church might become one: one as the body of Christ, not through compromise of doctrine and dogma, but through unity under the person of Jesus Christ, unity amidst our diversity. This sense of oneness does not require any church to dismiss its unique expression as Christ's body, but calls each one to appreciate and embrace the variety and beauty of the church worldwide and throughout history.

Convergence churches appreciate the gifts that each stream of the church provides to the whole. The call of CM churches is to "be one," to move together in presenting a people united under Christ to reach a hurting world.

### 4. The Blending in the Practice of All Three Streams Is Evident, Yet Each Church Approaches Convergence from a Unique Point of View.

A church does not necessarily have to change its identity when it becomes a part of a convergence movement. Most convergence churches have a dominant base, one particular expression of the church that regulates the others. They can still look very Episcopalian, Orthodox, Baptist, Nazarene, independent charismatic, and so on, while including additional elements of worship and ministry from other streams.

Three different types of convergence churches seem to be most common today: blended churches, inclusion churches, and network churches. *Blended churches* have maintained their original identity, denominational connection, and theological distinctives. From this base they add to their worship and ministry practices and elements from the other two streams. While most often found among liturgical/sacramental churches, blended churches are found in evangelical and charismatic streams as well. Overland Park Church of the Nazarene, in the Kansas City metroplex, is involved in convergence, yet remains strongly identified with its denominational heritage.

*Inclusion churches* are those which have undergone a metamorphosis through their involvement in the convergence movement. Primarily from charismatic or evangelical backgrounds, these churches have found themselves so closely identifying with another stream of the church that they have realigned themselves; some have even become a part of liturgical/sacramental denominations. Church of the King in Valdosta, Georgia, mentioned above, is probably the best-known inclusion church of recent years.

*Networked churches* are churches which, having become a part of the CM, have left their former associations but chosen to remain independent. Their connections are based on strong relationships with other like-minded congregations. Most networked churches have come out of the charismatic stream.

### 5. An Interest in Integrating Structure with Spontaneity in Worship.

As God's Spirit continues to move powerfully in the world, new wineskins (structures) are required to contain the power and potential of God's new wine. Most Christian futurists expected these new wineskins to take the form of more open and spontaneous churches with a de-emphasized structure. The spirit of independence so characteristic of North American Christians especially, suggests that this would be like pouring wine into a fish net!

God's holy fire is now being kindled in furnaces of faith where liturgical forms, once considered lifeless, are no longer creating the fear of moving into error. Liturgies are being reintroduced into the church to bring a balance in worship among all the elements Scripture revealed as necessary for worshiping God in spirit and truth. The word "liturgy" literally means the "work of the people." Through the introduction of liturgical elements, worship becomes the work of the body in praise, repentance, the hearing of the Word, and the celebration of Christ's death and resurrection. Within these forms room can always be found for the spontaneous moving of the Spirit.

The historic creeds of the church, especially the Apostle's Creed and the Nicene Creed, are once again giving the body of Christ the foundational roots of orthodoxy. *The Book of Common Prayer* and other liturgical resources are also being blended with spontaneous praise and worship in convergence churches. The Lord's Supper is being celebrated with a greater understanding of the sacredness of the event, and churches are following the Christian year and liturgical calendar more consistently as a means of taking congregations on an annual journey of faith. All of these expressions give local fellowships a greater sense of connection with the church worldwide and with the church through history.

**6. A Greater Involvement of Sign and Symbol in Worship.** The contemporary church has begun to reclaim the arts for Christ. Signs and symbols point beyond themselves to a greater truth and serve as contact points for apprehending inward spiritual reality. Banners and pageantry have found a new place in the church. Crosses and candles now adorn processionals in some churches that, for years, had looked on pageantry as the death-knell of a vital faith. Crosses and Christian art are appearing in contexts where they had been absent before. Pastors from formerly "free church" backgrounds are now wearing clerical collars and vestments in worship celebrations. The collar serves as a sign of the spiritual reality of being yoked with Christ—of identifying with and speaking to the church as a whole.

**7. A Continuing Commitment to Personal Salvation, Biblical Teaching, and the Work and Ministry of the Holy Spirit.** Some who watch the new direction of CM from the evangelical or charismatic sidelines are still skeptical. They are concerned that convergence churches are abandoning their heritage, and that the values of biblical infallibility and personal conversion will be lost or compromised in pursuit of the liturgical/sacramental side of the Christian heritage. Often this concern arises out of negative prior personal experiences with certain expressions of the church or from stereotypes. Those watching from the liturgical/sacramental side are equally as concerned about their churches' embrace of more conservative or "fundamentalist" expressions of faith and practice.

The convergence movement is definitely not the abandonment of a stream but a convergence of streams. The work of God is inclusive, not exclusive, bringing forth from each tributary those things which he has authenticated. Such issues as evangelism, missions, and the work of ministry by the power of the Spirit remain intact in this journey. The Spirit's power continues to be released in marvelous ways in people's lives, bringing about conversion, healing, release from bondages, and change in the direction of life.

The church's rich and vital heritage in the power and primacy of the scriptural Word has been more completely undergirded as churches give more time in worship to the corporate reading of the Bible. This practice fulfills Paul's admonition to Timothy to "devote yourself to the public reading of Scripture, to preaching and to teaching" (1 Tim. 4:13).

Ironically, on Sunday mornings more Scripture is usually read in a traditional liturgical service than in most evangelical or charismatic gatherings.

## Future Trends

It appears that the future of the church will be greatly affected by the convergence movement. Walls between groups and denominations are already becoming veils which can be torn open, giving those from the different branches of the church greater opportunity to experience one another's faith and practice. We can suggest some things to expect by way of future developments.

As the convergence movement expands, mainline denominations will find their numbers reinforced and their churches revitalized. As people who are aware of the power of ancient forms of Christian worship join these churches, their devotion will be contagious, reawakening the spiritual life of those who have lost their enthusiasm.

Formal and informal educational tracks in the various streams can now become much broader in scope, addressing issues that traditionally have been emphasized in other sections of the church, such as sacramental theology and practice, rites of initiation, patrology, the work of the Holy Spirit, evangelism, and outreach.

The convergence movement will open up greater opportunities for shared facilities and ministry. The architecture and layout of newly designed churches will be more accommodating to the worship elements of the different streams of Christian tradition. Approaches to ministry will also converge, allowing a greater diversity of churches to work together for evangelism, discipleship, social action, and body life.

The Old Testament's final verses (in English versions) contain the promise that the spirit of Elijah will turn the hearts of the fathers to the children and the hearts of the children to their fathers. While this passage has been used in recent years to focus on the need to return to family values, we see another application: the expression of hope that a new spirit in the church will turn the hearts of this generation of believers back toward the apostolic fathers and others who formed and fashioned vital faith in the centuries following the ascension of Christ. These leaders envisioned and worked for a Christianity that was orthodox and durable, generation upon generation, operating in loyal adherence to the revelation of Christ for his church. The church of the twentieth century now eagerly looks back to these fathers of faith and discovers new life in the forms and structures God built in their midst.

**Randy Sly and Wayne Boosahda**

## 159 • THE SEEKERS' SERVICE/BELIEVERS' WORSHIP MOVEMENT

*A central feature of the seekers' service/believers' worship movement is the clear distinction it makes between outreach services (called seekers' services) and services designed for believers (believers' worship). This approach to renewal, pioneered by Willow Creek Community Church in South Barrington, Illinois, now commands a worldwide following.*

Willow Creek Community Church began with a vision for a new relevance for God's church today. It originated from a small youth group in South Park Church in Park Ridge, Illinois, a northwest suburb of Chicago. This high school group was called Son City.

Bill Hybels, a student at Trinity College in Deerfield, Illinois, in the early 1970s, began developing Son City for unbelievers and Son Village for believers. With him was a core of committed students who shared his vision for reaching their friends with the gospel in new ways. Within a few years, the ministry numbered in the hundreds.

After his graduation from college, Hybels, in conjunction with Dr. Gilbert Bilezikian, who at that time taught at Trinity College, and the group of men and women that led Son City, developed the Willow Creek Church. Their aim was to expand the outreach to include the parents of the young people with whom they ministered in Son City. Their larger purpose and approach was threefold. First, they wanted to create and maintain a biblical community similar to what the church originally experienced, as recorded in the book of Acts. Hybels and the others did not want to "reinvent the wheel," but to make it roll more smoothly. Second, they aimed to reach the unchurched seekers, who realized there was something more to life than they had experienced. This could not be done, they felt, using the same worship format most churches used; innovation was required. Third, they were committed to the view that the cause of Christ is worthy of full devotion. This involved not only a commitment to win lost souls to Christ and make disciples of them,

but also a commitment to doing these things in attractive and polished ways. From the very beginning, Willow Creek's music and drama ministries—the backbone of its outreach to seekers, along with Hybels' practical and down-to-earth teaching—were marked by high professional standards.

For several years the church met in a suburban movie theater (from which it derived its name "Willow Creek"), an ideal environment for avoiding the "churchy" feeling that might intimidate the very group Hybels and his associates were trying to reach. During this time the leadership made a basic distinction between nontraditional seekers' services on weekends and "new community" services for believers in midweek. The team surveyed their suburban target group to assess what was essential, and what was not, in attracting new believers. They wanted to remove any social or traditional church barrier which would keep people away.

Today Willow Creek Church continues to create a "safe" atmosphere in which to challenge and confront the seeker concerning his or her need for God's salvation. Weekend worship continues to be something of a stage production, with minimal congregational involvement in singing or other liturgical actions. The large congregations and the theater format enable new attendees to slip into the crowd in more comfortable anonymity, until they come to feel more "at home" with the Christian faith. When the offering is received, the leader emphasizes that visitors are the church's guests and should not feel obligated to contribute. A more intense worship session, attended by the growing body of believers who form the core group of the church, is held in midweek.

Over the years, as attendance grew from hundreds to thousands, a "campus" was erected in South Barrington, Illinois, not far from where the church started, on land donated by an enthusiastic supporter. The church structure has no overt Christian symbols; from the outside it looks like a corporate headquarters or a large high school, and the auditorium has the ambiance of a theater. There are six services a week, with a total of more than 20,000 in attendance. Many of the original leaders still play an important part in Willow Creek Church. Nearly 300 full- and part-time staff members work with hundreds of volunteers involved in almost ninety different ministries. A variety of events take place every day and on most evenings. Another unarticulated goal has been reached: the church certainly is lived in.

Steve Burdan

## 160 • BIBLIOGRAPHY ON WORSHIP RENEWAL IN THE 20TH CENTURY

Dayton, Donald, ed. _"The Higher Christian Life":_ _Sources for the Study of the Holiness, Pentecostal,_ _and Keswick Movements._ New York: Garland, 1985. A bibliographic overview of all Holiness and Pentecostal movements, their theology, and their worship.

Robeck, Cecil M., Jr., ed. _Charismatic Experiences in History._ Peabody, Mass: Hendricksen Publishers, 1985. This book is a collection of essays on the charismatic experience. While it touches on particular historical periods, it is not a history or an exposition on the development of the charismatic experience throughout history. Articles deal with the charismatic experience in the New Testament, on historical figures such as Origen, and on movements such as the Pentecostal Revival of 1906.

Shephard, Lancelot, ed. _The People Worship: A History of the Liturgical Movement._ New York: Hawthorn Books, 1967. Explores the history of the Liturgical Movement; investigates the fundamental ideas of the liturgical revival, the advances made by the liturgical movement, and the documents of liturgical renewal.

Taylor, Michael J., ed. _Liturgical Renewal in the Christian Churches._ Baltimore: Helicon Press, 1967.

Webber, Robert. _Signs of Wonder._ Nashville: Abbott Martyn Press, 1992. This book develops the historical trends in Western culture and in the church that precipitated the rise of the Convergence Movement of worship. Webber discusses convergence in the context of Sunday worship, the arts, the Christian year, the sacraments, and areas of related ministry.

# PART THREE

# Historic Models of Worship

# ✤ EIGHT ✤

# Pre-Reformation Liturgies

This section provides the reader with an overview of the major liturgies and worship orders from the early church through the nineteenth century. (Twentieth-century models are found in Volume 3.)

Each article in Part 3 is has three distinctive features: Introduction, Text or Order or Worship, and Commentary. Each model is preceded by a brief introduction that puts the selection into its historical setting. For clarity, the text (or order of service) and the commentary are preceded by the words "Text" or "Commentary," respectively. The commentary provides insight into the worship and experience of the worshiping community. The material is arranged in a roughly chronological order so that the reader may gain a sense of the development of worship from the early church to the beginning of the twentieth century.

Worship of the early church period followed the forms of worship that emerged in the New Testament period, namely that of Word and Table. In the first three centuries, worship was simple and plain in comparison to the elaborate ceremonial that developed in the fourth and fifth centuries and that continued to develop in the Middle Ages.

In this chapter, ancient Christian forms of worship are described in the Didache, Justin Martyr, and The Apostolic Tradition attributed to Hippolytus. The more complex and elaborate worship of the later periods of history are illustrated in the Byzantine and Roman texts.

If we presented all the texts of this period of history, the material would take up volumes and volumes of books. The five texts with commentary included here, however, are sufficient to provide the reader with a sense of pre-Reformation worship.

## 161 ✦ THE DIDACHE (A.D. 100)

*The Didache probably represents the type of small Christian group that met in the region of Syria, perhaps outside of the city of Antioch. By the fifth century, this hilly countryside was dotted with small churches and baptistries, but in the late first century there were probably no buildings specifically designated as churches. Christianity was still a proscribed religion, and the Christians of a village or rural area gathered after work. Although they did not necessarily meet in secret, they certainly did not publicize their gathering loudly.*

### ——————— Introduction ———————

Sunday was a workday, and the Christians gathered after work for a potluck meal, known throughout the Mediterranean world as the *agape,* and for the Eucharist (literally, the thanksgiving), which was the ongoing celebration of the command of Jesus to break the bread and drink the cup in remembrance of him (1 Cor. 11:26). While the Agape-meal and the Eucharist were celebrated together, as early as the time of the *Didache,* Christian communities were distinguishing between the *agape* and the Eucharist, which was only for the baptized.

The description that follows is an imaginative reconstruction of what a first-century Christian service might have looked like. Many details of such a service remain unknown.

Text: *This is how to give thanks. First in connection with the cup:*

We give you thanks, our Father for the holy vine of David your servant, which you have made known to us through Jesus, your servant. Unto you be glory forevermore.

Commentary: After a full day of work on Sunday, the Christians of a small Syrian village gather for their weekly meeting in the house of their wealthiest member. The generosity of this elder in their community has made it possible to fit all forty members of the community together in the large courtyard and adjoining great room, built like all Syrian houses with a long, walled courtyard running along the south side of the home. Individually and in family groups, the community arrives at the locked gate leading from the dirt road into the paved courtyard, being admitted after knocking at the door by one of the local elders who receives their contribution of food and wine for the meal to come. Each person stops first at the fountain in the courtyard, where they wash their hands, face and feet, assisting those who are too young or too old to reach the water themselves. Making their way to the large room, the newcomers greet the other members of the community as they anxiously draw closer to meet the visiting teacher, an apostle visiting from the city of Antioch. Eventually, everyone crowds into the large room or along the covered portico, finding a cushion or rug on which to sit. Each group of eight or ten people is gathered around common pots of food, with baskets of flat bread which will serve as the dishes. At one end of the room, the visiting teacher sits on a cushion at a low table, talking with the host of the gathering.

Eventually one of the leaders calls the people to silence by intoning a psalm, which is sung alternating between the people and the leader. The words are known by heart to the gathered community. As the psalm draws to a close, the people rise, standing in prayer with their arms raised up.

**Text:**

> As this broken bread was scattered over the hills and then, when gathered, became one, so may your church be gathered from the ends of the earth into your kingdom. For yours is the glory and the power through Jesus Christ forevermore.

**Commentary**: After everyone has risen and stands attentive in prayer, the visiting prophet raises a large cup filled with wine and begins a prayer of thanks to God for the goodness of the earth and the gifts which come from God. The singsong chant, which provides the vehicle for the spontaneous prayer of the visiting teacher, is sung in the same way as the Jewish chants of meal blessings. He praises God for vines and vineyards and for the church, which is the vine grown since the time of David and revealed through Jesus. As he draws to a close, he hands the cup to the host standing next to him, resting his tired arms and signaling to the people to conclude the prayer with their sung consent to what has been done. Led once again by the same leader who began

the psalm, the community sings the acclamation: "To you be the glory forevermore," praising God with their own voices.

**Text**: *Let no one eat and drink of your Eucharist but those baptized in the name of the Lord; to this, too, the saying of the Lord is applicable: Do not give what is sacred to the dogs.*

**Commentary**: After the cup is returned to the low table, the visiting leader picks up a large loaf of bread and begins to chant a prayer over it, praising God for the goodness of the fields and the bounty represented by the loaf of bread. The single loaf of bread becomes a representation of the community gathered to pray on this Sunday evening. Like the grain which had once grown over the hillsides around their village and was then brought to a common threshing mill, they also have gathered in this meeting from various places and professions to become one worshiping community. The temptation to look around the room at this point in the prayer is always too great—it is easy to see in the variety of faces around the room the very image of the gathered church now being formed into a single entity. The prayer also calls the community to focus on the future; on that time when the church will be gathered together at the second coming for which everyone prays three times a day: "your kingdom come, your will be done."

As the prophet lowers the bread to the table, the community again sings their consent to the prayer by acclaiming: "For yours is the glory and the power through Jesus Christ forevermore."

**Text**: *After you have taken your fill of food, give thanks as follows:*

> We give you thanks, O holy Father, for your holy name which you have enshrined in our hearts, and for the knowledge and faith and immortality which you have made know to us through Jesus, your servant. To you be the glory forevermore.

**Commentary**: The members of the community standing near the visiting teacher bring cups and plates to the low table and begin to pour the wine from the large cup into the smaller ones. Others break the loaf of bread into smaller pieces to fit on the plates. In later centuries, the presider would proclaim "holy things for holy people" at this point, but even in this ancient church, all those present are reminded by their very presence and participation that they are the baptized, perhaps remembering their own baptismal experience, which was most likely celebrated as an adult.

After preparing the bread and cup of wine, the leaders of the local community, men and women chosen to serve because of their faith, wisdom, and perhaps because of their suffering for the name of Jesus, begin to move among the gathered Christians, distributing the bread and the wine to everyone present.

After everyone present has finished the bread and wine, people begin to return to their cushions and rugs, gathering around the common food pots and bread baskets. When the leader invites all to eat, everyone begins with great gusto—it is getting late and those who have had very little to eat this day, especially the poor who depend on these potluck meals for sustenance, rush into the food. The business of eating and drinking quiets the talk for a while, but as the food disappears and everyone feels comfortably full, the noise level rises and the people share the problems and joys of the past week with each other. Gradually, the dishes are cleared and cleaned in the fountain outdoors, the crumbs are shaken from the rugs and cushions, and the attention of the community members focuses once more on the visiting prophet, who has been regaling those within hearing distance during the meal with tales of the Christian heroes of Antioch in the face of sporadic persecutions by civil authorities.

**Text:**

Lord almighty, you have created all things for the sake of your name, and have given food and drink to all to enjoy that they may thank you. But to us you have given spiritual food and drink and eternal life through Jesus, your servant [or "child"].

**Commentary:** As the last of the dishes are cleaned and the last drop of wine is drunk (whether a specific "psalm leader" existed in the time of the _Didachē_ is doubtful), someone signals to the people to stand, and the prayer stance of outstretched arms is again adopted.

**Text:**

Above all, we give you thanks because you are mighty. To you be glory forevermore.

**Commentary:** The teacher continues the prayer of thanksgiving, focusing more particularly on God, revealed through the work and person of Jesus the Christ. Again, the gathered Christians are reminded of their own baptism, recalling the anointing with oil which "Christed" them, giving them the name of their adopted family. The response of the people, "to you be the glory forever," rings through the room.

**Text:**

Remember, O Lord, your church: Deliver it from all evil, perfect it in your love. Make it holy, and gather it together from the four winds into your kingdom which you have made ready for it. For yours is the power and the glory forevermore.

**Commentary:** The prayer continues, acknowledging the divine creation of all things, in contrast to the Gnostic groups who deny the goodness of creation and claim another god created the material realm. But the high point of the prayer is coming: In addition to all created goodness, God is now to be praised for providing the means to eternal life through Jesus. The spiritual food and drink which is the center of the Eucharist would be called the "medicine of immortality" by the bishop of Antioch, Ignatius, fifty years later. The seeds of his expression are already here in this gathering and in the prayer chanted by the leader.

**Text:** _May grace come and this world pass away!_

Hosanna to the God of David.

**Commentary:** As this long prayer reaches its culmination, recalling the chants of great feasts in the Jewish calendar, God is proclaimed as mighty, and the confident acclamation of the people gives them courage and strength to meet the challenges of the coming week. If God is truly the Lord of all and they are part of God's family, then surely they will be able to trust in God's continuing presence regardless of what confronts them.

**Text:**

If anyone is holy, let him come; if anyone is not, let him be converted.

**Commentary:** The prayer turns to petition for the church and for the return of Jesus. The prayer is expressive of the people's identity as the church—not a building, but a gathered group of the baptized, formed into one body like the one loaf of bread. This part of the prayer also reminds people that the church is larger than their small community; it is all the small communities of Christians scattered in the four winds who are united in prayer on this day and will be drawn together on the last day.

This last part of the longer prayer of thanksgiving ends with the same acclamation, sung with more elaboration than before. As this acclamation ends, a series of acclamations are sung back and forth between the visiting apostle and the people, expressing the belief of all Jewish Christians that the promised Messiah had indeed come. The leader in turn sings, reminding all present that not only is peace among themselves necessary, but that the gift of faith is given to people when they least expect it, and that the gift of faith demands a response to God.

**Text**: *Maranatha*
Amen.

**Commentary**: The dialogue ends with the acclamation, "Come, Lord (Jesus), let it be so!" Even today in this congregation there were people who had known the disciples of Jesus, and one old woman who had even heard Jesus himself speak. Because of her intimate connection with God, she is revered as highly as any elder, and her prayer of "Maranatha" has special poignancy: She longed to see Jesus once again, just as she had as a young woman.

**Text**: *But permit the prophets to give thanks as much as they wish.*

*On the day of the Lord, come together, break bread, and give thanks, having first confessed your sins, that your sacrifice may be pure. But let none who has a quarrel with his companion join with you until they have been reconciled, that your sacrifice may not be defiled. For this is that which was spoken by the Lord: "In every place and at every time offer me a pure sacrifice; for I am a great king, says the Lord, and my name is wonderful among the nations."*

**Commentary**: At the ending of the prayer, the visiting teacher from Antioch begins to greet the members of the community individually, moving among the gathering, blessing babies, congratulating new parents, and especially welcoming the newly baptized. The local leaders of the community—those who gathered the food, saw to it that the widows and orphans were fed, and organized the weekly *agape* and Eucharist—move with the Antiochene apostle through the crowd, introducing him to the members. Some of the Christians embrace his scarred hands and arms, injuries received when he was imprisoned and tortured for refusing to deny

Christ. His witness to the Messiah and his knowledge of Scripture, what later generations would call the Old Testament, make him a revered leader. When he leads the community in prayer, his spontaneous words, proclaimed within the structure of prayers inherited from Judaism, are recognized to be prophetic and true, representative of his faith and his personal experience of the Lord.

As evening turns into dark night, the members of the church begin to gather their children and belongings and prepare to go home. Tomorrow is another workday and it is getting late. The visiting apostle will stay the night at the home of the host, spending the next morning sharing news of the church in Antioch, such as the letters being read in Sunday gatherings in Antioch along with readings from Scripture, before moving on to a neighboring village where another group of Christians live.

The cool of the night is filled with the quiet sounds of people whispering good night, and a single voice humming the melody of acclamation proclaiming that eternal power and glory belongs to God alone.

**Text**: *Didache 9–10, 14*

Lizette Larson-Miller

## 162 ✦ Justin Martyr: The *First Apology*

*Justin Martyr was a Christian catechist living in Rome who was martyred, along with several of his students, in the mid-second century. His First Apology, written in the style of a classical speech of defense, was addressed to the household of the non-Christian Emperor Antoninus Pius, defending the new faith and arguing for their conversion to Christianity.*

### ———— Introduction ————

In Chapters 61–67, Justin described aspects of Christian worship, primarily to clarify for non-Christians that the worship services were neither orgies nor cannibalistic rites, two accusations leveled against early Christians. Justin carefully avoided words that carried connotations of pagan worship, such as *priest,* and strived to convince his readers that the Christians who gathered in the liturgy were morally upright and responsible citizens. In the course of his description, Justin preserved a picture of second-century worship among his Greek-speaking community in Rome. His weekly liturgy was composed of a reading service together with a Eucharist, the first clear indication of such a worship form.

**Text:** And on the day called Sunday there is a meeting in one place of those who live in cities or the country . . .

**Commentary:** The community of believers that gathered in the home of Justin the teacher was one of several small Christian communities spread throughout the city of Rome. Each small community may have known of the others, but they worshiped in individual groups based on familial connections, language and nationality, or their relationship to the teacher who may have first communicated to them the gospel of Jesus the Christ. Most of those gathering on this Sunday evening spoke Greek, and many of them were recent immigrants from the regions of Cappadocia, Palestine, and Samaria like their teacher Justin.

The choice of Sunday for a meeting day was no accident; Justin himself wrote that Sunday had a double significance: It was the "first day, on which God transformed darkness and made the universe," and it was also the day on which "Jesus Christ our Saviour rose from the dead." These Christians gathered to celebrate both divine events, remembering the blessings of creation, as they had done in their Jewish childhood, and the weekly remembrance of the death and resurrection of Jesus, which made all creation new.

As the work day ended for the Christians, they gathered quietly at the home of Justin, who lived above a shopkeeper named Martinus, in a typical Roman apartment building. With living quarters as close as they were in Rome, the comings and goings of the students of Justin, as well as the weekly gatherings for liturgy, were certainly not a secret to the neighbors, and the very act of gathering was risking arrest and possibly death.

**Text:** . . . And the memoirs of the apostles (which are called Gospels) or the writings of the prophets are read as long as time permits. When the reader has finished, the president in a discourse urges and invites [us] to the imitation of these noble things.

**Commentary:** The worship began with readings from Scripture—the Law and prophets of the Hebrew Bible—or from the recently circulated accounts of Jesus' death and resurrection, passed on through the followers of Jesus' disciples. Listening to the same stories from Scripture with which they

had grown up, many in the community remembered their Jewish roots and felt at home. For the Greek members who had grown up with stories of Greek and Roman gods, however, the stories of Scripture were new and unusual, and the explanation which always followed was helpful to their understanding.

One of Justin's jobs as the teacher of the community was to keep the rolls on which the Scriptures were written and to gather the stories of Jesus and the letters between Christian communities. Part of the reason that this Sunday gathering was in his house was because he was the keeper of the books and had the room to store them. The reader chosen for the day read from this collection of Justin's, standing at an upright table with an assistant who helped with the rolls of Scripture. When the readings were done (they were done when the president signaled that he had heard enough!), the president—one of the elders of the community—began an explanation of the readings, first interpreting the readings from the Hebrew Scripture with regard to the prophecies of Christ and the fulfillment in Jesus, and then applying this interpretation and the stories of Jesus to the lives of the gathered Christians.

The president did not have the training and education that a catechist like Justin had. What he could share was the experience of being a Christian for much of his life, surviving persecution and imprisonment while sharing the wisdom of living a life in imitation of Christ.

**Text:** Then we all stand up together and offer prayers.

**Commentary:** In response to the inspiring words of the president who had urged the imitation of the acts of Jesus in each person's life, the community rose up from the floor, which was spread with rugs, to offer prayers. Standing with uplifted hands, they prayed as a baptized community, confident that their prayers for the world and for the wider church would be heard by the gracious God remembered in the readings. In the prayers, they remembered especially those of their own community who were sick or dying and the two members who had been arrested for professing Christ, handed over by non-Christian family members.

**Text:** On finishing the prayers we greet each other with a kiss.

**Commentary:** After the prayers were completed, all of the baptized Christians acknowledged the presence of the Spirit in each other by sharing a kiss, the sign of the presence of the Spirit of God in each person. It was this kiss—exchanged on the lips because of its identification with the breath of God in the creation stories—which had so scandalized the critics of Christianity and had led to stories of Christian gatherings being no more than excuses for orgies. For the gathered Christians, however, the kiss was not a scandal but a sign of the pure love of God and a physical reminder of the unity of the community as it moved towards sharing communion.

**Text:** When we have finished . . . bread is brought, and wine and water, and the president similarly sends up prayers and thanksgivings to the best of his ability, and the congregation assents, saying the Amen.

**Commentary:** Certain members of the community had brought the bread and wine for the Eucharist, and as the exchange of the kiss of peace was completed, the freshly baked bread and homemade wine were brought to the table standing in the front of the room. A pitcher of water was brought from the back so that the strong red wine of the Roman countryside could be softened a bit by the addition of some water.

After the plate and cup had been arranged on the table, the same leader who had related the lives of the gathered community to the readings proclaimed in their midst, offered a prayer of thanksgiving to God for the gifts which had been given to all those present. Chanting in the style associated with the telling of epic poems, the president recounted the works of God for which God was being blessed, including the central act of the sending of the Son of God for the salvation of all. Following a structure inherited from Jewish tradition, the president thanked God in his own words and asked that the Spirit of God come down on all those gathered in the room. At the conclusion of his chanting, the community added their assent to all that had been said by singing "Amen," or "so be it," one of several Hebrew words directly borrowed by these Greek-speaking Christians.

**Text:** The distribution, and reception of the consecrated (eucharistized) [elements] by each one takes place, and they are sent to the absent by the deacons.

**Commentary:** At the end of the prayer of thanksgiving, all the people came forward to receive the consecrated bread and wine, gathering around the deacons who supervised the distribution. After all had received a small chunk of bread and drunk from the single large cup, the remaining bread and wine was given to the two deacons who would bring it to the sick members of the community and to the two who were in prison, awaiting martyrdom. The very act of gathering the remaining bread and wine and watching the president blessing the two deacons as they went on their way reminded all those present how very close the threat of arrest was to them and how precious this time together had been.

**Text:** Those who prosper, and who so wish, contribute, each one as much as he or she chooses to. What is collected is deposited with the president, and he takes care of orphans and widows, and those who are in want on account of sickness or any other cause, and those who are in bonds, and the strangers who are sojourners among [us], and, briefly, he is the protector of all those in need.

**Commentary:** As the members of this small community prepared to leave, those who had extra clothing, food, or money left it with the president to distribute where he thought it would be needed. They knew that in a society where there were few nets to catch those unable to feed themselves, these gifts were a matter of life and death for some. As the gifts were brought up to the president, he gently acknowledged each person, proud that the prayer offered by the community bore fruit in such tangible ways.

After bidding farewell to each other, the members of the community returned to their own homes: some to servants' quarters in elaborate palaces, some to family homes filled with non-believers, and others to humble dwellings on the outskirts of Rome. But all left praying that everyone would remain safe until the next Sunday when they would gather once again with their new family, born in baptism and sustained by Word and Eucharist.

Lizette Larson-Miller

## 163 • THE APOSTOLIC TRADITION OF HIPPOLYTUS (A.D. 215)

_The Apostolic Tradition, a church order which was compiled sometime in the third century and attributed to Hippolytus of Rome probably contains a text of a complete eucharistic prayer, or anaphora. Although much of the text may have been typical of the eucharistic prayers in use in Rome at the time, some scholars suggest that it reflects the way in which a conservative bishop may have wished the Eucharist were celebrated._

### Introduction

The study of this prayer in the twentieth century, and its application to the worship of the church at the table, has revolutionized the way the Eucharist is celebrated today. This classic prayer has influenced the shape and content of the new prayers of thanksgiving in contemporary liturgical and non-liturgical churches. It sets the words of institution within the context of a prayer which gives thanks to God, tells the story of salvation, offers sacrifice, calls upon the Spirit, and gives glory to God. The following is a Eucharist celebrated immediately after the consecration of a new bishop.

Text: _And when he has been made bishop, all shall offer the kiss of peace, greeting him because he has been made worthy. Then the deacons shall present the offering to him; and he, laying his hands on it with all the presbytery, shall give thanks saying:_

The Lord be with you.
_And all shall say:_
**And with your spirit.**
Up with your hearts.
**We have them with the Lord.**
Let us give thanks to the Lord.
**It is fitting and right.**

Commentary: This ancient dialogue builds on Boaz's words to the reapers (Ruth 2:4). And it assumes that, for those whose hearts are in God's presence, giving thanks makes good sense.

Text: _And then he shall continue thus:_

We render thanks to you, O God, through your beloved child Jesus Christ, whom in the last times you sent to us as saviour and redeemer and angel of your will; who is your inseparable Word, through whom you made all things, and in whom you were well pleased. You sent him from heaven into the Virgin's womb; and, conceived in the womb, he was made flesh and was manifested as your Son, being born of the holy Spirit and the Virgin. Fulfilling your will and gaining for you a holy people, he stretched out his hands when he should suffer, that he might release from suffering those who have believed in you.

Commentary: The word for "child" may also mean "servant." The focus is upon Jesus, through whom we pray, and because of whom we give thanks. "Angel" means "messenger." Here, unlike many later prayers, there is slight mention of creation. God's goal is the creation and redemption of a people. And to this end, the "Word" is made flesh, as Jesus is born of Mary through the work of the Spirit. Strong verbs recite what has happened: sent, made, born, manifested, stretched, and release. Redemption is a "release" from captivity, and it requires, and overcomes, "suffering."

Text: And when he was betrayed to voluntary suffering that he might destroy death, and break the bonds of the devil, and tread down hell, and shine upon the righteous, and fix a term, and manifest the resurrection, he took bread and gave thanks to you, saying, "Take, eat; this is my body, which shall be broken for you." Likewise also the cup, saying, "This is my blood, which is shed for you; when you do this, you make my remembrance."

Commentary: What matters is not that he was "betrayed," or even his "suffering," but his choice to save. And in that saving, he is victorious. He overwhelms the ancient enemies: death, devil, and hell. In this context, his meal with his disciples is crucial to the story of redemption, as his body is broken and his blood is shed. And when we "do this," we are summoned, across time, into the presence of him who suffered for us.

Text:

Remembering therefore his death and resurrection, we offer to you the bread and the cup, giving you thanks because you have held us worthy to stand before you and minister to you. And we ask that you would send your holy Spirit upon the offering of your holy Church; that, gathering her into one, you would grant to all who partake of the holy things (to partake) for the fullness of the holy Spirit for the strengthening of faith in truth, that we may praise and glorify you through your child Jesus Christ, through whom be glory and honour to you, with the holy Spirit, in your holy Church, both now and to the ages of ages. Amen.

**Commentary**: "Remembering . . . we offer." We offer nothing of our own, except what we have been given. And even to be allowed to do this is cause for us to be grateful. Those who are grateful are free to ask; and Christians, as they offer thanks, call upon the Spirit to create unity among them, and to help them grow in faith, that their praise may be completed in Christ.

This table prayer, which is addressed to God, through his child Jesus, in the fullness of the Spirit, culminates with doxology ("words of praise"), to which all give consent by saying "Amen."

**Text**: (Geoffrey J. Cuming, ed., *Hippolytus: A Text for Students* [Bramcote, Notts., UK: Grove Books, 1976], 10–11.)

John Burkhart

## 164 ✦ THE BYZANTINE LITURGY (NINTH CENTURY)

*The Byzantine Liturgy is the product of a complex evolution that began before the time of Christ. Like its Western counterpart, the eucharistic service of the Eastern Orthodox churches consists of two parts. The first, the Liturgy of the Word, developed from the services of the Jewish synagogue. The second, the Liturgy of the Faithful, evolved from the prayer of blessing or b<sup>e</sup>rakah of the Passover and other Jewish religious meals.*

### Introduction

Originally the Liturgy of the Word and the Liturgy of the Faithful were two separate services. By the fourth century, the two services had been combined. This is possibly due to the influence of the church in Jerusalem where, according to the pilgrim Egeria, the people gathered at Golgotha for the Liturgy of the Word and processed to the tomb of Christ for the Liturgy of the Faithful. Since other communities had only one church building, they imitated the church of Jerusalem by celebrating both services in the same place.

The Byzantine liturgy belongs to the West Syrian family of liturgies and is related to the third-century *Apostolic Tradition,* the fourth-century service found in Book VIII of *The Apostolic Constitutions,* and the *Liturgy of St. James* in use in Jerusalem by the fifth century. Although its roots are in Antioch,

it reached its final form in Constantinople, the capital of the East Roman or Byzantine Empire. The great influence of the imperial city eventually led all churches of the East that adhered to the Council of Chalcedon to conform to its liturgical usage. In 1194 Theodore Balsamon, the Patriarch of Antioch and noted expert on canon law, declared that all Orthodox must follow the liturgical traditions of Constantinople. Today all but a few Western Rite Eastern Orthodox as well as several groups of Eastern Rite Roman Catholics follow the Byzantine liturgy. Since the liturgy of the Eastern church underwent only a few changes following the ninth century, much of the commentary below also applies to the contemporary eucharistic service of the Orthodox church.

By the end of the fourth century, the imperial church used two *anaphoras,* or prayers of consecration, the central prayer of the liturgy. One bore the name of St. John Chrysostom, Bishop of Constantinople (398–404), the other that of St. Basil, Bishop of Caesarea (370–379). Although some scholars have questioned this tradition, contemporary scholarship leans toward the opinion that both played a major role in compiling the texts attributed to them. It is probable that St. Gregory of Nazianzus introduced the liturgy of Cappadocia as revised by St. Basil, his close friend, when he became Bishop of Constantinople in 380. It is also likely that St. John Chrysostom revised the liturgy of Antioch, his home, for use in Constantinople when he became its Bishop in 398. During the ninth century, the church of Constantinople used the Liturgy of St. Basil on most Sundays, reserving the shorter Liturgy of St. John Chrysostom for weekday celebrations. Thus our commentary will focus on the Liturgy of St. Basil.

Although it is possible to reconstruct the eucharistic service of Constantinople from the homilies of St. John Chrysostom or the seventh century *Mystagogia* of St. Maximus the Confessor, the *Barberini Codex* contains the earliest text of the Byzantine liturgy. Written in southern Italy between 788 and 789, this important document contains the text of the Liturgies of St. John Chrysostom and St. Basil, the Liturgy of the Presanctified Gifts and several other services. Unfortunately, the *Barberini Codex* only contains the prayers of the celebrant and omits the rubrics, litanies, antiphons, and other hymns. However, with the help of other sources such as a commentary on the liturgy written by St. Germanus, Patriarch of Constantinople between 715 and 730, it is possible to obtain a fairly close picture of the Divine Liturgy as celebrated in the imperial church during the ninth century.

The major theme of the Byzantine liturgy is the entrance of the faithful into the kingdom of God. The clergy and faithful also considered the liturgy a sacrifice or offering. As the principal act of worship of the church, it was a sacrifice of praise and thanksgiving. It was also the offering of bread and wine as symbols of the offering of creation to God by a grateful people. The believers of ancient Byzantium also considered the Eucharist a remembrance of the sacrifice of Christ. Finally, the faithful offered themselves to God by their participation in the liturgy.

The biblical accounts of the worship of heaven contained in the sixth chapter of Isaiah and the book of Revelation had great influence on the development of Byzantine worship, which conscientiously imitated the worship of heaven. The building itself became an image of heaven. The robes of the clergy became images of the robes worn by the elders or presbyters during heavenly worship as portrayed in Revelation. Since both Isaiah and Revelation mention incense, it played a prominent role in Byzantine worship as a symbol of the sweetness of the kingdom of God and of the prayers of the saints ascending to heaven.

Just as the worship of Judaism and biblical texts describing worship in heaven greatly influenced the worship of the early church, the architecture of the biblical temple and synagogue also played a major role in the development of ecclesiastical architecture in the Eastern church. The earliest church buildings in Syria contain the same arrangement as the temple and synagogue. The area for the reading of the Scriptures became the pulpit or _ambon_. The seat of Moses evolved into the throne for the bishop. The Holy of Holies that contained the Ark of the Covenant in the temple and the scrolls of the Law in the synagogue became the sanctuary containing the altar or Holy Table. Significantly, Arabic-speaking Orthodox Christians refer to the sanctuary as the Heikel, from the Hebrew word for the Holy of Holies. In Constantinople, ecclesiastical architecture reached its highest development in Hagia Sophia, the Church of the Holy Wisdom, built by the Emperor Justinian in the sixth century. A vast domed structure, the Church of Holy Wisdom set the pattern for all subsequent churches in the Eastern church. There were no pews, only a few seats for the elderly and infirm, as the faithful stood during the service, the men divided from the women. A large platform, the ambon, for the reading of the Scriptures, stood at the center of the nave. At the eastern end of the cathedral, a waist-high barrier with three doors, the ancestor of the modern iconostasis, separated the sanctuary from the nave. A path, the _bema,_ also separated from the nave by waist-high barriers, led between the ambon and the sanctuary. A marble table, the altar or Holy Table, stood at the center of the sanctuary, which ended in an apse containing a series of semicircular steps, the _synthronon,_ which provided seating for the clergy during readings and sermons. A circular building, the _skeuophylakion,_ or sacristy, stood northeast of the main church.

Believers in ancient Byzantium considered the church building an image or icon of the kingdom of God. The dome represented the vault of the heavens. The image of Christ the Almighty, or Pantrocrator, in the dome symbolized Christ ruling over the universe, especially his church, an image of the kingdom of God. The mosaics and paintings portrayed the saints and the entire company of heaven, which mystically joined the faithful for the celebration of the Eucharist, the banquet of the kingdom of God. The barrier between the nave and the sanctuary, symbolized the mystery of the Eucharist and the division between heaven and earth. The Holy Table at the center of the sanctuary, which represented heaven, was an image of the throne of God.

The bishop, or patriarch who presided over the Eucharist, symbolized Christ, the true minister of the sacrament. The priests symbolized the twelve apostles, and the deacons and altar servers, the angels of heaven. Originally the clergy wore formal attire of a gentleman of the fourth century. However, as styles changed, they continued to dress in the traditional manner for services, leading to the development of specialized vestments. By the ninth century, the robes of the clergy had gained symbolic meaning. The bishop and priests wore an inner gown, the _sticharion,_ symbolizing the robe of baptism. Over it they wore a stole, the _epitrachelion,_ with both ends fastened together with a hole for the head, signifying the robe of Aaron and the cloth by which Christ was tied as he was taken to the cross. The large cape-like vestment, the _phelonion,_ symbolized the cross carried by Christ to his Passion. On this, as a symbol of his role as chief shepherd, the bishop wore a large woolen stole, the _omopho-_

*rion,* wrapped over his neck as a shepherd would wrap a wounded lamb around his neck as he carried it to safety. Deacons wore the *sticharion* with a thin stole, the *orarion,* which symbolized the wings of angels. Thus the celebrant, whether patriarch, bishop, or priest, symbolized Christ standing before the throne of God, while the deacons symbolized the angels who act as messengers between heaven and earth.

By the ninth century, commentators began to interpret the liturgy as an icon in words and action of the mystery of salvation through Christ. St. Maximus the Confessor in the seventh century and St. Germanus built on earlier works by St. Cyril of Jerusalem (315–386) the Pseudo-Dionysius in the fifth or sixth century, and Theodore of Mopsuestia (*c.* 350–427), to interpret every part of the service as an image of some aspect of the saving activity of Christ. As a result of their veneration of pictorial icons as a manifestation of the presence of Christ or the saint on the icon, the believers saw the liturgy as a means to transcend time and space to enter the kingdom of heaven and the presence of the saving acts of Christ. When they entered the church, they mystically left the sinful world and entered the presence of God in heaven. When they kissed the Gospel Book, it was as if they had kissed Christ himself. When they touched the robes of the clergy during the Great Entrance, it was as if they had touched the seamless robe of the Savior. Thus, although we use the word "symbol" in English, it should be understood that to the clergy and faithful of ancient Constantinople, a symbol was not something unreal, but an image through which ultimate reality could be perceived.

Meanwhile, an emphasis on mystery spread from Syria to Constantinople. Curtains in the ancient Syrian churches hid the high points of the service from the eyes of the people, to show the sacred and mysterious nature of the Eucharist. Although there apparently was no curtain in Constantinople during the ninth century, this stress on mystery led the clergy to say many prayers of the service in a low voice. By the fourteenth century this practice would lead to the expansion of the barrier between the sanctuary and the nave into the modern iconostasis. As a result, the deacon assumed an important role as a bridge between the faithful and the mystery taking place at the altar by standing outside the sanctuary as he called the faithful to pay attention during important parts of the service and led them in a series

of hymns and litanies while the celebrant said the prayers inside the sanctuary.

By the ninth century, the Divine Liturgy consisted of several sections. These were

I. The Rite of Preparation
II. The Liturgy of the Word or Synaxis
   a. The Antiphons
   b. The Entrance of the clergy
   c. The Readings
   d. The Dismissal of the catechumens
III. The Liturgy of the Faithful
   a. The Prayers of the faithful
   b. The Great Entrance
   c. The Kiss of Peace and Creed
   d. The Anaphora
   e. The Lord's Prayer and Communion
   f. The Final Prayers and Dismissal

## The Divine Liturgy of St. Basil

The text below is a reconstruction of the Liturgy of St. Basil as celebrated in Constantinople in the ninth century. Since the ancient texts and commentaries are incomplete, some parts of the contemporary Orthodox liturgy are included although they are not found in ninth-century manuscripts. It is highly possible that they were a part of the liturgy by the ninth century, although they may have been added later. The translations used come from texts authorized for use by the Antiochian Evangelical Orthodox Mission, with additions from other service books of the Antiochian Archdiocese.

**Text:**
THE RITE OF PREPARATION
*Before the beginning of the Liturgy, the clergy gather in the sacristy to vest and prepare the bread and wine.*

*After a deacon gives the bread to a priest, he cuts it with the lance and then makes the sign of the cross over it with the lance and says:*

He was led as a sheep to the slaughter. And as a spotless lamb is dumb before his shearer . . .

*As he puts the bread on the diskos, the priest says:*

. . . so opened he not his mouth. In his humiliation his judgment was taken away. And for his generation, who shall declare it? For his life is taken away from the earth.

*As he pours water and wine in the chalice, the priest says:*

One of the soldiers with a spear pierced his side; and immediately there came forth blood and water; and he that saw it bore witness, and his witness is true.

*The priest then says:*

There are three that bear witness, the Spirit and the water and the blood, and the three are one. Now and ever and unto ages of ages. Amen.

*The priest censes the gifts and says:*

O God our God, who did send forth the heavenly Bread, the food of the whole world, our Lord and God Jesus Christ, our Savior and Redeemer and Benefactor, blessing and sanctifying us: Bless this Oblation and receive it upon your altar above the heavens. Remember, as you are good and love mankind, those who brought this offering, and those for whom they brought it; and preserve us blameless in the celebration of your holy Mysteries; for sanctified and glorified is your most honorable and majestic name, of the Father and of the Son, and of the Holy Spirit; now and ever and unto ages of ages. Amen.

**Commentary**: Originally a deacon prepared the gifts. However, by the ninth century a priest prepared them. The church considered Isaiah 54:7-8 a prophecy of the crucifixion of Christ. The small lance symbolized the spear that the soldier thrust in the side of Christ. By the ninth century, the water and wine symbolized the water and blood that flowed from the side of Christ as is seen by the quote from St. John 19:34-35. Thus the Rite of Preparation had become a symbol of the sacrificial death of Christ. The Rite of Preparation, or *Proskomedia*, became more elaborate until it reached its present form by the fourteenth century.

**Text:**
### THE ANTIPHONS

*While the faithful wait for the entrance of the celebrant, they sing the antiphons. Before each antiphon one of the priests prays the prayer of the antiphon.*

**Commentary**: At times, the faithful gathered at a church or other suitable site in the city for a short service of prayers and intercession and processed to the church being used for the liturgy. During the procession, chanters sang psalms and the people responded with short, easily remembered refrains.

Eventually, they began to chant psalms and refrains, pausing for three prayers as they waited for the arrival of the clergy and the beginning of the liturgy. By the ninth century, the Psalms were considered a commemoration of the Old Testament prophecies of the coming of Christ.

**Text:**
### The First Antiphon

*Deacon:* Let us pray to the Lord.
**People:** Lord, have mercy.
*Priest:* O Lord our God, Whose power is unimaginable and Whose glory is inconceivable, Whose mercy is immeasurable and Whose love for mankind is beyond all words, in Your compassion, O Lord, look down on us and on this holy house, and grant us and those who are praying with us the riches of Your mercy and compassion. For to You are due all glory, honor and worship, to the Father and to the Son and to the Holy Spirit, now and ever and unto ages of ages.
**People:** Amen.

*The people then sing Psalm 91 with the following refrain:*

Through the prayers of the Mother of God, O Savior, save us.

### The Second Antiphon

*Deacon:* Let us pray to the Lord.
**People:** Lord, have mercy.
*Priest:* O Lord our God, save Your people and bless Your inheritance. Guard the fullness of Your Church, sanctify those who love the beauty of Your House, glorify them by Your divine power and do not forsake us who hope in You. For Yours is the dominion and the Kingdom and the power and the glory of the Father and of the Son and of the Holy Spirit, now and ever and unto ages of ages.
**People:** Amen.

*The People then sing Psalm 92 with the following refrain:*

O Son of God, Who rose from the dead, save us who sing to You, Alleluia!

**The Third Antiphon**

| | |
|---|---|
| *Deacon:* | Let us pray to the Lord. |
| **People:** | **Lord, have mercy.** |
| *Priest:* | O Lord, Who have given us the grace to pray together in peace and harmony, and Who promise to grant the requests of two or three who agree in Your Name, fulfill even now the petitions of Your servants as is best for us, giving us in this age the knowledge of Your truth, and in the age to come, eternal life. For You are good, O our God, and You love mankind, and we send up glory to You, to the Father and to the Son and to the Holy Spirit, now and ever and unto ages of ages. |

*The People then sing Psalm 93 with the following refrain:*

O Only-begotten Son and Word of God, who is immortal, yet did deign for our salvation to be incarnate of the holy Theotokos and ever-virgin Mary, and without change was made man; and was crucified also, O Christ our God, and by your death did Death subdue; who are one of the Holy Trinity, glorified together with the Father and the Holy Spirit: save us.

**Commentary**: Although usually attributed to the Emperor Justinian, (483–565) some consider Severus (c. 465–538) the Monophysite Patriarch of Antioch, the author of the hymn "Only-begotten Son of God." In any case, it entered the service around 536 and is a summary of the doctrine of the incarnation of Christ as perfect God and perfect man.

Originally, the faithful waited outside the church or in the narthex for the arrival of the clergy. When the clergy entered the nave, the faithful followed, symbolizing the entrance into the kingdom of God. By the ninth century, the faithful had already gathered in the nave before the beginning of the service. The clergy, led by a deacon carrying the Gospel Book, began the Liturgy with a solemn entrance through the nave into the sanctuary accompanied by altar servers bearing the cross, candles, and incense during the chanting of the Third Antiphon. By the ninth century, this Entrance, the origin of the contemporary Little Entrance, symbolized the beginning of the public ministry of Christ. The dea-con placed the Gospel on the Holy Table, symbolizing the enthronement of Christ. The clergy then assumed their seats on the *synthronon,* a symbol of the ascension of Christ.

**Text:**

**The Entrance.** *While the people sing the third antiphon, the celebrant and other clergy stand before the doors leading from the narthex into the nave for the prayer of the Entrance:*

| | |
|---|---|
| Celebrant: | (*in a low voice*) O Sovereign Lord, our God, Who appointed in heaven the orders and armies of angels and archangels for the service of Your glory, grant that the holy angels may enter with us, to serve and glorify Your goodness with us. For to You are due all glory, honor, and worship, to the Father and to the Son and to the Holy Spirit, now and ever and unto ages of ages. |

*Then led by a deacon carrying the Gospel Book, the clergy enter in procession through the nave into the sanctuary accompanied by altar servers bearing the cross, candles, and incense as the people complete the hymn, "O Only-begotten Son. . . ." The celebrant and other clergy enter the sanctuary and take their seats on the* synthronon.

## THE LITURGY OF THE WORD

The Liturgy of the Word is also called the *Synaxis,* which means "gathering" or "assembly." Orthodox considered the church a eucharistic assembly. By entering the church building to assemble for worship, the faithful symbolically left the sinful world to enter the kingdom of God.

### The Great Litany and Trisagion

*A deacon stands outside of the sanctuary to lead the people in the Great Litany.*

**Commentary**: Ultimately stemming from the Prayer of Intercession of the Jewish service, the litany form of prayer was fully developed by the time of the *Apostolic Constitutions.* Originally chanted by the deacon with responses by the faithful, following the readings and sermon, the Great Litany had moved to a position following the Entrance and before the *Trisagion* sometime during the ninth century. Meanwhile, the clergy prayed the prayer of the *Trisagion.*

Text:

| | |
|---|---|
| *Deacon:* | In peace, let us pray to the Lord. |
| **People:** | **Lord, have mercy.** |
| *Deacon:* | For the peace from above and for the salvation of our souls, let us pray to the Lord. |
| **People:** | **Lord, have mercy.** |
| *Deacon:* | For the peace of the whole world, for the stability of the holy churches of God, and for the union of all, let us pray to the Lord. |
| **People:** | **Lord, have mercy.** |
| *Deacon:* | For this holy house and for all who enter with faith, reverence and the fear of God, let us pray to the Lord. |
| **People:** | **Lord, have mercy.** |
| *Deacon:* | For our Bishop *(N.)* for the honorable priests and deacons in Christ, and for all the clergy and the people, let us pray to the Lord. |
| **People:** | **Lord, have mercy.** |
| *Deacon:* | For this country and for every authority and power within it, let us pray to the Lord. |
| **People:** | **Lord, have mercy.** |
| *Deacon:* | For this city, for every city and country and for the faithful living in them, let us pray to the Lord. |
| **People:** | **Lord, have mercy.** |
| *Deacon:* | For seasonable weather, for an abundance of the fruits of the earth, and for peaceful times, let us pray to the Lord. |
| **People:** | **Lord, have mercy.** |
| *Deacon:* | For those who travel by land, air, and sea, the sick and suffering, those under persecution and for their deliverance, let us pray to the Lord. |
| **People:** | **Lord, have mercy.** |
| *Deacon:* | For our deliverance from all affliction, anger, danger, and need, let us pray to the Lord. |
| **People:** | **Lord, have mercy.** |
| *Deacon:* | Help us, save us, have mercy on us and keep us, O God, by Your grace. |
| **People:** | **Lord, have mercy.** |
| *Deacon:* | Remembering our most holy, most pure, most blessed and glorious Lady, the Mother of God, and Ever-virgin Mary, with all the saints, let us commit ourselves and each other and all our life unto Christ our God. |
| **People:** | **To You, O Lord.** |
| *Celebrant:* | (*in a low voice*) O Holy God, Who rest in the saints, Who with the Trisagion Hymn are praised by the Seraphim, glorified by the Cherubim and worshipped by all the heavenly powers, Who out of nothing brought all things into being, Who created man in Your image and likeness and adorned him with every gift of Your grace, Who give wisdom and understanding to anyone asking for them, and Who do not disregard the sinner, but have appointed repentance for salvation, Who have made us Your humble and unworthy servants, even at this hour, to stand before the glory of Your holy altar, and to offer You the worship and praise due to You: accept, O Lord, from the mouths of us sinners the Trisagion Hymn and visit us in Your goodness. Forgive us every transgression, whether voluntary or involuntary. Sanctify our souls and bodies, grant that we may worship You in holiness all the days of our life, through the intercessions of the holy Mother of God and of all the saints who have pleased You from the beginning. |
| | (*aloud*) For You are holy, O our God, and we send up glory to You, to the Father and to the Son and to the Holy Spirit, now and ever . . . |
| *Deacon:* | . . . and unto ages of ages. |
| **People:** | **Holy God, Holy Mighty, Holy Immortal One, have mercy on us.** |
| | **Holy God, Holy Mighty, Holy Immortal One, have mercy on us.** |
| | **Holy God, Holy Mighty, Holy Immortal One, have mercy on us.** |
| | **Glory to the Father and to the Son and to the Holy Spirit. Now and ever and unto ages of ages. Amen. Holy Immortal One, have mercy on us.** |
| | **Holy God, Holy Mighty, Holy Immortal One, have mercy on us.** |

**Commentary**: Originally sung during the Entrance, the Thrice-Holy Hymn, or *Trisagion,* dates at least back to the time of Patriarch Proclus (434–446). According to popular legend, while the patriarch led the people in prayers for deliverance from an earthquake, a young boy was carried up into heaven, where he heard the angels singing this hymn. Thus, the faithful believed that they joined the choirs of heaven when they sang the *Trisagion,* another indication of the view of the Eucharist as an ascent to heaven and a participation in the worship of the angels.

**Text:**
**The Readings**

**Commentary**: There were originally readings from the Old Testament, the Epistles, and the Gospels. However, only the Epistle and Gospel remained by the ninth century. The *Prokeimenon,* a short verse from the Psalms sung before the Epistle, is a remnant of the Psalm sung between the Old Testament and Epistle readings. St. Germanus considered the *Prokeimenon* a symbol of the prophecies of the coming of Christ and the Gospel a symbol of the revelation of God through Christ. As the deacon carried the Gospel to the ambon, the faithful venerated the book as a way to venerate Christ Himself, symbolized by the elaborately decorated book.

**Text:**

| | |
|---|---|
| *Deacon:* | Let us attend! |
| *Celebrant:* | Peace be to all. |
| *People:* | **And to your spirit.** |

*The Reader then chants the* Prokeimenon.

| | |
|---|---|
| *Deacon:* | Wisdom! |
| *Reader:* | The Reading from the Epistle of the holy Apostle *(N.)* to the *(N.).* |
| *Deacon:* | Let us attend! |

*The reader then reads the Epistle.*

| | |
|---|---|
| *Celebrant:* | Peace be to you who read. |

*The People chant verses from the Psalms with the refrain:*

**Alleluia, Alleluia, Alleluia.**

*Meanwhile the deacon censes the Gospel Book on the Holy Table and then carries it accompanied with incense, candles and the cross to the ambon for the reading of the Gospel.*

| | |
|---|---|
| *Deacon:* | Wisdom! Let us listen to the holy Gospel. |

| | |
|---|---|
| *Celebrant:* | Peace be to all. |
| *People:* | **And to your spirit.** |
| *Deacon:* | The reading from the holy Gospel according to St. *(N.)* |
| *People:* | **Glory to You, O Lord, glory to You.** |
| *Deacon:* | Let us attend! |

*The deacon then reads the Gospel.*

| | |
|---|---|
| *People:* | **Glory to You, O Lord, glory to You.** |

**The Sermon**
**The *Ektenia* of Fervent Supplication**

**Commentary**: This Litany is called "of Fervent Supplication" because of the triple response, "Lord, have mercy".

**Text**: *A deacon stands outside of the sanctuary to lead the people in the* Ektenia *of Fervent Supplication.*

| | |
|---|---|
| *Deacon:* | Let us say with our soul and with our mind, let us say: O Lord almighty, the God of our fathers, we pray thee, hearken and have mercy. |
| *People:* | **Lord, have mercy. Lord, have mercy. Lord, have mercy.** |
| *Deacon:* | Have mercy upon us, O God, according to thy great goodness, we pray thee hearken and have mercy. |
| *People:* | **Lord, have mercy. Lord, have mercy. Lord, have mercy.** |
| *Deacon:* | Again we pray for pious and Orthodox Christians; for our Celebrant *(N.);* for Priests, deacons, and all other clergy; and for all our brethren in Christ. |
| *People:* | **Lord, have mercy. Lord, have mercy. Lord, have mercy.** |
| *Deacon:* | Again we pray for mercy, life, peace, health, salvation, and visitation for the servants of God *(N.N.),* and for the pardon and remission of their sins. |
| *People:* | **Lord, have mercy. Lord, have mercy. Lord, have mercy.** |
| *Deacon:* | Again we pray for the blessed and ever-memorable founders of this holy temple; and for all our fathers and brethren, the Orthodox departed this life before us, who here and in all the world lie asleep in the Lord; and for the Orthodox ser- |

vant(s) of God departed this life _(N.N.)_, and for the pardon and remission of their sins.

_People:_ **Lord, have mercy. Lord, have mercy. Lord, have mercy.**

_Deacon:_ Again we pray for those who bear fruit and do good works in this holy and all-venerable Temple; and for all the people here present who await thy great and rich mercy.

_People:_ **Lord, have mercy. Lord, have mercy. Lord, have mercy.**

_Celebrant:_ _(in a low voice)_ O Lord our God, accept this fervent supplication of your servants, and have mercy upon us according to the multitude of your mercy; and send down your compassions upon us and upon all your people, who await the rich mercy that comes from you.

_(aloud)_ For you are a merciful God who loves mankind, and to you we ascribe glory to the Father and to the Son and to the Holy Spirit, now and ever and unto ages of ages.

_People:_ **Amen.**

## The Litany of the Catechumens

_A deacon stands outside of the sanctuary to lead the people in the Litany of the Catechumens._

_Deacon:_ Pray to the Lord, you catechumens.
_People:_ **Lord, have mercy.**
_Deacon:_ You faithful, pray unto the Lord for the catechumens, that the Lord will have mercy on them.
_People:_ **Lord, have mercy.**
_Deacon:_ That He will teach them the word of truth.
_People:_ **Lord, have mercy.**
_Deacon:_ That He will reveal to them the Gospel of righteousness.
_People:_ **Lord, have mercy.**
_Deacon:_ That He will unite them to His Holy, Catholic and Apostolic Church.
_People:_ **Lord, have mercy.**
_Deacon:_ Help them; save them; have mercy upon them; and keep them, O God, by your grace.
_People:_ **Lord, have mercy.**

_Deacon:_ You catechumens, bow your heads unto the Lord.
_People:_ **To you, O Lord.**
_Celebrant:_ _(in a low voice)_ O Lord our God, Who dwell in the heavens and have regard for all Your works: Look upon your servants the catechumens, who have bowed their necks before You. Give them Your light yoke; make them honorable members of Your holy Church; count them worthy of the laver of regeneration, the remission of sins, and the robe of incorruption, in the knowledge of You, our true God.

_(aloud)_ That with us they may glorify Your all-honorable and majestic name, of the Father and of the Son and of the Holy Spirit, now and ever and unto ages of ages.

_People:_ **Amen.**

## The Dismissal of the Catechumens

_Deacon:_ Catechumens depart. As many as are catechumens, depart. Let none of the catechumens remain.

**Commentary**: Since ancient times, the church considered the Eucharist too sacred for non-Christians. Significantly, St. Cyril, the fourth-century Bishop of Jerusalem, did not describe either the rite or the significance of the Eucharist to those receiving instruction until after they had been baptized. Thus those preparing for baptism, the catechumens, left the assembly following the Liturgy of the Word.

Text:
## THE LITURGY OF THE FAITHFUL
### The First Prayer of the Faithful

_Deacon:_ Let us pray to the Lord.
_People:_ **Lord, have mercy.**
_Celebrant:_ You, O Lord have shown us this great mystery of salvation, You have accounted us, the humble and unworthy servants, worthy to be ministrants of your holy Altar. Enable us with the power of your Holy Spirit for this service, that standing uncondemned before your holy glory, we may offer unto you a sacrifice of praise; for you are he that works all

things in all men; grant, O Lord, that our sacrifice may be acceptable and well pleasing in your sight, for our own sins, and for the errors of the people; for unto you are due all glory, honor, and worship; to the Father and to the Son and to the Holy Spirit, now and ever and unto ages of ages.

*People:* Amen.

## The Second Prayer of the Faithful

**Commentary:** Until the Middle Ages, a deacon repeated the Great Litany in its original location.

**Text:**

*Deacon:* In peace, let us pray to the Lord.

**People:** Lord, have mercy.

*Deacon:* For the peace from above and for the salvation of our souls, let us pray to the Lord.

**People:** Lord, have mercy.

*Deacon:* For the peace of the whole world, for the stability of the holy churches of God, and for the union of all, let us pray to the Lord.

**People:** Lord, have mercy.

*Deacon:* For this holy house and for all who enter with faith, reverence, and the fear of God, let us pray to the Lord.

**People:** Lord, have mercy.

*Deacon:* For our Bishop *(N.)* for the honorable priests and deacons in Christ, and for all the clergy and the people, let us pray to the Lord.

**People:** Lord, have mercy.

*Deacon:* For this country and for every authority and power within it, let us pray to the Lord.

**People:** Lord, have mercy.

*Deacon:* For this city, for every city and country, and for the faithful living in them, let us pray to the Lord.

**People:** Lord, have mercy.

*Deacon:* For seasonable weather, for an abundance of the fruits of the earth, and for peaceful times, let us pray to the Lord.

**People:** Lord, have mercy.

*Deacon:* For those who travel by land, air, and sea, the sick and suffering, those under persecution and for their deliverance, let us pray to the Lord.

*People:* Lord, have mercy.

*Deacon:* For our deliverance from all affliction, anger, danger, and need, let us pray to the Lord.

*People:* Lord, have mercy.

*Deacon:* Help us, save us, have mercy on us and keep us, O God, by Your grace.

*People:* Lord, have mercy.

*Deacon:* Remembering our most holy, most pure, most blessed and glorious Lady, the Mother of God, and Ever-virgin Mary, with all the saints, let us commit ourselves and each other and all our life unto Christ our God.

*People:* To You, O Lord.

*People:* Lord, have mercy.

*Celebrant:* *(in a low voice)* O God, who in pity and compassion has visited our lowliness; who has set us, thy humble and sinful and unworthy servants, before your holy glory, to minister at your holy Altar: Strengthen us by the power of your Holy Spirit for this service, and grant us utterance in the opening of our mouth, to invoke the grace of your Holy Spirit upon the gifts about to be set before you.

*(aloud)* That guarded always by your might we may ascribe glory to you: to the Father and to the Son and to the Holy Spirit, now and ever and unto ages of ages.

*People:* Amen.

*Meanwhile, the clergy leave their seats and gather around the Holy Table, over which they spread a large cloth, the* eiliton.

**Commentary:** By the ninth century the *eiliton* had become a symbol of the winding sheet placed on the body of Christ for his burial.

**Text:**
## The Great Entrance
## The Hymn of the Cherubim

*The people chant Psalm 23:7-10 with The Hymn of the Cherubim as a refrain.*

**Let us, who mystically represent the Cherubim, and who sing the Thrice-Holy Hymn to the Life-**

creating Trinity, lay aside all earthly cares that we may receive the King of all, who comes invisibly upborne by the Angelic Hosts. Alleluia. Alleluia. Alleluia.

Commentary: The Hymn of the Cherubim is another indication of the view of the Eucharist as a participation in the worship of heaven. The Emperor Justinian II ordered its singing in about 573.

Text: _The celebrant washes his hands and says the Prayer of The Hymn of the Cherubim._

_Celebrant:_ _(in a low voice)_ No one bound by fleshly desires and pleasures is worthy to approach or come near or minister before You, the King of glory. For to serve You is great and awesome, even to the Heavenly Powers themselves. Yet because of Your unspeakable and immeasurable love for mankind, You became man without undergoing change or alteration. And taking the title High Priest, You, as Lord of all, have committed to us the celebration of this liturgical and unbloody sacrifice. For You alone, O Lord our God, rule over all things in heaven and earth, You Who are seated upon the throne of the Cherubim and are Lord of the Seraphim and King of Israel, Who alone are holy and rest in the saints. Therefore I implore You, Who alone are good and ready to hear: Look upon me, Your sinful and unprofitable servant, and cleanse my soul and heart from an evil conscience. And enable me by the power of Your Holy Spirit, clothed with the grace of the priesthood, to stand before this, Your holy Table, and to consecrate Your holy and spotless Body and precious Blood. For to You I come bowing my neck, and I pray to You: Do not turn away Your face from me, nor reject me from among Your children, but make me, Your sinful and unworthy servant, worthy to offer these Gifts to You. For You alone are the Offerer and the Offered, the Receiver and the Distributed, O Christ our God,

and we send up glory to You, together with Your Father Who is without beginning, and Your all-holy, good, and life-giving Spirit, now and ever and unto ages of ages. _Amen._

_Meanwhile, the deacons bring the bread and wine in procession through the nave to the sanctuary, escorted by candles, incense, and the liturgical fans. After they place them on the Holy Table, the veils are placed over them, and they are censed._

Commentary: Originally a simple utilitarian act, the Great Entrance had assumed major significance by the ninth century. The elaborate procession became one of the high points of the Liturgy. When present, the emperor met the procession and escorted it to the sanctuary. The faithful touched the vestments of the clergy, as the woman with the hemorrhage touched the robe of Christ. Sometimes, parents would place their children in the path of the procession so that the clergy would step over them. Popular devotion during the Great Entrance was so great that Patriarch Eutychinus (552–555) warned the faithful lest they worship unconsecrated the bread and wine. By the ninth century, the faithful considered the Great Entrance an image of the procession of Christ to Calvary. The liturgical fans symbolized the Seraphim. The placing of the vessels on the Holy Table represented the entombment of Christ. The small veils symbolized the burial cloths of Christ and the large veil, the stone before the tomb of Christ. The incense symbolized the Holy Spirit and the spices used to anoint the body of the dead Savior.

Text:

_Celebrant:_ _(in a low voice)_ Remember me, brother and fellow minister.

Commentary: The dialogue following the Entrance did not take its modern form until the Middle Ages. However, from ancient times the celebrant asked for the prayers of his fellow ministers.

Text:

_Deacon:_ _(in a low voice)_ May the Lord God remember your priesthood in His Kingdom.

_Celebrant:_ _(in a low voice)_ Pray for me, my fellow minister.

_Deacon:_ _(in a low voice)_ May the Holy Spirit

descend on you, and the power of the most High overshadow you.

Celebrant: *(in a low voice)* May the Holy Spirit Himself minister together with us all the days of our life.

Deacon: *(in a low voice)* Remember me, holy Master.

Celebrant: *(in a low voice)* May the Lord God remember you in His Kingdom always, now and ever and unto ages of ages.

*The celebrant then prays the prayer of the* Prothesis.

Celebrant: *(in a low voice)* O Lord our God, Who have created us and brought us into this life; Who have shown us the ways to salvation, and have given us the revelation of heavenly mysteries; You have appointed us to this service in the power of Your Holy Spirit; graciously grant us, O Lord, to be ministers of Your New Covenant, and servants of Your holy mysteries. Through the greatness of Your mercy, accept us as we approach Your holy altar, so that we may be worthy to offer to You this spiritual and unbloody sacrifice for our own sins and for the errors of the people. Receive it upon Your holy and ideal altar above the heavens as sweet fragrance, and send down upon us in return the grace of Your Holy Spirit. Look upon us, O God, and behold this our service. Accept it as You accepted the gifts of Abel, the sacrifices of Noah, the whole burnt offerings of Abraham, the priestly offices of Moses and Aaron, and the peace offerings of Samuel. Even as You accepted this true worship from the hands of Your holy apostles, O Lord, so now in Your goodness, accept these gifts from the hands of us sinners. Count us worthy to serve without offense at Your holy altar, so that we may receive the reward of wise and faithful stewards on the awesome day of Your just retribution. Through the mercies of Your Only-

begotten Son, with Whom You are blessed, together with Your all-holy, good, and life-giving Spirit, now and ever and unto ages of ages. Amen.

## The Kiss of Peace

Celebrant: Peace be to all.

**People:** **And to your spirit.**

Deacon: Let us love one another that with one accord we may confess:

**People:** **Father, Son, and Holy Spirit, Blessed Trinity, Consubstantial, Co-eternal, Undivided Trinity.**

*The clergy and people then exchange the kiss of peace.*

**Commentary:** The clergy and faithful exchanged the kiss of peace within their own rank: clergy with clergy, men with men, and women with women. The kiss of peace is a symbol that all must leave all animosity behind them as they unite in love with the company of heaven as they worship at the throne of God.

**Text:**
**The Creed**

Deacon: The Doors! The Doors! In wisdom, let us attend!

**Commentary:** The cry, "The doors, the doors," is a reminder that the doors to the church must be closed as only the faithful may experience the mystery of the Eucharist. By the ninth century, the removal of the veils had become a symbol of the removal of the stone before the tomb of Christ. As all sang the Niceno-Constantinopolitan Creed, the clergy waved the *aer* over the elements. Originally a utilitarian act to keep insects away, this became a symbol of the earthquake that accompanied the resurrection of Christ.

**Text:** *The celebrant removes the veils over the gifts. The clergy then wave them over the gifts while the people recite the Creed.*

**People:** **I believe in one God, the Father Almighty, Maker of heaven and earth, and of all things visible and invisible; And in one Lord Jesus Christ, the Son of God, the Only-begotten, Begotten of the Father before all worlds; Light of Light, Very God of Very God, Begotten, not made; of one essence with the**

Father, by Whom all things were made: Who for us men and for our salvation came down from heaven, was incarnate of the Holy Spirit and the Virgin Mary, and was made man; And was crucified also for us under Pontius Pilate, and suffered and was buried; And the third day He rose again, according to the Scriptures; And ascended into heaven, and sits at the right hand of the Father; And He shall come again with glory to judge the living and the dead, Whose Kingdom shall have no end. And I believe in the Holy Spirit, the Lord, and Giver of Life, Who proceeds from the Father, Who with the Father and the Son together is worshipped and glorified, Who spoke by the Prophets; And I believe in One Holy, Catholic, and Apostolic Church. I acknowledge one Baptism for the remission of sins. I look for the Resurrection of the dead and the Life of the world to come. Amen.

**Commentary**: Peter the Fuller, the Monophysite Patriarch of Antioch (470), introduced the Creed in the Liturgy in Antioch as a sign of his orthodoxy. Patriarch Timothy of Constantinople (511–518), also a Monophysite, added the Creed to the Liturgy as a demonstration of his own orthodoxy.

**Text:**

**The Anaphora of St. Basil**

*Deacon:* Let us stand well! Let us stand with fear! Let us attend that we may offer the holy offering in peace.

*People:* **An offering of peace! A sacrifice of praise!**

*Celebrant:* The grace of our Lord Jesus Christ, the love of God the Father and the communion of the Holy Spirit be with you all.

*People:* **And with your spirit.**

*Celebrant:* Let us lift up our hearts.

*People:* **We lift them up unto the Lord.**

*Celebrant:* Let us give thanks unto the Lord.

*People:* **It is fitting and right.**

**Commentary**: This dialogue dates at least as far back as the third-century *Apostolic Tradition*. It may stem from the dialogue at the beginning of the prayer of blessing (*bᵉrakah*) of the Passover and other religious meals in the Jewish tradition. The faithful are reminded that they must leave behind the concerns of the world as they elevate their hearts and minds to heavenly things, as they prepare for the most sacred moments of the Liturgy. The celebrant invites the faithful to give thanks to the Lord, as the Eucharist is the great thanksgiving for the mystery of salvation.

**Text:**

*Celebrant:* (*in a low voice*) O truly existing One, Master, Lord, God, almighty and adorable Father, how right it is, and befitting the majesty of Your holiness, to praise You, to sing to You, to bless You, to worship You, and to glorify You. You alone are truly God, and we offer You this spiritual worship with a humble spirit and a contrite heart. You have given us the knowledge of Your truth. Who is worthy to speak of Your mighty deeds, or make all Your praises heard? O Master of all things, Lord of heaven and earth, and of all creation, both visible and invisible, You are seated upon the throne of glory and behold the depths. You are without beginning, invisible, incomprehensible, indescribable, changeless. O Father of our Lord Jesus Christ, the great God and Savior, our Hope, Who is the image of Your goodness, the seal equal to its model, Who shows You in Himself: the Father, Living Word, true God before all ages, Wisdom, Life, Sanctification, Power, true Light: Through You the Holy Spirit was manifested, the Spirit of truth, the gift of adoption, the pledge of our future inheritance, the first-fruits of eternal good things, the life-giving Power, the fountain of holiness; through whom every rational and spiritual creature is made capable to worship You and give You eternal glorification, for all things are Your servants. You are praised by the angels, the archangels, the thrones, the dominions, the principalities, the authorities, the powers, and the many-eyed cherubim. The seraphim are around You, each having six wings: with two they veil their face, with two their feet; and with two they fly, continually crying out to one another with mouths that do not grow tired, in praises which are never silent,

*(aloud)* singing, proclaiming, shouting the hymn of victory:

**People:** **Holy! Holy! Holy! Lord of Hosts! Heaven and earth are filled with Your glory. Hosanna in the highest! Blessed is He Who comes in the Name of the Lord! Hosanna in the highest!**

**Commentary:** The reference to the company of heaven and the Thrice-Holy Hymn, stemming in part from Isaiah 6:3, are manifestations of the belief that the clergy and faithful join the worship of the angels around the throne of God in heaven during the Liturgy. It ends with the words "the crowd shouted," from Psalm 118:25–26, as Christ entered Jerusalem, as the faithful prepare to welcome Christ who comes through the Eucharist.

**Text:**

*Celebrant:* *(in a low voice)* With these blessed powers, O Master and lover of mankind, we sinners also cry aloud and say: You are Holy, truly most Holy, and there is no limit to the majesty of Your holiness. You are just in all Your works, for in righteousness and true judgment, You have ordered all things for us. When You had created man by taking dust from the earth and honored him with Your own image, O God, You placed him in the paradise of delight, promising him eternal life and the enjoyment of everlasting good things in the observance of Your commandments. But when man disobeyed You, the true God Who created him, and was led astray by the deceit of the serpent, and died in his own transgressions, You banished him, in Your righteous judgment, from paradise into this world. You caused him to return to the earth from which he was taken, yet provided for him the salvation of regeneration in Your Christ Himself. For You did not turn away forever from the creature You made, O Good One, and You did not forget the work of Your hands. Through the tender compassion of Your mercy, You visited us in manifold ways: You sent us the prophets; You worked mighty wonders through Your saints who were pleasing to You in every generation. You have spoken to us through the mouths of Your servants the prophets, foretelling to us the salvation to come. You gave us the law to help us; You appointed angels to guard us. And when the fulness of time came, You spoke to us through Your Son Himself, by Whom You also made the ages. He is the Radiance of Your glory and the Image of Your Person. He upholds all things by the word of His Power. He did not think it robbery to be equal to You, God and Father. He was God before the ages, yet He appeared on earth and lived among men. He took flesh from a holy Virgin; He emptied Himself, taking the form of a slave. He conformed Himself to the body of our lowliness in order to conform us to the image of His glory. For as by man sin entered into the world, and by sin, death, it pleased Your Only-begotten Son, Who is in Your bosom, God and Father, Who was born of a woman, the holy Mother of God and Ever-virgin Mary, Who was born under the law, to condemn sin in His flesh, so that we who died in Adam might be brought to life in Him Your Christ. He lived as a citizen in this world, and gave us commandments of salvation. He released us from the waywardness of idols and brought us into the knowledge of You, the true God and Father. He won us for Himself as His own chosen people, a royal priesthood, a holy nation. After purifying us with water and sanctifying us with the Holy Spirit, He gave Himself over in exchange to death, in which we were held captive, sold by sin. After descending into hell through the cross, that He might fill all things with Himself, He loosed the bonds of death; He rose on the third day and opened to all flesh the path of resurrection from the dead, since it was not possible for the Author of Life to be dominated by corruption. So He became the firstfruits of those who sleep, the firstborn from among the dead, that He might truly be the first of all things. He ascended into heaven and sits at the right hand of Your majesty on high, and He will come to render to every one according to his works. And as a memorial of His saving passion, He has left us these things, which we have presented to You according to His command. For when He was about to go forth to His voluntary, blameless, and life-giving death, on the night in which He gave Himself for the life of the world, He took bread into His holy and spotless hands, and when He had presented it to You, His God and Father, He gave thanks, blessed, sanctified, broke it, and

*(aloud)* gave it to His holy disciples and apostles, saying: Take, eat, this is my body which is broken for you, for the remission of sins.

*People:* Amen.
*Celebrant:* *(in a low voice)* Likewise He took the cup of the fruit of the vine and mingled it, gave thanks, blessed and sanctified it, and gave it to His holy disciples and apostles, saying:

*(aloud)* Drink of this, all of you! This is my blood of the new covenant, shed for you and for many, for the remission of sins.

*People:* Amen.
*Celebrant:* *(in a low voice)* Do this as a memorial of Me, for as often as you eat this

Bread and drink this Cup, you announce My death and confess My resurrection. Therefore, O Master, mindful of His saving passion and life-giving cross, His burial for three days and resurrection from the dead, His ascension into heaven and sitting at Your right hand, O God and Father, and His glorious and awesome second coming,

*(aloud)* we offer You Your own, from what is Your own, for everyone and for everything.

**Commentary**: The memorial of the sacrifice of Christ, or *amamnesis,* is a feature of all ancient liturgies. It is a reminder that the Eucharist is a memorial of the passion of Christ.

**Text**:

*People:* We praise You. We bless You. We give thanks to You, O Lord. And we pray unto You, our God.

### The *Epiklèsis*

While the celebrant said the Anaphora in a low voice, the people sang hymns related to the meaning of the central prayer of the Liturgy.

*Celebrant:* *(in a low voice)* Therefore, all-holy Master, we also, Your sinful and unworthy servants, whom You have considered worthy to serve at Your holy Altar, not because of our own righteousness, for we have nothing good on earth, but because of Your mercies and compassion, which You have so richly poured out on us, now approach Your holy altar with boldness, and presenting the signs of the holy Body and Blood of Your Christ, we beg You and call upon You, O Holy of Holies, by the favor of Your goodness, to cause Your Holy Spirit to descend upon us and upon these gifts now offered,
*Deacon:* Bless Master, the Holy Bread.
*Celebrant:* that He may show us this Bread to be the precious Body of our Lord, God, and Savior, Jesus Christ.
*Deacon:* Amen. Bless Master the Holy Cup.
*Celebrant:* And this Cup to be the precious

Blood of our Lord, God, and Savior Jesus Christ.

*Deacon:* Amen. Bless both, Master.

*Celebrant:* Shed for the life of the world.

*Deacon:* Amen. Amen. Amen.

**Commentary:** All stood or prostrated themselves in silent awe as the celebrant prayed the *Epiklesis,* an invocation of the Holy Spirit to descend and transform the bread and wine into the Body and Blood of Christ. Although the Eastern church, which emphasized the role of the Holy Spirit in the mystery of the Eucharist, avoided a rationalistic explanation of the exact nature of the change, all believed that the bread and wine became the actual body and blood of the risen Christ.

### The Commemoration of the Departed and Living

*Celebrant:* *(in a low voice)* And unite all of us to one another, who partake of the one Bread and the one Cup in the communion of the one Holy Spirit. Grant that none of us will partake of the holy Body and Blood of Your Christ for judgment and condemnation. Instead, may we find mercy and grace with all the saints that have been pleasing to You in all the ages: the ancestors, the fathers, the patriarchs, the prophets, the apostles, the preachers, the evangelists, the martyrs, the confessors, the teachers, and every righteous spirit perfected in the faith,

*(aloud)* especially with our most holy, most pure, most blessed and glorious lady, the Mother of God, Ever-virgin Mary.

**Commentary:** The commemorations are a remnant of the *diptychs,* originally read by a deacon.

**Text:** *A deacon censes the gifts, while other deacons wave the fans. Meanwhile the celebrant blesses the* antidoron.

*People:* In you rejoices, O full of grace all creation, the angelic hosts, and the race of men, O hallowed Temple and super-sensual Paradise, glory of Virgins of whom God was incarnate and became a little child, even our God who is before all ages; for he made your womb a throne, and yours he made more spacious than the heavens. In you rejoices, O full of grace, all creation. Glory to you.

**Commentary:** Originally a utilitarian act to drive away insects, the fans became a symbol of the seraphim and cherubim, who fly around the throne of God in heaven. The hymn to the *Theotokos* ("God-bearer"), or *Megalynarion,* entered the Byzantine Liturgy around the turn of the sixth century. The people began to sing it to fill the time taken for the commemorations when the celebrant began to say the anaphora in a low voice. The *antidoron,* which means "instead of the gifts," is the bread that remained after the preparation. It was blessed for distribution to the faithful.

**Text:**

*Celebrant:* *(in a low voice)* May we also find grace and mercy with the holy prophet, forerunner and baptist John, the holy apostles worthy of all praise, St. *(N.)* whose memory we celebrate, and with all Your saints. Through their prayers, be pleased to protect us, O God. We offer You this spiritual worship for the salvation, protection, and remission of sins of the servants of God *(N.N.).* Remember all those who have fallen asleep before us in the hope of resurrection to eternal life, especially *(N.N.),* and grant them rest, O our God, in a place of light where there is no sighing or sorrow, where the light of Your countenance shines. Again we entreat You: Remember, O Lord, Your Holy, Catholic, and Apostolic Church, from one end of the inhabited earth to the other, and grant peace to her whom You have purchased with the precious Blood of Your Christ, and strengthen this holy house until the end of the world. Remember, O Lord, those who have brought You these gifts, those for whom, by whom, and in whose intention they were brought. Remember those who bring tithes and offerings and do good works in Your holy churches and those who remember the poor; grant them in exchange Your heavenly riches and gifts: give them heavenly things in return for earthly things, incorruptible things for corruptible things. Remember, O Lord, those who are in the deserts, mountains, caves and pits of the earth. Remember, O Lord, those who live in virginity, godliness, asceticism, and holiness of life. Remember, O Lord, this country and all those in civil authority: grant them a secure and lasting peace; speak good things to their hearts concerning Your Church and all Your people, so that in the serenity they will provide us, we may live a calm and peaceful life in all godliness and holiness. Remember, O Lord, every principality and authority, our brethren who serve in the government and the armed forces. Preserve the good in their goodness, and make the wicked good through Your goodness. Remember, O Lord, the people here present and those who are absent for an honorable reason. Have mercy on them and on us according to the multitude of Your mercy. Fill their houses with all good things; preserve their marriages in peace and harmony; bring up their children, guide their youth; strengthen their elderly; encourage the faint-hearted; reunite the separated; lead back the wayward and unite them to Your Holy, Catholic, and Apostolic Church. Deliver those who are afflicted by unclean spirits; sail with those who are at sea; accompany those who travel by land or by air; defend the widows; protect the orphans; free the captives; heal the sick. Remember, O God, those who are under persecution, in courts, in mines, in exile, in harsh labor, and those in any kind of tribulation, need, or distress. Remember, O Lord our God, all those who have need of Your great compassion,

those who love us, those who hate us, and those who have asked us in our unworthiness to pray for them. Be mindful of all Your people, O Lord our God, and pour out Your rich mercy upon all of them, granting them all the petitions which are for their salvation. And remember, O God, all those whom we have not remembered through ignorance, forgetfulness, or the multitude of names, for You know the name and age of each, even from his mother's womb. For You, O Lord, are the help of the helpless, the Savior of the afflicted, the haven of the voyager, the physician of the sick. Be all things to all men, for You know each one and his request, his household, and his need. Deliver this city, O Lord, and every city, land, town from famine, plague, earthquake, and shipwreck, flood, fire, sword, foreign invasion, and civil war.

_(aloud)_ Among the first, remember O Lord, Our Bishop _(N.)_ and grant him to Your holy churches for many years in peace, safety, honor, health, and in rightly teaching the word of Your truth.

**Commentary:** When the deacon ceased to read the _diptychs_ aloud, the commemoration of the chief bishop of the see evolved to fill the void.

**Text:**

| | |
|---|---|
| _Deacon:_ | And remember also those men and women whom each of us has in mind. |
| _People:_ | _And all Your people._ |
| _Celebrant:_ | _(in a low voice)_ Remember, O Lord, every Orthodox bishop who rightly teaches the word of Your truth. Remember me also, O Lord, in my unworthiness, according to the multitude of Your mercies; forgive my every transgression, both voluntary and involuntary. Do not take away the grace of Your Holy Spirit from these gifts here presented on account of my sin. Remember, O |

Lord, the presbytery, the diaconate in Christ, and every order of the clergy. Let none of us who stand about Your holy altar be put to confusion. Visit us with Your goodness, O Lord; manifest Yourself to us in the richness of Your mercies. Grant us seasonable and healthful weather; send gentle showers upon the earth so that it may bear fruit. Bless the crown of the year with Your goodness. Cause schisms in the churches to cease. Put an end to the attacks of the unbelievers; quickly bring to an end the rise of heresy by the power of Your Holy Spirit. Receive us all into Your Kingdom, consecrating us as children of the light and children of the day. Grant us Your own peace and Your own love, O Lord our God, for You have given all things to us.

This petition is found originally in the fourth century *Apostolic Constitutions* (VIII. 12.40–42).

> *(aloud)* And grant that with one mouth and one heart we may glorify Your all-honorable and majestic Name, of the Father and of the Son and of the Holy Spirit, now and ever and unto ages of ages.

*The celebrant blesses the people as he says:*

Celebrant: And may the mercies of our Great God and Savior Jesus Christ be with you all.

*People:* *And with your spirit.*

### The Litany Before the Lord's Prayer

*A deacon stands outside of the sanctuary to lead the people in the Litany Before the Lord's Prayer.*

Deacon: Calling to remembrance all the Saints, again and again in peace, let us pray to the Lord.

*People:* **Lord, have mercy.**

Deacon: For the precious Gifts that have been offered and sanctified, let us pray to the Lord.

*People:* **Lord, have mercy.**

Deacon: That our God, who loves mankind, receiving them upon his holy, heavenly, and ideal Altar for an odor of spiritual fragrance, will send down upon us in return his divine grace and the gift of the Holy Spirit, let us pray to the Lord.

Deacon: For our deliverance from all affliction, anger, danger, and need, let us pray to the Lord.

*People:* **Lord, have mercy.**

Deacon: Help us, save us, have mercy on us and keep us, O God, by Your grace.

*People:* **Lord, have mercy.**

Deacon: That this whole day may be perfect, holy, peaceful, and sinless, let us ask of the Lord.

*People:* **Grant this, O Lord.**

Deacon: For an angel of peace, a faithful guide and guardian of our souls and bodies, let us ask of the Lord.

**Commentary:** The mention of the angels during this litany is yet another indication of the belief that the clergy and faithful joined in the worship of heaven during the Liturgy.

**Text:**

*People:* **Grant this, O Lord.**

Deacon: For pardon and remission of our sins and transgressions, let us ask of the Lord.

*People:* **Grant this, O Lord.**

Deacon: For all that is good and profitable for our souls and for peace in the world, let us ask of the Lord.

*People:* **Grant this, O Lord.**

Deacon: That we may spend the remainder of our life in peace and repentance, let us ask of the Lord.

*People:* **Grant this, O Lord.**

Deacon: For a Christian end to our life, painless, blameless, and peaceful, and for a good defense before the dread judgment seat of Christ, let us ask of the Lord.

*People:* **Grant this, O Lord.**

Deacon: Asking for the unity of the Faith and the communion of the Holy Spirit, let us commend ourselves and each other and all our life unto Christ our God.

*People:* **To you, O Lord.**

Celebrant: And make us worthy, O Lord, that with boldness and without condemnation, we may dare to call upon You, the heavenly God as Father and say:

*People:* Our Father, who art in heaven, hallowed be Thy Name. Thy Kingdom come, Thy will be done on earth as it is in heaven. Give us this day our daily bread, and forgive us our trespasses, as we forgive those who trespass against us; and lead us not into temptation, but deliver us from evil.

*Celebrant:* For Thine is the Kingdom and the power and the glory of the Father and of the Son and of the Holy Spirit, now and ever and unto ages of ages.

*People:* Amen.

### The Prayer at the Bowing of the Head

*Celebrant:* Peace be to all.
*People:* And to your spirit.
*Deacon:* Let us bow our heads to the Lord.
*People:* To You, O Lord.
*Celebrant:* *(in a low voice)* O Master, Lord, the Father of compassions and God of every consolation: Bless, sanctify, guard, strengthen, and defend those who have bowed their heads to You. Withdraw them from every evil deed; apply them to every good work; and graciously grant that without condemnation, they may partake of these, Your most pure and life-creating Mysteries, for the remission of their sins, and unto the communion of the Holy Spirit.

*(aloud)* Through the grace and compassion and love for mankind of Your Only-begotten Son, with Whom You are blessed, together with Your all-holy, good, and life-giving Spirit, now and ever and unto ages of ages.

*People:* Amen.

### The Elevation

**Commentary:** Sometime after the fifth century the celebrant began to elevate the consecrated bread. Originally a call to the faithful to prepare for communion, the elevation became a symbol of the lifting up of Christ's body on the cross. The celebrant then broke the bread to prepare it for distribution

during Holy Communion. A part of the Eucharist from the very beginning, this too took on a symbolic meaning as an image of the sacrifice of Christ on the cross.

**Text:**

*Celebrant:* *(in a low voice)* Hear us, O Lord Jesus Christ our God, from Your holy dwelling place and from the glorious throne of Your Kingdom, and come to sanctify us, You Who sit on high with the Father and are here invisibly present with us. And make us worthy by Your mighty hand to be given Your most pure Body and precious Blood and through us to all Your people.

*Deacon:* Let us attend!
*Celebrant:* The holy Gifts for holy people!
*People:* One is holy. One is holy. One is the Lord Jesus Christ. To the glory of God the Father. Amen.

*The celebrant then breaks the consecrated bread and places portions of it in the Chalice as he says:*

*Celebrant:* *(in a low voice)* For the fullness of the Holy Spirit.

*The celebrant then pours warm water, the* zeon, *into the Chalice.*

**Commentary:** The origin of the warm water, or *zeon* is unknown. Some believe that it began in Cappadocia to keep the wine from freezing. Others argue that it stems from the *Aphthartodocetae,* an extreme form of Monophysitism, that taught that the blood and water that flowed from the side of Christ was warm because the body of Christ remained incorrupt even in death. In any case, it was an established custom by the middle of the sixth century, when the Armenian Catholicos Moses II stated that he would not drink warm wine in Constantinople.

**Text:**

### The Communion

*During Communion a psalm is sung.*

**Commentary:** The faithful of ancient Constantinople took Holy Communion very seriously. They believed that they received the actual body and blood of the risen Christ. Therefore they prepared themselves by strict fasting and through special prayers. In time they would consider the sacrament so sacred that they began to receive Holy Communion only a few times a year. Originally the clergy placed the consecrated bread in the crossed hands of the faithful and then gave them the chalice. By the ninth century, the clergy placed the consecrated bread in the chalice and administered Communion to the laity with a spoon.

Text: *Following Communion, the celebrant blesses the people as he says:*

Celebrant: O God, save Your people and bless Your inheritance.

People: **Amen. Let our mouths be filled with your praise, O Lord, that we may sing of your glory: for you have permitted us to partake of your holy, divine, immortal, and life-giving Mysteries. Establish us in your Sanctification, that all the day long we may meditate upon your righteousness. Alleluia, alleluia, alleluia.**

### The *Ektenia* of Thanksgiving

*A deacon stands outside of the sanctuary to lead the people in The* Ektenia *of Thanksgiving.*

Deacon: Let us attend! Having received the holy, most pure, immortal, heavenly, life-giving, and awesome Mysteries of Christ, let us worthily give thanks to the Lord.

People: **Lord, have mercy.**

Deacon: Help us, save us; have mercy on us; and keep us, O God, by your grace.

People: **Lord, have mercy.**

Deacon: Asking that the whole day may be perfect, holy, peaceful, and sinless, let us commend ourselves and each other and all our life unto Christ our God.

Celebrant: *(in a low voice)* We thank You, O Lord our God, for the participation in Your holy, pure, immortal, and heavenly Mysteries, which You have given us for the welfare and sanctification and healing of our souls and bodies. O Master of all, grant that the communion of the holy Body and Blood of Your Christ may be for us unto a faith which cannot be put to confusion, a love unfeigned, an increase of wisdom, the healing of soul and body, the repelling of every adversary, the fulfillment of Your commandments, and an acceptable defense at the awesome judgment seat of Your Christ.

*(aloud)* For You are our sanctification, and we give glory to You, to the Father and to the Son and to the Holy Spirit, now and ever and unto ages of ages.

People: **Amen.**

Celebrant: Let us go forth in peace.

People: **In the Name of the Lord.**

### The Prayer Behind the Ambon

*The clergy then process out of the Church. When they reach the ambon, the celebrant pauses for the Prayer Behind the Ambon.*

Deacon: Let us pray to the Lord.

People: **Lord, have mercy.**

Celebrant: O Lord, Who bless those Who bless You, and sanctify those who put their trust in You: save Your people and bless Your inheritance. Protect the whole body of Your Church, and sanctify those who love the beauty of Your house. Glorify them by Your divine power and do not forsake us who hope in You. Give peace to Your world, to Your churches, to the priests, to our civil authorities and to all Your people. For every good gift and every perfect gift is from above, coming down from You, the Father of Lights; and to You we send up glory, thanksgiving, and worship, to the Father and to the Son and to the Holy Spirit, now and ever and unto ages of ages.

People: **Amen.**

(Adapted from the Antiochian Orthodox Christian Archdiocese of North America, *Service Book of the Holy Eastern Orthodox Catholic Church and Apostolic Church* [New York, 1975].)

## Conclusion

Although it had reached most of its present form by the ninth century, the development of the text of Byzantine Liturgy continued through the Middle Ages. The preparation of the bread and wine was expanded and proceeded by the *Kairon,* or prayers of the clergy, before entering the sanctuary and a set of vesting prayers. The Great Litany moved to the beginning of the service and disappeared from the Prayers of the Faithful. Little Litanies introduced the second and third prayers of the antiphons. The Litany before the Lord's Prayer was duplicated following the Great Entrance. The text of the Liturgy reached its contemporary form by the publication of the *Diataxis* by Patriarch Philotheus of Constantinople (1354–1376). Changes in architecture also influenced the development of the Byzantine Liturgy. In smaller churches, the sacristy moved from outside the building to an area in the sanctuary to the left of the Holy Table. Thus the Entrances became processions from inside the sanctuary through the nave and back to the sanctuary. The barrier between the nave and the sanctuary became the iconostasis as icons were placed on the barrier, reaching its final form in Novgorod in the fourteenth century. The symbolic interpretation of the Liturgy also developed further, especially through the commentary of St. Nicholas Cabasilas, also in the fourteenth century.

John Warren Morris

## 165 • THE ROMAN CATHOLIC MASS (1570)

*Although the Roman Mass, standardized by directives of the Council of Trent (1570), is technically a post-Reformation document, it is not an innovation but rather the summation of the medieval development of western Catholic worship. Consequently the mass below is presented as part of the pre-Reformation liturgies as an example of ancient Catholic worship.*

─────── **Introduction** ───────

The English text which appears below is a translation of the Low Mass of the Latin Rite which was used from 1570 until the reforms following the Second Vatican Council, which began in 1962. The Roman Mass comprises two classes of material: the "ordinary" of the Mass, those parts that remain constant through all the seasons and celebrations of the church year, and the "proper" of the mass, those parts that vary according to the season, the Sunday of the year, or the particular commemoration of the day. In the Low Mass, the "ordinary" parts (*Kyrie eleison, Gloria, Credo, Sanctus, Benedictus* and *Ag-*

*nus Dei*) were recited, whereas in the High Mass these would be sung by a choir or a *schola cantorum.* The Low Mass grew out of the medieval practice at the monastery of Cluny, where the priest was directed to read the sung portions in the absence of musicians. The text we read dates from the time of Pope Pius V in the wake of the Council of Trent in 1568. This rite endured with almost no change until the Second Vatican Council, which called for the revision of the missal in light of the historical and liturgical studies of the first part of this century. The word "Mass" comes from the last words of the rite where the priest dismissed the people with the words, "*ite, missa est,*" meaning "Go, this is the dismissal" or "Go, you are sent." The book that governed the proper performance of the rite of the eucharistic liturgy was therefore called the Missal.

It is important to understand the genesis and use of the Roman Missal to appreciate how the Roman rite enjoyed such great stability while suffering liturgical stagnation for almost four hundred years. Briefly the earlier medieval period was very fertile in liturgical production, a fact attested to by Joseph Jungmann, *The Mass of the Roman Rite,* and by Gregory Dix, *The Shape of the Liturgy.* Throughout the Middle Ages, there was a great proliferation of new and diverse prayers. Popular devotional prayers, as well as prayers to accompany the feasts of different saints, found their place in the Roman Missal. Medieval piety was nourished heavily by liturgical allegory, whereby invented and oftentimes fanciful meanings were overlaid upon the liturgical actions and words. The faithful, unable to participate directly in the Mass, were encouraged to pray the *Paternoster* in Latin, or in the vernacular if Latin were an impossibility for them. New prayers and hymns were composed and incorporated into prayerbooks to be recited and sung during Low Mass. For the illiterate, the recitation of communal prayers, such as the rosary, was the appropriate participation of the faithful.

On the other hand, the Middle Ages witnessed the development of a eucharistic theology strongly sacrificial in nature, which determined the role of the presider as the sacerdotal offerer of the sacrifice. This idea made the Mass more of an exercise of private devotion of the priest. The theology stressed that each Mass was in itself a good and holy work and a new act of Christ himself through which he applied his sacrifice of redemption. The medieval theology tended to accentuate the privileged place of the priest, which led to certain liturgical abuses.

Before the Missal was compiled, the rites of the church were scattered throughout a number of liturgical books such as the sacramentary, lectionary, and antiphonary, which were consolidated into this one book for the use of the priest in accomplishing his private Mass.

Pope Gregory VII (1073–1085) tried to correct the sad ecclesial situation, marked by gross illiteracy of the clergy, by instituting a reform that included the liturgy. His ambitious program tried to restore the clerical mores as well as ecclesiastical discipline. The Gregorian reform, rather than truly reforming the liturgy, turned out to be a type of instruction given to the clergy so that they would know and recognize better the parts of the Mass, especially the canonical and liturgical rules. The final result of this reform was a movement of unification of the liturgy.

It would be mistaken, however, to assume that absolute uniformity was achieved by the Gregorian reform. In Spain, for example, the liturgy of the Latin Rite entered with great difficulty, gradually supplanting the old Mozarabic rites. The Spanish bishops in the northern dioceses of Spain found a way to implant the official Roman rite by using monks from foreign lands. Little by little, the Roman rite gained ground in the Iberian peninsula, first in Aragon in 1071, then moving towards Castille in 1078. At the Council of Burgos in 1085, the local rite disappeared in favor of the official Latin rite, except for the cities of Valencia and Toledo, where special indulgence was granted to preserve the old Mozarabic rite.

In Italy, an independent rite associated with St. Ambrose flourished in the city of Milan. All attempts to suppress this rite in favor of religious and political unity and liturgical uniformity in the West were thwarted. The success of the Gregorian reform, however, is attributed to two principal causes: the work of Franciscan mendicants in the thirteenth century and the influence of the printing press in the fifteenth century.

The Franciscan order, founded by St. Francis of Assisi in the thirteen century, brought about two results regarding the Mass, namely abbreviation and unification. Formerly in Rome two kinds of liturgies coexisted. The basilica liturgy was known for its conservative and traditional quality, while the curial liturgy, which had been adapted to the needs of the papal chapel which moved about frequently, was much less traditional. The papal chapel adopted the missal, containing all the readings and prayers in one consolidated book, because these could be transported more easily. This later led to the adoption of the missal in an abbreviated form over the use of many different liturgical books. At the beginning of the thirteenth century, Innocent III officially established the Office of the Curia. The mendicant friars of St. Francis, renowned for their itinerant preaching, spread its use throughout Europe. In a papal decree of the Franciscan Pope Nicholas III, the abbreviated and simplified Mass supplanted the ancient basilica liturgy. In spite of the resistance at the basilicas of St. Peter and St. John Lateran, the new missal was rapidly adopted with only minor adaptations of the local churches who maintained the celebrations of local saints within the liturgical year. Shortly thereafter, by another official decree, the calendar of the saints was made universal for the church, unifying the Roman liturgy even more.

In the fifteenth century, the invention of the printing press by Gutenberg aided in the widespread diffusion of the Roman Missal. This also lead to the disappearance of many liturgical elements which formerly had been conserved in the independent ancient rites. Prior to the printing press, the liturgical books had been copied by hand, which was slow and costly, but allowed for regional differences in the contents of the missal. The first printed missals appeared in 1457 in Constance, the diffusions center for the Rhenish region. Later, in 1474, the first Roman Missal was published in Milan and the following year in Rome. Other European capitals—like Paris, Lyons, Salisbury, Strasbourg, and Venice—followed suit and undertook the task of printing and distributing the new missal, contributing to even more widespread uniformity according to the Roman usage.

A few notable exceptions to the liturgical simplification and uniformity can be found among the monastic and religious orders. The Dominicans, apparently heavily influenced by the basilica-style liturgy, launched their own reform of the liturgy between 1228 and 1238. The Cistercian Order had derived their liturgy from the important reformed Benedictine Abbey of Cluny, which conserved Franco-Roman usages. In 1618 they abandoned their ritual for the newly adopted Missal of Pius V. Other orders, such as the Premonstratensians and the Carmelites, blended their ancient liturgies with later liturgical customs.

The need for liturgical reform, especially of the Roman Missal, was recognized from the time of Pope Pius II (1458–1464). During the pontificate of Sixtus IV, several feeble attempts at reform were enacted, especially in the area of liturgical chant at the celebrated Sistine Chapel (1473). Sixtus was formerly the Superior General of the Franciscan Order and favored Franciscan liturgical usage. For many historical reasons, it was necessary to wait for the Council of Trent in the sixteenth century for the long-needed liturgical reform.

The liturgists, whose task it was to reform the Roman Missal, exhibited three distinct tendencies: humanist, traditionalist, and classicist. Acting on a mandate by Pope Leo X (1513–1521), the liturgical reformers first revised the hymns, having determined that this area had been impoverished by music of very poor taste. They produced a work which was almost completely new and brought about the flowering of the great age of polyphony. Beyond the musical dimension, several reforms were introduced to improve the liturgy: clarification of the legislation in liturgical matters through the use of rubrics (directions written in red ink); reformation of the Sunday cycle; revision of all the texts of the Mass, eliminating historical accretions to the liturgy of dubious origin and value; and simplification of certain historical additions, which would aid in a better execution of the liturgy.

Various synods and regional councils sought more changes which would touch fundamental questions of liturgical reform. Partially in response to these requests, as well as to the demands of the Reformers North of the Alps and of the German Emperor Ferdinand I and the French King Charles IX, the Council of Trent, in its first session (1545–1547), undertook a larger reform of the liturgy. This program was approved during the second session (1547–1552) but was not fully implemented until the last session (1562–1563). The general tenets of Trent called for liturgical uniformity, while upholding the rights for individual diocesan usages which were more than 200 years old.

Authorized by the twenty-fifth session of the council, Pope Pius IV began to promulgate the necessary decrees to insure the Tridentine reforms. The formation of a liturgical commission in 1564 was soon thereafter suspended, later to be reestablished in 1566. The next pope, Pius V, completed the work of Trent. The newly revised missal appeared in 1570

and contained several important points: simplification of the feasts of saints in order to reemphasize the priority of the Sunday cycle; suppression of numerous octaves (eight-day observances of certain feasts); and clarification of the rubrics.

Although the Mass text fixed by the Council of Trent endured for almost four hundred years, liturgical art and architecture, music, and vessels continued to develop and change throughout the centuries. It would be impossible to describe the typical setting and celebration, since this varied from place to place and from century to century. A helpful study of these ancillary dimensions can be found in Edward Foley's *From Age to Age* (Chicago: Liturgy Training Publications, 1991). In spite of these subtle changes, the impression that most Catholics had was of the invariability and timelessness of the Roman Rite. The fact that the performance of the liturgy was limited to the priests and servers rendered the faithful mere spectators and fostered the idea that the Mass was a fixed monument. The liturgy was considered as "a finished art-product, as a wondrous work of the Holy Spirit, and it is forgotten that in the service of this higher master, human hands had been at work through the centuries, probing and fumbling and, not always very happily, endeavoring to make the eternally incomplete as fit for its purpose as they could" (Jungmann, *The Mass of the Roman Rite,* vol. 1, 158). One consequence of this mistaken notion of the unchangeability of the Mass has provoked the reaction of some Catholics who do not accept the recent reform of the liturgy promulgated by Vatican II.

The participation of the faithful was hindered for several reasons. First, the Latin language rendered most people incapable of following the action, let alone participating in the parts of the service designated as the people's response. Altar servers, therefore, responded in the name of the people. At the time of the Council of Trent, it became apparent that even many priests did not know Latin sufficiently to understand what they were praying. One of the tasks of Trent, therefore, was seminary reform, to ensure that seminarians would understand the Latin texts. Second, the attitude that the Mass was the sole property of the priest-presider fostered the notion that the faithful would be better served by prayer books and rosary beads to occupy their time during the Mass. One significant attempt to render the Latin Mass more intelligible by the faithful was the personal missal, where the Latin text was juxtaposed with a translation in the vernacular. The personal missal was not, however, intended to foster active participation on the part of the faithful, but rather was a means for them to follow passively the liturgical action. The introduction of the private missal met with negative reaction and the translation of the Latin prayers into the vernacular was forbidden. The intention of the church legislation in this prohibition was to retain a veil of mystery around the Mass.

The Tridentine Missal delineated several different parts of the eucharistic liturgy, yet one can broadly uncover a liturgical shape comprised of four parts: the Mass of the Catechumens, the Offertory, the Canon, and the Communion. In the preface of the missal, in the section entitled "Ritus Servandus," detailed instructions are given to the priest as to the celebration of the Mass, beginning with the manner in which he is to prepare himself while vesting and how he is to proceed to the altar. These instructions go into greater detail, delineating all the various parts of the Mass, but in the interest of brevity and clarity, the four-part division mentioned above is helpful.

**Text:**

**Order of Low Mass**

Mass of the Catechumens

*When the priest enters, those present rise and remain standing until he descends to the foot of the altar to begin Mass. They then kneel throughout the Mass except during the two Gospels, when they stand; but usage permits them to sit from the Offertory to the beginning of the Preface, and after the giving of Holy Communion until the reciting of the Communion antiphon.*

**Commentary:** The Mass of the Catechumens derives its name as a vestige of the liturgy of the early church when the catechumen (those preparing for Christian initiation) were still undergoing a lengthy period of preparation called the catechumenate. Since the catechumens were not yet initiated to the table, they could remain only for the liturgy of the Word before being dismissed. Gradually from the fourth century onwards, especially after the Edict of Milan in 313 C.E., the practice gradually moved away from adult baptism as normative to infant baptism. Although the practice changed, the liturgical division gives testimony to this historical fact.

**Text:** *The priest crosses himself and says aloud:*

In the name of the Father, and of the Son, and of the Holy Ghost. Amen.

I will go up to the altar of God.

*The server responds:*

Server: To God, the giver of youth and happiness.

*Then, except in the Masses of Passiontide and of the Dead, the celebrant and server say alternately Psalm 42:1-5.*

**Commentary:** Roughly the first half of the Mass consists of some preparatory rites and the Liturgy of the Word. The purpose of the Liturgy of the Catechumens was to evoke several sentiments. The feeling of penitence and contrition are the object of the *Confiteor* (Confession), the *Aufer a nobis* ("Take away from us our iniquities"), the *oramus te* ("we pray thee, Lord") and the *Kyrie eleison* ("Lord, have mercy"). The *Gloria* Hymn creates a feeling of adoration and gratitude. Finally the sense of supplication, found in the variable collect prayers, prepares one for the Epistle, Gospel, and Creed.

**Text:**

O God, sustain my cause; give me redress against a race that knows no piety; save me from a treacherous foe and cruel.

Server: Thou, O God, art all my strength, why hast thou cast me off? Why do I go mourning, with enemies pressing me hard?

Celebrant: The light of thy presence, the fulfillment of thy promise, let these be my escort, bringing me safe to thy holy mountain, to the tabernacle where thou dwellest.

Server: There I will up to the altar of God, the giver of youth and happiness.

Celebrant: Thou art my own God, with the harp I hymn thy praise.

Soul, why art thou downcast, why art thou all lament?

Server: Wait for God's help; I will not cease to cry out in thankfulness: My champion and my God!

Celebrant: Glory be to the Father, and to the Son, and to the Holy Ghost.

| | |
|---|---|
| _Server:_ | As it was in the beginning, is now, and ever shall be, world without end. Amen. |
| _Celebrant:_ | I will go up to the altar of God. |
| _Server:_ | To God, the giver of youth and happiness. |

_The priest crosses himself, saying:_

| | |
|---|---|
| _Celebrant:_ | Our help is in the name of the Lord. |
| _Server:_ | Who made heaven and earth. |

_Then he bows low and says:_

I confess to almighty God, to blessed Mary, ever-virgin, to blessed Michael the archangel, to blessed John the Baptist, to the holy apostles Peter and Paul, to all the saints, and to you, brethren, that I have sinned exceedingly in thought, word, and deed;

_He strikes his breast three times, saying:_

through my fault, through my own fault, through my own most grievous fault. Therefore I beseech the blessed Mary, ever-virgin, blessed Michael the archangel, blessed John the Baptist, the holy apostles Peter and Paul, all the saints, and you, brethren, to pray to the Lord our God for me.

| | |
|---|---|
| _Server:_ | May almighty God have mercy upon you, pardon your sins, and bring you to everlasting life. |
| _Celebrant:_ | Amen. |

_The server repeats the Confession:_

I confess to almighty God, to blessed Mary, ever-virgin, to blessed Michael the archangel, to blessed John the Baptist, to the holy apostles Peter and Paul, to all the saints, and to you, father, that I have sinned exceedingly in thought, word, and deed;

_He strikes his breast three times, saying:_

through my fault, through my own fault, through my own most grievous fault. Therefore I beseech the blessed Mary, ever-virgin, blessed Michael the archangel, blessed John the Baptist, the holy apostles Peter and Paul, all the saints, and you, father, to pray to the Lord our God for me.

| | |
|---|---|
| _Celebrant:_ | May almighty God have mercy upon you, pardon your sins, and bring to you everlasting life. |
| _Server:_ | Amen. |

_All cross themselves as the priest says:_

May the almighty and merciful Lord grant us pardon, absolution, and remission of our sins.

| | |
|---|---|
| _Server:_ | Amen. |

_He bows his head and continues:_

| | |
|---|---|
| _Celebrant:_ | Thou wilt relent, O God, and bring us to life. |
| _Server:_ | And thy people will rejoice in thee. |
| _Celebrant:_ | Show us they mercy, Lord. |
| _Server:_ | And grant us they salvation. |
| _Celebrant:_ | Lord, heed my prayer. |
| _Server:_ | And let my cry be heard by thee. |
| _Celebrant:_ | The Lord be with you. |
| _Server:_ | And with you. |
| _Celebrant:_ | Let us pray. |

_Then, as he goes up to the altar, he says silently:_

Take away from us our iniquities, we entreat thee, Lord, so that, with souls made clean, we may be counted worthy to enter the Holy of Holies: through Christ our Lord. Amen.

**Commentary**: Ascending to the altar, usually elevated by a few steps, the priest places the covered chalice and paten on a linen cloth called the corporal at the center of the altar in front of the tabernacle. The entire liturgy will be celebrated with the priest's back to the people.

**Text**: _Bowing down, he says:_

We pray thee, Lord, by the merits of thy saints whose relics are here . . .

_He kisses the altar in the middle._

. . . and of all the saints, that thou wilt deign to pardon all my sins. Amen.

_The priest now makes the sign of the cross, and, standing at the Epistle corner, begins the Introit, which will be found in the Mass proper to the day._

After kissing the altar, he proceeds to the left side (Epistle side) and reads the Introit.

_When the Introit is finished he returns to the middle of the altar and recites the_ Kyrie _in alternation with the server._

Afterwards the priest returns to the middle at the lowest altar step, where he and the servers (acolytes) say the prayers at the foot of the altar. These prayers include the double Confession and the nine-fold _Kyrie eleison_. These strongly penitential elements found their proper place in the preparatory rite during the Middle Ages when penitential practices abounded in the church.

*Celebrant:*    Lord, have mercy.
*Server:*       Lord, have mercy.
*Celebrant:*    Lord, have mercy.
*Server:*       Christ, have mercy.
*Celebrant:*    Christ, have mercy.
*Server:*       Christ, have mercy.
*Celebrant:*    Lord, have mercy.
*Server:*       Lord, have mercy.
*Celebrant:*    Lord, have mercy.

*The* Gloria, *which follows, is omitted when the vestments are black or violet, in votive Masses (other than the votive Masses of Angels, and of our Lady when said on a Saturday), and in certain other Masses where its omission is directed in the rubrics.*

**Commentary**: On Sundays outside of Advent and Lent and on special feast days during the week, the *Gloria* is said, followed by a special prayer called the *collect,* which varies according to the liturgical feast or season. The opening rites are punctuated with numerous genuflections and altar kissings as prescribed by the rubrics of the Missal.

**Text**:

Glory be to God on high, and on earth peace to men who are God's friends. We praise thee, we bless thee, we adore thee, we glorify thee, we give thee thanks for thy great glory: Lord God, heavenly King, God the almighty Father, Lord Jesus Christ, only-begotten Son; Lord God, Lamb of God, Son of the Father, who takest away the sins of the world, receive our prayer; thou who sittest at the right hand of the Father, have mercy upon us. For thou alone art the Holy One, thou alone art Lord, thou alone art the Most High: Jesus Christ, with the Holy Spirit: in the glory of God the Father. Amen.

*The priest turns to the people and says:*

*Celebrant:*    The Lord be with you.
*Server:*      And with you.

*He then moves to the Epistle side and says:* Oremus. *After this he recites one or more Collects, to the first and last of which the server responds:*

Amen.

**Commentary**: The Epistle is read at the right side of the altar, followed immediately by the gradual, tract, alleluia, or sequence. The gradual and the tract are psalm-based texts, the former consisting of two verses as a kind of vestige of the responsorial psalm,

the latter, a section of a psalm used to replace the alleluia during Lent. On special feast days, a sequence, a strophic Latin poem, is added to the alleluia. Only four sequences from the Middle Ages survived the liturgical reform of Pius V following the Council of Trent.

**Text**: *The Epistle is now read, and at its close, the server responds:*

*Server:*      Thanks be to God.

*The priest then recites the Gradual (or during Eastertide the Alleluia) and the Tract, when one is prescribed. These, the Collect, and the Epistle are to be found in the Mass proper to the day.*

*The missal is now moved to the Gospel side, while the priest, bowing at the middle of the altar, says silently:*

Cleanse my heart and my lips, almighty God, who didst cleanse the lips of the prophet Isaiah with a live coal. In thy gracious mercy, deign so to cleanse me that I may be able to proclaim fitly thy holy Gospel: through Christ our Lord. Amen.
Lord, grant a blessing.
The Lord be in my heart and on my lips, so that I may fitly and worthily proclaim his Gospel. Amen.

**Commentary**: The missal is next transferred to the left side where the Gospel will be proclaimed with the priest facing diagonally, half-facing the people. This is also accompanied by numerous signs of the cross and acts of reverence.

**Text**: *Then, facing the book, he says:*

*Celebrant:*    The Lord be with you.
*Server:*      And with you.

*He now makes the sign of the cross upon the book, and all cross themselves on forehead, lips, and breast while he says:*

A passage from (or The beginning of) the holy Gospel according to *(N.).*
*Server:*      Glory to thee, Lord.

*The priest then reads the Gospel, which will be found in the Mass proper to the day; after which the server answers:*

Amen.

**Commentary**: After the proclamation of the Gospel, the missal with its stand is moved to the middle of the altar, from where the Credo will be said every

Sunday and on special feasts. If there is to be a sermon, the priest ascends into the pulpit.

**Text**: _The celebrant kisses the book and says:_

Celebrant: Through the Gospel words may our sins be wiped away.

_If there is to be a sermon, it is delivered after the reading of the Gospel._

**Commentary**: The sermon, which had almost completely disappeared from the Mass in the early Middle Ages, was revived by the mendicant preaching orders. Since this was the only part of the Mass in the vernacular, the sermon constituted a point of intersection with the faithful, who to this point had been following the Mass with a personal missal, when permitted, or praying privately. At various historical periods in certain geographical locations, the sermon became a central focal point of the liturgy. The pulpit was often located in the middle of the nave of the church, so that people might hear better, given the absence of electronic assistance. It was fairly common for the priest to disrobe from the chasuble, the outer, colorful vestment, when leaving the sanctuary to give the sermon. This fact gave the strong impression that the sermon was not an essential part of the liturgy, but more of a time-out. For this reason, the content of the sermon did not necessarily reflect the readings of the day, but took on the air of a morality talk.

**Text**: _The priest then returns to the middle of the altar and says the Creed, if so directed in the Mass proper to the day._

I believe in one God, the almighty Father, maker of heaven and earth, maker of all things visible and invisible. I believe in one Lord Jesus Christ, only-begotten Son of God, born of the Father before time began; God from God, light from light, true God from true God; begotten, not made, one in essence with the Father, and through whom all things were made. For us men, and for our salvation (_here all genuflect_), he came down from heaven, took flesh of the Virgin Mary by the action of the Holy Spirit, and was made man. For our sake too, under Pontius Pilate, he was crucified, suffered death, and was buried. And the third day he rose from the dead, as the scriptures had foretold. And he ascended to heaven where he sits at the right hand of the Father. He will come again in glory to judge the living and the dead; and his reign will have no end. I believe too in the Holy Spirit, Lord and life-giver, who proceeds from the Father and the Son; who together with the Father and the Son is adored and glorified; who spoke through the prophets. And I believe in one holy, catholic, and apostolic Church. I acknowledge one baptism for the remission of sins. And I look forward to the resurrection of the dead, and the life of the world to come.
Amen.

**OFFERTORY**

The second part of the Mass, called the Offertory, reflected the eucharistic theology so prevalent since the Middle Ages.

_The priest turns to the people and says:_

Celebrant: The Lord be with you.
Server: And with you.
Celebrant: Let us pray.

_He then recites the Offertory, which is to be found in the Mass proper to the day._

**Commentary**: The priest first recites an offertory verse, based upon a text from Scripture, usually from the Psalms. These prayers, called the "super oblata," underscore the sacrificial notion of the Mass, signified by the word _oblation,_ and they are found in the Mass Propers which change according to the feast and the liturgical season. The purpose of these verses is to make a transition from the Liturgy of the Catechumens into the eucharistic Prayer. The choice of scriptural text heightens the sense of offering of the paschal victim for the salvation of the whole human race, as well as the offering of the Christian people together with Christ, the principal victim.

**Text**: _He now takes the paten with the host, which he offers up, saying:_

Holy Father, almighty, everlasting God, accept this unblemished sacrificial offering, which I, thy unworthy servant, make to thee, my living and true God, for my countless sins, offences, and neglects, and on behalf of all who are present here; likewise for all believing Christians, living and dead. Accept it for their good and mine, so that it may save us and bring us to everlasting life.
Amen.

**Commentary**: Then unveiling the chalice and paten, the priest raises the elements of bread and wine, individually reciting prayers which underline the action of a propitiatory offering for sins. According to liturgical custom, it was a serious sin for one to be late for Mass, but the sin was considered mortal if the chalice and paten were already uncovered when the latecomer arrived.

**Text**: *Moving to the Epistle side, the priest now pours wine and water into the chalice. He blesses the water, saying:*

O God, by whom the dignity of human nature was wondrously established and yet more wondrously restored, grant that through the sacramental use of this water and wine we may have fellowship in the Godhead of him who deigned to share our manhood, Jesus Christ, thy Son, our Lord, who is God, living and reigning with thee in the unity of the Holy Spirit, for ever and ever. Amen.

*He returns to the middle of the altar and offers up the chalice, saying:*

We offer thee, Lord, the chalice of salvation, entreating thy mercy that our offering may ascend with a sweet fragrance in the presence of thy divine majesty for our salvation and for that of all the world. Amen.

*Bowing slightly, he continues:*

Humbled in spirit and contrite of heart, may we find favour with thee, Lord, and may our sacrifice be so offered in thy sight this day that it may please thee, Lord our God.

*He then stands erect and invokes the Holy Spirit, making the sign of the cross over the bread and wine:*

Come, thou sanctifier, almighty, everlasting God, and bless these sacrificial gifts, prepared for the glory of thy holy name.

**Commentary**: A prayer addressed to the Holy Spirit with the sign of the cross over the elements precedes the washing of the hands accompanied with the recitation of Psalm 25. Every gesture is carefully measured so that, in the case of the hand washing, the priest presses his thumbs and forefingers together, extending only them for washing. This indicates that this is not a true ablution, but one for the sake of ritual purity.

**Text**: *The priest now goes to the Epistle side, where he washes his hands, reciting Psalm 25:6-12:*

With the pure in heart, I will wash my hands clean and take my place among them at thy altar, Lord, listening there to the sound of thy praises, telling the story of all thy wonderful deeds. How well, Lord, I love thy house in its beauty, the place where thy own glory dwells! Lord, never count this soul for lost with the wicked, this life among the bloodthirsty: hands ever stained with guilt, palms ever itching for a bribe! Be it mine to guide my steps clear of wrong: deliver me in thy mercy. My feet are set on firm ground; where thy people gather, Lord, I will join in blessing thy name.

*The* Gloria Patri *is omitted in the Masses of Passiontide and of the Dead.*

Glory be to the Father, and to the Son, and to the Holy Ghost. As it was in the beginning, is now, and ever shall be, world without end. Amen.

*Then, returning to the middle of the altar, the priest says:*

Holy Trinity, accept the offering we here make to thee in memory of the passion, resurrection, and ascension of our Lord Jesus Christ; in honour, too, of blessed Mary, ever-virgin, of blessed John the Baptist, of the holy apostles Peter and Paul, of the Martyrs whose relics are here, and of all the saints. To them let it bring honour, to us salvation; and may they whom we are commemorating on earth graciously plead for us heaven: through the same Christ our Lord. Amen.

**Commentary**: A prayer to the Most Holy Trinity to bless and receive the offerings of the entire church follows, with specific mention made of the connection between this offering and the passion, resurrection, and ascension of Christ. The prayer hearkens back to the earlier confession of sins with the mention of various saints.

**Text**: *The priest then asks the prayers of the people, turning towards them as he says the first two words aloud, then facing the altar:*

Pray, brethren, that my sacrifice and yours may find acceptance with God the almighty Father.

*Server:* May the Lord accept the sacrifice at your hands, to the praise and glory of his name, for our welfare also, and that of all his holy Church.

*Celebrant:* Amen.

**Commentary:** Turning to the people, the priest next invites them to pray that his sacrifice and theirs may find acceptance with God. Only the first two words of the invitation are spoken aloud, "Pray, Brethren," and the servers pick up the relay by responding on behalf of the people. In the English translation, it is difficult to tell whether the sacrifice of the priest is distinct from that of the people, but the Latin speaks of it in the singular indicating that this one sacrifice is offered by the priest in the name of all.

**Text:** *He now says one or more Secret prayers. Their number and order are those of the Collects. At the end of the last he says aloud:*

| | |
|---|---|
| *Celebrant:* | For ever and ever. |
| *Server:* | Amen. |

**Commentary:** Facing back towards the altar, the priest next prays quietly one or more variable prayers found in the Mass proper to the specific feast or season. These prayers are called the Secrets because they were said silently. These prayers lead to the preface concluded by the angelic hymn, "Holy, holy, holy." The prefaces are also variable, prescribed by the Mass proper to the day. The structure of the beginning dialogue between priest and servers is a good indication of the dialogical nature of the Roman liturgy, albeit reduced to a vicarious participation of the people through the responses of the servers. The attitude of priest and people is two-fold: They offer themselves with Christ, the eternal victim, and with the preface, they herald the great sacrificial action itself.

**Text:**
THE CANON

*He then begins the Preface.*

**Commentary:** The Canon is the third part of the liturgy, referring to the consecratory prayer of blessing, which contains the account of the Last Supper. The eucharistic prayer was invariable and unique, summoning the church to join the Angels and Saints, especially the Incarnate Word, in thanking God, in proclaiming God's holiness, in imploring God's help for the church, and especially those assisting at the Sacrifice. Unfortunately the fact that this prayer was said quietly, accompanied by a host of complicated and obscured gestures, did not insure any participation by the people other than as passive spectators. A somewhat detailed description of the rubrics, or actions to be done by the priest

when reciting the canon will serve as an example. The celebrant first looks up to the cross, extends and lifts his hands, then looks down while joining his hands. Next he bows, laying his hands on the altar and begins the eucharistic prayer silently. Clearly we are in the presence of high drama with every stage direction being spelled out in great detail by the rubrics of the missal. Three-signing of the cross with the right hand over the chalice and paten accompany the words "bless these + offerings, these + oblations, these + holy, unblemished sacrificial gifts," indicated by red crosses in text.

The priest then bows while remembering those for whom he prays during the liturgy. The priest, united in fellowship with the Blessed Virgin, with the Holy Apostles, Martyrs and all the Saints, becomes one with Christ who at the Last Supper commanded this action, "Do this in memory of me."

Spreading his hands over the elements in an action usually associated with summoning the Holy Spirit, he prays that the bread and wine might become a peace offering. This action is signaled by the ringing of bells by the server.

Three more signs of the cross accompany the consecratory prayer "to make this offering wholly + blessed, a thing + consecrated and + approved." Then he makes the sign of the cross over the bread as he says "Body" and another over the wine as he says "Blood."

Taking the bread next into his hands, he enters into the Institutional Narrative, recalling the actions of Christ at the Last Supper. Every gesture is carefully monitored by the Missal. As he says "lifting his eyes toward heaven," he looks up to the cross positioned high above the altar and at once looks down. "Giving thanks," he bows, and at the word "blessed," he again makes the sign of the cross over the host held in his left hand. Continuing on, he says in a low voice, while looking at the host, "For this is my body." When the words have been said, without delay he stands erect, then genuflects on the right knee and elevates the host over his head for all present to see.

Similarly with the wine, he takes the chalice into his hands and, bowing over it, says quietly the words of institution, once again blessing the cup at the appropriate cue, and elevates the cup over his head for all to see. The attitude of the priest and the assembled people is one of adoration, uniting their lives to that of Christ. Although the complexity of the liturgical gesture was not fully visible to the assembled people, they are aware that this action is to be reenacted in memory of Christ.

**Text:**

*The Preface to the Canon*

*The celebrant, with hands laid upon the altar, says or chants:*

| Celebrant: | The Lord be with you. |
|---|---|
| Server: | And with you. |
| Celebrant: | Let us lift up our hearts. |
| Server: | We lift them up to the Lord. |
| Celebrant: | Let us give thanks to the Lord our God. |
| Server: | That is just and fitting. |

*Any special Preface prescribed in the Mass proper to the day will be found in the section of special Prefaces. On Sundays which have no special Preface, that of the Holy Trinity is said, and on weekdays, unless otherwise directed, the Common Preface.*

### PREFACE OF THE HOLY TRINITY

Just it is indeed and fitting, right, and for our lasting good, that we should always and everywhere give thanks to thee, Lord, holy Father, almighty and eternal God; who with thy only-begotten Son and the Holy Ghost art one God, one Lord, not one as being a single person, but three Persons in one essence. Whatsoever by thy revelation we believe touching thy glory, that too we hold, without difference or distinction, of thy Son, and also of the Holy Spirit, so that in acknowledging the true, eternal Godhead, we adore in it each several Person, and yet a unity of essence, and a co-equal majesty; in praise of which the Angels and Archangels, the Cherubim too and the Seraphim, lift up their endless hymn, day by day, with one voice singing:

### THE COMMON PREFACE

Just it is indeed and fitting, right, and for our lasting good, that we should always and everywhere give thanks to thee, Lord, holy Father, almighty and eternal God, through Christ our Lord. It is through him that thy majesty is praised by Angels, adored by Dominations, feared by Powers; through him that the heavens and the celestial Virtues join with the blessed Seraphim in one glad hymn of praise. We pray thee let our voices blend with theirs as we humbly praise thee, singing:

### SANCTUS

*Here the bell is rung thrice.*

**Commentary:** To help the congregation in their devotional response, bells, either in the church tower or hand bells rung by a server, signal the solemnity of the moment.

**Text:**

Holy, holy, holy art thou, Lord God of hosts. Thy glory fills all heaven and earth. Hosanna in high heaven! Blessed be he who is coming in the name of the Lord. Hosanna in high heaven!

*The celebrant, bowing low over the altar, says silently:*

And so, through Jesus Christ, thy Son, our Lord, we humbly pray and beseech thee, most gracious Father, to accept and bless these offerings, these oblations, these holy, unblemished sacrificial gifts. We offer them to thee in the first place for thy holy Catholic Church, praying that thou wilt be pleased to keep and guide her in peace and unity throughout the world; together with thy servant our Pope *(N.)*, and *(N.)* our Bishop, and all who believe and foster the true Catholic and Apostolic faith.

**Commentary:** Once again, a triple sign of the cross accompanies the blessing of the sacrifice that is "pure +, holy +, and unblemished +" as well as two more signs of the cross, one over "the sacred Bread of everlasting life" and the other over "the Cup of eternal salvation."

**Text:**

Remember, Lord, thy servants *(N.)* and *(N.) (here the celebrant makes silent mention of those for whom he wishes to pray)*, and all here present. Their faith and devotion are known to thee. On their behalf we offer, and they too offer, this sacrifice in praise of thee, for themselves and for all who are theirs, for the redemption of their souls, for the hope of safety and salvation, paying homage to thee, their living, true, eternal God.

United in the same holy fellowship, we reverence the memory, first, of the glorious, ever-virgin Mary, Mother of our God and Lord Jesus Christ, and likewise that of thy blessed apostles and martyrs Peter and Paul, Andrew, James, John, Thomas, James, Philip, Bartholomew, Matthew, Simon, and Jude; of Linus, Cletus, Clement, Sixtus, Cornelius, Cyprian, Laurence, Chrysogonus, John, and Paul, Cosmas and Damian; and of all thy saints. Grant for the sake of their merits and prayers that in all things we may be guarded and helped by thy protection: through the same Christ our Lord. Amen.

_The bell is rung once as the celebrant spreads his hands over the bread and wine. He continues:_

And so, Lord, we thy servants, and with us thy whole household, make this peace offering, which we entreat thee to accept. Order our days in thy peace, and command that we be rescued from eternal damnation and numbered with the flock of thy elect: through Christ our Lord. Amen. We pray thee, God, be pleased to make this offering wholly blessed, a thing consecrated and approved, worthy of the human spirit and of thy acceptance, so that it may become for us the Body and Blood of thy dearly beloved Son, our Lord Jesus Christ.

_He takes the host in his hands and consecrates it, saying:_

He, on the day before he suffered death, took bread into his holy and worshipful hands, and lifting up his eyes to thee, God, his almighty Father in heaven, and giving thanks to thee, he blessed it, broke it, and gave it to his disciples, saying: Take, all of you, and eat of this:

For this is my body.

_The bell is rung thrice as he genuflects, shows the Sacred Host to the people, and genuflects again._
_He now consecrates the wine, saying:_

In like manner, when he had supped, taking also this goodly cup into his holy and worshipful hands, and again giving thanks to thee, he blessed it and gave it to his disciples, saying: Take, all of you, and drink of this:
For this is the chalice of my blood, of the new and everlasting covenant, a mystery of faith. It shall be shed for you and many others, so that sins may be forgiven.

_He genuflects, saying:_

Whenever you shall do these things, you shall do them in memory of me.

_He then shows the chalice to the people, genuflecting after doing so. The bell is again rung thrice. He continues:_

Calling therefore to mind the blessed Passion of this same Christ, thy Son, our Lord, and also his resurrection from the grave, and glorious ascension into heaven, we thy servants, Lord, and with us all thy holy people, offer to thy sovereign majesty, out of the gifts thou hast bestowed upon us, a sacrifice that is pure, holy, and unblemished, the sacred Bread of everlasting life, and the Cup of eternal salvation.

Deign to regard them with a favourable and gracious countenance, and to accept them as it pleased thee to accept the offerings of thy servant Abel the Just, and the sacrifice of our father Abraham, and that which thy great priest Melchisedech sacrificed to thee, a holy offering, a victim without blemish.

**Commentary**: Next he bows low over the altar and prays as a humble servant before Almighty God, kissing the altar when he speaks about the sacrifice. More signs of the cross are made over the eucharistic elements which accompany the words "Body" and "Blood," and the priest signs himself at the words "every grace and heavenly blessings."

**Text**: _Bowing low over the altar, he says:_

Humbly we ask it of thee, God almighty: bid these things be carried by the hands of thy holy angel up to thy altar on high, into the presence of thy divine majesty. And may those of us who by taking part in the sacrifice of this altar shall have received the sacred Body and Blood of thy Son, be filled with every grace and heavenly blessing: through the same Christ our Lord. Amen.

Remember also, Lord, thy servants _(N.)_ and _(N.)_, who have gone before us with the sign of faith and sleep the sleep of peace.

_Here the celebrant makes silent mention of those dead for whom he wishes to pray._

To them, Lord, and to all who rest in Christ, grant, we entreat thee, a place of cool repose, of light and peace: through the same Christ our Lord. Amen.

_Striking his breast, and raising his voice as he says the first three words, he continues:_

**Commentary**: When the priest prays for "thy sinful servants," he strikes his breast, while recalling a list of saints in whose company he seeks to be admitted, provided that his sins be forgiven.

**Text:**

To us also, thy sinful servants, who put our trust in thy countless acts of mercy, deign to grant some share and fellowship with thy holy apostles and martyrs: with John, Stephen, Matthias, Barnabas, Ignatius, Alexander, Marcellinus, Peter, Felicity, Perpetua, Agatha, Lucy, Agnes, Cecily, Anastasia, and all thy saints. Into their company we pray thee to admit us, not weighing our deserts, but freely granting us forgiveness: through Christ our Lord.

It is ever through him that all these good gifts, created so by thee, Lord, are by thee sanctified, endowed with life, blessed, and bestowed upon us.

*The celebrant makes the sign of the cross thrice over the chalice with the Sacred Host and twice between the chalice and himself, then raises the Host and chalice slightly, saying meanwhile:*

Through him, and with him, and in him, thou, God, almighty Father, in the unity of the Holy Spirit, hast all honor and glory,

**Commentary:** Yet again, more signs of the cross accompany the prayer over "all these good gifts" which are "+ sanctified, + endowed with life, + blessed" by God. Immediately the priest makes the sign of the cross thrice with the Host over the chalice, as he prays "through + him and with + him and in + him. . . ." Still holding the chalice in the same way with the left, he makes the sign of the cross twice over the altar cloth between himself and the chalice, as he continues, "Thou, God, almighty + Father, in the unity of the Holy + Spirit," then elevating the Host and chalice together a little above the altar, he finishes "hast all honor and glory."

**Text:** *Replacing the Host and chalice upon the altar, he then chants or says aloud:*

Celebrant:   World without end.

**Commentary:** As one might gather, the choreography of the liturgical prayer was terribly complicated, demanding the careful attention of the priest. In the short span of the eucharistic prayer, one can sense the redundancy of the liturgical gestures with the multiple signs of the cross, genuflections, and bows. Yet all these gestures were stringently governed by the rubrics in the Missal, giving hardly any room for personal expression and devotion. Furthermore, since the priest had his back to the people, almost

all the liturgical gestures were totally obscured from the view of the worshiping assembly.

**Text:**

Server:        Amen.
Celebrant:   Let us pray. Urged by our Saviour's bidding, and schooled by his divine ordinance, we make bold to say:
Our Father, who art in heaven, hallowed be thy name. Thy kingdom come. Thy will be done, on earth as it is in heaven. Give us this day our daily bread. And forgive us our trespasses, as we forgive those who trespass against us. And lead us not into temptation:
Server:        But deliver us from evil.
Celebrant:   *(silently)* Amen.

## COMMUNION

**Commentary:** The *Our Father* begins the preparation for communion. During the Middle Ages, the reception of communion was often limited to the priest. Given the strong penitential piety of the age, most people felt unworthy to receive the body and blood of the Lord. This sense of spiritual awe, linked to personal unworthiness, lead to the practice of "ocular communion." Stories circulate in which people would rush from church to church to see the elevation of the eucharistic elements and immediately depart as though they had seen the Devil. Because the priest had his back to the people, blocking the public view, people would cry out to him to lift the host higher so that they could see. There are other stories suggesting that in certain churches in England, people would drill holes into the churches so that they could peek in at the elevation. These facts contributed to the widespread practice of composing special musical pieces for the elevation. One consequence of this eucharistic piety was manifested in adoration of the Host in special vessels called *monstrances*. To combat many of these liturgical abuses and to encourage more frequent communion of the faithful, the Fourth Lateran Council (1215 C.E.) imposed that all people receive the Eucharist at least once a year during the Easter season.

**Text:** *Taking the paten in his right hand, he continues silently:*

Deliver us, we pray thee, Lord, from every evil, past, present, and to come, and at the intercession of the blessed and glorious ever-virgin Mary, Mother of God, of thy blessed apostles Peter and

Paul, of Andrew, and of all the saints (*he crosses himself with the paten and kisses it* ), be pleased to grant peace in our time, so that with the help of thy compassion we may be ever free from sin and safe from all disquiet.

*He then breaks the Sacred Host over the chalice, saying:*

Through the same Jesus Christ, thy Son, our Lord, who is God, living and reigning with thee in the unity of the Holy Spirit:

*He concludes the prayer aloud:*

Celebrant:	World without end.
Server:	Amen.

*He makes the sign of the Cross thrice with a particle of the Sacred Host over the chalice, chanting or saying aloud:*

Celebrant:	The peace of the Lord be always with you.
Server:	And with you.

*Then he drops the particle into the chalice and continues silently:*

May this sacramental mingling of the Body and Blood of our Lord Jesus Christ be for us who receive it a source of eternal life. Amen.

*He strikes his breast three times as he says aloud:*

Lamb of God, who takest away the sins of the world, have mercy on us.

Lamb of God, who takest away the sins of the world, have mercy on us.

Lamb of God, who takest away the sins of the world, give us peace.

*After this he says silently:*

Lord Jesus Christ, who didst say to thy apostles: I leave peace with you; it is my own peace that I give you: look not upon my sins but upon thy Church's faith, and graciously give her peace and unity in accordance with thy will: thou who art God, living and reigning for ever and ever. Amen.

*At Solemn Mass the kiss of peace is given here. The celebrant gives the kiss to the deacon and says:*

Peace be with you.

*The deacon responds:*

And with you.

*Next the deacon gives the kiss, with the same salutation and response, to the subdeacon, who passes it on to the clergy in choir, who in turn give it to one another.*

*The celebrant now says:*

Lord Jesus Christ, Son of the living God, who, by the Father's will and the cooperation of the Holy Spirit, didst by thy death bring life to the world, deliver me by this most holy Body and Blood of thine from all my sins and from every evil. Make me always cling to thy commandments, and never allow me to be parted from thee: who with the selfsame God the Father and the Holy Spirit art God, living and reigning for ever and ever. Amen.

Let not the partaking of thy Body, Lord Jesus Christ, which I, unworthy as I am, make bold to receive, turn against me into judgment and damnation, but through thy loving-kindness, let it safeguard me, body and soul, and bring me healing: thou who are God, living and reigning with God the Father in the unity of the Holy Spirit, world without end. Amen.

I will take the Bread of Heaven, and will call upon the name of the Lord.

*He takes the two pieces of the Sacred Host in his left hand. Then, saying the opening words audibly each time, and striking his breast with his right hand as he does so, he says thrice:*

Lord, I am not worthy that thou should enter beneath my roof, but say only the word, and my soul will be healed.

**Commentary:** The double communion in the Tridentine liturgy remained as a vestige of earlier eucharistic practice, where the priest would first receive, but the second communion for the faithful was not always in force. The council of Trent reiterated the legislation of Lateran IV regarding the frequent reception of the Eucharist but not always to great avail. The strong sacrificial and penitential piety left a trace on the eucharistic piety whereby the congregation envisaged itself as offering itself in acts of homage. This could be accomplished in adoration as well as reception of the Host. They would make entreaties that the eucharistic bread would deliver them from all evil and bring about the pardon of their sins.

**Text:** *The bell is rung as he says these words, and those of the congregation who are to communicate go to the altar rails.*

*The celebrant crosses himself with the Sacred Host, saying:*

The Body of our Lord Jesus Christ preserve my soul for everlasting life. Amen.

*He then receives the Host.*

*After a short pause the celebrant collects any fragments of the Host that may be on the corporal, and puts them into the chalice, saying:*

What return shall I make to the Lord for all that he has given me? I will take the chalice of salvation and invoke the names of the Lord. Praised be the Lord! When I invoke his name I shall be secure from my enemies.

*Crossing himself with the chalice, he says:*

The Blood of our Lord Jesus Christ preserve my soul for everlasting life. Amen.

*He drinks the contents of the chalice.*

*If any wish to communicate, the Confession is now repeated by the deacon or server:*

I confess to almighty God, to blessed Mary, ever-virgin, to blessed Michael the archangel, to blessed John the Baptist, to the holy apostles Peter and Paul, to all the saints, and to you, father, that I have sinned exceedingly in thought, word, and deed:

*He strikes his breast three times, saying:*

through my fault, through my own fault, through my own most grievous fault. Therefore I beseech the blessed Mary, ever-virgin, blessed Michael the archangel, blessed John the Baptist, the holy apostles Peter and Paul, all the saints, and you, father, to pray to the Lord our God for me.

*The celebrant turns to the people and says aloud:*

May almighty God have mercy upon you, pardon your sins, and bring you to everlasting life.
*Server:* Amen.

*All cross themselves as he says:*

May the almighty and merciful Lord grant you pardon, absolution, and remission of your sins.
*Server:* Amen.

*The celebrant, taking the ciborium from the altar, holds up a consecrated Host and says:*

Behold the Lamb of God, behold him who takes away the sins of the world.

*Then he says three times:*

Lord, I am not worthy that thou shouldst enter beneath my roof, but say only the word, and my soul will be healed.

**Commentary**: Just before receiving communion, the words of the centurion are reiterated, protesting the unworthiness of the recipients and begging humble pardon. The communion unites the priest and people most intimately with Christ, and through him with the very life of the Trinity.

*He then goes to the altar rails and gives Holy Communion, saying to each communicant:*

The Body of our Lord Jesus Christ preserve your soul for everlasting life. Amen.

*When all have communicated, he returns to the altar and replaces the ciborium in the tabernacle.*

*The congregation may now sit. Wine is poured into the chalice; the celebrant drinks it, and says:*

That which our mouths have taken, Lord, may we possess in purity of heart; and may the gift of the moment become for us an everlasting remedy.

*Wine and water are poured into the chalice over the fingers of the celebrant, who dries them with the purificator, saying silently:*

May thy Body, Lord, which I have taken, and thy Blood, which I have drunk, cleave to every fibre of my being. Grant that no stain of sin may be left in me, now that I am renewed by this pure and holy sacrament; who livest and reignest, world without end. Amen.

*He then drinks the wine and water, after which, at High Mass, the subdeacon dries the inside of the chalice with the purificator. He then lays it across the chalice and places on it the paten and pall. Then he veils the chalice and takes it to the credence. If there is no subdeacon, the celebrant dries and veils the chalice and leaves it in the middle of the altar. The celebrant now goes to the Epistle side and says the Communion antiphon, which will be found in the Mass proper to the day. Then he goes to the middle of the altar, and, turning to the people (who at High Mass stand, but at Low Mass kneel), says or chants:*

*Celebrant:* The Lord be with you.
*Server:* And with you.

*After which he reads one or more Postcommunion prayers. Their number and order are those of the Collects. Before the first and second of these prayers he says or chants:* Oremus; *and at the end of the first and last the server or choir responds:* Amen.

**Commentary**: The variable prayer after communion (Postcommunion) thanks God for this inestimable gift, followed by the blessing of the Triune God.

**Text**: _Coming back to the middle of the altar, the celebrant turns to the people and says or chants:_

> Celebrant:    The Lord be with you.
> _Server:_        And with you.

_Then, if it is a day upon which the Gloria has been said, the deacon turns to the people and chants, or at Low Mass, the celebrant says aloud:_

> Go, this is the dismissal.
> _Server:_        Thanks be to God.

_In the Masses of Holy Saturday and Easter week, the words_ alleluia, alleluia, _are added, thus:_

> Go, this is the dismissal; alleluia, alleluia.

_If the Gloria has not be said, the deacon or celebrant chants or says instead:_

> Let us bless the Lord.
> _Server:_        Thanks be to God.

_Bowing before the altar, the celebrant says silently:_

> May the tribute of my humble ministry be pleasing to thee, Holy Trinity. Grant that the sacrifice which I, unworthy as I am, have offered in the presence of thy majesty may be acceptable to thee. Through thy mercy, may it bring forgiveness to me and to all for whom I have offered it: through Christ our Lord.
> Amen.

_He kisses the altar, and all kneel as he gives the blessing, saying:_

> Almighty God bless you: the Father, the Son, and the Holy Ghost.
> _Server:_        Amen.

_The congregation rises when, at the Gospel side, he says:_

> Celebrant:    The Lord be with you.
> _Server:_        And with you.

_He then makes the sign of the cross upon the altar, and all cross themselves on forehead, lips, and breast, as he says:_

> The beginning of the holy Gospel according to John.

_Or, if the second Gospel is that of a commemoration:_

A passage from the holy Gospel according to _(N.)_.
> _Server:_        Glory to thee, Lord.

_He then reads the Gospel, John 1:1-14:_

At the beginning of time the Word already was; and God had the Word abiding with him, and the Word was God. He abode, at the beginning of time, with God. It was through him that all things came into being, and without him came nothing that has come to be. In him there was life, and that life was the light of men. And the light shines in darkness, a darkness which was not able to master it. A man appeared, sent from God, whose name was John. He came for a witness, to bear witness to the light, so that through him all men might learn to believe. He was not the Light; he was sent to bear witness to the light. There is one who enlightens every soul born into the world; he was the true Light. He, through whom the world was made, was in the world, and the world treated him as a stranger. He came to what was his own, and they who were his own gave him no welcome. But all those who did welcome him, he empowered to become the children of God, all those who believe in his name; their birth came, not from human stock, not from nature's will or man's, but from God. _Here all genuflect._ And the Word was made flesh and came to dwell among us; and we had sight of his glory, glory such as belongs to the Father's only-begotten Son, full of grace and truth.
> _Server:_        Thanks be to God.

**Commentary**: The last Gospel recalls the glory of the Incarnate Word who dwells within the body of the church and whom all the participants carry to the world in which they live.

(Text from _Liturgies of the Western Church,_ ed. Bard Thompson [Cleveland, Ohio: World Publishing Co., 1962], 55–89; transcribed from _The Missal in Latin and English,_ being the text of the _Missale Romanum_ with English rubrics and a new translation.)

### ——————— Conclusion ———————

Due to the unintelligibility of the Latin Mass to the majority of the faithful, they depended heavily upon prayer books, which would help evoke the proper sentiments at the appropriate moments in the Mass. Music was also a key element for stimulating the proper feelings. Of course, a more complete study would reveal that the prayers and the musical styles changed according to the changes in the spiritual and cultural modes of the various centuries.

In conclusion, one can look at the enactment of the Mass on three levels. In the sanctuary of the church, the priest and servers engaged in a fixed form of liturgical prayer, the only variations in the order being the predetermined variable prayers. All gestures and words were carefully governed by the Roman Missal, which even indicated how far apart the priest's hands should be while praying. The more solemn the occasion, the more ornate were the vestments and the more incense was used to create a sense of the celestial action. In the body or the nave of the church, the faithful watched, listened, smelled, but passively participated as spectators of this heavenly affair. By use of personal missals, the literate could follow the action, much like the way a modern operagoer would use a libretto. Otherwise people used other means of popular piety, especially the rosary. In the loft, the choir would accompany the action, always being careful to their cues by way of bells, gestures, or certain key words. The principle of progressive solemnity applied to them as well since the choice of the setting of the Mass could be determined by the liturgical feast. Often the priest would continue his part, speaking silently as the missal demanded, while the choir provided a rich aural background. Each actor, or group of actors, knew what was expected of them, but there was little intersection of dramatic action or dialogue.

Concerning the development of sacred music, the musical setting of a Mass became the standard repertory of any serious composer. Since the ordinary parts were fixed texts, composers took great liberties in setting them. By the late eighteenth century, some musical settings clearly went beyond liturgical use, and the musical piece was destined for the concert hall. A clear example of this is the *Missa Solemnis* of Beethoven. Josef Jungmann was sharply critical of the overall liturgical musical development in the post Tridentine period: "It sometimes happened that this church music, which had fallen more and more into the hands of laymen, forgot that it was meant to serve the liturgical action. As a result of this, the music often fitted very poorly into the liturgical setting. And since this latter was but little understood, and because esthetic consideration began to hold sway, the liturgy was not only submerged under this ever-growing art but actually suppressed, so that even at this time there were

festival occasions which might best be described as church concerts with liturgical accompaniment" (*Mass of the Roman Rite* [New York: Benziger, 1959], vol. 1, 149).

A more conscious attempt to promote active participation came from certain communities of Europe and in the nineteenth century, when the German *Singmesse* was introduced, and in the early twentieth century, when the *missa dialogata* or *missa recitata* was tried. In these experimental rites, the congregation was encouraged to learn the Latin responses. But these attempts at fuller liturgical participation for the faithful were not widespread.

In spite of Trent's intention to provide a pure Roman Missal, historical accretions did creep into the Mass. In 1833, the call came from the French Benedictine Dom Prosper Gueranger to rid these liturgical books of any arbitrary additions and return the Roman Rite to its noble purity. This signaled the beginning of the Catholic Restoration, which would grow into the liturgical movement of the late nineteenth and early twentieth centuries. A crack in the liturgical ossification was detected in 1949 and in 1952, when Pope Pius XII called for the restoration of the Easter Vigil. A few years later in 1956, the International Congress for Pastoral Liturgy met at Assisi, and in 1959, the Conference for Liturgy and Missions met a Nijmegen. Within a short decade, new reforms were demanded by the Second Vatican Council to return the liturgy to its pristine understanding as the "public work" of the whole people of God.

Michael S. Driscoll

## 166 • Bibliography on Pre-Reformation Liturgies

Deiss, Lucien. *Springtime of the Liturgy.* Collegeville, Minn.: Liturgical Press, 1979. Here are the actual sources of liturgy—explanations, descriptions, and liturgies from the early church.

Jasper, R. C. D., and G. J. Cuming, *Prayers of the Eucharist: Early and Reformed,* 2d ed. New York: Oxford University Press, 1980. Studies in the history of worship through an examination of liturgies. This work presents and comments on forty liturgies from early Christians through the Book of Common Prayer, 1662. An invaluable aid for anyone who wishes to study the historic texts of the Eucharist.

Liesel, Nikolaus. _The Eucharistic Liturgies of the Eastern Churches._ Collegeville, Minn.: Liturgical Press, 1963. This volume contains the complete liturgies of the various parts and actions of the liturgy. Liturgies include Coptic Rite, Ethiopic Rite, Syrian Rite, Malankarese Rite, Maronite Rite, Greek Rite, Melkite Rite, Russian Rite, Ruthenian Rite, Chaldean Rite, Malabarese Rite, and the Armenian Rite.

Thompson, Bard. _Liturgies of the Western Church._ Cleveland: World Publishing Co., 1962. This invaluable work contains the full liturgies of the church through the Reformation era. Among the liturgies of interest to the study of Roman Catholic worship is the full Latin (and English translation) of the Roman Rite.

# NINE

# Reformation Models of Worship

*The sixteenth-century Reformers regarded the worship model of the Roman Catholic church in varying ways. The liturgies of Luther and of the Anglican church retained more elements of the Catholic Mass. Calvin and Hubmaier made more radical attempts to "purify" worship and discarded much of the Catholic liturgy. Unfortunately, none of the Reformers had available to them the knowledge of ancient Christian worship accessible to scholars today. Nevertheless, the Reformers sought to remain faithful to what they believed to be appropriate worship in keeping with Scripture and Scripture-based traditions.*

## 167 ✦ LUTHER: *FORMULA MISSAE*: ORDER OF MASS AND COMMUNION FOR THE CHURCH AT WITTENBERG (1523)

*Luther's* Formula Missae, *written after his break with Rome, did not suggest a wholescale reform of the Catholic mass. Rather, Luther cautiously suggested ways of adapting the Mass for use in local congregations and also proposed ways to make it more relevant to the common people.*

### Introduction

Martin Luther (1483–1546) came reluctantly to liturgical change. In the midst of growing enthusiasm for reformation, he was afraid that any liturgical dictum from his hand would be quickly snatched up, widely printed, and applied as a new law. He did not want anyone saying, "This proposal Luther writes is the only true way to do Christian worship." Rather, he believed that liturgical change depended upon actual pastoral circumstances and that it always had to be preceded by education and accompanied by love. Furthermore, if only the gospel of Christ was clearly preached, the character of the ceremonies hardly mattered. His own taste, like that of the common people he meant to serve, seems to have run generally toward the conservation of visually dramatic ceremony and the encouragement of good, participatory music.

Finally, asked repeatedly by his friends and irritated by the widespread use of liturgies created by his enemies, he had to act. In 1523, he published his *Formula Missae,* the "Order of Mass and Communion for the Church at Wittenberg." He would return to the task in 1526 with his "German Mass."

In the same years, he also published two different proposals for doing baptism and two essays about what is important in worship. But the first of these works, the *Formula,* is the one which has had the greatest and longest-lived influence among Lutherans and the one which stands at the root of North American Lutheran liturgy. It is the text which, in edited form, is printed here.

There are three important things to note about this text. In the first place, it is not a liturgy. Luther, in fact, never produced an actual liturgy. This text is neither a service book nor a manual of liturgical prayers. Rather, it is an essay discussing how to use evangelically the traditional liturgy and liturgical books of the church. It is that discussion which is important to Luther, not the imposition of a particular set of prayers. He is concerned with the order of things and their meaning in that order. Indeed, the best of the Lutheran tradition continues to be a discussion about the meaning and evangelical use of catholic material, not the production of required texts.

In the second place, the essay is about "how we do it in *Wittenberg*." Luther knows that other congregations and cities may take his pattern as their own, but he wants to avoid the unthinking application of a new law. Liturgy, while it receives universal material and traditions, is always local, always done here, in our particular way. And Luther wants any liturgical change to be preceded by teaching and preaching. Change must be for the sake of the clarity of the gospel, not because of the authority of the preacher.

In the third place, the liturgy which Luther here

envisions is celebrated _in Latin_. Luther calls for a sermon in the language of the people, but here he is still proposing a liturgy in the old language of the church, sung by the priest and a choir, with the people sometimes entering in, if they knew the chant. Later, he would interweave vernacular hymnody with this Latin rite, and then he would see the old liturgical texts brought over into singable German. But, for now, he uses a Latin mass, sung in a church with an educated choir. He could, of course, count on such a choir being present in Wittenberg, a university town with scholars at every level.

The reader, then, ought to imagine a medieval parish or collegiate church in Wittenberg. The old statues and stained glass are all still in place. There is a choir of schoolboys and university students near the altar, at the east end of the building. There is a great crucifix over the altar. Candles are burning. The people are seated on benches or standing against the walls. There is a high pulpit against one wall, in the midst of the people. And the clergy are mostly vested in the old mass vestments, although the preacher may very well be wearing a black university gown.

**Text:** Grace and peace in Christ to the venerable Doctor Nicholas Hausmann, bishop of the church in Zwickau, saint in Christ, from Martin Luther.

Until now I have only used books and sermons to wean the hearts of people from their godless regard for ceremonial; for I believed it would be a Christian and helpful thing if I could prompt a peaceful removal of the abomination which Satan set up in the holy place through the man of sin [Matt 24:15; 2 Thess. 2:3-4]. Therefore, I have used neither authority nor pressure. Nor did I make any innovations. For I have been hesitant and fearful, partly because of the weak in faith, who cannot suddenly exchange an old and accustomed order of worship for a new and unusual one, and more so because of the fickle and fastidious spirits who rush in like unclean swine without faith or reason, and who delight only in novelty and tire of it as quickly, when it has worn off. Such people are a nuisance even in other affairs, but in spiritual matters, they are absolutely unbearable. Nonetheless, at the risk of bursting with anger, I must bear with them, unless I want to let the gospel itself be denied to the people.

But since there is hope now that the hearts of many have been enlightened and strengthened by the grace of God, and since the cause of the king-dom of Christ demands that at long last offenses should be removed from it, we must dare something in the name of Christ. For it is right that we should provide at least for a few, lest by our desire to detach ourselves from the frivolous faddism of some people we provide for nobody, or by our fear of ultimately offending others, we endorse their universally held abominations.

Therefore, most excellent Nicholas, since you have requested it so often, we will deal with an evangelical form of saying mass (as it is called) and of administering communion. And we will so deal with it that we shall no longer rule hearts by teaching alone, but we will put our hand to it and put the revision into practice in the public administration of communion, not wishing, however, to prejudice others against adopting and following a different order. Indeed, we heartily beg in the name of Christ that if in time something better should be revealed to them, they would tell us to be silent, so that by a common effort we may aid the common cause.

We therefore first assert: It is not now nor ever has been our intention to abolish the liturgical service of God completely, but rather to purify the one that is now in use from the wretched accretions which corrupt it and to point out an evangelical use.

**Commentary:** Luther's work is addressed to one of his friends, the pastor of a congregation in a neighboring town. He calls this pastor "bishop" because he believes the pastor and presider in any Christian congregation is the present occupant of the New Testament office of bishop and is more important than the regional princes and hierarchs which the medieval church called "bishop." He continues to use this title for the local pastor throughout this document.

Luther expresses his hesitations about doing liturgical work at all. He wants no innovations, no faddism. He wants no offense to the weak. He wants no universal rule which _he_ determines. Nonetheless, against these fears, he decides to "dare something in the name of Christ."

Any reader of Luther quickly discovers the passion, vigor, and earthiness of his language. He is hard on his opponents and colorful in his condemnations. He is equally passionate in his care for the people and his descriptions of the Gospel. This is not a measured and moderate theological treatise, such as one would have later from the hand of John Calvin.

Luther plans not only to write about the liturgy but to see it actually done in Wittenberg. He is not sure it should be done this way elsewhere, and he pleads for better work to be made known.

This last paragraph states the central Lutheran liturgical principle: not the invention of a new liturgy, even a supposedly "biblical" one, but the purification and evangelical use of the old liturgy.

**Text:** First, we approve and retain the introits for the Lord's days and the festivals of Christ, such as Easter, Pentecost, and the Nativity, although we prefer the Psalms from which they were taken as of old. But for the time being we permit the accepted use. And if any desire to approve the introits (inasmuch as they have been taken from Psalms or other passages of Scripture) for apostles' days, for feasts of the Virgin and of other saints, we do not condemn them. But we in Wittenberg intend to observe only the Lord's days and the festivals of the Lord. We think that all the feasts of the saints should be abrogated, or if anything in them deserves it, it should be brought into the Sunday sermon. We regard the feasts of Purification and Annunciation as feasts of Christ, even as Epiphany and Circumcision. Instead of the feasts of St. Stephen and of St. John the Evangelist, we are pleased to use the office of the Nativity. The feasts of the Holy Cross shall be anathema. Let others act according to their own conscience or in consideration of the weakness of some—whatever the Spirit may suggest.

Second, we accept the Kyrie eleison in the form in which it has been used until now, with the various melodies for different seasons, together with the Angelic Hymn, Gloria in Excelsis, which follows it. However, the bishop may decide to omit the latter as often as he wishes.

Third, the prayer or collect which follows, if it is evangelical (and those for Sunday usually are), should be retained in its accepted form; but there should be only one. After this the Epistle is read. Certainly the time has not yet come to attempt revision here, as nothing unevangelical is read, except that those parts from the Epistles of Paul in which faith is taught are read only rarely, while the exhortations to morality are most frequently read. The Epistles seem to have been chosen by a singularly unlearned and superstitious advocate of works. But for the service, those sections in which faith in Christ is taught should have been given preference. The latter were certainly considered more often in

the Gospels by whoever it was who chose these lessons. In the meantime, the sermon in the vernacular will have to supply what is lacking. If in the future the vernacular be used in the mass (which Christ may grant), one must see to it that Epistles and Gospels chosen from the best and most weighty parts of these writings be read in the mass.

Fourth, the gradual of two verses shall be sung, either together with the Alleluia, or one of the two, as the bishop may decide. But the Quadregesima graduals, and others like them that exceed two verses, may be sung at home by whoever wants them. In church we do not want to quench the spirit of the faithful with tedium. Nor is it proper to distinguish Lent, Holy Week, or Good Friday from other days, lest we seem to mock and ridicule Christ with half of a mass and the one part of the sacrament. For the Alleluia is the perpetual voice of the church, just as the memorial of His passion and victory is perpetual.

**Commentary:** The liturgy begins. The choir is singing the *Introit,* that old fragment of a psalm which is a shortened version of the entrance psalm originally used in the Roman Mass. Luther would like to recover the whole psalm, but for now the traditional introits stay in place. While the choir is singing, a procession enters, perhaps from the sacristy door on the side, perhaps from the great western door. Candles and a cross lead the way and the vested clergy follow, moving through the building and up to the altar.

In Wittenberg, this day is probably a Sunday, though it may be one of the days of the year which are regarded as "feasts of Christ": i.e., Christmas, New Year's Day (Circumcision), Epiphany, the Purification (February 2), Annunciation (March 25), Ascensino, or Transfiguration (August 6). While at this point Luther is proposing elimination of the Saints' days, the example of the saints as believers should be brought into the Sunday sermon nearest their old observances.

When the procession concludes, with the presiding priest, the "bishop," standing before the altar, facing east, the choir takes up the chant of the ninefold *Kyrie* ("Lord have mercy, Christ have mercy, Lord have mercy"), using one of the old chant tones. Many of the people may join in this singing.

Then the presider intones, "*Gloria in Excelsis Deo,*" "Glory be to God on high," and the choir continues singing this old Roman rite entrance hymn.

Finally the entrance is completed with the presider, still facing the altar in the east, intoning the *collect* which the old mass formularies appointed for this particular Sunday. This is the prayer of the day, the prayer which sums up and concludes the entrance into worship.

Many of the people will have been standing throughout this entrance. Now they will be seated, though some will continue to mill around and others will be standing against the walls. The presider, still standing to one side at the altar but now facing the people, reads a passage from one of the Epistles in Latin. In a few years, here, this passage will be read in German and may be read from the pulpit. In spite of Luther's critique, Lutherans for the most part continued to read the old appointed readings, even when they shifted to reading in German. No matter what the reading, however, the teaching of "faith in Christ" was to be the business of the sermon.

The lesson finished, the choir takes up the chant again. They sing the traditional verses between the readings, the Gradual or the Gradual and Alleluia. Forbidden by Luther, they do not sing the longer versions of these, nor do they usually sing the Latin hymn, the so-called sequence which may sometimes follow here on great feasts. In spite of Luther, they generally continue to suppress Alleluia during Lent.

Text: Fifth, we allow no sequences or proses unless the bishop wishes to use the short one for the Nativity of Christ: "*Grates nunc omnes.*" There are hardly any which smack of the Spirit, save those of the Holy Spirit: "*Sancti Spiritus*" and "*Veni sancte spiritus,*" which may be sung after breakfast, at Vespers, or at mass (if the bishop pleases).

Sixth, the Gospel lesson follows, for which we neither prohibit nor prescribe candles or incense. Let these things be free.

Seventh, the custom of singing the Nicene Creed does not displease us; yet this matter should also be left in the hands of the bishop. Likewise, we do not think that it matters whether the sermon in the vernacular comes after the Creed or before the introit of the mass; although it might be argued that since the Gospel is the voice crying in the wilderness and calling unbelievers to faith, it seems particularly fitting to preach before mass. For properly

speaking, the mass consists in using the Gospel and communing at the table of the Lord. Inasmuch as it belongs to believers, it should be observed apart (from unbelievers). Yet since we are free, this argument does not bind us, especially since everything in the mass up to the Creed is ours, free and not prescribed by God; therefore it does not necessarily have anything to do with the mass.

Eighth, that utter abomination follows which forces all that precedes in the mass into its service and is, therefore, called the offertory. From here on almost everything smacks and savors of sacrifice. And the words of life and salvation [the Words of Institution] are imbedded in the midst of it all, just as the ark of the Lord once stood in the idol's temple next to Dagon. And there was no Israelite who could approach or bring back to the ark until it "smote his enemies in the hinder parts, putting them to a perpetual reproach," and forced them to return it—which is a parable of the present time. Let us, therefore, repudiate everything that smacks of sacrifice, together with the entire canon and retain only that which is pure and holy, and so order our mass.

After the Creed or after the sermon, let bread and wine be made ready for blessing in the customary manner. I have not yet decided whether or not water should be mixed with the wine. I rather incline, however, to favor pure wine without water; for the passage, "Thy wine is mixed with water," in Isaiah 1 [:22] gives the mixture a bad connotation.

Pure wine beautifully portrays the purity of gospel teaching. Further, the blood of Christ, whom we here commemorate, has been poured out unmixed with ours. Nor can the fancies of those be upheld who say that this is a sign of our union with Christ; for that is not what we commemorate. In fact, we are not united with Christ until he sheds his blood; or else we would be celebrating the shedding of our own blood together with the blood of Christ shed for us. Nonetheless, I have no intention of cramping anyone's freedom or of introducing a law that might again lead to superstition. Christ will not care very much about these matters, nor are they worth arguing about. Enough foolish controversies have been fought on these and many other matters by the Roman and Greek churches. And though some direct attention to the water and blood which flowed from the side of Jesus, they prove nothing. For that water signified something entirely different from what they wish that mixed water to signify. Nor was it mixed with blood. The symbolism does not fit, and the reference is inapplicable. As a human invention, this mixing [of water and wine] cannot, therefore, be considered binding.

**Commentary:** While the choir is singing, a procession forms again, the cross and candles being carried into the midst of the people, preceded by a cleric carrying incense and followed by another carrying a Gospel Book and by the presider. All the people stand to receive this procession. In the midst of the church, the procession gathers into a group around the book, and the presider then chants the appointed passage from one of the four Gospels. Though the candles and incense are sometimes omitted, they are not here. Indeed, in the dark church, the candles are often needed to read the text of the book. And this text is always chanted. Even later, when the Gospel would come to be read in German rather than Latin, the "Gospel tone" was used for the reading. This sung text is able to make itself heard, reverberating into all the corners of the old stone church.

As the procession then makes it way back to the eastern end of the church, the choir takes up chanting the Nicene Creed, and the presider (or, sometimes, another priest, vested in the habit of a monastic teacher at the university) turns aside to climb into the pulpit which is near the people. When the creed is finished, the preacher begins the sermon. On some occasions, this vernacular preaching may be the first thing to occur, before the singing of the Introit. Such a placement continues the medieval practice of the friars, but Luther now gives this free-floating sermon an evangelical interpretation. And he sums up the whole of this first part of the mass, this chanting and reading of Scripture and preaching, in the phrase "using the gospel." But today in Wittenberg—and ordinarily—this use of the gospel takes place in the classic order: After the readings, which the preacher first repeats in the vernacular, the sermon makes the gospel of Jesus Christ available to be used by faith.

What follows now is the greatest Lutheran break with the medieval mass. The several prayers which the priest would recite at the preparation of the Table ("the little canon" of the offertory) and at the consecration of the elements (the "Roman canon" or the "great canon" of the mass) are simply excised. For Luther, all these texts stank of sacrifice, as if the Supper were something we were giving to God, not God to us. The preparation of the Table

occurs, rather, in silence, and the prayer over bread and cup is reduced to elegant simplicity. What the people see, however, is essentially unchanged. They never took part in these prayers, in any case: The prayers were recited by the priest alone, *sotto voce* or even silently, facing the altar, and the people never had the book in which they were written. So, while the priest comes down out of the pulpit and begins to approach the altar, clerics near the altar are unveiling the chalice, spreading the corporal (the great linen cloth on which the vessels will stand), and bringing bread and wine from the side table (the "credence"). Today, only wine is used, as Luther counseled. No water usually is added to the chalice, though that is still sometimes done, albeit without the medieval prayers which used to accompany it.

**Text:**

II. The bread and wine having been prepared, one may proceed as follows:

The Lord be with you.
*Response:*    And with thy spirit.
Lift up your hearts.
*Response:*    Let us lift them to the Lord.
Let us give thanks unto the Lord our God.
*Response:*    It is meet and right.

It is truly meet and right, just and salutary for us to give thanks to Thee always and everywhere, Holy Lord, Father Almighty, Eternal God, through Christ our Lord . . .

III. Then:

. . . Who the day before he suffered, took bread, and when he had given thanks, brake it, and gave it to his disciples, saying, Take, eat; this is my body, which is given for you.

After the same manner also the cup when he had supped, saying, This cup is the New Testament in my blood, which is shed for you and for many, for the remission of sins; this do, as often as ye do it, in remembrance of me.

I wish these words of Christ, with a brief pause after the preface, to be recited in the same tone in which the Lord's Prayer is chanted elsewhere in the canon so that those who are present may be able to hear them, although the evangelically minded should be free about all these things and may recite these words either silently or audibly.

IV.   The blessing ended, let the choir sing the Sanctus. And while the Benedictus is being sung, let the bread and cup be elevated according to the customary rite for the benefit of the weak in faith who might be offended if such an obvious change in this rite of the mass were suddenly made. This concession can be made especially where, through sermons in the vernacular, they have been taught what the elevations means.

V. After this, the Lord's Prayer shall be read. Thus, let us pray: "Taught by thy saving precepts . . ." The prayer which follows, "Deliver us, we beseech thee . . ." is to be omitted together with all the signs they were accustomed to make over the host and with the host over the chalice. Nor shall the host be broken or mixed into the chalice. But immediately after the Lord's Prayer shall be said, "The peace of the Lord," etc., which is, so to speak, a public absolution of the sins of the communicants, the true voice of the gospel announcing remission of sins, and therefore the one and most worthy preparation for the Lord's Table, if faith holds to these words as coming from the mouth of Christ himself. On this account, I would like to have it pronounced facing the people, as the bishops are accustomed to do, which is the only custom of the ancient bishops that is left among our bishops.

**Commentary:** The presider now stands at the prepared altar. Turning toward the people, he begins the prayer at the Table—or "the blessing"—by the ancient exchange with people, sung according to the ancient tone. Many of the people know the Latin response and reply together with the choir. Then, turning toward the east, toward the bread and cup, the presider lifts his hands in the old posture of prayer and begins the thanksgiving.

The thanksgiving quickly comes to the recitation of the account of the Supper, and at the mention of bread and cup, the presider slightly lifts the paten (the plate for the wafer-form bread) and chalice in turn. Unlike medieval practice, this entire prayer, though simple and brief, is sung aloud in the old chant tone of the Lord's Prayer so the people can hear it.

After the presider concludes Christ's words over the cup, the choir begins to sing the Sanctus and Benedictus:

> Holy, holy, holy Lord God of Sabbaoth, heaven and earth are full of your glory. Hosanna in the highest. Blessed is he who comes in the name of the Lord. Hosanna in the highest.

While they are so singing, the priest lifts the bread and cup well over his head, so the people can see them, so they can behold these concrete signs of the mercy of God in Christ. Many of the people fall to their knees before this sight, just as they have done all their lives. Luther's theology of the real presence of Christ "in, under, and with" the elements enables the churches following him to retain the elevation, as long as the people understand its significance.

The paten and chalice are then replaced on the altar and the presider sings, "Taught by your saving precept, we make bold to say," whereupon he begins to chant the Lord's Prayer in the traditional tone. Today, the choir and many of the people join him. In the following way is the Lutheran canon of the mass is concluded:

> dialogue,
> thanksgiving and words of Christ,
> Sanctus with elevation, and
> Lord's Prayer.

With these words and ceremony, the promise of Christ is claimed, a thanksgiving prayer is said, and the Table is blessed.

None of the medieval prayers which followed at this point, mostly prayers for forgiveness and for a good reception of communion, are recited. Rather, the priest turns to the people and greets them with the fragment of the ancient kiss of peace which still survives: He says, "The peace of the Lord be with you always." A few voices answer with the traditional response: "And also with you." They have been taught that this mutual greeting is the very voice of the gospel, announcing the forgiveness of sins, and that trusting this voice is enough of a preparation for a worthy communion.

**Text:** Then, while the Agnus Dei is sung, let him [the bishop] communicate, first himself and then the people. But if he should wish to pray the prayer, "O Lord Jesus Christ, Son of the living God, who according to the will of the Father," etc., before communing, he does not pray wrongly, provided he changes the singular "mine" and "me" to the plural "ours" and "us." The same thing holds for the prayer, "The body of our Lord Jesus Christ preserve me (or thy) soul unto life eternal," and "The blood of our Lord preserve thy soul unto life eternal."

VII. If he desires to have the communion sung, let it be sung. But instead of the _complenda_ or final collect, because it sounds almost like a sacrifice, let the following prayer be read in the same tone: "What we have taken with our lips, O Lord . . ." The following one may also be read: "May thy body which we have received . . . (changing to the plural number) . . . who livest and reignest world without end." "The Lord be with you," etc. In place of the *Ite missa,* let the *Benedicamus domino* be said, adding Alleluia according to its own melodies where and when it is desired. Or the *Benedicamus* may be borrowed from Vespers.

VIII. The customary benediction may be given, or else the one from Numbers 6 [:24-27], which the Lord himself appointed:

> "The Lord bless us and keep us. The Lord make his face shine upon us and be gracious unto us. The Lord lift up his countenance upon us, and give us peace."

Or the one from Psalm 67 [:6-7]:

> "God, even our God shall bless us. God shall bless us; and all the ends of the earth shall fear him."

I believe Christ used something like this when, ascending into heaven, he blessed his disciples [Luke 24:50-51].

The bishop should also be free to decide on the order in which he will receive and administer both species. He may choose to bless both bread and wine before he takes the bread. Or else he may, between the blessing of the bread and of the wine, give the bread both to himself and to as many as desire it, then bless the wine and administer it to all. This is the order Christ seems to have observed, as the words of the Gospel show, where he told them to eat the bread before he had blessed the cup [Mark 14:22-23]. Then is said expressly, "Likewise also the cup after he supped" [Luke 22:20; 1 Cor. 11:25]. Thus you see that the cup was not blessed until after the bread had been eaten. But this order is [now] quite new and allows no room for those prayers which heretofore were said after the blessing, unless they would also be changed.

**Commentary:** Then the choir begins to sing the *Agnus Dei* ("Lamb of God, you take away the sins of the world, have mercy on us, grant us peace"), while the presider communes himself and the people begin to come forward to kneel at the altar rail and receive Communion themselves. They are given both the bread and the cup, the former by the presider and the latter by another cleric. Today, these words are used at the distribution:

> The body of our Lord Jesus Christ preserve your soul into life eternal; and the blood of our Lord preserve your soul unto life eternal.

Luther's reflections on a different order (prayer over the bread then distribution of the bread followed by prayer over the cup and distribution of the cup) remain only a literary conjecture for now, although later this rather awkward idea will be tried occasionally.

When the choir has finished the Agnus Dei and when they themselves have communed, they take up the chant of a passage of Scripture, called "the communion," properly appointed for the day in the old missals. The presider, meanwhile, consumes what remains of the bread and wine and cleanses the vessels. When the choir has finished, he chants these prayers, facing the altar:

> What we have taken with our lips, O Lord, may we receive with pure minds, and from a temporal gift may it become for us an everlasting remedy. May the body and blood which we have received cleave to our inmost parts. And grant that no stain of sin may remain in us whom this pure and holy sacrament has refreshed, O God, who lives and reigns, world without end. Amen.

The mass then comes quickly to a conclusion with the rites of Dismissal. Facing the people, the priest exchanges the greeting with them again. He then chants, "Let us bless the Lord," the choir and some of the people responding, "Thanks be to God." Then he extends his hands and intones the benediction. He and the other clerics leave and the people begin to move toward the door.

**Text:** Thus we think about the mass. But in all these matters we will want to beware, lest we make binding what should be free, or make sinners of those who may do some things differently or omit others. All that matters is that the Words of Institution should be kept intact and that everything should be done by faith. For these rites are supposed to be for Christians, i.e., children of the "free woman" [Gal. 4:31], who observe them voluntarily and from the heart, but are free to change them how and whenever they may wish. Therefore, it is not in these matters that anyone should either seek or establish as law some indispensable form. . . . Further, even if different people make use of different rites, let no one judge or despise the other, but every man be fully persuaded in his own mind [Rom. 14:5]. Let us feel and think the same, even though we may act differently. And let us approve each other's rites lest schisms and sects should result from this diversity in rites. . . . For external rites, even though we cannot do without them—just as we cannot do without food or drink—do not commend us to God, even as food does not commend us to him [1 Cor. 8:8]. Faith and love commend us to God. Wherefore here let the word of Paul hold sway, "For the kingdom of God is not meat and drink; but righteousness, and peace, and joy in the Holy Ghost" [Rom. 14:17]. So the kingdom of God is not any rite, but faith within you, etc.

**Commentary**: Again Luther states the central principal: It is _we_ who need ritual, like we need food and drink, not _God_ who requires it. Therefore, the liturgy should rightly be traditional, but it must also be evangelical, a use of the gospel and a reception of Christ's gift. The details of the ceremony must never be made into a new law.

(Text excerpted from "An Order of Mass and Communion for the Church at Wittenberg, 1523," in _Luther's Works,_ vol. 53: _Liturgy and Hymns,_ ed. by Ulrich S. Leupold [Philadelphia: Fortress Press, 1965], 19–31.)

Gordon Lathrop

## 168 ✦ CALVIN: _THE FORM OF CHURCH PRAYERS,_ STRASSBURG LITURGY (1545)

_Although there is considerable diversity within the Reformed community, it is fair to say that the ideas of John Calvin strongly influenced Reformed worship practice. Calvin's Strassburg Liturgy is presented below._

——————— **Introduction** ———————

**Definition of Calvinist.** It is often assumed that "Calvinist" and "Reformed" are synonymous, but in fact the Reformed tradition includes considerable diversity. The most important streams within the Reformed family of churches are usually called Zwinglian and Calvinist, for the two most outstanding leaders, Ulrich Zwingli in Zurich and John Calvin in Geneva. One of the critical issues in the sixteenth century was who could share in the Lord's Supper together; Zwinglians and Calvinists agreed upon intercommunion in 1549, but there continued to be a variety of theological and practical differ-

_Martin Luther. This is a facsimile of a woodcut portrait of Luther that appeared on the title page of his pamphlet_ The Babylonian Captivity of the Church, _published in 1520 by the Johann Press in Strassburg._

ences within this family of Reformed churches, particularly in ecclesiology and the liturgy.

**Calvinist Worship and Liturgy in Context.** Although their descendants have sometimes forgotten it, sixteenth-century reformers were very deeply concerned about worship and they devoted an immense amount of time, thought, and care both to the theology and the practice of worship. Indeed, the primary purpose of much reform was to bring the church back to the right worship of God, according to God's will. The negative task of attacking what they perceived as a perversion of worship was normally only a necessary first step toward the goal of a pure worship which would glorify God and serve human salvation. There was no universal agreement on what exactly was the right and pure worship of God, and the process of discerning what was wrong and what should be put in its place took time and effort. Even where there was general agreement in principle, there were diversities in practice, particularly when it came to embodying worship in liturgical acts.

The liturgy which is called "Calvinist" is not the work of one person but of a community, though John Calvin gave the service his own particular impress, and his influence was very important in the spread of this liturgy. The Sunday service of Word and Sacrament is the fruit of many years of study, reflection, and practical experimentation on the part of a considerable number of church leaders, especially Martin Bucer and colleagues in Strassburg, in contact with other reformers across the whole spectrum of theological opinion. The liturgy published here also did not remain frozen, though it continues to be one of the best expressions of worship in the sixteenth-century Calvinist tradition.

**Theological Principles.** Calvin's liturgy was clearly shaped by certain biblical principles and influenced by what was known of early church practice. Calvinists believed that there are some elements which are necessary for a rightly formed liturgy, and they read Acts 2:42 as a summary of the first Christians' worship: "the teaching of the apostles, the breaking of bread, fellowship/*koinonia,* and prayers." Calvinists generally understood this biblical pattern to mean that liturgy should include the Word/Gospel purely preached, the sacraments rightly administered, prayer (both spoken and sung), and the expression of communal love, for example in the kiss of peace or almsgiving.

**Liturgical Practice.** Early Calvinists were not as literalistic as some of their descendants; they did not read the Bible as a book of liturgical rubrics. In different circumstances, it was possible to have different practical expressions of the essentials, and early Calvinists were prepared to alter details to fit historical or pastoral situations. Such changes must not be made simply to be entertaining or creative; the fundamental basis for reshaping the precise order is practical concern for how the right worship of God is best expressed in a given community (usually a region, not different congregations of the same city).

The church's liturgy does not belong to the pastors, though those specially trained in the necessary knowledge (Bible, theology, history) are the proper leaders in formulating the community's worship. One way of illustrating the minister's role is through his dress, which was simply the ordinary street dress (outer garment) of an educated man. The "Genevan

gown" was originally intended not to distinguish the minister from any other lay-educated person (physicians and lawyers wore the same thing); the academic gown did emphasize the importance of a learned ministry among Calvinists, since the chief task of a pastor was to proclaim the gospel using every gift of mind as well as heart. Calvin himself was very conscious of the heart, though some Calvinists have focused narrowly on the mind.

**The Development of Calvin's Liturgy.** The form of Calvin's Sunday service printed here is his "Strassburg liturgy." After his first ministry in Geneva ended in 1538, Calvin was for three years the pastor of a French-speaking refugee congregation in the German-speaking city of Strassburg. Here Calvin associated with Bucer and others, and was much influenced by the Strassburg German liturgy which had been developing over the previous fifteen years.

Calvin was particularly impressed with the singing in Strasbourg, and his first liturgical publication (1539) was a small French Psalter containing twenty-two pieces: Psalms translated by the gifted French poet Clement Marot or by Calvin himself, and Simeon's Song, the Decalogue, and the Apostles Creed, set to music. Later, as more of Marot's translations became available, Calvin replaced his versions with Marot's; Calvin's colleague in Geneva, Theodore Beza, translated the rest of the Psalms and published the complete Psalter for the first time in 1562. After 1539, the Psalter and the Calvinist liturgy were normally printed together.

It is generally thought that Calvin published a version of his French Sunday service during his Strassburg pastorate, perhaps in 1540, but no copy of this exists, and its precise contents remain unclear. The first extant texts of Calvin's service were published in 1542: one in Strassburg by his successor as pastor in the French congregation, one by Calvin himself in Geneva, where he had returned in the autumn of 1541. The two editions of 1542 were somewhat different, since Calvin had been obliged to modify his text for the Genevan situation. Another edition of the Strassburg text, with more changes (which tended to combine elements of the two 1542 editions), was published in 1545, and editions of the Genevan service, with minor modifications, appeared during Calvin's lifetime (1547, 1549, 1552, 1553, 1559, 1561) and later. The text followed here is Strassburg 1545, with the most important variants noted in the commentary.

One final word about the order: Calvin expressed clearly that he wanted to see the service of Word and the service of the Lord's Supper celebrated weekly. He could accept a monthly celebration, however, because he believed that people needed time to prepare for a right participation in the Supper, and in Strassburg, Calvin's congregation celebrated the Supper monthly. The Word and the service of the Supper were not printed in a block, since the sacrament was not celebrated every time there was a service of the Word. (Besides the Sundays when the sacrament was not celebrated, there were weekday services of the Word, the most important being the days of prayers.) Here the order of the printed text has been slightly altered to present the whole service as it might have been experienced.

**Text:**
**The Form of Church Prayers**
_On Sunday morning the following form is generally used._

Our help is in the name of the Lord, who made heaven and earth. Amen.

**Commentary:** The text is Psalm 124:8, the usual greeting in Calvinist services. In Strassburg the minister is probably at the Table; in Geneva, already in the pulpit.

**Text:**
Confession

My brethren, let each of you present himself before the face of the Lord, and confess his faults and sins, following my words in his heart.

O Lord God, eternal and almighty Father, we confess and acknowledge unfeignedly before thy holy majesty that we are poor sinners, conceived and born in iniquity and corruption, prone to do evil, incapable of any good, and that in our depravity we transgress thy holy commandments without end or ceasing: Wherefore we purchase for ourselves, through thy righteous judgment, our ruin and perdition. Nevertheless, O Lord, we are grieved that we have offended thee; and we condemn ourselves and our sins with true repentance, beseeching thy grace to relieve our distress. O God and Father most gracious and full of compassion, have mercy upon us in the name of thy Son, our Lord Jesus Christ. And as thou dost blot out our sins and stains, magnify and increase in us

day by day the grace of thy Holy Spirit: that as we acknowledge our unrighteousness with all our heart, we may be moved by that sorrow which shall bring forth true repentance in us, mortifying all our sins, and producing in us the fruits of righteousness and innocence which are pleasing unto thee; through the same Jesus Christ &c.[Our Lord. Amen.]

**Commentary:** People kneel for the confession. In place of traditional individual confessions, Calvinists made confession a corporate act of the church as a body. Calvinists begin worship with the recognition of sinfulness because humans can only approach God rightly if they acknowledge what they are: sinners in need of God's grace in Christ.

**Text:** _Now the Minister delivers some word of Scripture to console the conscience; and then he pronounces the Absolution in this manner:_

Let each of you truly acknowledge that he is a sinner, humbling himself before God, and believe that the heavenly Father wills to be gracious unto him in Jesus Christ. To all those that repent in this wise, and look to Jesus Christ for their salvation, I declare that the absolution of sins is effected, in the name of the Father, and of the Son, and of the Holy Spirit. Amen.

**Commentary:** Calvin instructs the pastor to pronounce an appropriate text of Scripture. Bucer offers several examples: John 3:16; 3:35-36; Acts 10:43; 1 Tim. 2:1-2. For Calvinists, the power of forgiveness is attached to the Gospel, not particular persons, and Christians may confess to each other and have the promise of forgiveness, though the minister of the Word is the usual bearer of the Gospel and therefore of the Word of forgiveness. Genevans insisted on omitting the scriptural verses and absolution, probably because they associated these with the priestly monopoly on absolution in Roman Catholic tradition.

**Text:** _Now the Congregation sings the first table of the Commandments, after which the Minister says:_

The Lord be with us. Let us pray to the Lord.

Heavenly Father, full of goodness and grace, as thou art pleased to declare thy holy will unto thy poor servants, and to instruct them in the righteousness of thy law, grant that it may also be inscribed and impressed upon our hearts in such wise, that in all our life we may endeavor to serve and obey none beside thee. Neither impute to us at all the transgressions which we have committed against thy law: that, perceiving thy manifold grace upon us in such abundance, we may have cause to praise and glorify thee through Jesus Christ, thy Son, our Lord. Amen.

**Commentary**: The 1542 Strassburg text says "the people sing"; in 1545 the words "the first table of the law" are added—possibly simply expressing what had been the content of the singing, though this cannot be proved. Geneva omitted the Decalogue until 1549, then sang it after the sermon; here, between the confession and the prayer before the sermon, they sang a psalm. The first table (Num. 20:2-11) expresses how to worship and love God; the second concerns love of neighbor (Num. 20:12-17). The Decalogue may well have been placed after the confession and absolution because in Calvinist understanding, the most important use of the Law (in Calvin studies called "the third use of the Law") is to show the forgiven sinner what a regenerate life looks like.

**Text**: *While the congregation sings the rest of the commandments, the Minister goes into the pulpit; and then he offers prayers of the type which follows.*

[*Collect for Illumination*]

We call upon our heavenly Father, Father of all goodness and mercy, asking Him to cast the eye of His mercy on us His poor servants, not imputing to us the many faults and offenses which we have committed, by which we have provoked His wrath against us, but [instead] seeing us in the face of His Son, Jesus Christ our Lord, as He has established Him as Mediator between Him and us. Let us pray that, as the whole plenitude of wisdom and light is in Him, He may guide us by His Holy Spirit to the true understanding of His holy teaching, and may make it bear in us all the fruits of righteousness, to the glory and exaltation of His Name and the instruction and edification of His church. And we will pray to Him in the name and the favor of His beloved Son Jesus Christ, as we have been taught by Him, saying: Our Father who art in heaven, [hallowed be thy name; thy kingdom come, thy will be done, as in heaven so also on earth. Give us today our daily bread. Forgive us our debts as we forgive our debtors. Lead us not into temptation but deliver us from evil. For thine is the kingdom and the power and the glory, forever. Amen.]

**Commentary**: The invocation of the Holy Spirit before the Bible reading and sermon was at the minister's discretion; Strassburg gives this example, Geneva simply lists key points. (Author's translation.)

**Text**:
[Scripture reading and sermon]

**Commentary**: The Bible reading and sermon are not described in Calvin's service, though Bucer gives a few instructions. Reformed theologians rejected the lectionary because they saw it as having treated Scripture in a very selective way, and they wanted people to hear the whole Bible proclaimed. Following the practice of John Chrysostom and others, Reformed pastors normally preached straight through a Biblical book, the system called "continuous reading" (*lectio continua*). At special times, such as Easter, Pentecost, and Christmas, Calvin would interrupt whatever series he was doing to preach on the appropriate biblical texts. He also envisioned interrupting a series for sermons on the Lord's Supper (though probably this would not apply regularly if the Supper were celebrated frequently).

Normally, the pastor would read from the Bible, taking up the text where he had left off at the previous sermon and reading the number of verses he thought he could cover. Calvin's sermons probably lasted about an hour, though many of his colleagues were less restrained and he took some of them to task for going on too long. Usually the Sunday morning text was a Gospel, occasionally an Epistle. On Sunday afternoons, Calvin preached on the Psalms or Epistles; on weekdays, the text was usually Old Testament. (Preaching services were held frequently in Reformed cities: at least several days a week, and often daily.) Calvin's sermons (all extant ones were preached in Geneva) were biblical exposition and application. The text was explained verse by verse; the content was much like Calvin's commentaries (lectures to future pastors) but suited to the education of his audience. One of the marked characteristics of the sermons is the application and/or exhortation for each person to apply to herself or himself what the Bible teaches.

Text: *At the end of the Sermon, the Minister, having made exhortations to prayer, commences in this manner.*

Almighty God, heavenly Father, thou hast promised to grant our requests which we make unto thee in the name of thy well-beloved Son, Jesus Christ our Lord: by whose teaching and that of His apostles we have also been taught to gather together in His name, with the promise that He will be in the midst of us, and will be our intercessor with thee, to obtain all those things for which we agree to ask on earth.

First we have thy commandment to pray for those whom thou hast established over us as rulers and governors; and then, for all the needs of thy people, and indeed of all mankind. Wherefore, with trust in thy holy doctrine and promises, and now especially that we are gathered here before thy face and in the name of thy Son, our Lord Jesus, we do heartily beseech thee, our gracious God and Father, in the name of our only Saviour and Mediator, to grant us the free pardon of our faults and offenses through thine infinite mercy, and to draw and lift up our thoughts and desires unto thee in such wise that we may be able to call upon thee with all our heart, yea agreeably to thy good pleasure and only-reasonable will.

Wherefore we pray thee, O heavenly Father, for all princes and lords, thy servants, to whom thou hast intrusted the administration of thy justice, and especially for the magistrates of this city. May it please thee to impart to them thy Spirit, who alone is good and truly sovereign, and daily increase in them the same, that with true faith they may acknowledge Jesus Christ, thy Son, our Lord, to be the King of kings and Lord of lords, as thou has given Him all power in heaven and earth. May they seek to serve Him and to exalt His kingdom in their government, guiding and ruling their subjects, who are the work of thy hands and the sheep of thy pasture, in accordance with thy good pleasure. So may all of us both here and throughout the earth, being kept in perfect peace and quietness, serve thee in all godliness and virtue, and being delivered and protected from the fear of our enemies, give praise unto thee all the days of our life.

We pray thee also, O faithful Father and Saviour, for all those whom thou hast ordained pastors of thy faithful people, to whom thou hast intrusted the care of souls and the ministry of thy holy Gospel. Direct and guide them by the Holy Spirit, that they be found faithful and loyal ministers of thy glory, having but one goal: that all the poor, wandering, and lost sheep be gathered and restored to the Lord Jesus Christ, the chief Shepherd and Prince of bishops, so that they may grow and increase in Him daily unto all righteousness and holiness. Wilt thou, on the contrary, deliver all the churches from the mouths of ravening wolves and from all mercenaries who seek their own ambition or profit, but never the exaltation of thy holy name alone, nor the salvation of thy flock.

We pray thee, now, O most gracious and merciful Father, for all men everywhere. As it is thy will to be acknowledged the Saviour of the whole world, through the redemption wrought by thy Son Jesus Christ, grant that those who are still estranged from the knowledge of Him, being in the darkness and captivity of error and ignorance, may be brought by the illumination of thy Holy Spirit and the preaching of thy Gospel to the straight way of salvation, which is to know thee, the only true God, and Jesus Christ whom thou hast sent. Grant that those whom thou hast already visited with thy grace and enlightened with the knowledge of thy Word may grow in goodness day by day, enriched by the spiritual blessings: so that all together we may worship thee with one heart and one voice, giving honor and reverence to thy Christ, our Master, King, and Lawgiver.

Likewise, O God of all comfort, we commend unto thee all those whom thou dost visit and chasten with cross and tribulation, whether by poverty, prison, sickness, or banishment, or any other misery of the body or affliction of the spirit. Enable them to perceive and understand thy fatherly affection which doth chasten them unto their correction that thy may turn unto thee with their whole heart, and having turned, receive full consolation and deliverance from every ill.

Finally, O God and Father, grant also to those who are gathered here in the name of thy Son Jesus to hear His Word (and to keep His holy Supper), that we may acknowledge truly, without hypocrisy, what perdition is ours by nature, what condemnation we deserve and heap upon ourselves from day to day by our unhappy and disordered life. Wherefore, seeing that there is nothing of good in us and that our flesh and blood cannot inherit thy kingdom, may we yield ourselves completely, with all our love and steadfast faith, to thy dear Son, our Lord, the only Saviour and Redeemer:

To the end that He, dwelling in us, may mortify our old Adam, renewing us for a better life, *by which thy name, according as it is holy and worthy, may be exalted and glorified everywhere and in all places, and that we with all creatures may give thee true and perfect obedience, even as thine angels and heavenly messengers have no desire but to fulfill thy commandments. Thus may thy will be done without any contradiction, and all men apply themselves to serve and please thee, renouncing their own will and all the desires of their flesh. *In this manner, mayest thou have lordship and dominion over us all, and may we learn more and more each day to submit and subject ourselves to thy majesty. In such wise, mayest thou be King and Ruler over all the earth, guiding thy people by the sceptre of thy Word and the power of thy Spirit, confounding thine enemies by the might of thy truth and righteousness.

*And thus may every power and principality which stands against thy glory be destroyed and abolished day by day, till the fulfillment of thy kingdom be manifest, when thou shalt appear in judgment.

*Grant that we who walk in the love and fear of thy name may be nourished by thy goodness; and supply us with all things necessary and expedient to eat our bread in peace. Then, seeing that thou carest for us, we may better acknowledge thee as our Father and await all good gifts from thy hand, withdrawing our trust from all creatures, to place it entirely in thee and thy goodness.

*And since in this mortal life we are poor sinners, so full of weakness that we fail continually and stray from the right way, may it please thee to pardon our faults by which we are beholden to thy judgment; and through that remission, deliver us from the obligation of eternal death in which we stand. Be pleased, therefore, to turn aside thy wrath from us, neither impute to us the iniquity which is in us; even as we, by reason of thy commandment, forget the injuries done to us, and in instead of seeking vengeance, solicit good for our enemies.

*Finally, may it please thee to sustain us by thy power for the time to come, that we may not stumble because of the weakness of our flesh. And especially as we of ourselves are so frail that we are not able to stand fast for a single moment, while, on the other hand, we are continually beset and assailed by so many enemies—the devil, the world, sin, and our own flesh never ceasing to make war upon us—wilt thou strengthen us by thy Holy Spirit and arm us with thy grace, that we may be able to resist all temptations firmly, and preserve in this spiritual battle until we shall attain full victory, to triumph at last in thy kingdom with our Captain and Protector, Jesus Christ our Lord.

**Commentary**: This prayer is primarily intercessory, concluding with a paraphrase of the Lord's Prayer (here marked with asterisks for: Your Name be hallowed, Your kingdom come, Your will be done, Give us our daily bread, Forgive our sins, Lead us not into temptation but deliver from evil). Note that the daily bread is physical, earthly food; the model prayer is concerned with all matters, including the ordinary nourishment of this life. The 1542 Strassburg text does not have the paraphrase, but after the recitation of the Lord's Prayer, the minister is instructed to explain it to the people. There is a significant addition to this prayer in 1559, intercession for those Christians who are being persecuted for their faith.

**Text**:
[The Manner of Celebrating the Lord's Supper]
Rubric prefixed to the Supper service:

"It is proper to observe that on the Sunday prior to the celebration of the Lord's Supper, the following admonitions are made to the people: first, that each person prepare and dispose himself to receive it worthily and with such reverence that it deserves; second, that children may certainly not be brought forward unless they are well instructed and have made profession of their faith in church; third, that if strangers are there who may still be untaught and ignorant, they proceed to present themselves for private instruction. On the day of the Lord's Supper, the Minister touches upon it in the conclusion of his Sermon, or better, if there is occasion, preaches the whole Sermon about it, in order to explain to the people what our Lord wishes to say and signify by this mystery, and in what way it behooves us to receive it."

**Commentary**: In the Strassburg text the Supper service is also prefaced by an essay explaining the meaning and character of the Supper and the whole service. This essay includes references to the giving of alms for the poor, and Calvinists considered _koinonia_ (fellowship, communion) or love a necessary part of right worship (see Introduction). There are no rubrics in Calvin's service, however, to indicate when the alms collection was to be made. The medieval "offertory" was the presentation of the host and wine for the sacrifice of the Mass, so Protestants eliminated it (see below). Most instituted a collection for the poor, but often did not include it in their rubrics. It is fairly clear that Calvin collected alms during the Supper service in Strassburg, and he certainly believed it should be done, but this alms collection cannot easily be assigned a precise place in the order.

The minister moves from pulpit to table. In Geneva the minister recited the creed in the name of the people. Geneva gives no instructions about preparing the table, though it was probably done at this point. The simple language—or omission—was intended to lessen the ceremonial focus on the material elements (and the idea of sacrifice).

**Text**: _Then, after the accustomed prayers have been offered, the congregation, in making the confession of the faith, sings the Apostles Creed to testify that all wish to live and die in the Christian doctrine and religion. Meanwhile, the minister prepares the bread and wine on the table. Thereafter he prays in this fashion:_

Inasmuch as we have made confession of our faith to testify that we are children of God, hoping therefore that He will take heed of us as a gracious Father, let us pray to Him saying:

Heavenly Father, full of all goodness and mercy, as our Lord Jesus Christ has not only offered His body and blood once on the Cross for the remission of our sins, but also desires to impart them to us as our nourishment unto everlasting life, we beseech thee to grant us this grace: that we may receive at His hands such a great gift and benefit with true sincerity of heart and with ardent zeal. In steadfast faith, may we receive His body and blood, yea Christ Himself entire, who, being true God and true man, is verily the holy bread of heaven which gives us life. So may we live no longer in ourselves, after our nature which is entirely corrupt and vicious, but may He live in us to lead us to the life that is holy, blessed, and everlasting: whereby we may truly become par-

takers of the new and eternal testament, the covenant of grace, assured that it is thy good pleasure to be our gracious Father forever, never reckoning our faults against us, and to provide for us, as thy well-beloved children and heirs, all our needs both of soul and body. Thus may we render praise and thanks unto thee without ceasing and magnify thy name in word and deed.

Grant us, therefore, O heavenly Father, so to celebrate this day the blessed memorial and remembrance of thy dear Son, to exercise ourselves in the same, and to proclaim the benefit of His death, that, receiving new growth and strength in faith and in all things good, we may with so much greater confidence proclaim thee our Father and glory in thee; through the same Jesus Christ, thy Son, our Lord, in whose name we pray unto thee, as He hath taught us.

Our Father which art in heaven, [hallowed be thy name. Thy kingdom come, thy will be done, as in heaven so also on earth. Give us today our daily bread. Forgive us our debts as we forgive our debtors. Lead us not into temptation but deliver us from evil. For thine is the kingdom and the power and the glory, forever. Amen.]

**Commentary**: Note the emphasis on real communication of Christ's body and blood and benefits. For Calvinists, the Lord's Supper is a gift which God gives to the church, not a sacrifice which the church offers to God.

**Text**: _Then the Minister says:_

Let us hear how Jesus Christ instituted His holy Supper for us, as St. Paul relates it in the eleventh chapter of First Corinthians:

I have received of the Lord, he says, that which I have delivered unto you: That the Lord Jesus, on the night in which he was betrayed, took bread: And when He had given thanks, He brake it and said, Take, eat, this is my body which is broken for you: this do in remembrance of me. After the same manner, when He had supped, He took the cup saying: This cup is the new testament in my blood: this do ye, as oft as ye drink it, in remembrance of me. For as often as ye eat this bread and drink this cup, ye do proclaim the Lord's death till He come. Therefore, whosoever shall eat this bread and drink of this cup unworthily shall be guilty of the body and blood of the Lord. But let a man examine himself and so let him eat of this bread and drink of this cup. For whosoever eateth and drinketh unworthily, taketh his own condemnation, not discerning the Lord's body.

**Commentary:** 1 Corinthians 11:23-29. Also in Geneva; Strassburg 1542 has only verses 23-26.

**Text:**

We have heard, my brethren, how our Lord observed His Supper with His disciples, from which we learn that strangers and those who do not belong to the company of His faithful people must not be admitted. *Therefore, following that precept in the name and by the authority of our Lord Jesus Christ, I excommunicate all idolaters, blasphemers, and despisers of God, all heretics and those who create private sects in order to break the unity of the Church, all perjurers, all who rebel against father or mother or superior, all who promote sedition or mutiny; brutal and disorderly persons, adulterers, lewd and lustful men, thieves, ravishers, greedy and graspy people, drunkards, gluttons, and all those who lead a scandalous and dissolute life. I warn them to abstain from this Holy Table, lest they defile and contaminate the holy food which our Lord Jesus Christ gives to none except they that belong to His household of faith.

Moreover, in accordance with the exhortation of St. Paul, let every man examine and prove his own conscience to see whether he truly repents of his faults and grieves over his sins, desiring to live henceforth a holy life according to God. **Above all, let him see whether he has his trust in the mercy of God and seeks his salvation wholly in Jesus Christ and, renouncing all hatred and rancor, has high resolve and courage to live in peace and brotherly love with his neighbors.

***If we have this witness in our hearts before God, never doubt that he claims us as His children, and that the Lord Jesus addresses His Word to us, to invite us to His Table and to give us this holy Sacrament which He imparted to His disciples.

And yet, we may be conscious of much frailty and misery in ourselves, such that we do not have perfect faith, but are inclined toward defiance and unbelief, or that we do not devote ourselves wholly to the service of God and with such zeal as we ought, but have to fight daily against the lusts of our flesh. Nevertheless, since our Lord has granted us the grace of having His Gospel graven on our hearts so that we may withstand all unbelief, and has given us the desire and longing to renounce our own wishes that we may follow His righteousness and His holy commandments: let us be assured that the sins and imperfections which remain in us will not prevent Him from receiving us and making us worthy partakers of this spiritual Table. For we do not come here to testify that we are perfect or righteous in ourselves. On the contrary, by seeking our life in Jesus Christ we confess that we are in death. Know, therefore, that this Sacrament is a medicine for the poor sick souls, and that the only worthiness which our Lord requires of us is to know ourselves sufficiently to deplore our sins and to find all our pleasure, joy, and satisfaction in Him alone.

Above all, therefore, let us believe those promises which Jesus Christ, who is the unfailing truth, has spoken with His own lips: He is truly willing to make us partakers of His body and blood, in order that we may possess Him wholly and in such wise that He may live in us and we in Him. And though we see but bread and wine, we must not doubt that He accomplishes spiritually in our souls all that He shows us outwardly by these visible signs, namely, that He is the bread of heaven to feed and nourish us unto eternal life. So, let us never be unmindful of the infinite goodness of our Savior who spreads out all His riches and blessings on this Table, to impart them to us. For in giving Himself to us, He makes a testimony to us that all that He has is ours. Therefore, let us receive this Sacrament as a pledge that the virtue of His death and passion is imputed to us for righteousness, even as though we had suffered them in our own persons. May we never be so perverse as to draw away when Jesus Christ invites us so gently by His Word. But accounting the worthiness of this precious gift which He gives, let us present ourselves to Him with ardent zeal, that He may make us capable of receiving it.

To do so, let us lift our spirits and hearts on high, where Jesus Christ is in the glory of His Father, whence we expect Him at our redemption. Let us not be fascinated by these earthly and corruptible elements which we see with our eyes and touch with our hands, seeking Him there as though He were enclosed in the bread or wine. Then only shall our souls be disposed to be nourished and vivified by His substance when they are lifted up above all earthly things, attaining even to heaven and entering the Kingdom of God where He dwells. Therefore let us be content to have the bread and wine as signs and witnesses, seeking the truth spiritually where the Word of God promises that we shall find it.

**Commentary**: Strassburg 1542 only gives a rubric, instructing the minister to excommunicate impenitent sinners, exhort all to a proper participation, and then the minister, the deacon, and the people receive communion. Calvin is usually remembered for his excommunication of the unworthy, and unworthiness is usually understood morally. In fact, one might be suspended from the Lord's Supper as easily for ignorance as for improper behavior. The participation in the Supper requires at least a minimum understanding of the Gospel and faith (see above). Here the moral does come to the fore (*), but note that the most important thing about worthiness is not moral purity but trust in God's mercy and loving relationships with one's neighbor (**). This becomes particularly evident (***) in the description of who is welcomed—not the perfect, but those who recognize their need and trust only God.

**Text**: _That done, the Minister, having informed the people that they are to come to the holy table in reverence, good order, and Christian humility, first partakes himself of the bread and wine, then administers them* to the deacon, and subsequently to the whole congregation, saying:_

Take, eat, the body of Jesus, which has been delivered unto death for you.

_And the deacon offers the cup, saying:_

This is the cup of the new testament in the blood of Jesus, which has been shed for you.

**Commentary**: Asterisk indicates "it" changed to "them." Geneva 1542 simply says "ministers" distribute the bread and wine to the people; from other sources we know that the pastor was assisted by deacons and elders. The words of delivery are not found in Strassburg 1542 or Geneva. Having deacons give the cup was a common patristic practice

adopted by Calvinists. The deacons meant here are those whose primary work was the care of the poor and afflicted and whose other activity in the liturgy was the collection of alms.

**Text**: _Meanwhile, the congregation sings the Psalm: "Louange et Grace" (Praise and thanks)._

**Commentary**: "Praise and grace" are the opening words of Psalm 138. In Geneva during the communion, people sang psalms or heard some appropriate part of Scripture read.

**Text**: _The thanksgiving after the Supper:_

Heavenly Father, we offer thee eternal praise and thanks that thou hast granted so great a benefit to us poor sinners, having drawn us into the Communion of thy Son, Jesus Christ our Lord, whom thou hast delivered to death for us, and whom thou givest us as the meat and drink of life eternal. Now grant us this other benefit: that thou wilt never allow us to forget these things; but having them imprinted on our hearts, may we grow and increase daily in our faith, which is at work in every good deed. Thus may we order and pursue all our life to the exaltation of thy glory and the edification of our neighbor; through the same Jesus Christ, thy Son, who in the unity of the Holy Spirit liveth and reigneth with thee, O God, forever. Amen.

**Commentary**: According to Calvinist understanding, thanksgiving is the right sacrifice we offer to God, and gratitude, a key to worship.

**Text**: _After thanks has been given, the Canticle of Simeon is sung: "Maintenant Seigneur Dieu" (Now, Lord God)._

**Commentary**: Luke 2:29-32. The Song of Simeon does not appear in the Genevan liturgy until 1549.

**Text**: _Then the Minister dismisses the congregation by pronouncing the Benediction used on Sunday._

The Lord bless you and keep you. The Lord make His face to shine upon you and be merciful unto you. The Lord lift up His countenance upon you and keep you in virtuous prosperity. Amen.

**Commentary**: Numbers 6:24-26. This was the normal dismissal in all Calvin's liturgies, daily as well as Sunday.

Elsie McKee

## 169 • THE TRADITIONAL ANGLICAN LITURGY (1662)

*The Reform of the liturgy in England began in 1540 under the leadership of Thomas Cranmer. The Book of Common Prayer was revised again in 1552, and a final revision was completed in 1662. The service below is from the 1662 Book of Common Prayer.*

———————— **Introduction** ————————

Soon after Henry VIII's break with the papacy, efforts toward liturgical reform began to gain momentum in England. It was not until 1549, however, after Edward VI had ascended the throne, that the first comprehensive reformed liturgy was issued. The principles upon which this book was based were spelled out in the order called on in the old service books and in the Act of Uniformity for the first revision of *The Book of Common Prayer.* These documents state that the first *Book of Common Prayer* was (1) "grounded upon the Holy Scripture," (2) "agreeable to the order of the primitive [i.e., early] church," (3) designed to be unifying to the realm, and (4) intended for the edification of the people. Thomas Cranmer, the Archbishop of Canterbury, was its chief architect. In compiling the book, he made use of various sources, including writings of early church fathers, English reformation formularies, German church orders, Qui-

*John Calvin. A portrait of the leader of the Swiss Reformation.*

nones's revised breviary, Eastern liturgies, Gallican rites, and various uses of the medieval Roman rite.

The 1549 book was not well received. It was too conservative for some, too radical for others, and too open to diverse interpretations to encourage uniformity. *The Clerk's Book,* published that same year, contained some revisions. Marbeck's [Merbeck's] commissioned musical setting contained further changes. The rubrics were widely disregarded. It was too radical for the Devonshire rebels, for such bishops as Bonner, Thirlby, and Gardiner, and for priests who continued the use of old service books or who "counterfeited Masses." On the other hand, it did not go far enough in its revisions to satisfy the Norfolk rebels, or continental reformers such as Martin Bucer and Peter Martyr who had come to England and had been given positions of prominence in the universities, or the Anabaptists, or some of the clergy and bishops such as Hooper and Knox.

The second *Book of Common Prayer* (1552) is sometimes spoken of as a radical plot foisted upon the people. It was, in fact, in many ways a compromise and an effort to arrive at a middle way or *via media.* With Mary's accession to the throne and the restoration of Roman Catholicism and the medieval Sarum use in England, religious exiles carried the 1552 book to the continent where it was revised by the exiles in Frankfurt and Geneva. After the accession of Elizabeth, with the return of the exiles, pressure mounted for the establishment of a liturgy more closely akin to those of the continental reformers. However, the 1552 book was again imposed with only a few changes. When James VI of Scotland came to the throne as James I of England, he was confronted by Puritans with the Millenary Petition, which called for a number of changes in the rites and ceremonies of the church. The resultant Hampton Court Conference (1604) made few concessions. At the time of the Restoration, despite efforts of Puritans to force more radical change on the one hand and of Laudians (followers of Archbishop Laud, who attempted to force the return of high churchmanship and ritual catholicity on the nation) on the other, relatively few changes were made in the 1662 revision.

**The Architectural Setting.** The first *Book of Common Prayer* assumed a style of architecture in which the nave and chancel were divided by a screen. The congregation would occupy the nave for the daily offices and the Ante-Communion (the liturgy of the Word portion of the eucharistic rite) and, at the offertory, move into the chancel to place their alms in the "poore menes boxe." Those who would receive Communion remained in the chancel, where the celebrant, _"standing humbly afore the middes of the Altar,"_ would proceed with the rite. For the use of the nave for liturgies of the Word and the chancel for the liturgy of the sacrament, there was precedent among both Lutherans and Calvinists on the continent.

In Lent 1550, John Hooper, preaching before the court, expressed a wish that the magistrates "turn the altars into tables." On St. Barnabas's Day, June 11, a table was set up in place of the high altar at St. Paul's Cathedral in London, and that summer Bishop Ridley exhorted the clergy and wardens to set up an "honest table" in each church in the diocese. In November the council commanded each bishop to give orders that altars be taken down and tables set up instead. The tables were normally placed in the midst of the chancel with their long sides parallel to the north and south walls. The 1552 _Book of Common Prayer_ consistently referred to it as a "table" or as "God's board," not once calling it an "altar." The priest was to stand "at the north side" and the congregation to gather around. The Elizabethan settlement called for the table, with a cover of "silk, buckram or other such like," to stand in the place of the old altar except when the communion is to be celebrated. These "carpets" varied in color; there was no attempt to follow a color sequence. Some more affluent churches had different frontals for festal and ordinary use, and some had black for use in Lent or on occasions of national mourning. For celebrations of the Eucharist, the table was to be covered with a fair linen cloth (reaching down almost to the floor on all four sides) and to stand in the midst of the chancel or in the body of the church if the chancel could not accommodate the communicants. In many places, the table stayed at all times in the midst of the chancel because of the inconvenience of moving it or because of theological considerations. In some churches seating for the communicants was provided on two, three, or all four sides of the chancel. A tablet containing the Decalogue was to be put up on the east wall over the table. Often the tablet(s) contained the Apostles' Creed and the Lord's Prayer as well. Altar rails came into use early in the seventeenth century. Originally the rails were not used for the administra-

tion of communion but for the protection of the costly hangings and to keep the table from being used as a desk, or as a repository for hats, or for other profane purposes. In some cases, the new rails surrounded the table in the midst of the chancel, but generally they extended across the chancel to protect the altar when it was placed at the east end, either altar-wise or table-wise. Eventually communicants would begin to kneel at the rails for the receiving of communion. In exceptional circumstances, candles were placed on the table, but normally nothing was placed on the table except the books, vessels, and elements necessary for a eucharistic celebration.

Fonts were typically made of stone, set near the door, and large enough for the immersion of infants, though those of puritan persuasion sometimes used a basin and substituted pouring or sprinkling for immersion.

Occupying an important position in the nave, typically against the north wall, was a triple-decked pulpit, which was often enhanced by hangings and by cushions for the books. On the lowest level was the desk for the clerk, a lay assistant who led the people in their responses and, if there was no choir, in the metrical psalms and hymns. Behind this, on a higher level, was the desk for the officiant, at which he read the daily offices and typically the Ante-Communion. On a yet higher level was the pulpit for the preaching of sermons. In some churches a pew near the pulpit was designated as the "churching pew" for use at the rite then called "The Churching of Women," more recently the "Thanksgiving of Women after Childbirth."

In the churches of the period, the pews in the nave were generally arranged in such a way that most people faced the pulpit. In parish churches where there was a choir, it generally occupied a gallery in the west end or over the rood screen. Smaller churches often had instead a "singers' pew," typically in the west end. If we can judge by later practice, the congregation often turned to face the choir during psalms, hymns, or anthems.

**The Vestments.** The first _Book of Common Prayer_ (1549) had designated that for the Eucharist the celebrant wear _"a white Albe plain, with a vestement [chasuble] or Cope,"_ and that assisting priests or deacons were to wear _"Albes with tunacles."_ For other rites, the clergy were to wear a surplice. The use of a hood with the surplice was recommended for preaching and for general use by the clergy in cathedral or collegiate churches. A bishop, when celebrating the Eucharist or executing *"any other publique minystracyon shall have upon hym, besyde his rochette, a Surples or albe, and a cope or vestment, and also his pastorall staffe."* The 1550 ordination rites specified that a candidate for ordination as a deacon or priest be vested in a *"a playne Albe,"* and that a candidate for ordination as a bishop and the presenting bishops be vested in *"Surples and Cope."* The ordination rites had been out only a day or two when Hooper, who was soon thereafter nominated to the bishopric at Gloucester, preached before the king denouncing the vestments.

In the 1552 *Book of Common Prayer,* a rubric preceding Morning Prayer dealt with vesture: *"And here is to be noted, that the minister at the tyme of the Comunion and all other tymes in his ministracion, shall use neither albe, vestment, nor cope: but being archbishop or bishop, he shall have and wear a rochet; and being a preest or deacon, he shall have and wear a surplice onely."* Exiles on the continent during Mary's reign rejected the use of the surplice.

The 1559 revision replaced the 1552 rubric on vestments with one which reads: *"And here is to be noted, that the Minister at the tyme of the comunion and at all other tymes in his ministracion, shall use such ornamentes in the church, as were in use by aucthoritie of parliament in the second yere of the reygne of king Edeard the VI."* The rubric was apparently designed to restore the use of eucharistic vestments, but it did not have that effect. Archbishop Parker's "Advertisements" of 1566 simply ordered the use of a cope by the celebrant, the gospeller, and the epistoler at celebrations of the Eucharist in cathedral and collegiate churches, and of a surplice and hood at other services and for preaching. In other churches, the minister was to wear the surplice for all rites. These regulations were not universally followed. In many places a black gown was worn for preaching and often for presiding or assisting at the services.

**Ceremonial Actions.** The 1549 *Book of Common Prayer* prescribed little ceremonial. In the eucharistic prayer, the celebrant was to make signs of the cross over the bread and wine during the epiclesis and to take the bread and the cup in his hands at the Institution Narrative. Baptism included a signation, vesting with the "Crisome," and an anointing. The marriage rite included the giving of a ring and specified a sign of the cross with each of the two blessings. Visitation of the Sick provided for an optional anointing. Though few ceremonial actions were required, the only rubric that explicitly forbade an old action was printed immediately after the Institution Narrative: *"These wordes before rehersed are to be saied, turning still to the Altar, without any eleuacion or shewing the Sacrament to the people."* Among the "Notes" at the end of the book is one which reads, *"As touching, kneeling, crossing, holding up handes, knocking upon the brest, and other gestures: they may be used or left as every mans deuocion serueth without blame."* Though some priests were accused of "counterfeiting Masse" rather than using the book in the way in which it was intended to be used, many found the retention of even these few required ceremonial actions objectionable.

The 1552 book dropped all indications for the use of the sign of the cross except for the signation in baptism, all directions for any manual acts in the eucharistic prayer, and all references to anointing. The 1549 book had not specified the posture for receiving Communion, and in some places people received while seated. The 1552 book specified kneeling as the posture, but explained in a rubric that this did not imply *"anye reall and essencial presence there beeying of Christ's naturall fleshe and bloude."* The 1559 revision dropped this rubric but retained the direction to kneel. The 1549 book had retained the use of wafers which were to be put in the communicants' mouths by the priest. The 1552 book allowed use of bread *"such, as is usuall to bee eaten at the Table wyth other meates,"* and this was to be put into the communicants' hands rather than their mouths. Provisions regarding ceremonial actions were not changed in the 1559 revision, but the Royal Injunctions published that year directed that "whensoever the name of Jesus shall be in any lesson, sermon, or otherwise in the church pronounced, that due reverence be made."

Among the issues raised in the Millenary Petition presented to King James, April 1603, were the use of the signation in baptism and the ring in the marriage rite and bowing at the name of Jesus.

A committee appointed by the House of Lords in 1641 listed "innovations" that had arisen. These pointed to some of the changes in practice among those of the so-called Laudian school. Among the "innovations" were turning the table altar-wise and calling it an altar, bowing toward the table, putting candlesticks on it, compelling communicants to receive at the rails, turning east for the creed and prayers, offering of bread and wine by the hand of the churchwardens or others "before the consecration," standing for the hymns (canticles) and the Gloria Patri, and carrying children from baptism to the table, "there to offer them up to God."

**The Music.** There is evidence that in some places plainsong settings and polyphonic settings for the old Latin texts were adapted for the new English texts at the time of or even before the appearance of the first _Book of Common Prayer_ in 1549. In _The booke of Common praier noted_ [London, 1550] John Marbeck [Merbecke], organist at the royal chapel at Windsor, provided simple music, one note per syllable, partly adapted from plainsong and partly original, for almost all of the texts of the daily offices, the eucharistic rite, and the burial rites. When the 1552 revision appeared, Marbeck's settings fell out of use because of changes in the texts. The rubrics of the 1552 book allowed for the singing of certain portions of the rites "in a plain tune after the manner of distinct reading."

Clement Marot had produced metrical versions of psalms which were sung to popular tunes in the French court. This was imitated in England. Thomas Sternhold began to translate the Psalms, generally in "Ballad Metre" or "Common Metre." Nineteen of these were published in 1547. After Sternold's death, John Hopkins in 1549 published this collection with an additional eighteen metrical versions by Sternhold and seven of his own. There is no evidence, however, that these were used in liturgical services prior to the accession of Mary and the suppression of the _Book of Common Prayer._

Congregations of English people in exile during the reign of Mary published revised and expanded versions of the Sternhold and Hopkins Psalter, with tunes from German and French sources, including tunes now commonly known as PSALM 42, OLD 100TH, OLD 112TH [VATER UNSER], OLD 113TH, OLD 124TH, OLD 134TH [ST. MICHAEL], COMMANDMENTS, LE CANTIQUE DE SIMEON [NUNC DIMITTIS], and ERHALT UNS, HERR, and with other tunes apparently never before published (for example, OLD 148TH). These congregations in exile, following the examples of continental churches, began to make use of metrical versions of the Psalms and other liturgical texts in the services.

Elizabeth's Royal Injunctions of 1559 allowed a hymn at the beginning and end of services. In 1562 _The Whole Booke of Psalmes, collected into Englysh metre_ was first printed. This Psalter, which continued to be published into the nineteenth century, contained metrical versions of Sternhold and Hopkins or others of every psalm and of several Prayer Book texts (the Veni Creator, the canticles, the Lord's Prayer, the Decalogue, the Athanasian and Apostles' Creeds). It also contained several hymns, including two which were translations from German. From 1566 the title page described these metrical psalms and hymns as being allowed before and after sermons as well as before and after the daily offices. One of the hymns (124 lines in length) was for use at the time of the ministration of Communion.

During the reigns of Elizabeth and the Stuarts, plainsong, anthems, and new polyphonic service music was used by choirs in cathedrals, royal chapels, college chapels, and a few parish churches with endowed choirs. The music in the typical parish church, however, was largely confined to the metrical psalms and hymns of the Sternhold and Hopkins psalter. With a few tunes repeated, a proper tune was appointed for each text—sixty-seven tunes in the fullest edition (1570). In the typical parish church, the psalms and hymns were normally led by a clerk without the benefit of a choir or any instrument. They were apparently sung at a fast clip and with a pronounced rhythm, for they were derided by some as "Genevan jigs."

Later in the reign of Elizabeth, the fashion turned toward slower singing and shorter tunes. Among tunes that are still in use WINDSOR and SOUTHWELL were apparently first printed in Damon's 1579 edition of the psalter. East's (Est's, Este's) 1592 version introduced several new tunes, including CHESHIRE and WINCHESTER OLD. Ravenscroft's 1621 edition was the first to print with the texts of the Sternhold and Hopkins psalter some tunes from the Scottish psalters, including DUNDEE, MARTYRS, ST. DAVID'S, and YORK, as well as a tune from Archbishop Matthew Parker's Psalter, THE EIGHTH TUNE ['TALLIS' CANON]. Ravenscroft also introduced other tunes, including BRISTOL, DURHAM, MANCHESTER, and OLD 104TH.

**The Rites.** The prayer books called for Morning and Evening Prayer to be said daily by all priests and deacons. A minister in charge of a parish was to say them in the church or chapel, after having tolled a bell "that suche as be disposed maye come to heare Goddes worde, and to praie with hymn." The attendance of all in the parish was expected on Sundays and major holy days. On Sundays, Wednesdays, and Fridays, Morning Prayer was followed by the Litany, and on Sundays and major holy days, by Ante-Communion, if not the whole of the eucharistic rite.

Early in the reign of Elizabeth, the singing of a metrical psalm or hymn was allowed before the beginning of Morning Prayer. The 1552 revision directed Morning Prayer to begin with a penitential section (for which there was precedent in Calvinistic liturgies), which consisted of a scriptural sentence and an exhortation calling to repentance, a general confession lined out by the minister (for which the congregation was to kneel), and a declaration of forgiveness to which the people were to respond "Amen."

The elements which followed the opening penitential section were mostly derived from the old rites of Matins, Lauds, and Prime. The minister was to say "wyth a loude voyce" the shorter form of the Lord's Prayer. A short series of versicles and responses which incorporated the Gloria Patri introduced the psalmody. Psalm 95 (*Venite*) was to be said or sung daily except on Easter Day itself when two brief anthems from the New Testament (Romans 6:9-11 and 1 Corinthians 15:20-22) were to be used instead. The *Venite* was to be followed by a selection from the Psalms. Proper psalms were appointed for Christmas Day, Easter Day, Ascension Day, and Whitsunday (Pentecost). The Prayer Book provided a table which divided the psalms between Morning and Evening Prayer over the period of a month. As opposed to the medieval systems, this meant that even those who came to church only on Sundays would be exposed to the whole psalter every seven months, but particular psalms might come up at very inappropriate times (Psalms 144–150 on Ash Wednesday or the First Sunday in Lent, for example, or Psalms 50–55 on a festal day such as Epiphany, Trinity Sunday, or All Saints).

In some places, the Psalms were sung to plainsong tones, sometimes with a *fauxbourdon,* from which Anglican chant evolved early in the seventeenth century. The Psalter was not bound with the early prayer books, and in most places, the Psalms appointed would have been read by the minister or the clerk, or the minister and the clerk would have alternated verse by verse (if we can judge by the printing of alternate verses in italics or in a different font in some of the Elizabethan special forms). Each psalm was followed by the Gloria Patri.

The Psalms were followed by the reading or singing *"in a plain tune after the maner of distinct reading,"* of a chapter from the Old Testament and one from the New Testament. To assure that the Old Testament "except certain bokes and chapiters, whiche be least edifyeng" would be read once each year, the lectionary was arranged according to the civil calendar rather than the church year. Depending upon the date of Easter, post-resurrection material from John and Acts might be read in Lent, or the account of the Passion in Eastern season. A particularly weak point of the system was that those who attended church only on Sundays and Holy Days would often get lessons from the Old Testament which made little sense out of context. At the 1559 revision, proper Old Testament lessons were appointed for the Sundays and Holy Days, but proper New Testament lessons were provided for only three Sundays: Easter, Pentecost, and Trinity Sunday. The chapter from the Old Testament might be read by either the minister or the clerk; that from the New Testament was apparently normally read by the minister.

The chapter from the Old Testament was followed by the saying or singing of one or the other of two canticles, *Te Deum* or *Benedicite omnia opera.* Since the alternative canticle was from the Apocrypha its use was avoided by those of Puritan persuasion. The chapter from the New Testament was followed by either the Song of Zechariah (*Benedictus*) or Psalm 100 (*Jubilate Deo*). Those of Puritan persuasion favored the *Jubilate Deo,* believing that it was not proper for others to appropriate the singing of the Song of Zechariah (or the Songs of Mary or of Simeon, the first of the alternatives that followed the lessons at Evening Prayer). The appointed place for baptism was between the New Testament lesson and the canticle which followed.

On major feasts and on certain saints' days, the Athanasian Creed would be said or sung immediately after the canticle following the second lesson. On most days, however, the canticle would be followed immediately by the Apostles' Creed, which was to be said by all, standing. The creed was followed by the _Kyrie_ and the short form of the Lord's Prayer, said by all, kneeling. The minister was then to resume a standing position for versicles and responses and three collects, the collect of the day and two that were said daily throughout the year, a collect for peace and a collect for grace. Where there was a choir, an anthem often followed this third collect. In other places, a metrical psalm or hymn may have been sung.

On Sundays, Wednesdays, and Fridays, Morning Prayer was followed by the Litany, said kneeling. This may have been followed by an anthem or a metrical psalm or hymn. This is the point in the Sunday morning service at which women would have been "churched" and couples would have been married.

Cranmer's ideal was communion every Sunday and Holy Day, but he did not approve of a Eucharist at which only the priest received. There had to be a _"good noumbere"_ to receive with the priest, _"And yf there be not above twentie persons in the Parishe of discretion to receive the communion: Yet there shal be no Communion, excepte foure, or three at the least communicate wiyth the Prieste."_ Persons not used to receiving more than once a year, and then typically from the reserved sacrament immediately after private confession, did not immediately embrace frequent communions. In many parishes, there was a celebration once a month or even less frequently, yet to keep the ideal of every Sunday communion before the people the Ante-communion was to be said every Sunday.

**Text:**
THE EUCHARISTIC RITE OF _THE BOOK OF COMMON PRAYER,_ 1662

_[The Eucharist would be immediately preceded by Morning Prayer and Litany]_
PSALM 100 [Tate and Brady] (_Tune:_ OLD HUNDREDTH):

> With one consent let all the earth
> To God their cheerful voices raise;
> Glad homage pay with awful mirth,
> And sing before him songs of praise.
>
> Convinc'd that he is God alone
> From whom both we and all proceed;
> We, whom he chooses for his own,
> The flock that he vouchsafes to feed.

> O enter then his temple gate,
> Thence to his courts devoutly press,
> And still your grateful hymns repeat,
> And still his Name with praises bless.
> For he's the Lord, supremely good,
> His mercy is for ever sure:
> His truth, which always firmly stood,
> To endless ages shall endure.

THE LORD'S PRAYER (_Priest alone; the people kneeling_):

> Our Father which art in heaven,
> Hallowed be thy Name.
> Thy kingdom come.
> Thy will be done in earth as it is in heaven.
> Give us this day our daily bread.
> And forgive us our trespasses,
> As we forgive them that trespass against us.
> And lead us not into temptation;
> But deliver us from evil. _Amen._

COLLECT (_Priest_):

> Almighty God, unto whom all hearts be open, all desires known, and from whom no secrets are hid; Cleanse the thoughts of our hearts by the inspiration of thy Holy Spirit, that we may perfectly love thee, and worthily magnify thy holy Name; through Christ our Lord. _Amen._

Despite the fact that the prayer book directed that Ante-communion begin with the priest standing at the north side of the table, it seems typically to have been read from the same place as Morning Prayer. The priest alone said the short form of the Lord's Prayer, followed by a prayer that later came to be known as the Collect for Purity, elements that had been part of the priest's private preparation in late medieval rites and the 1549 prayer book.

THE DECALOGUE (_Priest: the people, still kneeling, respond after each commandment_):

> God spake these words, and said; I am the Lord thy God: Thou shalt have none other gods but me.
>
> **Lord, have mercy upon us, and incline our hearts to keep this law.**

> Thou shalt not make to thyself any graven image, nor the likeness of anything that is in heaven above, or in the earth beneath, or in the water under the earth. Thou shalt not bow down to them, nor worship them: for I the Lord thy God am a jealous God, and visit the sins to the fathers

upon the children, unto the third and fourth generation of them that hate me, and show mercy unto thousands in them that love me, and keep my commandments.

> **Lord, have mercy upon us, and incline our hearts to keep this law.**

Thou shalt not take the Name of the Lord thy God in vain: for the Lord will not hold him guiltless, that taketh his Name in vain.

> **Lord, have mercy upon us, and incline our hearts to keep this law.**

Remember that thou keep holy the Sabbath-day. Six days shalt thou labour, and do all that thou hast to do; but the seventh day is the Sabbath of the Lord thy God. In it thou shalt do no manner of work, thou, and thy son, and thy daughter, thy man-servant, and thy maid-servant, thy cattle, and the stranger that is within thy gates. For in six days the Lord made heaven and earth, the sea, and all that in them is, and rested the seventh day: wherefore the Lord blessed the seventh day, and allowed it.

> **Lord, have mercy upon us, and incline our hearts to keep this law.**

Honour thy father and thy mother; that thy days may be long in the land, which the Lord thy God giveth thee.

> **Lord, have mercy upon us, and incline our hearts to keep this law.**

Thou shalt do no murder.

> **Lord, have mercy upon us, and incline our hearts to keep this law.**

Thou shalt not commit adultery.

> **Lord, have mercy upon us, and incline our hearts to keep this law.**

Thou shalt not steal.

> **Lord, have mercy upon us, and incline our hearts to keep this law.**

Thou shalt not bear witness against thy neighbour.

> **Lord, have mercy upon us, and incline our hearts to keep this law.**

Thou shalt not covet thy neighbour's house, thou shalt not covet thy neighbour's wife, nor his servant, nor his maid, nor his ox, nor his ass, nor any thing that is his.

> **Lord, have mercy upon us, and write all these thy laws in our hearts, we beseech thee.**

PRAYER FOR THE RULER [one of two alternatives] (*Priest*):

Let us pray.

Almighty and everlasting God, we are taught by thy holy Word, that the hearts of Kings are in thy rule and governance, and that thou dost dispose and turn them as it seemeth best to thy godly wisdom: We humbly beseech thee so to dispose and govern the heart of *(N.),* thy servant, our *King* and Governour, that, in all *his* thoughts, words, and works, *he* may ever seek thy honour and glory, and study to persevere thy people committed to *his* charge, in wealth, peace, and godliness: Grant this, O merciful Father, for thy dear Son's sake, Jesus Christ our Lord. *Amen.*

THE COLLECT OF THE DAY [Fourth Sunday after the Epiphany] (*Priest*):

O God, who knowest us to be set in the midst of so many and great dangers, that by reason of the frailty of our nature we cannot always stand upright; Grant to us such strength and protection, as may support us in all dangers, and carry us through all temptations; through Jesus Christ our Lord. *Amen.*

THE EPISTLE (*Priest*):

The Epistle is written in the thirteenth Chapter of Romans beginning at the first Verse.

THE GOSPEL (*Priest, the people standing*):

The holy Gospel is written in the eighth Chapter of Saint Matthew, beginning at the twenty-third Verse.

THE NICENE CREED

**Commentary:** The ninefold Kyrie of Western medieval rites and the 1549 prayer book, from 1552 on, was replaced by the recitation by the priest of the Ten Commandments. For this the priest and people knelt. The people responded after the first nine, "Lord, haue mercye upon us, and encline our hearts to kepe this lawe," and after the tenth, "Lord haue mercye upon us, and write al these thy lawes in our hearts, we beseche thee." The priest then stood to say the collect of the day and one or the other of two prayers for the monarch. Cranmer had only slightly modified the Epistle and Gospel lectionary of the Sarum Missal. Both lessons were read by the priest, one immediately after the other, apparently typically from the middle level of the pulpit. The Gospel was followed immediately by the Nicene

Creed. It was not until the 1662 revision that the people were directed to stand for the Gospel and creed.

**Text:**
HYMN
SERMON OR HOMILY
Psalm 117

**Commentary:** The Sternhold and Hopkins metrical psalter provided a forty-line hymn, "A Prayer to the Holy Ghost, To be sung before the Sermon." Selections from the metrical psalms were probably often used instead. The Elizabethan Injunctions provided a bidding prayer for use before sermons. If there was no sermon, the priest was directed to read one of the official homilies. These homilies were written to promote and explain the changes in liturgy and theology that the Reformation had brought. The sermon was often followed by a metrical psalm.

**Text:**

ANNOUNCEMENT OF HOLY DAYS AND FASTING DAYS WITHIN THE FOLLOWING WEEK, AND OTHER AUTHORIZED ANNOUNCEMENTS.

OFFERINGS FOR THE POOR AND OTHER OFFERINGS [_gathered by the Deacons, Churchwardens, or others and brought to the Priest who is to "present and place" them upon the holy Table; while the offerings are being received, the Priest reads sentences from the Scriptures_]:

Let your light so shine before men, that they may see your good works, and glorify your Father which is in heaven [Matt. 5:16].

Lay not up for yourselves treasure upon the earth; where the rust and moth doth corrupt, and where thieves break through and steal: but lay up for yourselves treasures in heaven; where neither rust nor moth doth corrupt, and where thieves do not break through and steal [Matt. 6:19-20].

Whatsoever ye would that men should do unto you, even so do unto them; for this is the Law and the Prophets [Matt. 7:12].

Not everyone that saith unto me, Lord, Lord, shall enter into the Kingdom of heaven; but he that doeth the will of my Father which is in heaven [Matt. 7:21].

Zaccheus stood forth, and said unto the Lord, Behold, Lord, the half of my goods I give to the poor; and if I have done any wrong to any man, I restore four-fold [Luke 19:8].

Who goeth a warfare at any time of his own cost? Who planteth a vineyard, and eateth not of the fruit thereof? Or who feedeth a flock, and eateth not of the milk of the flock? [1 Cor. 9:7].

If we have sown unto you spiritual things, is it a great matter if we shall reap your worldly things? [1 Cor. 9:11].

THE PLACING UPON THE TABLE OF THE BREAD AND WINE BY THE PRIEST

**Commentary:** After the sermon the priest was to remind the people of the holy days and fasting days in the week following. The priest initiated the presentation of alms (and other offerings on occasion) by reading one or more of a series of scriptural sentences, most of which were exhortations to give to the poor or to support the ministers. Apparently in many places, the minister continued reading the sentences until the people had finished placing their offerings in plates held by the wardens or others, who stood near the entrance to the chancel which contained the poor box into which they would then deposit the offerings. In other places, however, after a sentence or two had been said, an anthem may have been sung or the metrical psalm or hymn that was allowed after the sermon. The 1549 prayer book had directed that the bread and wine be placed on the table at this point, and that direction was restored in 1662. The intervening prayer books said nothing about when this was to be done. The old practice may have continued in many places, but in most places apparently the bread and wine were placed on the altar by the clerk before the rite and covered with a second large linen table cloth, presenting an appearance which reminded people of some suppers prepared beforehand in private homes.

**Text:**
PRAYER FOR THE CHURCH (_Priest_):

Let us pray for the whole state of Christ's Church militant here in earth.

Almighty and ever-living God, who by thy holy Apostle hast taught us to make prayers, and supplications, and to give thanks, for all men; We humbly beseech thee most mercifully [to accept our alms and oblations] and to receive these our prayers, which we offer unto thy Divine Majesty;

beseeching thee to inspire continually the universal Church with the spirit of truth, unity, and concord: And grant, that all they that do confess thy holy Name may agree in the truth of thy holy Word, and live in unity, and godly love. We beseech thee also to save and defend all Christian Kings, Princes, and Governours; and specially thy Servant *(N.),* our King; that under *him* we may be godly and quietly governed: And grant unto *his* whole Council, and to all that are put in authority under *him,* that they may truly and indifferently minister justice, to the punishment of wickedness and vice, and to the maintenance of thy true religion, and virtue. Give grace, O heavenly Father, to all Bishops and Curates, that they may both by their life and doctrine set forth thy true and lively Word, and rightly and duly administer thy holy Sacraments: And to all thy people give thy heavenly grace; and especially to this congregation here present; that, with meek heart and due reverence, they may hear, and receive thy holy Word; truly service thee in holiness and righteousness all the days of their life. And we most humbly beseech thee of thy goodness, O Lord, to comfort and succor all them, who in this transitory life are in trouble, sorrow, need, sickness, or any other adversity. And we also bless thy holy Name for all thy servants departed this life in thy faith and fear; beseeching thee to give us grace so to follow their good examples, that with them we may be partakers of thy heavenly kingdom: grant this, O Father, for Jesus Christ's sake, our only Mediator and Advocate. *Amen.*

**Commentary**: After the offerings came a general intercession, partly derived from Latin and German sources, a prayer "for the whole state of Christ's Church militant here in earth." If there was to be no celebration of the Eucharist, the rite ended with one or more of five collects printed after the rite, and possibly a metrical psalm or hymn.

**Text:**
EXHORTATION (*Priest*).

Dearly beloved in the Lord, ye that mind to come to the holy Communion of the Body and Blood of our Saviour Christ, must consider how Saint Paul exhorteth all persons diligently to try and examine themselves, before they presume to eat of that Bread, and drink of that Cup. For as the benefit is great, if with a true penitent heart and lively faith we receive that holy Sacrament; (for then we spiritually eat the flesh of Christ, and drink his blood; then we dwell in Christ, and Christ in us; we are one with Christ, and Christ with us;) so is the danger great, if we receive the same unworthily. For then we are guilty of the Body and Blood of Christ our Saviour; we eat and drink our own damnation, not considering the Lord's Body; we kindle God's wrath against us; we provoke him to plague us with diverse diseases, and sundry kinds of death. Judge therefore yourselves, brethren, that ye be not judged of the Lord; repent you truly for your sins past; have a lively and steadfast faith in Christ our Saviour; amend your lives, and be in perfect charity with all men; so shall ye be meet partakers of these holy mysteries. And above all things, ye must give most humble and hearty thanks to God, the Father, the Son, and the Holy Ghost, for the redemption of the world by the death and passion of our Saviour Christ, both God and man; who did humble himself, even to the death upon the Cross, for us, miserable sinners, who lay in darkness and the shadow of death; that he might make us the children of God, and exalt us to everlasting life. And to the end that we should alway remember the exceeding great love of our Master, and only Saviour, Jesus Christ, thus dying for us, and the innumerable benefits which by his precious blood-shedding he hath obtained to us; he hath instituted and ordained holy mysteries, as pledges of his love, and for a continual remembrance of his death, to our great and endless comfort. To him therefore, with the Father and the Holy Ghost, let us give (as we are most bounden) continual thanks; submitting ourselves wholly to his holy will and pleasure, and studying to serve him in true holiness and righteousness all the days of our life. *Amen.*

**Commentary**: If there was to be a celebration of Communion, the priest was to say one or more of three lengthy exhortations. The first, the work of Peter Martyr, was for use if the people are "negligent to come to the holy Communion." The second was designed for those with troubled consciences and points to the option of private confession. The third, always to be said, is a warning against unworthy reception of the sacrament. The last two exhortations, and the penitential order which follows, are largely dependent upon the *Consultation,* the

German Church Order of Hermann von Wied, Archbishop of Cologne, the liturgical portion of which was prepared by Martin Bucer.

**Text**:
INVITATION (*Priest*):

Ye that do truly and earnestly repent you of your sins, and are in love and charity with your neighbours, and intend to lead a new life, following the commandments of God, and walking from henceforth in his holy ways; Draw near with faith, and take this holy Sacrament to your comfort; and make you humble confession to Almighty God, meekly kneeling upon your knees.

GENERAL CONFESSION [*All kneel, and the General Confession is then said "in the name of all"*]:

Almighty God, Father of our Lord Jesus Christ, Maker of all things, Judge of all men; We acknowledge and bewail our manifold sins and wickedness, Which we, from time to time, most grievously have committed, By thought, word, and deed, Against thy Divine Majesty, Provoking most justly thy wrath and indignation against us. We do earnestly repent, And are heartily sorry for these our misdoings; The remembrance of them is grievous unto us; The burden of them is intolerable. Have mercy upon us, Have mercy upon us, most merciful Father; For thy Son our Lord Jesus Christ's sake, Forgive us all that is past; And grant that we may ever hereafter Serve and please thee In newness of life, To the honour and glory of thy Name; Through Jesus Christ our Lord. *Amen.*

ABSOLUTION (*Priest, standing*):

Almighty God, our heavenly Father, who of his great mercy hath promised forgiveness of sins to all them that with hearty repentance and true faith turn unto him; Have mercy upon you; pardon and deliver you from all your sins; confirm and strengthen you in all goodness; and bring you to everlasting life; through Jesus Christ our Lord. *Amen.*

Hear what comfortable words our Saviour Christ saith unto all that truly turn to him.

Come unto me all that travail and are heavy laden, and I will refresh you [Matt. 11:28].

So God loved the world, that he gave his only begotten Son, to the end that all that believe in him should not perish, but have everlasting life [John 3:16].

Hear also what Saint Paul saith.

This is true saying, and worthy of all men to be received, That Christ Jesus came into the world to save sinners [1 Tim. 1:15].

Hear also what Saint John saith.

If any man sin, we have an Advocate with the Father, Jesus Christ the righteous; and he is the propitiation for our sins [1 John 2:1-2].

**Commentary**: The penitential section which followed the exhortation consisted of a bidding to confession, a general confession, an absolution, and four scriptural sentences which came to be known as the Comfortable Words. Apparently in many places from 1552, the clergy and people entered the chancel at the end of the bidding, "Drawe nere and take this holy Sacramente to youre comfort," though in other places they may have entered the chancel at the time of the offering, as was directed in the first *Book of Common Prayer*. At the point at which those planning to receive communion entered the chancel, the others probably left the church. The communicants were instructed to kneel for the general confession, which was said by one of the communicants or by one of the ministers "in the name of all." If we can judge by some eighteenth century manuals, the people remained kneeling for the absolution but then stood for the Comfortable Words.

**Text**:
Lift up your hearts;

**Answer:**   **We lift them up unto the Lord.**
*Priest:*   Let us give thanks unto our Lord God.
**Answer:**   **It is meet and right so to do.**
*Priest:*   It is very meet, right, and our bounden duty, that we should at all times, and in all places, give thanks unto thee, O Lord, Holy Father, Almighty, Everlasting God.

[Preface of Epiphany]

Therefore with Angels and Archangels, and with all the company of heaven, we laud and magnify thy glorious Name; evermore praising thee, and saying, Holy, Holy, Holy, Lord God of hosts, heaven and earth are full of thy glory: Glory be to thee, O Lord most High. Amen.

*Priest:*   *(kneeling)* We do not presume to come to this thy Table, O merciful Lord, trusting in our own righteousness, but in thy manifold and great mercies. We are not worthy so much as to gather up the crumbs under thy Table. But thou art the same Lord, whose property is always to have mercy: Grant us therefore, gracious Lord, so to eat the flesh of thy dear Son Jesus Christ, and to drink his blood, that our sinful bodies may be made clean by his body, and our souls washed through his most precious blood, and that we may evermore dwell in him, and he in us. *Amen.*

THE PRAYER OF CONSECRATION (*Priest, standing*):

Almighty God, our heavenly Father, who of thy tender mercy didst give thine only Son Jesus Christ to suffer death upon the cross for our redemption; who made there (by his one oblation of himself once offered) a full, perfect, and sufficient sacrifice, oblation, and satisfaction, for the sins of the whole world; and did institute, and in his holy Gospel command us to continue, a perpetual memory of that his precious death, until his coming again; Hear us, O merciful Father, we most humbly beseech thee; and grant that we receiving these thy creatures of bread and wine, according to thy Son our Saviour Jesus Christ's holy institution, in remembrance of his death and passion, may be partakers of his most blessed Body and Blood: who, in the same night that he was betrayed, [*Here the Priest is to take the Paten into his hands*] took Bread; and, when he had given thanks, [*And here to break the Bread*] he brake it, and gave it to his disciples, saying, "Take, eat, [*And here to lay his hand upon all the Bread*] this is my Body which is given for you: Do this in remembrance of me. Likewise after supper he [*Here he is to take the Cup into his hand*] took the Cup; and, when he had given thanks, he gave it to them, saying, Drink ye all of this; for this [*And here to lay his hand upon every vessel (be it Chalice or Flagon) in which there is any Wine to be consecrated*] is my Blood of the New Testament which is shed for you and for many for the remission of sins: Do this, as oft as ye shall drink it, in remembrance of me. *Amen.*

THE ADMINISTRATION OF THE SACRAMENT (*the people kneel to receive*):

The Body of our Lord Jesus Christ, which was given for thee, preserve thy body and soul unto everlasting life, Take and eat this in remembrance that Christ died for thee, and feed on him in thy heart by faith with thanksgiving.

The Blood of our Lord Jesus Christ, which was shed for thee, preserve thy body and soul unto everlasting life. Drink this in remembrance that Christ's Blood was shed for thee, and be thankful.

(*The Priest covers what remains with a linen cloth.*)

HYMN

**Commentary**: The traditional *sursum corda* (the "Lift up your hearts") dialogue introduced the Preface and Sanctus. Proper Prefaces were provided for insertion at Christmas, Easter, and Ascension [and from 1552, their octaves], for Whitsunday (Pentecost) [and from 1552, the six days following], and for Trinity Sunday. From 1552 the Preface was followed by a prayer later called the Prayer of Humble Access, which had served in the 1548 Order of the Communion and in the 1549 prayer book as a pre-Communion devotion. For this prayer, the priest was to kneel. There is no direction to this effect, but later practice would lead one to believe that the priest, when he stood back up, normally removed the second tablecloth which covered the elements which had been prepared. The form which followed, later referred to as the Prayer of Consecration, begins with a section with no precedent in historic eucharistic prayers but is dependent on Reformation formularies concerning the one sacrifice of Christ upon the cross and the Eucharist as a "perpetuall memorye of that his precious death." This was followed by a petition for worthy reception. Epicletic elements in the 1549 petition had been edited out in 1552. This petition led into the Institution Narrative. There were no directions in the prayer book concerning manual actions, but the priest probably continued to take the bread and the cup into his hands, as he had been directed to do in the 1549 book and would be directed to do in the 1662 book. If we can judge from altar practice, he probably broke the bread for distribution at the words "he brake it." Late Western medieval eucharistic piety had been based on adoration of the sacrament at the Institution Narrative, which had come to be seen as the moment of consecration. The 1549 prayer book had attempted to substitute a piety centered in the communal receiving of the sacrament for a eucharistic piety centered in seeing the conse-cration of the sacrament. The 1552 and subsequent books placed the act of receiving right at what in the late middle ages had been the ultimate point of devotion. Through much of the seventeenth and eighteenth centuries, the priest administered com-munion by moving among the people kneeling in the chancel. To each person he said a sentence of administration. From 1559 the sentence consisted of two parts. The first half of each sentence was the sentence of administration in the 1548 Order of the Communion and the 1549 *Book of Common Prayer.* It was a Lutheran amplification of an earlier form, "The body (bloud) of our Lorde Jesus Christe whiche was geuen (shed) for thee, and be thanke-full." The second half expressed a reformed under-standing of the real presence of Christ, stressing that it was "in your hearts" and not "with your teeth" that one feeds on Christ by faith. For the receiving of communion, the people were to kneel, though in some places they sat or stood instead. During the time of the ministration of communion, or after people had begun to receive at the rails as "tables" were moving to and from the rail, portions of "A Thanksgiving after the receiving of the Lord's Sup-per" from the Sternhold and Hopkins psalter, or some other metrical hymn or psalm, may have been sung.

**Text:**

THE LORD'S PRAYER (*the people repeating every petition after the priest*):

Our Father, which art in heaven, Hallowed by thy Name. Thy kingdom come. Thy will be done in earth, As it is in heaven. Give us this day our daily bread. And forgive us our trespasses, As we forgive them that trespass against us. And lead us not into temptation; But deliver us from evil: For thine is the kingdom, The power, and the glory, For ever and ever. Amen.

PRAYER [One of two alternatives] (*Priest*):

O Lord and heavenly Father, we thy humble ser-vants entirely desire thy fatherly goodness merci-fully to accept this our sacrifice of praise and thanksgiving; most humbly beseeching thee to grant, that by the merits and death of thy Son Jesus Christ, and through faith in his blood, we and all thy whole Church may obtain remission of our sins, and all other benefits of his passion. And here we offer and present unto thee, O Lord,

ourselves, our souls and bodies, to be a reason-able, holy, and lively sacrifice unto thee; humbly beseeching thee, that all we, who are partakers of this holy Communion, may be fulfilled with thy grace and heavenly benediction. And although we be unworthy, through our manifold sins, to offer unto thee any sacrifice, yet we beseech thee to accept this our bounden duty and service; not weighing our merits, but pardoning our offences, through Jesus Christ our Lord; by whom, and with whom, in the unity of the Holy Ghost, all honour and glory be unto thee, O Father Al-mighty, world without end. *Amen.*

GLORIA IN EXCELSIS (*Priest*):

Glory be to God on high, and in earth peace, good will towards men. We praise thee, we bless thee, we worship thee, we glorify thee, we give thanks to thee for thy great glory, O Lord God, heavenly King, God the Father Almighty.

O Lord, the only begotten Son Jesus Christ; O Lord God, Lamb of God, Son of the Father, that takest away the sins of the world, have mercy upon us. Thou that takest away the sins of the world, have mercy upon us. Thou that takest away the sins of the world, receive our prayer. Thou that sittest at the right hand of God the Father, have mercy upon us.

For thou only art holy; thou only are the Lord; thou only, O Christ, with the Holy Ghost, art most high in the glory of God the Father. *Amen.*

THE BLESSING (*Priest*):

The peace of God, which passeth all understand-ing, keep your hearts and minds in the knowledge and love of God, and of his Son Jesus Christ our Lord: and the blessing of God Almighty, the Fa-ther, the Son, and the Holy Ghost, be amongst you and remain with you always. *Amen.*

[*The people having departed, the clergy (assisted by others, if necessary) consume what remains with-out carrying it from the building.*]

**Commentary:** After the people had received Com-munion, the priest was to line out the Lord's Prayer (until 1662, the shorter form) with the people re-peating each petition after him. He was then to say one or the other of two prayers. The first was an abridged form of the final paragraph of the 1549 eucharistic prayer, later commonly called the "self-oblation." This form contained phrases from the

Roman canon, the liturgy of St. Basil, Hermann's *Consultation,* and a quotation from Romans 12:1. The second was a revised form of the fixed postcommunion prayer of the 1549 book which replaced the proper postcommunion prayers of the medieval rites, many of which contained theological sentiments unacceptable to Cranmer.

The rite concluded with the *Gloria in Excelsis* and the blessing. The *Gloria in Excelsis* was moved to this position in 1552, possibly because Calvinistic rites normally followed communion with a metrical psalm in imitation of the hymn sung after the Last Supper (Mark 14:26). Early Lutheran liturgical books concluded rites with blessings, and one dependent on Hermann's *Consultation* was provided in the 1548 *Order of the Communion* and the *Book of Common Prayer.* After the blessing, a metrical psalm or hymn may have been sung.

---------------- **Conclusion** ----------------

The 1549 *Book of Common Prayer* did not specify what was to be done with elements which remained after the administration of communion except that (following some German Lutheran precedents) on the day of a celebration they might be used for the Communion of the Sick. The 1552 revision specified that *"yf any of the bread or wine remayne, the Curate* [i.e., the person in charge of the cure] *shal have it to hys owne use."* It was not until the 1662 revision that what remained was to be consumed by the priest and other communicants and not taken out of the church.

Through the authorization of this eucharistic liturgy, a basic pattern of Anglican worship was established in the mid-sixteenth century which would not be radically altered until the Victorian period.

Marion Hatchett

## 170 • ANABAPTIST: HUBMAIER'S "A FORM FOR CHRIST'S SUPPER" (1527)

*The liturgy below is of an Anabaptist group in Waldshut. Unlike other Anabaptists, this community was not on the run, but settled in a place where the people enjoyed greater freedom of worship. These Anabaptists were also led by a minister who was a liturgical scholar.*

*Balthasar Hubmaier. Likeness of a drawing made c. 1606 by Christoffel Van Sichem and found in a series of engravings of Anabaptist leaders. The historical basis of the drawing is in question.*

---------------- **Introduction** ----------------

Balthasar Hubmaier (circa 1480–1528) was the most highly trained of Anabaptist theologians. He matriculated under Johannes Eck at the University of Freiburg and then assumed his mentor's chair in biblical studies in 1510. In 1512 he followed Eck to the University of Ingolstadt where he earned a doctorate. In 1516 he became dean of the cathedral in Regensburg where he developed a reputation for fiery preaching. In 1521 he became the parish priest in Waldshut. Hubmaier's interest in liturgy flourished in his years there. He refers to the ceremonial which he added to the Mass during that time. Waldshut lay in the Austrian-controlled territory of south Germany where mass movements in favor of local political and religious autonomy were afoot.

By 1523, Hubmaier had embraced the Reformation and was caught up in Zwingli's reform initiatives at Zurich. His contributions to the Zurich Disputation of 1523 on worship and images show that he was by then an articulate participant in the radical movement. He and several younger thinkers, like Conrad Grebel, pushed the reform of the church beyond what Zwingli would sanction. But unlike the other Anabaptists, Hubmaier held that a believers' church could still be a territorial church, publicly sanctioned and supported.

This fact is significant for the present discussion because it means that Hubmaier was creating liturgies for a church in which the majority of the population participated, though, according to his plan, only if they personally confessed Christ and accepted the responsibilities of membership. In addition to this service of the Lord's Supper, Hubmaier also wrote a baptismal service and one for fraternal admonition. While the Anabaptist community at Waldshut was part of a new order trying to overthrow an old one, it was not a band of refugees worshiping on the run or at least on the sly. Nor were they, like most other Anabaptist congregations, made up of people whose intensely personal piety burst the framework of any formal structure of worship. It is probably that this difference in liturgical expression was due not only to the more settled character of Hubmaier's churches but also to the fact that they were led by a liturgical scholar.

It is evident from "A Form for Christ's Supper" that Hubmaier was aware of what he was doing and that is expressed the unusual political and theological commitments he had made. A fixed liturgical form is nicely woven together with an openness to charismatic expression. And repeated references to the inward disposition of the worshiper show the decisive significance the author attributed to the faith of the participant.

From references throughout Hubmaier's writings at the time, it may be assumed that his service for the breaking of bread was created at Waldshut, though it was not published until he moved to Nicolsberg, Moravia to give his experiment of a territorial church of believers a second chance. Waldshut was located in the middle of the area where the Peasants War was fought. So, even though the Anabaptists were for a time officially tolerated, the population was constantly under threat by its worried Austrian overlords. Thus, the people must have come to church with a mixture of excitement and insecurity. On the one hand, the common people were really determining their own religious destiny; on the other hand, their radical experiment and the movement of which it was a part were viewed by the Austrian crown not only as heretical but also as seditious.

Hubmaier's community was apocalyptic in that the intensity of faith asked for by Hubmaier knew no limits: Every baptized believer was asked to be faithful unto death. Just as Christ gave up his life for us, so we ought to give up ours for others in suffering love. That is the promise that makes the bread and wine into a true Lord's Supper, according to Hubmaier. Though the circumstances, initially, were outwardly settled, Hubmaier (and perhaps those with whom he made common cause) knew that the experiment of the common folk went against everything the people on top stood for. He knew that wolves would soon come to prey on his sheep.

Radical peasant protests were in the air during Hubmaier's years as an Anabaptist leader in Waldshut. So, people came to church to reenlist in the cause of Christ as the cause of the common person. The liturgy was theirs in two significant ways. Personally, each one was free to speak after the sermon as the Spirit gave utterance. Socially, the form of worship was determined locally by a pastor the people had chosen.

**Text:** The brethren and sisters who wish to hold the table of the Lord according to the institution of Christ, (Matt. 26:26ff.; Luke 22:19ff.; Mark 14:22ff.; 1 Cor. 11:23ff.), shall gather at a suitable place and time, so there may be no division, so that one does not come early and another late and that thereby evangelical teaching is neglected. Such the apostles desired when they asked Christ, "Master, where wilt thou that we prepare the Passover lamb?" Then he set for them a certain place. Paul writes, "When you come together . . . etc.," (1 Cor. 11:20ff). Then they should prepare the table with ordinary bread and wine. Whether the cups are silver, wood, or pewter, makes no difference. But those who eat should be respectably dressed and should sit together in an orderly way without light talk and contention (1 Pet. 3:3; Eph. 4:29; Heb. 12).

**Commentary:** Hubmaier is in the process of socializing the people to their new worship life. At the beginning, and throughout the liturgy, there are admonitions about everything from promptness to the disposition of the heart which should accompany each part of the service. Hubmaier's own commentary is woven together with rubrics and the text itself.

**Text:** Since everyone should begin by accusing himself and confessing his sins and recognizing his guilt before God, it is not inappropriate that the priest first of all should fall on his knees with the church and with heart and mouth say the following words:

> "Father we have sinned against heaven and against thee" (Luke 15:21). We are not worthy to be called thy children. But speak a word of consolation and our souls will be made whole. God be gracious to us sinners (Luke 19:1ff). May the almighty, eternal and gracious God have mercy on all our sins and forgive us graciously, and when he has forgiven us, lead us into eternal life without blemish or impurity, through Jesus Christ our Lord and Savior. Amen.

**Commentary:** Once the congregants are settled, the "priest" leads them in confessing their sins. He prays with them and together with the people asks God to "have mercy on all our sins." Here it is not a priest offering absolution to a penitent congregation, but a fellow believer seeking absolution in their company. This was a revolutionary experience for sixteenth century Christians.

**Text:** Now let the priest sit down with the people and open his mouth, explaining the Scriptures concerning Christ (Luke 24:31), so that the eyes of those who are gathered together may be opened, which were still somewhat darkened or closed, so that they may recognize Christ, who was a man, a prophet, mighty in works and teaching before God and all people, and how the highest bishops among the priests and princes gave him over to condemnation to death, and how they crucified him, and how he has redeemed Israel, that is, all believers. The priest shall also rebuke those who are foolish and slow to believe all the things that Moses and the prophets have spoken, that he may kindle and make fervent and warm the hearts of those at the table, that they may be afire in fervent meditation of his bitter suffering and death in contemplation, love, and thanksgiving, so that the congregation with its whole heart, soul, and strength calls out to him.

> Stay with us, O Christ! It is toward evening and the day is now far spent. Abide with us, O Jesus, abide with us. For where thou art not, there everything is darkness, night, and shadow, but thou are the true Sun, light, and shining brightness (John 8:12). He to whom thou doest light the way, cannot go astray.

On another day the servant of the Word may take the 10th or 11th chapter of Paul's First Epistle to the Corinthians, or the 13th, 14th, 15th, 16th, or 17th

chapter of John. Or Matthew 3 or Luke 3 on changing one's life, Sirach 2 on the fear of God, or something else according to the opportuneness of the time and persons. No one shall be coerced herein, but each should be left free to the judgment of his spirit. But there must be diligence so that the death of the Lord is earnestly proclaimed, so that the people have a picture of the boundless goodness of Christ, and the church may be instructed, edified, and led, in heartfelt, fervent, and fraternal love, so that on the last day we may stand before the judgment seat of Christ with the accounts of our stewardship (Luke 16:8), and shepherd and sheep may be held together.

**Commentary:** Next the Scriptures are opened to the people concerning Christ so "that they may be afire in fervent meditation of his bitter suffering . . ." A puzzling comment concerning the procedure follows. What does the text mean when it says, "On another day the servant of the Word may take [another chapter]"? It might mean, in line with Mennonite tradition, that the first gathering is a preparatory service on the day before communion. It might also mean that on another Sunday a different set of suggested texts would be appropriate sources for the proclamation.

**Text:** Now that the death of Christ has been proclaimed, those who are present have the opportunity and the authority to ask, if at any point they should have some misunderstanding or some lack (1 Cor. 14:26ff); but not with frivolous, unprofitable, or argumentative chatter, nor concerning heavenly matters having to do with the omnipotence or the mystery of God or future things, which we have no need to know, but concerning proper, necessary, and Christian items, having to do with Christian faith and brotherly love. Then one to whom something is revealed should teach, and the former should be quiet without any argument and quarreling. For it is not customary to have conflict in the church. Let women keep silence in the congregation. If they want to learn anything, they should ask their husbands at home, so that everything takes place in orderly fashion (1 Cor. 11:14). After the sermon, anyone who lacks understanding may ask for it, and anyone who is given a revelation may teach it.

**Commentary:** Apparently, this freedom for spontaneous expression had been taken advantage of: People had turned to chatter, speculation, and quarreling; Hubmaier saw fit to warn them against this abuse of freedom. One can imagine the thrill, if not also the bewilderment, of being invited to speak in church as an individual with particular needs and insights when formerly only conformity had counted. It would not be hard to get carried away!

**Text:** Let the priest take up for himself the words of Paul (1 Cor. 11), and say:

> Let every one test and examine himself, and let him thus eat of the bread and drink of the drink. For whoever eats and drinks unworthily, eats and drinks judgment upon himself, as he does not discern the body of the Lord. And if we thus judge ourselves, we would not be condemned by the Lord.

Now such examination comprises the following: First, that one believes, (Matt. 26:26ff.; Mark 13:22ff.; Luke 22:19f.; 1 Cor. 11:24ff.), utterly and absolutely that Christ gave his body and shed his crimson blood for him on the cross in the power of his words, as he said: "This is my body, which is given for you, and this is my blood, which is shed for you for the forgiveness of his sins."

Second: Let a person test himself, whether he has a proper inward and fervent hunger for the bread which comes down from heaven, from which one truly lives, and thirst for the drink which flows into eternal life, to eat and drink both in the spirit, faith, and truth, as Christ teaches us in John 4; 6; and 7. If the spiritual eating and drinking does not first take place, then the outward breaking of bread, eating and drinking is a killing letter (2 Cor. 3:6; 1 Cor. 11:29), hypocrisy, and the kind of food and drink whereby one eats condemnation and drinks death, as Adam did with the forbidden fruit of the tree in Paradise (Gen. 3:6).

Third: Let one also confirm himself in gratitude, so as to be thankful in words and deeds toward God for the great, overabundant, and unspeakable love and goodness that he has shown him through his most beloved Son, our Lord Jesus Christ (John 3:16; Rom. 8:32). Namely that he now gives praise and thanks from the heart to God. Further, that he be of an attitude and ready will to do for Christ his God and Lord in turn as he had done for him. But since Christ does not need our good deeds, is not hungry, is not thirsty, is not naked or in prison, but heaven and earth are his and all that is in them, therefore he points us toward our neighbor, first of all to the members of the household of faith, (Matt. 25:34ff.; Gal. 6:10; 1 Tim. 5), that we might fulfill the works of this our gratitude toward them physically and spiritually, feeding the hungry, giving drink to the thirsty, clothing the naked, consoling the prisoner, sheltering the needy. Then he will be ready to accept these works of mercy from us in such a way as if we had done them unto him. Yea, he will say at the last judgment, "I was hungry and you fed me. I was thirsty and you gave me drink. I was naked, in prison, and homeless, and you clothed me, visited me, and housed me" (Matt. 25). He says, "I, I, I, me, me, me." From this it is certain and sure that all the good that we do to the very least of his, that we do to Christ himself. Yea, he will not let a single drink of cool water go unrewarded (Matt. 10:42). If one is thus inclined toward his neighbor, he is now in the true fellowship of Christ, a member of his body, and a fellow member with all godly persons (Col. 1:4).

Fourth: So that the church might also be fully aware of a person's attitude and will, one holds fellowship with her in the breaking of bread, thereby saying, testifying, and publicly assuring her, yea, making to her a sacrament or a sworn pledge and giving one's hand on the commitment that one is willing henceforth to offer one's body and to shed one's blood thus for one's fellow believers. This one does not out of human daring, like Peter (Matt. 26:33), but in the grace and power of the suffering and the blood shed by our Lord Jesus Christ, his (i.e., meaning Peter's) only Savior, of whose suffering and death the human being is now celebrating a living commemoration in the breaking of bread and the sharing of the chalice.

This is the true fellowship of saints (1 Cor. 10:16). It is not a fellowship for the reason that bread is broken, but rather the bread is broken because the fellowship has already taken place and has been concluded inwardly in the spirit, since Christ has come into flesh (John 4:27). For not all who break bread are participants in the body and blood of Christ, which I can prove by the traitor Judas (Matt 26:25). But those who are partakers inwardly and of the spirit, the same may also worthily partake outwardly of this bread and wine.

A parable: We do not believe because we have been baptized in water, but we are baptized in water because we first believe. So David says: "I have believed, therefore I have spoken" (Ps. 116:10; Matt. 16:16; Acts 8:30). So every Christian speaks equally: "I have believed, therefore I have publicly confessed that Jesus is Christ, Son of the living God, and have thereafter had myself baptized according to the order of Christ, the high priest who lives in eternity." Or: "I have fellowship with Christ and all his members (1 Cor. 10:16), therefore I break bread with all believers in Christ according to the institution of Christ." Without this inner communion in the spirit and in truth, the outward breaking of bread is nothing but an Iscariotic and damnable hypocrisy. It is precisely to this fellowship and commitment of love that the Supper of Christ points, as a living memorial of his suffering and death for us, spiritually signified and pointed to by the breaking of bread, the pouring out of the wine, that each one should also sacrifice and pour out his flesh and blood for the other. Herein will people recognize that we are truly disciples of Christ (John 13; 14; 15; 16; 17). All of the words which Christ spoke about the Last Supper tend toward this. For just as water baptism is a public testimony of the Christian faith, so is the Supper a public testimony of Christian love. Now he who does not want to be baptized or to observe the Supper, he does not desire to believe in Christ to observe the Supper, he does not desire to believe in Christ nor to practice Christian love and does not desire to be a Christian. How much someone cares about the flesh and blood, that is about the suffering and death of Christ Jesus, about the shedding of his crimson blood, about the forgiveness of sins, about brotherly love and communion in God the Father, the Son, and the Holy Ghost, yea the communion of the whole heavenly host and the universal Christian church outside of which there is no salvation, just this much he should care about the bread and the wine of God's table. Not that here bread and wine are anything other than bread and wine; but according to the memorial and the significant mysteries for the sake of which Christ thus instituted it. If now one had no other word or Scripture, but only the correct understanding of water baptism and the Supper of Christ, one would have God and all his creatures, faith and love, the law, and all the prophets. So whoever makes a mockery of the Supper of Christ, the Son of Man will mock before God and his angels. So much for self-examination.

**Commentary:** It is interesting that the self-examination is not concerned with a long list of proscribed attitudes or behaviors (as might be expected from the rigor of the Pledge of Love we find later in the service) but with matters of the heart.

Do I believe "utterly and absolutely" that Christ gave his body and blood for me? Do I hunger for that bread which comes down from heaven? Am I grateful for the fact that I am loved?

**Text:** Since now these ceremonies and signs have to do completely and exclusively with fraternal love, and since one who loves his neighbor like himself is a rare bird, yea even an Indian phoenix on earth, who can sit at the supper table with a good conscience? Answer: One who has thus taken to heart and has thus shaped himself in mind and heart and senses inwardly that he truly and sincerely can say, "The love of God which he has shown to me through the sacrifice of his only-begotten and most-beloved Son for the payment my sins (John 3:16; 1 John 4:9; Rom. 8:32), of which I have heard and been certainly assured through his holy Word, has so moved, softened, and penetrated my spirit and soul that I am so minded and ready to offer my flesh and blood, furthermore so to rule over and so to master it, that it must obey me against its own will, and henceforth not take advantage of, deceive, injure, or harm my neighbor in any way in body, soul, honor, goods, wife, or child, but rather to go into the fire for him and die, as Paul also desired to be accursed for his brethren and Moses to be stricken out of the book of life for the sake of his people" (Rom. 9:3; Exod. 32:32). Such a person may with good conscience and worthiness sit at the Supper of Christ.

You say: "This is humanly impossible." Answer: Certainly for the Adamic human nature. But all things are possible to the Christian (Mark 9:23), not as persons, but as believers, who are one with God and all creatures, and are (except for the flesh) free and independent of themselves. For God works such willing and doing in his believers (Phil. 2:14), through the inward anointing of his Holy Spirit, so that he stands in complete freedom to will and to do good or evil. The good one can do is through the anointing of God. The evil comes from one's own innate nature and impulse, which evil will one can, however, master and tame through the grace given by God (Deut. 30:1ff.; Gen. 4:17; Rom. 10; Matt. 19; John 1:12).

It is not sufficient that sin be recognized through the law, nor that we know what is good or evil. We must bind the commandments on our hand, grasp them, and fulfill them in deeds (Deut. 6:8; Matt. 11:30; John 3). To do this is easy and a small thing to the believer, but to those who walk according to the flesh, all things are impossible. Yet the believing and newly born person under the gospel is still also [a person] under the law. He has just as many trials as before, or even more. He finds (however holy he may be) nothing good in his own flesh, just as Saint Paul laments the same with great seriousness regarding the conflict and the resistance of the flesh (Rom. 7:18). Nevertheless the believer rejoices and praises God that the trial is not and cannot be so great in him, but that the power of God in him, which he has received through the living Word which God has sent, is stronger and mightier (1 Cor. 10:13; Rom. 8:11). He also knows certainly that such resistances, evil desires, and sinful lusts of his flesh are not damning for him if he confesses the same to God, regrets them, and does not follow after them, but reigns and rules mightily over the restless devil of his flesh (1 Cor. 9:27), strangles, crucifies, and torments him without letup; holds in his rein, does not do his will, cares little that breaks his neck (Exod. 34:20). So every one who is a Christian acts and behaves so that he may worthily eat and drink at the table of the Lord.

Know thou further, righteous Christians, that to fulfill the law it is not enough to avoid sins and die to them. Yea, one must also do good to the neighbor, (Ps. 37). For Christ not only broke the bread, he also distributed it and gave it to his disciples. Yea, not only the bread, but also even his own flesh and blood. So we must not only speak the word of brotherly love, hear it, confess ourselves to be sinners, and abstain from sin, we must also fulfill it in deeds, as Scripture everywhere teaches us.

Forsake evil and do good (Ps. 37).

Brethren, work out your salvation (Phil. 2:12).

While we have time, let us do good, for the night comes when no man can work (Gal. 6:9).

Wilt thou enter into life, keep the commandments (Matt.19:17).

For not those who hear the word are righteous before God, but those who do the law will be justified (Rom. 2:7).

Not all those who say to me, Lord, Lord, will enter into the kingdom of the heavens, but he who does the will of my Father who is in heaven, will enter into the kingdom of heaven, says Christ, and adds: Everyone who hears my words and does them, he shall be likened unto a wise man who built his house upon a rock. But everyone who hears my word and does it not shall be likened to a fool who built his house on sand (Matt. 7:21-27).

In sum: God requires of us the will, the word, and the works of brotherly love, and he will not let himself be paid off or dismissed with words (Matt. 15; Luke 8:21; Rom. 8:1; Luke 17; Isa. 64:5ff.; Col 2:10; Ps. 32:1f.; Rom. 4:5; 5; 7; 8). But what innate weaknesses and imperfections constantly are intermingled with our acts of commission and omission because of our flesh, God—thanks to the grace of our Lord Jesus Christ—will not reckon to our eternal condemnation; for in Christ we have all attained perfection, and in him we are already blessed. What more do we lack?

Since now believers have inwardly surrendered themselves utterly to serve their fellow members in Christ at the cost of honor, goods, body, and life, yea even to offer their souls for them to the point of hell with the help of God; therefore, it is all the more needful sincerely to groan and pray to God that he may cause the faith of these new persons to grow; also that he may more deeply kindle in them the fire of brotherly love, so that in these two matters, signified by water baptism and the Lord's Supper, they might continually grow, mature, and persevere unto the end.

Here shall now be held a time of common silence, so that each one who desires to approach the table of God can meditate upon the suffering of Christ and thus with Saint John rest on the breast of the Lord. After such silence, the "Our Father" shall be spoken publicly by the church, reverently, and with hearts desirous of grace as follows (Matt. 6:9ff.; Luke 11:2ff.):

Our Father who art in heaven,
Hallowed by thy name
Thy kingdom come,
Thy will be done on earth as in heaven.
Give us today our daily brad.
Forgive us our debts as we forgive our debtors.
Lead us not into temptation but deliver us from
  evil.
Amen.

**Commentary:** That part of the service must have evoked openness and tenderness in its hearers. Then comes the great "but." Christ does not need our love expressed to him in a mystical way; he bids us love him in our neighbor. Only the one who desires to love Christ in the person of the neighbor is ready to meet him in the Supper. This is the gist of Hubmaier's theology of worship and his belief about the Lord's Supper. The fulfillment of the sacrament is to pour out one's flesh and blood for the other. Without this pledge, it is all hypocrisy.

How might people have felt in the face of this challenge? Relieved that someone finally said that you can't call yourself a Christian if you don't put your money where your mouth is? Or crushed by the extremity of the challenge?

Appropriately for Hubmaier's purposes, silence follows to allow intimate meditation on Christ. He describes the contemplation as a resting on the breast of the Lord. Silence was so important to Hubmaier because it afforded worshipers an opportunity to internalize the words of the liturgy. This concern for the coincidence of outer words and inner commitment gained in significance the further left one went on the Reformation spectrum. The radical reformers feared that in the mass, liturgy was more an expression of religious conformity than personal conviction. Hubmaier wanted to be existentially radical and liturgically conservative: He sought worshippers who know Christ and his way personally, yet he valued their collective expression in continuity with the tradition. The silence is broken by the most traditional of all Christian formulations, the Lord's Prayer.

**Text**: Now the priest shall point out clearly and expressly that the bread is bread and the wine, wine and not flesh and blood, as has long been believed.

**Commentary**: Lest the people's minds still harbor false teaching on the Eucharist, the priest is to instruct them "that the bread is bread."

**Text**: Brothers and sisters, if you will to love God before, in, and above all things, in the power of his holy and living Word, serve him alone (Deut. 5; 6; Exod. 20), honor and adore him and henceforth sanctify his name, subject your carnal and sinful will to his divine will which he has worked in you by his living Word, in life and death, then let each say individually:

I will.

If you love your neighbor and serve him with deeds of brotherly love (Matt. 25; Eph. 6; Col. 3; Rom. 13:1; 1 Pet. 2:13ff.), lay down and shed for him your life and blood, be obedient to father, mother, and all authorities according to the will of God, and this in the power of our Lord Jesus Christ, who laid down

and shed his flesh and blood for us, then let each say individually:

I will.

If you will practice fraternal admonition toward your brethren and sisters (Matt. 18:15ff.; Luke 5; Matt. 5:44; Rom. 12:10), make peace and unity among them, and reconcile yourselves with all those whom you have offended, abandon all envy, hate, and evil will toward everyone, willingly cease all action and behavior which causes harm, disadvantage, or offense to your neighbor, [if you will] also love your enemies and do good to them, and exclude according to the Rule of Christ (Matt. 18) all those who refuse to do so, then let each say individually:

I will.

If you desire publicly to confirm before the church this pledge of love which you have now made, through the Lord's Supper of Christ, by eating bread and drinking wine, and to testify to it in the power of the living memorial of the suffering and death of Jesus Christ our Lord, then let each say individually:

I desire it in the power of God.

So eat and drink with one another in the name of God the Father, the Son, and the Holy Spirit. May God himself accord to all of us the power and the strength that we may worthily carry it out and bring it to its saving conclusion according to his divine will. May the Lord impart to us his grace. Amen.

**Commentary**: So that their praise of God might be spiritually and theologically authentic, the worshipers are not asked to make a true moral response to the Supper in the Pledge of Love. It is a fine balancing act: the prayers are full of gratitude and grace, the exhortations full of challenges and demands. But after communion the balance is lost. The liturgy becomes moralistic, filled with praise and warnings. The closing blessing is too concise to return the focus to Christ.

**Text**: The bishop takes the bread and with the church lifts his eyes to heaven, praises God, and says:

We praise and thank thee, Lord God, Creator of the Heavens and earth, for all thy goodness toward us. Especially hast thou so sincerely loved us that thou didst give thy most-beloved Son for us unto death so that each one who believes in him may not be lost but have eternal life (John

3:16; 1 John 4:9; Rom. 8:32). Be thou honored, praised, and magnified now, forever, always and eternally. Amen.

Now the priest takes the bread, breaks it, and offers it into the hands of those present, saying:

The Lord Jesus, in the night in which he was betrayed, took the bread, gave thanks, and broke it, and said: "Take, eat. This is my body, which is broken for you. Do this in my memory." Therefore, take and eat also, dear brothers and sisters, this bread in the memory of the body of our Lord Jesus Christ, which he gave unto death for us.

Now when everyone has been fed, the priest likewise takes the cup with the wine and speaks with lifted eyes:

"God! Praise be to thee!"

and offers it into their hands saying:

Likewise the Lord took the vessel after the Supper and spoke: "This cup is a new testament in my blood. Do this, as often as you drink, in memory of me." Take therefore also the vessel and all drink from it in the memory of the blood of our Lord Jesus Christ, which was shed for us for the forgiveness of our sins.

When they have all drunk, the priest says:

As often as you eat the bread and drink of the drink, you shall proclaim the death of the Lord, until he comes (1 Cor. 11:26).

Now the church is seated to hear the conclusion.

**Commentary:** How would the people have felt as they returned from church to everyday life? Some of them must have rejoiced in the fact that they were being made the subjects of their own destiny; they were assured that they—simple people who had had no say in their own lives—were the body of Christ, able to extend the incarnation into a hostile world. Others must have been overwhelmed by the expectations placed on them, fearing—as the liturgy warns in its words of dismissal—that a millstone might be tied around their neck.

**Text:** Most dearly beloved brethren and sisters in the Lord. As we now, by thus eating the bread and drinking the drink in memory of the suffering and shed blood of our Lord Jesus Christ for the remission of our sins, have had fellowship one with another (1 Cor. 10:17; 12:12; Eph. 4:4; Col. 1:3; Eph. 1; 4; 5), and have all become one loaf and one body,

and our Head is Christ, we should properly become conformed to our Head and as his members follow after him, love one another, do good, give counsel, and be helpful to one another, each offering up his flesh and blood for the other. Under our Head Christ we should all also live, speak, and act honorably and circumspectly, so that we give no offense or provocation to anyone (Matt. 18; Mark 9; Luke 17; 1 Cor. 8; Rom. 14). So that also those who are outside the church might not have reason to blaspheme our Head, our faith, and church, and to say: "Does your Head Christ teach you such an evil life? Is that your faith? Is that your baptism? Is that your Christian church, Supper, and gospel, that you should lead such an ungodly and shameful life in gluttony, drunkenness, gambling, dancing, usury, gossip, reviling, cursing, blasphemy, pride, avarice, envy, hate and wrath, unchastity, luxury, laziness, and frivolity? (Matt. 18:6). Woe, woe to him who gives offense! It would be better for him that a millstone should be hung around his neck and he should be cast into the depth of the sea. Let us rather take upon ourselves a righteous, honorable, and serious life, through which God our Father who is in heaven may be praised.

Since our brotherly love requires that one member of the body be also concerned for the other, therefore we have the earnest behest of Christ (Matt. 18:14ff.), that whenever henceforth a brother sees another erring or sinning, that he once and again should fraternally admonish him in brotherly love. Should he not be willing to reform nor to desist from his sin, he shall be reported to the church. The church shall then exhort him a third time. When this also does no good, she shall exclude him from her fellowship. Unless it should be the case that the sin is quite public and scandalous; then he should be admonished also publicly and before all, so that the others may fear (1 Cor. 5:1; 1 Tim. 5:20; Gal. 2:11).

Whereupon I pray and exhort you once more, most dearly beloved in Christ, that henceforth as table companions of Christ Jesus (Luke 22:15), you henceforth lead a Christian walk before God and before men. Be mindful of your baptismal commitment and of your pledge of love which you made to God and the church publicly and certainly not unwittingly when receiving the water and in breaking bread. See to it that you bear fruit worthy of the baptism and the Supper of Christ, that you may in the power of God satisfy your pledge, promise, sacrament, and sworn commitment (Matt. 3:8; Luke 3:8). God sees it and knows your hearts. May our Lord Jesus Christ, ever and eternally praised, grant us the same. Amen.

Dear brothers and sisters, watch and pray lest you wander away and fall into temptation (Matt. 24:42; 25:15; Luke 16). You know neither the day nor the hour when the Lord is coming and will demand of you an accounting of your life. Therefore watch and pray. I commend you to God. May each of you say to himself, "Praise, praise, praise to the Lord eternally!"

Arise and go forth in the peace of Christ Jesus. The grace of God be with us all.
Amen.

## Truth Is Unkillable: Hubmaier on the Lord's Supper

To the noble Lord Buriano of Cornitz, my gracious sovereign.
Grace and peace in Christ, noble and Christian Lord.

The majority of people who stand by the gospel recognize that bread is bread and wine, wine in the Lord's Supper, and not Christ (Acts 1:9; Mark 16:19; Heb. 1:3; 12:2; Matt. 22:44; Ps. 110). For the same ascended into heaven and is sitting at the right hand of God his Father, whence he will come again to judge the living and the dead. Precisely that is our foundation, according to which we must deduce and exposit all of the Scriptures having to do with eating and drinking. Thus Christ cannot be eaten or drunk by us otherwise than spiritually and in faith. So then he cannot be bodily the bread either but rather in the memorial which is held, as he himself and Paul explained these Scriptures (Luke 22; 1 Cor. 11). Whoever understands them otherwise does violence to the articles of our Christian faith. Yet the restless Satan has invented another intrigue to hold us in his snare. Namely, that such a Lord's Supper should be established without a prior water baptism, something which again Scripture cannot suffer. When the three thousand men and Paul had been instructed in the Word and believed, only thereafter did they break bread with the brethren (Acts 2:41ff.; Acts 9). For as faith precedes love, so water baptism must precede the Lord's Supper. So that Your Grace may know in what form the Lord's Supper is celebrated in Nicolsburg, I have had it printed, for the praise of God, the honor of Your Grace, and the salvation of all believers in Christ, so that no one might think that we fear the light or that we are unable to give reasons for our teaching and actions. May Your Grace be commended to God and graciously accept from me this written token of respect, through my dear brother Jan Zeysinger,

Your Grace's willing [servant]
Balthasar Huebmor [Hubmaier], etc.

### Conclusion

The Reformation was a time in which drastic correctives were applied to conventional patterns of church life. Hubmaier was among those who did their utmost for people to know that Christ "died for all, so that those who live might live no longer for themselves, but for him who died and was raised for them" (2 Cor. 5:15). This double theme fills "A Form for Christ's Supper."

Some of its moralism derives from Hubmaier's intense desire to retain but purify liturgical worship. For him to be satisfied with an order of service, it had to make the goal of the Christian life unequivocally clear. In doing this, Hubmaier was perhaps more extreme but of the same mind as other contemporary liturgical reformers such as Martin Bucer and Thomas Cranmer. One sees this similarity especially in the exhaustive exhortations to those preparing to come to the Lord's Table. This comparison should remind us that while his gathering for the breaking of bread bears the marks of Hubmaier's and Anabaptism's distinctives, it also reflects the age in which he lived. For all of them, this preparation replaced the no less serious act of individual confession before a priest in the old church. Hubmaier was using liturgy to teach and persuade. It sounds as if this service was written for a congregation which was not yet as fully converted as its pastor thought it should be.

A large part of the lasting value of "A Form for Christ's Supper" is its corrective, and therefore, incomplete state. The service exemplifies the tensions faced by anyone trying to hold together form and spirit, grace and works. Even though the commentary woven throughout the service shows how mightily the author strove to give forgiveness and obedience their due, the service fell into a kind of perfectionism, perhaps because the sacrament itself had become primarily a human act. Because of Hubmaier's fear of sacramentalism, the validity of the ceremony depended on the intensity and purity of the human response. But Hubmaier's service stands as a warning against every attempt to use liturgy to smooth out the rough demands of the Gospel; it invites us to grapple as he did to give voice to the whole counsel of God.

John Rempel

## 171 ❖ BIBLIOGRAPHY ON REFORMATION MODELS OF WORSHIP

### Lutheran
Lehmann, Helmut, ed. _Luther's Works._ Vol. 35: _Word and Sacrament I._ Philadelphia: Muhlenberg, 1960; and vol. 53: _Liturgy and Hymns._ Philadelphia: Muhlenberg, 1965.

### Reformed
Bornert, René. _La réforme protestant du culte a Strasbourg au XVIe siècle (1523–1598): Approche sociologique et interpretation théologique._ Leiden: E. J. Brill, 1981. Authoritative discussion of development of liturgical reform in Strasbourg over the course of the 16th century.

Bucer, Martin. _De Regno Christi,_ 1551. Translated in Wilhelm Pauck, ed., _Melanchthon and Bucer._ Library of Christian Classics, 19. Philadelphia: Westminster Press, 1969.

Bucer, Martin. _Censura Martine Buceri super libro sacrorum._ Alcuin Club Collection, 55. Great Wakering, UK: Mayhew-McCrimmon, 1974. Bucer's comments on the 1549 _Book of Common Prayer,_ which probably contributed to its revision.

Calvin, John. "Draft Ecclesiastical Ordinances," 1541, and "Short Treatise on the Lord's Supper," 1541, in J. K. S. Reid, ed., _Calvin: Theological Treatises._ Library of Christian Classics, 22. Philadelphia: Westminster, 1954.

Old, Hughes Oliphant. _The Patristic Roots of Reformed Worship._ Zurich: Thelogischer Verlag, 1975. Treats the Reformed tradition generally but pays little attention to other Protestants. Much detail on the Lord's Supper.

_____. _The Shaping of the Reformed Baptismal Rite in the Sixteenth Century._ Grand Rapids: Eerdmans, 1992. Treats the Reformed rite in the context of Luther and first-generation Anabaptists.

_____. _Worship: Guides to the Reformed Tradition._ Atlanta: John Knox, 1984. A general discussion of Reformed worship, but concentrates on 16th century.

Pahl, Irmgard, ed. _Coena Domini I: Die Abendmahlsliturgie en der Reformationskirchen im 16./17. Jahrhundert._ Frieburg, Switzerland: Univcrsitatsverlag, 1983. Brief but detailed analyses of the Lord's Supper services of 16th-17th century Protestants; articles are in language of liturgy.

van de Poll, G. J. _Martin Bucer's Liturgical Ideas._ Groningen: Van Gorcum, 1954. Although dated, it remains the only book-length English study.

Zwingli, Ulrich. "On Baptism" and "On the Lord's Supper," in G. W. Bromiley, ed., _Zwingli and Bullinger._ Library of Christian Classics, 24. Philadelphia: Westminster, 1953.

### Anabaptist
Dyck, C., ed. _The Writings of Dirk Philips._ Peabody, Mass: Hendricksen Publishers, 1991. Dirk was the closest colleague and systematizer of the thought of the formative early leader of northern Anabaptism, Menno Simons. No one in the first generation of the movement dealt as extensively with the sacraments, especially the Lord's Supper. Dirk was a sacramentarian for whom sacraments were outer assurances of inward states.

Fast, H., ed. "Gemeinsame Ordnung der Glieder Christi" in _Der Lunke Fluegel Der Reformation,_ vol. 4. Bremen: Carl Scheuneman, 1962. This description of the worship pattern of early Swiss Anabaptism sets forth the acts of worship and offers devotional comments about how to observe them. However, it contains no texts.

_Het Offer des Heeren,_ 1562. This is the oldest Anabaptist hymnal. Its main theme is faithfulness under persecution. Psalm texts are also included.

Klaassen, W. _The Writings of Pilgram Marpeck._ Scottdale, Pa.: Herald Press, 1978. Marpeck was the most sacramental and incarnational among Anabaptist writers. He sought to transcend both the sacramentalist and spiritualist interpretations of "ceremonies," claiming that faith was necessary to the dynamic of sacramental reality but that where faith and Spirit were present, matter could unite believers with Christ.

Krebs, M., and H. Rott, eds. _Quellen zur Geschichte der Täufer,_ vol. 7, Elsass 1. Gütersloh: Gerd Mohn, 1959. Mostly transcripts of court hearings and public disputations in which the Anabaptists were pressed to describe their worship and belief about sacraments. The most substantive piece is the debate between Martin Bucer and Pilgram Marpeck.

Loserth, J., ed. *Pilgram Marpecks Antwort auf Kaspar Schwenkfelds Beuteilung des Buches der Bundebezeugung von 1542.* Wien: Carl Fromme, 1929. A voluminous record of the debate between Marpeck, the most sacramental and incarnational of the Anabaptists, and Schwenkfeld, the most consistent advocate of spiritualism. As the debate unfolds, Marpeck sees that the spiritualistic tendency of the Reformation, if taken to Schwenkfeld's extreme, would remove all outer evidence of God's work, including the visible church. Out of this encounter comes a sophisticated apology for sacraments based on the prolongation of the incarnation in the church, worked out in exquisite detail in relation to the Lord's Supper.

Muralt, L., and W. von Schmidt, ed. *Quellen zur Geschichte der Täufer in Der Schweitz,* vol. 1. Zürich: S. Hinzel, 1952. Transcripts of court hearings in which Anabaptists explain their ordinances as acts of community and often denounce the worship practices and sacramental beliefs of Catholicism and even other forms of Protestantism.

Pipkin, W., and J. Yoder, eds. *Balthasar Hubmaier.* Scottdale, Pa.: Herald Press, 1989.

# TEN

# Post-Reformation Models of Worship

Between 1600 and 1900 a variety of new movements grew out of the Reformation. Believers within each of these movements expressed their faith in slightly different forms of worship. This chapter presents these forms of worship in their historical context, arranges them chronologically, and provides text and commentary. However, except for Wesley's liturgy, extended texts are not available, for most Protestant groups abandoned written texts in favor of extemporaneous prayers and forms of worship. Consequently this section contains orders of worship along with commentaries that explain the order and the experience of the worshiping community. Twentieth-century models for renewing worship are found in Volume 3.

## 172 ✦ AN AMERICAN PURITAN MODEL OF WORSHIP

*From the landing of the Mayflower through the American Revolution, the majority of free-church clergy probably spent more time interacting with worshipers around the Communion table than they did preaching from pulpits. The services that follow reflect Puritan worship as well as the general approach to worship in the separatist congregations—Baptist, Congregational, Independent.*

———— **Introduction** ————

At the Communion table, close to the worshiping congregation, the clergy often presided with lay leaders. Standing at the table with the people, clergy began the service with prayers of thanksgiving and later led prayers of intercession incorporating concerns spoken out or written by laity. All continued to stand for singing led by laity. Often from the table, clergy read the Scriptures interspersed with exegesis so that the Word would be heard truly and actively. Then the clergy went into the pulpit to give their sermons, applying the Bible to any of a wide range of issues related to God's kingdom on earth. Immediately after the sermon, as worship continued, they came down from the pulpit and sat at the table to answer the congregation's questions and hear witnessing by laity who were free to agree or disagree with what was said in the sermon. From the table, clergy gave thanks and gave the bread and

wine to lay leaders who distributed Communion to the people. After more singing, the people often gave their offerings at the table. Communion was celebrated as often as each Sunday or at least once a month.

Darrell Todd Maurina

Text:

*Prayers of Thanksgiving and of Intercession*

All stood for prayer with hands lifted above their heads in the biblical manner enjoined in 1 Timothy 2:8; and the prayers were all extemporaneously spoken, whether by the pastor, teacher, or others.

*Singing of Psalms*

All stood to sing a psalm before (and sometimes after) the time devoted to opening of Scripture, sermon, exhortations, and questions. As some of the Psalms have as many as 130 lines, it would take 15 minutes to sing some (and twice that long if lined out). (Since our service is reflective of 18th century worship as well as 17th we will be singing the music of Isaac Watts as well as the Psalms.)

*Reading, Expounding and Preaching the Word*

Cotton notes that there was no dumb reading of Scripture; for the reading of Scripture included expounding. In expounding to aid understanding, the reader of Scripture would make brief comments between the lines of Scripture, with extended comments just before and immediately following the Scripture reading.

During the sermon, members of the congregation took notes. From these, parents would later question their children on the matter of the sermon. Also, from such notes, small study groups would later in the week discuss the sermons with both those who had been present and others who had been unable to attend the service.

### Exhorting and Questioning by Laity

After preaching and returning to his seat, the ordained or lay leader of worship called upon "any other of the Brethren whether of the same Church or any, to speak a word of Exhortation to the people." The time of exhorting was accompanied by questioning of the minister on the matter of the sermon.

### Celebrating the Lord's Supper

Cotton wrote of "celebrating" the Lord's Supper and noted that they administered it "once a month at least" in the Sunday morning worship. "After the celebration of the Supper, a Psalm of thanksgiving is sung (according to Matt. 26:30) and the church is dismissed with a blessing."

Doug Adams[17]

## 173 ✦ JOHN COTTON'S NEW ENGLAND CONGREGATIONAL MODEL OF WORSHIP

*In his book* The Way of the Churches of Christ in New England, *John Cotton, a leading Congregational pastor of the first generation of American colonists, provided a detailed description of worship practices in New England. Although conclusive evidence is lacking, it appears that English Congregationalists used the same basic order.*

——————— **Introduction** ———————

This version of Cotton's description, with modernized spelling and capitalization, is taken from Bryan Spinks's *Freedom or Order?* (Allison Park, Pa.: Pickwick Publications, 1984), 34–36.

**Text**: First when we come together in the church according to the Apostle's direction (1 Tim. 2:1) we make prayers and intercessions and thanksgivings for ourselves and for all men, not in any prescribed form of prayer, or studied liturgy, but in such a manner, as the Spirit of grace and of prayer

*John Cotton. A portrait of the New England Puritan leader.*

(who teaches all the people of God what and how to pray, Rom. 8:26-27) helps our infirmities, we having respect therein to the necessities of the people, the estate of the times, and the works of Christ in our hands.

**Commentary**: Congregational worship opened with items more commonly referred to as pastoral prayer rather than beginning with an invocation or opening prayer. This is an example of the Puritan unwillingness to make even minor emendations to what they viewed as the Scriptural directives for worship.

**Text**: After prayer, either the Pastor or Teacher, reads a chapter in the Bible, and expounds it, giving the sense, to cause the people to understand the reading, according to Nehemiah 8:8. And in sundry churches the other (whether Pastor or Teacher) who expounds not, he preaches the Word, and in the afternoon the other who preached in the morning does usually (if there be time) read and preach, and he that expounded in the morning preaches after him.

**Commentary**: Congregationalists detested what they called "dumb reading" without comment. Based on Ephesians 4:11, the Puritans viewed the teaching eldership as divided into two offices: the "pastor" who labored in exhortation and the "teacher" who labored in doctrinal explication. This "expounding" was a brief exegetical discourse on the Scripture passage being read, either in the form of a running commentary or a summary following the reading.

**Text**: Before sermon, and many times after, we sing a Psalm, and because the former translation of the Psalms, does in many things vary from the original, and many times paraphrases rather than translates; beside diverse other defects (which we cover in silence) we have endeavored a new translation of the Psalms into English meter, as near the original as we could express it in our English tongue, so far as for the present the Lord has been pleased to help us, and those Psalms we sing, both in our public churches, and in private.

**Commentary**: The sermon here indicated was generally expected to occupy at least an hour and often more. Early Congregationalists sang the Psalms exclusively, as was the general Reformed practice until the English Congregationalist Isaac Watts introduced free paraphrases of the Psalms and actual hymns into Reformed worship in the mid-1700s. The new translation referred to by Cotton is the _Bay Psalm Book_. The first book printed in the English Colonies, it is a very literal translation of the Psalms from Hebrew into English meter.

**Text**: The seals of the covenant (to wit, the sacrament of Baptism and the Lord's Supper) are administered, either by the Pastor or by the Teacher; . . . . Both the sacraments we dispense . . .

**Commentary**: The Lord's Supper was normally celebrated in the morning service. The offering, any baptisms, and any "relations" (public professions of faith) would be made in the afternoon.

**Text**: . . . The Lord's Supper to such as neither want knowledge nor grace to examine and judge themselves before the Lord. Such as lie under any offense publicly known, do first remove the offense, before they present themselves to the Lord's Table; according to Matthew 5:23, 24. The members of any

church, if any be present, who bring letters testimonial with them to our churches, we admit them to the Lord's Table with us . . . . The prayers we use at the administration of the seals, are not any set forms prescribed to us, but conceived by the minister, according to the present occasion, and the nature of the duty in hand . . . . The Lord's Supper we administer for the time, once a month at least, and for the gesture, to the people sitting; according as Christ administered it to his disciples sitting (Matt. 26:20, 26) who also made a symbolic use of it, to teach the church their majority over their ministers in some cases, and their judicial authority, as co-assessors with him at the Last Judgment (Luke 22:27-30), which makes us to look at kneeling at the Lord's Supper, not only as an adoration devised by men, but also as a violation by man of the institution of Christ, diminishing part of the counsel of God, and of the honor and comfort of the church held forth in it.

In time of the solemnization of the Supper, the minister having taken, blessed, and broken the bread, and commanded all the people to take and eat it, as the body of Christ broken for them, he takes it himself, and gives it to all that sit at table with him, and from the table it is reached by the deacons to the people sitting in the next seats about them, the minister sitting in his place at the table.

**Commentary**: The historic Congregational "church order," the Cambridge Platform, specifies "closed" Communion in which the Lord's Table is limited to members of a particular local church and those bearing letters from other churches certifying their membership in good standing (Cambridge Platform 13:7-9, 15:2:4-5). The text here represents the effort to "fence the table," by warning unrepentant sinners not to participate. Infant baptism, not mentioned in this particular description of worship, was treated in the same manner. Since baptism was a sign of a covenant promise to raise a child in the nurture and admonition of the Lord (rather than a sacrament which itself brought children to salvation, or a mere rite of passage), it was only administered to children of church members. Since only those showing fruits of conversion were admitted to membership, the church could charitably assume that these were capable of training the child in the Christian faith.

**Text**: After they have all partaken in the bread, he takes the cup in like manner, and gives thanks anew (blesses it), according to the example of Christ in the Evangelist, who describes the institution (Matt. 26:27; Mark 14:23; Luke 22:17). All of them in such a way as sets forth the elements, not blessed together, but either of them apart; the bread first by itself, and afterwards the wine by itself; for what reason the Lord himself best knows, and we cannot be ignorant, that a received solemn blessing, expressly performed by himself, does apparently call upon the whole assembly to look again for a supernatural and special blessing in the same element also as well as in the former; for which the Lord will be again sought to do it for us.

After the celebration of the Supper, a Psalm of thanksgiving is sung, (according to Matt. 26:30) and the church dismissed with a blessing.

**Commentary**: The double consecration of the elements should be noted. While now a common practice in some Protestant churches, it was controversial at the time. The Congregationalist did not attempt to explain the reasons for the double consecration beyond noting that it was prescribed in the Word of God.

Darrell Todd Maurina

## 174 &#x2666; The *Westminster Directory*

*In 1643, following the outbreak of civil war in England between the Puritan-controlled Parliament and the Anglican King Charles I, Parliament commissioned 150 ministers and lay leaders to draft a new confession, catechism, worship service, and form of government for England. Although this body, later known as the Westminster Assembly of Divines, was predominantly Presbyterian, almost a dozen Congregationalists were invited. This body produced the first Westminster Directory.*

### Introduction

The Westminster Assembly first began work on replacing the Anglican *Book of Common Prayer* in the belief that both Presbyterians and Congregationalists shared compatible views of worship. One Congregationalist was elected to the nine-member subcommittee on liturgical matters.

As late as the end of the nineteenth century, the Congregational historian Williston Walker could say that this order of worship "is substantially the one that has been used in conservative Presbyterian and Congregational churches for generations." The

word "substantially," however, is significant. The Congregationalists did take exception to certain parts of the *Directory*. Plus, a number of compromises within the *Directory* itself reflect division in the Assembly. Furthermore, some descriptions of New England church services from decades after its adoption bear a much closer resemblance to the service described by John Cotton than to the *Directory*. In general, Congregationalists eventually came to follow the form of the *Directory* with some modifications.

In the actual *Directory* text, each item is accompanied by an extended explanation, similar to Cotton's. Notes are appended in this explanation only when necessary for clarity or when Congregational practice differed from that of Presbyterians.

**Text**:
Call to Worship (Prefacing)

**Commentary**: The Congregationalists argued that "all prefacing was unlawful; that according to 1 Timothy 2:1, it was necessary to begin with prayer, and that in the first prayer we behooved to pray for the King." See "Prayer before the Sermon" below.

**Text**:
Prayer of Approach
Psalm Reading
Old Testament Chapter
New Testament Chapter

**Commentary**: Ordinarily, entire chapters of books were read. Some Congregationalists sang a psalm between one or more of the readings to aid in concentration. The *Directory* notes that if comment (Cotton's "expounding") is to be made on the Scripture, it is to be done after a chapter is read, not while it is read.

**Text**:
Psalm (sung)
Prayer Before the Sermon

**Commentary**: In most Reformed liturgies, this item indicates a simple prayer for the delivery of the sermon. In a compromise with the Congregationalists, the type of prayers specified in 1 Timothy 2:1 are listed here so they can be prayed fairly early in the service if not at the very beginning. The *Directory* also specified that some petitions could be deferred until after the sermon, which allowed for the Presbyterian preference for having the primary prayer after the sermon.

**Text:**
Sermon
General Prayer

**Commentary:** The General Prayer was the prayer and thanksgiving for all things not coming under the headings of Prayer of Approach or Prayer Before the Sermon. When the petitions of the Prayer Before the Sermon were deferred, the General Prayer was termed the Long Prayer and was so described until well into the twentieth century.

**Text:**
Lord's Prayer

**Commentary:** Many Congregationalists protested that the Lord's Prayer was a model for prayer rather than a specific set prayer. The Anglican liturgy prescribed multiple uses of the Lord's Prayer and was condemned by the Congregationalists as requiring "vain repetitions" contrary to the Word of God. The _Directory_ declared that it was not a mere model and "recommended" its use.

**Text:**
Psalm (sung)
Blessing

**Order of the Lord's Supper**

**Commentary:** The celebration of the Lord's Supper was "judged to be convenient" following the morning sermon. The frequency of administration was left up to each church; but a preparatory sermon or midweek lecture was to be made if administration was not weekly.

**Text:**
Exhortation

**Commentary:** A brief explanation of the benefit of the sacrament.

**Text:**
Warning

**Commentary:** Fencing of the table by warning unrepentant sinners not to participate.

**Text:**
Invitation

**Commentary:** Encouragement of those who "labor under the sense of burden of their sins" to participate.

**Text:**
Words of Institution: 1 Corinthians 11:23-27, followed by optional explanation.

**Commentary:** From the Gospels or 1 Corinthians 11:23-27.

**Text:**
Prayer, Thanksgiving, or Blessing of the Bread and Wine

**Commentary:** Note the single blessing to which the Congregationalists objected.

**Text:**
**Fraction and Delivery:** "According to the holy institution, command, and example of our blessed Savior Jesus Christ, I take this bread, and, having given thanks, I break it, and give it unto you. [Delivery to the communicants] Take ye, eat ye; this is the body of Christ which is broken for you: do this in remembrance of Him . . . . According to the institution, command, and example of our Lord Jesus Christ, I take this cup, and give it unto you; [Delivery to the communicants] This cup is the New Testament in the blood of Christ, which is shed for the remission of the sins of many: drink ye all of it."

**Commentary:** Presbyterian practice was to have the communicants sit at a central table. Congregationalists regarded this as unnecessary and sat in their pews. The _Directory_ allows either option.

**Text:**
Exhortation
Solemn Thanksgiving
Collect for the Poor: "The collection for the poor is so to be ordered, that no part of the public worship be thereby hindered."

Darrell Todd Maurina

## 175 • A Baptist Model of Worship

_Baptists emerged from a variety of Separatist congregations in seventeenth-century England. While Baptists disagreed theologically on the issue of predestination, they eventually came to share the same form of worship. Like the Congregationalists, Baptists looked to the Bible for their liturgical guidance. At the same time, early Baptists strongly emphasized the leading of the Spirit in worship and avoided a strict structuring of the Sunday service. As the texts below make clear, Baptist liturgical patterns began to solidify on both sides of the Atlantic by the eighteenth century._

## Introduction

As Baptists developed in England in the seventeenth century, they worshiped in a variety of ways (see Origins of Baptist Worship), but by the end of the century a prevalent pattern had formed. The "Churchbook" of the congregation at Paul's Alley, Barbicon (London), illustrates that pattern.

## Seventeenth-Century Baptists

Text:
A MODEL OF BAPTIST WORSHIP, 1695
ORDER OF SERVICE
Psalm
Prayer
Scripture
Sermon(s)
Prayer
   [LORD'S SUPPER
   Homily and Exhortation
   Blessing the Bread
   Words of Institution
   Receiving the Bread
   Blessing the Wine
   Words of Institution
   Receiving the Wine]
Psalm (hymn)
Benediction

A layman selected by the congregation began the service by reading a psalm. In some congregations he read it. In others he "read" it by "lining it out" for the congregation to sing after him to a known psalm tune.

A time of prayer followed. The layman prayed, and others could follow him in a general time of prayer. The layman then read a portion of Scripture.

After reading his text, the minister preached, the sermon lasting as long as an hour. The minister concluded with prayer directed toward the application of the sermon.

Then a psalm was read or sung (as at the beginning of the service), although in some churches a hymn was sung. An intense controversy over whether hymns could be sung arose during this period. Eventually, however, following the leadership of the London Baptist pastor Benjamin Keach, almost all Baptist congregations adopted the singing of hymns, and hymns became a significant part of Baptist worship. The minister pronounced a benediction to conclude the service.

Usually one Sunday each month, often in an afternoon or evening service, the congregation celebrated the Lord's Supper after the minister's sermon and prayer. The minister took his place behind the table at the front of the congregation and began with a brief homily on the meaning of the Supper and exhorted the members to receive it properly. He gave thanks for the bread; then taking it in his hands and saying the words of institution, he broke it as he said the words, "This is my body, broken for you." He partook of the bread, gave to the deacons for them to partake, and the deacons distributed the bread to the members, who remained in their seats, while the minister said appropriate words of distribution. They repeated the same pattern for the wine. This pattern would remain virtually unchanged during the first three centuries of Baptist life, although in many congregations the frequency decreased to once each quarter during the late eighteenth and nineteenth centuries.

## Eighteenth-Century Baptists

Text:
**Regular Baptists.** The Baptists who came to America from England brought the aforementioned pattern of worship with them and modified it according to their own experience. These Baptists who followed this somewhat more structured pattern came to be called Regular Baptists, distinguishing them from Baptists who had developed later with a less-structured style of worship.

An example of the Regular Baptists was Morgan Edwards, a product of the Baptist college at Bristol, England. Edwards was pastor of the First Baptist Church, Philadelphia. With history as an avocation, Edwards visited Baptists up and down the east coast collecting statistics on congregations and materials regarding their theology and practices. His *Customs of Primitive Churches,* 1768, provides evidence for reconstructing Regular Baptist worship in the latter part of the eighteenth century.

MODEL OF REGULAR BAPTIST WORSHIP, 1768
ORDER OF SERVICE
Call to Worship
Prayer
Scripture
Prayer
Singing

Preaching
Prayer
Singing
   [Lord's Supper]
Offering
Benediction

The call to worship could be a brief word spoken by the minister or the singing of a hymn by the congregation. The minister followed it with a brief prayer of invocation.

The minister then read a portion of Scripture, which provided the larger context from which his sermon text would be taken. The main prayer in the worship service followed. In this lengthy prayer, the minister addressed all the needs of the congregation.

The Lord's Supper normally was celebrated once each month either before or after the offering. It followed the pattern of the English Baptists cited earlier.

**Separate Baptists.** Although the Regular Baptists began Baptist work in America, during the eighteenth century another Baptist group evolved out of the revivals of the Great Awakening. Known as Separate Baptists because of their origins out of Separate Congregationalism during and following the revivals, these Baptists' roots were clearly evident. Whereas the Regulars were more prominent in the cities and towns of the East and relatively more formal and structured in worship, the Separates were more prevalent in frontier regions, especially in the West, and more informal and openly evangelistic in tone.

Because of their informality, lack of structure, and disinterest in chronicling their worship, no materials have been preserved to guide in reconstructing a definitive Separate Baptist worship. However, by piecing together information from Separate Baptist writings and journals, the following speculative model emerges.

MODEL OF SEPARATE BAPTIST WORSHIP, *c.* 1770
ORDER OF SERVICE
Hymn(s)
Prayer
Sermon(s)
Prayer
Exhortation(s)

Hymn(s)
   [Lord's Supper]

Separate Baptists began their worship with singing. Sometimes they sang one hymn, at other times several hymns or choruses.

The minister led a time of prayer which followed, but the pattern of prayer varied. Sometimes only the minister prayed; at other times several joined in. The Separates were criticized because of the emotional nature of many of the prayers and because women often prayed during this part of the service.

The Separates used a unique preaching style which was characterized as emotional and noisy, and which evoked an emotional response in the hearers. People cried out, expressed their emotions physically, or exhorted others around them.

After a prayer at the close of the sermon, the minister came down from the pulpit and walked among the congregation exhorting persons to prayer and repentance. He then joined with persons who knelt to pray for the state of their souls. Sometimes others joined in the exhorting as well.

Separate Baptists concluded the service with singing. On occasion the exhorting continued while people sang. It is not surprising that critics often called their services disorderly and chaotic.

With their entire concept of worship focused upon conversion of sinners, the Lord's Supper did not hold an important place for the Separates, but they observed it because Christ commanded it. When they did observe it, they placed it at the end of the service after everything else was finished. The Lord's Supper was held infrequently, most commonly on a quarterly basis—the same pattern used by other American Baptists.

## Nineteenth-Century Baptists

Text: During the nineteenth century the Regular Baptist and Separate Baptist patterns merged, with the resulting Baptist worship patterns exhibiting clear marks of both strands. In 1870 John A. Broadus set forth a clear example of this merger in his renowned text on preaching, *On the Preparation and Delivery of Sermons*. Although the work is obviously about preaching, Broadus devotes the last chapter to elements the preacher must consider in worship, saying that preaching is an act of worship and must take place within the overall context of worship.

Because he was a native of Virginia and a long-time professor of preaching at the Southern Baptist Seminary, Broadus was clearly aligned with the more structured worship of the Regular Baptists. Yet, his delineation of elements of Baptist worship practice showed the influence of the Separate Baptists. Thus Broadus' chapter on worship was one of the clearest indications that these two strands which formed the foundation for modern Baptist worship had finally merged. Although Broadus provided no order of service, by reading his descriptions of the liturgical elements and piecing the parts together, the reader can clearly discern Broadus' vision of Baptist worship.

The worship model and the commentary are based on the work of Broadus. It is supplementary with other works of the period which address the various elements of worship.

MODEL OF BAPTIST WORSHIP, 1870
ORDER OF SERVICE
Choral Call to Worship
Invocation
Hymn of Worship
Devotional Scripture Reading
Hymn of Devotion
Principal Prayer
Hymn of Preparation
Sermon
Prayer
Final Hymn
Offering
　[Lord's Supper]
Benediction

The service began with a call to worship. As choirs developed in Baptist congregations, either the choir sang an anthem or the congregation sang a suitable hymn.

The prayer following the call to worship invoked God's presence in the worship service. It was usually short but could be longer on occasion.

After the invocation a hymn of worship was sung which might relate closely to the sermon and the service as a whole. It could be a hymn of praise or rejoicing, or thanksgiving; the essential element was that it promote a sense of worship. The lines of the hymns were usually read to the congregation just prior to their singing them. In some instances this was done due to a lack of hymnals, but it also made the congregation reflect more thoughtfully on the words of the hymn. In more informal services, the worship leader might say a few words about the origin of the hymn, its tune, or its meaning for the congregation.

The devotional reading of Scripture followed the first hymn. This Scripture passage was not necessarily connected with the sermon, but was devotional in tone drawing the listener to God. Passages from the Psalms were particularly favored, but any selection could be used. On occasion the worship leader might preface the reading with some well-chosen remarks to explain the reading, to awaken interest, or to promote a devotional context.

The next hymn was a hymn of devotion. Sometimes it was left out so that the prayer followed the Scripture reading, but if used, it would carry the devotional tone from the reading to the prayer.

The prayer at this point was the major prayer for the worship service. It was often quite long; in fact, Broadus warns about its being too long. It began with invocation, adoration of God, and thanksgiving. It then moved to confession and prayer for forgiveness. After petition for renewed dedication and for help for current needs, the prayer concluded with intercessions, both general and specific.

Immediately preceding the sermon, a hymn was sung to help prepare the congregation. It could be sung by the congregation or by the choir. Broadus felt it was better for the choir and congregation to sing somewhat familiar hymns rather than for the choir to sing anthems which would be unfamiliar. He clearly believed that the primary function of a choir was to lead the congregation in singing.

The sermon normally was twenty-five to thirty-five minutes in length, although occasionally it was as short as fifteen or as long as forty-five minutes. The text was often read prior to beginning the sermon, but it could be read at a later point. Broadus stressed that the length of the sermon should be coordinated with the elements of the service so that the worship service did not often go beyond the normal time for ending.

The prayer following the sermon was usually short and focused on the main objective of the sermon, yet it could be extended on occasion if the situation seemed to merit it.

The final hymn applied the sermon and formed a conclusion for the service. Broadus, however, pointed out that for many churches following the revival tradition, to always make this an "invitation" hymn, inviting persons to come to the front to make a public profession of faith in Christ or to become members of the church.

The offering was often the last item in the service prior to the benediction. It was sometimes called a "collection for the poor" or a "collection for the necessities of the saints."

The benediction was sometimes preceded by a few sentences of prayer appropriate to the theme of the worship service. The minister then concluded with a benediction.

In some churches the Lord's Supper continued to be celebrated once each month, but many churches changed to a quarterly observance. It either preceded or followed the offering, using the same pattern Baptists had used since the seventeenth century.

## Bibliography

There are no secondary works providing models of Baptist worship; therefore, material must be gleaned directly from primary sources. Since Baptists did not use service books, one must consult material in churchbooks, journals, and historical accounts. However, there are a few works that give some attention to elements and patterns of Baptist worship. For the seventeenth century, the best description and rationale for some elements of Baptist worship is found in Thomas Grantham, _Hear the Church_ (1688). The best eighteenth-century resource is Morgan Edwards, _Customs of Primitive Churches_ (1768). Although Edwards was a Regular Baptist, he visited Separate Baptist churches and gave some account of their worship in his _Materials Toward a History of Baptists_. Although many nineteenth-century resources provide pieces of information, the best single resource is Broadus' _On the Preparation and Delivery of Sermons_ (1870).

G. Thomas Halbrooks

## 176 • A QUAKER MODEL OF WORSHIP

_The worship of the Friends is rooted in silence. The people wait upon the Holy Spirit, who in the silence moves them in worship, where they meet God._

## Introduction

In calm and cool and silence once again
I find my old accustomed place among
My brethren, where, perchance no human tongue

Shall utter words; where never hymn is sung,
Nor deep-toned organ blown, nor censer swung.

Nor dim light falling through the pictured pane!
There, syllabled by silence, let me hear
The still small voice which reached the prophet's ear;
Read in my heart a still diviner law
Than Israel's leader on his tables saw . . .

(John Greenleaf Whittier, "First-Day Thoughts")

Quaker writers like John Greenleaf Whittier have left us vivid descriptions of the traditional Quaker meeting for worship in which worshipers assemble in disciplined silence and holy expectancy, to wait—without prearranged singing, Bible reading, prayers or sermon—for the movement of God's spirit. And as they wait, they pray—

Recall my wandering fancies, and restrain
The sore disquiet of a restless brain . . . .

(Whittier, ibid.)

As the silence of the gathered meeting deepens, it draws a profound response from the worshiper:

. . . when I came into the silent assemblies of God's people, I felt a secret power among them, which touched my heart, and as I gave way unto it, I found

_George Fox. A portrait of the founder and leader of the Quaker movement._

the evil weakening in me, and the good raised up, and so I became thus knit and united unto them, hungering more and more after the increase of this power and life. . . .

(Robert Barclay, quoted in Eleanore Price Mather, *Barclay in Brief* [Wallingford, Pa: Pendle Hill Pamphlet, 1948]).

There is no pastoral leadership in Quaker worship. Each worshiper centers down in personal prayer and meditation. Worship proceeds with mystical communion and spoken ministry as individual worshipers are led by the Spirit to speak or pray.

> Lowly before the Unseen Presence knelt
> Each waiting heart, til haply, some one felt
> On his moved lips the seal of silence melt.
>
> Or, without spoken words, low breathings stole
> Of a diviner life from soul to soul,
> Baptizing in one tender thought the whole.

The spirit of God moves, and worshipers are

> wrapped in a sense of unity and of Presence such as quiets all words and enfolds [them] within an unspeakable calm and interknittedness within a vaster life.

(Thomas Kelly, *The Eternal Promise* [New York: Harper & Row, 1966]).

Worship continues undirected and uninterrupted—"for silence and words have been of one texture, one piece" (Kelley)—until an elder quietly stands and turns to greet those near him.

> When shaken hands announced the meeting o'er.
> The friendly group still lingered near the door,
> Greeting, inquiring, sharing all the store
>
> Of weekly tidings . . . .
>
> And solemn meeting, summer sky and wood,
> Old, kindly faces, youth and maidenhood,
> Seemed, like God's new creation, very good.
>
> And greeting all with quiet smile and word,
> Pastorius went his way. The unscared bird
> Sang at his side; scarcely the squirrel stirred
>
> At his hushed footstep on the mossy sod;
> And wheresoe'er the good man looked or trod,
> He felt the peace of Nature and of God.

(John Greenleaf Whittier, "The Quaker Meeting," 1868, in Joseph Walton, *Incidents Illustrating the Doctrine and History of the Society of Friends* [Philadelphia: Wm. H. Pile's Sons, 1897]).

Warren Ediger

## 177 • A Methodist Model of Worship: John Wesley's *Sunday Service*

*The service below is strongly dependent on the 1662* Book of Common Prayer.

### Introduction

Wesley was an Anglican priest and organized the Methodists into small groups for prayer, Bible study, and worship. These groups would continue to worship in Anglican parishes on Sunday.

**Text:**
The Order for the Administration of the Lord's Supper

*The Table at the Communion-time, having a fair white Linen Cloth upon it, shall stand where Morning and Evening Prayers are appointed to be said. And the Elder, standing at the Table, shall say the*

*John Wesley. A likeness of the tireless and charismatic leader of the evangelical revival and founder of the Methodist church.*

*Lord's Prayer, with the Collect following the People kneeling.*

**Commentary**: Early Methodists often worshiped in rather plain settings. Their society room or preaching house was generally a multipurpose room of simple construction: it may have been a barn, school, factory, or theater which was converted to the cause of the revival. Wesley's Chapel, on City Road, London, with its rose-colored marble columns and white lacquered woodwork, was the exception to this pattern. In most instances, rather than ornate surroundings and lofty cathedral music, the liturgy, sermon, congregational song, and sacrament marked off sacred space by creating a sense of the presence of God and communion among Christians. Ironically, this *Sunday Service* does not designate where the Wesleyan hymns were to be used in the liturgy, but they certainly were utilized as congregational song formed an important part of early Methodist worship.

The liturgical furniture is specifically called a "table" so that it cannot be construed as an "altar" where sacrifice could occur. The model of table fellowship is based on Jesus' parables about the "great feast" and his institution of the Lord's Supper at the table of his last meal.

**Text**:

Our Father, who art in Heaven, Hallowed be thy Name; Thy Kingdom come; Thy will be done on earth, as it is in heaven; Give us this day our daily bread; And forgive us our trespasses, as we forgive them that trespass against us; And lead us not into Temptation, but deliver us from evil. *Amen.*

**Commentary**: The Lord's prayer functions as an invocation. It is a familiar prayer; since most of the early Methodists were Anglicans, it was prayed thrice daily as a part of their personal spiritual discipline. Its presence at the head of the service calls to mind God's fatherhood, holiness, and sovereign will. The prayer reminds the petitioner of his or her call to be submissive to the divine will (which is reinforced by the act of kneeling), as well as the deep and constant need to both ask for and to bestow forgiveness. The petition about freedom from temptation and deliverance from evil fits well with Methodism's emphasis upon "scriptural holiness" or "Christian perfection."

**Text**:
**The Collect**

Almighty God, unto whom all hearts be open, all desires known, and from whom no secrets are hid; cleanse the thoughts of our hearts by the inspiration of thy Holy Spirit, that we may perfectly love thee, and worthily magnify thy holy Name, through Christ our Lord. *Amen.*

**Commentary**: Praying the first clause, along with the elder, causes the congregation to reflect upon the experience of living one's life as being always "open to God." Because "all hearts are open" and "no secrets are hid" from God, the second clause and petition comes with deep urgency: "cleanse the thoughts of our hearts." Methodists sought "circumcision of the heart," a renewing of the inner person by the Holy Spirit, so that one wills God's will and loves with God's love. The Collect reinforces this experience through its petition that we "may perfectly love" God and "worthily magnify" God's holy name.

**Text**: *Then shall the Elder, turning to the People, rehearse distinctly off the TEN COMMANDMENTS: and the People still kneeling shall, after every Commandment, ask God Mercy for their Transgression thereof for the Time past, and Grace to keep the same for the Time to come, as followeth:*

*Minister:* God spake these words, and said, I am the Lord thy God:
Thou shall have none other gods but me.

*People:* **Lord, have mercy upon us, and incline our hearts to keep this law.**

*Minister:* Thou shalt not make to thyself any graven image, nor the likeness of any thing that is in heaven above, or in the earth beneath, or in the water under the earth. Thou shalt not bow down to them, nor worship them; for I the Lord thy God am a jealous God, and visit the sins of the others upon the children, unto the third and fourth generation of them that hate me, and shew mercy unto thousands in them that love me, and keep my commandments.

*People:* **Lord, have mercy upon us, and incline our hearts to keep this law.**

*Minister:* Thou shalt not take the Name of the Lord thy God in vain: for the Lord will not hold him guiltless that taketh his Name in vain.

*People:* **Lord, have mercy upon us, and incline our hearts to keep this law.**

*Minister:* Remember that thou keep holy the Sabbath-day. Six days shalt thou labour, and do all that thou hast to do; but the seventh day is the Sabbath of the Lord thy God: in it thou shalt do no manner of work, thou, and thy son, and thy daughter, thy man-servant, and thy maid-servant, thy cattle, and the stranger that is within thy gates. For in six days the Lord made heaven and earth, the sea, and all that in them is, and rested the seventh day; wherefore the Lord blessed the seventh day, and hallowed it.

*People:* **Lord, have mercy upon us and incline our hearts to keep this law.**

*Minister:* Honour thy father and thy mother, that thy days may be long in the land which the Lord thy God giveth thee.

*People:* **Lord, have mercy upon us, and incline our hearts to keep this law.**

*Minister:* Thou shalt do no murder.

*People:* **Lord, have mercy upon us, and incline our hearts to keep this law.**

*Minister:* Thou shalt not commit adultery.

*People:* **Lord, have mercy upon us, and incline our hearts to keep this law.**

*Minister:* Thou shalt not steal.

*People:* **Lord, have mercy upon us, and incline our hearts to keep this law.**

*Minister:* Thou shalt not bear false witness against thy neighbour.

*People:* **Lord, have mercy upon us, and incline our hearts to keep this law.**

*Minister:* Thou shalt not covet thy neighbour's house, thou shalt not covet thy neighbour's wife, nor his servant, nor his maid, nor his ox, nor his ass, nor any thing that is his.

*People:* **Lord, have mercy upon us, and incline our hearts to keep this law.**

**Commentary:** This litany of prayer focuses the congregation's attention upon transgression and forgiveness. It makes specific the "trespasses"

regretted in the Lord's Prayer, and since genuine repentance demands amendment of life, each reflection ends with a petition for God's mercy as well as for the resolve "to incline our hearts to keep this law."

Wesley's willingness to walk the congregation through the deep waters of their specific transgressions was characteristic of his own resolve to give strict account of his life. This litany also emphatically confronts one with the utter seriousness of one's sin. The congregation remains on their knees, acting out contrition and humility through bodily posture. In an age when many people were "triflers with sin," Wesley wanted the Methodists to take serious account of their sins so that they might not only be forgiven, but also healed from their bent to sinning.

Christian life, for Wesley, was a life that was victorious over sin; it was therefore necessary and important to know what sin was, and to resolve and seek spiritual assistance to turn from it.

**Text:** *Then shall follow this Collect.*

Let us pray.

Almighty and everlasting God, we are taught by thy holy word, that the hearts of the Princes of the earth are in thy rule and governance, and that thou dost dispose and turn them as it seemeth best to thy godly wisdom; we humbly beseech thee so to dispose and govern the hearts of the Supreme Rulers of these United States, our Governors, that in all their thoughts, words, and works, they may ever seek thy honour and glory, and study to preserve thy people committed to their charge, in wealth, peace, and godliness. Grant this, O merciful Father, for thy dear Son's sake, Jesus Christ our Lord. *Amen.*

**Commentary:** The prayer on behalf of the "Princes of the earth" and "Supreme Rulers of these United States" continues the congregation's reflection upon the law of God (see Rom. 13, and 1 Pet. 2:13ff.), as well as concrete submission to God's will as it is worked out in the world, through God's ordained agents. Yet submission gives way to intercession as the congregation prays that their leaders will seek to glorify God, and thereby to preserve the people "in wealth, peace, and godliness."

**Text:** *Then shall be said the Collect of the day. And immediately after the Collect, the Elder shall read the Epistle, saying,*

The Epistle [or, The Portion of Scripture appointed for the Epistle] is written in the ＿＿＿ Chapter of ＿＿＿＿＿＿＿＿ beginning at the ＿＿＿＿ Verse.

_And the Epistle ended, he shall say._

Here endeth the Epistle.

_Then shall he read the Gospel (the People all standing up), saying,_

The holy Gospel is written in the ＿＿＿ Chapter of ＿＿＿＿＿ beginning at the ＿＿＿＿ Verse.

**Commentary:** As the liturgy turns to the "Collect of the day," we are reminded of Methodism's debt to the _Book of Common Prayer,_ and to a lectionary of Scripture texts which moved the congregation through the entire Bible, in an orderly fashion, over the course of three years. The "Collect of the day" tailored the _Sunday Service_ to the liturgical year.

**Text:** _Then shall follow the Sermon._

**Commentary:** John and Charles Wesley often preached extemporaneously, giving a line by line exposition that was heavily seasoned with basic Christian doctrine and ethical injunctions. Their published sermons provide good examples of the content of Wesleyan preaching, but they obviously cannot preserve original urgency with which they were delivered.

The sermon's location in the _Sunday Service,_ following the Scripture readings, suggests that the sermon is an application of the Word of God, and a vehicle through which the Word of God speaks afresh, by power of the Holy Spirit, through the words of the preacher. The sermon is an application and vehicle of the Word, but it is not the culmination of the _Sunday Service._

**Text:** _Then shall the Elder say one or more of these Sentences._

(The elder may choose from:
Matt. 5:16; 6:19-20; 7:12, 21;
Luke 19:8;
1 Cor. 9:7; 9:11; 9:13-14;
2 Cor. 9:6-7;
Gal. 6:6-7; 6:10;
1 Tim. 6:17-19;
Heb. 6:10; 13:16;
1 John 3:1-3;

Tob. 4:8-9;
Prov. 19:17;
Psalm 41:1)

**Commentary:** The Scripture sentences pronounced after the sermon exhort congregations to actualize the spoken Word through holy, merciful, and charitable living. The selection of texts is broad enough to cover any eventuality arising from the lectionary readings and the sermon. Several of these sentences were probably read solemnly, as the offering was being taken, instead of the organ interlude that is more familiar in modern churches. These sentences applied as exhortations to obedience and faithfulness set the offering in its appropriate context; offering of money was to be understood as a response to the word of God, an acting out of the gospel.

The liturgy specifies two applications for the offering: "alms for the poor" and "devotions of the people." Methodism's advocacy for the poor was both deeply felt and necessary, because of the economic status of many of the early Methodists. Many people lived in or on the edge of poverty, and practical sustenance was a regular ministry of the Methodist societies. For Wesley to describe the various ministries of the congregation as "devotions" is also rather instructive; it reminds us that these too are acts rendered unto God. They are acted prayers of intercession and sanctification.

**Text:** _While these Sentences are in reading, some fit person appointed for that purpose, shall receive the alms for the poor, and other devotions of the people, in a decent Basin, to be provided for that purpose; and then bring it to the Elder who shall place it upon the Table._

_After which done, the Elder shall say:_

Let us pray for the whole state of Christ's Church militant here on earth.

Almighty and everliving God, who, by thy holy Apostle, hast taught us to make prayers and supplications, and to give thanks for all men; We humbly beseech thee most mercifully . . . to receive these our prayers, which we offer unto thy Divine Majesty; beseeching thee to inspire continually the universal Church with the spirit of truth, unity, and concord: and grant that all they that do confess thy holy Name, may agree in the truth of thy holy word, and live in unity and godly love. We beseech thee also to save and defend all Christian Kings, Princes, and Governors; and especially thy Servants the Supreme Rulers of these United States; that under them we may be godly and quietly governed: and grant unto all that are put in authority under them, that they may truly and indifferently administer justice, to the punishment of wickedness and vice, and to the maintenance of thy true religion and virtue. Give grace, O heavenly Father, to all the Ministers of thy Gospel, that they may both by their life and doctrine set forth thy true and lively word, and rightly and duly administer thy holy Sacraments. And to all thy people give thy heavenly grace; and especially to this Congregation here present; that with meek heart and due reverence they may hear and receive thy holy word, truly serve thee in holiness and righteousness all the days of their life. And we most humbly beseech thee of thy goodness, O Lord, to comfort and succor all them, who in this transitory life are in trouble, sorrow, need, sickness, or any other adversity. And we also bless thy holy Name, for all thy servants departed this life in thy faith and fear; beseeching thee to give us grace so to follow their good examples, that with them we may be partakers of thy heavenly kingdom. Grant this, O Father, for Jesus Christ's sake, our only Mediator and Advocate. *Amen.*

**Commentary:** This prayer for "the whole state of Christ's Church" returns again to Jesus' deeds in the upper room where the Lord interceded for his disciples in the immediate context of his Supper (John 17). Wesley's "catholic spirit" shows through here since the prayer is for the entire Christian Church, not for the Methodists alone. It also reminds us that the Methodist movement began as a society of Christians drawn from a variety of churches. For the Elder to describe this church as "militant here on earth" reminds us that the church is, through the various agents enumerated, actively engaged in a victorious struggle against evil and injustice.

The enumeration of specific persons prayed for is as broad as the introduction to the intercession implies; it turns the congregation's heart and mind to consider the service of political, civil, and religious leaders. This approach weaves the many spheres of Christian life into one broad cloth; it reminds us that the various offices each have their own purview and service, yet they each in their way are avenues of service and vehicles through which God's Word and kingdom are made manifest. Those

who suffer and those who succor them are mentioned as special objects of prayerful intercession. The departed saints of the congregation are remembered as examples of "faith and fear"; but our intercession is not for those who already have their reward, but for we who need "grace so to follow their good example."

**Text:** *Then shall the Elder say to them that come to receive the Holy Communion.*

Ye that do truly and earnestly repent of your sins, and are in love and charity with your neighbours, and intend to lead a new life, following the commandments of God, and walking from henceforth in his holy ways; Draw near with faith, and take this holy Sacrament to your comfort; and make your humble confession to Almighty God, meekly kneeling upon your knees.

**Commentary:** The invitation to the Lord's Table is addressed to all repentant sinners, who are being reconciled to God and to neighbor, and who "intend to lead a new life." Wesley esteemed the Eucharist as a "converting and confirming sacrament." Wesley, and the Methodists after him, believed that communion was a place where the earnest seeker could meet Christ with saving and strengthening import. It must be remembered, however, that in Wesley's time very few in England would not have been baptized; it is extremely doubtful that John Wesley intended the giving of the Lord's Supper to unbaptized persons. The Elder's preparatory words ready the communicants for reconciliation and new life with God through faith in Christ: "Repent," "intend to lead a new life," "draw near in faith," and "make your humble confession to Almighty God." Thus, through this sacramental act, the liturgy extends to us the comforts of the Gospel and fellowship with the risen Christ.

**Text:** *Then shall this general Confession be made by the Minister in the name of all those that are minded to receive the Holy Communion, both he and all the people kneeling humbly upon their knees, and saying,*

Almighty God, Father of our Lord Jesus Christ, Maker of all things, Judge of all men; We acknowledge and bewail our manifold sins and wickedness, Which we from time to time most grievously have committed, By thought, word, and deed, against thy Divine Majesty, provoking most justly thy wrath and indignation against us. We do earnestly repent, and are heartily sorry for these our misdoings; The remembrance of them is grievous unto us. Have mercy upon us, have mercy upon us, most merciful Father; For thy Son our Lord Jesus Christ's sake, forgive us all that is past; And grant, that we may ever hereafter serve and please thee in newness of life, To the honour and glory of thy Name, Through Jesus Christ our Lord. _Amen._

Commentary: The petitioner feels the awesomeness of almighty God and the depth of his or her unworthiness; our sins are "manifold," "grievous," and have been permeated into every sphere of our lives—"in thought, word, and deed." Our sins have provoked the "wrath and indignation" of almighty God. We are sinners in the hands of an angry God, completely undone because of the depth of our corruption, and God's infinite knowledge of our wrong. Our repentance must be "earnest" and it must run as deep as our former falseness. We feel an awesome sense of our guilt and a familiar sorrow because of our willful wanderings from the Father of our love. The petition ends with pleas for mercy and forgiveness for the sake of Christ as well as for amendment ("newness") of life.

Text: _Then shall the Elder say,_

O Almighty God, our heavenly Father, who of thy great mercy hast promised forgiveness of sins to all them that with hearty repentance and true faith turn unto thee; Have mercy upon us; pardon and deliver us from all our sins, confirm and strengthen us in all goodness, and bring us to everlasting life, through Jesus Christ our Lord. _Amen._

Commentary: The Elder's intercession for the congregation emphasizes the same constitutive elements requested in the corporate confession. Having prayed for themselves and each other—and subsequently receiving the intercession of the Elder—the congregation has moved through confession and repentance and now awaits the renewal and reconciliation which the Lord's Supper both symbolizes and effects.

Text: _Then all standing, the Elder shall say,_

Hear what comfortable words our Saviour Christ saith unto all that truly turn to him:

Come unto me, all ye that are burdened and heavy-laden, and I will refresh you. _Matt. 11:28._

So God loved the world, that he gave his only-begotten Son, to the end that all that believe in him, should not perish, but have everlasting life. _John 3:16._

Hear also what St. Paul saith:

This is a true saying, and worthy of all men to be received, That Christ Jesus came into the world to save sinners. _1 Tim. 1:15._

Hear also what St. John saith:

If any man sin, we have an Advocate with the Father, Jesus Christ, the righteous: and he is the propitiation for our sins. _1 John 2:1, 2._

Commentary: These scriptural sentences are "comfortable words," because in announcing them afresh in the context of confession, repentance and faith, we hear in the Elder's words God's voice of acceptance. The sentences assure the congregation that those who have made sincere confession and repentance shall certainly have forgiveness through faith in the grace of Christ. We feel that a burden of sin is lifted off our shoulders, and we are filled with joy and gratitude.

Text: _After which the Elder shall proceed, saying,_

_Lift up your hearts._
_Answ._ We lift them up unto the Lord.
_Elder._ Let us give thanks unto our Lord God.
_Answ._ It is meet and right so to do.

_Then shall the Elder say,_

It is very meet, right, and our bounden duty, that we should at all times, and in all places, give thanks unto thee, O Lord, Holy Father, Almighty, Everlasting God.

Commentary: This litany of thanks encourages the congregation to "lift up your hearts"; they are forgiven and reconciled, their hearts are no longer downcast and penitent. Because of the annunciation and reality of God's will to save, it is "meet and right" to thank God with elevated hearts.

Text: _Here shall follow the proper Preface, according to the Time, if there be any especially appointed; or else immediately shall follow;_

Therefore with Angels and Archangels and with all the company of heaven, we laud and magnify thy glorious Name, evermore praising thee, and saying, Holy, holy, holy, Lord God of hosts, heaven and earth are full of thy glory. Glory be to thee, O Lord most high. Amen.

## Proper Prefaces

### *Upon Christmas-day*

Because thou didst give Jesus Christ thine only Son to be born as at this time for us, who, by the operation of the Holy Ghost, was made very man, and that without spot of sin, to make us clean from all sin. Therefore with Angels, etc.

### *Upon Easter-day*

But chiefly we are bound to praise thee for the glorious Resurrection of thy Son Jesus Christ our Lord: for he is the very Paschal Lamb, which was offered for us, and hath taken away the sin of the world; who by his death hath destroyed death, and by his rising to life again, hath restored to us everlasting life. Therefore with Angels, etc.

### *Upon Ascension-day*

Through thy most dearly beloved Son, Jesus Christ our Lord; who, after his most glorious Resurrection, manifestly appeared to all his Apostles, and in their sight ascended up into heaven, to prepare a place for us, that where he is, thither we might also ascend, and reign with him in glory. Therefore with Angels, etc.

### *Upon Whitsunday*

Through Jesus Christ our Lord; according to whose most true promise the Holy Ghost came down, as at this time, from heaven with a sudden great sound, as it had been a mighty wind, in the likeness of fiery tongues, lighting upon the Apostles, to teach them, and to lead them to all truth; giving them both the gift of divers languages, and also boldness, with fervent zeal, constantly to preach the Gospel unto all nations, whereby we have been brought out of darkness and error, into the clear light and true knowledge of thee, and of thy Son Jesus Christ. Therefore with Angels, etc.

### *Upon the Feast of Trinity*

Who are one God, one Lord: not only one person, but three persons in one substance. For that which we believe of the glory of the Father, the same we believe of the Son, and of the Holy Ghost, without any difference or inequality. Therefore with Angels, etc.

*After each of which Prefaces shall immediately be said,*

Therefore with Angels and Archangels, and with all the company of heaven we laud and magnify thy glorious Name, evermore praising thee, and saying, Holy, holy, holy, Lord God of hosts, heaven and earth are full of thy glory. Glory be to thee, O Lord most high. *Amen.*

**Commentary**: The three-fold cry of "holy" blends our thanksgiving for reconciliation with praise for the perfections and majesty of God. The "Proper Prefaces" again fit the *Sunday Service* into the liturgical calendar. Just as the introductory praise reminded us that "heaven and earth are full of the glory of God," so now we are reminded, through attention to the major Christian festivals, that the Incarnation, Resurrection, Ascension, bestowal of the Holy Spirit, and the tri-unity of God are manifestations and demonstrations of that same glory.

**Text**: *Then shall the Elder, kneeling down at the Table, say, in the Name of all of them that shall receive the Communion, this Prayer following; the People also kneeling:*

We do not presume to come to this thy Table, O merciful Lord, trusting in our own righteousness, but in thy manifold and great mercies. We are not worthy so much as to gather up the crumbs under thy table. But thou are the same Lord, whose property is always to have mercy: Grant us therefore, gracious Lord, so to eat the flesh of thy dear Son Jesus Christ, and to drink his blood, that our sinful bodies may be made clean by his body, and our souls washed through his most precious blood, and that we may evermore dwell in him, and he in us. *Amen.*

**Commentary**: The Elder approaches the Communion table as a representative of the congregation. His prayer of approach reminds all that they must come to the Lord's Table deeply aware of their unworthiness and equally aware of God's great mercy. Wesley's Anglican heritage contributes to the sacramental realism; partaking in faith, the bread and wine are to us the flesh and blood of Jesus Christ. The effects of faith-filled partaking are not only forgiveness and renewal (since we are "made clean" and "our souls washed"), but also union with the risen Christ—"that we may . . . dwell in him, and he in us."

**Text**: *Then the Elder shall say the Prayer of Consecration, as followeth:*

Almighty God, our heavenly Father, who, of thy tender mercy, didst give thine only Son Jesus

Christ to suffer death upon the cross for our redemption; who made there (by his oblation of himself once offered) a full, perfect, and sufficient sacrifice, oblation, and satisfaction for the sins of the whole world; and did institute, and in his holy Gospel command us to continue a perpetual memory of that his precious death until his coming again; hear us, O merciful Father, we most humbly beseech thee, and grant that we, receiving these thy creatures of bread and wine, according to thy Son our Saviour Jesus Christ's holy institution, in remembrance of his death and passion, may be partakers of his most blessed Body and Blood: who, in the same night that he was betrayed, took bread; and when he had given thanks, he brake it, and gave it to his disciples, saying, Take, eat; this is my Body which is given for you: Do this in remembrance of me. Likewise, after supper, he took the cup; and when he had given thanks, he gave it to them, saying, Drink ye all of this; for this is my blood of the New Testament, which is shed for you, and for many, for the remission of sins: Do this, as oft as ye shall drink it, in remembrance of me. *Amen.*

Commentary: The Prayer of Consecration focuses our attention upon the historical and theological reality of Christ's death on our behalf. The belief in the saving efficacy of Jesus' death is reinforced through a series of traditional phrases: his death is "once offered" and need not be repeated. It is "a full, perfect and sufficient sacrifice" so that we need bring nothing more than faith in Christ before God for the covering of our sins. It is an "oblation," or offering, which Jesus willingly made for us. Jesus' death was a "satisfaction," which means that God's just penalty against sinners has been paid by a sinless substitute. And finally, Jesus' death is not for himself alone or for a few. Rather it has such power and significance that it covers the "sins of the whole world."

The prayer does not specifically consecrate or set apart the Communion elements (bread and wine) through a special transformation; the congregation is the focus of this prayer of consecration. Reflecting upon the deep significance of Jesus' death, and the reality of our forgiveness, we dedicate ourselves to God through participation in the Lord's Supper. Thus this new relationship ("covenant") brings Christ's life into our lives. The bread and wine are set apart through our faith; they remain unchanged, but by faith they are received as emblems of Jesus' body and blood.

The second section of the Prayer of Consecration turns our attention to Jesus' establishment of the Lord's Supper. The "gospel command" is found in the Lord's words: "Do this . . . in remembrance of me. . . . For whenever you eat this bread and drink this cup, you proclaim the Lord's death until he comes" (1 Cor. 11:25-26). The Elder's liturgical re-enactment of Jesus breaking the bread and the blessing of the cup makes our remembrance vivid and tangible. The minister speaks Jesus' words to the congregation: "Take, eat . . . Drink ye all of this . . ." and thereby proclaims the gospel to us. These sacramental signs of bread and wine testify to the remission of our sins through Jesus' broken body and shed blood.

Text: *Then shall the Minister first receive the Communion in both kinds himself, and then proceed to deliver the same to the other Ministers in like manner, (if any be present) and after that to the People also, in order, into their Hands. And when he delivereth the Bread to anyone, he shall say,*

The Body of our Lord Jesus Christ, which was given for thee, preserve thy body and soul unto everlasting life. Take and eat this in remembrance that Christ died for thee, and feed on him in thy heart by faith with thanksgiving.

*And the Minister that delivereth the Cup to any one shall say,*

The Blood of our Lord Jesus Christ, which was shed for thee, preserve thy body and soul unto everlasting life. Drink this in remembrance that Christ's Blood was shed for thee, and be thankful.

Commentary: The minister receives and offers communion in "both kinds," in that both bread and wine are offered and received. With the Protestant reformers, (and in contrast to Roman Catholic rites of the same era) Wesley affirmed the equality and unity of all Christians before God by stipulating communion be offered and received by all.

The words for offering the bread make Christ's sacrifice very tangible for us; "the Body of our Lord Jesus Christ . . . ," and we take bread into our hands. Once again, the Methodist rite is more concerned with the transformation of the Christian through the Lord's Supper, than with a transformation of the elements.

The second sentence shows how the sacrament

bridges time and space with the saving effectiveness of Christ's death: we "take and eat . . . in remembrance" of Christ's death in the historical past. This taking and remembering enables us to "feed on him . . . by faith with thanksgiving." In a similar way, the taking of the cup calls to mind the shedding of Christ's blood, and evokes thankfulness on our part.

**Text**: *If the consecrated Bread or Wine be all spent before all have communicated, the Elder may consecrate more, by repeating the Prayer of Consecration. When all have communicated, the Minister shall return to the Lord's Table, and place upon it what remaineth of the consecrated Elements, covering the same with a fair Linen Cloth. Then shall the Elder say the Lord's prayer, the People repeating after him every Petition.*

**Commentary**: That the prayer is also understood to consecrate the Communion elements is clear from the treatment accorded them here. The bread and the wine are set apart for sacramental use. But they are not said to be "holy," nor are they elevated, bowed to, or shown special veneration.

**Text**:

> Our Father who art in Heaven, Hallowed be thy Name; Thy kingdom come; Thy will be done on Earth, As it is in Heaven: Give us this day our daily bread; And forgive us our trespasses, As we forgive them that trespass against us; And lead us not into temptation; But deliver us from evil: For thine is the Kingdom, and the Power, and the Glory, For ever and ever. *Amen.*

**Commentary**: The congregation's recitation of the Lord's Prayer reminds us that the Lord's Supper is "communion," communion with Christ, and with Christians. The act of praying together establishes both aspects of our communion. The prayer, as an act of devotion and commitment, is also an appropriate response to God's bestowal of himself to us through the offering of his Son.

**Text**: *After which shall be said as followeth:*

> O Lord and heavenly Father, we thy humble servants desire thy Fatherly goodness mercifully to accept this our sacrifice of praise and thanksgiving; most humbly beseeching thee to grant that, by the merits and death of thy Son Jesus Christ, and through faith in his blood, we and all thy whole Church may obtain remission of our

sins, and all other benefits of his passion. And here we offer and present unto thee, O Lord, ourselves, our souls and bodies, to be a reasonable, holy, and lively sacrifice unto thee; humbly beseeching thee that all we who are partakers of this holy Communion, may be filled with thy grace and heavenly benediction. And although we be unworthy, through our manifold sins, to offer unto thee any sacrifice, yet we beseech thee to accept this our bounden duty and service; not weighing our merits, but pardoning our offences, through Jesus Christ our Lord; by whom, and with whom, in the unity of the Holy Ghost, all honour and glory be unto thee, O Father Almighty, world without end. *Amen.*

**Commentary**: The communicants respond to the gift of Christ's sacrifice by offering up "this our sacrifice of praise and thanksgiving." The magnitude of God's gift, made tangible for us through the bread and wine, elicits heartfelt thanks and adoration. The petition to "obtain the remission of our sins" is based in the merits of Christ's death, and not in our participation in the Lord's Supper. The reference to "all other benefits of his passion" reminds us that Jesus' suffering and death on our behalf unlocks riches of a relationship we can have with God, which defies enumeration. The sacrifice of our praise is fittingly followed by the sacrifice of ourselves; just as Christ gave himself to us, and for us, so now we give ourselves ("souls and bodies") and whole lives ("bounden duty and service") to Christ.

The phraseology of "not weighing our merits, but pardoning our offences," creates a sense of humility and penitence because of our failings. It also creates an important juxtaposition between the "merits of Christ" and "our merits"; the former are reconciling and life-giving, the latter are utterly worthless.

**Text**: *Then shall be said,*

> Glory be to God on high, and on earth peace, good-will towards men, We praise thee, we bless thee, we worship thee, we glorify thee, we give thanks to thee for thy great glory, O Lord God, heavenly king, God the Father Almighty.
>
> O Lord, the only-begotten Son Jesus Christ; O Lord God, Lamb of God, Son of the Father, that takest away the sins of the world, have mercy upon us. Thou that takest away the sins of the

world, have mercy upon us. Thou that takest away the sins of the world, receive our prayer. Thou that sittest at the right hand of God the Father, have mercy upon us.

For thou only art holy, thou only art the Lord, thou only, O Christ, with the Holy Ghost, art most high in the glory of God the Father. *Amen.*

**Commentary**: This glorious annunciation puts the angels' words announcing Christ's birth (Luke 2:13-14) into our own mouths. It is a fitting reminder that through the Lord's Supper and through our communion with Christ in newness of life, Christ has come again among his people. The next clause of praise is formed on words and imagery borrowed from the prologue of John's gospel (John 1:1-17). It reminds us that our sins, and those of the whole world, are genuinely borne away by Jesus. But Jesus is no longer upon the cross of his sacrifice, he has ascended on high ("at the right hand of God the Father") to his place of glory, dominion, and intercession for us. The triune ascription of holiness ("only thou art holy") reminds us that the Father, Son, and Holy Spirit are one God, and that each have their role to play in our salvation and in our relationship with God.

**Text**: *Then the Elder, if he see it expedient, may put up an Extempore Prayer; and afterwards shall let the People depart with this Blessing:*

May the peace of God, which passeth all understanding, keep your hearts and minds in the knowledge and love of God, and of his Son Jesus Christ our Lord; and the blessing of God Almighty, the Father, the Son, and the Holy Ghost, be amongst you, and remain with you always. *Amen.*

**Commentary**: Extempore prayer was an important part of the Wesleyan tradition. One can well imagine that there were extensive, personal prayers made at this juncture. The benediction (drawn from Phil. 4:7) invokes a deep and enduring sense of God's peace upon the "hearts and minds" of the communicants, to the end that they are kept in the knowledge and love of God. Peace with God and an enduring sense of God's presence were certainly gifts given in the Lord's Supper, and they are the best gifts with which one can leave the worship service. Once again, the final blessing is tripartite, and it emphasizes the enduring effects of these sa-

cred moments ("be among us and remain with you always").

(Text: John Wesley, "The Order for the Administration of the Lord's Supper" from *The Sunday Service of the Methodists in North America* [1784], published in Bard Thompson, *Liturgies of the Western Church* [Cleveland: The World Publishing Company, 1961].)

John R. Tyson

## 178 ✦ A Salvation Army Model of Worship

*The earliest record of a Salvation Army worship service is found in the publications of William and Catherine Booth's London East End ministry that began in the late 1860s.*

***William Booth.*** *This is a likeness of the portrait presented in 1856 to Booth by his friends in Sheffield in appreciation of his labors there and in other parts of the country.*

———————— **Introduction** ————————

The organization that would become The Salvation Army in 1878 commenced its ministry in July 1865 in a series of tent meetings in the East London district of Whitechapel (Robert Sandall, *The History of the Salvation Army, Vol. 1: 1865–1878* [London: Thomas Nelson, 1947], 37).

The format of these early day services was modeled on the "free and easy" nineteenth century Methodist song service. These unstructured services included a combination of extemporaneous prayer, hymns, numerous personal testimonies, and often a concluding sermon.

**Text:** The first recorded example that provides the details of these services are found in *The East London Evangelist,* the monthly periodical that William Booth first published October 1868 as a record of the "Christian Work Among the People" of his East London Christian Mission. The March 1869 issue includes a reprint of a report from *The Revival,* another religious periodical of the 1860s:

> On the afternoon of Sunday, January 31, I was able to see some of the results of William Booth's work in the East of London by attending his experience meeting, held in the New East London Theatre. Probably about 500 were present, though many came late. The meeting commenced at three, and lasted one hour and a half. During this period forty-three persons gave their experience, parts of eight hymns were sung, and prayer was offered by four persons. After singing Philip Phillips' beautiful hymn, "I Will Sing for Jesus," prayer by Mr. Booth and two others, a young man rose, and told of his conversion a year ago last Tuesday, thanking God that he had been kept through the year.
>
> A negro of the name of Burton interested the meeting much by telling of his first open-air service, which he had held during the past week in Ratcliff Highway, one of the worst places in London. He said, when the people saw him kneel in the gutter, engaged in prayer for them, they thought he was mad.
>
> Hymn, "Christ, He Sits on Zion's Hill."
> A young man under the right-hand gallery having briefly spoken, one of Mr. Booth's helpers, a genuine Yorkshire man, named Dimaline, with a strong voice and a hearty manner, told of the open-air meetings, the opposition they encountered, and his determination to go on, in spite of all opposition from men and devils.
>
> A middle-aged man on the right, a sailor, told how he was brought to Christ during his passage home from Columbo. One of the Dublin tracts, entitled "Johns Difficulty," was the means of his conversion.
>
> A young man to the right having told how, as a backslider, he had recently been restored, a cabman said he had a deal to talk about. The Lord had pardoned his sins. He used to be in the public-houses constantly, but he thanked God he ever heard William Booth, for it led to his conversion.
>
> Three young men on the right then spoke. The first, who comes five miles to these meeting, told how he was lost through the drink, and restored by the gospel; the second said he was unspeakably happy; and the third said he would go to the stake for Christ.
>
> A middle-aged man in the centre spoke of his many trials. His sight was failing him, that of one eye having gone entirely, but the light of Christ shone brilliantly in his soul.
>
> Hymn, "Let us walk in the light," etc.
> Two sailors followed each other. The first spoke of his conversion through reading a tract while on his way to the Indies four months ago. The other said he was going to sea next week, and was going to take some Bibles, hymns, and tracts with him to see what could be done for Christ on board. He thought the conversion of sailors was fulfilling the passage, "The abundance of the sea shall be converted unto Thee."
>
> Hymn, "I believe I shall be there, And walk with Him in White."
> A young man of the name of John, sometimes called, "Young Hallelujah," told of his trials while selling fish in the streets, but he comforted himself by saying, "Tis better on before." He had been drawn out in prayer at midnight on the previous night, and had dreamed all night that he was in a prayer meeting. He was followed by another, a converted thief, who told how he was "picked up," as he termed his conversion, and of his persecutions daily while working in a shop with twenty unconverted men.
>
> A man in the centre, who had been a great drunkard, said, "What a miserable wretch I was till the Lord met with me. I used to think I could not do without my pint a day, but the Lord pulled me right back out of a public-house into a place of worship." (Gawin Kirkham, "An Afternoon with William Booth," *The East London Evangelist* [March 1, 1869], 89–90).

The report continues in a similar vein for several more pages (the portion reproduced here is only one-third of the whole account), and concludes:

Mr. Booth offered a few concluding observations, and prayed. The meeting closed by singing: I will not be discouraged, for Jesus is my Friend.

Richard E. Holz

## 179 • A Revival Model of Worship: Charles G. Finney

_No orders of service from either of Charles G. Finney's pastorates are extant. However, orders of service from the First Church in Oberlin, Ohio, are available from the pastorate of Finney's successor, James Brand, dating from the 1890s—a full twenty-five years after Finney's retirement. In addition, sermon notes (c. 1850) from Finney's son-in-law, James Monroe, containing order-of-service outlines, are also available. The orders of service described in Monroe's notes correspond to the orders of service observed at First Church of Oberlin nearly a half-century later. We can, therefore, have a certain amount of confidence that the order of service given below (a hybrid developed from Monroe's notes and the First Church orders) is similar to the liturgy employed during Finney's tenure._

### Introduction

There is nothing different or new about this order of service; it resembles that of many American churches with nonliturgical, low-church traditions. (Finney's own religious background was Presbyterian.) The novelty is not so much in the order, but in the way in which the various elements of the service were expressed.

Text:
Prelude

Usually on the organ, although at times a small orchestra was employed. The Prelude was designed to set the mood of the service, to prepare the worshipers for the sermon—to soften their hearts for the touch of the Holy Spirit.

Invocation
Doxology

The place of the Doxology in the liturgy seems to have been flexible. Its alternate placement is denoted by an asterisk (*).

Anthem

Here we notice a substantial difference from the traditional model of worship. Revivalism brought the choir to the fore, not only physically (from the balcony to the nave), but liturgically. Whereas earlier the choir had been used to help lead congregational participation through song, the choir now had a specific role in the liturgy, derived from its role in the revival meeting. The anthem was a musical mini-sermon of sorts, a message in song directed at the hearts of the congregation.

Finney reportedly loved music because it touched him personally. Choral music at First Church ranged from arrangements of popular hymns to more traditional pieces such as the "Hallelujah Chorus." The issue with Finney was not whether a musical piece was or was not traditional, but whether it produced a "heart-felt" response to the gospel.

Scripture Reading

A passage tied to the topic of the sermon.

Prayer

An extended prayer, containing praise and adoration, thanksgiving, and addressing the various needs of the congregation. In the revival services a prayer such as this addressed particular persons by name and prayed for their salvation. A certain amount of these emphases probably remained in Finney's pastoral services.

(*) Doxology
Hymn

As in the revival meetings, hymns were frequently directed at the needs of the sinner. Through the hymns' lyrics, the sinner's attention would be directed to his or her sinfulness, and consequent need of repentance. Although usually associated with later revivalists, Fanny Crosby's hymns reflect the prevailing sentiment:

> _Pass me not, O gentle Savior—Hear my humble cry!_
> _While on others Thou art calling, Do not pass me by._

Offering
Sermon

While Finney's revival sermons lasted up to two hours, Sunday, pastoral sermons probably were shorter. Given, however, their substantial length in manuscript outline, they were substantially longer than modern sermons, and were probably close to one hour. Their topics ranged widely, from exhortations on elements of the Christian life to the amelioration of social ills (most notably the abolition of slavery and advocacy of temperance). Characteristic of Finney's sermons were his passionate, pleading delivery and his pedagogical approach which rooted all points in the individual Christian's need for holiness, or full consecration to Christ. The pursuit of such a holy life was squarely on the shoulders of the individual person who must choose, of his or her own volition, to follow Christ.

Altar Call

By no means a regular occurrence on Sundays for Finney, the addition of an altar call demonstrates his new approach to worship. While it shows the change from a Calvinist to an Arminian soteriology (which has become standard in much of modern American Protestantism), the inclusion of an altar call also demonstrates the change in ecclesiology noted above.

Prayer

For Finney, the final prayer was one last opportunity to reinforce the message of the sermon to the individuals in the congregation, often asking God to "drive home" the message, and "melt hard hearts." Finney often employed agricultural imagery ("breaking up the fallow ground") which spoke much more poignantly to his rural parishioners than to the residents of the modern urban age.

Hymn

Usually of slower tempo, providing one last opportunity for the penitent to respond.

(*Doxology)
Benediction

James Peck

## 180 ◆ ADVENTIST MODEL OF WORSHIP

*Early Adventist worship was simple, informal, and vigorously nonliturgical. When the first church Manual was adopted, reluctantly, in 1883, it made no mention how regular worship services should be conducted. It did, however, lay down some guidelines for the "ordinances of the Lord's house," meaning the Lord's Supper and the accompanying footwashing service. Indeed, the earliest mention of an order of service for Adventist churches appears to be in a book published in 1906 by a prominent Colorado pastor, H. M. J. Richards.*

──────── **Introduction** ────────

This order of service is presented below. Scattered hints in earlier sources mention such elements as "prayers, singing, exhortation, and preaching" (see D. M. Canright, "A Few Thoughts About Meetings," *Review and Herald*, vol. 28 [Oct. 30, 1866], 173).

Text:
Silent Prayer
Opening Hymn
Public Prayer
Hymn
Sermon
Hymn
Benediction

**Commentary:** The minister enters the pulpit and kneels for a few moments in silent prayer to God. All the people bow their heads and unite with their minister in silent prayer, imploring the Divine blessing upon the services of the hour. Then the minister announces the opening hymn, then all stand and join in singing. After this the minister and all the people kneel in prayer, while he leads them in a public extemporaneous prayer of moderate length and appropriate to the needs of the people and subject of the sermon. Usually a second hymn is then sung, and the sermon follows this. The service is concluded by another hymn sung by the entire congregation, after which the benediction is pronounced by the minister. (H. M. J. Richards, *Church Order* [Denver: Colorado Tract Society, 1906], 64).

Even this order of service was not ironclad. Richards allowed for some variations, such as "special music," including sacred solos, duets, quartets, or anthems; and also occasionally "a short Scripture reading at some time before the sermon; and at times a short prayer is introduced after the sermon, when the Spirit so directs." Richards' only concession to liturgical propriety was his insistence that no announcements intrude on the worship service and that the benediction be pronounced by an ordained minister. Ten years earlier the same reservation had been expressed, describing a benediction as "a blessing pronounced upon the congregation. In doing this the minister usually raises his hands and blesses the congregation in the name of the Lord, pronouncing grace, mercy, and peace upon them. This function . . . ought to be confined to ministers of the gospel." (G. C. Tenney, "To Correspondents, #68" *Review and Herald* 73 [March 31, 1896], 202).

Ronald D. Graybill

## 181 ✦ An African-American Model of Worship

*We find diversity in the worship practices of African-Americans. This diversity results from differences in points of entry into and acceptance of the Christian faith, as well as denominational distinctions. However, there is a common history and heritage rooted in the religious life of Africans enslaved in America. There is sufficient documentation for the genesis of unique African-American worship styles in the imposed marginalization of Africans in America. For a people whose slave existence was partially supported by Scripture, it was necessary for a new form of Christianity to be shaped. The "new" religion represented a fusion of a number of worldviews, beliefs, and practices: African, Judeo-Christian, Euro-American, and African-American.*

### Introduction

Although they had some exposure to Euro-American worship practices, slaves generally found this form of worship both depressing and oppressive. The message of the gospel preached was often designed to keep slaves under oppressive control. Parameters set by slave holders limited natural response to God by a people who needed freedom in order to express their faith. Opportunities were not provided for communal fellowship in worship which was so basic to a people who valued kinship and community. In such an unfriendly, nonspiritual environment, African-American worshipers were forced to find a separate time and place (sacred space) for freedom in worship. Their hunger to hear the Good News without the hypocritical slants given in worship planned for slaves was part of the empowerment which propelled them away from Euro-American established worship.

The first attempts at separate worship in locations where the slave system was most oppressive were necessarily clandestine and risky. Nevertheless, slaves developed a religious life of their own in which ritual action could evolve. In the secrecy of brush arbors (also referred to use as "bush harbors," and "bus harbors") and "designated" cabins, slaves indigenized Christianity. Such places were later referred to as "invisible institutions" to distinguish them from visible or legal places of worship.

The earliest liturgical shaping occurred in late evening prayer and praise meetings which often lasted all night. In privacy, slaves could meet, respond to, and interact with Jesus who had walked a similar path. Struggles, sorrows, and pains which the slaves experienced could be poured out with confidence to one who listened with compassion. The joy of simply being alive and able to meet together "just one more time" provided profound hope for freedom in this world. Preachers, who were licensed only by virtue of their "call" by the Holy Spirit and approved by the slave community, provided gospel messages of freedom and exhorted the worshipers to seek personal encounters with God in Jesus the Christ. The gathered community helped in the spontaneous shaping of the worship through their propensity to "move with the Spirit."

Since worship was initially clandestine and informal, the flow of services was never exactly the same everywhere. Elements of worship and a basic rhythmical flow can be determined, however, from slave narratives as well as from diaries and letters of observers. What is readily apparent is that African-American worship was truly the "work of the people" enabled by the Holy Spirit. In most, if not all, services, the community involved itself in singing, praying, preaching, shouting, and communal fellowship. There is also evidence of calls to worship, community concerns (as a part of the time of gathering), and personal confessions of sin as a part of individual testimonies (most often in relation to conversions).

In early African-American worship the manner and style of the execution of the elements were perhaps as important as what was done. In a way, manner and matter, or content, were inseparable. This is not to say that the work of the people (the liturgy) was a haphazard exercise. It does affirm the *élan vital* of the African inheritance which allows worshipers to "see" and understand through all of the senses—the total being. One does not listen simply through the ears alone; one does not see simply through eyes only; and one's emotions can be animated by intellect, reason, and intuitive sight. Directions in the flow of the service depended upon the worshiping "moment" and all that this entails. One element was not void of other elements, and music and bodily movement were often combined with all elements.

The order which follows is based on a composite of information received from slave narratives, the oral tradition, current practices rooted in the early slave period, and written records, diaries, and letters from the eighteenth and nineteenth centuries. This order represents the first common model of African-American worship, out of which other unique models incorporating denominational practices have emerged.

**Text:**

**Call to Worship.** The "call to worship" started long before services began, usually announcing the time and place in words of songs which had dual or multiple meanings. Slaves would understand that songs such as "Steal Away to Jesus," "Get you Ready There's A Meeting Here Tonight," and "Over My Head" might have been calls to meeting or calls to escape. Either would have meant freedom from the current situation, in spite of the danger of getting caught. Certain words in the "call" might have also identified the sacred space and time for worship, since it was often necessary to change either or both.

**A Time of Gathering.** There is sufficient evidence that slaves might have spent a portion of time at the beginning of worship "reconnecting" and establishing the sacred space. They would inquire about the state of health of each person gathered, what they had been doing since the last meeting, and the whereabouts of the family. They sang, greeted, and embraced each other as they continued in worship.

**Singing.** The response to God in song reflected the African propensity to engage the whole self in prayer, expression of belief, attitude, and commitment. Very soft singing was apparently an extension of the call to worship, as the gathering community reconnected and became centered so that worship could take place. Words and music were shaped spontaneously, or were carried over from their oral memories of psalms and hymns heard in Euro-American worship. The sound of slave singing has been described as wild, weird, plaintive, sorrowful, and sad.

In music and song slaves were lifted closer to God and to each other as they struggled to live in their situations created by a harsh slave system. Singing at worship and at work helped to ease pains, and connected the sacred-secular dimensions of life. Singing served a symbolic linguistic function as a common means of communicating the faith and hope of an oppressed, marginalized people. Spirituals, the first religious music created by African-Americans, communicated a spiritual depth when sung and heard that even non-Blacks recognized as powerful.

**Prayer.** Prayer seems to have been especially important in worship, and also signaled a new level in the dynamics of the flow. The first of these prayers were later labeled "invocations." They are filled with thanksgiving to God for allowing people to be there "clothed in their right minds." In keeping with the African tradition, there were prayers of adoration, praise, thanksgiving, intercession, and petition. Prayers after the sermon would often "drive home" the message of the sermon, or exhort the congregation to live "so God could use them." It was not unusual for conversions to take place in the midst of prayers, as people continued to respond to the Word. Liberation, freedom, and deliverance were natural themes of prayers.

**Preaching.** The word of God preached, heard, and experienced in a free (albeit clandestine) worshiping environment was the foundation of the Invisible Institution. The reality of the presence of Jesus, the Word incarnate, was evident in sermon, song, and prayer. In separate environments the good news of liberation, salvation, and sanctification for *ALL* was quite clear. It was important that the preacher as divine deliverer of the Word, was responding to a call from God, was knowledgeable of the Bible, and had the ability to communicate with the community. Like the African *griot* or story teller, the preacher was able to hold the attention of the people and engage them in dialogue. The role of the preacher as priest, pastor, prophet, diviner, and "chosen" leader (both by God and the people) converged during the time for preaching. Whatever else the people expected during these clandestine gatherings, nothing was more important than the preached "word from the Lord." Although preaching styles varied, an intoned or musical delivery style was quite common. This style encouraged dialogue that would evolve into a new song.

**Shouting.** Shouting in worship, including involuntary physical movements, is one way that a person responds emotionally to the encounter, movement, and enabling power of the Holy Spirit. Such physical response, described as religious ecstasy or "getting happy," also may have involved uncontrollable screams, yells, and vocal utterances called "speaking in tongues." Shouting could occur during preaching, praying, singing, or the delivery of emotional personal testimonies. Although shouting occurred with individuals, the community was affected by this emotional expression as it participated with the individual emphatically, or as others' emotions were so aroused that they, too, would shout.

**Conversions.** Slaves were often inhibited from adapting to the external world set by the narrow parameters of slavery except on a superficial level. Psychological release from uncertainty, necessary cleansing, and regeneration could happen through the experience of worship and (for some) through conversion. The desire for personal status and affirmation could be realized in such forms as visions, dreams, and imagination where individuals could be convinced of their worth. These forms of behavior were unleashed when there was a "knockdown" conversion experience. For the slaves, conversion was the overcoming of a struggle to recognize God in Jesus Christ, and the ultimate awareness that God had already freed him or her to walk in God's glory. Since for some the state of "not knowing" or not having had a personal encounter was sinful, the convert would identify his or her experience as a release from sin. Shouting was quite often linked with the emotional conversion experience, as evidence of the fire of the "Holy Ghost" burning inside. Shouting was part of the evidence of conversion—or an outward demonstration of the inner joy of a divine creative encounter.

**Testimonies.** If time permitted, the people offered personal testimonies in worship, an act which had a definite impact on the corporate community. All could claim the experiences and learn from them, so that they were enabled to walk together in the testimonies of others.

**Singing.** There is little evidence of an exact form for closing worship except that there was singing and sometimes a prayer. One can speculate that many of the clandestine meetings were abruptly ended if there was evidence of an outsider approaching. Prayers and songs attest to some words of parting which served as a benediction:

> Lord, make me more Holy . . .
> Until we meet again.

> Lord, make me more faithful . . .
> Until we meet again.
> Lord, make me more loving . . .
> Until we meet again.

Melva Wilson Costen

## 182 • A Restoration Model of Worship

_Until the rise of the Stone-Campbell movement on the American frontier, the restoration movement that began in Britain was so fissiparous in spirit that much diversity in worship was inevitable. Eventually, however, a primitive model of worship based on the second chapter of Acts prevailed._

### Introduction

The restoration movement can be traced to the departure by John Glass from the Church of Scotland in 1728. His son-in-law, Robert Sandeman, started several small churches in Scotland which patterned their worship in such a way as to _restore_ the order of the church described in the book of Acts. Yet another branch of this movement began when James and Robert Haldane started an independent church in Edinburgh in 1799 as well as a seminary in Glasgow.

As Sandemanean and Haldanean influence spread, Thomas Campbell and his family started attending services in the Haldane church southwest of Belfast, Ireland. Campbell, a Presbyterian preacher, was impressed by the ideas of the Haldanes. His son Alexander, eventually became the most articulate advocate of restoration ideas.

In 1807 Thomas Campbell set sail for the United States. Arriving in western Pennsylvania, he found that religious freedom and the separation of church and state had resulted in unbridled sectarianism. Moreover, only one adult in ten belonged to a church and attended worship regularly. Sectarianism was an obstacle to evangelism: Therefore, Thomas Campbell declared, "The Church of Christ upon earth is essentially, intentionally, and constitutionally one." Furthermore, he claimed, "Division among Christians is a horrid evil fraught with many evils." Unity among Christians, he said, should be based on love and on a simple effort to follow the Scriptures alone in faith and practice.

At about the same time in Kentucky, Barton W. Stone was leaving the Presbyterian church for similar reasons. Those who followed his lead simply called themselves "Christians," and they also based a plea for Christian unity on the standard of restoring the faith and practice of the church to a New Testament pattern.

Although no absolute rules were set down by restoration leaders for an order of worship, churches in this movement looked to Acts 2:42 for a model of how the New Testament church worshiped.

**Text:**

1. Invocation
2. One or two hymns
3. Reading of Scriptures
4. Prayer
5. Hymn
6. Sermon
7. Invitation hymn
8. Lord's Supper
9. Hymn
10. Benediction

**Commentary:** To overcome the formalism of the Church of Scotland in the late 1700s, *restoration worship* followed a variety of practices. Resistance to prim ceremonialism attracted pioneers on the American frontier in the early 1800s. Farmers in western Pennsylvania, western Virginia, Ohio and Kentucky had little use for protocol in worship: What they wanted was substance. They considered prescribed prayers less meaningful than impromptu petitions from the lips of a lay elder. Imposed liturgies satisfied these pioneers less than informal services improvised for the circumstances of each congregation.

Nevertheless, part of restoring worship to a New Testament pattern was doing all things "decently and in order" as Paul encouraged in 1 Corinthians 14:40. One thing was certain: the Lord's Supper would be observed weekly, and that practice became a normative and identifying feature of the movement. Moreover, restorationists understood the Lord's Supper as a symbolic memorial of the self-giving sacrifice of Jesus Christ, which revealed God's unconditional love in history, and which continues to show forth God's forgiving grace. A leader, usually a lay elder (most frontier churches functioned without ordained ministers), took the bread and cup, offered a simple prayer of thanks, broke the bread, and gave the bread and cup to the congregation to share with one another.

In the language of Acts 2:42, "the fellowship"

(*koinonia*) implied a partnership with other Christians. Thus, a weekly collection of tithes and alms for the work of the church and the relief of the poor played an important role. This offering was integrally related to the Communion service.

Scriptures and sermons almost always were from the New Testament, which they considered not only a more recent, but a brighter disclosure of the light of divine truth than the Hebrew Scriptures. The Bible was understood as a set of facts which, if clearly set forth, would be seen the same way by everyone. The New Testament came to be seen as a "constitution" for the Christian life.

Salvation was considered a legal kind of transaction, so the purpose of the sermon was to convict—not by means of emotional enticement, but by the use of reasonable common sense. Clear, simple communication was more important than theological refinement. The sermon became more evangelistic due to the situation of preaching to the many who were unchurched; often sermons led to an invitation to Christian discipleship. Those who responded to such a call were received into the church as members based on a simple confession of faith in Christ and baptism by immersion. They were not tested for correct beliefs, nor obliged to describe a personal religious experience, nor required to pass a vote of the congregation.

An issue that divided churches in this movement by 1900 was whether instrumental music should be used. In pioneer churches, musical instruments often were unavailable. But singing was very important. Ephesians 5:19 and Colossians 3:16 were understood as promoting congregational singing both as an expression of praise and as a means for building up faith among believers.

*Philip V. Miller*

## 183 • A Holiness Model of Worship

*The Holiness Movement did not readily record its liturgy. Worship followed a common pattern familiar to its members. A reporter describing a camp meeting in Quinebaug, Connecticut, wrote: "Meetings were held from day to day, after the usual order." The scarcity of printed orders of worship makes exploration of this topic difficult. There are, however, some prose descriptions of portions of worship that provide sufficient information to reconstruct a typical revivalistic, camp meeting service.*

## Introduction

The last fifteen years of the nineteenth century were marked by controversy within the Holiness Movement. Some had chosen to "come-out" of older denominations in which holiness, in their minds, was not preached and practiced. Others relied upon holiness associations to carry on the work. These associations were established to provide means of proclaiming the Wesleyan doctrine of holiness. Meetings were arranged so that they did not conflict with the services of the established churches. These associations became increasingly interdenominational, and served as havens for persons who were in conflict with those who did not share the same understanding of this doctrine. Within a very few years, independent churches were formed from members of the holiness associations who had either "come-out" or had been removed from membership in the older denominations. These independent churches organized camp meetings and banded together for support and fellowship.

*Beulah Christian* was an interdenominational periodical published in the 1890s from Providence, Rhode Island. The masthead of the paper quoted a portion of 1 Thessalonians 5:23 ("the very God of peace sanctify you wholly"). The Holiness Movement rallied around this verse and others like it. This periodical was devoted to promulgating the message of holiness, and specifically to spreading the doctrine of entire sanctification. It included topical articles, news, and schedules of various camp and holiness association meetings, and testimonials to spiritual experience. The "Camp Meeting Calendar" in the issue of July 1896, listed no less than forty-seven different camp meetings for the months of July through September alone. The list included meetings from Great Falls, Montana, to Marshall, Texas, to Rock, Massachusetts. These meetings were generally a week to ten days in length. Camp meetings and camp meeting worship was in abundant supply.

We know that singing was a part of camp meeting services because of announcements which included this element. Participants in the meeting were expected to bring their own songbooks. In *Beulah Christian* (July, 1896), an announcement of the Douglas (Mass.) Camp Meeting read: "Rev. B. Caradine, and many other prominent ministers will be present. Rev. A. Hartt will lead the singing. *Voice of Triumph* will be used." The announcement of a different camp meeting in the same issue informed attenders: "Mr. and Mrs. D. O. Chapman will lead the singing. Bring *Voice of Triumph* and *Good News in Song*." Congregational singing, however, was not the only singing that occurred. At the Rock, Massachusetts Camp Meeting in August of 1896: "Bro. Lee was on hand to sing." "I feel the fire burning in my heart," and "I've just come from the fountain, Lord." Singing was characterized by freedom of expression and spontaneous emotion. As one reported: "There was great liberty in the Spirit, and at times the songs and shouts of victory would for some moments sweep over the meeting. Glory to God forever!" Camp meetings, however, cannot be caricatured simply as shouting and emotional frenzies. One reported: "Interest was manifested at times by an impressive stillness, and again by shouts and other unmistakable demonstrations of joy." Another writer attempted to squelch some of the inaccurate stories of the physical manifestations which accompanied the camp meeting: "The truth of the matter is that there was a noticeable lack of undue excitement in the meeting."

*Beulah Christian* (May, 1897) recorded the order of a service which was characteristic of camp meetings:

> In the evening, Bro. R. S. Robson of Boston, sang, "When I see the blood I will pass over you." After prayer, and while the congregation were [sic] singing, "Rivers of Love," a wave of glory came upon the people, and shouts of holy triumph were heard from many who were in touch with God. Rev. C. H. Bevier preached a sermon full of holy inspiration, from Ezekiel's vision of the river. On invitation at the close, a large number were at the altar, who gave evidence of finding real victory in God.

Preaching, concluded by a call to conversion or commitment, was the climactic part of every worship service. Often when no mention was made of the other elements of the service, the effects of preaching were reported. Preaching was "earnest," "soul-stirring," and often lengthy. Although the duration of the sermon was infrequently mentioned, *Beulah Christian* (May, 1897) reported: "At three, Rev. G. W. Wilson preached. For two hours, the people gave rapt attention to the mighty words of life."

An invitation to a camp meeting in Danielson,

Connecticut in August of 1897 accurately summarized the purpose and design of revivalistic worship. "The design of these meetings is the conversion of sinners, the entire sanctification of believers, and the promotion of genuine Christian life and efficiency." This was the character of worship in the camp meeting tradition of the late nineteenth-century Holiness Movement.

Brad Estep

## 184 • BIBLIOGRAPHY ON POST-REFORMATION WORSHIP

**General Works on the Origins and History of Protestant Worship from 1600–1900.**

Davies, Horton. *Worship and Theology in England.* 5 vols. Princeton: Princeton University Press, 1961–1970. The purpose of this five volume series is to give an account of worship and the theology that undergirds it from the Reformation to the middle of the twentieth century. This masterful and thorough work is written out of the conviction that the worship of the church rather than this or that theologian gives the deepest clue to the interior life of the church. The emphasis is not only an Anglican worship, but the worship of the Puritans and separatists. Music and architecture are treated as revelatory of worship patterns.

White, James F. *Protestant Worship: Traditions in Transition.* Louisville: Westminster/John Knox Press, 1989. A comprehensive historical treatment of the worship of nine communities of worship: Lutheran, Reformed, Anabaptist, Anglican, Separatist and Puritan, Quaker, Methodist, Frontier, and Pentecostal.

Willimon, William. *Word, Water, Wine, and Bread.* Valley Forge, Pa: Judson Press, 1980. A brief but excellent overview beginning with the Jewish heritage and following through on the early church, the medieval era, the Reformation, and modern eras.

**Puritan and Free Church Worship (Baptist; Congregationalists; Separatists)**

Adams, Doug. *Meeting House to Camp Meeting: Toward a History of American Free Church Worship From 1620 to 1835.* Saratoga, N.Y.: Modern Liturgy Resource Publications, 1981. Adams amply details seventeenth-century Puritan worship, and its heir, eighteenth-century Congrega-

tional worship. Particularly interesting and useful is his reconstruction of and commentary on a seventeenth-century Puritan service, using Cotton Mather's model.

Beebe, David Lewis. The Seals of the Covenant: The Doctrine and Peace of the Sacraments and Censures in the New England Puritan Theology Underlying the Cambridge Platform of 1648. Th.D. dissertation, Pacific School of Religion, 1966.

Cotton, John. A Modest and Cleare Answer to Mr. Bell's Discourse of Set Forms of Prayer. London: n.p., 1642.

———. Singing of Psalms, A Gospel Ordinance. London: n.p., 1650.

Davies, Horton. *The Worship of the American Puritans, 1629–1730.* New York: Peter Lang, 1990. Puritan worship has had a decided impact on the Free Church worship of American Christianity. This book deals with the pioneering type of worship that was biblically based, that introduced extemporaneous prayer, expressed the priesthood of all believers and encouraged lay piety. All aspects of Puritan worship is covered—praise, prayer, sacraments, marriages and funerals, ordination, architecture and more.

Miller, Perry. *The New England Mind.* New York: Macmillan, 1939. American Puritanism is an inexhaustible mine for historians. Among the numerous volumes available, Perry Miller's account provides the foundation for further study.

Miller, Perry, ed. *The American Puritans, Their Prose and Poetry.* Garden City, N.J.: Doubleday, 1956.

Miller, Perry, and Thomas H. Johnson, eds. *The Puritans.* New York: American Book Co., 1938. A thorough collection of primary materials, edited and with an introduction. Although the volume may overwhelm those desiring only an acquaintance with the Puritans, reading even a few of these period pieces engenders a deeper appreciation of the Puritan ethos.

**Presbyterian & Reformed**

Baird, Charles. *The Presbyterian Liturgies: Historical Sketches.* Grand Rapids: Baker, 1960. The work was originally written in 1866. It traces Presbyterian worship from Calvin through John Knox, the Scottish Liturgy, the early Puritans, Baxter and others. No actual liturgies are provided.

Barkley, John M. *The Worship of the Reformed Church*. Richmond: John Knox Press, 1967. This helpful work provides an exposition and critical analysis of the eucharistic, baptismal, and confirmation rites in the Scottish, English-Welsh, and Irish Liturgies.

Brillioth, Ynvge. *Eucharistic Faith and Practice, Evangelical and Catholic*. London: SPCK, 1930. Argues that the Reformation was a rediscovery of the Eucharist, but that since the time of the Reformation the story of the Eucharist has been one of decline. Sketches the history of the Eucharist and argues for its recovery.

Davies, Horton. *The Worship of the English Puritans*. London: Dacre Press, 1948. A study of the free church tradition of worship, with an attempt to show the relevance of Reformed worship for today. Addresses a wide variety of issues including the relationship of free church worship to liturgical worshipers.

DeJong, Gerald. *The Dutch Reformed Church in the American Colonies*. Grand Rapids: Eerdmans, 1978. A study of the Reformed church in America, with comments on the ministry and on the church architecture.

Donnelly, Marion C. *The New England Meeting House of the Seventeenth Century*. Middletown, Conn.: Wesleyan University, 1968. The worship of meetinghouses in various periods of English history are treated in depth.

Earle, Alice Morse. *The Sabbath in Puritan New England*. Lima, Ohio: CSS Press, 1896. This is more than a study of the Sabbath. It is a discussion of Puritan worship that deals with the New England meetinghouse, its seating, pews, length of service, the singing of psalms and many more matters of interest in Puritan worship.

Edwards, Jonathan. *Thoughts on the Revival of Religion in New England*. New York: American Tract Society, n.d. This work argues that the revival is a work of God and should be promoted. It also addresses some errors, such as lay exhorting and the mismanagement of the singing of the praises of God.

Hollifield, Brooks E. *The Covenant Sealed: The Development in Old and New England 1570–1720*. New York: Oxford University Press, 1974. A study in the sacramenture debates in England and New England among the Puritans. These debates demonstrate how seriously the Puritans took sacramental understanding and practice.

Melton, Julius. *Presbyterian Worship in America: Changing Patterns Since 1787*. Richmond: John Knox Press, 1967. This book traces the divergent practices stemming from two very different convictions about worship. On the one hand were those convinced that worship should only follow the specific guidelines of Scripture; others argued worship could be influenced by changing cultural attitudes and needs. The history of Presbyterian worship is brought into the twentieth century.

Spinks, Bryan. *Freedom or Order: The Eucharistic Liturgy in English Congregationalism*. New York: Pilgrim Press, 1984. This work presents actual liturgies of English congregationalism between 1645 and 1980.

Nichols, James Hasting. *Corporate Worship in the Reformed Tradition*. Philadelphia: Westminster Press, 1968. A study of the intent and practice of worship among the Reformers and post-Reformation developments in the Reformed tradition. The study includes chapters on Puritanism, pietism, and evangelicalism.

### Quaker Worship

Barclay, Robert. *The Inner Life of the Religious Societies of the Commonwealth*, 3d ed. London: n.p., 1879. An extensive examination of the origins and beliefs of the Friends.

Green, Thomas F. *Preparation For Worship*. London: George Allen & Unwin, 1952. The author argues for a preparation of worship that arises out of a willingness to wait on the Spirit.

Moon, James H. *Why Friends Do Not Baptize With Water*. Philadelphia: The Leeds and Biddle Company, n.d. Argues that the baptism taught by Jesus is only a baptism of the Spirit.

Nicholls, G. L., ed. *The Journal of George Fox*. Cambridge: Cambridge University Press, 1952. Primary source material in which George Fox, the leader of the Quakers, expresses his view of worship.

Steere, Douglas V. *Where Words Come From*. London: George Allen & Unwin, 1955. A Swarthmore College lecture in which the author argues for the ability to feel words as the ground of true conversation and of prayer and worship.

Tellack, William. *George Fox, The Friends and the Early Baptists*. London: S. W. Partridge & Co., 1868. This work presents a comprehensive description of the life of George Fox and traces the doctrines of the Friends back to the early Baptists.

Woolman, John. *Worship.* A Pendle Hill pamphlet. Wallingford, Pa.: Pendle Hill, n.d. John Woolman was an eighteenth-century leader of the Quaker movement and a radical social reformer. Woolman saw worship at the center of life and society and argued for an inward stillness and humility in outward living.

### Adventist

Stevens, James L. *Worship Among the Pioneers: A Study of the Religious Meetings of the Early Seventh-Day Adventists.* Niles, Mich.: Adventist Heritage Center, 1977. A brief but very helpful exploration into the origins of Advent worship. While there are no orders of worship, there are several descriptions which are insightful.

White, Ellen G. *Testimonies to Ministers.* Omaha: Pacific Press Publishing Association, 1923. This work contains instructions to ministers including advice on preaching and material that relates to worship.

### Camp Meeting and Revival Worship

Finney, Charles Grandison. *Lectures on Revivals of Religion.* Ed. by William G. McLaughlin. Cambridge, Mass.: Belknap Press of Harvard University Press, 1960. While this work does not address worship as such, it does speak to the shape of revival and to the place of prayer and preaching in a revival service.

Gay, Ralph Gerald. "A Study of the American Liturgical Revival, 1825–1860." Unpublished Ph.D. dissertation, Emory University, 1977. Gay demonstrates that revivalists approached liturgy in a distinct and novel fashion, and argues that they established these approaches in a new cultus.

Johnson, Charles. *The Frontier Camp Meeting.* Dallas: Southern Methodist University Press, 1955. This work addresses the camp meetings of the trans-Allegheny west in the first four decades of the nineteenth century. It explains how this Kentucky revival weapon of Presbyterian origin became largely the property of the church of John Wesley, utilized by the circuit rider to extend Methodism.

Sizer, Sandra S. *Gospel Hymns and Social Religion: The Rhetoric of Nineteenth-Century Revivalism.* Philadelphia: Temple University Press, 1978. Although Sizer's work concentrates primarily on later revival hymnody—D. L. Moody and his con-temporaries—it illustrates the interplay of music within the revival service and the development of distinct revival hymns.

Weiss, Ellen. *City in the Woods: The Life and Design of an American Camp Meeting on Martha's Vineyard.* New York: Oxford University Press, 1987. A detailed examination of a particular camp meeting, with discussion of the setting and the message.

### Holiness

Hunter, Harold D. *Spirit-Baptism: A Pentecostal Alternative.* Lanham, Md.: University Press of America, 1983. The purpose of this work is to explore exigetical and historical studies to determine the validity of the classical Pentecostal argument for a distinct work of the Spirit.

Synan, Vinson. *The Holiness-Pentecostal Movement in the United States.* Grand Rapids: Eerdmans, 1971. A solid study of the rise, development, and theology of the many Holiness churches that have emerged in America.

### Restoration Worship

Campbell, Alexander. *The Christian System in Reference to the Union of Christians and the Restoration of Primitive Christianity as Plead by the Current Reformation.* St. Louis: Christian Publishing Company, 1839. Argues for a return to the first three centuries of the church, including its worship.

Gates, Erratt. *The Early Relations and Separation of Baptists and Disciples.* Chicago: Christian Century, 1904. This work explores the work of Alexander Campbell and the origins of the restoration movement.

Richesin, L. Dale, and Larry D. Bouchard. *Interpreting Disciples: Practical Theology in the Disciples of Christ.* Fort Worth: Texas Christian University Press, 1987. Addresses all the areas of the life of the church, including that of worship.

Watkins, Keith. *The Breaking of Bread: An Approach to Worship for the Christian Churches.* Nashville: Broadman Press, 1966. This work probes the origins of Discipleship worship and applies that worship to the worship of Disciples today.

### Methodist

Baker, Frank. *From Wesley to Asbury: Studies in Early American Methodism.* New York: Oxford

University Press, 1976. A study in the historical development of Methodist life, thought, and worship.

Bishop, John. _Methodist Worship in Relation to Free Church Worship._ New York: Scholars Studies Press, 1975. This book contains material very difficult to find. It explores the origin of free church worship dealing with matters such as Praise, Prayers, the Lessons, the Sermon and the Sacraments. Another equally valuable section deals with the origin, development and practice of Methodist worship.

Bowmer, John C. _The Sacrament of the Lord's Supper in Early Methodism._ Fort Worth: Dominion Press, 1951. A thorough study of the origin and development of Methodism, with particular emphasis on the understanding and practice of the Lord's Supper.

Hilderbrandt, Franz, and Oliver A. Beckerlegge, eds. _The Works of John Wesley._ Vol. 7: _A Collection of Hymns for the Use of the People Called Methodist._ London: Oxford University Press, 1983. A critical edition of the 1780 Methodist hymnal.

Tripp, David. _The Renewal of the Covenant in the Methodist Tradition._ London: Epworth Press, 1969. A study of the renewal of the covenant in its historical setting and in its worship context.

White, James F. _John Wesley's Prayer Book._ Cleveland: DSL Publications, 1991. A facsimile of the 1784 _Sunday Service,_ with introduction.

**African-American Worship**

_Adventures of Charles Ball, a Black Man._ New York: J. S. Taylor, 1837. Reprinted as _Fifty Years in Chains._ New York: Oxford University Press, 1970. Accounts of worship rituals, including descriptions of slave funerals, with comments and thoughts from the vantage of a slave.

Allen, William F., Charles Pickard Ware, and Lucy Garrison, eds. _Slave Songs of the United States._ New York: A. Simpson and Co., 1867. A collection of 136 songs compiled by the authors in 1867. Valued historically as the first published collection of slave songs. The preface includes sketchy but helpful information on worship practices and singing styles of the nineteenth century.

Berry, Mary Frances, and John W. Blassingame. _Long Memory: The Black Experience in America._ New York: Oxford University Press, 1982. A scholarly synthesis of recent research on black history,

black ritual, and its significance for family life are highlighted in Chapter 3, "Family and Church: Enduring Institutions."

Clarke, Erskine. _Wrestlin' Jacob: A Portrait of Religion in the Old South._ Richmond: John Knox Press, 1979. A recounting of the story of the quest for dignity and freedom among black slaves in the antebellum South. Excellent vignettes of slave worship.

Jones, Charles Colcock. _The Religious Instruction of the Negroes in the United States._ Savannah: Thomas Purse, 1842. Historical sketch of the religious instructions of black Americans from 1620 to 1842, with catechism and other doctrinal statements that white religionists taught newly converted blacks.

Haynes, Leonard L. _The Negro Community within American Protestantism: 1619–1844._ Boston: Christopher Publishing House, 1953. A significant documentation by the grandson of slaves that highlights the evidence of community among black slaves within the Protestant tradition. Provides evidence of the overt rejection of Christianity by certain African slaves.

Herskovits, Melville. _The Myth of the Negro Past._ Boston: Beacon Press, 1958. One of the earliest scholarly documentations of evidence of the survival of African influences in worship practices of black Americans.

Higginson, Thomas Wentworth. _Army Life in a Black Regiment._ Boston: Fields, Osgood and Co., 1869. Reprint. Boston: Beacon Press, 1962. A frequently quoted source that documents the life of black servicemen in the Union Army. Examples of the "Shout," a ritual both in the content of worship and in informal gatherings of slaves and ex-slaves, are described with much detail.

Lyell, Charles. _A Second Visit to the United States of America,_ 2 vols. New York: Harper and Brothers, 1849. These volumes provide rare glimpses inside black worshiping congregations in the South and support evidence that Muslim slaves from Africa continued the customs of Islam.

McClain, William B. _Black People in the Methodist Church._ Cambridge, Mass.: Schenkman Publishing Co., 1984. The history of blacks in the Methodist Church from the baptism of two (nameless) converts in 1758 to the present day, with brief examples of worship practices and significant religious pioneers.

McIntyre, Paul. *Black Pentecostal Music in Windsor.* Ottawa, Ontario: National Museum of Man, 1976. A well-documented history of blacks in southwestern Ontario, descendants of former slaves who went to Canada from the United States prior to the Civil War. Equally well documented are liturgical practices of the Church of God in Christ in Canada.

Rivers, Clarence Joseph. *This Far by Faith: American Worship and Its African Roots.* Washington, D.C.: National Office of Black Catholics, 1977. An anthology of major papers presented during a conference in 1977 on "Worship and Spirituality in The Black Community."

Scherer, Lester B. *Slavery and the Churches in Early America, 1619–1818.* Grand Rapids: Eerdmans Publishing Co., 1975. A scholarly account of the history of blacks during slavery, the Christianization process, and the attitudes of various Protestant church members in this process. Examples of the oppressive sermonizing and baptismal vows required provide insight into the need for separate worshiping places and different worship rituals.

Smith, Warren Thomas. *Harry Hoosier: Circuit Rider.* Nashville: Upper Room Books, 1981. A bibliography of "Black Harry," a Methodist circuit preacher par excellence in the colonial period.

Wade, Richard C. *Slavery in the Cities: The South, 1820–1860.* New York: Oxford University Press, 1964. An excellent source providing a glimpse into black worship styles in southern cities.

Weatherford, Willis D. *American Churches and the Negro.* Boston: Christopher Publishing House, 1957. Historical presentation with detailed accounts of attitudes of major Protestant denominations, Quakers, and Roman Catholics.

Wesley, Charles H. *Richard Allen: Apostle of Freedom.* Washington, D.C.: Associated Press, 1935. An autobiography of one of the leading preachers of the eighteenth and nineteenth centuries, a moving force in the establishment of the A.M.E. Church.

Turner, H. W. *History of an African Independent Church,* 2 vols. London: Oxford University Press, 1967. This work studies the phenomena of the African Independent Church of the prophet-healing type known as *aladura* (praying) churches in Western Nigeria.

Wilmore, Gayraud S. *Black Religion and Black Radicalism: An Interpretation of the Religious History of Afro-American People,* 2d ed. Maryknoll, N.Y.: Orbis Books, 1983. While providing a scholarly treatment of the history of black religion and the black church, the author highlights the inseparable bond between religious beliefs and rituals and the psychological realities of daily existence.

Wimberly, Edward P., and Anne Streaty Wimberly. *Liberation and Human Wholeness: The Conversion Experience of Black People in Slavery and Freedom.* Nashville: Abingdon Press, 1986. A meticulously documented study utilizing the voices of slaves and free Afro-Americans to examine conversion experiences vis-à-vis psychological, theological, and social cultural world from 1750 to 1930. Provides a fascinating look at religio-mystic human liberation from the perspective of a unique African-American coming to Christ.

Woodson, Carter G. *The History of the Negro Church.* Reprint. Washington, D.C.: Associated Press, 1972. One of the earliest scholarly presentations of the history of the black church in America.

# PART FOUR

# Theologies of Worship

# Approaches to the Theology of Worship

*Theology is a reflective discipline. That is, people who do theology reflect on the truth of Scripture and the insights of the church in a systematic way. Systematic reflection on worship results in a theology, or rather, theologies of worship. In this section, theologians of various Christian traditions reflect on their worship and attempt to articulate the words and actions of this worship in a systematic form.*

*Interpreters bring their own experience to the subject they interpret. One who constructs a theology of worship is not exempt from this hermeneutical method. Personal perspectives can often illuminate the broad and varied patterns of Christian worship. This chapter offers three views on the theology of worship: a liturgical approach, a free-church perspective, and a charismatic interpretation.*

## 185 • DEFINING THE TASK OF A THEOLOGY OF WORSHIP

*The following article underscores how the theology of worship has been neglected by many Christians and challenges believers to find new hope and power in the vision of the Christus Victor.*

The topic of worship is not only timely, it is urgent. There is a widespread sense among Christians in North America that all is not well with the church, that we need a new sense of direction, a new dynamism.

In particular, we need something that will capture the imagination and enthusiasm of young adults. The institutional loyalty that many older Christians grew up with is no longer evident among young people. Many of them are walking away from the church, not necessarily because they are hostile to religion, not because they object to the teachings or standards of the church, but because they just don't sense any particular value in participating in the Christian community. They see it as an option for those who want it, but certainly not a necessity for their own lives. There is a growing sense that we need a revitalization of church life, something to convey the excitement that being a Christian involves. What we need is a new understanding of worship.

### Worship and Ecclesiology

Our need for a theology of worship is part of a much larger need for a doctrine of the church.

Ecclesiology, as the doctrine is sometimes called, is the most underdeveloped aspect of Protestant thought. Protestant evangelicals have had a lot to say about the doctrine of human beings and the person and work of Christ, as well as the doctrine of revelation, which has received considerable attention through numerous discussions about biblical inspiration. So, when you look through the standard list of Christian doctrines to see what Protestants have been interested in, the work done in the area of ecclesiology is remarkably thin.

Even as part of a doctrine of the church, a full-fledged theology of worship itself is no small undertaking. It would have to include a theology of preaching, a theology of prayer, and a sacramental theology as well.

Besides a theology of worship, with all it entails, a comprehensive doctrine of the church must also include a theology of ministry. The controversy over women's ordination shows how much thinking we still have to do about this important topic. And perhaps most important of all, we need a theology of the Spirit. According to the New Testament, the church is the community of the Spirit, life in

Christ is life in the Spirit, and worship is impossible without the presence of the Spirit.

Several factors seem to mitigate a Protestant evangelical theology of worship. One might be our preoccupation with the mission of the church. This tends to make our times together occasions for planning, for organization, for motivational speeches, but not for devotional or celebration. Similarly, if we are preoccupied with the teachings of the church, then our times together will become occasions for indoctrination.

Of course, the church has a mission and the church has a message, and both deserve all the attention we can give them. But there is more to the Christian life than these things. In worship, the church—the community of the Spirit—brings to vivid expression its entire experience of salvation in Jesus Christ, with adoration, devotion, and celebration.

### Worship and Theology

A second point concerns the connection between worship and theology. We need to recognize both as important activities in the Christian community. If worship is the heart's love for God, theology is the mind's love for God; both are responses to God.

In addition, there is a reciprocal relation between theology and worship. Our worship affects our theology, and our theology affects our worship. On the one hand, theology has its roots in worship. It rises out of our experience with God. As one thinker puts it, "Theology has its basis in the experience of prayer." (Heinrich Ott, *God* [Richmond: John Knox, 1974], 95.) So, theology is one of the forms worship takes.

There is an ancient tradition of what we might call "worshipful reflection" or perhaps "theological worship." I am referring, of course, to the venerable idea of faith seeking understanding. For Anselm, the great medieval theologian, adoration found expression in careful thinking. "I do not seek to understand that I may believe," he said, "but I believe in order to understand. . . . So Lord, who dost give understanding to faith, give me . . . to understand that thou art as we believe." (*Saint Anselm: Basic Writings,* trans. S. N. Deane [LaSalle, Ill.: Open Court, 1966], 7.)

The relation moves in the other direction, too: theology can have an important effect on worship. What we come to believe about God and his relation to us cannot fail to affect the way we respond. Un-

fortunately, there are ways of looking at God that make it impossible for people to worship. And people who have different views of God will have different worship experiences. Those who are preoccupied with what God expects of them and those who are preoccupied with what God has done for them will have worship experiences that are radically different. Good theology and good worship go hand in hand. You can't ever have one without the other.

### Worship and Our Particular Theologies

It is one thing to assert that our worship should reflect our theology, but just how our theology should shape our worship experience is not easy to say. A series of sermons on distinctive denominational themes, for example, is no guarantee that the worship experience of the congregation will be somehow distinct.

In response, some may feel that particular denominations should *not* strive to be unique in their worship. Worship, they say, is one place in church life where we can reach beyond denominational boundaries and affirm solidarity with other branches in the body of Christ. But to achieve any significant theology of worship, however, we need to do more than emphasize particular denominational doctrines. We need to achieve a fundamental transformation in our perspective on the Christian life. We need something like a revolution, a paradigm shift, a new model or metaphor for what it means to be a Christian. If theology as such is truly significant, it will have more than ideas and practices to offer the world. It will have a powerful vision of what Christianity means. And this will have an inevitable effect on the central experience of worship.

Let me conclude with one possibility for theology-to-worship transformation. This is the familiar theme of *Christus Victor,* the idea that the entire universe is engulfed in a conflict whose central acts unfold in the history of God's people. I first sensed the potential of *Christus Victor* for worship several years ago when I heard a lecture on the work of Christ as a dramatic victory over the great powers that oppose and enslave human lives—the powers of sin, death, and the devil. It occurred to me that this was a viewpoint the whole church could embrace with enthusiasm.

Consider the exciting possibilities such a vision

opens up—the motifs of liberation, celebration, joy, and peace, for example. Think of the tension and drama that such a vision of human history conveys. Here is an idea with real power to transform worship. To a great extent we have left that comprehensive, overarching theme on the theological shelf. The time has come to bring it into the arena of concrete life where personal commitments and values are shaped. The time has come to infuse our worship with the exciting perspectives the _Christus Victor_ message contains.

In the _Christus Victor_ theme lies an ecclesiology—the church as the people of Christ's victory over the powers; a theology to free the mind to worship as it reflects on the implication of such a vision; a theology for worship that affirms worship as a celebration of the historic dethronement of the powers; an eschatological vision of the world freed from the powers; and a present awareness of God's power at work in worship to free the worshiper and ultimately all creation from the domain of the powers. In this task lies the promise of a theology of worship.

## 186 ✦ MODELS OF LITURGICAL THEOLOGY

_In our pluralistic world, it is often necessary to consider several perspectives to gain a complete picture of a concept or object. Theology has been similarly affected by this multicultural, multidimensional approach. As this article points out, we benefit from studying many different models as we attempt to understand the theology of liturgy._

We have moved beyond a theological world where we could point to a theological giant such as Barth or Tillich as the way to view our relationship with God, as Protestants tended to do. Nor is there any such thing as _the_ catholic theology as many Roman Catholic theologians one time presupposed. This became clear when Avery Dulles wrote his foundational book, _Models of the Church_ (1974), soon to be followed by his _Models of Revelation_. Sally McFague picked up the same approach in her _Models of God_ (1987). It has been no different for liturgical theology.

Since liturgical theology is part of the larger discipline of theology, it is going to take its approach from the reigning theological systems. Some liturgical theologies have chosen to stay within the parameters of a more classical kind of theology such as Thomistic or Barthian, but most, when they reach the level of systematic theology, tend to be rather eclectic. It seems only logical that an approach within the field of theology which has proven to be helpful should be employed to place liturgical theology in conversation with its theological neighbors.

Theologians learned from scientists that the use of models can remove many of the obstacles that are present when one attempts to make connections between two or more closely defined systems. To employ models of theology is to take seriously the fact that we cannot adequately describe reality; we can only interpret it. We do not provide photographs of God, sin, and grace. But we can find analogies which will allow us to speak about these spiritual realities. Models allow the conversation to take place.

Models are like windows. They are a way of viewing some event, in this case, the liturgical celebration. We know that if we have only one window in our house and the only world we see is the one viewed through the single window, that such a view can only be a distortion. But it is many windows and the many views through those windows which make it possible for us to sense and know more deeply the world outside of us. If we limit ourselves to one window, usually the one which supports our bias, we have severely restricted our grasp of life.

Rather, we need several windows, several models, just as we need several self images if we are going to live humanly. Those people who live under the imperialism of only one view of themselves, whether it be man or woman, teacher or student, mother or father, rich or poor, endanger their very growth as human beings. Much of the stunted growth that is part of our liturgical experience and that of assemblies all over the world is due to a single, dominating self-image of the liturgy. By expanding our windows on the liturgy through use of models, we can enrich our liturgical experiences and insights.

### The Institutional Model

What one sees when one peers through this window is the visible rite with all of its structure, procedure, and format. Here the emphasis is on the ritual itself in terms of what can be perceived through the human senses. This does not mean that this model sees liturgy only as empty ritualism, but the stress is on the proper ordering of worship. Rubrics would still be important in this approach and the liturgical assembly resembles more that of a pyramid. In this model one knows who is in charge, who is conducting the worship and how that person is differentiated from the congregation.

This stress on structure and procedure is not to be construed as negative since all good ritual needs structure as well as that liminal quality which takes people beyond and below those structures. The model, however, does imply that the way that the liturgical assembly is organized is the way that our relationship with God is structured. When this model dominates, it produces a very distorted view of Christianity.

At liturgy the worshiper is the privileged recipient of grace. One of the purposes of worship is to assist the congregant to continue on the way to God along certain established lines so that there is some security about the movement to salvation. In this approach one knows who is on that path and who is not. Looking at the assembly is like looking at the blueprints of a building. Everything is clearly delineated.

Through this window we see liturgy more as something legislated by the church rather than a community at celebration. There is a strong emphasis on doing the liturgy in a proper way and often the criteria for that takes precedence over the experience of the worshipers. The liturgy is to be received as something unchanging, a gift from the tradition handed down to be entered into on its own terms. Most readers will recognize this model as one which has dominated many of our assemblies over the years.

## The Mystery Model

This is the Easter model because of all the models, the mystery one celebrates the paschal mystery most explicitly. This model developed out of the theology of one of the first liturgical theologians of the twentieth century, Odo Casel, O.S.B., who maintained that in the liturgical celebration we do more than merely commemorate Christ or produce his real presence. Rather it is Christ and his saving mysteries, that is, Christ in his activity, which is made present. The mobilizing image here is that of the church in an act of remembering. Through its thanksgiving in its liturgical actions the Christian community effectively recalls the whole Christ so that event is actually present in the liturgical celebration itself. It is a model which attempts to explain how the cross is made contemporary in a way which

is more than mere recall. The liturgical notion of *anamnesis* is the way in which this model still lives on in liturgical theology today. For Casel, the liturgy and its relationship to Christ remains always a mystery, but this mystery is an event which can be reactualized in the present liturgical assembly.

What this model does is to introduce a sense of realism into the liturgical rite. The liturgical year is not some kind of biography of the life of Christ, but in each feast some aspect of the mystery is made contemporaneous in a unique way. In the liturgy salvation is made visible because the liturgy itself is visible. And while the saving activity of Christ is transcendent and eternal, yet the worship of the church exists in time and so Christ continues to act in time.

## The Sacramental Model

This is the model of the liturgical community above all else. The Pauline language of the body of Christ finds its best home in this model. As in the mystery model salvation seeks perceptibility, but now the emphasis is on the assembly as the locus of God's salvific action. This is the more mainline model that has been dominant in much of liturgical theology after the Second Vatican Council. It presupposes that the church is a sacrament and that the liturgy of the church is the way that the church expresses this sacramentality.

This model does not stress the individual sacraments but rather it places the emphasis on the incarnational character of the Christian community and its worship. Whereas the institutional model stressed the visible structures of church and liturgy and the mystery model highlighted the reality of the salvation found in those structures, this model points to the hidden level of grace beneath the structures which brings this liturgical event together to become the body of Christ. This is probably the most communal of all the models. Here one speaks of the communion of grace that exists among the members of the congregation. Here reference is made to the power of the Holy Spirit who brings together all worshipers to become the people of God. The restoration of the catechumenate in the church is an example of a pastoral implication of the power of this model of liturgy.

## The Proclamation Model

While this model has been operative throughout the history of the liturgy, it had become the dominant Protestant model after the Reformation. Here the Word of God has prime place. In our relationship with God and so in liturgy, God proclaims and we respond. Jesus Christ is God's perfect proclamation and our perfect response. It is the Word of God which creates the church and makes present the saving event of Christ.

The pattern of the liturgy is proclamation and response because that is the pattern of God coming into our lives. And here proclamation means far more than the proclaiming of a text. The full kerygmatic power of the gospel comes into play because this proclamation creates a world. It calls people to decision. One may refuse to make a decision in terms of the word, but the call to decision is always there.

In the liturgy the word and response structure makes of liturgy a dialogic event, one which places great value on communication. Dialogue is characteristic of human interchange. For such interchange to be meaningful the parties involved must be humanly present to one another. This human presence takes place through language. Jesus Christ is the language of God. Communicative human language is not the mere transmitting of information. It sets one up for an encounter, a deepening of relationships, and a challenge to one's presuppositions. And all this communication takes place within the rhythmic pattern of the liturgy which is where the language of God becomes concrete.

### The Process Model

This model was developed out of Alfred North Whitehead's process philosophy which has been very important in American theology. This way of thinking stresses relationality and creativity or novelty. There is a sense in which God and the world are one, or better, are at one. This is not to identify God and the world but rather to say that the only world we have is the world of our God and the only God we have is the one of our world. Of all the models the process one emphasizes the immanence of God. God is working in our world luring it ever more toward Godself.

Another key category of process thought is becoming. The basis of reality is that which changes, not that which remains the same. That is why novelty and creativity are such values in this system. The implications for liturgical theology is that liturgy is an event which is ever becoming, always on the way, constantly redefining itself in terms of the world around it, the environment in which its own life takes place. For this reason, a main image of the liturgy which emerges from this model is that of the worshiping community on the way, the assembly on pilgrimage.

When one gazes through this process window one sees a liturgical celebration which is very much connected with the larger world. It incorporates into its ritualization the contemporary values of society such as growth and development. Process liturgies try to take seriously the language of the liturgical texts and songs, namely, that God is deeply affected by what we do and truly cares for us. God does not remain immutably aloof, but both God and Christ change and grow with the worshipers themselves. Change is built into the very structure of the rites, and the prayer of the symbolizing community is directed toward the future.

### The Therapeutic Model

If the sacramental model is based on the role of the incarnation in our lives, the therapeutic model intensifies this incarnate character. This model, sometimes called the humanizing model, begins with the presupposition that human growth is synonymous with growth in union with God. Thus, this theological view pays particular attention to the stories of celebrating Christians. Rather than using explicitly religious images and categories to speak of the divine reality in human life, therapeutic liturgy employs the language of ordinary human experience to articulate the mystery that is at the heart of all liturgy. God is not alien to the humanizing process.

Liturgy's task here is one of clarification. God is always up to something in our world. Salvation is always going on. But often this is not noticed. It remains hidden. But liturgical assemblies can know what is going on because their liturgies unveil for them these deeper processes. And the community does this primarily through its story telling. In their songs and prayers and taking, blessing, breaking, and sharing action of the Eucharist they retell the great story of the Passover of Jesus Christ. This provides the members of the assembly the opportunity to place their smaller, often deficient, stories into the larger incorporating story of Jesus Christ.

### The Liberation Model

Many of the themes that one would find in the various forms of contemporary liberation theology will be echoed in this model. It is certainly about experiencing the kingdom of God through the breaking down of barriers that cause human division and inequality. It calls for the reform of sinful structures, and challenges the worshipers to join with the poor and oppressed in realistic ways to promote greater justice. Looking through this window one sees a liturgy that does justice.

It is in terms of the model that the worship of the church is seen as a prophetic event. But this is more than mere intellectual persuasion. The liturgy is the place where one's affections and emotions are to be transformed so that imaginative ways can be found to bring about this restructuring of society and the conversion of the members of the congregation. The kingdom of justice reaches into the most pedestrian dimensions of our lives and just worship pays attention to hospitality in the assembly, inclusive language in the liturgical texts, equality of women with men in the ministerial roles, and team effort in liturgical planning.

Liturgy is not, however, like some recipe book for the world's problems. Rather, it is like a dress rehearsal for the kingdom. When the liberation model is present in a celebration it becomes, albeit for only an hour on Sunday, the place where we play at being at home in the kingdom. That is, for this short period of time, the usual divisions in life and the barriers to full humanity disappear and we act as if the kingdom has truly arrived. These obstacles will all reappear at the church door when we leave the space of worship, but we will have experienced briefly what that kingdom of God is like.

In summary, liturgical models are theological models. They are useful instruments to discern the nature of any ritual celebration. But they are not more than that. Liturgy itself remains a mystery.

The apostle Paul put it best, "Now we see but a poor reflection as in a mirror; then we shall see face to face. Now [we] know in part; then [we] shall know fully, even as [we are] fully known" (1 Cor. 13:12).

James Empereur

## 187 • LITURGICAL WORSHIP: ENACTMENT OF SALVATION HISTORY

*For those who approach worship from a liturgical and sacramental point of view, Christian worship is an action which recalls the events of the history of salvation. This recollection,* *which is based on biblical models of worship, is not simply an intellectual remembering; it becomes an actual participation in the saving event through forms of worship empowered by the Holy Spirit and received in faith.*

A fundamental principle of New Testament theology is that all salvation history is recapitulated and "personalized" in Jesus. Nothing is clearer than the fact that everything in sacred history—event, object, sacred place, theophany, cult—has quite simply been assumed into the person of the Incarnate Christ. He is God's eternal Word (John 1:1, 14); his new creation (2 Cor. 5:17; Gal. 6:15; Rom. 8:19ff.; Rev. 21–22) and the new Adam (1 Cor. 15:45; Rom. 5:14); the new Pasch and its lamb (1 Cor. 5:7; John 1:29, 36; 19:36; 1 Pet. 1:19; Rev. 5ff.); the new covenant (Matt. 26:28; Mark 14:24; Luke 22:20; Heb. 8–13), the new circumcision (Col. 2:11-12), and the heavenly manna (John 6:30-58; Rev. 2:17); God's temple (John 2:19-22), the new sacrifice, and its priest (Eph. 5:2; Heb. 2:17–3:2; 4:14–10:14); the fulfillment of the Sabbath rest (Col. 2:16-17; Matt. 11:28–12:8; Heb. 3:7–4:11) and the messianic age that was to come (Luke 4:16-21; Acts 2:14–36). Neither the list nor the references are exhaustive. He is

*Jesus the Conqueror. The Abae Chi Rho symbol contains the letter N, meaning* nika *or [Jesus] conquers. The theme of Christ as victor over sin is an expression of the victory of Christ over the powers of evil, a theme expressed in the ancient liturgies of the church.*

quite simply "all, and in all" (Col. 3:11; this verse and all subsequent biblical quotations are from the Revised Standard Version), "the Alpha and the Omega, the first and the last, the beginning and the end" (Rev. 22:13; cf. 1:8; 21:6). All that went before is fulfilled in him: "For since the law has but a shadow of the good things to come instead of the true form of these realities" (Heb. 10:1); and that includes cultic realities: "Let no one pass judgment on you in questions of food and drink or with regard to a festival or a new moon or a sabbath. These are only a shadow of what is to come; but the substance belongs to Christ" (Col. 2:16-17).

This is seminal for any theology of Christian worship. The Old Testament temple and altar with their rituals and sacrifices are replaced not by a new set of rituals and shrines, but by the self-giving of a person, the very Son of God. _Henceforth, true worship pleasing to the Father is none other than the saving life, death and resurrection of Christ._ And our worship is this same sacrificial existence in us. Paul tells us, "Just as we have borne the image of the man of dust, we shall also bear the image of the man of heaven" (1 Cor. 15:49; cf. Phil. 2:7-11; 3:20-21; Eph. 4:22-24), the risen Christ, "image of the invisible God, the first-born of all creation" (Col. 1:15; cf. 2 Cor. 4:4), who conforms us to his image through the gift of his Spirit (2 Cor. 3:18; Rom. 8:11ff., 29). For St. Paul, "to live is Christ" (Phil. 1:21), and to be saved is to be conformed to Christ by dying to self and rising to new life in him (2 Cor. 4:10ff.; 13:4; Rom. 6:3ff.; Col. 2:12-13, 20; 3:1-3; Gal. 2:20; Eph. 2:1ff.; Phil. 2:5ff.; 3:10-11, 18-21) who, as the "last Adam" (1 Cor. 15:45) is the definitive form of redeemed human nature (cf. 1 Cor. 15:21-22; Rom. 5:12-21; Col. 3:9-11; Eph. 4:22-24). Until this pattern is so repeated in each of us that Christ is indeed "all in all" (Col. 3:11), we shall not yet "complete what is lacking in Christ's afflictions for the sake of his body, that is, the church" (Col. 1:24). For we know "the power of his resurrection" only if we "share his sufferings, becoming like him in his death" (Phil. 3:10).

Far from being a fourth-century innovation, edification and personal sanctification and the intimate relation of liturgy to everyday life are the essence of the New Testament message concerning the new cult. Indeed, for St. Paul liturgy _is_ Christian life. Never once does he use cultic nomenclature (liturgy, sacrifice, priest, offering) for anything but a life of self-giving, lived after the pattern of Christ. When

he does speak of what we call liturgy, as in 1 Corinthians 10–14, Ephesians 4, or Galatians 3:27-28, he makes it clear that its purpose is to build up the body of Christ into that new temple and liturgy and priesthood, in which sanctuary and offerer and offered are one. For it is in the liturgy of the church, in the ministry of word and sacrament, that the biblical pattern of recapitulation of all in Christ is returned to the collectivity and applied to the community of faith that will live in him.

To borrow a term from the biblical scholars, the liturgy is the on-going _Sitz im Leben_ of Christ's saving pattern in every age, and what we do in the liturgy is exactly what the New Testament itself did with Christ: it applied him and what he was and is to the present. For the _Sitz im Leben_ of the Gospels is the historical setting not of the original event, but of its telling during the early years of the primitive church. Do not both New Testament and liturgy tell us this holy history again and again as a perpetual anamnesis? Note that this is not kerygma, as it is often mistakenly called. Kerygma is the preaching of the Good News in order to awaken the response of faith in the new message. But the kerygma written down and proclaimed in the liturgical assembly to recall us to our commitment to the Good News already heard and accepted in faith, even though we "know them and are established in the truth" (2 Pet. 1:12), is anamnesis, and that is what we do in liturgy. We make anamnesis, memorial, of this dynamic saving power in our lives, to make it penetrate ever more into the depths of our being, for the building up of the body of Christ:

> That which was from the beginning, which we have heard, which we have seen with our eyes, which we have looked upon and touched with our hands, concerning the word of life—the life was made manifest, and we saw it, and testify to it, and proclaim to you the eternal life which was with the Father and was made manifest to us—that which we have seen and heard we proclaim also to you, so that you may have fellowship with us; and our fellowship is with the Father and with his Son Jesus Christ. And we are writing this that our joy may be complete. (1 John 1:1-4)

It seems to me, then, that the eschatological expectation vs. sanctification of life dichotomy arose long before the fourth century, _pace Dix,_ and was solved by the apostolic church. But it was not solved by abandoning New Testament eschatology, which sees

Christ as inaugurating the age of salvation. What was abandoned was the mistaken belief that this implied an imminent parousia. But that does not modify the main point of Christian eschatology, that the end time is not in the future but *now.* And it is operative now, though not exclusively, through the anamnesis in word and sacrament of the dynamic present reality of Emmanuel, "God-with-us," through the power of his Spirit in every age.

In the Gospels the transition to this new age of salvation history is portrayed in the accounts of the post-resurrection appearances of Jesus. They introduce us to a new mode of his presence, a presence that is real and experienced, yet quite different from the former presence before his passover. When he appears he is not recognized immediately (Luke 24:16, 37; John 21:4, 7, 12). There is a strange aura about him; the disciples are uncertain, afraid; Jesus must reassure them (Luke 24:36ff.). At Emmaus they recognize him only in the breaking of the bread—and then he vanishes (Luke 24:16, 30-31, 35). Like his presence among us now, his presence to the disciples is accessible only through faith.

What these post-resurrection accounts seem to be telling us is that Jesus is with us, but not as he was before. He is with us and not with us, real presence and real absence. He is the one whom "heaven must receive until the time for establishing all that God spoke by the mouth of his holy prophets from of old" (Acts 3:21), but who also said "I am with you always, until the close of the age" (Matt. 28:20). It is simply this reality that we live in the liturgy, believing from Matthew 18:20 that "where two or three are gathered in my name, there am I in the midst of them," yet celebrating the Lord's Supper to "proclaim the Lord's death until he comes" (1 Cor. 11:26) in the spirit of the early Christians, with their liturgical cry of hope: Maranatha! "Amen. Come, Lord Jesus!" (Rev. 22:20).

So the Jesus of the apostolic church is not the historical Jesus of the past, but the heavenly Priest interceding for us constantly before the throne of the Father (Rom. 8:34; Heb. 9:11-28) and actively directing the life of his church (Rev. 1:17–3:22 and *passim*). The vision of the people who produced these documents was not directed backwards, to the "good old days" when Jesus was with them on earth. We see such nostalgia only after Jesus' death, before the resurrection appearances give birth to Christian faith.

The church did keep a record of the historical events, but they were reinterpreted in the light of the Resurrection and were meant to assist Christians to grasp the significance of Jesus in their lives. That this was the chief interest of the New Testament church, the contemporary, active, risen Christ present in the church through his Spirit, can be seen in the earliest writings, the epistles of St. Paul, which say next to nothing about the historical details of Jesus' life.

It is this consciousness of Jesus as the Lord not of the past but of contemporary history that is the aim of all Christian spirituality and liturgical anamnesis. Christian vision is rooted in the gradually acquired realization of the apostolic church that the parousia was not imminent and that the eschatological, definitive victory won by Christ must be repeated in each one of us, until the end of time. And since Christ is both model and source of this struggle, the New Testament presents both his victory and his cult of the Father as ours: just as we have died and risen with him (Rom. 6:3-11; 2 Cor. 4:10ff.; Gal. 2:20; Col. 2:12-13, 20; 3:1-3; Eph. 2:5-6), so, too, it is we who have become a new creation (2 Cor. 5:17; Eph. 4:22-24), a new circumcision (Phil. 3:3), a new temple (1 Cor. 3:16-17; 6:19; 2 Cor. 6:16; Eph. 2:19-22), a new sacrifice (Eph. 5:2), and a new priesthood (1 Pet. 2:5-9; Rev. 1:6; 5:10; 20:6). This is why we meditate on the pattern of his life, proclaim it, preach it, celebrate it: to make it ever more deeply our own. This is why the apostolic church left us a book and a rite, word and sacrament, so that what Christ did and was, we may do and be, in him. For this reason, sacred history is never finished: it continues in us.

## The Newness of Christian Ritual

I think it fair to say that this New Testament vision of cult is something startlingly, radically new. Of course human beings have always gathered to express themselves in ritual, so when Christians do so they are not inventing something new. What *is* new is the *vision* they are expressing.

Ritual itself is simply a set of conventions, an organized pattern of signs and gestures which members of a community use to interpret and enact for themselves and to express and transmit to others, their relation to reality. It is a way of saying what we are a group in the full sense of that *are,* with our past that made us what we are, our present in which we live what we are, and the future we hope to be. Ritual, then, is ideology and experience in action, the celebration or interpretation-through-action of our human experience and how we view it.

Human societies have used ritual especially to express their religious outlook, their universal system for relating to the ultimate questions of life. A religion is different from a personal philosophy of life in that it is a *shared* perspective, a common outlook on reality. As such it depends on *history,* on the group's collective remembrance of things past, of events that have been transformed in the collective memory of the community into key symbolic episodes determinative of the community's being and self-understanding.

This is the basis of ritual behavior. For it is through the interpretation of its past that a community relates to the present and copes with the future. In the process of ritual representation, past constitutive events are made present in ritual time, in order to communicate their force to new generations of the social group, providing thus a community of identity throughout history.

In primitive, natural religious systems the past was seen as cyclic, as an ever-repeating pattern of natural seasons. Rituals were celebrations of this cycle of autumn, winter, spring, harvest—of natural death and rebirth. But even at this primitive stage men and women came to see these natural rhythms as symbols of higher realities, of death and resurrection, of the perdurance of human existence beyond natural death.

So even natural religious ritual is not just an interpretation of experience but implies a reaching for the beyond, for an ultimate meaning in the cycle of life that seemed to be an ever-recurring circle closed by death. The discovery of history was a breakthrough in this process: life was seen to have a pattern that extended beyond the closed cycles of nature, of life and death. Time acquired a new meaning, and human ritual was transformed from a way of interpreting *nature* into a way of interpreting *history.*

Thus, events in the past came to acquire a universal symbolic value in the mind of the community: in fact, these events were so fundamental that they actually created and constituted the community's very identity. By celebrating these events ritually, the community made them present again and mediated to its members their formative power. Of course these were usually events of salvation, of escape from calamity and death, and it was but one further step for them to become transformed in the collective memory of the group into symbols of God's care and eternal salvation.

This is what happened with Israel. What makes Israelite liturgy different from other rituals is revelation. The Jews did not have to *imagine* that their escape from Egypt was a sign of God's saving providence: he *told* them so. When they celebrated this Exodus ritually in the Passover meal, they knew they were celebrating more than the universalization of a past event in the historical imagination of their poets and prophets. The covenant with God which they reaffirmed ritually was a permanent and hence ever present reality because God had said so.

Here we encounter a basic difference between Judeo-Christian worship and other cults. Biblical worship is not an attempt to contact the divine, to mediate to us the power of God's intervention in past saving events. It is the other way around. It is a worship of the already saved. We do not reach for God to appease him; he has bent down to us.

With Christian liturgy we take another step in our understanding of ritual. As in the Old Testament, we, too, celebrate a saving event. For us, too, the meaning of this event has been revealed. But that is where the parallel ends. For Old Testament ritual looked forward to a promised fulfillment; it was not only an actualization of the covenant, but the pledge of a yet unrealized messianic future. In Christianity, what all other rituals strain to achieve has, we believe, already been fulfilled once and for all by Christ. Reconciliation with the Father has been accomplished eternally in the mystery of his Son (2 Cor. 5:18-19; Rom. 5:10-11). The gap is bridged forever through God's initiative.

So Christian worship is not how we seek to contact God; it is a celebration of how God has touched us, has united us to himself and is ever present to us and dwelling in us. It is not a reaching out for a distant reality but a joyful celebration of a salvation that is just as real and active in the ritual celebration as it was in the historical event. It is ritual perfected by divine realism; ritual in which the symbolic action is not a memorial of the past, but a participation in the eternally present salvific Pasch of Christ.

Christian liturgy, therefore, publicly feasts the mystery of our salvation already accomplished in Christ, thanking and glorifying our God for it so that it might be intensified in us and communicated to others for the building up of the church to the perpetual glory of God's holy name.

## Liturgy: A Work of the Church

So liturgy is an activity of the church. It is one of the ways the church responds in praise, surrender, thanksgiving, to the call of God's revealing, saving word and deed. This eternal doxology is a response to something, and it is important to note that this divine action itself is not extrinsic to the liturgy but an integral part of it. Liturgy is not just our response; it is also the eternally repeated call. It is both God's unending saving activity and our prayerful response to it in faith and commitment throughout the ages.

Liturgy, then, is much more than an individual expression of faith and devotion and infinitely more than a subjective expression of "where we're at" or "where we're coming from," as contemporary American slang puts it. It is first and foremost an activity of God in Christ. Christ saves through the ages in the activity of the body of which he is the head. He does this in the word that calls us to conversion to him and union with him and to reconciliation with one another in him. He creates and nourishes and heals and restores this life in the water and oil and food of sacrament, and joins his prayer to ours to glorify the Father for those gifts. And all this is liturgy.

Liturgy then is the common work of Christ and his church. This is its glory. It is also what makes possible the extraordinary claims the church has made about the nature of Christian worship. Our prayers are worthless, but in the liturgy Christ himself prays in us. For the liturgy is the efficacious sign of Christ's saving presence in his church. His saving offering is eternally active and present before the throne of the Father. By our celebration of the divine mysteries, we are drawn into the saving action of Christ, and our personal self-offering is transformed into an act of the body of Christ through the worship of the body with its head. What men and women have vainly striven for throughout history in natural ritual—contact with the divine—is transformed from image to reality in Christ.

Of course, Christ, through the Spirit, does all these things apart from the liturgy, too—all this calling and healing and nourishing and saving and praying in us and with us. Then what is so special about the liturgy? Certainly not its efficaciousness, for God is always efficacious in all he does. The obstacles come from us. What is special about the liturgy is that it is a *visible* activity of the *whole* church. Indeed, in a certain sense church is church only in liturgy, for a gathering in its fullest sense is a gathering only when it is gathered! Liturgy therefore is different from private prayer and other means and vehicles of grace and salvation in that it is a "symbol," a symbolic movement both expressing what we are and calling us to be it more fully. It is a celebration of the fact that we have been saved in Christ, and in the very celebration that same saving mystery of Christ is offered to us again in anamnesis for our unendingly renewed acceptance and as everlasting motive for our song of joyful thanks and praise: "He who is mighty has done great things for me, and holy is his name!" (Luke 1:49).

We do all this together because we *are* a "together," and not just individuals. Christian salvation is by its very nature "church," a "gathering," a one body of Christ, and if we do not express this, then we are not what we proclaim to be. Redemption in the New Testament is a coming together, a solidarity in the face of the evil of this world. It necessarily leads to community because only in common can new human values be effectively released and implemented. Christ came not just to save individuals, but to change the course of history by creating the leaven of a new group, a new people of God, paradigm of what all peoples must one day be. In the Acts of the apostles the life of this group is sustained in *gatherings,* and its basic dynamic is toward unity: that they may be one in Jesus, that they may love one another as Jesus has loved them and as the Father loves Jesus, is the will and prayer of Jesus in the Last Discourse in John's Gospel (15:9ff., 17:20ff.). This is the remedy for hate and divisiveness and enmity, the products of egoism that is the root of all evil.

Unless seen in this broader context of the whole of life, what the community does in its synaxes does not make much sense, for liturgy is not an end in itself. It is only the means and expression of a life together in Christ. It is that which is primary: A common life of mutual support and generosity, of putting self second so that others can be first. Prayer in common is one of the means to this unity, part of the group's cement, as well as its joyful celebration of the fact that inchoatively, if not perfectly, this unity exists already.

So it is toward *life* that worship is always directed. We see this in 1 Cor. 11–14 and Matt. 5:23-24. We see it in the *Didache* 14:1–2: "And on the Lord's day of the Lord, after you have gathered, break bread and offer the Eucharist, . . . But let no one who has a quarrel with his neighbor join you until he is reconciled, lest your sacrifice be defiled." A few years later, around A.D. 111–113, we see it in the garbled account of a Christian assembly in the letter of the pagan governor Pliny to the emperor Trajan, during a time of persecution in the Roman Empire. Pliny had interrogated Christians concerning their private gatherings, which had brought them under suspicion after Trajan's edict forbidding _hetaeriae_ or secret meetings. Pliny obviously did not comprehend the information he had received from them. But he did understand that these Christian assemblies involved commitment to a covenant with stringent ethical implications:

> They insisted, however, that their whole fault or error consisted in the fact that they were accustomed to gather before daylight on a fixed day to sing a hymn to Christ as God and to bind themselves mutually, by means of a religious vow, not to any crime, but rather not to commit any theft or robbery or adultery, nor to go back on their word, nor to refuse to return a loan when it is demanded back. (Plinius Minor, _Ep._ 10, 96:7)

We see it in the questions asked the _baptizandi_ in Hippolytus, _Apostolic Tradition_ 20:

> And when those who are to receive baptism are chosen, let their life be examined: did they live good lives when they were catechumens? Did they visit the sick? Have they done every kind of good work? And when those who sponsored them bear witness to each: "He has," let them hear the gospel.

In short, the touchstone of our liturgy is whether or not it is being lived out in our lives. Is the symbolic moment symbolizing what we really are? Is our sacred celebration of life a sign that we truly live in this way?

In taking this perspective we are doing precisely what we saw the New Testament do with the mystery that is Christ: we recall it, make anamnesis of it, as a medium for encountering this mystery anew, so that we might see it as it is, the model and source of what we must be. But its purpose is not merely didactic. Its blazing light serves not only to illumine our deficiencies. It also burns away our darkness and draws us into its divine light.

Liturgy then has precisely the same dynamic as the New Testament and also contains my response to it. To appropriate an expression of Mark Searle,

just as the Bible is the saving Word of God in the words of human beings, so the liturgy is the saving deeds of God in the actions of men and women. And both have the same end: that we might respond to the call and live it. Indeed, in a sense liturgy is more inclusive than the Scriptures, for it comprises both the saving Word _and_ the saving actions of God, and our response to both. But just as the Word and deeds of God are seen here in sacramental form, but are present to us at every moment, symbolized but not exhausted in the ritual movement, so, too, my ritual response is but the symbolic movement of what must be the response of my every moment, with God's help.

For liturgy is a present encounter. Salvation is now. The death and resurrection of Jesus are past events only in their historicity, that is, with respect to us. But they are eternally present in God, who has entered our history but is not entrapped in it, and they have brought the presence of God among us to fulfillment in Jesus, and that enduring reality we encounter at every moment of our lives. The past memorialized is the efficacious saving event of salvation now, re-presented in symbol. In the risen Lord, creation is at last seen as what it was meant to be, and Christ is Adam, that is, all humankind.

So the Jesus we recall is the fulfillment of all that went before. But this fulfillment of the past is directed at the future. For just as Christ has become everything and fulfilled all, so for us to be fulfilled, we must become him. And we can do this only by letting him conform us to himself, to his pattern, the model of the new creation. It is this remaking of us into a new humanity that is the true worship of the New Law. The old cult and priesthood have been replaced by the self-offering of the Son of God, and our worship is to repeat this same pattern in our own lives, a pattern we celebrate in symbol when we gather to remember what he was and what we are to be.

To express this spiritual identity, St. Paul uses several compound verbs that begin with the preposition _syn_ (with): I suffer with Christ, am crucified with Christ, die with Christ, am buried with Christ, am raised and live with Christ, am carried off to heaven and sit at the right hand of the Father with Christ (Rom. 6:3-11; Gal. 2:20; 2 Cor. 1:5; 4:7ff.; Col. 2:20; Eph. 2:5-6). This is one of Paul's ways of underscoring the necessity of personal participation in redemption. We must "put on Christ" (Gal. 3:27), and assimilate him, somehow experience with God's grace the principal events by which Christ has saved us and repeat them in the pattern of my own life. For by undergoing them he has transformed the basic human experiences into a new creation. How do we experience these events? In him, by so entering into the mystery of his life so that each can affirm with Paul: "I have been crucified with Christ; it is no longer I who live, but Christ who lives in me" (Gal. 2:20).

This is what Christian life, our true liturgy, is all about. Our common worship is a living metaphor of this same saving reality, not only representing and re-presenting it to us constantly in symbol to evoke our response in faith and deed, but actively effecting it in us through the work of the Holy Spirit, in order to build up the body of Christ into a new temple and liturgy and priesthood in which offerer and offered are one.

This is what I mean when I say that all liturgy is anamnesis. It is not just a psychological reminiscence, not just a remembering, but an active and self-fulfilling prophecy in which by the power of God we become what we celebrate, while at the same time thanking and glorifying him for that great gift.

2 Peter 1:12-16 says:

> Therefore I intend always to *remind* you of these things, though you know them and are established in the truth that you have. I think it is right . . . to arouse you by way of *reminder.* . . . And I will see to it that after my departure you may be able at any time to *recall* these things. For we did not follow cleverly devised myths when we made known to you the power and coming of our Lord Jesus Christ, but we were eye-witnesses of his majesty.

Liturgy also reminds us of the powerful deeds of God in Christ. And being reminded we remember, and remembering we celebrate, and celebrating we become what we do. The dancer dancing is the dance.

Robert Taft[18]

## 188 • FREE-CHURCH WORSHIP: ASCRIBING WORTH TO GOD

*Free-church worship occupies a middle position between the liturgical/sacramental forms of worship and the informal worship of many charismatic churches. Whereas free churches may follow a formal order of service, their worship does not conform to historic Eucharist-centered liturgies. This worship has three objectives: to speak to God, to listen to God, and to respond to God—a sequence based on the ancient biblical structure of proclamation and response. This style of worship is found in evangelical and fundamental churches as well as in many mainline Protestant congregations. Many Pentecostal churches also use a free-church format in their Sunday morning services.*

Worship is the ascription of worth to God for who he is and what he does—just as the psalmist expresses it:

> Ascribe to the Lord, O families of nations,
>  ascribe to the Lord glory and strength.
> Ascribe to the Lord the glory due his name.
>  (Psalm 96:7-8)

Ascribing to God the glory due his name—by our words and our deeds, is basic to a Christian lifestyle. The first statement that should be made about worship is that it isn't turned on and off when we enter the "worship center" each Sunday. We cannot compartmentalize our lives into a worship day and six others. Worship is, indeed, a way of life. Every word and every action of every day should bring glory to God. Despite imperfection, this should be our daily ambition.

Giving the Lord the glory due his name includes offering to him the sacrifice of praise—that is, the fruit of lips which acknowledge that he is Lord (Heb. 13:15). It also includes doing deeds of mercy and compassion in his Name (Heb. 13:16), presenting our bodies as living sacrifices (Rom. 12:1), having our minds renewed by the Word of God (Rom. 12:2), giving offerings of talents, time, and treasures (2 Cor. 8–9). These and other activities are actions which honor him and which happen throughout our days, not only in our public or corporate services of worship and instruction.

The Scriptures tell us (John 4:23-24) that God desires our honesty before him. He wants us to worship him with understanding (our intellect), and with the heart (loving him). But true worship includes actions as well as thoughts and emotions. We understand with our mind and heart, but we act by our will. Facts and feelings must come together resulting in actions which bring honor to our Lord. Of course, he already knows all there is to know, and he already sees our hearts; so it is not as if we could reveal to him anything that might surprise or enlighten him. Worship is really a spiritual exercise, our spirit to his; but it must also be expressed materially. A right heart-relationship with God brings about right attitudes in the mind, resulting in activities that would please him and honor him.

The critical key to all this activity, word and deed, is a heart in tune with God, made righteous before him by the blood of the Lamb. Until a person has been reconciled to God through his Son, Jesus Christ, any words one might utter or deeds one might do in his name are as nothing to him—maybe noticeable by men and women, perhaps very good for the human race, but as far as God is concerned, "dead works."

## Gathering for Worship

If this is true of every aspect of daily life, it also holds true for our corporate times of worship when the body of Christ gathers to focus minds, hearts, and wills on God. Ascribing to God the glory due his name is basic to these experiences.

Many phrases have been used in defining this activity: admiring God's character, delighting in God's works, declaring God's worth, celebrating God, responding to God, honoring him. All of these fall into the broad definition: *worship is the ascription of worth to God for who he is and what he does.* It is telling God what we think of him. It's saying, "Thank you, Lord God, for who you are and the ways you show yourself real to me. I appreciate you." It is honoring him by doing things that help us declare his worth: singing to him and of him, exalting his name and his character, praying, learning more about him as we read the Scriptures, recounting his works on behalf of his people throughout history, telling and celebrating the story of redemption, and so on.

As God's truth is taught and Jesus Christ is lifted up to draw people to himself, even the sermon is an act of worship. In reading and understanding the Scriptures, we are taught how to honor God in our lives, and we learn more and more about who he is and what he has done—the proofs of his character. Although we learn of God primarily by our study of Scripture, we also find reinforcement of his eternal attributes in sharing with each other his activity in our own lives. Our contemporary experience affirms that he is the same God to whom the Bible testifies. For that we praise and thank him. The more we learn about him and his works, the more we

have for which to thank him, to sing his praises, and to declare his worth.

## Worship Is Giving

Worship is God-oriented. He is the object of our affections. Our attitude should never be "what's in this for me?" as it was in the case of the priests we read of in the book of Malachi, or the New Testament Pharisees. It must always be "What can I give you today, Lord? What can I do to please you?" It is the attitude of Mary, the friend of Jesus who even cleaned and anointed his dirty feet. We *give* to God the glory due his name. Are human needs met in so doing? Absolutely. God has always been known as the greatest giver, and he has promised to meet the needs of his people. In fact, he first gave, and our worship is a response to his activities on our behalf. Our communion with him always satisfies our basic human needs, but need-fulfillment should never be the primary motivation for worship.

To know God personally and actively to participate in adoring him are our two fundamental areas of need. As we grow in our knowledge of him and closeness to him, we find that our worship takes on new significance and meaning. Our worship is governed by what we believe about its object. We *need* to know him more. Then we can be more conscientiously involved in giving him the praise he deserves and desires. Worshipers cannot be mere spectators, but must be participants. We *need* to ascribe worth to the God we know, because of who he is and what he has done. "To know him and to make him known": may seem to some a rather trite and even "hyper-spiritual" phrase, but it is truth! (cf. John 4:22; Phil. 3:10; 1 Chron. 16:24; Ps. 105:1)

## What Happens in Worship?

Communication with almighty God is not the same as with humans. We could never reduce that spiritual union to the level of our finite understanding. Fortunately, God knows that! And because he designed us, he knew from the beginning that our communion with him would be very special to us and to him. God does not sit in heaven on a throne merely listening to people talk to him about their fears, desires, needs, wants, sins. He also answers. We speak, but so does he. He hears, and so must we.

Worship includes speaking, listening, and responding. We actively give God glory, telling him what we think of him; we listen to him speak to us—

through the Word of God taught, but also by his Holy Spirit and at *his* discretion; and then we must respond to what has been said to us. Those are the rudiments of communication: speak, listen, respond. Often we speak too much and listen indifferently, and then we do nothing in response to what we hear because we really don't care. In our worship, we must speak openly about our great God. We must hear what he has to say to us—as individuals and as a body, and we must then respond to whatever he told us. In planning a worship service, whether personal or corporate, those three elements must be present: Speak to God—we tell him how much we adore him; listen to God—we study the Word and do not harden our hearts to its truth; respond to God—we do whatever we must to fulfill his commands. Our response in worship can be both immediate and lasting. An immediate response at the close of a worship service might be a song, the giving of offerings, communion or baptism, or many other things planned as a specific response to what has already happened. But the key to living as God's people is in the *lasting* response we make. "How do I live this out during the next week?" Every preacher should be prepared to offer suggestions on how this message from God can be followed up on Monday through Saturday, helping the people carry the beauty of Sunday's fellowship and worship back to the workplace. The result will be evangelism and new souls in the kingdom. If God's people will honestly continue to worship and serve him during the week, they will be noticed and believed, and God will be pleased and glorified.

A great example from Scripture of this immediate and lasting response is seen in the Israelites as they dedicated the temple in Jerusalem and invoked God's presence and blessing (2 Chronicles 5–7). After the people lifted their voices to God in adoration—"You are great! Your love endures forever!" and after God visited his people and let them know he was pleased, the people responded by further praise, falling on their faces in awe and celebrating God's presence with great joy. That was an immediate response to their encounter with him that day. But the listening response (cf. chapter 7) was that they went home rejoicing, sharing with others the good things they had experienced, living holy lives—changed people! Both in their public meeting and in their personal daily living they honored God, *ascribing worth to him for his being and his works.*

## The Result of Worship: Changed Lives

A life of honest and true worship affects everyone: church leaders, laypersons, and even unbelievers. If we truly connect with God in times of corporate worship, not only will that aspect of our lives change, but so will our everyday activities with a freshness and vitality which transcend the mundane.

Here are just a few examples of how people were changed when they decided to worship God according to the pattern set forth here. Genesis 35 records that God told Jacob to take his people and move from Shechem to Bethel. Jacob informed the clan that they were to go together to worship the living God at Bethel—to build an altar and to settle there. The people agreed and when they realized they would be in God's presence, they knew they had to mend their ways. So they brought to Jacob the many idols representing foreign gods that had crept into their lives along the way. Everyone renewed his or her vow to 'El 'Elohei Yisra'el—the mighty God of Israel. Lives were changed.

More than four centuries later Moses informed the Israelites that God had decided to make a covenant with them and that he had invited Moses to the top of the mountain to receive the remaining details. The people decided that the Lord was indeed their God. Although they had faltered along the way, they responded with great determination, saying, "Everything the Lord has said we will do" (Exod. 24:3). Lives were changed.

Nehemiah 8 tells about the exiles who returned to Jerusalem from Babylon after the completion of the wall. Ezra took out the Book of the Law and read it in their hearing. All the people listened attentively, and when Ezra praised the Lord, the people lifted their hands and, shouted "Amen! Amen!" and then bowed down and worshiped the Lord with their faces to the ground (Neh. 8:5-6). Lives were changed.

After the dedication of the temple in Jerusalem (2 Chron. 5–7), the people returned to their home villages "joyful and glad in heart for the good things the Lord had done . . ." (7:10). 1 Kings 8:66 adds that the people blessed the king as they left. The people had such an encounter with God that they responded in joyous praise and righteous living. Lives were changed.

Acts 4 says that Peter and John and their friends

worshiped God by raising their voices to him in prayer, including praises and petition. After they prayed (verse 31), the place where they were meeting was shaken; they were all filled with the Holy Spirit, and they spoke the Word of God boldly. Because of a dynamic and meaningful connection with almighty God, lives were changed.

The real "bottom line" of worship is to know that God is pleased. But an important by-product is that in worshiping him "in spirit and in truth" we are affected and changed: we come to a better knowledge of who he is; we experience anew his love, grace, and power; we are renewed, refreshed, revived; we become doers of the Word, not just hearers; Christ's church around the world is expanded because we serve him by sharing his love with others; we are gladly obedient to all he wants us to be and do, honoring him in all of life—ascribing to the Lord the glory due his name.

In summary, worship is the ascription of worth to God for who he is and what he has done.

God alone should be the object or focus of my praise and adoration.

My attitude is "I'm here to give myself to you, Lord."

My most central needs are to get to know him better and then actively participate in telling him that I appreciate and adore him.

Although others will help me in this, the major responsibility is mine.

I must talk to God, listen to him, and respond to whatever he says.

The worship I give him with others on Sunday helps and motivates me to continue honoring him throughout the week. At the same time, the experiences I bring with me on Sunday from the week past become times to recount his blessings, his goodness, and his eternal faithfulness.

Timothy Mayfield

## 189 • CHARISMATIC WORSHIP: RESPONDING TO THE SPIRIT

*Worship, for Pentecostal and charismatic Christians, is an expression of the experience and empowerment of the Holy Spirit—an event which for many brings the Scriptures to life and continuously incarnates Jesus Christ in his church. The release of a life of praise, of intercession, and of spiritual gifts for ministry takes place in the setting of the body of Christ at worship.*

Although tongues and interpretation are an important manifestation of the Spirit in the worship of Pentecostals, emphasis is also placed broadly on others gifts of the Spirit, including those of healing and prophecy. The modern Pentecostal movement originated in revivals which occurred in Kansas, Los Angeles, and other places early in the twentieth century. As Pentecostalism came to be perceived as a "dangerous" influence in denominational churches, those who had experienced the revival were often forced to leave their congregations. The formation of Pentecostal churches and denominations was the result. This never seemed to be an explicit goal of Pentecostals, who wished primarily to revitalize their existing churches from within. The emerging bodies did, however, play into holiness movement thinking, and thus even those Pentecostal churches which did not spring from holiness movement roots have often grown from both of these traditions.

On the other hand, the term *charismatic* carries more generic connotations. Its use has come into vogue more recently, removing the stigma of Pentecostalism from charismatics. In charismatic churches there is a wider variety of understandings regarding the gifts of the Spirit. Charismatics may not be as dogmatic as classical Pentecostals about the need for particular manifestations of these gifts (i.e., tongues) as signs that a person has truly received the Holy Spirit. Emphasis on the spiritual gifts and their use is even more broadly based than with Pentecostals. Thus we can say that all Pentecostals are charismatic but not all charismatics are Pentecostal. Whereas the classical Pentecostal movement has provided Pentecostals with their own churches—even their own denomination—charismatics tend more often to remain in their original denominational churches unless their congregation is antagonistic to their presence.

Can there be such a thing as a theology of charismatic worship? Given the pluralistic profile of faith among charismatic worshipers, what is the starting point or central theme for a consistent theology of charismatic worship? Once discovered is this theology going to be very different from liturgical theologies developed by Christians in the past? And finally, if we *can* develop a viable theology of charismatic worship then what sorts of changes in thinking, behavior, public orders of worship, and overall lifestyle would it suggest? The starting place for a theology of charismatic worship should be the common ground of charismatic experience, moving from there to a theology of Christ and the Holy Spirit.

### ——— From Experience to Exegesis ———

The Latin maxim *lex orandi lex credendi* applies to the development of a charismatic theology of worship. This phrase enunciates the conviction that liturgical experience precedes theology in most cases, and that therefore our creeds or beliefs grow more out of our prayer and worship life than the other way around. In reality, of course, experience and belief are continually honing one another, and constants such as the Scriptures provide norms. But because experience is so important to human existence, the way in which worship is conducted can reinforce, shape, or challenge a person's beliefs.

Charismatics *are* charismatics because they have had a specific *experience.* This experience is a vital encounter with Jesus Christ and the Holy Spirit. Although it is necessary to maintain that all Christians must have contact with the Holy Spirit in order to be Christians, the vitality of charismatic experience, whether sporadic or ongoing, affects lives deeply. We should not be too quick to say that this experience is a dimension *added* to the relationship with God shared by all Christians. Rather, we would suggest it is a *fuller* experience of normative Christian existence—one charismatics believe is available to all. Theologically this fullness has far-reaching implications for the gathered worshiping community.

The unfortunate term "full gospel" has been used by Pentecostals and charismatics for years as a way of describing what they believe they have received in their experience, but this term implies that those Christians who rely on the written Word of God alone are somehow missing the mark—that they do not have the whole gospel. We must respect the fact that many charismatics and Pentecostals genuinely feel that those who do not share their *experience* of God are missing out on something good. We also must respect the fact that their experiences are not invalid. At the same time, we must also emphasize

that exclusivity is not of the Holy Spirit—that just as the spiritual gifts themselves differ, so do perceptions and God-given experiences and that it is only by the work of the Holy Spirit in peoples' lives that they are drawn to relationship with God in Jesus Christ in the first place. The gentleness, humility, and unity which are characteristic of the Holy Spirit imply that terms like "full gospel," while well-intended, are inappropriate.

What characteristics of the charismatic experience are shared by all, to one degree or another? These generally cross denominational lines, and most are not unique to charismatics.

First, the Word of God is central to any lasting encounter with God as a Christian, for Christ is the Word of God. The Scriptures are our most reliable reference to this Word today. Charismatics typically have a highly developed personal devotional life which centers on the Word of God and prayer, though these devotions may take on various styles in different church traditions.

Second, openness to the prompting and moving of the Holy Spirit both in oneself and in others is also essential. Scriptural statements like "the Holy Spirit, whom the Father will send in my name, will teach you all things" (John 14:26), and "the anointing you received from him remains in you, and you do not need anyone to teach you. But as his anointing teaches you about all things and as that anointing is real, not counterfeit—just as it has taught you, remain in him" (1 John 2:27), are taken very seriously. While their implications must be nuanced, the point is that charismatics often feel directives from the Holy Spirit which they believe are consistent with the Word of God.

Third, evangelism, a strong desire to reach others with the gospel message on the love of Christ, and a concern for their own personal holiness is characteristic of charismatics.

Fourth, charismatics also see the need for and legitimacy of exercising the power and authority of Christ and his name in intercession, whether in prayer, healing, exorcisms, evangelism, or general Christian concern. These qualities of charismatic life will find their corresponding expression in public charismatic worship. By means of *Lex orandi lex credendi* charismatics interpret the Scriptures, the world, their Lord, and each other through the experience of the Holy Spirit with which they have been blessed by God.

## In Christ, in the Spirit

"Spirit Christology" aptly describes the practical ecclesiology of a charismatic community at worship. Many consider Christology and ecclesiology to be fields of thought that are essentially separate and distinct from one another, but the unity of Christ and the church, is one issue that resounds in charismatic thinking and practice. It also calls for some radical rethinking of ministry in charismatic communities. But this will be discussed later. Foregoing any discussion of "high or low Christology," we simply affirm what seems evident in the Gospel accounts of Jesus' baptism that Christ was dependent upon the Holy Spirit to empower him to live out his ministry on earth as God and man. But there is a very important connection to the church here, for Christ made it clear that he must return to the Father so that the Holy Spirit—the helper, the Paraclete—could come and fill those who were to continue his ministry here on earth.

Theologically speaking, the incarnation is ongoing today. The church is a continuation of Christ, his body in the world, filled and empowered by the Holy Spirit. It is Word-become-flesh just as he is. Just as Mary's simple openness to the Holy Spirit allowed for the conception and birth of Jesus Christ, so the church when she is receptive to the Holy Spirit conceives and brings forth Christ in the world today. There is one difference which is quite obvious to all: But while the church differs radically from Jesus Christ in its lack of perfect obedience and submission to the triune God, it is also radically the same. Its members are members of Christ. Christ himself has made them so. They are new creations conceived, if you will, by the Holy Spirit. These Christlike lives continue only because of the ongoing presence and ministry of the Holy Spirit.

Charismatics are typically very much in tune with the idea of their total and complete dependence on the person of the Holy Spirit. Just as Christ was and is the "anointed one," so the body of Christ continues in this same anointing. One cannot truly be in Christ without the anointing of the Holy Spirit. What this means, and what implications derive from such a statement, are items for discussion among charismatics. One struggle for charismatics, particularly those with "holiness" backgrounds, is the attempt to strike a balance between being and becoming. That is, it is the question of how sanctification relates to salvation and ministry and how

much of the human response to God's initiative can be indulged without lapses into legalism and human traditions which go beyond the Scriptures in an effort to maintain the new law of love. By faith Christians must affirm that they have been made members of Christ as grace is freely bestowed upon us by God, not because of anything they are or do or have done. However, we seldom live the lives we claim we have been given in Christ. Much of the reason for this must relate to the human will and the need daily to live out the death of our baptisms in order to become fully regenerate.

But this too is only made possible by the empowerment of the Holy Spirit. Too often Christians with "holiness" backgrounds interpret the gift of the Holy Spirit as something which makes us holy by giving us the power to keep the commandments. This idea takes a giant leap backwards from the reality of Christ's fulfillment of the law and the prophets. It is also a brand of holiness which very selfishly focuses on one's personal acquisition of holiness rather than the purpose for which holiness has been given. This purpose is ministry—reaching a lost world with the love and healing of Christ. Instead of separating God's people from the world to a point where interaction with non-Christians is tainted with suspicion and antagonism, true holiness frees us from the bondage that prevents us from ministering to others as Christ did. The goal of holiness is not one we consciously aim for, but one we are given. Now we spend our lives growing into the fullness and the reality of this gift, all the while as we are ministering as Christ in the world. The Spirit-filled life is a dichotomy. Christians are becoming what they already are, and they already are what they are still becoming. The Holy Spirit is what makes both realities possible in peoples' lives. God freely gives to humans the holiness he demands of us, and our responses to God's love are as much a part of his initiative as the Incarnation—in fact they *are* Incarnation.

More specifically, in the setting of public charismatic worship, Christ's presence is felt and made manifest. Some have even summed up the phenomenon of charismatic worship with the term "manifest presence." Presence is clearly an issue in charismatic worship. Even in large crowds of worshipers, intimacy with the person of Christ is made evident as people worship in the Spirit.

People, too, must be present in worship. This does not mean simply that people have to be there physically, in the room; it means they must be making themselves fully present to God even as he is making himself really and fully present to them. In short, people must be honest in order to experience true worship. Part of worshiping in spirit and in truth is being truthful with God and ourselves about our own fallenness. One of the functions of God's Word is to confront us with God himself, to humble us by comparison with God's holiness, continually to keep our fallenness before us so that we may throw ourselves upon the mercy of God's grace realizing, like Paul, that no matter how much good we think we are doing, we are still no better than the chief among sinners. Worshiping in spirit and in truth also means that people must make themselves really and fully present to one another, for it is precisely through people that Christ ministers to our needs. This is one way of walking in the light. Christ in others can often illuminate dark portions of our lives that are hidden even to ourselves. Living the light of Christ lovingly in community is an encouragement to everyone to grow in the Lord and keep the body growing. In this way Christ's presence may be felt as profoundly in the kiss of peace as in the Eucharist, and inroads to healing can be made in down-to-earth ways.

Although things are slowly changing, liturgical traditions have historically thought of the culmination of Christ's presence in the worshiping community in terms of *epiklēsis,* the "calling down" of the Holy Spirit during the eucharistic prayer to make Christ present in the Eucharist—in the elements of bread and wine and in the gathered community of worshipers. This understanding has, however, the potential of limiting the idea of the real presence of Christ in worship to a kind of Sunday-morning-eucharistic piety. A similar concept, and just as limiting in its own way, is the Pentecostal tradition of a sort of implicit *epiklēsis* of the Word. At some point in the reading of Scripture, or preaching the speaker (or pastor) reaches a level of anointing where the Word is considered almost to speak for itself; the speaker often becomes very animated, and congregational response is heightened to include uninhibited praise and thanksgiving accompanied in many cases by shouting, clapping, and dancing. Here Christ is felt to have made himself manifest in the spoken Word, and an effort is made by the pastor to discover what is the specific "word" God has for his people that day.

Another practice that is prevalent in many Pente-

costal and holiness traditions is the altar call. This, too, is a point of culmination in terms of presence and the anointing of the Spirit. The practice stems from revival and evangelistic meetings where the goal was to bring into the fold of the church the unbelieving and "backsliders." In Pentecostal and charismatic churches, however, this altar call is often still performed even though there may be few if any unbelievers present. Its purpose has been shifted to the bestowing of the "baptism in the Holy Spirit" (which is seen as a form of Christian initiation) and to ministering to those who wish to rededicate their lives to the Lord.

All three of these practices are, in their proper contexts, fitting and can be positive experiences for the churches in which they occur. But if the presence of Christ or the ministry of the Holy Spirit in the worship of Christians is limited to these three— *epiklēsis* in Eucharist, *"epiklēsis* of the Word," or the altar call—then the full power of Christ's presence in his people is shackled.

For the charismatic, the idea that the Lord inhabits the praises of his people says much. This is because for those who truly are charismatic all of life has become Eucharist; all of life has become a praise response to God's initiative of love. The gathered praises of God's people voiced on Sunday mornings are only symptomatic of a lifelong reality of praise, for by the power of the Holy Spirit every day has become the Lord's day, every day a day of death and resurrection, every day a day of healing and restoration. Charismatic communities can be thought of as "epicletic communities," for the lives of people have become instruments for constantly calling upon the Holy Spirit to come and transform into new creation everything that the believer is, says, does, and touches.

## Praise, Power and Mission

*Epiklēsis* leads naturally to intercession. With intercession we touch on two distinct practices associated with charismatic worship. One is the traditional intercessory prayer time. This may be conducted differently in various churches, but most Christian traditions have in their public worship a time of intercessory prayer. For liturgical charismatics intercession occurs in the prayers of the people prior to Eucharist; for Assembly of God, Pentecostal, or other similar traditions there is typically a time when the pastor leads in intercession for prayer requests that have been made known to him or her, or when people may voice concerns and be prayed for immediately.

The second type of intercession is effected by the praises of God's people. This concept derives both from a theology of liturgical prayer in Christ and from Old Testament models of warfare conducted by giving praise to God. The essence of Christ is God's intercession on behalf of his creation, and the same thing may be said of the nation of Israel in Old Testament times. In ancient Israel and in Christ, God intercedes on behalf of humankind. Both Israel and Christ embodied God's saving presence in the world. This can also be said of the church today. As the Lord inhabits the praises of his people and as human lives become lives of worship and response to God in praise and obedience, intercession takes place. By virtue of their openness to the Holy Spirit, charismatics feel compelled to bring the rest of their life into harmony with their prayer life. God often calls upon his people to bring about the changes he desires. Far from being mere abandonment to the spiritual "high" of the moment, worship calls forth responsibility.

The praises of God's people have intercessory impact on the cosmic level as well. As people respond to God in obedience and open themselves to the transforming power of the Holy Spirit, the powers of evil in the world are exorcised and put on the defensive. Obedience to God is the most powerful weapon the Christian is given, for Satan is the personification of disobedience. Christ in contrast _was and is_ obedience. We who are members of Christ, who daily die to sin and the old order that we may be found in him, have been caught up in Christ's obedience as well. This is not because of what we can do as humans, but it is a gift lovingly bestowed upon us by God, who wishes to make us his children once more. Because Christ _is_ obedience, and because Christ _is_ intercession incarnate, the praises of those who constitute his body in the world are intercessory in nature. More than one Old Testament story relates how the praises of Israel offered to God in obedience resulted in military victory against insurmountable human odds. This is the same power and authority which Christ uses in the lives of his people to transform the world. The enemies faced by those who obey God through their participation in Christ may be conquered by his praises. Malignant spiritual forces that empower disobedient lives are overwhelmed by the opposing forces acting in obedience to God.

Sadly, for many people who call themselves charismatic, power has become an end in itself, and much of the rhetoric of power heard from preachers is little more than self-indulgent emotionalism designed to whip congregations into feeling powerful and then release them into the world to do nothing at all for the kingdom of God.

The whole point of empowerment by the Holy Spirit is it given for the sake of mission. If the worship of the charismatic is the daily life in which Christ is revealed and realized, then evangelism, social action, healing, and spiritual warfare are also going to be daily occurrences. Too often "mission" is depicted as a very limited concept where the emphasis is on verbal evangelism or going to a remote part of the world to reach people for Christ. Unfortunately, when our idea of mission is this small, people are reached with a message, but not necessarily with Christ. The mission of bringing Christ to the world is more than merely speaking the message of the gospel to those who have not heard it before; it is bringing Christ himself to others by touching them as he would touch them. If the only thing the lost are receiving from us in the name of Christ is a message, then they are not really getting the message at all. For charismatics Christ is all and in all. Worship and mission are one.

## The Gifts and the Body

Again, the point of empowerment by the Holy Spirit is mission. This idea must be applied to the gifts of the Spirit as well. The point of spiritual gifts is ministry to and edification of the body so that it can do its job. Spiritual gifts are not given as rewards for having achieved a level of holiness, rather they are bestowed by God in order to help the body move toward the complete holiness to which it is called in Christ. This is why Paul stresses that the gift of tongues, must be made understandable by all, so that all may benefit. Gifts are given _for_ the body, and not just _to_ it.

Unity is an issue in this context as well as in the context of ministry. The uniqueness of the various gifts of the Spirit often overshadows the implied unity which is needed to give them meaning and maximum effect. Often churches in which spiritual gifts are expressed are also plagued by disagreements, divisiveness, and infighting. But such division in the body only means that the gifts are being improperly applied, to the body as a whole. In Romans 12, 1 Corinthians 12, and Ephesians 4 Paul talks about both the gifts of the Spirit and the unity of the body. The gifts make unity necessary in order for maturity to result. Diversity and unity must go together. In fact, our God-given uniqueness should automatically draw us together as we realize that each of us needs what the others in the body have been given by God, and that others need what we have been given. It is only pride which declares that one gift is more important than others, and Paul speaks to this problem as well.

It seems curious, then, that anyone should ever have claimed that one particular gift of the Spirit must be manifested in order to prove that a Christian has received the Holy Spirit. In Romans 12 Paul states "as in one body we have many members, and all the members do not have the same function, so we, though many, are one body in Christ, and individually members one of another. Having gifts that differ according to the grace given to us, let us use them" (vv. 4-6, RSV). It is never implied that all should have any one of the gifts, but rather that grace is given to each person differently. This is even more explicit with Paul's list of rhetorical questions in 1 Corinthians 12, where he asks, "Are all apostles? Are all prophets? Are all teachers? Do all work miracles? Do all possess gifts of healing? do all speak with tongues? Do all interpret?" (vv. 29-30, RSV).

With the emphasis on the plurality of the gifts and the need for all of them for the upbuilding of the body of Christ, there also seems to be a gross inconsistency in most charismatic churches regarding ministry. The position of "pastor," as it is expressed in today's churches, is more a historical phenomenon than a biblical one. The gift of pastoring or shepherding people may or may not occur in a person who is also able to preach or teach or heal, and so on. Likewise it should be recognized that good teachers are not always good counselors or evangelists. Nevertheless, today's pastors in many churches are required to perform all these functions. The assumption seems to be that if one is "anointed enough" to be a pastor, then God will supply all the gifts as they are needed in the ministry. The problem is that the calling of pastor does *not* result from an *amount* of anointing, but from a specific kind of anointing like that experienced by every other member of the body.

Today's charismatic churches suffer greatly from the American phenomena of individualism, self-sufficiency, and lack of commitment beyond lip-service. Many Christians think like Americans before they are inclined to think as Christians. "Freedom" is drummed into us from birth. No one can make us do anything we don't want to, because we are Americans. People can believe whatever they want to believe. Unfortunately for God's work in the world, charismatics are no exception. The result is that we often think that the most important thing about being a Christian is what a person believes. Even conversion to Christianity has become for many merely a decision that has to be made, instead of an entire change of life and orientation which affects everything we do and everyone to whom we relate.

Ministry is the work of the whole body of Christ, not just that of the pastor. People may enter the body of Christ—become Christians—because they are needy, but ultimately there will be work to which these people are called. It is ironic that pastors of charismatic churches end up doing more of everything singlehandedly than pastors of most churches, for here it should be most obvious to people that the whole body needs to minister. Perhaps there is need for greater organization in ministry. For example, ministry teams could be established in which people with different gifts would lead the worship and administer the various ministries of the churches in a more balanced manner. There is no place in the body of Christ for the personality cults that many charismatic or Pentecostal churches have become.

What is perhaps the biggest puzzle, however, is the exclusivity with which many charismatics look upon Christians of denominations or leanings different from their own. Some even go as far as to assume that Christians of other "non-charismatic" denominations are not Christians at all. It is commonplace in churches of this type, to hear on a missions emphasis Sunday that an entire nation has only a handful of Christians, even though the country is 95 percent Roman Catholic.

"There is one body and one Spirit . . . one Lord, one faith, one baptism; one God and Father of all, who is over all and through all and in all" (Eph. 4:4-6). Why then are we not more eager to maintain the unity of the Spirit in the bond of peace? If members of Christ are truly united with their head, Christ himself, then they must be at peace with one another, walking in love, imitating Christ who gave himself. This is not true simply of the local church body, but of the body of Christ in the entire world.

It is no mistake that there is a marked symmetry between the story in Genesis regarding the tower of Babel, the beginning of different languages and the division in humankind, and the story of the day of Pentecost. At Babel, languages were imposed to divide, to keep sinful humans from becoming like God. At Pentecost, languages were given to reunite what had been divided for too long, to restore sinful humans not only to the unity with God that was intended from the beginning, but also to each other. The point is that as long as Christians are divided, they are violating the spirit of prayer displayed in John 17. There Christ links the Holy Spirit directly to unity among all who believe in him when he says, "As you, Father are in me, and I in you, so also may they be in us, that the world may believe that you sent me. The glory which you gave me I have given them, that they may be one, as we are one, I in them and you in me, may they be perfectly one. Then the world will know that you have sent me, and that you loved them as you loved me (vv. 21-23, New English Bible).

Unity in the Body of Christ may declare to the world more effectively that Christ is who he says he is than any sermon. Disunity has no place among those who claim to be charismatic Christians, for the Holy Spirit desires that we be like Christ in our daily dying to ourselves. We who want to know Christ and the power of his resurrection and the sharing of his sufferings by becoming like him in his death have no place judging others.

## Conclusion

For the charismatic Christian, all of life is worship. Because of Christ's gift of redemption and the Holy Spirit who allows us to participate in God himself, we are caught up in a mystery and are empowered to convey this mystery in ministry just as Jesus Christ did in the flesh. He conveys this mystery in our flesh by the Holy Spirit.

Charismatics look forward to the day when all will stand in God's presence and together with angels and archangels and all the company of heaven sing, "Holy, holy, holy Lord, God of power and might, heaven and earth are full of your glory. Hosanna in the highest. Blessed is he that comes in the name of the Lord. Hosanna in the highest!"

Our calling here, however, is to remain steadfast, living in _this_ world and declaring that someday is now, that heaven is here, that we are blessed to be in Christ, who is one with the Father. God's presence is where we are already standing.

Gregory Wilde

# Theologies of Worship Among the Churches

*Christian churches experience both unity and diversity. For example, churches express the unity of their faith in the common confession of the Apostles' Creed, while their adherence to a particular confession, such as the Augsburg Confession, the Westminster Confession, or the Anglican Thirty-Nine Articles, sets them apart from other groups.*

*Unity and diversity also characterize worship. What the churches hold in common is baptism, the proclamation of the Word, and the Service of the Table. How the churches interpret and practice these common elements of worship differ from denomination to denomination. These differences demonstrate the rich variety of insights among Christians about their common heritage of worship. Below are expressions of that variety.*

## 190 • A ROMAN CATHOLIC THEOLOGY OF WORSHIP

*The centerpiece of Roman Catholic theology of worship is the life, death, and resurrection of Jesus Christ, which is celebrated in worship.*

The whole of Christian life takes its meaning from that which alone gives meaning to everything: the incarnation, life, death and resurrection of Christ Jesus. This Paschal Mystery is the basis of any theology of Christian worship that takes the New Testament as its starting point. Until recently, however, Roman Catholic theology, like that of the Reformation churches, has suffered from the assumptions of medieval cosmology and scholastic philosophy. These assumptions continue to have their impact upon the concrete understanding and practice of the sacraments, especially Initiation and the Eucharist. The impact of historical studies upon the understanding of Scripture and other ecclesial documents not only provides for a richer integration of biblical data and subsequent church practice, but also gives strength to ecumenical theology.

### Worship in the New Testament

All salvation history—every event, object, sacred place, theophany, cult—has been assumed into the person of Jesus of Nazareth, the incarnate Word of God. This Anointed One is God's eternal Word (John 1:1, 14); the new creation (2 Cor. 5:17; Gal. 6:15; Rom. 8:19ff.; Rev. 21–22) and the new Adam (1 Cor. 15:45; Rom. 5:14); the new Pasch and its Lamb (1 Cor. 5:7; John 1:29, 36; 19:36; 1 Pet. 1:19; Rev. 5ff.); the new covenant (Matt. 26:28; Mark 14:24; Luke 22:20; Heb. 8–13), the new circumcision (Col. 2:11-12), and the heavenly manna (John 6:30-58; Rev. 2:17); God's temple (John 2:19-22), the new sacrifice, and its priest (Eph. 5:2; Heb. 2:17–3:2; 4:14–10:14); the fulfillment of the Sabbath rest (Col. 2:16-17; Matt. 11:28–12:8; Heb. 3:7–4:11) and the messianic age that was to come (Luke 4:16-21; Acts 2:14-36). "Let no one pass judgment on you in questions of food and drink or with regard to a festival or a new moon or a sabbath. These are only a shadow of what is to come; but the substance belongs to Christ" (Col. 2:16-17, RSV).

The Old Testament temple cult (worship) with its rituals and sacrifices is not replaced by another set of sacrifices and rituals, but by the sacrifice of Christ (Heb. 8–9), that is, the free response of the Word made flesh to the Father by the power of the Spirit. Therefore, the only true worship pleasing to God is the saving life, death and resurrection of Christ. Christian worship is Christ's total response of worship into which we have been grafted by the power of the Spirit to the glory of the Father.

In his letter to the Romans (chapters 6–8) St. Paul

presumes the existence of a rite by which persons are made Christians and comments on the meaning and consequence of baptism. *Being grafted into the death of the Lord by the power of the Spirit,* that is, being conformed to Christ in the activity by which humanity is justified, implies that Christian worship, obedience, and faith are a singular gift which precedes human choice; that is, by the one Spirit, we have been grafted into the perfect act of humanity before God, the perfect act of worship.

This union with the crucified and risen Lord is permanent, since it is Christ the Lord who baptizes in and through the church. Therefore, in the time of the church, Christ cannot be separated from the members of his body. This gift of insertion into Christ conforms the Christian to the triune life of God (because of the divinity of the Word) and to all humanity (because of the human nature of Christ). However, baptism constitutes a specific kind of relation to Christ, that is, a relationship with other Christians in the activity by which God had redeemed the world. In this sense, the church is the sacrament of salvation whose purpose is to proclaim the kingdom of God to the world.

Such insertion into Christ does not preclude the need for the free human decision of worship, obedience, and faith on the part of the baptized according to their ability. However, the weakness of human nature means that we can refuse to worship; and that refusal to worship is sin. Therefore, while the saving act of Christ on the cross is the sufficient source of all salvation, and in baptism that gift of salvation and worship is given with no need for repetition, the gift must be continually accepted and celebrated in human history in the liturgy of the sacraments, especially the celebration of the Sunday Eucharist.

### Liturgy, the Public Worship of the Church

One is baptized into the corporate reality of the church—Christ and his body. This is a worship of the Father by the power of the Spirit. Hence, for St. Paul liturgy is primordially the worship which is the gift of the Christian life. Paul does not use words like liturgy, sacrifice, priest, or offering for anything but the life of Christ and a life lived by that norm. The reality of being in Christ is the norm for Christian gatherings which we call public worship or liturgy (1 Cor. 10–14, Eph. 4, or Gal. 3:27-28).

*Leitougia* describes Zechariah's service in the temple (Luke 1:23), the collection of money for missions and the poor (2 Cor. 9:12), Ephaphroditus' fellowship with Paul (Phil. 2:30), as well as the total response of Christ to the Father by his death on the cross (Heb. 8:6). In other words, personal and communal prayer, service to the world, fellowship and communion with one another are not radically separate activities, but the concrete expressions of the single response of our entire being which has been grafted by the Spirit into the "once-for-all" sacrifice (self-gift) of Christ to God on the cross (Heb. 10:10). The chief rites of the church, that is, the sacraments, are the concrete expressions of the social need to actualize what has been given, that is, to build up the body of Christ into that new temple and liturgy and priesthood, in which sanctuary and offerer and offered are one.

Service to word and sacrament are service to the Word made flesh, the "Christed" Word, never to be separated from humanity in virtue of his humanity, and never separated from the members of his body the church for the sake of proclaiming the kingdom. At liminal moments in life, Christ in his body, the church, speaks the saving word to a given situation. From this viewpoint the sacraments are not contrived or 'merely of ecclesial origin,' for Christ cannot be separated from the body. The sacraments of the church are precisely acts of worship of the body, each mirroring a facet of the mystery of Christ in which the church lives and moves and has its being.

Having been initiated into Christ with the consequence of intimate union with the members of his body, the celebration of the weekly Eucharist is the most intense manner by which Christians call to mind their origin, the sacrifice (total self-offering) of Christ; their present state, being "in Christ," and their future hope, the fulfillment of all things in Christ. This intimate union of Christians with Christ is the basis for the celebration of the Eucharist, where the sacrifice of Christ is offered in *anamnesis.*

In Catholic conviction and theology, *anamnesis* (making memorial) of the sacrifice of Christ is, therefore, not simply a psychological acknowledgment that Christ died on the cross so that individuals may be moved by that death in the present, nor is the Mass a repetition of the sacrifice of Christ on the cross (even though corrupt practices may have led to that conclusion). When the church in the eucharistic Prayer prays: "Father, calling to mind the death your Son endured for our salvation . . . we offer you in thanksgiving this holy and living sacrifice," it does so in the conviction that precisely because it is grafted into Christ's sacrifice, it offers to God that one same sacrifice of praise, and a repetition of the original sacrifice.

When the church baptizes, the baptism needs to be done once because it is Christ who baptizes. In the weekly celebration of the Eucharist, in contrast the church makes memorial of the saving act of God in Christ which is its origin, its judgment, its consolation, and its hope: Christ crucified and risen, from whom it cannot be separated. In response to this unearned gift of salvation, grateful praise is the only response. The Eucharist is the sacrifice of praise, the perfect act of worship, because it is Christ who offers it, the same Christ in whom the church dwells.

As the human sciences indicate, ritual itself is a set of conventions, an organized pattern of signs and gestures which members of a community use to interpret and enact themselves and to transmit to others. Ritual confirms their relation to reality. Such is the case for the chief rites of the church known as the liturgy of the sacraments. They are always subject to reform, as the *Constitution on the Sacred Liturgy*, issued by the Second Vatican Council proclaimed.

Theresa Koernke

## 191 • An Orthodox Theology of Worship

*Orthodox worship emphasizes the mystical presence of Jesus Christ, a presence that is experienced as the infusion of Jesus' life in the believer.*

The church is primarily a worshiping community constituted by the very presence of God's embracing love. Established by the redeeming action of God, sustained and vivified by the Holy Spirit, the church at prayer is always being constituted and actualized as the body of Christ. Through worship in general and the sacraments in particular the faithful experience a personal relationship with God, who infuses his life in them.

Worship is the soul of Orthodoxy and the lead to her mind. Replete with biblical readings, imagery, and expressions, the liturgical texts set forth the church's authentic and living tradition in doxological form. Through the church's worship the faithful are in constant touch with the fundamental truths

of the faith. Worship informs, reforms and transforms the believer. The life and character of Orthodox Christians, in large measure, is shaped and formed by the worship of the church. As a window on God and the created order, worship enlivens faith as well as the social consciousness of the church. It is the great school for Christian living. It is an encounter with the living God. Thus it becomes the agent for the renewal of the human personality and the empowerment for godly praxis.

Orthodox worship is paschal in character and essentially eschatological in spirit. While rehearsing continuously the mighty acts of God in history, Orthodox worship joyously celebrates the kingdom of God already come and already given as the very pledge of salvation through the incarnation, death, resurrection, and ascension of Jesus Christ. The church is always oriented towards the future, towards the age to come, Orthodox Christians draw their identity from Christ and his kingdom. Through worship and especially the sacraments, the faithful participate in the saving acts of Christ and experience continually the presence of the Holy Spirit, who bestows the resurrectional life..

The rituals of the church embody her vision of the new life, confirm the presence of divine grace, and communicate salvation and sanctification. The embodiment of spiritual realities in material forms is rooted in the mystery of the Incarnation and based on the belief of the ultimate redemption and transfiguration of the cosmos.

The essential elements and basic structures of Orthodox worship are rooted in the liturgical practices of the apostolic church. Ritual and text developed gradually over the course of many centuries. The Byzantine or Constantinopolitan Rite constitutes the final unification of liturgical usage of the Orthodox church. This rite represents both the intermingling of cathedral and monastic practices, as well as the remarkable reception, assimilation, and synthesis of the liturgical riches of Eastern Christianity.

The church's order of prayer is made up of many parts, including the following major components: (a) sacramental rites and services and eucharistic liturgies; (b) a daily office; (c) a calendar of feasts and fasts; (d) a lectionary system; and (e) a distinctive arrangement of liturgical space and use of liturgical gestures and art forms.

**Sacraments.** The sacraments prepare the faithful for the future life, but they also make that life real, here and now. The sacraments give the faithful powers by which to draw near to Christ and his kingdom. These powers are dynamic and are meant to be developed by each person. They are neither magical nor mechanical operations. The full effectiveness of the sacramental life is made manifest to a greater or lesser degree by the spiritual awareness, faith, and devoutness of the participants. Salvation is accomplished by God with the collaboration of humankind. This collaboration is called synergy.

The sacraments are founded upon the words and actions of Christ and are, in a particular and special way, a continuation and extension of his saving ministry. In them we encounter Christ and experience as well our true and eternal mode of being.

The Orthodox church recognizes seven sacraments: baptism, chrismation, Eucharist, penance, priesthood, marriage, and anointing of the sick. Among the sacraments, baptism and the Eucharist hold a preeminent position.

Preparation for the kingdom begins with our baptism and chrismation. It is sustained and advanced through the Eucharist. The Eucharist, which lies at the center of the church's life, is her most profound prayer and principal activity. It is at one and the same time both the source and summit of her life. In the Eucharist the church manifests her true nature and is continuously changed from a human community into the body of Christ, the temple of the Holy Spirit, the people of God. The Eucharist imparts life and the life it gives is the life of God.

The Divine Liturgy is the sacred rite by which the Orthodox church celebrates the sacrament of the Eucharist. The Divine Liturgy is structured around two solemn entrances, the reading and exposition of Holy Scripture, the great eucharistic prayer which includes the consecration of the eucharistic elements, and the distribution of Holy Communion. The Orthodox church has three eucharistic liturgies: the Divine Liturgies of St. John Chrysostom and St. Basil, and the Pre-Sanctified Gifts, the latter being celebrated only during the Lenten season and part of Great and Holy Week.

**The Daily Office.** The liturgical cycle moves on four interrelated planes: the day, week, month and year. Its goal is to incorporate the faithful into the mystery of Christ, in order to transform ordinary time into the decisive moment of salvation. Each day has the possibility to be a day of grace and each year to be a year of the Lord.

The daily prayer cycle of worship is comprised of the following services: Vespers, Compline, Midnight, Orthros, and the Hours (First, Third, Sixth and Ninth). Of these, Vespers and Orthros, the evening and morning services respectively, are preeminent.

The services of the daily office have their roots in the devotional practices of the early Christians and in the communal worship of the monastic communities. Each service of the daily office has a particular theme and sometimes a sub-theme, based on some aspect of the Christ-event. The services, and especially the Vespers and Orthros, also contain festal elements which concentrate on particular moments of sacred history and/or commemorate the lives of saints and other memorable events in the life of the church. The services draw attention to God's saving presence in history and the lives of human beings.

**Feasts and Fasts.** The weekly festal cycle begins with the observance of the Lord's Day (Sunday). The principal activity of the church on Sunday is to assemble for the celebration of the Divine Liturgy. Sunday is a day of rejoicing, inasmuch as it constitutes a weekly commemoration of Christ's resurrection.

In continuity with ancient Christian practices, the church, with some exceptions, observes a fast on Wednesdays and Fridays of each week.

The succession of feasts and fasts of the liturgical year vary in importance and are usually divided into two large categories: "movable" and "fixed." The movable are related to the celebration of Pascha (Easter), while the fixed feasts occur on the same date each year. Each feast, whether of universal or local importance, is celebrated with the Divine Liturgy, since the Eucharist constitutes the perpetual festival of the church.

Pascha, which commemorates the resurrection of Christ, is the oldest, most venerable, and preeminent feast of the church. It lies at the very center and heart of the liturgical year. Christ's passion, death, and resurrection constitute the essence of his redemptive work. The solemn celebrations of Holy Week and Pascha are centered on these events.

Holy Week is preceded by a forty-day Lenten period, called the Great Fast. Through a series of special Lenten observances and penitential rites, the church affirms the power and value of repentance and the vitality and truth of the Christian life.

Besides Pascha, the Orthodox festal calendar contains twelve other great feasts which highlight events in the life of Christ and the Theotokos, including: the Annunciation, Christmas, Theophany, Palm Sunday, Ascension, Pentecost, and the Transfiguration.

In addition to the weekly fast and Great Lent, the liturgical year contains other periods and days of fasting. Christmas, for example, is preceded by a period of fasting.

Fasting is integrally related to prayer and almsgiving. It is not understood as a meritorious act, nor as an exercise in self-denial. It is rather an act which gives expression to and affirms the words of the Lord, "man shall not live by bread alone, but by every word that proceeds from the mouth of God" (Matt. 4:4, RSV). Thus, fasting is seen primarily as an increase in spiritual awareness, obedience to and love for God's commandments, a transformation of the passions through self-control, and acts of charity.

The service books used in the worship of the church fall into four main categories. The first category contains only one book, the *Typikon,* which is the book of directives and rubrics which regulate the order of the divine services for each day of the year. The second includes the books which contain the priestly prayers and petitions for all the divine services, the sacraments and other rites. These are the *Euchologion* and its derivatives the *Small Euchologion, Archieratikon, Hieratikon* and *Diakonikon.* The third category includes the books which contain the fixed and variable elements of the daily office. The *Horologion* contains the fixed elements of the daily office and other miscellaneous services and material. The *Great Octoechos* (or *Parakletike*) contains the hymns of the daily services throughout the week and is structured on a recurring cycle of eight weeks and tones. The *Triodion* contains the hymns for the daily office of the Pre-Lenten and Lenten seasons and Great and Holy Week. The *Pentaekostarion* contains the hymns of the daily office for the Paschal period. The *Menaia* is a collection of twelve volumes, one for each month of the year. They contain the divine services for the fixed or immovable feasts of the liturgical year.

The hymns of the Orthodox church are more doctrinal than lyrical in nature. Each hymn is set to one of the eight tones which comprise the musical idiom of the church.

The fourth category includes the books which contain the readings from Holy Scripture. These are the *Evangelion,* which contains the text of the four Gospels arranged in sections and pericopes, in the order in which they are read throughout the year; the *Apostolos,* which contains the pericopes from the Acts and the Epistles for the whole year; and the *Psalter,* which contains the Psalms divided into twenty sections as well as the nine biblical odes; and the *Prophetologion* which once contained the prescribed readings of the Old Testament. These last readings are no longer contained in this separate liturgical book, but have been distributed into one or another of the liturgical books mentioned above which contain the text for a given service with assigned Old Testament readings.

**Liturgical Space.** The traditional church building or temple has several distinctive features and characteristics. Its purpose is to reflect the power and beauty of the transfigured world and to give tangible evidence to the principle of communion. Through the use of domes, arches, and apses, together with a well-defined iconographic scheme, and the use of light and measurements that take into account human proportions and dimensions, the temple manifests the embracing love of God and gives expression to the church's view of man and the world.

The temple is divided into three main sections: the narthex, nave and sanctuary. The *ambon* or pulpit is located in the nave near the sanctuary. The holy Table or Altar is situated in the center of the sanctuary. The sanctuary is slightly raised and is set apart from the nave by the *iconostasis* (or icon screen).

Icons play an important role in the worship of the church and in private personal devotion. The icon depicts persons and events of sacred history and brings before the faithful the transfigured world. The icon teaches and elevates. More importantly, however, it safeguards a proper understanding of the Incarnation and bears witness to the sanctification and transfiguration of the cosmos.

*Alkiviadis C. Calivas*

# 192 • A LUTHERAN THEOLOGY OF WORSHIP

*Lutheran worship calls people to faith again and again through the proclamation of the Gospel through Word and*

_Table. In this service, God acts and the people respond. In form, Lutheran worship is both evangelical and Catholic._

The pattern of Lutheran worship becomes clear—even exciting—once one perceives that its meaning is dependent on a series of paradoxes. Lutherans desire to be _evangelical_ in their worship, to see to it that everything serves to proclaim the Good News of Jesus Christ. They also desire to be _catholic,_ to be part of the great tradition of liturgical acts which unite most Christians through the ages and throughout the world. And they believe that being truly catholic is the surest way to be evangelical and that being evangelical is at the center of being catholic.

Or, to say it in another way, Lutherans fiercely resist making something required in worship which ought to be free, as if God would only be happy if we were to do a certain ceremony in a certain way. The gospel of Christ sets us free from trying to please God with our worship patterns. But Lutherans also fiercely resist making "freedom" required, as if the only truly Christian worship were made up on the spot. Such "freedom" in worship is frequently full of hidden tyrannies—the tyranny of the moment, of current taste, of the leader, or of hidden and unexplored patterns. It is not God who needs our liturgies; _we_ need good rituals, in order to be called to faith again and again. We are also free to be in communion with the Christian past, to use all the good gifts which come down to us through the history of Christian worship.

Indeed, some of those gifts which come down to us are so important that we simply cannot do without them. The _Scripture_ which is read in the church is that collection of writings which Christians came to regard as authoritative and as appointed for public reading. We cannot do without it. And the core events of Lutheran worship are none other than those things which the churches have anciently done and passed on, believing them to be gifts from God: the _washing_ which Christians do in Jesus' name, the _preaching_ of Christ as the meaning of the Scriptures, the announcement of the _forgiveness of sins,_ and the _meal_ which the church has always held as full of Christ's presence and promise. Lutherans believe these very concrete, earthly gifts—water, a book, people speaking God's promise, bread and wine—are the "means of grace," the way God gives us the Holy Spirit, (which is God's own self), and so leads us to faith. We cannot live, we certainly cannot

be Christians, without them. So there is no "Lutheran worship" in which these "means of grace" are not central.

But then we are back to another paradox. _We_ do these things. We receive and enact these traditions. We evangelically criticize and rearrange these traditions. We do these things not to please God but because we need them. But, finally, in and through these things, it is _God_ who acts. Lutherans believe that the principal service done in "the worship service" on Sunday morning is not our service to God but, astoundingly, God's service to us. God speaks in the words we speak and sing to each other, especially as those words are faithful to Christ, who is the meaning of the Scripture. And God acts in the washing and the meal we hold, especially as those concrete acts are faithful to the gospel. These things from Christian tradition are central to Lutheran worship because they have to do with Jesus Christ, because they are under the promise of Christ or are "instituted" by Christ. Indeed, for Lutherans, the trust that God acts through our actions and is encountered in "earthly stuff" is directly related to the trust in God's full presence to the world in the human existence of the man Jesus. The paradoxes of Christian worship correspond to the paradox of the identity of Christ.

The "official" way in which Lutherans express this free tradition or bound freedom, this evangelical catholicism, is found in their confessional definition of the church:

> It is also taught among us that one holy Christian church will be and remain forever. This is the assembly of all believers among whom the gospel is preached in its purity and the holy sacraments are administered according to the gospel. For it is sufficient for the true unity of the Christian church that the gospel be preached in conformity with a pure understanding of it and that the sacraments be administered in accordance with the divine word. It is not necessary for the true unity of the Christian church that ceremonies of human institution should be observed uniformly in all places. (_Augsburg Confession,_ Article VII)

At their best, then, Lutherans love old worship traditions but are always criticizing them, asking how they can better serve the gospel of Christ. Along with the central traditions of the "means of grace," they also receive less important but deeply useful traditions. They observe Sunday as the day of meeting, the day for the Lord's Supper. They keep Easter and Christmas and the old cycles of observances which came to surround these feasts. They mark some saints' days. They use a traditional lectionary. They use the old western texts for the Mass and they chant parts of these liturgical texts. They use traditional vestments for the leaders of the liturgy and for those being baptized. Indeed, this love of tradition can sometimes extend to things that are less useful: Lutherans are frequently conservative, even in the nonessentials, and suspicious of change.

Yet, a Lutheran liturgy may occur with none of these secondary traditions. Lutherans believe that the traditions themselves are simply ways that the gospel was unfolded in a variety of historical circumstances. Such "inculturation" needs to continue. In communities of non-European cultural traditions, for example, patterns of music, leadership, and vesture for worship may be very different. What will make these liturgies "Lutheran" will be the centrality of the "means of grace" in the service and the accent on God's mercy through Christ in the preaching.

Hymn singing is also central. One of the major ways in which the Lutheran reformation welcomed change into medieval liturgical practice was the vigorous encouragement of vernacular singing by all the people in the liturgy. This took place in the sixteenth century, well before *hymns*—as distinct from *psalms*—were welcomed in most other Protestant circles. It is still a key Lutheran characteristic, showing us yet another paradox: Lutheran liturgy gives a serious and important role to the pastor as the leader of the liturgy. But Lutheran liturgy is also seriously intent on the participation of all the people. Even where the old liturgical texts are not communally chanted or where a variety of lay leadership roles have not been encouraged, participation will be strongly evident in the singing of hymns. Hymns are not just a nice thing to do before one gets on to the sermon. They belong to the core of any Lutheran liturgy.

But then we are at the final paradox. Almost all of these things—the centrality of Scripture, baptism and the Lord's Supper; an evangelical recovery of old tradition; an accent on both strong leadership and strong participation; the use of hymnody—are found widely in the Christian world today. They belong to the characteristics of the ecumenical liturgical movement. Thus, while they are tied to the identifying marks of Lutheran worship, they are by no means a Lutheran possession. Indeed, in another sense, there *is* no unique Lutheran worship. The worship of Lutherans is rather a reception by them of the pattern of worship among catholic Christians, together with its ongoing questions and renewals. Lutherans see that pattern, applied nonlegalistically, as the best vehicle for the gospel to which they are devoted. Finally, the best Lutheran worship is not narrowly Lutheran at all, but catholic and evangelical, universally recognized by Christians and always centered in the God who is known in Jesus Christ.

Gordon Lathrop

## 193 ✦ A Reformed Theology of Worship

*Reformed worship focuses on the majesty of God's transcendence and the frailty and sinfulness of humans. Reformed worship captures, proclaims, and enacts the gospel.*

Two somewhat contradictory images might be used to introduce the theology of Reformed worship: the majestic vision and call of Isaiah in the temple (Isa. 6:1-8), and the depiction of the high-pulpited Congregational church in Melville's *Moby Dick*. Disparate as these images might seem at first glance, both, like the depictions of the worship of the redeemed in the book of Revelation, assume the majesty and the transcendence of God, even in the white simplicity of a New England church. The historic trail of Reformed and Presbyterian worship has always emphasized God's majesty and power and the frailty of humanity in approaching him.

Central to Calvin and his followers was the proclamation of the Word. The Word declared through Scripture and even more than for Luther, stood at the center of worship. God was transcendent, all-powerful: viz., the *Westminster Shorter Catechism*: "God is a Spirit, infinite, eternal, and unchangeable, in His being, wisdom, power, holiness, justice, goodness and truth." This is why early Reformed worship, both in Geneva and in Scotland, always had near its beginning a general confession or penitential psalm, to demarcate who the worshiper was, relative to God. This Calvinistic (and Augustinian) sense of the sovereignty of God is the "ground bass" of this worship, and although the awe of Isaiah might be present, it swiftly yields to a search for the divine will expounded in the Word and submits in human obedience to the Word's commission.

As in the book of Revelation, the Word is Jesus Christ, but Reformed worship (partly in reaction to elements of the medieval Mass perceived by Protestants as fanciful) eschewed the pageantry of the Revelation worship scenes, though the Christ was still the center and the source of its word. Church historians speak of the passion of people of the Reformation for sermons, and such was indeed the case. Worship is not to be "creative art," _pace_ much of modern Protestant and Catholic experimentation. To use the metaphor of Dr. D. H. Hislop (_Our Heritage in Public Worship_, Edinburgh, 1935), Reformed worship contains more of the "downward" motif than the "upward," although the Reformed insistence, from Calvin on, for sung psalms and hymns encourages the latter. The "upward" was held in check so that the focus would not be on the worshiper and on his or her feelings, but on him who is worshiped and on his Word to the worshiper.

The classic Reformers, which would include Calvin, Bucer, Oecolampedius, Beza, Farel, Zwingli, and Knox, all sought a weekly celebration of the Lord's Supper, which they viewed as an apostolic custom, as part of regular Sunday morning service. It was expected that Communion would be received in both kinds by all repentant worshipers on each occasion of celebration. This would have radically increased the frequency of individual Communion from the prevailing pre-Reformation custom, in which individuals might commune once a year or even less often. Calvin was thwarted in his hopes, however, by the governing laity in his church, who supported quarterly observance of the Lord's Supper. Similar compromises seem to have been made by other Reformers as well. (When the sacrament was not celebrated, the service ended where the prayer of consecration would have occurred, with a concluding hymn and benediction.) In Reformed churches a common loaf was used, broken for their own portions by the worshipers, and a common cup was passed. Many congregations gathered around tables for the reception of the elements, maintaining the aspect of a covenant meal rather than a sacrifice. These Reformers generally used a set prayer of consecration in the Lord's Supper, and most assumed some form of the Real Presence in the sacrament. Calvin clearly emphasized Jesus' presence through his Word, made apparent at the words of institution, "_This is my body . . . ; this is my blood . . . ._" Zwingli, on the other hand, saw the

Real Presence more in the memory of the gathered community.

The Reformers used prayer books of varying degrees of complexity. The prayers of the invocation at the beginning of the service and the great prayer of intercession further along would be from a prayer book; but a time, usually after the sermon, was allotted for free prayer by the minister. John Knox' _Book of Common Order_ for the Scot's kirk was largely modeled on Calvin's Genevan _Form of Prayers_, but also showed some awareness of the Anglican _Book of Common Prayer_.

Significant differences began to develop by the 17th century between the English-speaking churches of the Reformed family and the Continental ones. The Puritan Revolution in England and Scotland, culminating in the Westminster Assembly (1643) during Cromwell's rule, saw the more liturgical Scots' kirk making common cause with the Puritan party among Anglicans and even some English Congregationalists. The Anglican Puritans were skeptical of liturgy and the English Congregationalists were hostile towards it; but the Scots were political enough to compromise in liturgical matters. This led to significant decline in both liturgy and liturgical theology in Scottish Presbyterianism and its later American forms, as well as in American colonial Puritanism. In similar fashion, the five "evangelical holidays" observed until then fairly uniformly in the various Reformed churches (Christmas, Good Friday, Easter, Ascension, and Pentecost) were neglected or proscribed in the Puritan era in England, Scotland, and America. In contrast, descendants of Continental Reformed churches in North America stayed closer to their Calvinistic roots, although some of their more evangelical offshoots tended to adopt Puritan anti-liturgical practices.

Advent and Lent were generally discouraged by the Reformers as being non-Biblical. Their penitential slant appeared too close to a doctrine of salvation by works and the possibility of pre-Reformation abuses to which such a theology had given rise. Similarly, saints' days and prayers to saints were eliminated by the Reformers, but the church was encouraged in sermons to remember with thanks and emulation the faithful witnesses and teachers across the centuries of church history.

Early Reformed worship encouraged the historic three lessons (Old Testament, Epistle, and Gospel), usually with several sung psalms. While some lectionaries were used, a more primary emphasis gradually became reading and preaching through a complete book at a time (or three books concurrently, as above). Since the preacher might want to spend longer on one passage than another, the result was the decline of set lectionaries, allowing greater expository freedom to the individual minister. Scripture was all inspired by God, of course, but little time was generally spent on the more arcane or tribal portions of books like Leviticus and Numbers. The progression through one or more books of the Bible would be interrupted for church holidays or other occasional major events in the life of the community.

With the reduction in the observance of feasts and seasons came a richer observance of the Lord's Day as a weekly celebration of the Resurrection. No other major Christian tradition can compare with the richness of the use of Sunday by the Reformed, Presbyterian and Puritan traditions which would have decried our modern Sabbath excursions to shopping malls, professional sporting events, and weekend resorts.

Dr. Hughes Oliphant Old, leading contemporary Presbyterian worship scholar, in his superb review of Reformed worship (*Worship That is Reformed According to Scripture* [Atlanta: John Knox Press, 1984]), cites five essentials of this worship: it is according to Scripture; it is in the name of Christ; it is the work of the Holy Spirit; the fruits of the Spirit in holiness and love flow from it, not vice versa; and it edifies or builds up the church.

The Reformed understanding of baptism redeveloped the biblical and Augustinian sense of *covenant*. Baptism is not the final step in sanctification, completing a longer period of catechumenate, as happened at various times in church history and as the Anabaptists wished to restore. Such would put the emphasis on man's holiness, approaching a works salvation, rather than emphasizing God's grace through his covenant in Jesus Christ. Instead, baptism was the initiation into God's covenant family, the church, the body of Christ on earth. Growth in holiness following baptism was expected, from the grace of this covenant relation with Christ. For infants, this would mean later catechetical instruction and public confession of faith prior to welcome to the Lord's Supper, usually near the age of twelve. All the Reformers developed thorough and theologically incisive catechisms for this purpose. Baptism as a covenant of the family of Christ was always to be done in a service of public worship. It was a

continuation of the Old Testament covenant of circumcision. The Holy Spirit was truly given in the baptism, which was seen as a sign and symbol of something present, not something absent. No other anointing, use of oils, etc., was to be included, for nothing more was needed save the biblical pouring of the water of baptism with the use of the biblical Trinitarian formula.

Similarly, the Lord's Supper was seen as a covenant meal, with antecedent covenant meals noted in both Old and New Testaments. The Lord was indeed present with his people in the Supper, but his presence was not narrowly localized in the bread and the wine. Again, the Supper was a covenant sign of his presence, not merely a memory of something or someone absent. It was to be celebrated, however, as simply and directly as Jesus himself did with his disciples. This lessened the sense of mystery of the medieval Mass and the Orthodox liturgies, but it strengthened the sense of the power and presence of the Word known through the Scriptures. The eucharistic motif and the praise motif were found in the sung psalms (or sometimes hymns), and in the great prayer of intercession, where the whole history of salvation—Creation, Fall, Incarnation, and redemption—was remembered. "Holy mysteries" would not, however, be an apt phrase for the Reformed Lord's Supper.

Only baptism and the Lord's Supper were considered sacraments in the Augustinian sense, but the propriety of some other seven sacraments was recognized, and these were retained as ordinances of the church.

One final note can be added concerning trends of the late 20th century, particularly in the Presbyterian Church (USA). Perhaps as a result of the ecumenical movement, perhaps as a search for more beauty and mystery and drama in worship, this denomination has sought to recover or redeem some pre-Reformation practices. These are reflected in theological or practical suggestions or enablements in the "Directory for Worship," adopted in 1989 as part of that church's constitution. There are now six new official but voluntary worship resource books on baptism, the service for the Lord's Day (Eucharist), marriage, funeral services, daily prayer, and special services. Some of the suggested variations from past Reformed tradition include anointing with oil at baptism and confirmation for the sick, the renunciation of evil in the baptismal service, and certain other phraseological or liturgical actions which most of the early leaders of the Reformed tradition had rejected. At the same time the increasing success of special interest groups in the denomination has forced other changes in areas such as language, worship, psalmody, hymnody, and even Scripture to achieve "politically correct" ends, so much so that the 1990 Presbyterian Hymnal has been called "the p.c. P.C. (USA) Hymnal." It is too early to say whether the use of liturgy to achieve politically correct thinking (whether in language or other matters) will succeed or will increase mainstream alienation. Whatever one's political persuasion, however, it is clear that this change in the Presbyterian and Reformed understanding of worship turns it into humanity's tool to achieve humanistic goals and is far distant from the high Reformation concept of worship infused by the Word from the mouth of God.

Stanley Niebruegge

# 194 ✦ An Anglican/Episcopal Theology of Worship

_Anglican worship emphasizes the incarnational and sacramental motifs of the Christian faith. God was embodied in Jesus Christ. Thus, in worship the church incarnates in a visible and tangible form the embodiment of God in Jesus Christ for the salvation of the world._

The Episcopal church, like the other national and regional churches which comprise the Anglican Communion, does not have an official theology of worship. It does have an official practice set forth in _The Book of Common Prayer_ in its various editions from 1549 until the present. Anglican theology of worship is derived from its official liturgical practice.

In _The Book of Common Prayer_ of 1979 the American Episcopal Church says, "The Holy Eucharist, the principal act of Christian worship on the Lord's Day and other major Feasts, and daily Morning and Evening Prayer . . . are the regular services of public worship in this Church." (_Book of Common Prayer_, 13). The pattern of worship there set forth is daily prayer, preferably in common, and the weekly celebration of a service of Word and Sacrament.

Anglican theology has often been described as incarnational or sacramental and this is especially true of its theology of worship which uses the words and actions of an "outward and visible" rite

_The Chi Rho Symbol._ _This ancient symbol is the abbreviation of the word "Christ." In the ancient world, Jesus' name was spelled_ ΧΡΙΣΤΟΣ _in Greek. By taking the first two letters of the word, an abbreviation was made of the name of Jesus. Because the first two letters are Chi_ (X) _and Rho_ (P), _the symbol assumed the name of the first two letters. Numerous examples of the Chi Rho symbol are found in the catacombs and on early coins, lamps, and pottery._

as the symbol and the means of entering into an "inward and spiritual" relationship with God in Christ (_Book of Common Prayer_, 857). Worship is therefore embodied. It is something that we do, not only with our minds but with our entire being. We stand, we sit, we kneel, we bow, we lift our hands and our voices. We look, we listen, we sing, we speak, we remain silent. We smell and we taste. What often appears to be an undue concern with the external aspects of worship by Anglicans, however badly it may be expressed in particular cases, derives from this central theological conviction that it is by entering into the symbolic activity of the liturgy that we are drawn by the action of the Holy Spirit into the very center of the divine mystery, there to lay all that we have and are and hope to be before the throne of grace as members one of another in Jesus Christ.

It is in the coming together of the people of God to hear the Word and celebrate the sacraments that we become the body of Christ, that Christ our Head becomes present in our midst, and that we participate in his paschal victory over death. Christ's promise to be present in the midst of the assembly "where two or three are gathered in my name," (Matt. 18:20, RSV) stands as the primary foundation of worship, which is a corporate activity of the Christian people in which we encounter the living God. Its principal parts include the reading and proclamation of the Word, prayer in Jesus' name, and the celebration of the sacraments, of which baptism and holy Communion are the chief.

In worship we as a gathered community remember the mighty acts of God in Christ by which we are saved, in all their power, virtue, and effect, and offer our lives—"our selves, our souls and bodies" (*Book of Common Prayer,* 336) to God in praise and thanksgiving. This very act contains elements of penitence for sin, acknowledgment of our own unworthiness, and fervent petition and intercession for the needs of all humanity, including ourselves and those we love, for it is only as we are spiritually united to Christ in the power of his risen life and through the activity of the Holy Spirit that we are emboldened to make this response to the divine initiative.

In baptism we are reborn by water and the Spirit to new life as the children of God, passing over with Christ through death to life, and in holy Eucharist the *anamnesis* (commemorative celebration) of the sacrifice of Christ makes us partakers of the benefits of Christ's death and resurrection. As our bodies are fed by the bread and wine over which we have given thanks in obedience to Christ's command, "Do this in remembrance of me," (Luke 22:19; 1 Cor. 11:24), so our souls are nourished by the body and blood of Christ and we are united with him and with one another in his mystical body.

From this theological center, worship moves out to the celebration of this saving mystery in the daily praise of Morning and Evening Prayer and its application to the critical moments in the lives of individual Christians in pastoral offices such as marriage, ministry to the sick, rites of reconciliation, and burial services, drawing every aspect of life into unity with God in Christ through the church, so that all may be offered in union with the perfect self-offering of Christ. It is from this center that we receive, in turn, the power of Christ's victory, so

that we may become what St. Paul declares us to be (1 Cor. 12:27)—the body of Christ in the world.

Leonel E. Mitchell

## 195 ◆ A BAPTIST THEOLOGY OF WORSHIP

*Although Baptists seek to develop a worship rooted in Scripture, they are more inclined to rely on general principles for guiding worship rather than on literalist models of worship based on Scripture texts alone.*

All Baptist theology begins with a consideration of Scripture; this is no less true for a theology of worship. In developing their theology and practice of worship, Baptists have considered numerous Scripture passages related to worship, including Moses' encounter with God in Sinai (Exod. 33–34); Isaiah's call (Isa. 6); Jesus in the synagogue in Nazareth (Luke 4:16-30); Jesus' words to the Samaritan woman (John 4:19-24); the various accounts of the Last Supper (especially 1 Cor. 11:23-26); numerous references to worship in the early church; and even heavenly worship (Rev. 4–5).

Consideration of Scripture has also led Baptists to recognize that true worship involves service in all of life. Whether individual or corporate, correct liturgical practice of any kind cannot substitute for a faith relationship with God through Christ or for right Christian living. Rather, worship is integrally related to both theology and ethics. In general Baptists have sought to follow instead the basic principles regarding worship that they discerned in Scripture. They have done so for both individual and corporate worship, but here we will focus our consideration on the corporate dimension.

Corporate worship means congregational worship. With a concept of the gathered church and an emphasis on the priesthood of all believers, Baptists have stressed that there is no division between clergy and laity. Thus in worship what the congregation does is as important as what the minister does.

Their stress on preaching and the lack of any fixed liturgy have at times undermined congregational participation, but Baptists have tried to compensate in various ways. They have called on laypersons to pray and to lead parts of the service. They have emphasized congregational singing and used responsive reading of Scripture. More recently they have sought to recover the importance of the offering of their gifts and have printed congregational responses and unison prayers in their orders of worship for Sunday morning. The "invitation" to make a profession of faith, which grew out of nineteenth century revivalism, is often used to call the entire congregation to commitment. Baptists are also increasing congregational participation through their recovery of the importance of Communion.

For Baptists, Christian worship is encounter with God. It is dialogue—revelation and response. God engages in self-disclosure to human beings and we respond to that revelation. The revelation can be conveyed through Scripture reading, preaching, hymns, baptism, and Communion. An important aspect of the response is praise and thanksgiving, for in worship we gather to celebrate the mighty acts of God in creation and redemption. The response can be expressed through hymns, offering of gifts, prayers, congregational readings and responses, and time of commitment. Thus worship is always directed toward God. It is an end in and of itself; it is never a means to an end, no matter how worthy that end might be.

Such worship of God must always allow freedom for the movement of God's Spirit. Although worship must be done "decently and in order" and liturgical elements may be freely used, there can be no fixed liturgy. The Spirit must be free to move in the midst of the congregation. This also means that worship should be relatively simple. There should be no complexity that stands between the laity and God, no liturgical obscurity that makes it difficult to experience God's presence. This mysterious sense of God's presence is not under the control of liturgy. God's Spirit moves where it will, whether liturgical elements are freely used or not used. The mystery simply happens when the congregation is genuinely engaged in the worship of God.

Not only is worship directed toward God and open to the movement of the Spirit, it is also Christocentric. Christ is the focus of worship because Christ is the central expression of God's creative and redemptive action. Thus a major aspect of worship is proclaiming the Good News of God's action in Jesus Christ. Preaching is such an important element in worship because of this emphasis on proclaiming the Good News. The Good News in Christ provides the Christian hope for the future and the assurance of God's grace and presence for every need in the present.

Communion also focuses on the Good News in Jesus Christ. In response to the revivalistic emphasis

in the nineteenth century, for a period of time Baptist placed little emphasis on Communion. But through much of their history it has had an important place, and many churches are restoring its important role in worship. Communion proclaims God's action in Christ in the past. It proclaims the future hope of Christ's return. It proclaims Christ's presence in the hearts and minds of the gathered community in the present. It is a clear expression of Christian faith, hope, and love.

In conclusion, corporate worship is the congregation's communal encounter with God in which the people respond together to God's creative and redemptive action most fully revealed in Jesus Christ. Through this encounter God mysteriously makes available to the gathered community the reality of his salvation. The Baptist congregation worships, then, to hear of God's action on their behalf and to respond out of the depths of their own being, they worship to sense the mystery of God's presence in the midst of his people, and they worship to experience the power of God's grace and to be made whole.

G. Thomas Halbrooks

## 196 • AN ANABAPTIST THEOLOGY OF WORSHIP

_Anabaptists see the church as a radical body of believing disciples. Worship arises out of this community of faith and is simple and egalitarian. It recounts God's story of redeeming love through the ongoing experience of the community of faith._

Worship says _In the beginning God_ . . . and worship says, _Yes, God's actions are working out in our history for good._ Worship respects and recognizes the various vitalities by which we enjoy life, the various values that govern it, and the various visions which transform it. Anabaptist worshipers respond to such revelations. Worship is therefore the interaction of the revelation of God and the response of the people who follow Jesus. We bring the phenomena of our living into the phenomenon of the living Jesus. We carry our various realities in into the presence of God.

Anabaptists have a faith-vision that calls forth unique worship patterns. The Anabaptist vision is almost five hundred years old and includes Mennonites, Brethren, and various Baptist and Congregationalists with sixteenth-century Anabaptist theological roots. The faith components may look very similar to those of other faith families, but what distinguishes Anabaptism is a combination and a configuration of "ABC's":

A. Authority of Scriptures, not as a creed or code but as our stories and story to be believed and obeyed—that which forms and expresses our identity;
B. Baptism of believers (not infants) whereby one's own faith in God, much like one's love for another, evokes a public commitment;
C. Church as community of the transformed, a working out with others who are also a part of the body of Christ, thus a rejection of rugged individualism;
D. Discipleship of life, following Christ in imitation and participation;
E. Ethic of love in all relationships, an agape stance affirming even adversaries, seeking justice, building peace, reconciling relationships, confronting waste, living simply, honoring ecology, giving relief, sharing faith.

In worship Anabaptists are consciously and communally responding to God. The purpose of worship is, all at once expressing gratitude to God and renewing, reaffirming, and reforming all aspects of life according to the ABC's of faith.

## Worship and Liturgy

What does Anabaptist worship include and what does it look like? We've already alluded to the two necessary ingredients of divine expression and human experience—revelation and response. Simply put, worship is being present with Presence. We now examine three things that make liturgy happen in Anabaptist worship: experience, expression and environment.

**The Experiences We Have.** Worship includes actual *settings:* It is involvement, taking place in the active and concrete here and now: a blessing for this meal, going to church, a dedication for this child, a consideration of this question and that issue.

Worship has to do with wholeness of our various *separations* and *sectionings.* God gives us his peace, bringing harmony to our various dissonances. The biblical metaphor of the potter is telling: God taking clay and answering our song, "Spirit of the Living God, fall fresh on me, . . . mold me,

make me, . . . fill me, use me." Biblical precedents include the Corinthians' love feast fiasco, Jacob's wrestling with the Lord's angel, Mary's new vocation, Peter's awareness that Cornelius is "in." One cannot discard weekday and have weekend, or this pain and have that promise, or that brother and have this sister. Each fragment has a larger view, a larger setting, a greater dimension.

Worship has to do with all of our *struggles;* it takes them all seriously. Honest worship pays attention to our human conflicts; they are "tools at hand." Life-stages and life-developments are the stuff that make for worship. Anabaptist liturgy puts struggle where it belongs—in worship.

**The Expressions We Make.** With what symbols shall we tell the story—to us, to others, to God? *Language* comes in word and deed, helping us to praise, confess, commit, speak, and listen. In worship language is always inclusive. *Music* both glorifies God and builds the body of Christ through expression in thought and feeling. It uses a variety of styles. *Actions* can be natural and spontaneous as well as planned, as in the examples of drama and dance. Silence also speaks: it is the still small voice of quietness. *Preaching* is allowing the Scriptures and the sermon to address us and then to respond to the living God. The sermon also allows for congregational preaching expressing itself as incarnation into today's life and, therefore, as redemptive sign and event.

**The Environment We Need.** The preacher and liturgists do not need "to be up there." The best liturgical aid is people—seated in a semicircle allowing for a sense of community and communication. Visual aids (banners, paintings, free standing cross, an open Bible, a candle, a globe, a Communion cup) can powerfully suggest, "We now have met to worship thee." Biblical liturgy doesn't occur only in the meetinghouse. Worshipers meet also in Sunday school rooms and in living rooms. A lit candle on the table in business and committee meetings reminds us of our purpose.

## Worship and Rituals

The previous section shows that Anabaptist liturgies include the entire range of human experience. Here we see that all of life's pilgrimage is the stuff of ritual performance—the locus where God is met. Assembling with others on the first day of the week is a repeated action and sign of our worship of God.

Each Sunday service proclaims the giving of Christ anew. Sunday worship, like all repeated events, can deepen both revelation and response. Special acts of worship that signify God's self-giving, and our self-giving in return, are properly called sacraments. Anabaptists are suspicious of this word, however, because of the track record in which sacred things have been exploited—in instances in church history when sacraments have become cultic objects. In Anabaptist worship ordinance has replaced sacrament, a radical and far-reaching switch. Ordinances, rites and rituals are troublesome words for Anabaptists. "Performances" that God's people enjoy might be better received.

**Baptism** is initiation into the body of Christ, not only by believing in Jesus but in being part of the church. It marks the beginning of a pilgrimage of a lifelong journey of worship and witness. It is ordination into co-ministry with Jesus. It symbolizes cleansing and new life, an outward sign of new birth and new creation. Anabaptists practice believer's baptism (sometimes referred to as adult baptism)—an experience akin to marriage in that baptism is a service of two parties who have consciously fallen in love with the "ring" (the water) as sign and seal of that love relation.

**The Lord's Supper** engages in living memory; it implies being present for a living memorial. It promises that something more is coming, particularly as one opens oneself to "thy kingdom come, thy will be done." The future is present. Christ is present in the *taking* of the bread, which includes *our* "taking." Our openness to Christ, our attitude of acceptance whereby we hunger and thirst after the brooks of eternal life, make this time of taking a junction where we meet God and where we receive drink that satisfies and food that nourishes. If we eat and drink "all of it," we accept Christ's joy and pain, fulfillment and searching. We accept Christ's continued purposes for the world, and we enlist in that mission. We fine tune our motivation; we receive manna to carry on.

**Other Performances** include ordination, healing, reconciliation, marriage, death, agape meals, foot or hand washing, and the various markings (dedication service of a new home, a high school graduation, mortgage burnings, child dedications, and commissioning of teachers and officers).

### Worship and Living

It's a cliché in church bulletins—"Enter to Worship . . . Depart to Serve"—but a cliché rich in meaning for Anabaptists. Biblical, Anabaptist worship begins at church but does not end there; it pushes us into witness and work and then back again to worship where we can be revived. Liturgy means the work of the people (not, as commonly believed the assembling of the saints). What goes on in weekdays follows what goes on in their weekends—the rhythm of the church gathered and the church scattered. Accordingly, Anabaptist worship underscores the biblical learning that believers bring to the world. For Paul, liturgical worship was an exercise of work and witness (taking offerings to Jerusalem, a hoped-for missionary trip to Spain, witness to the high officials of government) (cf. Rom.15:9, 24-29, where the actual word "liturgy" is used). Later he designates as worship whatever we do as unto the Lord (1 Cor. 10:31).

### Conclusion

Anabaptist faith-vision and Anabaptist worship-practice go together. The faith of a Christian as a disciple—can be analogized as a *caravan,* a people "banded together to make common cause in seeking a common destination," whose existence is in a continual becoming, a following of its Lord on the way toward the kingdom. This vision is in contrast to a *commissary,* which has existence in its own being in maintaining its divinely given essence. The faith of *shalom*—God uniting and integrating holistically all the details of life's pilgrimages—is found in human experiences, expressions, environments, and life's repeated events. A life of faith is response to the living Word, to the Bible as central, not so much as a message-book but a voice-book, speaking not only *about* worship but also *as* worship, giving voice to the presence of the living God. Anabaptists are *at* worship as they meditate on its words—from Genesis to Revelation—experiencing the One who is the Way, the Truth, and the Life.

LeRoy E. Kennel

## 197 • A QUAKER THEOLOGY OF WORSHIP

*The roots of the traditional Quaker theology of worship are found in George Fox's experience of the Inner Light—that sense of the divine and direct working of Christ in the soul. He came to believe and subsequently taught that the same*

*experience is available to all. The purpose of worship, there-*
*fore, is to wait in silence and then respond to the presence*
*and power of God.*

The development of the Quaker theology of worship was driven by a deep dissatisfaction with the
mainstream of the Reformation, especially the
Puritan-dominated established Church of England.
They felt that the Reformers failed to properly emphasize the Spirit's freedom of movement and the
believers' dependence on the Spirit in worship.
They also accused the established church of ignoring or denying the priesthood of all believers in the
practice of worship and limiting it by the clergy's
central role in worship.

The Richmond Declaration of Faith (1887) captures the theology of traditional Quaker worship
when it declares that "worship is the adoring response of the heart and mind to the influence of the
Spirit of God. It stands neither in forms nor in the
formal disuse of forms; it may be without words as
well as with them, but it must be in spirit and in
truth."

Traditional Quaker worship emphasizes that true
worship takes place only when the Spirit of God
moves the hearts of those who are gathered for
worship and that silence, not planning, is one of the
surest means of guaranteeing the Spirit's freedom. It
emphasizes a firsthand encounter of the worshiper
with God in the context of a strong corporate mysticism. Privately or individually God speaks to the
community through individuals to whom he has
spoken.

The following statements outline the traditional
Quaker theology of worship:

1. Christ is present by his Spirit in every Christian
   in the gathered community.
2. The purpose of worship is for the gathered
   community to open itself, individually and
   collectively, to the presence of Christ through
   his Spirit.
3. The activity of worship is waiting, in disciplined, expectant silence, for the moving of
   the Spirit and then responding inwardly or
   with spoken ministry or prayer as the Spirit
   directs.
4. Christ's presence by the Spirit requires no mediation, so all externals, including words and
   forms, and all human activity are secondary.

Worship is totally dependent on divine activity
and not on human preparation. There is no
formal leadership.

5. The Spirit can speak to any or all in the gathered community. Therefore there are no distinctions between laity and clergy, male and
   female, slave and free.
6. God can speak through any or all in the gathered community. Since all—as believer
   priests—may minister to one another, there is
   no need for clergy.
7. The only essential baptism is the inward baptism of the Spirit; the only essential communion is spiritual communion. Christ did not
   intend that the sacraments found in the New
   Testament continue after his death.
8. Only spontaneous music is permitted—a portion of a psalm or a sung concern or word of
   witness. Quakers held that there was no New
   Testament example or teaching for "artificial
   musick."

Today Quaker worship assumes various forms,
many of which appear to be at variance with traditional Quaker theology. However, Francis Hall insists that genuine Quaker worship, regardless of its
form, continues to unite around the following:

1. Believers gather to worship God in spirit and
   in truth to sense the presence of and respond
   to the moving of the Spirit of God.
2. Jesus Christ is honored in worship. Worship
   arises from the Christ event and from Christ's
   role as the supreme revealer of the nature of
   God and transmitter of the Spirit of God.
3. True worship occurs when the Spirit of God
   moves worshipers' hearts.
4. Quaker worship is not bound by human
   forms. The Spirit is free, and hearts that open
   to the Spirit in worship will open also to the
   Spirit's freedom.
5. Silence is a genuine and important means of
   becoming open to God and one of the surest
   means of guaranteeing the freedom of the
   Spirit. So it is a part of Quaker worship—absolutely central for some, and at least an element
   in all genuine Quaker worship (Text from Francis B. Hall, ed., *Quaker Worship in North*

_America_ [Richmond, Ind: Friends United Press, 1978]).

Warren Ediger

## 198 ✦ A WESLEYAN THEOLOGY OF WORSHIP

_Wesleyan liturgical theology is deeply concerned to define worship as more than public acts. Worship has to do with all of life, with relationships, and with vocations. In deed and thought believers continually act out their relationship to Christ._

Christianity, as John Wesley describes it, is the method of worshiping God which has been revealed to us by Jesus Christ. Christ makes known the profusion of God's love for us, and faith ("the eyes of the newborn soul") apprehends this love. Faith involves us in a life of worship as we are drawn to adore and to imitate the God who has loved us. Thus "worship," in the Wesleyan tradition, encompasses not only public rituals and private devotions, but the Christian life in all its fullness.

Worship is much more than the simple awareness of God. In its most general sense, worship is adoration, the loving contemplation of God's holiness. Worship, says Wesley, brings us into the presence of God. Through it we "find such a near approach [to God] as cannot be expressed. [We] see him, as it were, face to face . . ." (_The Works of the Rev. John Wesley,_ vol. 1 [Grand Rapids: Baker Book House, 1979] 514. Subsequent references will be to _Works._) In the presence of this God we learn "to love him, to delight in him, to desire him, with all our heart and mind and soul and strength; to imitate him we love by purifying ourselves, . . . and to obey him whom we love . . . both in thought, and word, and work." (_Works,_ vol. 1, 544).

This sense of adoration and devotion before the presence of God found expression in the singing that characterized Methodist worship from its earliest days. Charles Wesley devoted his theological energies to setting Methodist doctrine to poetry and melody.

Worship invokes in the worshiper the whole drama of redemption including the call to repentance, the joy of knowing God as forgiving God, and the challenge of imitating Christ through holy living.

As a priest in the Church of England, Wesley was familiar with and generally at home in highly ritual-

ized forms of worship. As a young missionary to the English settlement at Savannah, Georgia, he pored over new translations of Eastern Orthodox liturgical texts and revised the Anglican prayer book based on his research. In the heyday of the Methodist revival, he advised his followers to attend Communion as often as possible, preferably daily (he personally received Communion 5 days a week on the average). He recommended the Anglican prayer book for personal devotions and provided a revised edition of it for American Methodists—i.e., the _Sunday Service._

Wesley distinguishes between the outward form of worship and its inward power, neither of which can be neglected. He criticizes nominal Christians for observing the forms of worship while neglecting the power of God's grace at work in them. To these he says "true religion is so far from consisting in forms of worship." (_Works,_ vol. 1, 219).

At the same time he criticizes believers who insist that "spiritual worship" makes the form of worship a matter of indifference and who ask "will it not suffice to worship God, who is a Spirit with the spirit of our minds?" (_Works,_ vol. 1, 532). To these Wesley insists that worship must engage our whole person and therefore, must include a disciplined use of the "means of grace," including public and private prayer, the Lord's Supper, Scripture reading, fasting, and small group nurture. Although forms and rituals can be abused, "let the abuse be taken way and the use remain. Now use all outward things; but use them with a constant eye to the renewal of your soul in righteousness and true holiness." (_Works,_ vol. 1, 545).

This unity of inward power and outward form enables Wesley to maintain a theology of worship which straddles the divide between a liturgical formality and formless subjectivism. Worship centers on the objective realities of God's presence and at the same time it draws the heart of the believer into a transforming relationship.

Wesley's discussion of the specific elements of worship indicates a thorough and consistent reinterpretation of liturgical forms in keeping with his theological commitment of visible holiness in believers.

Baptism represents the ordinary means by which we are initiated into the life of Christ. In speaking of infant baptism Wesley teaches a mild form of baptismal regeneration: "By baptism we are admitted into the Church, and consequently made members of Christ, its Head . . . By water then, as a means, the water of baptism, we are regenerated or born again." (*Works*, "A Treatise On Baptism," in vol. 10, 190–2).

Yet Wesley adapts this Anglican view to his evangelical commitments. He concludes, for instance, that although baptism is the ordinary means of initiation into the life of Christ, it is not necessary to salvation: "If it were, every Quaker must be damned which I can in no wise believe." (*Works*, vol. 26, ed. Frank Baker [Oxford: Clarendon Press, *c*. 1975], 36). In preaching to nominal Christians Wesley seems to dispense with baptismal objectivity altogether, chastening his listeners for assuming that baptism assures their salvation: "Lean no more on the staff of that broken reed, that ye were born again in baptism. Who denies that you were then made children of God . . . But notwithstanding this ye are now children of the devil." (*Works*, vol. 1, 430). Wesley calls those who have lived away their baptismal identity to rebirth in the Spirit.

Wesley's teaching on the Eucharist begins with a strong emphasis on the real presence of Christ. "He will meet me there, because he has promised so to do? I do expect that he will fulfil His word, that he will meet and bless me in this way." (*Poetical Works*, III, 203–4). We can come to the Lord's Table in the confidence that Christ will meet us there.

So confident was Wesley in Christ's presence that he speaks of the converting power of the Eucharist. "Ye are the witnesses. For many present know, the very beginning of your conversion to God (perhaps, in some, the first deep conviction) was wrought at the Lord's Supper." (*Journal*, vol. 2, ed., Nehemiah Curnock [London: Charles H. Kelly, n.d.], 360–61). Those who seek God may find him revealed to them here. The Lord's Supper stands as the chief means by which believers receive the grace of Christ and remained, for Wesley, an indispensable element in Christian living.

Wesley's one real innovation in worship was his Covenant Service which became an annual practice in the Methodist Societies after 1755. Wesley based his liturgy on a seventeenth-century Puritan service. The Covenant Service's prayers, responses, and solemn vows emphasized his vigorous program of moral and spiritual discipline.

For most of the eighteenth century, the Methodist Societies remained within the Anglican church. Therefore, in practice, Methodist worship rarely included sacramental elements. Methodists were instructed to receive the sacraments at their parish

churches, whereas the Methodist chapels were reserved for singing and preaching. As the Societies gained independence from the Church of England, and finally broke with it altogether (1795), these limitations came to shape Methodist worship especially in England. The tensions in Wesley's sacramental-evangelicalism generally relaxed in favor of more informal worship styles. These tendencies were only heightened by the independent culture of the North American frontier. In this century the influences of the student movement and liturgical renewal movement have led to a resurgence of liturgical formality and sacramental practice in Methodism.

*Mark Horst*

## 199 ◆ An African-American Theology of Worship

*African-American theology of worship arises out of a deep sense of oppression and a high anticipation of liberation. In worship, African-Americans experience the redeeming work of Jesus Christ, which liberates them from sin and the power of the Evil One.*

——————— **Introduction** ———————

When African-American Christians gather for worship, regardless of denominations, they share a mutual understanding of God's initiative in the call to worship. Although their experiences of God and life as a "marginalized" community of faith are varied, they share common needs and common perspectives on life. Worshipers come just as they are, in response to God's love and grace, to praise God, to offer thanks, to seek forgiveness and wholeness, and to probe the depths of God's divine mystery in an oppressive society. Worshipers come, well aware of the liberating power of God, seeking to be empowered by the grace of God, as their personhood is affirmed. The gathered redeemed fellowship— the *koinonia*—is the worshiping arena of the resurrected community of hope which will scatter as the *diakonia* empowered by the Holy Spirit to engage in mission and ministry in the world.

African-American Christians are by choice members of diverse communities of faith. There are historical African-American (or black) Protestant denominations and African-American congregations in Euro-American denominations. There are

Roman Catholics, as well as nondenominational bodies, and innumerable sects, small and large. The worship styles vary within and between denominations, so that African-American worshipers defy stereotypical descriptions of their styles of worship.

The theology of worship set forth here is based on a common history of a people who, having been called by many names, have chosen to call themselves "African-Americans." This name allows a people socially and politically marginalized by the dominant culture in America to claim two heritages: African and American.

African-Americans in worship proclaim a faith heritage which is a synthesis of African, African-American, and Judeo-Christian traditions. As sojourners, they have entered God's story at varying points in their lives, and they can together share their stories and God's story through the lens of familiar love relationships. The gathering itself bespeaks the human need to relate, understand, and interact in an environment where common needs, joys, struggles, and hopes can be shared. Corporate worship allows opportunities for personal and communal transformations to occur. The environment of worship is also conducive to the sharing of personal testimonies of transforming moments which might have occurred outside of worship.

Experiences of God in life, and meanings applied as a result of experiences, shape the lives of individuals and also help shape forms and styles of ritual action. Encounters with God, perceptions, beliefs, and attitudes which evoke responses are determined by the cultural context in which the faith is experienced. A basic theology of worship will necessarily explore the fact that God freely encounters humans contextually, wherever they are in the world. Enabled by the Holy Spirit, the human spirit is freed and opened to receive and objectify realities. In this way, people of African descent are able to know God implicitly before knowing about God.

For Africans in America during the horrid period of enforced slavery in a strange and alien land, the freedom to consciously transcend their finite existence was the only freedom that was naturally available to them. While functioning under the constraints of "bonded-servants-by-law," slaves were free to experience the power, love, and grace of a liberating God. The oral folk method of creating, re-creating, and disseminating songs provided for the slaves a means of shaping and recording

basic theological tenets unique to the African American experience.

## Foundations for Theological Reflections

It is necessary to set forth some foundational aspects of the African religious heritage in order to understand an African-American theology of worship. First and foremost, there is no monolithic African culture. Nor is there one established canon of religious beliefs and ritual practices for the whole continent of Africa. There are a plethora of societies, customs, cultures, languages, forms of social, political, economic, and religious institutions, which account for separate and distinct societal identities. Many societies had well-developed institutional structures and kingdoms dating back to the beginning of civilization. In spite of the diversity, however, there are shared fundamental worldviews which shape a basis understanding of life, ideals, virtues, symbols, modes of expression, and ritual actions, which give African peoples a common sense of identity. Basic primal worldviews are known to exist and remain operative as new worldviews and cultures emerge and take root.

Most African societies share the worldview that humans live in a religious universe. Thus, nature, natural phenomena, physical objects, and the whole of life are associated with acts of God. (See John S. Mbiti, *Concepts of God in Africa* [New York: Praeger, 1970], chapters 8–13.) Life is viewed holistically, and this perception is distorted if sacred and secular are compartmentalized. African ontology affirms a state of interrelated belongingness. One is considered fully human and whole in so far as one *BELONGS* to the divinely created universe, and lives in solidarity with, and akin to all that comprises the cosmos.

The North African heritage includes direct involvement in the shaping of Judeo-Christian theologies. Africans were vicariously involved from the time that Abraham came out of Ur and settled in Egypt through the time when the Christian church wrestled with faith statements. Africans were directly involved in the formulation of theological statements and creeds. Nine North Africans who were prominent theological leaders in these struggles included: Clement, Origen, Tertullian, Cyprian, Dionysius, Athanasius, Didymus, Augustine, and Cyril of Alexandria.

Many of the Africans who ultimately helped shape

the theology of African-American worship were enslaved and brought largely from the west coast of Africa, from northern Senegal to the southern part of Angola. Prevailing primal worldviews evident in African-American theologies of worship can be summarized as follows:

- God created an orderly world, and is dynamically involved in on-going creation throughout the world.
- Human beings are part of God's creation, and they are therefore divinely linked to, related to, and involved with all of creation. This cosmological perspective undergirds an understanding of beingness (ontology) which is relational and communal.
- Communal solidarity is expressed in terms of kinship in an extended family. This involves an "active" relationship with both the living and the "living dead" or those who have died and are in the living memory of the community. This concept is often explained as a vertical and horizontal community where those that live on earth are in communion with the saints.
- An understanding of the holistic "sacred cosmos" which is relevant for individual and communal life must be internalized if one is to find meaning and purpose in life.
- "Cosmic rhythm" is an embodiment of divine order, harmony, and permanence, and is the foundation for the "rhythm of life."
- Time is relative and cyclical, and is governed by the past and a broad understanding of the present. These two basic dimensions of time (past and present) are connected by a rhythm of natural phenomena which includes events which have occurred, and those which are taking place now and will occur immediately. John S. Mbiti is helpful in his observation that for the African "The Future is virtually non-existent as actual time, apart from the relatively short projection of the present up to two years hence." (John S. Mbiti, *African Religions and Philosophy* [New York: Anchor Doubleday, 1970], 27–28). Two Shahali terms, *Sas* and *Zamani,* are proposed by Mbiti to avoid the English linear conception of time as past, present and future. *Sasa,* the period of immediate concern for African peoples, has a sense of immediacy and nearness of time. Future events are likely to occur within the inevitable rhythm of nature, but can-

not constitute measurable time. *Zamani,* which encompasses an unlimited past, is not confined to the English conception of past since *Zamani* has its own past and also involves the present and an immediate future.

- Space and time are closely related experiential concepts in which the same word often used in either context to mean virtually the same thing. Space, like time, is relative, and must be experienced in order for there to be any indication of meaning. Just as *Samsa* includes contemporary life which people experience, space is determined by what is geographically near. Land, therefore, is sacred to African peoples, since it is the source of their existence and mystically binds them to those now dead and buried in the earth.

Africans generally understand and affirm the sacredness of God's creation, the harmonious structure of the cosmos, and the fundamental need for human wholeness. Ritual action is one of the ways to relate holistically to God and to God's world. Modalities of the sacred and of interrelational existence are revealed through the natural world and through cosmic rhythms which are called upon in rituals. In worship the divine connectedness is "activated" through symbols and symbolism. For instance, water, like the land, symbolizes the origin and sustenance of life. Water is often understood as synonymous with God the Creator whose presence and continual creation is evidenced in large bodies of water, flowing streams, and rain. Water is also symbolic of a means of death and new life. Contact with water signifies a return or re-incorporation of finite life into the creation process. Water is used in many rituals, especially rites of passage, to symbolize cosmical relatedness, death of the old, re-creation, regeneration, and purification. (see Melva Wilson Costen, "Roots of Afro-American Baptismal Practices," *Journal of the Interdenominational Center* 14 [Fall 1986–Spring 1987]: 23–42)

For African peoples, human responses through ritual actions are necessary in order to establish and maintain an ontological balance in a world fraught with negative and evil forces. Responses may be formal or informal, spontaneous or regularized, personal or communal. Certain divinely gifted individuals can determine particular forms of ritual action necessary at given "imbalances" or periods in the life of a community. These persons are identified by the community as "diviners" or "intermediaries," and are called upon to "intervene or behalf of the community," and to facilitate contact with divine spirits.

Worship is generally expressed vocally and physically rather than meditationally (Mbiti, _African Religions and Philosophy,_ 75). The corporate worship of God is more experiential than rationalistic, focusing upon the communal sharing of reality, rather than simply transmitting information. In traditional African religions, God's existence is not determined merely by a series of ideas which someone passes on to others. God exists simply because God can be experienced in all of creation. This is best expressed in an Ashanti proverb: "no one shows a child the Supreme Being," which means in essence that even children know God as if by instinct (Ibid., 38).

Since worship is basically a contextual-experiential response to the divine, symbols and symbolic forms common to the community provide the most expressive means of communication. Through symbols which often mirror or re-present sounds and movement in the natural environment, the community is able to express what might be difficult to verbalize. Various forms and styles of music, physical movement (dance), gestures, and familial unity are common symbols of African peoples. Elements of nature such as water, mountains, trees, large rocks, and certain animal life are also symbols of God's divine presence in the world. Just as in other traditions, symbols are born, adapted, and then die as new symbols emerge.

These, then are the theological foundations that were well ingrained in African peoples in diaspora as they continue their journey in God's story through Jesus the Christ.

## ───── Exposure to Christianity ─────

According to extant records, some Africans who would ultimately shape African-American theology were exposed to Christianity prior to their forced arrival in colonial America. Initial exposure was often limited to hasty baptisms in Africa in order to accommodate European laws regarding the capturing and enslaving of humans by other humans. "Emergency" baptisms are known to have occurred immediately before enslaved Africans were herded as cargo onto ships bound for the new colonies across the Atlantic Ocean.

Parents of the first African child baptized on American soil under the authority of the Church of England were an enslaved African couple "accidentally" brought to Jamestown, Virginia in 1619. This was the beginning of the history of reluctant attempts by Euro-Americans to Christianize slaves while holding them in bondage. This history of Christian paradoxes provides substantial evidence of the need for African-Americans to shape a theology free from hypocrisy.

The majority of Africans in colonial America were forced to remain bonded servants under a series of laws enacted by Euro-Americans. With the exception of a few single baptisms recorded in 1624 and 1641, the largest group of (20 black) congregants during this period were hardly noticed by recorders of liturgical history. There is sufficient documentation to ascertain that colonists were not in agreement as to the mental and spiritual capacity of African peoples. For those who held a low opinion of the African capacity to understanding Christian tenets, the tendency was to discourage the Christianization of slaves. Some planters suggested that those who became Christians became "sassy" and unmanageable.

Heated controversies hastened positive and negative theological conclusions among Christian Euro-American individuals and institutions in response to questions about the evangelization of slaves. It is of significance that the questions evoked by the controversy concerning the "status of baptized slaves" in regard to their freedom were fundamental theological questions. First and foremost, what denotes humanity? And who is equipped to determine which people created in the image of God are human and which are not? The next question had to do with the meaning of "engrafting into the body of Christ." Can anyone receive baptism in the name of the triune God and _not_ be considered part of the body of Christ? Is one portion of the body better or more worthy of inclusion? Is this determination left to the mercy of human beings?

These questions were solved in law courts in altered forms in order to solve a societal problem which the newly emerging United States had created for itself. Sacred and secular were clearly dichotomized in order to enact a series of laws which legalized the enslavement and dehumanized treatment of human beings by other humans. Baptism, it is was decided, did not free Africans from their obligations as bonded servants. Following these decisions the evangelization and baptism of Africans in America proceeded with great fervor, with baptized slaves continuing in their degrading, dehumanizing roles.

Full church membership was not initially granted to slaves by their oppressors, nor were they fully accepted as worshipers. Attendance at worship was permitted by generous planters who made sure that this "questionable" portion of the body of Christ would not be able to interact with them. Since African-Americans had no legal voice in matters that affected the shaping of worship, clandestine religious meetings were skillfully orchestrated by slaves. In secluded "brush harbors" in the woods, out of hearing range of the slave holders, slaves were free to share their faith experiences in an "Invisible Institution," the first African-American worshiping church. Faith experiences were shaped by core beliefs, existential struggles, and revised African-American versions of God's liberating activities with the Israelites and all persons who were willing to believe. An indigenous means of theologizing had been found.

The Great Awakening movement which engendered liberal and often unbridled enthusiasm in worship appealed to worshipers of African descent. Free and enslaved African-Americans participated enthusiastically in camp meeting worship, and concluded the evening when possible in brush harbors long after revivalists had pronounced the benediction. The praise of God was truly an offering of one's total self in sermons, songs, and prayers in sacred space identified by the African-Americans. Secluded worshipers remembered and reconnected with God's story as their journey was incorporated into the faith journey of Old Testament communities. Forms and styles of the elements of worship were fashioned out of the authentic expressions of an oppressed people.

Africans in America obviously did not arrive *tabula rasa,* nor were they unfamiliar with God's story. The Euro-American versions of God's story which they heard assumed that God had come only through Greco-Roman history. While the story of God incarnate in Jesus Christ canonized in the Bible may have been new to them, it was necessary to indigenize the Good News. Jesus of Nazareth, whose earthly journey was quite similar to that of the slaves, became in reality Jesus the Liberator. The worship of God in Jesus Christ in an oppressive church environment from the vantage point of segregated lofts and segregated pews was void of the liberating contextual-experiential so much needed

by an African people. They needed sacred space and time to foster spiritual progress unimpeded by the hypocritical motives of confused evangelizers.

The Holy Scriptures became for the slave the most important resource document from which a new theology could be shaped. It was of course necessary for slaves to apply a different hermeneutical principle as their journey, replete with struggles and suffering, became the lens through which the biblical stories could be seen. Long before slaves were able to read the Word of God as found in Scriptures for themselves, the liberation stories which they heard convinced them that this was the same God that they knew from experience. If God could free the Hebrew children, Daniel in the lion's den, Shadrach, Meshach, and Abednego from the fiery furnace, that same God could free them from the bondage of slavery. The Good News of God incarnate in Jesus Christ was a continuation of their journey with God into whose story they had entered. The coming of the Holy Spirit at Pentecost when people from a variety of cultures heard the gospel in their own language was equally available to them. The help provided to free them to learn to read the English language added another dimension to the slave's ability to interpret God's story as the first step toward shaping their own God talk.

## Theology of Worship in a New Key with Indigenized Harmonies

African-American theologizing is grounded in the African primal worldviews cited above. Finite beings are called to worship by God who freely calls whom God chooses, God enters the lives and experiences of a people and frees them consciously to continue in God's story. One historical way of documenting core beliefs about God in Jesus Christ is found in the slave songs. The gift of music and song remained available as the basic form of symbolic communication for an African people in diaspora. Theologizing for the slaves was not the "systematic" task of any one individual, but continued as a "folk-task" of the community.

While oral folk traditions are basic to the ongoing life of many cultures, the continuation of African traditional religions, and the shaping of new folk traditions in a new world was the basic means of survival for African-Americans. Reliance upon basic core beliefs transmitted orally undergirded the process of shaping new, dynamic cultures and also became pivotal modulation "chords" for shaping theology in a new key. The well-grounded concepts of God, humanity, life, and nature provided the ability to respond creatively to the realities and rhythms of new situations. Syncretisms evolved naturally without reliance upon council meetings for theological discourses and final theological decisions. Concepts of God in Africa emerged out of experiences. Greco-Roman descriptive terms such as omniscient, omnipresent, omnipotent, transcendent, and immanent were not used by Africans. Nevertheless, experience had taught that God was all knowing, all wise, eternal, everywhere, above and beyond all, yet present. These concepts are especially operative in worship.

The "divinely stolen" freedom of separate sacred space helped shape a doctrine of the church _ekklesia,_ truly called out by God. The estrangement and loneliness of slaves at the margins of a society which ostracized them were overcome in this arena as worshipers were made aware that they belonged to God and each other. The black church was initially formed as a liberating worshiping community. Its vitality has been sustained and continues to be perpetuated in proportion to the genuineness and continuity of authentic worship. The church functions as a living fellowship where wholeness of persons and communities is sought and found, prior to its functioning as an institution. Separate places of worship, initially in secret, where time and sacred space were relative, ultimately evolved into separate congregations of African-Americans. Having their own sacred space African-Americans can find their highest values as they praise God, under the power of the Holy Spirit. Herein, divine power is garnered and strength to survive is granted.

The Bible, God's Word in Scripture, has been and continues to be the major resource for shaping God-talk. Slaves relied heavily upon God's Word as they responded in worship and in life. In the evolution of worship over the centuries, biblical stories are foundational for African-American faith and spirituality. Initially steeped in the King James Version of the Bible, African-American worshipers are generally hesitant about questioning the language, even where the imagery has a negative effect upon them. There is a growing trend for congregations to listen more carefully to the language of newer translations introduced by pastors and other church leaders who are seminary graduates. Recent scholarly studies and contributions by African-

American liturgical, biblical, and music scholars are facilitating this process.

African-Americans have diverse opinions regarding the Bible. Common understandings include the biblical source as a record of divine history, a witness to the salvation that appeared in Jesus Christ, a record of human experiences which is relevant for today, and a source of truth concerning redemption and Christian living. The details of how this is understood are delineated by some denominations, and functional in the oral memories of others. Scripture does not always determine the content and sequence of elements of worship in all African-American congregations. Nevertheless, preaching is most often biblically based, and is a source of inspiration for worship.

African-Americans continue to respect the role of the black preacher, called of God as spiritual leader, prophet, priest, and divine instrument through which God's healing wholeness can take place. One of the gifts for which black preachers are noted is their ability to "tell the biblical story" and help bring the story to life for the gathered community. Like the African _griot_ (story teller and oral historian) the story telling process is supported and encouraged by the community in a "call-and-response" fashion. The major impetus for familial bonding takes place as the faith community dialogues openly with the preacher during the sermon and frees itself for communal fellowship which continues in music and other acts of worship.

During the period of slavery, preachers were often the most intellectual member of the community, and were therefore respected for their leadership abilities. Foundational materials for theologizing were presented by the preacher, and then shaped in folk-style by the congregants. The shaping often occurred in the words of songs, stylized and disseminated both in worship and during daily work activities of slaves. Some of the "stuff of everyday life" and nature found its way into the music of the church, thus continuing the African mode of blending sacred and secular as a means of worshiping God.

African-American religious ritual action is often reminiscent of the African heritage in content, symbols, and symbolism. The greatest similarity, however, is the dynamic nature of rituals and cultures, reflected in the ability of worshipers to react creatively to life situations and peak moments in worship. Styles and forms will vary according to the needs and expectations of the particular community, as well as the nature of worship generated by the experiences of worshipers. For African-Americans, worship as ritual action is basically forged and shaped as an anti-structural means of functioning in a society which has attempted to structure African-Americans out of the mainstream of society. (J. Randall Nichols, "Worship as Anti-Structure: The Contributions of Victor Turner," *Theology Today* 41 [January 1985]: 401–402; see also Victor W. Turner, *The Ritual Process: Structure and Anti-Structure* [Ithaca, N.Y.: Cornell University Press, 1963]). Worship services, whether contemplative or ecstatic, are Spirit-led, liminal experiences of God on the margin of society where social status is elevated above and beyond the assigned definitions imposed by the larger society. Under the power of God, responses in worship allow a vision of the Almighty which inspires, transforms, and makes one whole.

African-American worship is uniquely experiential and contextual, incorporating in varying ways the understanding of a personal, immanent, and transcendent God who is worthy of worship. Worshipers stand in awe of the *Mysterium Tremendum* of God's absolute presence, aware that God is trustworthy and "always on time." The worship of God is made possible through Jesus the Christ, the object of the Christian faith. As the living embodiment of one who divinely overcame oppression, Jesus the Christ, God incarnate, is the "meeting place" or altar, where an encounter with God can happen. While worship may take place anywhere that humans encounter Christ, it is in corporate worship that African-Americans walk and talk, sing and shout, and experience conversion in an acknowledgment of the true presence of the resurrected Christ among them. It is not uncommon for worshipers to address Jesus as God in prayers, songs, and sermons. Beyond the "Jesus Only" sects, one finds emphasis on the absolute oneness of these two persons in the Godhead especially among some Baptists and Pentecostal traditions.

A theology of African-American worship is also reflective of an understanding of the Holy Spirit as the dynamic of worship. The Spirit is personal and direct, and not merely an "atmosphere." The intimate, transforming power of the Holy Spirit enables salvation, life in the worship and work of the church, and fortification for mission and ministry. It is important in determining a theology of African-

American worship to acknowledge differences in denominational polity and theology which affect ritual action and verbal dialogue about the Holy Spirit. These distinctions are most apparent in reference to the Lord's Supper and baptism as delineated by various denominations.

The uniqueness of an African-American theology is the "liberation key" established in the tonality of the brush harbors, fanned and flamed first in African-American spirituals, and now also in black gospel music and "metered hymns." This key is clearly established and sounded in African primal world-views which led the early folk theologians to seek separate places of worship. From these well-established foundations the power of God is experienced the community of faith, which leads them to continue to talk and sing their core beliefs in the context of lived experiences. Even when denominational differences create an aura that is unique and distinct, the African-American community can find a common plane on which to attempt to "walk as they talk" out of the belief that a divinely liberated people should walk upright, for the power of God is available to all who believe.

Melva Wilson Costen

## 200 • A Restoration Theology of Worship

*Restoration theology of worship arises from the rejection of traditions and creeds in favor of Christ alone and Scripture alone. Consequently all thinking about worship is shaped from this premise.*

───────── **"No Creed but Christ!"** ─────────

Anthology of worship that would discuss the theology of the restoration movement, and of worship among the churches that have emerged from it, must first acknowledge an old but persistent dilemma. Persons long familiar with this movement tend to choke on the word "theology." They are reluctant to start talking about it, and when they do, they find they hold very diverse opinions. The late historian A. T. DeGroot explained the Disciple's reluctance to talk about theology by recalling that

. . . they were repelled by the church as they saw it—a church of medieval and post-reformation years, which had become so hypnotized by theological debate that it presented itself to the world as a fraternity for forensics, closely involved with politics. (A. T. DeGroot, _Disciple Thought: A History_ [Fort Worth: Texas Christian University, 1965], 23.)

A famous battle cry of the restoration movement was, "No creed but Christ!" Many churches were using formal statements of faith as tests of acceptance or inclusion—for membership, ordination, or both. Persons holding the right beliefs were in; those whose beliefs were in error were out. Because the founders of the restoration movement rejected this abuse of theology, many followers assumed theology was something to be avoided. Thus those with anti-intellectual tendencies justified their distrust of theology.

While Disciples continue to reject using theology as a test of orthodoxy or basis for membership, they realize its importance in clarifying beliefs for the sake of talking with Christians in other denominations. The purpose of theology was not to explain or defend a statement of faith but to express clearly what was believed.

When people join a church, they are asked, "Do you believe that Jesus is the Christ, the Son of the living God, and do you accept him as your Lord and Savior?" Even paraphrased, this question will almost reflect Peter's confession of faith (Matt. 16:16). It is a simple confession. The word "your" in the second clause stresses the _personal_ commitment entailed in giving a positive answer to the question. At the same time, it raises important _theological_ issues. Though this article does not explore the important question of Christology, an excellent study of this subject is William R. Barr's, "Christology in Disciples Tradition: An Assessment and a Proposal," in Kenneth Lawrence, ed., _Classic Themes of Disciples Theology_ ([Fort Worth: Texas Christian University Press, 1986], 9–27). If Jesus is "Christ" and "Savior," from what does he save us? In other words, what is sin ? And for what does Jesus save us? In other words, what is our hope and destiny ? If we call Jesus "the Son of the living God" and "Lord," what do we mean by "God", and what is the relationship between Jesus and God? In what way is Jesus human, and in what way divine? M. Eugene Boring's, _Truly Human/Truly Divine_ (CBP Press, 1984) a study of the Gospel of Mark, explores these questions in the light of current Disciples thought. As we discuss such matters, we appeal to some authority. Among all branches stemming from the Stone-Campbell restoration movement, this authority found in the Scriptures, "No book but the

Bible!" is a corollary to the cry of "No creed but Christ." However, the different branches of this movement differ noticeably in how the Bible is to be studied, understood, and applied.

In pondering such questions, Disciples and other descendants of the restoration movement want to know what the early thinkers of the movement had to say. Royal Humbert spent thirty years analyzing the writings of Alexander Campbell as found in _The Christian Baptist, The Millennial Harbinger,_ and several other sources. The product of his investigation was the _Compend of Alexander Campbell's Theology_ (St. Louis: Bethany Press, 1961). Humbert arranged Campbell's writings into twelve subject areas: "Faith and Reason," "The Bible," "Revelation," "God," "Christ as Lord," "The Holy Spirit," "Grace," "The Church," "The Means of Grace" (ordinances), "Man," "Christian Ethics," and "Eschatology." In this way, Humbert was able to show that Alexander Campbell, who never compiled a systematic theology, was nevertheless an influential theologian.

Alexander Campbell's prolific writings have had more impact on the theology of the restoration movement than those of any other author. However, during his long career, Alexander Campbell's ideas and attitudes changed in significant ways. His earlier period has been called iconoclastic; there was a negative emphasis to many of his writings in _The Christian Baptist._ During the years when he edited _The Millennial Harbinger,_ he took on a gentler and more optimistic tone. Because of these changes, it is possible to find two statements by Alexander Campbell on a single subject which directly contradict each other.

Similarly, although other reformers who cooperated with Campbell in the restoration movement may have agreed on the principal goal of restoring the faith and practice of the apostolic church as the basis for reaching Christian unity, they differed from him and each other in their convictions about that faith and practice. Consider, for example, the name for this body of believers. Thomas Campbell, Barton W. Stone, and Walter Scott all favored the simple name "Christians" or "Christian Church"; Alexander Campbell alone argued for the name "Disciples of Christ."

The point is, that people within this movement have valued freedom of opinion and diversity of thought. For this reason, generalizations about the theology of this movement are always too simplistic. Nevertheless, the following comments on four subjects relevant to worship suggest the type of theological conversation that is current among those who belong to the Christian Church (Disciples of Christ).

## The Bible

Professor Eugene Boring describes Alexander Campbell's view of the Bible as "both like and unlike all other books."

> It is like them in that the Bible is a human book by human authors, expressed in human words and ideas, and is therefore to be interpreted by the same grammatico-historical methods as all other books. But the Bible is unlike all other books in that it is a book of revealed propositional truths, divinely inspired in its entirety, and is therefore to be dealt with as in a different category from all other books. (Eugene Boring, "The Formation of a Tradition: Alexander Campbell and the New Testament," *The Disciples Theological Digest* 2:1 (1987): 5–62).

Campbell wanted biblical scholarship to be possible for the common reader, not limited to a professional elite. He laid out rules of interpretation that would free Scripture from fantastic, complicated, allegorical explanations, on the one hand, as well as from rationalistic solutions that did not allow the reader to listen for the voice of God speaking through the words of the Bible. He believed that some parts of the Bible shed more light than others. The stories of creation and the patriarchs are like starlight; the laws of Moses and the history of Israel are like moonlight; the story of the Christian church and the Epistles are like sunlight. The brightest light, judging from the number of references Campbell made to it, shines from the book of Hebrews.

Contemporary Disciples of Christ study the Bible with tools of historical and literary criticism. The Bible is not a book to be worshiped, but a library to be studied with the whole heart and mind as one seeks to find the will of God.

## The Church

Thomas Campbell's *Declaration and Address* challenged Christians to find in the New Testament a model of the primitive church that could be reproduced as a uniform standard. He said,

> The New Testament is as perfect a constitution for the worship, discipline, and government of the New Testament church, and as perfect a rule for the particular duties of its members, as the Old Testament was for the worship, discipline, and government of the Old Testament church, and the particular duties of its members.

Campbell was seeking to find in the New Testament a long-lost, simple solution to the dilemma of division among Christians. Such a solution was never found by Thomas Campbell, by his son Alexander, nor by those who joined them in the quest. Part of the problem, according to Professor Mark Toulouse, is that their reading of history was nostalgic rather than objective; the primitive church of the apostolic era could not provide a single, simple model, much less an ideal one. Moreover, their reading of the Bible as "a constitution" was mistaken. They were looking in the right place, but in the wrong way for something that was not to be found.

Nevertheless, they sincerely sought the voice of God instead of human authority for ordering the life and worship of the church. Thus they grasped a criterion by which to sift out the accretions that grew as the world sought to squeeze the church into its mold, and by which the church might be transformed by a renewal of minds seeking to discern the good and acceptable and perfect will of God. Perhaps the most significant fruit of their efforts was a renewed focus of worship around the Lord's Table.

## The Lord's Supper

Professor Keith Watkins introduced a book on the Lord's Supper for Disciples by saying, "The major act of Christian worship is a meal, a feast of joy where Jesus is the host and his people everywhere the guests" (Keith Watkins, *The Feast of Joy* [St. Louis: Bethany Press, 1977], 11). This statement implies three important points of theology.

First, the Lord's Supper is the essential element of worship. All followers of the Stone-Campbell restoration movement observe holy Communion every Lord's Day. Some, perhaps, have diminished the Lord's Supper so that it is less important than the preaching event. Even they, however, would not consider holding a Sunday morning worship service without breaking the bread and sharing the cup. A growing number of churches are giving greater emphasis than ever to the Lord's Table as the reason for gathering to worship.

Second, the Lord's Supper is a joyful event. It is a

thanksgiving dinner. At the Table we remember God's saving act in Jesus Christ and we rejoice. Remembrance, a key to worship, is not reliving the past, but re-experiencing in a fresh, relevant way the meaning of what took place in the past. Recent trends lead away from Communion as a grave time for private meditation (though it is deeply personal) and toward an appreciation of this moment as a time for community and celebration. For the Disciples of Christ, employing the chalice as an emblem or logo is a way of proclaiming to all Christians the call of Christ to unite around the Table.

Third, Jesus Christ serves as the unseen host at the Table. Because he is the one who extends the invitation to come, no human being or group has the license to refuse anyone who accepts that call. The Table is open to anyone. Informally, most members of this movement understand the invitation as a call for persons who have received baptism to renew the meaning of baptism at the Table. However, even in churches that practice "closed membership" (requiring immersion for membership), there is always an "open Communion" policy. Believing that Christ is the unseen host at the Table also addresses the question of the presence of Christ in the Lord's Supper.

--- **Baptism** ---

In ecumenical dialogue with other churches, Disciples of Christ have gained respect for other theologies of baptism. By continuing to look to the Scriptures, not for an ideal model or for proof of the right method of baptism, but for the real meaning of baptism, Disciples have grown in their understanding of this sacrament. Understood as a once-in-a-lifetime, unrepeatable act of God's grace, on the one hand, baptism also involves a human response to God's gracious act (Clark M. Williamson, _Baptism: Embodiment of the Gospel,_ The Nature of the Church: Study Series 4 [St. Louis: Christian Board of Publication, published for the Council on Christian Unity, 1989]).

Colbert Cartwright has said, "The fundamental question for us Disciples is not what we believe but in whom we believe." (Colbert S. Cartwright, _People of the Chalice_ [St. Louis: CBP Press, 1987], 69.) In this priority, all three major branches of the Stone-Campbell restoration movement can stand as one. Whether one interprets the Bible literally or by means of higher criticism, whether one shuns other "sects" or works for church union, the most important thing is to know Jesus Christ as Lord and Savior.

Philip V. Miller

## 201 • A HOLINESS-PENTECOSTAL THEOLOGY OF WORSHIP

_In the Holiness-Pentecostal tradition of worship, the key element is praise. Praise is not only the praise of song, but the praise of or testimony to God in this life. In worship, the Christian praises God for his character and for the deeds of salvation and healing God has wrought in the life of the worshiper._

For Pentecostal Christians worship has always focused on the public meeting when believers come together to praise the Lord. Praising the Lord is key, for, as they constantly remind themselves, the Lord "inhabit[s] the praise" (Ps. 22:3, NKJV) of his people. The actions that compose proper praise, however, have been various, falling somewhere between the freedom promised by Jesus and Paul, and the form implied in Paul's other statements that "the spirits of prophets are subject to prophets" (1 Cor. 14:32, RSV) and "let all things be done properly and in an orderly manner" (1 Cor. 14:40, NASB).

Unhappy with the alleged coldness and formality of the churches they left, or which asked them to leave, Pentecostals wanted nothing to do with liturgy. The intensity of their own Spirit baptism, which was accompanied by speaking in tongues (Acts 2:4) and other spiritual gifts (according to Charles Parham, the father of at least this part of Pentecostal doctrine), led them to expect a similar intensity of spirit in their public gatherings. "Come and see what the Lord will do for you" was a common invitation, along with "taste and see that the Lord is good" (Ps. 34:8). Nevertheless they unconsciously developed liturgies which met the twin demands of freedom and form in a variety of ways.

Pentecostal music is creative and expressive. It uses the musical idiom of popular culture: gospel song which tells a story about a person's response to God. "I came to Jesus weary, worn, and sad; He took my sins away." "Years I spent in vanity and pride, caring not my Lord was crucified." Choruses drawn from the Bible: "I will sing unto the Lord, for He hath triumphed gloriously, the horse and rider thrown into the sea" (Exod. 15). "I will bless the Lord at all times, His praise shall continually be in my mouth" (Ps. 34). Songs of praise; invitation, missionary, evangelistic, and revival songs; and seasonal hymns were all borrowed freely from American Protestant hymnology. For the distinctive experience of the Spirit, however, new songs and choruses were written: "O Lord, send the power just now"; "Jesus come and fill me now"; "Pentecostal fire is falling; praise the Lord it fell on me."

Musical instruments have always been important, usually as accompaniment for the singing, less often as praise in their own right. Salvation Army brass and drums, piano and organ, drum, tambourine, and guitar, all in the popular musical idiom are acceptable. Young worshipers accept modern styles first, modify them, and gradually incorporate them into worship in acceptable ways. There is no Pentecostal musical aesthetic except that which edifies the congregation.

Public prayer is not a distinct form, but is merely the individual praying in public, often with no inhibition to tone down the frankness. Intensity and spontaneity are the hallmarks of Pentecostal praying: written prayers according to Pentecostals are unspiritual. Private matters can be mentioned in public prayer without embarrassment because they are directed toward a loving Father; the town, the nation, and the world become part of the content as the one who is praying is led by the Spirit to intercede. If she or he is not so led, then it's all right because the Spirit is directing the prayer.

Prayer "in the Spirit" is not simply Spirit-directed prayer in the language of the worshipers; it is also prayer in a Spirit-given language, usually called "tongues" or " a tongue." Speaking in tongues occurs in two main forms: a message in tongues, during which others cease to pray aloud and being to listen, followed by an interpretation in the language of the worshipers; and praying in tongues while everyone is praying aloud, for which no interpretation is sought or expected. The latter use of tongues-speaking is sometimes called one's "prayer language," and is understood to be personally enriching (1 Cor. 14:4) and a kind of intercession that transcends all human limitations, since it is the Spirit praying perfectly through a person (Rom. 8:26-27). Prophecies are also appropriate prayer activities; these are short messages from anyone in the meeting which strengthen, encourage, and comfort the

worshipers (1 Cor. 14:3), but are not preceded by tongues-speech.

The Wesleyan testimony found its true descendants in Pentecostal testimony and preaching. Preaching is often extended testimony: "this is what God has done for me, and he will do it for you." Again, the measure is intensity and spontaneity, so much so that if singing or praying or congregational testimony last long enough, preaching is not necessary, or is thought to have been accomplished by the Spirit in the other parts of worship. In other countries, one or more sermons are simply added, since the meeting is not bound by time (as it increasingly is in Western Pentecostalism). Although Pentecostal faith is "better felt than telt [told]," (i.e., better experienced than explained) one who has experienced God's blessings had better tell others about them. Thus, the worship tends to be worshiper-centered rather than pulpit-centered. Since the preacher is presumed to have the greatest experience in the Spirit, however, worship tends to focus on him or her, at least as a prime example of what God is doing; thus, worship often focuses on the minister as star-performer.

The man or woman of God should lead by the Spirit. This is true in worship as well as in church life generally. Most American Pentecostals ordain women, and those who do not have welcomed them into every other position of leadership in the local church, though rarely into the highest positions. Spirit-leadership through a person, however, must be protected from willfulness. Here again, a tension is seen between "test[ing] the spirits to see whether they are from God" (1 John 4:1) and the formidable "Do not touch my anointed ones" (1 Chron. 16:22). The ancient rule which considered anyone who mentioned money while speaking "in spirit" an impostor (*Didachē* 11.12) exemplifies the enduring Pentecostal need for accountability (form) within the freedom of being led by the Spirit. Here, then, is congregational participation in cooperation with strong pastoral direction.

Worship in Pentecostal churches has followed Protestant forms and symbols until the recent spread of Catholic charismatic experience. One contribution of the latter to traditional Pentecostal worship is new songs and choruses. A second contribution is emphasis on the naturalness, rather than crisis, of beginning the life in the Spirit. This beginning is natural in the sense that Spirit experiences are for every Christian who already has the Spirit in him or her, and in the sense that redeemed human nature is capable of receiving and manifesting the gifts and graces of the Spirit if she or he knows how and is willing. Finally, Catholic charismatics remind all Pentecostals of the Christocentric purpose of all Pentecostal worship.

Protestant influences in worship are many. Places of worship have little ornamentation. The pulpit is centered and behind a conspicuous altar area. A baptismal tank for immersion and Communion table are present. Little use is made of symbols, whether colors, vestments, sculpture, or banners. However the cross (not crucifix) is often prominent, as is the dove. Scripture may be displayed, often a verse about the second coming of Christ, or "I am the Lord that healeth thee" (Exod. 15:26, KJV). Though the church year is ignored, national holidays have their place, with appropriate Protestant hymns, as well as Christian holidays such as Easter, Pentecost, Christmas, and rarely, Reformation Sunday. Common Sunday emphases are denominational programs, such as Servicemen's Day, Benevolence Day, and the important monthly Missionary Sunday.

Ordinances include Communion, called the Lord's Supper, usually celebrated monthly after the sermon in a lengthened service. Open Communion is the norm, and the theology is Zwinglian symbolism. Water baptism is less important and frequent in modern American practice than formerly; it is important and frequent elsewhere in the world. The gathering of tithes and offerings is indispensable to Pentecostal worship. Church marriages are usual, as are funerals. Babies are not baptized but are dedicated to God, without godparents, however.

American Pentecostal worship evolved out of late 19th century emphases among Holiness and other evangelical groups on salvation by faith, physical healing through prayer, an experience of the Spirit, subsequent to salvation, that sanctified the believer and empowered him/her for service, and the imminent second coming of Jesus to set up his kingdom. Worship forms compatible with such emphases were borrowed as needed from evangelical practice, and the union of Spirit with the spirits of an energized people caused the invention of new forms. The touchstones have remained practical (Does it edify the congregation?), biblical (Does the Bible refer to it?), and spiritual (Does it allow the Spirit to "have his way?").

Gary S. Liddle

## 202 • A Charismatic Theology of Worship

_A charismatic theology emphasizes a vital relationship with the Holy Spirit and the recovery of spiritual gifts, which are both experienced in worship._

Be filled with the Spirit. Speak to one another with psalms, hymns and spiritual songs. Sing and make music in your heart to the Lord, always giving thanks to God the Father for everything, in the name of our Lord Jesus Christ. (Eph. 5:18-20)

The charismatic movement is known primarily for its emphasis on the Holy Spirit and the restoration of the gifts (_charisma_) of the Spirit (that is, healing, prophecy, miracles, tongues, and so on.). However, one of the most important contributions of this movement to the church at large may be in the area of worship.

Although there may be debate as to exactly what it means to be a charismatic, there is very little debate about the primary evidence of being one: vigorous heartfelt worship. Paul indicates in Ephesians 5 that being filled with the Holy Spirit will be followed with psalms, hymns, and spiritual songs on our lips and melodious thanksgiving in our hearts. Since the role of the Holy Spirit is to glorify the Son (John 16:14), it is logical that a vital relationship with the Holy Spirit will result in a deepened desire to bring honor to Jesus through worship.

For many, the scene that comes to mind when "charismatic" is mentioned is that of an enthusiastic Christian with a transfigured face and lifted hands. Charismatics have given the church Scripture songs and choruses, guitars and drums, clapping and dancing, worship teams and banners, song sheets and overheads, worship seminars and conferences, as well as enthusiastic faith and infectious joy.

Why this stereotype has emerged is difficult to explain theologically, for there is considerable theological diversity among charismatics. Because the movement has sprung up in many different denominations, it has been affected by various historic traditions. A Catholic charismatic, for instance, would probably not share the same theology as a Baptist charismatic in every point. Both would say, however, that what they have in common is an experience of being filled with the Holy Spirit that has energized their walk with God and their worship of him.

This experience is similar to that of the disciples who met Jesus on the road to Emmaus. Even though they had previously learned much about him and had heard that he was alive, their eyes were opened and they really "saw" him. Their theology changed very little, but what they believed became living and real to them!

To understand better this phenomenon of charismatic worship, we will consider five principles of this style of worship and their theological foundations. First, the intervening presence of the Holy Spirit activates the priestly functions of worshipers. Second, worship involves the whole person—spirit, soul and body. Third, the act of worship is a progression into the manifest presence of God. Fourth, worship creates an atmosphere where God's power is revealed. And fifth, worship is more than singing—it is serving.

## The Activation of the Priesthood

You . . . are being built into a spiritual house to be a holy priesthood, offering spiritual sacrifices acceptable to God through Jesus Christ. (1 Pet. 2:5)

The energizing of the Holy Spirit could be described biblically as the anointing of a priest for priestly functions. According to 1 Peter 2:9, God's people are meant to be a royal priesthood declaring praises of the one who called us out of darkness into his marvelous light. In verse 5 of the same chapter, Peter explains that as we are being built together, we are becoming a holy priesthood to offer acceptable sacrifices. We *are* a priesthood made for praise (v. 9); we *are becoming* such a priesthood (v. 5). In other words, we are becoming what God has made us to be: a worshiping community. Those who are priests by position are becoming priests who really act like priests.

Old Covenant priests were born to be priests, but they did not carry out their priestly duties until they were anointed as priests (Exod. 29; Num. 8). Likewise, all Christians are part of a royal family of priests as a result of new birth. When we are filled with the Spirit, our priestly functions are activated and we find ourselves offering New Covenant sacrifices which include vocal praise (Heb. 13:15).

The understanding of the church as a priesthood

is certainly not unique to the charismatic movement. That was an emphasis fundamental to the Reformation. But these present day Spirit-filled worshipers are bringing a new understanding of what it means to be a priest. What is traditionally understood when we say that we are priests is that we no longer need another mediator besides Christ. As true as that is and as revolutionary as that may have sounded in Martin Luther's day, it is only a partial understanding of what it means to be a priest. Priests not only draw near to God, they minister to God. Priests offer sacrifices.

Jack Hayford, speaking of the priestly function of believers, says: "Five hundred years ago the issue was *relationship*—restoring personal access *to* God. Today, it is *worship*—revealing the potential of our praises *before* God" (Jack Hayford, *Worship His Majesty* [Waco, Tex.: Word Books, 1987], 88).

So for the charismatic, the Holy Spirit is the activator who takes us out of neutral and prompts the various expressions of worship. Worship, then, can be understood as the grateful sacrifices offered by activated priests discovering their ministry unto God.

## Spirit, Soul and Body

Love the Lord your God with all your heart and with all your soul . . . and with all your strength. (Mark 12:30)

One implication of this "activation" is that worship involves action. Charismatic worship is demonstrative. It is something you do. It is not passive. Charismatic worship includes hearty singing, lifting of hands, bowing, clapping, dancing, and shouting.

For the Spirit-filled worshiper, the Great Commandment—to love God with all of our spirit, soul, and body—is the reason behind all the activity. Worship is love for God expressed. Therefore, if we love God with all of our being—spirit, soul, and body—it follows that we will worship him with our whole being—spirit, soul, and body. Most traditions acknowledge the mental and spiritual aspects of worship. The charismatic makes sure we don't forget the physical and emotional elements of worship.

The charismatic Bible teacher and missionary Derek Prince, commenting on Romans 12:1, asks why God specified that the presenting of our *bodies* to God is worship. Why didn't he say to present our *hearts* or *minds?* Prince answers that for the Hebrews, the body was the container of the soul and spirit. The physical expression of worship, then, is not inferior to the spiritual expression of worship. It is the vehicle of spiritual worship. The physical act of lifting hands, for instance, is a token of the spiritual disposition of adoration and surrender. Dancing is the demonstration of great joy and gladness.

Closely related to the physical aspect of worship is the role of the emotions in worship. Being filled with the Spirit is more than a new understanding for the charismatic—it is an experience. Likewise, charismatic worship is not primarily an ordered mental process, but rather a spontaneous, spiritual encounter where emotions are not out of place. Charismatics are not ashamed of the emotional component of worship.

Placing greater value on the physical and emotional dimensions in worship greatly affects the musical style of charismatic worship. Most noticeable is the greater emphasis on rhythm in worship music. More than melody or harmony, rhythm corresponds to the physical side of human personality. A charismatic worship band is generally built around a rhythm section (piano or guitars, bass and drums) rather than around an organ. The organ doesn't easily accompany hand-clapping praise music.

The physical and emotional dimensions of charismatic worship heighten the spiritual dimension of worship. A practice unique to the charismatic movement is singing in the Spirit. Based on 1 Corinthians 14:15, this practice involves singing spontaneous words and melodies around a fixed chord or slowly moving chord progression. Sometimes referred to as free worship or open worship, this song form has affected regular congregational singing among charismatics. Replacing the longstanding style of four part vocal harmony, a free form approach to harmony and vocal lines has emerged among charismatics. This spontaneous quality of worship, along with a renewed desire for personal experience in worship, has created a burgeoning new library of contemporary, testimonial and simple-to-learn choruses. Thus, the vigorous nature of charismatic worship is rooted in Jesus' command to love God with one's whole being.

## Entering His Presence

Worship the Lord with gladness; come before him with joyful songs . . . Enter his gates with thanksgiving and his courts with praise. (Psalm 100:2, 4)

Another key to understanding charismatic worship is the presence of God. It doesn't take many visits to charismatic worship services to hear about "entering the presence of God." That phrase, those of us who have been taught that God is everywhere at all times, initially does not make sense. We cite Psalm 139:7: "Where can I go from your Spirit? Where can I flee from your presence?" or Matthew 28:20: "Surely I am with you always, to the very end of the age." These Scriptures indicate that God is equally present everywhere and always.

A charismatic understanding of God's presence distinguishes between his omnipresence (he is everywhere at all times) and his manifest presence (God is especially present at certain times and places). When David said that he could go nowhere to escape God's presence, he was referring to God's omnipresence. When he pleaded with God to not withdraw his presence (Ps. 51:11), he was talking about God's manifest presence. Jacob encountered the manifest presence at Bethel: "Surely the Lord is in this place, and I was not aware of it" (Gen. 28:16).

Taking this idea a step further, a charismatic believes that the acts of giving thanks and singing are gateways into God's manifest presence (Ps. 100:2, 4). Some authors distinguish between various dimensions of his manifest presence—outer court, holy place, and holiest of all (See Terry Law, _The Power of Praise and Worship_ [Tulsa: Victory House, 1985], 245).

Thus music is not incidental but fundamental to encountering God in a charismatic worship service. As a result, the worship leader (no longer just a "song leader") becomes a vital part of the church. His or her ability to lead worship affects the congregation's experience of God's manifest presence. New skills are sometimes required to know how to choose songs and connect them so as to create a progression into God's presence.

## Praise and Power

As they began to sing and praise, the Lord set ambushes against the men of Ammon and Moab and Mount Seir who were invading Judah, and they were defeated. (2 Chron. 20:22)

Closely related to the experience of entering God's presence with singing is the correlation between singing and experiencing God's power. Psalm 22:3 forms the basis of a commonly held conviction among charismatics that God sits enthroned on the praise of his people. Or, to extend the thought, our praise creates a throne from which God exercises his power and might. Using the typology of the priesthood, this demonstration of power is comparable to the fire with which God answered acceptable Old Covenant sacrifices (Lev. 9:24; Gen.15:17; 2 Chron. 7:1; see also Heb. 12:28-29).

Faith for miracles, healing, and deliverance from evil spirits seems to come more easily following vigorous worship. American evangelist T. L. Osborne regularly played the popular charismatic worship tape "All Hail King Jesus" for thirty minutes through loud speakers before his crusades in Africa and testified that miracles happened even before the preaching because of the atmosphere of power the worship music created. Jack Hayford, pastor and songwriter from California, prescribed regular singing to a woman in his church who was unable to have children. Based on Isaiah 54:1, the counsel was put into action and a year later the woman was a mother of a baby girl. Elisha called for a harpist before he prophesied (2 Kings 3:15). King Saul was relieved of the oppression of evil spirits when David played on his harp (1 Sam. 16:23). In the New Testament, Paul and Silas sang and prayed in prison when God answered with an earthquake (Acts 16:25-26).

Faith and worship are integrally connected. Abraham "was strengthened in his faith and gave glory to God" (Rom. 4:20-21). The relationship between faith and worship was articulated by an early church saying: *Lex orandi lex credenti*—we believe as we have worshiped. A Nigerian pastor commented on American Christianity with this comparison: "In America, you believe; in Nigeria, we worship."

### ———— Beyond the Song ————

Through Jesus, therefore, let us continually offer to God a sacrifice of praise—the fruit of lips that confess his name. *And do not forget to do good and to share with others, for with such sacrifices God is pleased* (Heb. 13:15-16, italics added for emphasis).

Finally, to complete our view of charismatic worship, we must move beyond the worship event to the life of worship. Charismatic worship is more than music and singing. It is vigorously living lives of sacrifice to God and service to others. Paul defined worship as presenting ourselves as living sacrifices (Rom. 12:1). The author of Hebrews commended God's people to vocal praise as well as good works (Heb. 13:15-16). Acceptable worship requires both.

This larger view of worship explains why the charismatic movement is noted for active involvement in ministries to the poor, the abused, the addicted, the brokenhearted, as well as in international missions. These ministries are in themselves acts of worship. Wholehearted worship in the Christian assembly, wherein we give gifts of praise to God, is a rehearsal for the life of worship which follows, wherein we give of ourselves to the needs of the world around us. If we are enthusiastic with the song, we most likely will be enthusiastic in our service.

Gerrit Gustafson

## 203 ◆ Bibliography on the Theology of Worship

Alexander, J. Neil. *Time and Community.* Washington, D.C.: Pastoral Press, 1990. This valuable work, written by a number of scholars, tackles liturgy and time, history and theology. The section on theology studies includes discussions on a search for theological roots, on how to be able to see liturgically, the Proclamation of Faith in the Eucharist, and the significance of community to worship.

Allmen, Jean Jacques von. *Worship: Its Theology and Practice.* London: Oxford University Press, 1965. A classic and acclaimed interpretation of worship from a Reformed point of view, yet based on contemporary liturgical scholarship of the early church.

Burkhart, John E. *Worship.* Philadelphia: Westminster Press, 1982. Protestant. Presbyterian professor draws from scholarly sources. Readable material on worship, the meaning of assembly, the meaning of Word and Table, and the relation of worship to social action and evangelism.

Brunner, Peter. *Worship in the Names of Jesus.* St. Louis: Concordia Publishing House, 1968. A definitive work on Christian worship in the congregation. Deals with the anthropological place of worship, the cosmological place of worship, worship as a service of God to the congregation, worship as the congregation's service before God.

Corbon, Jean. _The Wellspring of Worship._ New York: Paulist Press, 1988. Catholic. Marked by good scholarship. Addresses the mystery of the liturgy, the liturgy celebrated, and the liturgy lived.

Hardy, Daniel W., and David F. Ford. _Praising and Knowing God._ Philadelphia: Westminster Press, 1985. Protestant. Deals with the issue of praise, biblical praise, praise in the historical tradition, basic Christian existence as praise, evil, suffering and death, knowing God, Jesus in our praise, praise and prophecy with an appendix on the systematics of praise.

Kavanagh, Aidan. _On Liturgical Theology._ New York: Pueblo Publishing Co., 1984. Catholic. Popular but based on good scholarship. Lectures given in seminary settings. Addresses on the church and the world, and liturgy and theology.

Kilmartin, Edward J. _Christian Liturgy._ London: Sheed & Ward, 1988. Catholic. Scholarly. Addresses the theology of the sacraments with a concern for the recovery of mystery in worship.

Klaasen, Walter. _Biblical and Theological Bases for Worship in the Believer's Church._ Newton, Kans.: Faith and Life Press, 1978. A brief study of an Anabaptist view of worship. Deals with biblical directives, Anabaptist interpretation of biblical materials, and the meaning of the Bible and history for believer's worship.

Lathrop, Gordon W. _Holy Things: An Ecumenical Liturgical Theology._ Philadelphia: Fortress Press, 1993. Discusses liturgical meaning in a way that is both scholarly and devotional. The three parts address: (1) the ecumenical pattern of order of worship, (2) the ways meaning occurs in liturgy, and (3) practical and pastoral conclusions about worship and current human need.

Law, Terry. _The Power of Praise and Worship._ Tulsa: Victory House Publishers, 1985. A charismatic book on worship. Explores the relationship between worship and spiritual warfare, and emphasizes the principles and dimensions of praise.

Madigan, Shawn. _Spirituality Rooted in the Liturgy._ Washington, D.C.: Pastoral Press, 1988. Explores the relationship between the liturgy and spirituality through theological themes of creation and recreation.

Maxwell, Jack Martin. _Worship and Reformed Theology: The Liturgical Lessons of Mercersberg._ Allison Park, Pa.: Pickwick Publications, 1976. This work provides are interesting insight into the order and meaning of worship as espoused by the Mercersburg Reformers.

Price, Charles P., and Louis Weil. _Liturgy for Living._ New York: Seabury Press, 1979. A thoughtful presentation of Anglican worship. Explores the meaning of worship and the specific rites of the Episcopal church.

Schmemann, Alexander. _Introduction to Liturgical Theology._ Crestwood, N.Y.: St. Vladimir's Seminary Press, 1966. Orthodox. Scholarly. Addresses problems in eastern worship. Deals with the task and method of liturgical theology, the origin of the orthodox, the development of the orthodoxy, and the Byzantine synthesis.

_____. _For the Life of the World._ Crestwood, N.Y.: St. Vladimir's Seminary Press, 1973. Popular, but based on scholarly research. Addresses how worship is by definition and act a reality with cosmic, historical, and eschatological dimensions of Christian truth. Worship is seen not as mere piety but as an expression of worldview.

Schroeder, Frederick. _Worship in the Reformed Tradition._ Cleveland: United Church Press, 1966. Probes the approach of Reformed Christian to issues such as the theocentric nature of worship, sanctuary and altar, cultus and conduct, and the Eucharist.

Segler, Franklin M. _Christian Worship: Its Theology and Practice._ Nashville: Broadman Press, 1967. Addresses the meaning of worship, the means of expressing worship, planning and conducting worship, and other worship-related topics.

Senn, Frank C. _Christian Worship and Its Cultural Setting._ Philadelphia: Fortress Press, 1983. This clearly written work addresses the relation between worship and culture and argues against worship that is either irrelevant to culture or captivated by culture. The author presents guidelines for a worship that transforms culture and provides an experience of both transcendence and of human relevance.

Taft, Robert. _Beyond East and West: Problems in Liturgical Understanding._ Washington, D.C.: Pastoral Press, 1984. This work of extraordinary scholarship and depth introduces the student to a variety of subjects, from a theology of worship to difference between Byzantine and Catholic worship to structural studies of worship and the evolution of various liturgies.

Wainwright, Geoffrey. _Doxology: The Praise of God_

*in Worship, Doctrine, and Life.* New York: Oxford University Press, 1980. A systematic theology drawn from the experience of worship. Treats main themes such as God, Christ, Spirit, church, Scripture, creeds and hymns.

Webber, Robert. *Worship Old and New.* Grand Rapids: Zondervan Publishing Co., 1982. Protestant. Based on contemporary scholarship. An introduction to the biblical roots of worship, its historical development, an understanding of its theology, and a grasp of the relationship of worship to space, time, sound, and the world.

Williams, Benjamin D., and Harold B. Anstall. *Orthodoxy and Worship: A Living Continuity with the Synagogue, the Temple, and the Early Church.* Minneapolis: Life and Light Press, 1990. A highly readable defense of the orthodox liturgy; argues that of all liturgies, the eastern liturgy is rooted in the primitive worship of the church.

# PART FIVE

# New Directions
in Worship

# THIRTEEN

# Contemporary Documents on Worship Renewal

The twentieth century will no doubt be remembered as the era in which the church most vigorously addressed the renewal of worship. In this century, probably more research and writing centered on liturgy and worship have been produced than during any previous century.

Neoorthodox theology within North American mainline Protestantism following World War II led to a renewed interest in Reformation themes. Moreover, the rediscovery of the thinking of Luther, Calvin, Wesley, and others brought about change in the worship of several major denominations. Renewal came to the Roman Catholic church through the leadership of Pope John XXIII (1958–1963), who convened the Second Vatican Council; the Constitution on the Sacred Liturgy formulated by Vatican II set the stage for worship renewal not only within the Roman Catholic sphere but within other Christian communions as well. Equally significant has been the rise of the charismatic movement, a renewal that has spread throughout the world and into nearly every denomination. For the most part, denominations and local churches experiencing worship renewal have been influenced by one or more of these factors.

The most important twentieth-century document of worship renewal is the Roman Catholic Constitution on the Sacred Liturgy, the pronouncement from the second session (1963) of the Second Vatican Council. Many other statements and writings have echoed in various ways the themes set out in this document, affecting renewal in other Christian communities as well. This influence may be seen in the Protestant worship manifesto which follows, and to a degree in the subsequent statement, which reflects the concerns of the Pentecostal and charismatic traditions.

## 204 • A CATHOLIC STATEMENT: THE CONSTITUTION ON THE SACRED LITURGY

*On December 4, 1964, when Pope Paul VI promulgated the Constitution on the Sacred Liturgy, he spoke of worship as "the first [issue] to be examined and the first, too, in a sense, by reason of its intrinsic value and its importance in the life of the church." The influence of this, the most important document on worship in the twentieth century, has been felt around the world and in virtually every part of the body of Christ.*

### The Constitution on the Sacred Liturgy

Introduction

1. This Sacred Council has several aims in view: it desires to impart an ever increasing vigor to the Christian life of the faithful; to adapt more suit- ably to the needs of our own times those institutions that are subject to change; to foster whatever can promote union among all who believe in Christ; to strengthen whatever can help to call the whole of humanity into the household of the Church. The council therefore sees particularly cogent reasons for undertaking the reform and promotion of the liturgy.

2. For the liturgy, "making the work of our redemption a present actuality," most of all in the divine sacrifice of the Eucharist, is the outstanding means whereby the faithful may express in their lives, and manifest to others, the mystery of Christ and the real nature of the true Church. It is of the essence of the Church to be both human and divine, visible yet endowed with invisible resources, eager to act yet intent on contemplation, present in this world yet not at home in it; and the Church is all

these things in such wise that in it the human is directed and subordinated to the divine, the visible likewise to the invisible, action to contemplation, and this present world to that city yet to come, which we seek. While the liturgy daily builds up those who are within into a holy temple of the Lord, into a dwelling place for God in the Spirit, to the mature measure of the fullness of Christ, at the same time it marvelously strengthens their power to preach Christ, and thus shows forth the Church to those who are outside as a sign lifted up among the nations, under which the scattered children of God may be gathered together, until there is one sheepfold and one shepherd.

3. Wherefore the Council judges that the following principles concerning the promotion and reform of the liturgy should be called to mind and practical norms established.

Among these principles and norms there are some that can and should be applied both to the Roman rite and also to all the other rites. The practical norms that follow however, should be taken as applying only to the Roman rite, except for those that, in the very nature of things, affect other rites as well.

4. Lastly, in faithful obedience to tradition, the Council declares that the Church holds all lawfully acknowledged rites to be of equal right and dignity and wishes to preserve them in the future and to foster them in every way. The Council also desires that, where necessary, the rites be revised carefully in the light of sound tradition, and that they be given new vigor to meet the circumstances and needs of modern times.

## Chapter I
### General Principles for the Reform and Promotion of the Sacred Liturgy

### I. The Nature of the Sacred Liturgy and Its Importance in the Church's Life

5. God who "wills that all be saved and come to the knowledge of the truth" (1 Tim. 2:4), "who in many and various ways spoke in times past to the fathers by the prophets" (Heb. 1:1), when the fullness of time had come sent his Son, the Word made flesh, anointed by the Holy Spirit, to preach the Gospel to the poor, to heal the contrite of heart; he is "the physician, being both flesh and of the Spirit," the mediator between God and us. For his humanity, united with the person of the Word, was

the instrument of our salvation. Therefore in Christ "the perfect achievement of our reconciliation came forth and the fullness of divine worship was given to us."

The wonderful works of God among the people of the Old Testament were but a prelude to the work of Christ the Lord. He achieved his task of redeeming humanity and giving perfect glory to God, principally by the paschal mystery of his blessed passion, resurrection from the dead, and glorious Ascension, whereby "dying, he destroyed our death and, rising, he restored our life." For it was from the side of Christ as he slept the sleep of death upon the cross that there came forth the sublime sacrament of the whole church.

6. As Christ was sent by the Father, he himself also sent the apostles, filled with the Holy Spirit. Their mission was, first, by preaching the Gospel to every creature, to proclaim that by his death and resurrection Christ has freed us from Satan's grip and brought us into the paschal mystery of Christ: they die with him, are buried with him, and rise with him, they receive the spirit of adoption as children "in which we cry: Abba, Father" (Rom. 8:15), and thus become true adorers whom the Father seeks. In like manner, as often as they eat the supper of the Lord they proclaim the death of the Lord until he comes. For that reason, on the very day of Pentecost when the Church appeared before the world, "those who received the word" of Peter "were baptized." And "they continued steadfastly in the teaching of the apostles and in the communion of the breaking of bread and in prayers . . . praising God and being in favor with all the people" (Acts 2:41-47). From that time onward the Church has never failed to come together to celebrate the paschal mystery: reading those things "which were in all the Scriptures concerning him" (Luke 24:27); celebrating the Eucharist, in which "the victory and triumph of his death are again made present," and at the same time giving thanks "to God for his inexpressible gift" (2 Cor. 9:15) in Christ Jesus, "in praise of his glory" (Eph. 1:12), through the power of the Holy Spirit.

7. To accomplish so great a work, Christ is always present in his Church, especially in its liturgical celebrations. He is present in the sacrifice of the Mass, not only in the person of his minister, "the same now offering, through the ministry of priests, who formerly offered himself on the cross," but especially under the eucharistic elements. By his

power he is present in the sacraments, so that when a man baptizes it is really Christ himself who baptizes. He is present in his word, since it is he himself who speaks when the holy Scriptures are read in the Church. He is present, lastly, when the Church prays and sings, for he promised: "Where two or three are gathered together in my name, there am I in the midst of them" (Matt. 18:20).

Christ always truly associates the Church with himself in this great work wherein God is perfectly glorified and the recipients made holy. The Church is the Lord's beloved Bride who calls to him and through him offers worship to the eternal Father.

Rightly, then, the liturgy is considered as an exercise of the priestly office of Jesus Christ. In the liturgy, by means of signs perceptible to the senses, human sanctification is signified and brought about in ways proper to each of these signs; in the liturgy the whole public worship is performed by the Mystical Body of Jesus Christ, that is, by the Head and his members.

From this follows that every liturgical celebration, because it is an action of Christ and of his Body which is the Church, is a sacred action surpassing all others; no other action of the church can equal its effectiveness by the same title and to the same degree.

8. In the earthly liturgy we take part in a foretaste of that heavenly liturgy celebrated in the holy city of Jerusalem toward which we journey as pilgrims, where Christ is sitting at the right hand of God, a minister of the holies and of the true tabernacle, we sing a hymn to the Lord's glory with the whole company of heaven; venerating the memory of the saints, we hope for some part and fellowship with them; we eagerly await the Savior, our Lord Jesus Christ, until he, our life, shall appear and we too will appear with him in glory.

9. The liturgy does not exhaust the entire activity of the Church. Before people can come to the liturgy they must be called to faith and to conversion: "How then are they to call upon him in whom they have not yet believed? But how are they to believe him whom they have not heard? And how are they to hear if no one preaches? And how are men to preach unless they be sent?" (Rom. 10:14-15).

10. Still, the liturgy is the summit toward which the activity of the Church is directed; at the same time it is the fount from which all the Church's

power flows. For the aim and object of apostolic works is that all who are made children of God by faith and baptism should come together to praise God in the midst of his Church, to take part in the sacrifice, and to eat the Lord's Supper.

The liturgy in its turn moves the faithful, filled with "the paschal sacraments," to be "one in holiness;" it prays that "they may hold fast in their lives to what they have grasped by their faith;" the renewal in the Eucharist of the covenant between the Lord and his people draws the faithful into the compelling love of Christ and sets them on fire. From the liturgy, therefore, particularly the Eucharist, grace is poured forth upon us as from a fountain; the liturgy is the source for achieving in the most effective way possible human sanctification and God's glorification, the end to which all the Church's other activities are directed.

11. But in order that the liturgy may possess its full effectiveness, it is necessary that the faithful come to it with proper dispositions, that their minds be attuned to their voices, and that they cooperate with divine grace, lest they receive it in vain. Pastors must therefore realize that when the liturgy is celebrated something more is required than the mere observance of the laws governing valid and lawful celebration; it is also their duty to ensure that the faithful take part fully aware of what they are doing, actively engaged in the rite, and enriched by its effects.

12. The spiritual life, however, is not limited solely to participation in the liturgy. Christians are indeed called to pray in union with each other, but they must also enter into their chamber to pray to the Father in secret, further, according to the teaching of the Apostle, they should pray without ceasing. We learn from the same Apostle that we must always bear about in our body the dying of Jesus, so that the life also of Jesus may be made manifest in our bodily frame. This is why we ask the Lord in the sacrifice of the Mass that "receiving the offering of the spiritual victim," he may fashion us for himself "as an eternal gift."

13. Popular devotions of the Christian people are to be highly endorsed, provided they accord with the laws and norms of the Church, above all when they are ordered by the Apostolic See.

Devotions proper to particular Churches also have a special dignity if they are undertaken by mandate of the bishops according to customs or books lawfully approved.

But these devotions should be so fashioned that they harmonize with the liturgical seasons, accord with the sacred liturgy, are in some way derived from it, and lead the people to it, since, in fact, the liturgy, by its very nature far surpasses any of them.

## II. The Promotion of Liturgical Instruction and Active Participation

14. The Church earnestly desires that all the faithful be led to that full, conscious, and active participation in liturgical celebrations called for by the very nature of the liturgy. Such participation by the Christian people as "a chosen race, a royal priesthood, a holy nation, God's own people" (1 Pet. 2:9; see 2:4-5) is their right and duty by reason of their baptism.

In the reform and promotion of the liturgy, this full and active participation by all the people is the aim to be considered before all else. For it is the primary and indispensable source from which the faithful are to derive the true Christian spirit and therefore pastors must zealously strive in all their pastoral work to achieve such participation by means of the necessary instruction.

Yet it would be futile to entertain any hopes of realizing this unless, in the first place, the pastors themselves become thoroughly imbued with the spirit and power of the liturgy and make themselves its teachers. A prime need, therefore, is that attention be directed, first of all, to the liturgical formation of the clergy. Wherefore the Council has decided to enact what follows.

15. Professors appointed to teach liturgy in seminaries, religious houses of study, and theological faculties must be thoroughly trained for their work in institutes specializing in this subject.

16. The study of liturgy is to be ranked among the compulsory and major courses in seminaries and religious houses of studies; in theological faculties it is to rank among the principal courses. It is to be taught under its theological, historical, spiritual, pastoral, and canonical aspects. Moreover, other professors, while striving to expound the mystery of Christ and the history of salvation from the angle proper to each of their own subjects, must nevertheless do so in a way that will clearly bring out the connection between their subjects and the liturgy, as also the underlying unity of all priestly training. This consideration is especially important for pro-

fessors of dogmatic, spiritual, and pastoral theology and for professors of holy Scripture.

17. In seminaries and houses of religious, clerics shall be given a liturgical formation in their spiritual life. The means for this are: proper guidance so that they may be able to understand the sacred rites and take part in them wholeheartedly; the actual celebration of the sacred mysteries and of other, popular devotions imbued with the spirit of the liturgy. In addition they must learn how to observe the liturgical laws, so that life in seminaries and houses of religious may be thoroughly permeated by the spirit of the liturgy.

18. Priests, both secular and religious, who are already working in the Lord's vineyard are to be helped by every suitable means to understand ever more fully what it is they are doing in their liturgical functions; they are to be aided to live the liturgical life and to share it with the faithful entrusted to their care.

19. With zeal and patience pastors must promote the liturgical instruction of the faithful and also their active participation in the liturgy, both internally and externally, taking into account their age and condition, their way of life, and their stage of religious development. By doing so, pastors will be fulfilling one of their chief duties as faithful stewards of the mysteries of God; and in this matter they must lead their flock not only by word but also by example.

20. Radio and television broadcasts of sacred rites must be marked by discretion and dignity, under the leadership and direction of a competent person appointed for this office by the bishops. This is especially important when the service to be broadcast is the Mass.

## III. The Reform of the Sacred Liturgy

21. In order that the Christian people may more surely derive an abundance of graces from the liturgy, the Church desires to undertake with great care a general reform of the liturgy itself. For the liturgy is made up of immutable elements, divinely instituted, and of elements subject to change. These not only may but ought to be changed with the passage of time if they have suffered from the intrusion of anything out of harmony with the inner nature of the liturgy or have become pointless.

In this reform both texts and rites should be so drawn up that they express clearly the holy things they signify and that the Christian people, as far as possible, are able to understand them with ease and to take part in the rites fully, actively, and as befits a community.

Wherefore the Council establishes the general norms that follow.

## A. General Norms

22. §1. Regulation of the liturgy depends solely on the authority of the Church, that is, on the Apostolic See and accordingly as the law determines, on the bishop.

§2. In virtue of power conceded by the law, the regulation of the liturgy within certain defined limits belongs also to various kinds of competent territorial bodies of bishops lawfully established.

§3. Therefore, no other person, not even if he is a priest, may on his own add, remove, or change anything in the liturgy.

23. That sound tradition may be retained and yet the way remain open to legitimate progress, a careful investigation is always to be made into each part of the liturgy to be revised. This investigation should be theological, historical, and pastoral. Also the general laws governing the structure and meaning of the liturgy must be studied in conjunction with the experience derived from recent liturgical reforms and from the indults conceded to various places. Finally, there must be no innovations unless the good of the Church genuinely and certainly requires them; care must be taken that any new forms adopted should in some way grow organically from forms already existing.

As far as possible, marked differences between the rites used in neighboring regions must be carefully avoided.

24. Sacred Scripture is of the greatest importance in the celebration of the liturgy. For it is from Scripture that the readings are given and explained in the homily and that psalms are sung; the prayers, collects, and liturgical songs are scriptural in their inspiration; it is from the Scriptures that actions and signs derive their meaning. Thus to achieve the reform, progress, and adaptation of the liturgy, it is essential to promote that warm and living love for Scripture to which the venerable tradition of both Eastern and Western rites gives testimony.

25. The liturgical books are to be revised as soon as possible; experts are to be employed in this task and bishops from various parts of the world are to be consulted.

## B. Norms Drawn from the Hierarchic and Communal Nature of the Liturgy

26. Liturgical services are not private functions, but are celebrations belonging to the Church, which is the "sacrament of unity," namely, the holy people united and ordered under their bishops.

Therefore liturgical services involve the whole Body of the Church; they manifest it and have effects upon it; but they also concern the individual members of the Church in different ways, according to their different orders, offices, and actual participation.

27. Whenever rites, according to their specific nature, make provision for communal celebration involving the presence and active participation of the faithful, it is to be stressed that this way of celebrating them is to be preferred, as far as possible, to a celebration that is individual and, so to speak, private.

This applies with special force to the celebration of Mass and the administration of the sacraments, even though every Mass has of itself a public and social character.

28. In liturgical celebrations each one, minister or lay person, who has an office to perform, should do all of, but only, those parts which pertain to that office by the nature of the rite and the principles of liturgy.

29. Servers, readers, commentators, and members of the choir also exercise a genuine liturgical function. They ought to discharge their office, therefore, with the sincere devotion and decorum demanded by so exalted a ministry and rightly expected of them by God's people.

Consequently, they must all be deeply imbued with the spirit of the liturgy, in the measure proper to each one, and they must be trained to perform their functions in a correct and orderly manner.

30. To promote active participation, the people should be encouraged to take part by means of acclamations, responses, psalmody, antiphons, and songs, as well as by actions, gestures, and bearing. And at the proper times all should observe a reverent silence.

31. The revision of the liturgical books must ensure that the rubrics make provision for the parts belonging to the people.

32. The liturgy makes distinctions between persons according to their liturgical function and sa-

cred orders and there are liturgical laws providing for due honors to be given to civil authorities. Apart from these instances, no special honors are to be paid in the liturgy to any private persons or classes of persons, whether in the ceremonies or by external display.

## C. Norms Based on the Teaching and Pastoral Character of the Liturgy

33. Although the liturgy is above all things the worship of the divine majesty, it likewise contains rich instruction for the faithful. For in the liturgy God is speaking to his people and Christ is still proclaiming his gospel. And the people are responding to God by both song and prayer.

Moreover, the prayers addressed to God by the priest who presides over the assembly in the person of Christ are said in the name of the entire holy people and of all present. And the visible signs used by the liturgy to signify invisible divine realities have been chosen by Christ or the Church. Thus not only when things are read "that were written for our instruction" (Rom. 15:4), but also when the Church prays or sings or acts, the faith of those taking part is nourished and their minds are raised to God, so that they may offer him their worship as intelligent beings and receive his grace more abundantly.

In the reform of the liturgy, therefore, the following general norms are to be observed.

34. The rites should be marked by a noble simplicity; they should be short, clear, and unencumbered by useless repetitions; they should be within the people's powers of comprehension and as a rule not require much explanation.

35. That the intimate connection between words and rites may stand out clearly in the liturgy:

§1. In sacred celebrations there is to be more reading from holy Scripture and it is to be more varied and apposite.

§2. Because the spoken word is part of the liturgical service, the best place for it, consistent with the nature of the rite, is to be indicated even in the rubrics; the ministry of preaching is to be filled with exactitude and fidelity. Preaching should draw its content mainly from scriptural and liturgical sources, being a proclamation of God's wonderful works in the history of salvation, the mystery of Christ, ever present and active within us, especially in the celebration of the liturgy.

§3. A more explicitly liturgical catechesis should also be given in a variety of ways. Within the rites themselves provision is to be made for brief comments, when needed by the priest or a qualified minister; they should occur only at the more suitable moments and use a set formula or something similar.

§4. Bible services should be encouraged, especially on the vigils of the more solemn feasts, on some weekdays in Advent and Lent, and on Sundays and holy days. They are particularly to be recommended in places where no priest is available; when this is the case, a deacon or some other person authorized by the bishop is to preside over the celebration.

36. §1. Particular law remaining in force, the use of the Latin language is to be preserved in the Latin rites.

§2. But since the use of the mother tongue, whether in the Mass, the administration of the sacraments, or other parts of the liturgy, frequently may be of great advantage to the people, the limits of its use may be extended. This will apply in the first place to the readings and instructions and to some prayers and chants, according to the regulations on this matter to be laid down for each case in subsequent chapters.

§3. Respecting such norms and also, where applicable, consulting the bishops of nearby territories of the same language, the competent, territorial ecclesiastical authority mentioned in article 22, §2 is empowered to decide whether and to what extent the vernacular is to be used. The enactments of the competent authority are to be approved, that is, confirmed by the Holy See.

§4. Translations from the Latin text into the mother tongue intended for use in the liturgy must be approved by the competent, territorial ecclesiastical authority already mentioned.

## D. Norms for Adapting the Liturgy to the Culture and Traditions of Peoples

37. Even in the liturgy the Church has no wish to impose a rigid uniformity in matters that do not affect the faith or the good of the whole community; rather, the Church respects and fosters the genius and talents of the various races and peoples. The Church considers with sympathy and, if possible, preserves intact the elements in these peoples' way of life that are not indissolubly bound up with superstition and error. Sometimes in fact the Church

admits such elements into the liturgy itself, provided they are in keeping with the true and authentic spirit of the liturgy.

38. Provisions shall also be made, even in the revision of liturgical books, for legitimate variations and adaptations to different groups, regions, and peoples, especially in mission lands, provided the substantial unity of the Roman Rite is preserved; this should be borne in mind when rites are drawn up and rubrics devised.

39. Within the limits set by the *editio typica* of the liturgical books, it shall be for the competent, territorial ecclesiastical authority mentioned in article 22, §2 to specify adaptations, especially in the case of the administration of the sacraments, the sacramentals, processions, liturgical language, sacred music, and the arts. This, however, is to be done in accord with the fundamental norms laid down in this Constitution.

40. In some places and circumstances, however, an even more radical adaptation of the liturgy is needed and this entails greater difficulties. Wherefore:

§1. The competent, territorial ecclesiastical authority mentioned in article 22, §2 must in this matter carefully and prudently weigh what elements from the traditions and culture of individual peoples may be appropriately admitted into divine worship. They are to propose to the Apostolic See adaptations considered useful or necessary that will be introduced with its consent.

§2. To ensure that adaptations are made with all the circumspection they demand, the Apostolic See will grant power to this same territorial ecclesiastical authority to permit and to direct, as the case requires, the necessary preliminary experiments within certain groups suited for the purpose and for a fixed time.

§3. Because liturgical laws often involve special difficulties with respect to adaptation, particularly in mission lands, experts in these matters must be employed to formulate them.

### IV. Promotion of Liturgical Life in Diocese and Parish

41. The bishop is to be looked on as the high priest of his flock, the faithful's life in Christ in some way deriving from and depending on him.

Therefore all should hold in great esteem the liturgical life of the diocese centered around the bishop, especially in his cathedral church; they must be convinced that the preeminent manifestation of the Church is present in the full, active participation of all God's holy people in these liturgical celebrations, especially in the same Eucharist, in a single prayer, at one altar at which the bishop presides, surrounded by his college of priests and by his ministers.

42. But because it is impossible for the bishop always and everywhere to preside over the whole flock in his Church, he cannot do otherwise than establish lesser groupings of the faithful. Among these the parishes, set up locally under a pastor taking the place of the bishop, are most important: in some manner they represent the visible Church established throughout the world.

And therefore both in attitude and in practice the liturgical life of the parish and its relationship to the bishop must be fostered among the faithful and clergy; efforts must also be made toward a lively sense of community within the parish, above all in the shared celebration of the Sunday Mass.

### V. Promotion of Pastoral-Liturgical Action

43. Zeal for the promotion and restoration of the liturgy is rightly held to be a sign of the providential dispositions of God in our time, a movement of the Holy Spirit in his Church. Today it is a distinguishing mark of the Church's life, indeed of the whole tenor of contemporary religious thought and action.

So that this pastoral-liturgical action may become even more vigorous in the Church, the Council decrees what follows.

44. It is advisable that the competent, territorial ecclesiastical authority mentioned in article 22, §2 set up a liturgical commission, to be assisted by experts in liturgical science, music, art, and pastoral practice. As far as possible the commission should be aided by some kind of institute for pastoral liturgy, consisting of persons eminent in these matters and including the laity as circumstances suggest. Under the direction of the aforementioned territorial ecclesiastical authority, the commission is to regulate pastoral-liturgical action throughout the territory and to promote studies and necessary experiments whenever there is question of adaptations to be proposed to the Apostolic See.

45. For the same reason every diocese is to have a commission on the liturgy, under the direction of the bishop, for promoting the liturgical apostolate.

Sometimes it may be advisable for several dioceses to form among themselves one single commission, in order to promote the liturgy by means of shared consultation.

46. Besides the commission on the liturgy, every diocese, as far as possible, should have commissions for music and art.

These three commissions must work in closest collaboration; indeed it will often be best to fuse the three of them into one single commission.

### Chapter II
### The Most Sacred Mystery of the Eucharist

47. At the Last Supper, on the night he was betrayed, our Savior instituted the eucharistic sacrifice of his body and blood. He did this in order to perpetuate the sacrifice of the cross throughout the centuries until he should come again, and in this way to entrust to his beloved Bride, the Church, a memorial of his death and resurrection: a sacrament of love, a sign of unity, a bond of charity, a paschal banquet "in which Christ is eaten, the heart is filled with grace, and a pledge of future glory given to us."

48. The Church, therefore, earnestly desires that Christ's faithful, when present at this mystery of faith, should not be there as strangers or silent spectators; on the contrary, through a good understanding of the rites and prayers they should take part in the sacred service conscious of what they are doing, with devotion and full involvement. They should be instructed by God's word and be nourished at the table of the Lord's body; they should give thanks to God; by offering the immaculate victim, not only through the hands of the priest, but also with him, they should learn to offer themselves as well; through Christ the Mediator, they should be drawn day by day into an ever more perfect union with God and with each other, so that finally God may be all in all.

49. Thus, mindful of those Masses celebrated with assistance of the faithful, especially on Sundays and holy days of obligation, the Council makes the following decrees in order that the sacrifice of the Mass, even in its ritual forms, may become pastorally effective to the utmost degree.

50. The Order of Mass is to be revised in a way that will bring out more clearly the intrinsic nature and purpose of its several parts, as also the connection between them, and will more readily achieve the devout, active participation of the faithful.

For this purpose the rites are to be simplified, due care being taken to preserve their substance; elements that, with the passage of time, came to be duplicated or were added with but little advantage are now to be discarded; other elements that have suffered injury through accident of history are now, as may seem useful or necessary, to be restored to the vigor they had in the traditions of the Fathers.

51. The treasures of the Bible are to be opened up more lavishly, so that a richer share in God's word may be provided for the faithful. In this way a more representative portion of holy Scripture will be read to the people in the course of a prescribed number of years.

52. By means of the homily the mysteries of the faith and the guiding principles of the Christian life are expounded from the sacred text during the course of the liturgical year; as part of the liturgy itself therefore, the homily is strongly recommended; in fact, at Masses celebrated with the assistance of the people on Sundays and holy days of obligation it is not to be omitted except for a serious reason.

53. Especially on Sundays and holy days of obligation there is to be restored, after the gospel and the homily, "the universal prayer" or "the prayer of the faithful." By this prayer, in which the people are to take part, intercession shall be made for the holy Church, for the civil authorities, for those oppressed by various needs, for all people, and for the salvation of the entire world.

54. With article 36 of this Constitution as the norm, in Masses celebrated with the people a suitable place may be allotted to their mother tongue. This is to apply in the first place to the readings and "the universal prayer," but also, as local conditions may warrant, to those parts belonging to the people.

Nevertheless steps should be taken enabling the faithful to say or to sing together in Latin those parts of the Ordinary of the Mass belonging to them.

Wherever a more extended use of the mother tongue within the Mass appears desirable, the regulation laid down in article 40 of this Constitution is to be observed.

55. That more complete form of participation in the Mass by which the faithful, after the priest's communion, receive the Lord's body from the sacrifice, is strongly endorsed.

The dogmatic principles laid down by the Council of Trent remain intact. In instances to be specified by the Apostolic See, however, communion under both kinds may be granted both to clerics and religious and to the laity at the discretion of the bishops, for example, to the ordained at the Mass of their ordination, to the professed at the Mass of their religious profession, to the newly baptized at the Mass following their baptism.

56. The two parts that, in a certain sense, go to make up the Mass, namely, the liturgy of the word and the liturgy of the Eucharist, are so closely connected with each other that they form but one single act of worship. Accordingly this Council strongly urges pastors that in their catechesis they insistently teach the faithful to take part in the entire Mass, especially on Sundays and holy days of obligation.

57. §1. Concelebration, which aptly expresses the unity of the priesthood, has continued to this day as a practice in the Church of both East and West. For this reason it has seemed good to the Council to extend permission for concelebration to the following cases:

1. a. on Holy Thursday, both the chrism Mass and the evening Mass;

b. Masses during councils, bishops' conferences, and synods;

c. the Mass at the blessing of an abbot.

2. Also, with permission of the Ordinary, who is the one to decide whether concelebration is opportune, to:

a. the conventual Mass and the principal Mass in churches, when the needs of the faithful do not require that all the priests on hand celebrate individually;

b. Masses celebrated at any kind of meeting of priests, whether the priests be secular or religious.

§2.1. The regulation, however, of the discipline of concelebration in the diocese pertains to the bishop.

2. This, however, does not take away the option of every priest to celebrate Mass individually, not, however, at the same time and in the same church as a concelebrated Mass or on Holy Thursday.

58. A new rite for concelebration is to be drawn up and inserted into the Roman Pontifical and Roman Missal.

## Chapter III
## The Other Sacraments and the Sacramentals

59. The purpose of the sacraments is to make people holy, to build up the Body of Christ, and, finally, to give worship to God; but being signs they also have a teaching function. They not only presuppose faith, but by words and objects they also nourish, strengthen, and express it; that is why they are called "sacraments of faith." They do indeed impart grace, but, in addition, the very act of celebrating them disposes the faithful most effectively to receive this grace in a fruitful manner, to worship God rightly, and to practice charity.

It is therefore of the highest importance that the faithful should really understand the sacramental signs and should with great eagerness frequent those sacraments that were instituted to nourish the Christian life.

60. The Church has, in addition, instituted sacramentals. These are sacred signs bearing a kind of resemblance to the sacraments: they signify effects, particularly of a spiritual kind, that are obtained through the Church's intercession. They dispose to receive the chief effect of the sacraments and they make holy various occasions in human life.

61. Thus, for well-disposed members of the faithful, the effect of the liturgy of the sacraments and sacramentals is that almost every event in their lives is made holy by divine grace that flows from the paschal mystery of Christ's passion, death, and resurrection, the font from which all sacraments and sacramentals draw their power. The liturgy means also that there is hardly any proper use of material things that cannot thus be directed toward human sanctification and the praise of God.

62. With the passage of time, however, certain features have crept into the rites of the sacraments and sacramentals that have made their nature and purpose less clear to the people of today: hence some changes have become necessary as adaptations to the needs of our own times. For this reason the Council decrees what follows concerning the revision of these rites.

63. Because the use of the mother tongue in the administration of the sacraments and sacramentals can often be of considerable help for the people, this use is to be extended according to the following norms:

a. With article 36 as the norm, the vernacular may be used in administering the sacraments and sacramentals.

b. Particular rituals in harmony with the new edition of the Roman Ritual shall be prepared without delay by the competent, territorial ecclesiastical authority mentioned in article 22, §2 of this Constitution. These rituals are to be adapted, even in regard to the language employed, to the needs of the different regions. Once they have been reviewed by the Apostolic See, they are to be used in the regions for which they have been prepared. But those who draw up these rituals or particular collections of rites must not leave out the prefatory instructions for the individual rites in the Roman Ritual, whether the instructions are pastoral and rubrical or have some special social bearing.

64. The catechumenate for adults, divided into several stages, is to be restored and put into use at the discretion of the local Ordinary. By this means the tie of the catechumenate, which is intended as a period of well-suited instruction, may be sanctified by sacred rites to be celebrated at successive intervals of time.

65. With articles 37–40 of this Constitution as the norm, it is lawful in mission lands to allow, besides what is part of Christian tradition, those initiation elements in use among individual peoples, to the extent that such elements are compatible with the Christian rite of initiation.

66. Both of the rites for the baptism of adults are to be revised: not only the simpler rite, but also the more solemn one, with proper attention to the restored catechumenate. A special Mass "On the Occasion of a Baptism" is to be incorporated into the Roman Missal.

67. The rite for the baptism of infants is to be revised and it should be suited to the fact that those to be baptized are infants. The roles as well as the obligations of parents and godparents should be brought out more clearly in the rite itself.

68. The baptismal rite should contain alternatives. to be used at the discretion of the local Ordinary, for occasions when a very large number are to be baptized together. Moreover, a shorter rite is to be drawn up, especially in mission lands, for use by catechists, but also by the faithful in general, when there is danger of death and neither a priest nor a deacon is available.

69. In place of the rite called the "Order of Supplying What Was Omitted in the Baptism of an Infant," a new rite is to be drawn up. This should manifest more clearly and fittingly that an infant who was baptized by the short rite has already been received into the Church.

Similarly, a new rite is to be drawn up for converts who have already been validly baptized; it should express that they are being received into the communion of the Church.

70. Except during the Easter season, baptismal water may be blessed within the rite of baptism itself by use of an approved, shorter formulary.

71. The rite of confirmation is also to be revised in order that the intimate connection of this sacrament with the whole of Christian initiation may stand out more clearly; for this reason it is fitting for candidates to renew their baptismal promises just before they are confirmed.

Confirmation may be conferred within Mass when convenient; as for the rite outside Mass, a formulary is to be composed for use as an introduction.

72. The rite and formularies for the sacrament of penance are to be revised so that they more clearly express both the nature and effect of the sacrament.

73. "Extreme unction," which may also and more properly be called "anointing of the sick," is not a sacrament for those only who are at the point of death. Hence, as soon as any one of the faithful begins to be in danger of death from sickness or old age, the fitting time for that person to received this sacrament has certainly already arrived.

74. In addition to the separate rites for anointing of the sick and for viaticum, a continuous rite shall be drawn up, structured so that the sick person is anointed after confessing and before receiving viaticum.

75. The number of the anointings to be adapted to the circumstances; the prayers that belong to the rite of anointing are to be so revised that they correspond to the varying conditions of the sick who receive the sacrament.

76. Both the ceremonies and texts of the ordination rites are to be revised. The address given by the bishop at the beginning of each ordination or consecration may be in the vernacular.

When a bishop is consecrated, all the bishops present may take part in the laying on of hands.

77. The marriage rite now found in the Roman Ritual is to be revised and enriched in such a way that it more clearly signifies the grace of the sac-

rament and imparts a knowledge of the obligation of spouses.

If any regions follow other praiseworthy customs and ceremonies when celebrating the sacrament of marriage, the Council earnestly desires that by all means these be retained.

Moreover, the competent, territorial ecclesiastical authority mentioned in article 22, §2 of this Constitution is free to draw up, in accord with article 63, its own rite, suited to the usages of place and people. But the rite must always conform to the law that the priest assisting at the marriage must ask for and obtain consent of the contracting parties.

78. Marriage is normally to be celebrated within Mass, after the reading of the gospel and the homily and before "the prayer of the faithful." The prayer for the bride, duly emended to remind both spouses of their equal obligation to remain faithful to each other, may be said in the vernacular.

But if the sacrament of marriage is celebrated apart from Mass, the epistle and gospel from the nuptial Mass are to be read at the beginning of the rite and the blessing is always to be given to the spouses.

79. The sacramentals are to be reviewed in the light of the primary criterion that the faithful participate intelligently, actively, and easily; the conditions of our own days must also be considered. When rituals are revised, in accord with article 63, new sacramentals may also be added as the need for them becomes apparent.

Reserved blessings shall be very few; reservations shall be in favor only of bishops and Ordinaries.

Let provision be made that some sacramentals, at least in special circumstances and at the discretion of the Ordinary, may be administered by qualified laypersons.

80. The rite for the consecration to a life of virginity as it exists in the Roman Pontifical is to be revised.

A rite of religious profession and renewal of vows shall be drawn up with a view to achieving greater unity, simplicity, and dignity. Apart from exceptions in particular law, this rite should be adopted by those who make their profession or renewal of vows within Mass.

Religious profession should preferably be made within Mass.

81. The rite of funerals should express more clearly the paschal character of Christian death and

should correspond more closely to the circumstances and traditions of various regions. This applies also to the liturgical color to be used.

82. The rite for the burial of infants is to be revised and a special Mass for the occasion provided.

## Chapter IV
## The Divine Office

83. Christ Jesus, High Priest of the new and eternal covenant, taking human nature, introduced into this earthly exile the hymn that is sung throughout all ages in the halls of heaven. He joins the entire human community to himself, associating it with his own singing of this canticle of divine praise.

For he continues his priestly work through the agency of his Church, which is unceasingly engaged in praising the Lord and interceding for the salvation of the whole world. The Church does this not only by celebrating the Eucharist, but also in other ways, especially by praying the divine office.

84. By tradition going back to early Christian times, the divine office is so arranged that the whole course of the day and night is made holy by the praises of God. Therefore, when this wonderful song of praise is rightly performed by priests and others who are deputed for this purpose by the Church's ordinance or by the faithful praying together with the priest in the approved form, then it is truly the voice of a bride addressing her bridegroom; it is the very prayer that Christ himself, together with his Body, addresses to the Father.

85. Hence all who render this service are not fulfilling a duty of the Church, but also are sharing in the greatest honor of Christ's Bride, for by offering these praises to God they are standing before God's throne in the name of the Church, their Mother.

86. Priests engaged in the sacred pastoral ministry will offer the praises of the hours with greater fervor the more vividly they realize that they must heed St. Paul's exhortation: "Pray without ceasing" (1 Thess. 5:17). For the work in which they labor will effect nothing and bring forth no fruit except by the power of the Lord who said: "Without me you can do nothing" (John 15:5). That is why the apostles, instituting deacons, said: "We will devote ourselves to prayer and to the ministry of the word" (Acts 6:4).

87. In order that the divine office may be better and more completely carried out in existing circum-

stances, whether by priests or by other members of the Church, the Council, carrying further the restoration already so happily begun by the Apostolic See, has seen fit to decree what follows concerning the office of the Roman Rite.

88. Because the purpose of the office is to sanctify the day, the traditional sequence of the hours is to be restored so that once again they may be genuinely related to the hour of the day when they are prayed, as far as it is possible. Moreover, it will be necessary to take into account the modern conditions in which daily life has to be lived, especially by those who are called to labor in apostolic works.

89. Therefore, when the office is revised, these norms are to be observed:

 a. By the venerable tradition of the universal Church, lauds as morning prayer and vespers as evening prayer are the two hinges on which the daily office turns; hence they are to be considered as the chief hours and celebrated as such.

 b. Compline is to be so composed that it will be a suitable prayer for the end of the day.

 c. The hour known as Matins, although it should retain the character of nocturnal praise when celebrated in choir, shall be adapted so that it may be recited at any hour of the day; it shall be made up of fewer Psalms and longer readings.

 d. The hour of prime is to be suppressed.

 e. In choir the minor hours of terce, sext, and none are to be observed. But outside choir it will be lawful to choose whichever of the three best suits the hour of the day.

90. The divine office, because it is the public prayer of the Church, is a source of devotion and nourishment also for personal prayer. Therefore priests and all others who take part in the divine office are earnestly exhorted in the Lord to attune their minds to their voices when praying it. The better to achieve this, let them take steps to improve their understanding of the liturgy and of the Bible, especially the psalms.

In revising the Roman office, its ancient and venerable treasures are to be so adapted that all those to whom they are handed on may more fully and readily draw profit from them.

91. So that it may really be possible in practice to observe the course of the hours proposed in article 89, the psalms are no longer to be distributed over just one week, but over some longer period of time.

The work of revising the psalter, already happily begun, is to be finished as soon as possible and is to take into account the style of Christian Latin, the liturgical use of psalms, including their being sung, and the entire tradition of the Latin Church.

92. As regards the readings the following shall be observed:

 a. Readings from sacred Scripture shall be arranged so that the riches of God's word may be easily accessible in more abundant measure.

 b. Readings excerpted from the works of the Fathers, doctors, and ecclesiastical writers shall be better selected.

 c. The accounts of the martyrdom or lives of the saints are to be made to accord with the historical facts.

93. To whatever extent may seem advisable, hymns are to be restored to their original form and any allusion to mythology or anything that conflicts with Christian piety is to be dropped or changed. Also, as occasion arises, let other selections from the treasury of hymns be incorporated.

94. That the day may be truly sanctified and the hours themselves recited with spiritual advantage, it is best that each of them be prayed at a time most closely corresponding to the true time of each canonical hour.

95. In addition to the conventual mass, communities obliged to choral office are bound to celebrate the office in choir every day. In particular:

 a. Orders of canons, of monks and of nuns, and of other regulars bound by law or constitutions to choral office must celebrate the entire office.

 b. Cathedral or collegiate chapters are bound to recite those parts of the office imposed on them by general or particular law.

 c. All members of the above communities who are in major orders or are solemnly professed, except for lay brothers, are bound individually to recite those canonical hours which they do not pray in choir.

96. Clerics not bound to office in choir, if they are in major orders, are bound to pray the entire office every day, either in common or individually, following the norms in article 89.

97. Appropriate instances are to be defined by the rubrics in which a liturgical service may be substituted for the divine office.

In particular cases and for just a reason Ordinaries may dispense their subjects wholly or in part from the obligation of reciting the divine office or may commute it.

98. Members of any institute dedicated to acquiring perfection who, according to their constitutions, are to recite any parts of the divine office are thereby performing the public prayer of the Church.

They too perform the public prayer of the Church who, in virtue of their constitutions, recite any little office, provided this has been drawn up after the pattern of the divine office and duly approved.

99. Since the divine office is the voice of the Church, that is, of the whole Mystical Body publicly praising God, those clerics who are not obligated to office in choir, especially priests who live together or who meet together for any purpose, are urged to pray at least some part of the divine office in common.

All who pray the divine office, whether in choir or in common, should fulfill the task entrusted to them as perfectly as possible: this refers not only to the internal devotion of their minds but also to their external manner of celebration.

It is advantageous, moreover, that the office in choir and in common be sung when there is an opportunity to do so.

100. Pastors should see to it that the chief hours, especially vespers, are celebrated in common in church on Sundays and the more solemn feasts. The laity, too, are encouraged to recite the divine office either with the priests, or among themselves, or even individually.

101. §1. In accordance with the centuries-old tradition of the Latin rite, clerics are to retain the Latin language in the divine office. But in individual cases the ordinary has the power of granting the use of a vernacular translation, prepared in accord with article 36, to those clerics for whom the use of Latin constitutes a grave obstacle to their praying the office properly.

§2. The competent superior has the power to grant the use of the vernacular in the celebration of the divine office, even in choir, to nuns and to members of institutes dedicated to acquiring perfection, both men who are not clerics and women. The version, however, must be one that has been approved.

§3. Any cleric bound to the divine office fulfills his obligation if he prays the office in the vernacular together with a group of the faithful or

with those mentioned in 2, provided the text of the translation has been approved.

Chapter V
The Liturgical Year

102. The Church is conscious that it must celebrate the saving work of the divine Bridegroom by devoutly recalling it on certain days throughout the course of the year. Every week, on the day which the Church had called the Lord's Day, it keeps the memory of the Lord's resurrection, which it also celebrates once in the year, together with his blessed passion, in the most solemn festival of Easter.

Within the cycle of a year, moreover, the Church unfolds the whole mystery of Christ, from his incarnation and birth until his ascension, the day of Pentecost, and the expectation of blessed hope and of the Lord's return.

Recalling thus the mysteries of redemption, the Church opens to the faithful the riches of the Lord's powers and merits, so that these are in some way made present in every age in order that the faithful may lay hold on them and be filled with saving grace.

103. In celebrating this annual cycle of Christ's mysteries, the Church honors with special love Mary, the Mother of God, who is joined by an inseparable bond to the saving work of her Son. In her the Church holds up and admires the most excellent effect of the redemption and joyfully contemplates, as in a flawless image, that which the Church itself desires and hopes wholly to be.

104. The Church has also included in the annual cycle days devoted to the memory of the martyrs and the other saints. Raised up to perfection by the manifold grace of God and already in possession of eternal salvation, they sing God's perfect praise in heaven and offer prayers for us. By celebrating their passage from earth to heaven the Church proclaims the paschal mystery achieved in the saints, who have suffered and been glorified with Christ; it proposes them to the faithful as examples drawing all to the Father through Christ and pleads through their merits for God's favors.

105. Finally, in the various seasons of the year and according to its traditional discipline, the Church completes the formation of the faithful by means of devout practices for soul and body, by instruction, prayer, and works of penance and of mercy.

Accordingly the sacred Council has seen fit to decree what follows.

106. By a tradition handed down from the apostles and having its origin from the very day of Christ's resurrection, the Church celebrates the paschal mystery every eighth day, which, with good reason, bears the name of the Lord's Day or Sunday. For on this day Christ's faithful must gather together so that, by hearing the word of God and taking part in the Eucharist, they may call to mind the passion, the resurrection, and the glorification of the Lord Jesus and may thank God, who "has begotten them again into a living hope throughout the resurrection of Jesus Christ from the dead" (1 Pet. 1:3). Hence the Lord's Day is the first holy day of all and should be proposed to the devotion of the faithful and taught to them in such a way that it may become in fact a day of joy and of freedom from work. Other celebrations, unless they be truly of greatest importance, shall not have precedence over the Sunday, the foundation and core of the whole liturgical year.

107. The liturgical year is to be so revised that the traditional customs and usages of the sacred seasons are preserved or restored to suit the conditions of modern times; their specific character is to be retained, so that they duly nourish the devotion of the faithful who celebrate the mysteries of Christian redemption and above all the paschal mystery. If certain adaptations are considered necessary on account of local conditions, they are to be made in accordance with the provisions of articles 39 and 40.

108. The minds of the faithful must be directed primarily toward those feasts of the Lord on which the mysteries of salvation are celebrated in the course of the year. Therefore, the Proper of Seasons shall be given the precedence due to it over the feasts of the saints, in order that the entire cycle of the mysteries of salvation may be celebrated in the measure due to them.

109. Lent is marked by two themes, the baptismal and the penitential. By recalling or preparing for baptism and by repentance, this season disposes the faithful, as they more diligently listen to the word of God and devote themselves to prayer, to celebrate the paschal mystery. The baptismal and penitential aspects of Lent are to be given greater prominence in both the liturgy and liturgical catechesis. Hence:

a. More use is to be made of the baptismal features proper to the Lenten liturgy; some of those from an earlier era are to be restored as may seem advisable.

b. The same is to apply to the penitential elements. As regards catechesis, it is important to impress on the minds of the faithful not only the social consequences of sin but also the essence of the virtue of penance, namely, detestation of sin as an offense against God; the role of the Church in penitential practices is not to be neglected and the people are to be exhorted to pray for sinners.

110. During Lent penance should be not only inward and individual, but also outward and social. The practice of penance should be fostered, however, in ways that are possible in our own times and in different regions and according to the circumstances of the faithful; it should be encouraged by the authorities mentioned in article 22.

Nevertheless, let the paschal fast be kept sacred. Let it be observed everywhere on Good Friday and, where possible, prolonged throughout Holy Saturday, as a way of coming to the joys of the Sunday of the resurrection with uplifted and welcoming heart.

111. The saints have been traditionally honored in the Church and their authentic relics and images held in veneration. For the feasts of the saints proclaim the wonderful works of Christ in his servants and display to the faithful fitting examples for their imitation.

Lest the feasts of the saints take precedence over the feasts commemorating the very mysteries of salvation, many of them should be left to be celebrated by a particular Church or nation or religious family; those only should be extended to the universal Church that commemorate saints of truly universal significance.

## Chapter VI
### Sacred Music

112. The musical tradition of the universal Church is a treasure of inestimable value, greater even than that of any other art. The main reason for this preeminence is that, as sacred song closely bound to the text, it forms a necessary or integral part of the solemn liturgy.

Holy Scripture itself has bestowed upon sacred song and the same may be said of the Fathers of the Church and of the Roman pontiffs, who in recent times, led by St. Pius X, have explained more precisely the ministerial function supplied by sacred music in the service of the Lord.

Therefore sacred music will be the more holy the more closely it is joined to the liturgical rite, whether by adding delight to prayer, fostering oneness of spirit, or investing the rites with greater solemnity. But the Church approves of all forms of genuine art possessing the qualities required and admits them into divine worship.

Accordingly, the Council, keeping the norms and precepts of ecclesiastical tradition and discipline and having regard to the purpose of sacred music, which is the glory of God and the sanctification of the faithful, decrees what follows.

113. A liturgical service takes on a nobler aspect when the rites are celebrated with singing, the sacred ministers take their parts in them, and the faithful actively participate.

As regards the language to be used, the provisions of article 36 are to be observed; for the Mass, those of article 54; for the sacraments, those of article 63; for the divine office those of article 101.

114. The treasure of sacred music is to be preserved and fostered with great care. Choirs must be diligently developed, especially in cathedral churches; but bishops and other pastors of souls must be at pains to ensure that whenever a liturgical service is to be celebrated with song, the whole assembly of the faithful is enabled, in keeping with articles 28 and 30, to contribute the active participation that rightly belongs to it.

115. Great importance is to be attached to the teaching and practice of music in seminaries, in the novitiates and houses of study of religious of both sexes, and also in other Catholic institutions and schools. To impart this instruction, those in charge of teaching sacred music are to receive thorough training.

It is recommended also that higher institutes of sacred music be established whenever possible.

Musicians and singers, especially young boys, must also be given a genuine liturgical training.

116. The Church acknowledges Gregorian chant as distinctive of the Roman liturgy; therefore, other things being equal, it should be given pride of place in liturgical services.

But other kinds of sacred music, especially polyphony, are by no means excluded from liturgical celebrations, provided they accord with the spirit of the liturgical service in the way laid down in article 30.

117. The _editio typica_ of the books of Gregorian chant is to be completed and a more critical edition is to be prepared of those books already published since the reform of St. Pius X.

It is desirable also that an edition be prepared containing the simpler melodies for use in small churches.

118. The people's own religious songs are to be encouraged with care so that in sacred devotions as well as during services of the liturgy itself, in keeping with rubrical norms and requirements, the faithful may raise their voices in song.

119. In certain parts of the world, especially mission lands, people have their own musical traditions and these play a great part in their religious and social life. Thus, in keeping with articles 39 and 40, due importance is to be attached to their music and a suitable place given to it, not only in forming their attitude toward religion, but also in adapting worship to their native genius.

Therefore, when missionaries are being given training in music, every effort should be made to see that they become competent in promoting the traditional music of the people, both in schools and in sacred services, as far as may be practicable.

120. In the Latin Church the pipe organ is to be held in high esteem, for it is the traditional musical instrument that adds a wonderful splendor to the Church's ceremonies and powerfully lifts up the spirit to God and to higher things.

But other instruments also may be admitted for use in divine worship, with the knowledge and consent of the competent territorial authority and in conformity with article 22, §2, article 37 and article 40. This applies, however, only on condition that the instruments are suitable, or can be made suitable, for sacred use, are in accord with the dignity of the place of worship, and truly contribute to the uplifting of the faithful.

121. Composers, filled with the Christian spirit, should feel that their vocation is to develop sacred music and to increase its store of treasures.

Let them produce compositions having the qualities proper to genuine sacred music, not confining themselves to works that can be sung only by large choirs, but providing also for the needs of small choirs and for the active participation of the entire assembly of the faithful.

The text intended to be sung must always be consistent with Catholic teaching; indeed they should be drawn chiefly from holy Scripture and from liturgical sources.

International Committee
on English in the Liturgy[19]

## 205 • A Protestant Worship Manifesto

*This manifesto summarizes the themes of twentieth-century worship renewal and calls the Protestant community to action around twelve themes acceptable to the majority of worship leaders in the mainline Protestant tradition.*

A new Reformation of Word and sacrament is occurring in North American Protestantism. Yet so unnoticed has this movement been that it lacks a name. This inconspicuousness contrasts with the highly publicized liturgical reforms within Roman Catholicism since Vatican II. My purpose in this discussion is to delineate the contours of the movement, in the conviction that, although they are unpublicized, the goals for the reform of Protestant worship have reached a stage of consensus.

In the absence of a document such as the *Constitution on the Sacred Liturgy* of Vatican II, this Prot-

*The Nine-Pointed Star and the Nine Fruits of the Spirit. The fruits of the Spirit are based on Galatians 5:22. In Christian art they are depicted by a ninefold star, each point containing the name (or the letter) that symbolizes the gift:* Charitas, Gaudium, Pax, Longanimitas, Benignitas, Bonitas, Fides, Mansuetudo, *and* Continentia.

estant consensus is elusive. Indeed, it could be argued that the *Constitution* itself has provided the agenda for Protestant as well as Roman Catholic reform. But the *Constitution* dealt with a number of problems endemic to Roman Catholicism; many recent reforms go far beyond what that 1963 document envisioned.

My chief concern is with changes under way in churches at the center of the liturgical spectrum. Changes within the Episcopal and Lutheran churches (the liturgical right) are well known. Significant changes are also occurring on the liturgical left (Quakers, Pentecostals and, especially, the free-church tradition), but it is difficult to generalize about such disparate groups. My present concern is the liturgical center: the Reformed churches, Presbyterians, United Methodists, United Church of Canada and portions of the free-church tradition (United Church of Christ and Christian Church [Disciples of Christ]). In a rough, but convenient, way we may define the liturgical center in North American Protestantism as those churches that consider a service book normative for sacraments but never mandatory for the usual Sunday services. Within this framework, broad support exists for the reform of Protestant worship. I intend to articulate this increasingly evident, but as yet unformulated, consensus.

One does not necessarily do people a favor by changing the way in which they worship. Yet polls indicate that more than 66 per cent of Roman Catholics approve recent liturgical changes. Change in worship, as in any other human activity, is inevitable. But deliberate and carefully planned change in worship is a new phenomenon in North American Protestantism, just as it was unprecedented for Roman Catholics before Vatican II.

For change to be desirable, it has to be based on sound pastoral, theological and historical foundations. Only then can one act in confidence that the changes will be beneficial to the Christian people for whom they are designed. Criteria to judge changes are necessary so as to ensure that something more than personal preference is being promoted. Yet on major matters there seems to be remarkable agreement among those working for liturgical change.

One could designate the present movement as a "reformation of Word and sacrament." It is certainly an effort at reforming current practice in almost every aspect of worship. Or one might speak of it as the "renewal of worship" in the sense of efforts to infuse new vigor into it. Yet another dimension is represented by the phrase "recovery of worship." Much of the new is also very old. Many practices long dormant in Christian worship now seem relevant and useful. Greater knowledge of the first four Christian centuries has provided much impetus for recent reforms. Other possible terms could be revitalization of worship, or restructuring of worship.

The present movement is all that these terms indicate, and more. I shall try to delineate as concisely as possible twelve reforms generally advocated by almost all those working in this crusade, however it is labeled. Each reform will be presented in normative rather than descriptive terms. There seems to be sufficient agreement to state what should be done.

**1. Worship Should Be Shaped in the Light of Understanding It as the Church's Unique Contribution to the Struggle for Justice.** Protestantism has often identified preaching with prophetic ministry, and relegated the rest of worship to a priestly role, as if there were some distinction between these two aspects of ministry. Yet the weekly reiteration of the entire service (including the sermon) is the church's most-used method of shaping people for attitudes and acts of ecclesial and social justice. Although it is a by-product of worship, which exists for its own sake, constant exposure to words, action and roles within the worshiping community does more to reinforce a Christian's attitudes about justice than anything else the church does. Unfortunately, these same words, actions and roles can promote injustice as well as justice. Worship is a potent, possibly dangerous act, when it fails to do justice to all by being inclusive of all ages and races and both sexes.

Frequently the sacraments are more prophetic than preaching is. Baptism has long been recognized as the sacrament of equality (Gal. 3:27-28). Ordination of women is essentially a question of baptismal theology. Can one be baptized into Jesus Christ and not into his priesthood? Much has been made of the _koinonia_ or fellowship of the Lord's Supper (1 Cor. 10:16-17); more ought to be said about the Eucharist's exclusion of compromise with evil: "You cannot drink the cup of the Lord and the cup of demons too" (1 Cor. 10:21). The eschatological vision of the just reign of God which the Eucharist provides is far more radical than any human social program.

The chief contribution of worship to justice is

persistence, the ability to "hang in there." The need to worship, which we never outgrow or outlive, is recurring just as the struggle against evil is. As one who weekly receives God's self-giving through Word and sacrament, the Christian is enabled to give himself or herself for others in a struggle that outlasts each of us.

**2. The Paschal Nature of Christian Worship Should Resound Throughout All Services.** Baptism, grounded in the Easter event, starts the Christian life, and the same paschal joy echoes even in the service of Christian burial. Above all, Christian worship is rejoicing in what Christ has done for us, a form of God's self-giving in which the historical events are again offered to us. In worship, we experience anew the events of salvation history in terms of our own lives.

The penitential cloud of late medieval-Reformation worship continued to build in the neo-orthodox decades. Too often people go to church to be scolded rather than to experience the liberation of the divine. An opening prayer of confession sometimes does little more than suggest that worship is primarily about our failures rather than God's triumphs. An individualistic, introspective, subjective approach to worship makes it easy to forget that we have something far more important to focus on than our peccadilloes; we have the joyous Easter faith to proclaim. The proclamation and re-enactment of resurrection goes on week after week throughout the entire year.

**3. The Centrality of the Bible in Protestant Worship Must Be Recovered.** A curious link unites the worship of many liberal and fundamentalist congregations. Their use of Scripture in worship falls into the "when convenient" category. Scripture functions in the worship of thousands of Protestant congregations only as a means of reinforcing what the preacher wants to say. This use makes the Bible an optional resource rather than the source of Christian worship. It is forgotten that Scripture is read in worship not as a sermon text but as God's word to God's people. The sermon follows as a faithful exposition of what the Scriptures mean for our time. The new reforms encourage the reading of three lessons plus the singing of a psalm each week.

Reforms in this area have been the most successful, largely because of widespread use of the ecumenical lectionary. Unprecedented numbers of Protestant ministers have made the lectionary their organizing basis for the Sunday service. This is all the more striking in that, prior to 1970, such use was virtually nil to the liturgical left of Lutherans and Episcopalians. I was invited recently to speak to a ministerial association in a rural county in Indiana and was told not to mention the lectionary because most of those present would be Nazarene or Church of the Brethren preachers. But when I got there, the lectionary was all they wanted to talk about!

The discovery of the lectionary has had a major impact on preaching. A subtle form of oppression has been the subjection of the congregation to the preacher's own private canon of Scripture, which frequently excluded most of the Old Testament and much of the New. Conscientization has resulted in confrontation with all of Scripture. Use of the lectionary has meant a return to exegetical rather than topical or thematic preaching. And its use has surprised many preachers by making their preaching far more relevant than their own favorite thoughts, good advice, and *Reader's Digest* illustrations.

4. **The Importance of Time as a Major Structure in Christian Worship Must Be Rediscovered.** Many congregations are moving to a richer calendar as an unexpected by-product of the ecumenical lectionary. The calendar is the basic document of Christian worship, since it determines everything we do on a given Sunday. Those who use the ecumenical lectionary have discovered themselves following a common calendar shared by 80 million American Christians. For most churches it has almost doubled the festivals by adding occasions such as Baptism of the Lord, Transfiguration, and All Saints' Day. The new festivals are all christological events rather than human programs. At the same time, World Communion Sunday and Reformation Day are downplayed, along with promotional events.

Very important has been the discovery of the most dramatic part of Christian worship, Holy Week. Drama is intrinsic in Christian worship, not something added to it, and Holy Week is the climax of Christian drama. Holy Week is being celebrated in thousands of churches with an excitement unknown for centuries. Countless parishes have found popular a calendar that breaks the usual 11:00 A.M. Sunday structure with night services on special occasions: Christmas Eve, Ash Wednesday, Maundy Thursday, and Easter Eve. For millions, the liturgical year has become a major vehicle for living with Christ.

5. **All Reforms in Worship Must Be Shaped Ecumenically.** The widespread use of the lectionary and common calendar are the most important ecumenical developments of recent years. No one organized a national office or set up a committee to bring this about; pastors in towns and cities all over America simply began meeting to study the texts prescribed for worship. And laity learned of our oneness as they heard neighbors discuss sermons they had heard the previous Sunday. This is true grass-roots ecumenism.

Less obvious is the convergence of liturgical rites. Yet there are fewer and fewer distinctions between them, as different churches publish new versions. Bernard Cooke, the Roman Catholic theologian, is said to have remarked that he could use the new United Methodist eucharistic rite "without qualms." And Methodists certainly help themselves to much that is Roman Catholic.

The theological problems that have separated us in worship have been eliminated. A monk teaches worship at Yale; students in some Roman Catholic seminaries study worship from a Protestant textbook. I often wonder: "Why teach ecumenism when you can teach worship?" Differences, if they occur, are more apt to appear *within* churches. For example, a leading Roman Catholic liturgist refers to infant baptism as a "benign abnormality," while an *Instruction* from Rome defends the practice. But it is quite possible to teach liturgical theology today, making use of sources from every tradition, Orthodox to Quaker.

Much that has occurred is the result of borrowing with discernment. Even oriental rites and the practices and concepts of the Greek Orthodox have touched Western Christianity in crucial ways—the more reason for us to affirm and study the values of our own traditions so that we can offer them to others. An unexamined tradition often disappears simply because there is no one to expound it in the presence of one that is highly researched and articulated.

6. **Drastic Changes Are Needed in the Process of Christian Initiation.** This point is basic to current developments in worship and evangelization. Certain common themes seem to be emerging: initiation is an integral process that ought to be complete at one time in a person's life; God does not act to incorporate us into the body of Christ in halfway

fashion; what is done ought to be full and complete in itself.

Unfortunately, liturgical leaders have been forced to compromise in this area. Probably all of them would like to end present practices of confirmation and certainly to eliminate the term "confirmation." But there is a vast confirmation industry in the churches that is threatened by such suggestions. And so United Methodists, Lutherans, and Episcopalians were forced to compromise and retain the use of the term even though many now practice confirmation and communion of babies and children of any age. No longer do these acts seem contingent on us, but on God alone. A subtle form of ageism— the prejudice that children do not count until they think abstractly—is being assaulted from a theological basis.

The same churches also recognize the importance of human development and affirm that growth in Christian understanding is lifelong. Accordingly, rites for "affirmation," "reaffirmation," or "renewal" of what God has done for us in baptism have been published. The new Roman Catholic "Rite of Christian Initiation of Adults" has also attracted attention as a means of making the conversion of an adult an experience shared in community rather than an individual matter.

**7. High on the List of Reforms Is the Need to Recover the Eucharist as the Chief Sunday Service.** This is the most dramatic reform needed, as well as one of the most difficult to achieve, except where already present, as in the Christian Church (Disciples of Christ). Even many Lutherans and Episcopalians still experience resistance at this point. So desacralized has much of American Protestantism become that anything employing the physical and visible is suspect. The vast majority of Christian experience, past and present, witnesses to the value of weekly Eucharist, and study of our biblical and historical roots underscores this importance.

Yet to replicate the Lord's Supper on a weekly basis just as it is now celebrated monthly would be to court disaster. Until we develop genuine concern about the quality of celebration, greater frequency will reform little. Pastors need special sensitivity about the sign value of every aspect of these rites, not as a fussy rubrical matter but as a genuine pastoral concern that people better perceive and express what is ultimately real for them.

Two items need particular care. The eucharistic prayer, the central Christian doctrinal statement, must be rediscovered as prayerful proclamation. The pre-Vatican II rites of Roman Catholic and Protestant alike were woefully inadequate in this regard. And much work must be done to improve the method of distribution so that the people gather to stand, kneel or sit about the Lord's table, rather than remain in pews. We must discover how to act out fully the act of giving.

**8. Recovery of the Sense of God's Action in Other "Commonly Called Sacraments" Is Essential.** There is no Protestant consensus on just which sign-acts ought to be called sacraments, other than baptism, confirmation, and the Eucharist. This is as it should be, and was, for most of the church's history. But certain sign-acts provide the community the clearest experience of God's activity in its midst.

Reconciliation, formerly called "confession" or "penance," is an important part of the ministry of the sacraments. Eventually we may see quarterly or monthly public services of reconciliation. Public services of healing may also become common as we minister to whole persons rather than to disembodied souls. Ordination might as well be seen as a sacrament; it has kept sacramental characteristics in most churches.

Marriage and burial for Christians are special events of witness to God's self-giving in the midst of community. It is time to emphasize the special character of Christian marriage and Christian burial as these crucial passages are celebrated in the context of God's acts in the church.

**9. Music Must Be Seen in Its Pastoral Context as Fundamentally an Enabler of Fuller Congregational Participation.** It is frightening to analyze honestly how music functions in most Protestant churches. Usually it ranges from entertainment calculated to make palatable an otherwise bland service to innocuous Muzak used to fill in gaps and awkward moments. Gradually we are moving beyond a sense of "liturgical music" to a sense of "musical liturgy." Music thus used is seen as an integral part of the service rather than as gems of choral or instrumental music dropped into it. The problem with most choral music in Protestant worship is not that it is good or bad but that it is simply irrelevant. When it is not an integral part of the service, it cannot help being entertainment or background Muzak. The new lectionary benefits musicians as much as preachers by making integration of sung and spoken word much more readily achieved.

"Pastoral music," in contrast to "sacred music," is focused on helping the whole congregation express its worship with the fullest involvement. This means not that choral music should be eliminated but that such music is always a supplement to congregational song. Occasional sacred concerts, of course, are desirable, but they are never the model for the Sunday service. Musician and author Carlton Young said it well: "We tend to treat the choir as if it were the congregation; we should, instead, treat the congregation as if it were the choir." Renewed emphasis on hymnody, psalmody, and service music is encouraging.

One of the present frontiers is rediscovery of the Psalter. In most of our churches, responsive reading has vied with the pastoral prayer for being the dullest part of the service. One of the church's greatest treasures, the Psalter, is being rediscovered as song. Only the singing of it can do it justice. New methods of singing the Psalms themselves, rather than mangled paraphrases, have developed. These involve participation of choir or cantors and congregation. Suddenly we realize that choirs have been underused, relegated to anthem singing. Responsorial or antiphonal singing of the Psalms contributes far more to an integrated service than anthems used to camouflage the offering. The witness of the Psalms to God's saving actions in the context of the Psalms' fervent personal prayer adds an important dimension of participation.

**10. The Space and Furnishing for Worship Need Substantial Change in Most Churches.** If the quality of celebration is to be improved, frequently the very first step must be rearrangement of space. There are no possibilities for increasing the sign value of various acts if they cannot be seen. British theologian J. A. T. Robinson's pessimistic dictum that "the building will always win" may not be entirely true, but it tends to be so. We still see churches being designed as if nothing had happened in worship in the past twenty years—and in such churches, nothing is likely to happen in the next twenty. For worship of the incarnate God, space is a most important instrument.

To improve the quality of celebration, one must acknowledge people's visual, aural, and kinetic senses. Simplicity, utility, flexibility, and intimacy must characterize space designed for worship. This means, above all, careful examination of what the church does in each act of worship so as to provide the optimum physical setting for it.

Not much can be done for reforming baptism until candy-dish fonts are discarded in favor of those that make the washing audible and visible for the whole congregation. The font is our most feminine symbol; maybe that is why so many fonts are kept inconspicuous. The Lord's Table in many Protestant churches still must be pried loose from a wall and raised so that it can be used. Learning to use the altar-table would be a big step forward for many. When one sees an open Bible on the altar-table, one can almost be certain that neither is used in worship.

**11. No Reform of Worship Will Progress Far Until Much More Effort Is Invested in Teaching Seminarians and Clergy to Think Through the Functions of Christian Worship.** It is amazing how many clergy got through seminary without any serious reflection on and study of the church's most distinctive activity, its corporate worship. Those who need this help most are those least likely to realize it and seek it. Protestant seminaries have made major strides in teaching worship in the past decade. Nevertheless, in almost a fifth of our seminaries such instruction reaches only a meager number of students or none. Perhaps it is time to warn people planning to study for ordained ministry that if they are seriously interested in preparing for pastoral ministry they would do better to apply to a seminary which emphasizes worship studies. It is not difficult to determine in which seminaries worship instruction is presented to a significant number of students; lists of faculty are revealing.

For many pastors, educational gaps remain to be filled. Most denominations now offer workshops and various continuing education programs. Much is available in printed materials. The market for books about worship has grown remarkably in recent years. There is great opportunity here for the development of audiovisual resources, a natural medium for presentations on worship.

Strangely enough, clergy frequently have to catch up with the laity in this area. Courses on worship are now becoming common in undergraduate religion departments. Such courses provide one of the best ways of introducing Christianity—better than presenting it as an abstract system of doctrines. Laity frequently outnumber clergy at worship workshops. An uninformed minister is threatened by such people and often becomes more resistant to liturgical change. Only by learning can these insecurities be overcome.

**12. Finally, It Must Be Realized That Liturgical Renewal Is Not Just a Changing of Worship But Is Part of a Reshaping of American Christianity Root and Branch.** Liturgical renewal is not just window dressing, but a major force for justice, ecumenism, and rethinking of the whole Christian message and mission. It relates to and affects every part of the church's life. Liturgical renewal cannot coexist with the _status quo_ in most of these areas. It fits just as ill with liberals' negations as with conservatives' affirmations. Both seem to be inadequate reflections of the biblical and historical faith.

The "liturgical circle" begins by observing and listening to what the church does and says when it gathers for worship as the primary witness to what Christians believe, moves on to theological reflection on the meaning of these data, and then proceeds to reform worship so as to express these meanings more effectively. This liturgical circle provides methodology for a liturgical theology in which practice and theory are united.

Thus liturgical renewal is an important agent of change in American Protestantism. Although future historians will be able to isolate its most distinctive features with more precision and detachment than we can, we have the thrill of passionate engagement with the present as we reshape the church.

James F. White[20]

# 206 • A Pentecostal/Charismatic Manifesto

_The manifesto that follows addresses the worship life of traditional Pentecostal churches and that of charismatic churches in general. It distinguishes between changes basic to renewal and those that are more stylistic. It also focuses on the strengths and weaknesses of the Pentecostal and charismatic theology and practice of worship, and urges a reflective, biblical pursuit of worship renewal within this circle of churches. The author expresses a personal view and makes no claim to speak in behalf of Pentecostal or charismatic churches in general._

While worship renewal in mainstream Protestantism has been fairly intentional, in that it has resulted from theological reflection, the movement among Pentecostals and charismatics has taken a more un-

predictable course. Changes in worship patterns have been adopted more spontaneously, spreading from event to event and from church to church.

Enough common features have emerged, however, to disclose an identifiable trend. Included in this are elements such as singing led by praise-teams, extensive use of praise-choruses, sharply reduced use of the hymnal, increased physical expression such as clapping and raised hands, the congregational praise-chant, and in some churches the practice of rehearsed or spontaneous dance. Choral music is largely contemporary.

Benefits intrinsic to renewal include a recovery of emphasis upon the transcendence of God, with an accompanying emphasis upon singing _to_ God, not merely about Him. This recovery of the vertical dimension in worship may be the most significant aspect of Pentecostal-charismatic worship renewal, a feature achieved more through intuitive quest rather than through theological reflection. Another salutary result of worship renewal has been greatly increased congregational participation in sung praise and thanksgiving.

A serious defect of Pentecostal and charismatic worship is the lack of intense, in-depth biblical and theological reflection upon the nature of worship. As a result, worship tends to be a means to an end, whether that be church growth, personal fulfillment, or the defeat of God's enemies. Worship tends to become a utility or a self-absorbing "experience." Worship style is adjusted frequently to meet consumer appetites. Pragmatism wins over theology; that which attracts and holds a crowd is seen as that which God endorses. We should hasten to recognize that these ailments are all too common to our overall individualized American view of church life, as so many have observed.

I shall suggest several means by which the Pentecostal movement might participate in a more lasting, biblical renewal of worship.

**1. We Should See Our Worship as Christian, Occurring Within the Pentecostal-Charismatic Context—Not the Reverse.** We need to affirm and cherish those basic features which lie at the heart of Christian worship, regardless of special tradition. Our first question then should not be: "What makes worship Pentecostal or charismatic?" We need to ask: "What makes worship Christian?" We should reaffirm and celebrate those elements that are absolutely essential to Christian worship, practicing them in our own context. This is not a call to a bland eclecticism, nor a denial of so-called Pentecostal or charismatic distinctives. It is a call to join other evangelicals in recovering from historical amnesia and regaining a sense of continuity with the worshiping church through the ages, thus enriching our present experience.

**2. We Need to See the Vital Relationship Between Christian Worship and Christian Truth.** We are called to worship God in spirit and in truth; our way of worship is inseparable from our way of believing. Worship and belief, in other words, share a common hermeneutic; what we say in worship should harmonize with what we say in our other teaching. For example, if our worship is tainted by a triumphalism that obscures or denies our need of daily grace and mercy from God, then no amount of teaching on humility can compensate for that deviation from truth in worship. What we "say" through our worship-model may speak so loudly, our people may not hear our other declarations.

To ensure that all great redemptive truths are central to our worship, we need to restore more expanded and celebrative use of the Scriptures. It is only appropriate that those who defend a high view of biblical inspiration should demonstrate it by reading the Scriptures extensively and enthusiastically in worship. It should not be necessary to adopt the ecumenical lectionary to accomplish this high purpose, although we need to be informed by its scope. It is urgent that we gain that sense of God's Word to God's people which comes through regular reading of great, basic passages of the Old and New Testaments. These passages, read with uncontrived spiritual vigor, will resound in the memories and hearts of our children when most of our praise-choruses have faded.

**3. We Need to Maintain the Christological Focus, the "Paschal Center" of All Worship.** We gather around the crucified, risen and ever-living Lord Jesus Christ. Worship centers in what God has done for us in Christ, not in what we desire God to do for us today, nor in what we desire to do for God and for others. Although Christian growth, service and interpersonal care are inspired and enhanced by worship, they are not our direct pursuit in worship. Therefore, we need to affirm *an order of truth in worship,* in which we ensure that truth about God's steadfast covenant love and His saving acts in Christ are always central.

Since we do not adhere to a common liturgy, we need to apply ourselves with diligence to make certain that this theological focus emerges in our selection of music, scripture reading and other expressions. Each service should have its own way of declaring God's saving work. For example, hymns, songs and worship-choruses occurring early in the service need to express not only God's majesty but his loving, faithful acts of redemption. Those musical expressions which center on our response to God's action should follow later, providing that interaction between the declaration of truth and the response to truth which makes for vital worship. If our services are pointed in this central direction, we will have a happy, creative framework in which all spontaneous expressions can flourish.

Since most of our churches celebrate the Lord's Supper, or Holy Communion, no more frequently than monthly, we need the dynamic equivalent of what the Lord's Table declares within the framework of our regular worship services.

We also need to reexamine the content of our so-called praise-worship choruses, a body of more spontaneous music that celebrates the majesty of God, but often fails to emphasize the total redemptive story. We need to reinforce this music theologically. We should use with fresh inspiration the best of our older and newer hymnody, not as a concession to nostalgia or formality but as a confession of our love of sound theology in music.

To maintain this focus on Christ in our worship means that we will use structure not for the sake of dignity or "atmosphere," but for the sake of truth. The purpose of structure is to ensure that the vital truth about Jesus Christ as Savior and Lord resounds in our services. This calls for pastors to serve as theologians of the entire worship service, not merely of the sermon. This guidance task cannot be delegated to those who, however talented and creative, may be lacking in theological perspective. All musicians and other participants need to be informed by the central purpose of the worship service.

While we do not follow the traditional church year, which traces the events of the life of Christ, we have accumulated a miscellaneous civic-religious calendar of our own. All too often these varied emphases, many of which are promotional, encroach upon the vitality of our worship, and need to be reduced or purged. Far better that we celebrate the most vital seasons of the church year with spiritual enthusiasm, than spend time and energy on less important emphases. In addition to our celebration of Advent, Christmas and Easter, we can include other events of the life of Christ in our Scripture readings.

**4. We Need to Use Our Music More Purposefully Throughout the Service.** Music should assume its true role as a vital assistant to our entire worship, not merely as a "package" within the service. Music should enable us in our total response of love and thanksgiving to God as Creator and Redeemer, from the call to worship to our dismissal into the world for witness and service.

We need to correct a growing tendency to describe a certain more emotionally heightened section of the service as the "worship" portion. The idea is quite prevalent that during this section, generally devoted to praise-choruses and spontaneous prayer, worshipers gain a special presence of God. While it is true that we may experience deeper emotions during one portion of a service than at other times, we need to affirm that all of our worship is in the Lord's presence. And we need to employ one of the greatest means of worship, celebrative music, in all portions of the service.

This means that we should not dismiss our congregations immediately after the message, with scant opportunity to respond to God in song and prayer for what they have heard from the Word. For this response opportunity, we need the best of our hymns and a whole new variety of choruses that deal biblically and celebratively with our witness and mission in the world. Most of these latter expressions are yet to be written. We need to arrive as singing worshipers and depart as singing servants of God. We need a celebrative congruity in our services. This can be accomplished if we will combine spiritual zeal with strong theological direction.

**5. We Need to Recover a True Sense of Mystery in Christian Worship.** We should distinguish between mystical experience in worship and the central mystery of salvation as seen in God's historic saving acts in Jesus Christ. While the former is valid and biblical, the latter is also absolutely essential. We are not called to gather around mystical experience or a mystical atmosphere. Rather, we gather around the mystery of God incarnate. We do not celebrate first of all the degree to which we may sense the presence of God on a given day of worship. Rather, we celebrate above all the saving presence of God in our world.

Pentecostal and charismatic people have rightfully contributed to the idea that worship can be exciting. However, we also need to recognize that it is possible to have excitement without true Christian mystery. A recovery of a true sense of mystery, centered in the declarations of Scripture and touched by the Holy Spirit, is necessary for the preservation of genuine Christian excitement.

This calls for celebrative preaching, encompassed by celebrative singing and praying. It calls for a constant vein of doxology in our teaching and preaching. It means that we will not pose as experts, but as those who are participating in a great mystery of salvation. Our instruction on Christian living needs the fueling of the mystery of the cross, lest we fall into a sterile lecture-hall type of didacticism. It is remarkable too that in his how-to pastoral letters to Timothy and Titus, the apostle Paul constantly breaks into doxology. Such doxology-laced preaching and teaching surely should be within the genius of the Pentecostal movement, which celebrates openness to the Holy Spirit.

**6. We Need to Rediscover the Essence of the Kingdom of God in Our Worship.** We are called to worship as people who see the final, radical nature of the kingdom that has come to us in Christ and will come fully in his return. We worship as those who seek fulfillment of that kingdom, not merely escape from the woes of this life. In other words, we worship as an *eschatological people,* not merely as people who believe in some form of eschatology. As we worship we should pray that the kingdom may continue to come through our mission and service in the world. A wholesome, biblical view of the kingdom affirmed in our worship will help to deliver us from the self-absorption that is common to evangelicalism, including Pentecostalism, in our day.

**7. We Need to Rediscover a Deep Sense of Our Constant Need of the Grace of God.** Our historical emphasis upon the victorious personal Christian life needs to be held in a holy tension with a deepened sense of mercy and grace from God. And this emphasis needs to emerge, not only in Bible teaching, but in our regular worship services. How we will convey this renewed sense of God's mercy and grace within our context should be ours to explore. We need to learn anew, as Bonhoeffer emphasized, that the common link between Christians in worship is that they all have received a gift of mercy.

A movement that has exemplified spiritual excitement and vigor needs the constant and ultimate sustenance: that which comes from God's mercy and grace in Christ Jesus.

*Henry Jauhiainen*

## 207 • BIBLIOGRAPHY ON CONTEMPORARY WORSHIP DOCUMENTS

"Baptism, Eucharist and Ministry," *Faith and Order Paper No. 11.* Geneva, Switzerland: World Council of Churches, 1982. Here is an ecumenical document on the common faith and practice of the church around the world. This study of "Baptism, Eucharist and Ministry" is based on the teaching and practice of the early church.

Barauna, William, ed. *The Liturgy of Vatican II.* 2 vols. Chicago: Franciscan Herald Press, 1966. This work presents the nature and purpose of Vatican II to English-speaking people.

Bugnini, A., and L. Braga, eds. *The Commentary on the Constitution and on the Instruction of the Sacred Liturgy.* New York: Benziger, 1965. The *Constitution on the Sacred Liturgy* together with a commentary by a team of liturgical experts.

*Documents on the Liturgy 1963–1979: Conciliar, Papal and Curial Texts.* Collegeville, Minn: Liturgical Press, 1982. Numerous documents covering general principles, Eucharist, other sacraments and sacramentals, the divine office, the liturgical year, music, and art and furnishings.

McDonnell, Killian. *Presence, Power, Praise Documents on the Church Renewal.* Collegeville, Minn: Liturgical Press, 1980. 3 vols. The charismatic movement has made an impact on nearly every denomination throughout the world. This three-volume work presents a collection of documents that have been written regarding the charismatic movement have been collected. Volume 1 contains documents written between 1950–1974; volume 2 contains documents written between 1975–1979; and volume 3 contains documents written between 1973–1980. This is a comprehensive and even-handed drawing from sources in every denomination—Orthodox, Catholic, mainline Protestant, and evangelical Protestant. It is the most thorough source available for understanding the charismatic movement and the response of the various churches to charismatic Christian worship.

Simcoe, Mary Ann, ed. *The Liturgy Documents.* Chicago: Liturgy Training Publications, 1985. This work contains the major liturgical documents of the twentieth century, such as the *Constitution on the Sacred Liturgy,* documents on music, worship and environment in Catholic worship as well as lesser known documents of importance to worship renewal.

White, James F. *Documents of Christian Worship: Descriptive and Interpretive Sources.* Louisville: Westminster/John Knox Press, 1992. Two hundred sources and descriptions of worship from biblical times to the contemporary baptism, Eucharist, and ministry documents of 1982.

# ☙ **FOURTEEN** ❧

# Concerns for the Future of Worship

*Worship renewalists live by the Reformation axiom semper reformanda: the church must always be renewing itself. In advocating the need for worship and worshipers to be in continual renewal, renewalists recognize the pattern through which movements have moved historically. Normally a new movement becomes institutionalized within a generation, and in turn becomes in need of revitalization. The following entries call attention to the ongoing task of worship renewal.*

## 208 • AN ORTHODOX CONCERN

*Orthodox historians and theologians trace their tradition back to the apostolic faith of the early centuries of Christian history. This "living tradition" of apostolic Christianity, they hold, is preserved in the worship of today.*

Contemporary Christians typically ask the same question at their first visit to an Orthodox church: why does the liturgy follow such a set structure or order? Their assumption is often that worship in the New Testament was spontaneous. In fact the "order" of Orthodox liturgy has its very roots in the Scriptures, and the Orthodox Christian church has been worshiping this way, without major changes, for almost its entire life of nearly two thousand years.

Two words need to be kept in mind as one first experiences the Divine Liturgy of the Orthodox churches: "origin" and "changelessness." We should recall that the apostles and the first Christian disciples were fulfilled Jews. From their heritage, with its history of liturgical interaction with God, came the Jewish form of biblical worship, which supplied the origin and basic structure of Christian worship. For this reason we find a highly developed liturgical order in use even by the end of the first century, within sixty years of Christ's resurrection.

The second word is "changelessness." Perhaps the most striking and unique thing about Orthodox Christianity, especially in this age of rapid change— even change for its own sake—is its permanence and changelessness. It has been said that one of the distinctive characteristics of the Orthodox church is

its determination to remain loyal to the past, its sense of being in a living continuity with the church of ancient times. This commitment to protecting the gospel and keeping its message and its praise to God intact stems from the conviction that our faith is that which our Lord Jesus Christ delivered to us, to which we will add nothing and from which we will take nothing away. If we are going to be "apostolic," then we have to agree to belong to the same church that Christ founded. That church began in the first century, and in a sense all Christians must become Christ's contemporaries. The twentieth century is not an absolute norm, but the apostolic age is.

Within this changelessness there has indeed been change. But it has not been a change in the real nature or substance of the faith and practice of Orthodoxy. Rather, it has been a maturing and building upon an unchanging core or deposit of faith. Never changing for change's sake, we change only in order to remain the same. Orthodoxy has always been committed to the exhortation of St. Paul to Timothy to "guard what has been entrusted to your care" (1 Tim. 6:20). At the same time, there is a willingness to enhance our practice of worship in order to make it more heavenly, more spiritual, more edifying.

Benjamin D. Williams and Harold B. Austall[21]

## 209 • A CATHOLIC CONCERN

*The following author maintains that worship reflects the changing perceptions of people involved in the ongoing life of the world. It is imperative, therefore, that worship renewal be a continuous process; listening to the report of the social sciences is one way to promote renewal.*

**Liturgical Reform as Continuous Event.** During most of the church's history, liturgical reform has been characterized by fevered sprints after long periods of inactivity. This is as unhealthy for a social body as for an individual human body.

The liturgical reform following the Second Vatican Council has been an immense gift to Catholic Christian communities, in both form and vision. One example of these benefits has been the Rite of Christian Initiation for Adults. But there is no reason for complacency. It is not as though our life of worship has been fully and adequately updated, and we have only to enjoy it.

The church has long understood itself to be *semper reformanda,* in need of continual transformation. But it has not yet structured itself to provide for the future of worship through sustained and continuous research and committed, relentless experiment. It is our conviction that worship is sufficiently connected to the life of the world that the search for its best comprehension and best expression must be continual. What might this continuous and sustained exploration look like?

**Empirically Committed Theology.** Good theology has always been a faithful reflection of faith experience. Fidelity to experience is a touchstone of valid theological reflection. It is commonplace today to recognize that the human sciences are a report upon experience, and that theology must take serious cognizance of that report. An active relation between theology and the human sciences helps faith reflection keep firmly tied to experiential bases.

**Understanding as "Construction."** But there is a larger and perhaps more urgent consideration that compels theology to attend to the human sciences. The human sciences do not merely report upon experience, but they participate in the creation of the experience upon which they report. In a viewpoint widely held today, it is not that there is a kind of "objective" human nature upon which all the human sciences offer their varied perspectives, and against which they can be adjudicated for accuracy. Accurate knowledge is not a mirror of objective fact. Out of an interaction between someone who knows and something that is known, knowledge is con-

cretely constructed. What is constructed is not merely a formal resemblance between knower and known. The knowledge itself is a new "fact," getting some of its character from the subjectivity of the subject and some from the objectivity of the object. That "fact" is clothed with feeling, weighted with value, and replete with meaning. Human knowing does not find meaning ready made. Our quest for knowledge and meaning is always an active engagement in the social construction of reality.

The renewal of worship is tied to the conversation between theology and the social sciences because of the role each plays in constructing the world we inhabit. The conversation is too important to be left to happenstance.

**Playing with Possibility as an Act of Care.** Exploring possibilities for the renewal of liturgy involves "wondering into existence" new rituals, in order to exemplify the consequences of positions taken when theology and the human sciences converse seriously. Why not just offer theological reflection? Why wonder rituals into existence?

Only a small percentage of Catholics has studied the history or theologies of the Second Vatican Council. Yet the configuration of the Roman Catholic church is very different today because of that council. The differences are not just cosmetic. Even though most people have not systematically studied that council's presuppositions about the church and about human history, its perceptions have gradually seeped into our spiritual center. How has this occurred?

While there are multiple answers to this question, certainly one of the most crucial is the liturgy. Even though general absolution is not widespread, its possibility and occasional usage tell us a new story about the communal character of sin and grace. The transposition of the confession of sins from an anonymously dark little room to face-to-face interaction bespeaks a different sense of both community leadership (priest) and community membership (penitent). Removing the altar from the back wall so that it begins to look like a table in the midst of a community brings the notion of eucharistic meal to the forefront. Before long people want bread to look like bread again, and the sacred vessels to look like a plate and cup. The use of the words *chalice* and *paten* recedes. Once the language of worship becomes the vernacular, and people sing and pray more interactively, the language about the priest saying Mass begins to disappear. People and priest together celebrate the Eucharist; the priest does not "say Mass" alone. The point is that liturgy is one of the crucial places where a new perception of reality comes to the forefront.

The proffering of alternative ritual forms is a vivid way of "seeing" what kind of world the dialogue between the human sciences and sacramental and liturgical theology constructs. These alternatives help us feel what difference it all makes. The projection of possible scenarios is itself an act of hope. It is a way of taking care of a precious possession.

Regis A. Duffy[22]

## 210 • A MAINLINE PROTESTANT CONCERN

_Worship renewal is a corrective to the individualism of much Protestant worship. The liturgical movement is restoring the corporate nature of worship as well as the balance of Word and Table._

The liturgical movement addresses itself whole-heartedly to the problem of exaggerated individualism which has tended in the past two hundred years to reduce many Protestant churches to little more than private devotional assemblies. Its answer to pietism, rationalism, and liberalism is an attempt to restore the supernatural authority of revelation and the truly divine-human character of worship.

If leaders of renewal work to restore historical forms of worship, this is not because they derive some quaint delight in dabbling with antiquities. Rather, they see such liturgies as proclaiming the ancient faith in a truly magnificent manner. These liturgies proclaim that the worshiper is not an isolated soul in the sea of the saved, but an integral part of a community that witnesses to its faith and worships its God as a family. If the liturgical movement has an apostolic insistence to it, it is this: it wants to reclaim the disassociated Christian and put him or her squarely where the worshiper belongs: in the corporate Christian community.

If preaching has been overemphasized, at times to a sentimental extreme, there should be an attempt through liturgy to bring preaching within bounds and restore a proper balance to worship. Hence the many attempts to restore the sacrament of the Lord's Supper to the focal point of worship. The gospel is to be proclaimed in every worship service; nevertheless, the gospel can be proclaimed by sacrament

as well as by Word. Churches are returning to the conviction that the ideal Christian service is one that contains both elements; thus the message and deed of the redemptive act of God in Christ are not only proclaimed by word of mouth but are demonstrated before the eyes of the faithful through the sacramental action. Liturgists in all traditions are calling for more frequent celebrations of the Eucharist.

In general, the liturgical renewal, like all movements, is toward something. It is toward the corporate in worship, the sacramental in worship, and theological balance in worship. The movement in its best form maintains that Christianity is not a personal, private affair between the individual and God. Nor is the church conceived as a collection of individuals who happen to have a taste for religion. It sees Christianity and the church rather as a grand, corporate adventure inaugurated by the God-Man himself to league all mankind in intimate union with himself. Liturgical Christians are not people who live their lives in isolation. They look upon themselves as a family, true members of Christ, integral parts of his body, people lifted to a new level of creation where their lives must reflect in work and worship the belief of their unique containment in Christ. Liturgical Christians live as part of Christ's body and realize that they must, therefore, be in their portion what Christ is and was. Thus it is understandable why the liturgical Christian makes the Eucharist, the cause and expression of unity in Christ, an important part of his or her worship.

Michael J. Taylor[23]

## 211 • AN EVANGELICAL CONCERN

_Evangelicals are awakening to the need for worship renewal. True worship renewal does not come about through superficial measures, but through recognizing that worship studies are an essential discipline of Christian theology. Renewal grows out of attention to the biblical and historical sources of Christian worship and the provision of the Holy Spirit._

Trend watchers are telling us that worship is the emerging important issue in evangelical churches. Rumblings of discontent are already being heard in the church. Some are talking about boredom with sameness, others are concerned over the lack of relevance, and many feel the need to become worshipers but cannot find the words or concepts to

*Greek Cross and the Letter X. The meaning of this cross is found in the letter X, which stands for ΧΡΙΣΤΟΣ (Christ). Greek Christians use many variations of this cross.*

articulate their need, or signposts to direct this search. Unfortunately many evangelical seminaries are not prepared to offer our churches adequate leadership in worship.

I speak from experience. I graduated from three theological seminaries without taking a course in worship. Even though I was planning to become a minister, no one ever sat me down and said, "Look, worship is one of the most central aspects of your future ministry. Now is the time not only to learn all you can about the subject, but to become a worshiping person so you can offer mature leadership to your congregation." The simple fact is that my professors themselves knew little about the subject. My seminary education left me with the impression that the only important matter in morning worship was the sermon. All else was preliminary. Pick out a couple of hymns. Say a few prayers. Get through the announcements. Let the choir sing. And finally, what we all came for—the sermon! I say, shame!

It is my purpose to argue for something more than the mere inclusion of worship courses in the curriculum. What is needed within core seminary education is a recognition of worship as a necessary discipline among other disciplines. Unfortunately, in the curriculum of most evangelical seminaries

worship is relegated to the practical department and treated as a matter of technique and style. But worship in fact requires interdisciplinary study demanding expertise in biblical, historical, and systematic theology as well as the arts, practical skills, and personal spiritual formation. Thus worship, or more properly *liturgics,* is one of the more vigorous and demanding of the seminary disciplines. It must be taken off the back burner and given a central place in the seminary curriculum.

The study of liturgics would give us a methodology for renewal in worship. This methodology involves first the attempt to understand our present practice as the product of a particular past. Second, it involves rediscovery of our heritage: the model of worship contained in Scripture and the resources for worship developed by the church throughout her history, particularly in the early centuries. And third, it involves using this model and these resources as we seek to make our own worship more faithful.

## Understanding the Present

As children of the Reformation, we often get our theological bearings by looking to the Reformers. And this is not a bad place to begin in getting our liturgical bearings. My own study in this area yields two general observations. The first is that there is a radical difference between the worship of our sixteenth century evangelical predecessors and contemporary evangelical practice. The second is that Protestant-evangelical worship has followed the curvature of culture, rather than being faithful to the biblical, historical tradition of the church. A brief examination of these two theses is in order.

First, the gap between present evangelical worship and the practice of the Reformers can be seen easily through an examination of the Reformation liturgies. Pick up any of the liturgies such as Martin Luther's *Formula Missae* of 1523, Martin Bucer's *Strasbourg Rite* of 1539, John Calvin's *Form of Church Prayers* of 1542, or something as late as Richard Baxter's *The Reformation of the Liturgy* of 1661, and the difference can be readily seen. I find, for example, the five following characteristics in these liturgies: (1) an affinity with the liturgies of the ancient church; (2) an order that follows the pattern of revelation and Christian experience; (3) a significant emphasis on reading and hearing the Word of God; (4) a high degree of congregational involvement; and (5) a view of the Lord's Supper that affirms its mystery and value for spiritual formation.

By contrast, my experience in many evangelical churches is as follows: (1) a radical departure not only from the liturgies of the ancient church but those of the Reformation as well; (2) confusion about order; (3) minimal use of the Bible; (4) a low level of congregational involvement; and (5) a general indifference to the importance of the Lord's Supper.

How did this change occur? What are the cultural, social, religious and theological factors that contributed to these changes? How has the actual character of worship changed over the last several centuries? What do these changes mean for the corporate life of the church today?

It is not my intention fully to answer all these questions. Indeed, considerable historical work must be done in the evaluation of Protestant worship between 1600 and 1900 before a full and adequate answer is available. However, my preliminary work in this area leads to the second thesis: evangelicals have followed the curvature of culture. A few illustrations will illuminate this point.

As the meaning of worship became lost among various groups of Protestant Christians, the shape of worship was accommodated to the overriding emphasis within culture. For example, the first significant shift occurred with the introduction of the print media through the Gutenberg press. Protestantism, which can be characterized as a movement of the Word, led the way in the shift from symbolic communication of the medieval era to the verbal communication of the modern era. Because words were regarded as higher and more significant vehicles of truth than symbols, images, poetry, gesture, and the like, all forms of communication other than the verbal became suspect. Consequently, Protestant liturgies were not only word-centered but attached greater *religious* importance to the verbal content of worship.

A second shift occurred as the result of the Enlightenment. The concern for rational, observable, and consistent truth which grew out of the empirical method gradually influenced worship. The essential feature of worship was the sermon. All else sank into relative unimportance. In Puritan circles sermons were sometimes three hours in length with a break in the middle. They were often evangelical and theological dissertations that would be considered beyond the grasp or concern of the average lay person today.

Another shift in worship can be observed as a result of the rise of revivalism. The field preaching of the evangelists gradually replaced the morning service, making Sunday morning a time for evangelism. Although preaching still played a central part, one's focus shifted from information directed toward the intellect to an emotional appeal aimed at the will. The climactic point became the altar call to conversion, rededication, consecration to ministry, or work on the mission field.

Today another shift is taking place resulting from the current revolution in communications. The entertainment mentality which thinks in terms of performances, stages, and audiences has been making its appearance in local churches. Consequently, evangelical Christianity has produced its Christian media stars. Unfortunately some churches are following the trend by turning the worship time into a high-powered performance by musical groups, "superstar" preachers, dramatic groups, or anything intended to attract a bigger audience.

My concern is that this kind of evangelical worship represents not only a radical departure from historic Protestant worship, but also an accommodation to the trends of secularization. Worship, which should stand at the very center of our Christian experience, having been secularized is unable to feed, nourish, enhance, challenge, inspire, or shape.

How will change be brought about? Not simply by going back to the Reformers, but by critically appropriating their, and our, inheritance: worship defined and informed by Scripture and the ancient church. That is, we need to rediscover a biblical-theological model of worship, and reappropriate the means of worship of the early church.

## Restoring a Biblical-Theological and Historical Perspective on Worship

As evangelicals we must acknowledge that the true character of worship is not determined by people, but by God. Much of contemporary evangelical worship is anthropocentric. The biblical-theological view of worship, however, is that worship is not primarily for people, but for God. God created all things, and particularly the human person, for his glory. Thus, to worship God is a primary function of the church, the people who have been redeemed by God.

The meaning of the Greek word *leitourgia* is

"work" or "service." Worship is the work or service of the people directed toward God. That is, we do something for God in our worship of him. We bless God, hymn him and offer him our praise and adoration. But worship is not without reason. We worship because God has done something for us. He has redeemed us, made us his people, and entered into a relationship with us.

Consequently the biblical rhythm of worship is one of doing and responding. God acts, we respond. What God does and is doing happened in history and is now told and acted out as though it were being done again. The unrepeatable event is being repeated, as it were. And we are present responding in faith through words, actions, and symbols of faith.

There are two parts to this biblical-theological model of worship that need to be examined. First, worship is rooted in an event. Christian worship is grounded in God's action in Jesus Christ, which, although it occurred in the distant past, is now recurring through the Holy Spirit in the present. This event-character of worship is true in both the Old and New Testaments. In the Old Testament the event which gives shape and meaning to the people of God is the Exodus. It was in this historical moment that God chose to reveal himself as the Redeemer, the one who brought the people of Abraham, Isaac and Jacob up out of their bondage to Pharaoh with a strong arm. They then became his people, his *qahal,* the community of people who worship him as Yahweh. Thus the tabernacle, and later the temple, the feasts and festivals, the sacred year, the hymnic literature and psalms of thanksgiving revolve around the God who brought them up out of Egypt and made them his people.

The same is true in the New Testament. In the Christ-event God showed himself as the loving and compassionate one who came to free humankind from the kingdom of evil. In the birth, life, death, and rising again of Christ, Satan was vanquished. Christ showed himself Victor over sin, death, and the domain of hell. The worship of the primitive Christian community was a response to this event. Hymns, doxologies, benedictions, sermons, and symbols of bread and wine all flow from this event, and return to it in the form of proclamation, reenactment, remembrance, thanksgiving and prayer.

The second part of this biblical-theological model of worship is the understanding of the church as the response to the Christ-event. The church is the corporate body of Christ, and is the context in which the Christ-event is continuously acted out.

Thus the phenomena of the Christ-event does not stand alone. There is another event which happened simultaneously with it, an event intricately connected and inextricably interwoven with the Christ-event. It is the church, the new people of God, that people through whom the Christ-event continues to be present in and to the world. The church is the response to the Christ-event, a people whose very essence cannot be described or apprehended apart from that event. These are the people in whom Christ is being formed and without whom the fullness of Christ cannot be made complete. It is the *ekklēsia,* the worshiping community.

This biblical-theological model of worship—the central Christ-event made present and the church responding in celebration—is basic to worship renewal. The model is radically evangelical, yet I dare say it has been lost to our churches that have turned worship into a time for teaching, evangelizing, entertaining, or counseling. Methodologically worship renewal must begin with a fresh rediscovery of *Christus Victor* and the church as the community in whom the Christ-event is celebrated to the glory of God.

But beyond rediscovering this model, we need to recover that rich treasury of resources handed down to us by the experience of the church. I find American evangelicalism to be secularized in its attitude toward history. There is a disdain for the past, a sense that anything from the past is worn out, meaningless, and irrelevant. There seems to be little value ascribed to what the Holy Spirit has given the church in the past; it is all relegated to tradition and dismissed as form. At the same time, no critical examination is directed toward present distortions which have been elevated without thought to a sacred position. Evangelicals who want to reform their worship must therefore abandon their disdain of the historical, and return to a critical examination of the worship of the church in every period of history.

There is a normative content to worship that is found in the worship experience of the church everywhere, always and by all. This is the content of Word, Table, prayer, and fellowship (see Acts 2:43). Further, in the same way that the church has wrestled with its understanding of Christ and the Scripture through creeds, commentaries, systematic theologies and the like, so also the church has developed ways to do its worship. These include structural forms, written prayers, hymns, rules for preaching, the church year, the lectionary, and numerous symbolic ceremonies. Interestingly, in the early church these resources were being developed at the same time that creedal statements were coming into being. Yet, we evangelicals who affirm the Nicene and other ancient ecumenical creeds, and boast that we remain faithful to their intent, are pridefully neglectful of the liturgical forms and theological perception of worship shaped by some of the same church leaders.

Specifically we need to recognize that those who have gone before us, who have wrestled with the meaning and interpretation of the faith in creeds and liturgy, were women and men of faith. To accept the creeds on the one hand and neglect or even disdain the liturgies is contradictory and unwise. Orthodoxy was primarily given shape in the liturgy, and the creeds were originally part of the larger liturgical witness. We recognize that the early church was unusually gifted with the spiritual leadership of Justin, Irenaeus, Tertullian, Athanasius, John Chrysostom, and Augustine. Yet we neglect to study the worship of the church which reflects their faithfulness to Christ and the orthodox tradition.

Nevertheless the Scripture is still the judge of all liturgies. To be sure, there are liturgies which fail to hand down the orthodox tradition. Liturgies which reflect an Arian Christology, for example, or those medieval liturgies which clearly embrace a sacrificial notion of the Eucharist, must be judged by the orthodox tradition. But the task of critical evaluation of the older liturgies sharpens our ability to offer constructive and critical evaluation of contemporary worship. For without a knowledge of the worship experience of the church throughout history we are left without adequate tools either for critiquing contemporary worship or reconstructing a worship that is faithful to the Christian tradition.

In terms of tradition, we must be able to distinguish different levels and attach a corresponding scale of values to them. If we think in terms of a series of concentric circles, the apostolic tradition must be central. The apostolic tradition includes the Word, Table, prayers, hymns, benedictions, and doxologies. A second concentric circle includes those traditions which are universally accepted and practiced by Christians. This would include creeds, confession of sin, the kiss of peace, the Lord's Prayer, the *Gloria in Excelsis Deo,* and the church

year. In a third concentric circle we may place those traditions which are peculiar to a particular grouping of people such as the Orthodox church in the East, the Catholic church in the West, or one of the many Protestant denominations. Matters such as vestments (or no vestments), bells, architectural style, inclusion of the little entrance or the great entrance, musical tones and issues regarding kneeling, standing or raising hands during prayer may all be matters of cultural and stylistic preference. Finally, in a fourth circle, one may place those specific customs that are peculiar to a local congregation. Certainly, when we recognize the original impulses from which these ceremonies derive, we may see them for the most part as expressions of faith, witnesses to the importance attached to Christ and his redeeming work. Our task is not to be judgmental in a manner of spiritual superiority, but to dig beneath the traditions to recover the spiritual impulse that originally brought them forth. Then we, too, may share in the original dynamic that enlivened the telling and acting out of the Christ-event in another time and another place.

In sum, worship renewal needs to be rooted in a thoroughgoing biblical-theological understanding of Christ and the church. It needs to draw on all the resources available to the church derived through the continuous struggle of the church to be faithful to the tradition. The question is, what kinds of changes may occur in evangelical worship as a result of this methodological approach?

## Applying Biblical-Theological and Historical Methodology

Changes do not come easily in any aspect of the church. Worship is no exception. Nevertheless the approach proposed here will challenge evangelical worship in at least six areas.

First, it will challenge the *understanding* of worship. Evangelicals frequently exchange true worship for the substitutes mentioned in the first section. Those evangelicals who are thinking about worship tend to think almost exclusively in terms of worship as expressing God's worth. While it is essential to recover worship as directed toward God, it is equally important to rediscover the content of that worship. That content may be summarized this way: in worship we tell and act out the Christ-event. God is in this, doing the speaking and the acting. Consequently we respond to God and to each other, together with the whole creation, as we offer praise and glory to God.

Second, evangelicals will be challenged in the area of *structure*. Evangelical services often lack a coherent movement. There seems to be little, if any, interior rhythm. Historical worship, on the other hand, is characterized by a theological and psychological integrity. Theologically, worship is structured around God's revelation in Word and incarnation. This accounts for the basic structure of Word and Table. Psychologically the structure of worship brings the worshiper through the experience of his or her relationship with God. It follows the pattern of coming before God in awe and reverence, confession our sins, hearing and responding to the Word, receiving Christ in bread and wine, and being sent forth into the world.

Third, evangelicals will be challenged in a matter of *participation*. I find most evangelical worship to be passive and uninvolving. The worshiper sits, listens, and absorbs. But seldom does the worshiper respond. As in the medieval period, worship has been taken away from the people; it must be restored! Further, the participation of the people can be enhanced through the use of lay readers and preachers, congregational prayer responses, scripture responses, antiphonal readings, affirmations of faith, acclamations, the kiss of peace, and increased sensitivity to gestures and movement.

Fourth, a study of the past will sensitize evangelicals to the need to *restore the arts*. One of the great problems within the evangelical culture is a repudiation of the arts in general, and more specifically the failure to employ the arts in worship. This disdain toward the arts is deeply rooted in a view that consigns material things to the devil. The pietistic and fundamentalist backgrounds of modern evangelicalism are addicted to this erroneous view, a dualism that sets the material against the spiritual. Consequently art, literature, and music are frequently seen as the vehicles of evil, means through which people are lured away from spiritual realities to mundane physical attachments.

The repudiation of the material is in direct contradiction to the Incarnation and to the stand taken by the church against Gnosticism, a philosophy which denied that Jesus had come in the flesh. Consequently, the visible arts as well as theater, the dance, color, and tangible symbols have historically had a functional role in worship. Space, as in church

architecture, is the servant of the message. The design and placement of the furniture of worship such as the pulpit, table, and font bespeak redemptive mystery. The use of color, stained glass windows, icons, frescoes, and carvings are means by which the truths we gather around in worship are symbolically communicated. Worship not only contains elements of drama, but *is* a drama in its own right. It has a script, lead players, and secondary roles played by the congregation.

Fifth, evangelicals will be challenged to reconsider their view of *time*. We practice a secular rather than a sacred view of time. The restoration of the church year and preaching from the lectionary is a vital part of worship renewal. The liturgical calendar provides an opportunity for the whole congregation to make the life of Christ a lived experience. It is not merely an external covering of time, but the very meaning of time itself. During the church year we enter fully into the anticipation of Advent, the joy of Christmas, the witnessing motif of Epiphany, preparation for death in Lent, participation in the resurrection joy of Easter and the reception of Pentecost power. Surely it is an evangelical principle to live out the life of Christ. Practicing the church year takes it out of the abstract and puts it into our day-to-day life in the world.

Sixth, a recovery of true worship will restore the relationship between worship and *justice*. Worship affects our lives in the world. It is not something divorced from the concerns of the world. Because Christ's work has to do with the whole of life, so also worship which celebrates that life, death and resurrection relates directly to hunger, poverty, discrimination, and other forms of human suffering.

## Conclusion

In this study I have attempted to outline a methodology for worship renewal. My concern is that evangelicals who are now beginning to rediscover the theme of worship will offer a superficial approach to worship renewal. Our unexamined assumptions about worship could dull our hearing of Scripture. And our disdain for the past could prevent us from being open to the rich treasury of the historical understanding and practice of the church. This we must work together to change.

Robert E. Webber[24]

## 212 ✦ A CHARISMATIC CONCERN

_Charismatic Christians want to reclaim the fullness of the gospel, particularly the work of the Spirit that results in the experience of God's presence, the realization of the power of God in life, and the response of heartfelt praise._

The charismatic renewal is a prophetic renewal movement. To a large degree its prophetic protest and its renewal goals are directed to the churches. Directly or indirectly, those in the movement are saying that the churches need renewal. How do the churches react to this implied criticism? What does the renewal offer which so many in the churches find compelling?

There is general admission on the part of the churches that many Christians are living below their expected spiritual potential, and that persons who are drawn to the renewal are not the indifferent, but people who are genuinely and sincerely seeking a deeper and more meaningful spiritual life. The tendency to live below one's spiritual potential is due, in part, to the lack of a sense of reality in matters of faith, to an absence of the awareness of the presence of Christ in worship and daily life, and to a lack of joy, peace, and hope. There is an emptiness in the church's life which reveals itself in the daily life of its members. Ministers who lack nothing in education are wanting in warmth, personal conviction, and spiritual dedication. They preach the same message over and over, but no lives are changed. The hunger for God remains unsatisfied.

Christians are aware of the void which accompanies materialism and secularism, and of a dissatisfaction which expresses itself in a desire to be fed substantial food and to reach out to God in prayer and praise. Presence is a major category in the charismatic renewal. God is presence: here, now, real, a person, loving, acting. He is not the great absent One. Nor is he the God of yesterday who was present in power to the early church, but now leaves us simply to "grit our teeth" and hang on in the hope that God is around somewhere. One evidence that God is present and acting, say the charismatic churches, is the lives of those in the renewal which have been changed. How can one receive the gospel and remain unchanged? Is not _metanoia_ (repentance) the first demand of the Good News?

Obviously the charismatic renewal has an experience orientation, but there is no claim that experience exhausts New Testament witness. To place the whole of the biblical testimony under the dominance of religious experience would be falsification. In the renewal movement, it is recognized that one whose religious focus is dominated by religious experiences is a spiritual infant. But to excise religious experience from either the New Testament or from the Christian life is to impoverish them both. Both Old and New Testaments record charismatic experiences. Especially with regard to the reception of the Spirit, it seems clear that in the New Testament this event or process was experienced, evidenced, and often immediately perceived, not merely inferred. Experience is linked with enthusiasm, an essential feature of New Testament Christianity.

Beyond the New Testament witness there has been a fairly continuous and insistent tradition of charismatic experience, often disregarded by church historians and by the "main stream" of Christendom. We could make mention, for example, of Wesley's doctrine of the witness of the Spirit to the believer's spirit, which is the direct and immediate sense that one is God's child, the creation and object of his love. The experience of the presence of the Spirit is not sequestered for the few, but is the inheritance of every Christian. It cannot be standardized, but must be reclaimed afresh in every epoch.

To understand the presence and words of the Spirit, the Scriptures are normative; but the whole of Christian experience, both contemporary and historical, should be consulted. Obviously the experience of the Spirit and his coming to visibility in ministries and giftings has never been absent from the church. In the charismatic renewal, the revitalization of Christian lives is manifested in exterior phenomena (baptism in the Holy Spirit, healing, imposition of hands, tongues). This is due not only to the inherent charismatic nature of the church, but also in part to the eagerness with which contemporary Western culture encourages people to seek a personal experience of reality. The depersonalization of much of contemporary life has prompted believers to search for the personal dimensions of ultimate reality.

What must be recovered is the breadth of faith. The faith relationship is not exhausted by doctrinal statements. Within that relationship is a total response: intellect, will, memory, emotions, body, soul. It would be impossible to imagine an experience devoid of all emotional content, and it would be dangerous to exclude the emotions from the global assent of faith. What is offered to God in worship is the total person, including intellect and emotions.

Killian McDonnell[25]

## 213 ◆ A Praise-and-Worship Concern

*The worship style known as "praise and worship" may be described as a continuously flowing style in which more upbeat songs of celebration ("praise") are combined with, or lead into, slower songs or choruses of a more devotional nature ("worship"). The focus in praise and worship is on entering into the presence of the Lord and offering personal adoration to Him through corporate musical expression. Because the praise-and-worship movement is a relatively new worship tradition, its staying power and future direction is uncertain. This discussion provides helpful insight into these issues.*

### Five Current Trends in Praise and Worship

Praise and worship are causing a spiritual "explosion" in the hearts of believers around the nation. As I travel the country doing worship seminars, I have witnessed a fresh breath of new life being brought to birth by the Holy Spirit. Many churches are waking up to the power of God's presence through praise. God's people are experiencing individual and corporate growth through a revival of Biblical patterns for worship.

The following discussion cites ten current and future trends in praise and worship. It is offered in the conviction that praise and worship must always be more than another item in our order of service. They are vehicles through which God communicates with his people. In listing these trends, I am both describing what may be occurring in your church today, and challenging your church to press on into new areas of worship.

**1. Praise and Worship Stimulate New Life and Church Growth.** Praise and worship on a consistent basis stimulate enthusiasm and inject new life into our churches. It is an awesome thing when a depressed, discouraged believer is given an overcoming, victorious attitude through glorifying the Lord in song. Each individual believer, as he or she worships, enjoys refreshment and release. It is easy to ignore the obvious and innate power of praise and

worship to transform the heart and mind, an effect confirmed in Psalm 43:5: "Why are you so downcast, O my soul? Why so disturbed within me? Put your hope in God, for I will yet praise Him, my Savior and my God."

An unexpected benefit of genuine praise and worship which flow in the Holy Spirit is church growth. Many pastors have found their churches mushrooming as the result of adopting the flowing style of worship, and by integrating Scripture songs into their services. One reason for this is that good music inherently brings with it an uplifting experience. Once people come to a praise gathering, they are drawn back to enjoy it again and again. For church members, the variety of expressions in each service allows ample opportunity for every believer to release the personal outflow of his or her heart to the Lord. This release of the heart generates a spiritual satisfaction that refreshes and strengthens God's people.

**2. Praise and Worship Is an Ongoing Educational Tool.** The flow of praise and worship can be a major vehicle for educating and reeducating the church. Through the singing of God's Word in Scripture songs and choruses, people learn new passages from the Bible. By the very nature of today's contemporary worship styles, there is continual introduction of new songs. So believers, in a roundabout way, become educated in a variety of scriptural truths. Additionally, when worshipers take these songs home and sing them all week, the Scriptures are driven even deeper into their hearts. As Colossians 3:16 says, "Let the word of Christ dwell in you richly as you teach and admonish one another with all wisdom, and as you sing psalms, hymns and spiritual songs with gratitude in your hearts to God."

We are in the midst of a powerful revival, but most Christians don't even realize it. This revival is that of singing the Word of God using contemporary musical styles. Although the Psalms have been sung throughout Christian history, perhaps the Word of God as a whole has not been so commonly sung since the ancient biblical days when the fathers passed on to the next generation the Scriptures with musical interpretation.

**3. Praise and Worship Facilitate Spiritual Growth and Sensitivity.** As believers grow in spiritual sensitivity, there is an increase in the flow of spiritual gifts and in hearing God's voice daily. We are the people of God because we know God, primarily because we spend time with him. The more time spent in God's presence, the more sensitivity we have in spiritual things. 1 John 2:20, 27 tells us, "But you have an anointing from the Holy One, and all of you know the truth. . . . As for you, the anointing you received from him remains in you. . . . Just as it has taught you, remain in him."

The phrase of Hebrews 10:25 (KJV), "not forsaking the assembling of ourselves together. . . ." takes on new meaning in light of this truth. Consistent attendance at a worshiping church has definite long-term effects. Through continual participation in praise and worship services, a believer's spiritual sensitivity will become more fine-tuned. The result of greater spiritual sensitivity is usually sustained growth for a stronger Christian life.

**4. Praise and Worship Develop an Intimate Communion with the Lord.** Current worship songs are beginning to move our attention away from the "horizontal" songs of fellowship into the "vertical" aspect of one-on-one fellowship with the Lord. Previously, many of our praise-filled songs were directed to each other. As a church matures, more of its time is spent in ministering to the Lord in worship. People seem to have a greater need today to linger in God's presence rather than to sing songs to one another.

Worship services always contain a mixture of songs of fellowship, songs confessing our faith, and songs declaring God's character and deeds. These are combined with the choruses that lead us to a personal fellowship with the Lord, even in corporate settings. The types of songs used in a praise-and-worship service change fairly often as worship leaders look for the song mixture that will fit the spiritual needs of the church for that season. When the newer, free-flowing style of praise and worship becomes integrated into the service, it is important that the worship leader include some of the great traditional hymns also.

Our reminder is Psalm 108:1, 3: "My heart is steadfast, O God; I will sing and make music with all my soul. . . . I will praise you, O LORD, among the nations; I will sing of you among the peoples."

**5. Praise and Worship Have Brought a Restoration of Visible Expressions.** A rebirth of the use of outward motions in the church has occurred widely. The Bible is full of examples of actions in which the people of God give outward expression to that which is in their hearts. These actions include clapping, bowing and kneeling, dancing to the Lord and the lifting up of hands.

In the past, churches have usually been opposed to this kind of activity. For the most part, this opposition has been based on cultural experience or style. Now, praise-and-worship services have returned to a more biblical precedent rather than following cultural orientation. Admittedly, this is difficult for many people and many churches, because our experience says, "We've done it this way for years; why change now?" The answer is this: God deserves our best, and he is worthy of our all. If there are numerous creative ways to worship him, then let us utilize them to glorify his name.

This biblical type of praise includes the whole person—spirit, soul, and body. If we can shout and clap and get excited at athletic events, how much more should we be excited about Jesus our Savior, King of kings and Lord of lords? Psalm 47:1 invites us, "Clap your hands, all you nations; shout to God with cries of joy." Psalm 81:1-4 also says:

> Sing for joy to God our strength
> Shout aloud to the God of Jacob!
> Begin the music, strike the tambourine,
> Play the melodious harp and lyre.
> Sound the ram's horn at the New Moon,
> And when the moon is full, on the day of
>     our Feast;
> This is a decree for Israel,
> An ordinance of the God of Jacob."

## Five Future Trends

**1. Praise and Worship Will Be Used More for Evangelism and Outreach.** The church has not yet fully realized the power of praise and worship to reach the lost. It can restore those Christians who have been hurt, and recover those that have fallen away from the Lord. During a two-year period when I led a street team, we used a variety of tools to witness for Christ. Besides passing out tracts, we used praise and worship to attract and hold people's attention. It is amazing how many people will stop and listen to music, and even more amazing to see how the power of glorifying God can open up complete strangers to hear about Jesus.

In many communities, churches are teaming up for community-touching "Jesus parades." This type of parade may include floats, clowns, puppetry, a worship band, and a thematic message. In London, 15,000 people marched in parade-fashion to five different locations to pray for their city. At each location, as they walked from area to area, they would use praise and worship to sound forth their message: "Make way, make way, for the King of kings and Lord of lords." This allowed the focus of the outreach to be on honoring and giving glory to the name of the Lord. Many people, genuinely touched and saved, were added into local churches.

Surely we must not miss the opportunities we have. Psalm 57:9 testifies, "I will praise you, O LORD, among the nations; I will sing of you among the peoples."

**2. Praise and Worship Will Be Used More as a Vehicle for Prayer, Devotion, Intercession, and Warfare.** Praise and worship will increasingly be used on a corporate and individual basis for communing with the Lord and refreshing the awareness of his presence. Such a deeper flow in worship will allow a greater ability to discern God's will, because it will incorporate prayer into a worship setting. Hebrews 10:19-20 reminds us that "we have confidence to enter the Most Holy Place by the blood of Jesus, by a new and living way. . . ." Most of our prayer meetings begin with praise and worship. This is because praise and worship create one of the simplest forms of entrance into the presence of God. They combine the anointing of three different vehicles for contact with God: God's Word, God's Spirit, and God's music.

Praise and worship are also mighty weapons. Psalm 149:6-9 says:

> May the praise of God be in their mouths
> And a double-edged sword in their hands,
> To inflict vengeance on the nations
> And punishment on the peoples,
> To bind their kings with fetters,
> Their nobles with shackles of iron,
> To carry out the sentence written against them.
> This is the glory of all his saints.
> Praise the LORD.

When this passage is set in parallel with Ephesians 6, the message is very clear. The demonic kingdom can do very little to stop worshiping believers when they intercede for others and do warfare against devilish principalities and powers. The power of God's presence used in prayer and praise devastates the ranks of our enemies. It is not important to fully understand every part of this concept. What is important is that we put to use what we do know, allowing us to grow into the rest.

**3. Praise and Worship Will Activate More Conviction and Judgment.** When the presence of the Lord comes in a strong fashion it causes great searching of heart. It facilitates the application of the move of God, and enacts the judgment of God. I will never forget the time a rather large, intimidating man came forward and stood at the altar in the middle of the worship service. I walked down the stairs to the floor and asked if I could help him. His reply was, "I want what you guys got and I want it now!" I said "Yes sir!" and promptly prayed with him to be born again. Reflecting on the incident, I realized this man didn't really know how to say "I want to be saved" or "born again." But through the power of God's presence in praise and worship, he was drawn to the front for help. As our services increase in praise and worship, it will be a naturally supernatural occurrence that people coming to the altar during worship will be saved and filled with the Holy Spirit.

Consistently good worship services will have a similar effect on the church in terms of keeping believers' lives in order before the Lord. Our desire to be sanctified will increase as we deepen our times of worship to a holy God. We will strive more for the glory of his presence, even as the Old Testament saints did when they sanctified their physical temple to the Lord, as described in 2 Chronicles 5:11-14:

> The priests then withdrew from the Holy Place. All the priests who were there had consecrated themselves, regardless of their divisions. All the Levites who were musicians . . . stood on the east side of the altar, dressed in fine linen and playing cymbals, harps and lyres. They were accompanied by 120 priests sounding trumpets. The trumpeters and singers joined in unison, as with one voice, to give praise and thanks to the LORD. Accompanied by trumpets, cymbals and other instruments, they raised their voices in praise to the LORD and sang: "He is good; his love endures forever." Then the temple of the LORD was filled with a cloud, and the priests could not perform their service because of the cloud, for the glory of the LORD filled the temple of God.

**4. Praise and Worship Will Change Nations and Make History.** Praise and worship have the power to transform the hearts of men and women on such a large scale that an entire nation may be impacted. It is conceivable that, as more and more people enter into praise and worship and hear the word of prophecy with its note of warning as well as its promise of blessing upon an obedient people, a thrust might develop for change in the political arena. As increasing numbers of people in a nation come to know the Lord and are changed in heart, movements might arise to shift the governmental structure and philosophy from a Marxist or socialistic type to one that acknowledges and exalts the Lord.

If we would pray and seek God, I believe he would show us spiritual and social models that could make an impression even on third-world countries and economies. That very thing is recorded in 2 Chronicles 20:21-22, when King Jehoshaphat sent the Levitical singers out before the army of Judah. As they began to sing and to praise and confess the Lord, their enemies were routed. Because the people of God obeyed the word of the Lord, the nation's history and destiny were changed. In place of destruction, there was overwhelming victory.

**5. Praise and Worship Will Become a Movement for Unity Within the Body of Christ.** Praise and worship are a common ground for fellowship and unity, and will become more so. They are not meant to be a replacement for biblical or doctrinal foundations, but will, in fact, be a stronger gathering force which will cut across church and denominational lines. Many pastors are joining for multichurch gatherings in local civic auditoriums, bringing people together for a special night of worship, prayer, and fellowship. These events have become a major factor in removing walls between local churches, and in reducing the insecurity many Christians have about fellowship with those of other traditions.

For instance, in Champaign-Urbana, Illinois, seven to ten churches hold a "night of worship" three times a year on the fifth Sunday night of the month. Their pastors rotate in the various functions necessary to facilitate the flow of worship. Attendance varies from 600 to 800 at one of these events. Worshipers from each group have been inspired and renewed in vision for the growth of their home church. The event has also made it possible for the body of Christ to have a larger voice in the cities' political and legislative life; when a consensus is reached on an issue, these worshipers can begin to form a sizeable voting bloc. Few things can equal the one voice, one accord, and one heart such events help to create in witness to the community.

We have only seen the "tip of the iceberg" in praise and worship ministry. It is time for Christians prayerfully to consider the vastness of the power of praise and worship and the wonder of God's gift of music to us. If there is a lifestyle of praise and worship somewhere to be lived, let it start at my house with my person, the temple "not built by human hands" (2 Cor. 5:1). As Psalm 50:23 (NASB) puts it, "He who offers a sacrifice of thanksgiving honors Me; and to him who orders his way aright I shall show the salvation of God."

Kent Henry[26]

## 214 ◆ BIBLIOGRAPHY ON NEW DIRECTIONS IN WORSHIP

_Alternative Futures for Worship._ Collegeville, Minn.: Liturgical Press, 1987. Catholic. A seven-volume collaboration by a number of contemporary scholars. Examines social sciences, directed toward pastors. The seven volumes are:

Duffy, Regis, O.F.M., ed. _General Introduction._ Vol. 1. Examines the role of ritual and symbol, drawing on sociological and psychological studies.

Searle, Mark, ed. _Baptism and Confirmation._ Vol. 2. Examines baptism and confirmation as aspects of conversion process. Emphasis is on process and development. Draws on the social sciences.

Bernard, J. Lee, ed. _The Eucharist._ Vol. 3. Examines the Eucharist in relation to the human sciences—especially as the Eucharist pertains to church as intentional community. Sample liturgies.

Fink, Peter E., ed. _Reconciliation._ Vol. 4. Examines the act of reconciliation in light of psychology and applies reconciliation to groups as well as individuals. Contains excellent history of the rite. Sample liturgies.

Cooke, Bernard, ed. _Christian Marriage._ Vol. 5. Examines marriage in relation to socio-behavioral insights. Also contains excellent chapters on the history of marriage and the theology of marriage. Sample liturgies.

Cowan, Michael A., ed. _Leadership Ministry in Community._ Vol. 6. Examines various ministries in the church from the perspective of the social sciences. Excellent material on images of community, leadership, stewardship, empowerment, and theological assumptions and ministerial style. Sample liturgies.

Fink, Peter E., ed. *Anointing of the Sick*. Vol. 7. Examines the process of healing in light of the human sciences. Chapters on pastoral theology and anointing healing in the church. Sample liturgies.

Collins, Mary. *Worship: Renewal to Practice*. Washington, D.C.: Pastoral Press, 1987. Catholic. Based on scholarship. Addresses the renewal of worship, spirituality. The study of worship (rituals), the words of worship (inclusive language), the practice of worship (obstacles to liturgical creativity).

Fink, Peter C., and James M. Schellman, eds. *Shaping English Liturgy*. Washington, D.C.: Pastoral Press, 1991. This work, written in honor of Archbishop Dennis Hurley, contains articles on ritual reform, language and liturgy, culture and liturgy, justice and liturgy, lectionary and Scripture.

Kelsey, Morton. *Tongue Speaking: The History and Meaning of Charismatic Experience*. New York: Crossroad, 1981. A brief history from the day of Pentecost to the contemporary time with an approach to the meaning of tongues.

Last, Carl, ed. *Remembering the Future: Vatican II and Tomorrow's Liturgical Agenda*. New York: Paulist Press, 1983.

Martimort, A.-G. ed. *The Church at Prayer*. 4 vols. Collegeville, Minn.: Liturgical Press, 1986–1988. An excellent scholarly series of books addressing major issues of worship: The four volumes are *Principles of the Liturgy, The Eucharist, The Sacraments,* and *The Liturgy of Time.*

Micks, Marianne H. *The Future Present*. New York: Seabury Press, 1970. Protestant. Based on scholarly sources. The two major sections of this book deal with summoning the future and shaping the present. The author faces a variety of issues in the changing patterns of worship: motion and emotion, speaking and hearing, silence, hope, touch and feel, architectural space, taste and see, worship and action.

Newman, David R. *Worship as Praise and Empowerment*. New York: Pilgrim Press, 1988. Examines the origin of worship and argues for new discoveries of worship in the face of the loss of transcendence. Concludes with a protection of what can happen in a renewed worship.

Talley, Thomas J. *Worship: Reforming Tradition*. Washington, D.C.: Pastoral Press, 1990. Ecumenical. Scholarly. Examines major issues affecting worship renewal such as priesthood in baptism and ordination, sources and structure of the eucharistic prayer, healing, reconciliation, the primitive Pascha, origin of Lent, the Feast of All Saints, and the liturgical year.

Webber, Robert. *Signs of Wonder*. Nashville: Abbott Martyn Press, 1991. Protestant. Popular, but based on scholarship. Develops the six areas of current worship renewal (1) preconditions for worship renewal; (2) renewal of Sunday worship and preaching; (3) the place of music and the arts in worship; (4) the services of the Christian year; (5) sacraments, ordinances, and sacred actions of the church; (6) the relationship of worship to evangelism, social action, education, and spirituality.

# PART SIX

# Preparing for
# Worship Renewal

# ❧ 𝔽𝕀𝔽𝕋𝔼𝔼ℕ ❧

# Preconditions and Stages of Worship Renewal

*Although true worship renewal ultimately derives from divine initiative, there are a number of preparations a church can make to ready itself for God's action. This section discusses the preconditions, the principles, the psychology, and the challenges of worship renewal.*

*Because worship arises out of the gospel, congregations seeking the renewal of worship pay new attention to the gospel. This chapter speaks to several central issues addressed by churches involved in worship renewal: the restoration of Christus Victor; the recovery of the corporate nature of the church; the realization of community through small groups; and the release of every member's gift for ministry. The chapter concludes with a discussion of the stages of worship renewal.*

## 215 • THE RESTORATION OF *CHRISTUS VICTOR*

*The event which worship celebrates is the triumph of Jesus Christ over the powers of evil. This dethronement of evil lies at the heart of the gospel. Worship enacts and reenacts the great saving deeds of God in Jesus Christ; it brings the benefit of the victory of Christ over evil to the worshiping community and makes salvation and healing available to those who receive Jesus Christ by faith.*

### The Atonement in Worship and Theology

The New Testament reflects on the meaning of the life, death, and resurrection of Jesus in three ways. First the death of Jesus in particular, is interpreted in terms of the sacrificial worship of the Old Testament. The writer of Hebrews emphasizes that Jesus is the fulfillment of all the Old Testament sacrifices, that his sacrifice is a once-for-all sacrifice, and that it was a substitute for us (see Hebrews 7–10). This theme of *substitutional atonement* has been developed in worship throughout the history of the church and is reflected particularly in the Lord's Supper.

A second interpretation of the death of Jesus, one that is emphasized in Johannine thought in particular, is that Jesus' voluntary sacrifice of himself for the sins of the world was an act of love. Christians are urged to emulate this love of Jesus, as John writes: "This is how we know what love is: Jesus Christ laid down his life for us. And we ought to lay

down our lives for our brothers" (1 John 3:16). In Christian thought the interpretation and development of the atonement in terms of Jesus' death is called the *moral theory* or the *example theory* of the atonement. This theme has also been developed in worship, particularly in preaching.

The third interpretation of the death of Christ, and the one which has been most neglected since the Reformation until now, is the emphasis on Christ's victory over the devil, sin, and death. Paul gets at the very heart of this view of Jesus' death and resurrection when he says that "having disarmed the powers and authorities, he made a public spectacle of them, triumphing over them by the cross" (Col. 2:15). Gustav Aulen, in his book *Christus Victor,* speaks of the victory of Christ over evil as "the ruling idea of the atonement for the first thousand years of Christian history" (p. 21).

Unfortunately, the *Christus Victor* interpretation of the death of Christ which dominated the early church has been lost in the modern era. The rationalism of the age of the Enlightenment (1700–1950) was not able to support the supernatural understanding and experience of the Christian faith that *Christus Victor* implies. However, in the post-Enlightenment era in which we now live, renewalists, particularly in the charismatic arena, have recovered a *Christus Victor* gospel and its implications for a world very conscious of the powers of evil.

The recovery of *Christus Victor* in no way annuls the biblical teaching on the sacrifice of Christ or the love that impelled Jesus to the cross. Rather it complements these views to give us a full picture of the work of Christ. In sum, he gave himself as a sacrifice for sin (substitutional atonement) and thus gained the victory over sin (*Christus Victor*), leaving us an example of sacrificial love as the way to overcome evil (example theory).

### — *Christus Victor* in Biblical Thought —

The New Testament material concerning the victory of Christ over the powers of evil is extensive. However, we can organize this vast amount of material under several themes that will help us grasp more firmly the earliest Christian creed, the shout of victory expressed in the words, "Jesus is Lord"! (Acts 2:36). These themes are that Christ has bound Satan, has dethroned the powers of evil, and will utterly destroy these powers at the consummation. The consequence of Christ's work is that the powers are now limited and that we are called to live in the expectation of a restored creation.

**Christ Has Bound Satan and All Demonic Powers.** First, in a confrontation between himself and the Pharisees (Matt. 12:27-29), Christ makes the claim to have bound Satan. The occasion for the confrontation was the healing of a blind and mute man who was possessed by demons (v. 22). According to the Pharisees' interpretation, "It is only by Beelzebub, the prince of demons, that this fellow drives out demons" (v. 24). Rather than seeing Jesus as one who had power over the demonic, they saw him as subject to and even as an agent of the demonic. But Jesus, showing them the absurdity of this conclusion, argued that "if Satan drives out Satan, he is divided against himself" (v. 26). More importantly, Jesus categorically asks, "How can anyone enter a strong man's house and carry off his possessions unless he first ties up the strong man?" (v. 29).

The point made by Jesus is that he has power over the demonic because he had already entered into the domain of evil and found its source. The gospel writers pointedly accent the power of Jesus over Satan. Matthew sees the power of Jesus over evil as the fulfillment of Old Testament prophecies (Matt. 8:16-17), and coming as a result of the "Spirit of God" (12:28). Mark and Luke also testify that Jesus has power, even authority, over evil (Mark 1:21-28; Luke 9:37-43). The exercising of Christ's power over

Satan has the effect of restoring to wholeness a part of God's creation that has become demented, twisted, distorted, and corrupted by Satan. When Jesus casts out demons, heals the blind, causes the lame to walk, restores health, and raises the dead, he demonstrates that his purpose is to restore, renew, and recreate his universe.

In order to recreate the creation, it is first necessary for Christ to dethrone that power which is distorting the creation. Evil has been perverting the purposes of the structures of existence (which were created to provide order and meaning to the world), so they have to be dethroned in order to set the creation free from "its bondage to decay" (Rom. 8:21). This is accomplished through the death and resurrection of Jesus Christ.

**Through the Death and Resurrection of Jesus Christ, the Power of Satan Has Been Dethroned.** Paul expands the idea of God's victory over Satan in his letter to the Colossian church. He writes that Christ's death and resurrection has "disarmed" powers and authorities. The force of the word *disarm* is that of "taking away," like stripping a soldier of his guns, putting him in a position of vulnerability. So Christ's death has had the effect of exposing the deception that Satan exercises through the structures of existence. Christ is seen as Lord, not only over death, but over all other evil influences which seek to distort our lives.

The illusion that life or death, man-made religious observances, or human social regulations are ultimate is now exposed for the lie it is. Likewise all other aspects of the created order which people elevate to positions of ultimate authority are stripped of their power to deceive. Now people can be free from these illusions. It is no longer necessary to be bound by the power of a false understanding of the created order. Faith in Jesus Christ, who is the ultimate ruler over all of life, can break the twisting of political, economic, social, and moral structures into secular salvations. Because these secular salvations are disarmed, they can no longer exercise ultimate power in our life system and act as gods over our lives.

**In the Consummation, Satan's Influence Through the Powers of Evil Will Be Utterly Destroyed.** Third, although the influence of Satan, which he exercises through the powers (the structures of this world), has been overcome through the life, death, and resurrection of Christ, the final blow to Satan will not occur until the consummation of Christ's work in his second coming. Even though Jesus spoke of an "eternal fire prepared for the devil and his angels" (Matt. 25:41), a more elaborate development of the idea of Satan's ultimate destruction can be found in the thought of the early church.

In Paul's classic statement on the power of the resurrection over death (and the disintegration of the created order implied in the symbol of death), he reminds his readers that the end will come "after he has destroyed all dominion, authority and power. For he must reign until he has put all his enemies under his feet" (1 Cor. 15:24-25). More over, the apostle John, in his apocalyptic vision of the end times, declares that "the devil, who deceived them, was thrown into the lake of burning sulfur, where the beast and the false prophet had been thrown" (Rev. 20:10). These New Testament voices affirm the total destruction of Satanic forces and assure us that the work of Christ which is linked to the temptation (the binding of Satan) and to the cross (the overcoming of Satan) is concluded by the consummation (the final defeat of Satan).

**Between the Resurrection and the Consummation, the Power of Satan Is Limited.** It would be naive to conclude that Satan no longer has power in the world. He is still the master of deception. He still blinds the eyes of people to the truth. He still masterminds faith in false gods and creates messianic illusions which people follow to their own destruction. Yet his influence is limited, for Jesus has overcome him. "In this world you will have trouble," said Jesus, "But take heart! I have overcome the world" (John 16:33). In his first epistle, John ascribes this capacity to overcame to those who believe in Jesus: "For everyone born of God overcomes the world. This is the victory that has overcome the world, even our faith. Who is it that overcomes the world? Only he who believes that Jesus is the Son of God" (1 John 5:4-5).

Yet the overcoming is still not an established reality, as Paul indicates when he uses two words that mean "coming to nothing" and "expectation." The former word is used in his first epistle to the Corinthians: "We do, however, speak a message of wisdom among the mature, but not the wisdom of this age or of the rulers of this age, who are coming to nothing" (1 Cor. 2:6). The force of the word translated "coming to nothing" is "being put out of action." In the military sense, it means the war is over;

now the cleaning up of the final matters must occur. Guerrilla pockets may still exist, confrontation may still occur here and there; but the tide has been turned, the oppressor has been definitely routed, and it is only a matter of time until the end.

The second word, "expectation," describes the state of those who are to be released from the ravages of war. Paul uses this word in the Epistle to the Romans: "The creation waits in eager expectation for the sons of God to be revealed" (Rom. 8:19). This passage suggests a cosmic victory over a cosmic bondage. Satan has brought the entire creation under his dominion and influence, but that pervasive power has been so thoroughly broken that the entire creation—all the structures of existence—now experience an expectation of their release.

These passages point to the importance of preaching as the means by which Satan continues to be exposed to his defeat. For it is through faith in Jesus Christ (as the one who has defeated Satan and all his attempts to distort the creation) that the extent of Satan's activity is limited. Satan may continue to deceive some, perhaps many, but not all. Preaching Christ continually unmasks the power of Satan, for faith in Christ opens a person's eyes to the reality of Satan's deception. Whenever anyone believes in Christ, the limitation of Satan's power is unmasked.

**Creation Will Ultimately Be Reconciled to God.** It is a comfort to know that the contest between Satan and Christ will have an end, even as it had a beginning. Furthermore, as Paul states, the course of this cosmic conflict is under "the mystery of his will" and "according to his good pleasure." The will and pleasure of God are being fulfilled in Christ, whose purpose it is "to bring all things in heaven and on earth together under one head, even Christ" (Eph. 1:9–10). Paul mentions this same theme in his letter to the Corinthians, telling them that God has put "everything under him [Jesus Christ], so that God may be all in all" (15:28). For Paul, this means nothing less than the re-creation of the entire universe, including the structures of existence. Restoration of the structures is made more clear in his letter to the Colossians, when he tells his readers that it is God's purpose through Christ "to reconcile to himself all things, whether things on earth or things in heaven, by making peace through his blood, shed on the cross" (Col. 1:20).

In these passages, Paul does not imply that Satan and the fallen hosts which represent the demonic in this world will be reconciled to God. They are defeated and cast into the lake of fire (Rev. 20:1). What is redeemed, restored, and recreated is God's work of creation. In this sense, the new heavens and the new earth will be a restored paradise—the world as it was before the fall into sin.

It is this world view that lies behind a renewal of worship. The victory of Christ over the powers of evil, and all that is implied by that victory, are expressed in song, preaching, the eucharistic prayer, and the act of healing.

The emphasis on *Christus Victor* represents a shift from a juridical view of the atonement, in which the death of Christ is understood chiefly as a transaction satisfying the requirements of divine justice. This shift of focus has important implications for worship. When the atonement is seen as Christ's defeat of the powers of evil, worship becomes a dynamic experience through which Christ's victory is celebrated and its benefits and promises are made available to the congregation.

*Robert E. Webber*

## 216 • THE CHURCH AS COMMUNITY

*In the exodus event, God created a people and brought them into a covenant relationship. The covenant specified that Israelite worshipers display loyalty and faithfulness both to Yahweh, the King of the covenant, and to their fellow Israelites covenanted to that same King. In a corresponding way, God has created a people through the life, death, and resurrection of Jesus Christ; these people are bound together with him and with one another in a new covenant community. Jesus' commandment for this community, or church, is that they love him with their entire being, and their covenant brothers as themselves. It is out of this relationship with God and one's fellow believers that worship arises. Biblical worship is intended as a corporate expression of the covenant relationship.*

### The Church as a Body

In the liturgy there is a vertical movement, the out-going of the person to God; but there is also a horizontal movement. Liturgy is celebrated with others and the relationships between the members of the worshiping community are of the highest importance. Private acts of public worship are a contradiction in terms, as a statement in the Roman

Catholic *Constitution on the Sacred Liturgy* suggests: "Liturgical services are not private functions, but are celebrations of the Church, which is the sacrament of unity" (section 26). At the practical level all liturgical rites are arranged for the participation of the community. Rites enable people to relate to each other (the kiss, the handshake—both symbolic gestures) and also to the community. One can become part of the congregation and enter more deeply into its life. The sociologists tell us that for true community to exist there must be a face-to-face relationship. For the Christian this means that the members of the community are persons bound together by faith and love. In principle they are already related to one another. In the worshiping community this relationship is deepened and enhanced—or will be, if the members try to act as a community.

The Pauline teaching on the church as "body" emphasizes at once the closeness of the relationship between Christ and the people—they are members, limbs, of the body—and of the horizontal relationships between the members of the body (1 Cor. 12:12-31). In other words, perhaps more strongly than before, it is indicated that the priestly people is also a community, the community of Christ with which he has a vital relationship. He is the source of all its life; it is totally dependent on him as the branches of a tree are on its trunk (John 15:1-5). And the relationships of faith and love between its members are in the first instance created by Christ, though they are to be realized and strengthened by Eucharist, which is the sacramental sign of *koinonia* of communion, the union of minds and hearts in faith and love. If the church can be said to "make" the Eucharist, in a much deeper sense the Eucharist makes the church. But the depth and richness of the relationship is best seen in Ephesians 5, where Christ is said to be the head of the church of which he is also Savior; and this church is his bride (vv. 25-26), which he brought into existence by the "fragrant offering and sacrifice" that he offered to his Father (v. 2).

It is this people, then, the priestly people, the body of Christ and the community of Christ, who are the "subject" of liturgical celebrations. In other words, it is they who celebrate the liturgy, and the form of the liturgy must be of such sort as to make this possible. The Christian liturgy by its nature cannot be the monologue of a single participant. It is the action of a whole community.

J. D. Crichton[27]

## 217 ✦ UNITY THROUGH WORSHIP

*The community of faith is a place of worship. In worship, unity and healing recur as the church remembers that the community was born of a divine act of deliverance. As the church experiences community, it is renewed by that same gracious act.*

For ancient Israel, remembrance of divine grace was preserved by means of a sacred calendar that placed memory of the prevenient, gracious acts of God at the very heart of life. Once a year Israel recalled its deliverance from slavery at Passover and the Feast of Unleavened Bread; once a year thanks was given for the land and its harvest at the Feast of Weeks; once a year God's protection in the wilderness was commemorated in the Feast of Booths; and once a year the solemn fast of the Day of Atonement was observed.

The rhythm of the order God had established for the people of the covenant was also celebrated weekly, commemorating God's creation of the

*Canterbury Cross. This cross contains four hammer-like arms that spring from a square. It symbolizes the decisiveness of blows to hands, feet, and heart.*

world and Israel's release from bondage in Egypt, and reminding the people that they were a holy possession of their God. This rhythm in turn radiated outward in time to be marked by the observance in the seventh year of God's gift of the land, and in the fiftieth year of God's gift of freedom. This calendar lent a harmony to life, both by reminding Israel of the history of God's covenant relationship and by placing the community within the broader context of God's care for the entire created order.

Although the sacral calendar has fallen into neglect in many religious communities today, there is no question that much is lost when a people no longer symbolizes its communal life and the holy events of its past as parts of the much more encompassing order over which God reigns.

Only when its unity is rooted in its sense of devotion to the one true Sovereign can a community of faith transcend the webs of pettiness, parochialism, and self-interest that so rapidly belittle and destroy human fellowship. For only when a person's primary relationship, in the ultimate sense of the term, is to God, can the inordinate and unhealthy neediness and insecurity that blights our relationships with others be replaced by a genuine sharing predicated on a sense of wholeness dependent on no human, be it self or another, but on God's grace.

A community of faith that takes seriously the central theme of its heritage will therefore hold up before the world, by means of paradigms and symbols both old and new, the sole sovereignty of God as the only proven safeguard against the myriad penultimate loyalties that promise abundance but deliver death. To choose life is thus to submit to the only one who, as Creator of all life, is graciously willing and able to sustain the life and freedom of all. To choose life is to let go of all that holds the heart back from embracing that which alone possesses intrinsic worth, to relinquish all forms of bondage, and to find fulfillment in belonging to the order of life over which God reigns.

United in worship and reconciled with its God, the community of faith is restored to the health and wholeness that enables it to be a nucleus of health for the broader human community around it. Its own blessing and health are not gifts intended for it alone, but willed by God for all. And it is indeed in worship that the truth of God's absolute sovereignty brings into focus a vision of God's reign of peace and justice over all creation. This vision is the faith community's invitation to give expression to its devotion through a life of service in the world. And its experience of having its needs fulfilled by God in worship empowers it to speak out courageously against all that tears the fabric of the human family, and to ally itself with all peacemakers and agents of caring in the world.

Paul D. Hanson[28]

## 218 ◆ COMMUNITY THROUGH SMALL GROUPS

*The pervasive individualism of Western culture has broken down the sense of identity experienced through community. Nevertheless, the church in the post–World War II era has seen a resurgent interest in and recovery of community. Two promising models of community from which a strong worship is arising are the "basic communities" of South America and the small group movement.*

### Basic Communities of South America

One of the characteristics of non-modern society, whether it was of the simpler, tribal sort or of a more complex, civilized sort, was that the individual saw himself or herself in terms of the group. The group naturally tightened the bonds between individuals, creating close interdependence among them and regulating the nature of their social relationships from within. Whether the society was more simple and egalitarian or more hierarchical and stratified, the individual in non-modern society had an assigned place from birth. He or she was conditioned and limited somehow by the group, but also supported and sustained by the group. It cannot be said that this group (extended family, tribe, nation) was always a community in the sense of the word we use today, but there is no doubt that it did offer some of the features essential to any community: it personalized within the context of well-defined social relationships. Thus the individual was provided with identity and intelligibility.

The remote origins and roots of modernity were marked precisely by the breakdown of that paradigm, which took place relatively early in the Christian West. At the end of the twelfth century and throughout the thirteenth century, the individual was moving toward a position of autonomy in regard to the group. An important contributory factor was the changed relationship vis-à-vis the economic dimension at every level and the beginnings of the

modern market. The ties between individual and group were breaking down, opening up room for competition among individuals as isolated units. This lies at the root of modern society and finds concrete expression at every level: in the ideology of individualism, the economics of capitalism, and the politics of liberalism.

The full unleashing of this dynamic, which matured in the eighteenth and nineteenth centuries, has left us in the twentieth century with a society characterized by such traits as anonymity, extreme competition among individuals, and, most of all, a deterioration of social relationships, if not an outright perversion of them. All this has provided the bases and roots for new forms of domination and oppression. Converted into systems and invested with economic and political power, they crush the individual by various means and in various ways: e.g., by implementing impersonal bureaucratic rationalization; by atomizing the labor market; by dissociating work from family and group life; and by increasing migration, which accelerates the uprooting of individuals and cultural groups. In this general context we have seen a growing and widespread yearning for community from the middle of the nineteenth century on, but particularly since World War II.

The early church certainly viewed itself as a community, its point of departure being the first community composed of Jesus and the apostles he had gathered around him. The theme of the church as community was clearly explicated from Pentecost on: in the Acts of the Apostles; the writings of Paul, John, and James; and other works. Theology and exegesis would proceed to analyze and explore that thematic treatment from various angles. The church's early awareness of being a community began to fade markedly as time went on.

In South America, the Roman Catholic counterpoint to this loss of community was precisely the creation of "basic ecclesial communities." This new way embraces more fully the whole of life, and thus facilitates the creation of a community in the stricter sense. As one of their pastors has written:

In the present-day circumstances basic communities frequently manage to express various fundamental elements of Christian experience much better than parishes do. Basic ecclesial communities manage to facilitate a maximum of Christian life with a minimum of institutional structures. The missionary element of welcoming the divine word and bearing witness to the faith is sharply accentuated. There is the practical possibility of a pluralism suited to the desires and need of the community, which thus can experience the feeling of brotherhood and sisterhood in a more living way. In these basic communities people can fight peacefully for justice, better exercise Christian freedom in the free expression of the word, and live together in a less anonymous, hence more personal, way. In these base-level groups it is not rare to see the rise of new charisms and ministries dedicated to the build-up of community and service to the gospel message. New pastoral options also arise. The exclusivism bound up with territorial limits is overcome. By the same token, the evangelical Christ centrism characteristic of basic communities tends to purify popular religiosity, offering adults a practical form of catechumenate in the midst of real life. The very praxis of the sacraments takes on greater ecclesial relevance within these small communities. In and through basic communities, the work of priests is made enormously easier, lay participation in the apostolate finds a new space in reality, and the ecclesial community can more easily be the leaven of human reality.

Marcello de C. Azevedo[29]

## Home Cell Groups

The largest church in Christendom draws from an active adherent group of 625,000 for its various weekend worship services. But to the typical parishioner, the church is only about ten persons large.

Dr. Paul Yonggi Cho, founding pastor of Yoido Full Gospel Central Church in Seoul, Korea, has taught his people that the heartbeat of the church occurs through the "one another" ministry of small, home-based cells. These affinity-based, lay-pastored nurture groups are the center of the church's evangelism, discipleship, worship, prayer, and fellowship.

Corporate worship celebrations are still eminently important at the Yoido church. But they function more as conventions of cell groups than as large gatherings of individuals.

These large services radiate excitement. They are characterized by the festive qualities of a political rally or a recording-artist concert. What the feasts in Jerusalem were to the clans of Israel, the corporate worship of the Yoido church is to its home cell groups.

Yet, the congregation's sense of momentum, which regularly fills auditoriums and overflow rooms, cannot be traced solely to a charismatic speaker or talented music group. Rather, corporate worship exudes vitality because it brings together portions of more than 50,000 small, spiritual kinship groups that have each experienced the working of God during the week. The cell-driven church is at once small enough for intimacy and large enough for celebration.

The model of Yoido Full Gospel Central Church helps illustrate the burgeoning popularity of home-based small groups on all seven continents. In North America, for example, practically every church has, during the last two decades, elevated the priority of cell groups. Virtually all religious publishing houses now offer books and curriculums suitable for off-premises, lay-led small group gatherings.

Many factors contribute to this rising popularity of cell groups. With the widespread fragmentation of the nuclear family, many people are looking for a surrogate family. Others crave a personal touch in an ever increasingly high-tech society. Still others realize the need to establish reasonable spans of care in order to prevent leadership burnout—both of the laity and of clergy.

For these and other reasons, many churches now consider themselves to be a fellowship "with" cell groups. For them, whatever they consider to be the mission of the church—worship, evangelism, discipleship, prayer, fellowship, and the like—can occur both in the large meeting and in the small, with one reinforcing the other.

The leading-edge trend, however, goes further. It acknowledges that various-sized groups, such as cells, classes, congregations, and celebrations, are present in most churches, even if not officially recognized. As such, a social network of "cells" exists, though it may not be properly identified, resourced, encouraged, or supervised.

The trend of the future builds on that perception. It says that the effective church will see itself not as a fellowship "with" cells, but as a matrix "of" cells. The vibrancy and spiritual health of these cell-sized groupings is the engine used by the Holy Spirit to drive the church forward.

The church-"of"-groups concept is neither Korean nor limited to one particular style of worship. Its vital components—though not necessarily its identical outward forms—have been implemented in thousands of churches worldwide, spanning the spectrum of worship styles and traditions.

The cell-celebration concept is being implemented equally well in historically recent innovations (such as the seeker-sensitive church of the 1990s) as it was in the Wesleyan class meetings of the 1800s, or as it still is in the incense-burning high liturgy of a centuries-old Lutheran or Greek Orthodox setting.

Of North America's largest and most unchurched-sensitive churches, a significant number trace their growth to a new set of priorities: clergy focusing their energy on the development and empowerment of lay leadership for cell groups. A typical infrastructure involves each church staff member working with a small number of lay coaches. Each of them, in turn, supervises a few of cell group leaders. And each of them, likewise, sees to it that approximately ten people receive spiritual nurture.

These levels are sometimes connected according to life-state affinities ("youth," "young married," "single adults") and, in larger metropolises, by geographic zones. At each of the levels, the men and women involved are simultaneously training apprentices. That way, when growth opportunity calls for additional leadership, the necessary personnel are already prepared to be released.

This cell-drivenness factor has become so widespread that students of the church growth movement are now seeking categories for explaining and interpreting it. On the popular level the social theory is being called the "Cho model," "cell group church," "cell church movement" and the "cell-celebration" paradigm.

The theological jargon gaining the greatest popularity is the term *metachurch*. While large churches keep burgeoning until they become *mega* churches, the concept *meta*, meaning "change," communicates a radical paradigm shift. When examined structurally and philosophically, a metachurch, with its lay-tended cells, is as different from a traditional church of clergy-tended subcongregations as a butterfly after undergoing *meta*morphosis is different from a caterpillar.

Whatever the name, the phenomenon, which we believe traces its origins to the book of Acts, is undeniably linked to worship renewal and spiritual vitality. As goes the cell, so goes the church.

Carl F. George and Warren Bird

## 219 • RECOVERING THE GIFTS OF THE LAITY

*The significance of the release of spiritual gifts for worship has been rediscovered in the contemporary church. It is part of the recovery of the theology of the laity, the "people of God." Within the worshiping community, each member may contribute to the corporate life and celebration through the expression of his or her particular gift.*

One of the predominant and easily observed features of the contemporary movement for liturgical renewal has been the recovery of the ministry of the laity, together with the stress on the distribution of the gifts of the Holy Spirit throughout the body of Christ. This emphasis has been both a precondition and an effect of the renewal of liturgy. In churches where leadership of the service had long been virtually restricted to clergy, lay people have emerged in highly visible roles: reading the Scriptures, leading in prayer, assisting in the administration of the Eucharist or Lord's Supper, and performing other ministries of significance. Paradoxically, those denominations in which the laity have historically had a greater degree of participation in these aspects of worship are perhaps those least affected by the renewal movement of this century, no doubt because the more limited role of the minister in public worship has lowered the priority of liturgy as a theological concern.

## ——— Spiritual Gifts and the Body ———

The rise of lay visibility in worship has gone hand in hand with the recovery of the scriptural emphasis on the "peoplehood" of the community of faith. The English words "lay, laity" are derived from the Greek *laos*, "people," which the New Testament uses to designate those called into the new covenant. For example, Peter calls the church "a chosen people, a royal priesthood, a holy nation, a people [*laos*] belonging to God," using phrases borrowed from the Old Testament narrative of the Sinai covenant (1 Pet. 2:9; Exod. 19:6); he further stresses the concept of peoplehood in elaborating, "Once you were not a people [*laos*], but now you are the people [*laos*] of God" (2:10).

In the writings of Paul, the peoplehood or calling of the laity is expressed chiefly through the concept of the body of Christ, and it is in the context of the life of the body that Paul sets his discussion of the operation of the spiritual gifts (*charismata, pneumatika*). A major locus for Paul's treatment of the gifts is 1 Corinthians 12–14, where the apostle makes it clear throughout that the gifts of the members of the body are exercised not to promote the individual believer, but for the benefit of the body as a whole: "Now to each one the manifestation of the Spirit is given for the common good" (1 Cor. 12:7). Indeed, the "body" or "people" remains in focus wherever Paul discusses spiritual gifts. The differing endowments of the members of the body, he states, exist because "in Christ we who are many form one body, and each member belongs to all the others" (Rom. 12:5); the ministry gifts are given "to prepare God's people for works of service" (Eph. 4:12).

Paul offers several lists of gifts, the contents of which partially overlap. Those enumerated in Romans 12:6-8 may be termed the "serving gifts," which address the encouragement and corporate well-being of the assembly. Two series appear in 1 Corinthians 12: the "manifest gifts" which reveal the presence and power of the Holy Spirit (12:4-14), and the "administrative gifts" which facilitate the operation and activities of the church (12:28). The list in Ephesians 4:11-13 sets forth the "equipping gifts," which consist not of abilities but of _people_ given to the church by the ascended Christ for the enabling of others in ministry. These lists are evidently not intended to be comprehensive; the New Testament refers to other gifts and skills (especially those of service) exercised by members of the community.

From the New Testament descriptions of spiritual gifts, we can in general define a "gift" as _any activity or skill or even person which contributes to the church's ability to fulfill its mission of worship, witness and service,_ including those functions which add to the personal welfare and spiritual development of the members of the community. In this sense, "each one" (as Paul states) has one or more gifts, something to offer to the common good, and those gifts are regarded as conferred by the Spirit even when they coincide with what we today would regard as natural skills. C. Peter Wagner provides this definition: "A spiritual gift is a special attribute given by the Holy Spirit to every member of the body of Christ according to God's grace for use within the context of the body" (_Your Spiritual Gifts Can Help Your Church Grow_ [Ventura, Calif.: Regal Books, 1979], 42). Wagner catalogs and describes twenty-seven such gifts including martyrdom, celibacy, intercession, and others not specifically enumerated in the Pauline discussions. Clearly, when it comes to gifts which may be offered in the celebration of God's glory in worship, the list

could be extended to include skills in the liturgical arts, particularly in music, drama or choreography, and in architectural and other visual arts. The spectrum of such gifts is so broad that their practice cannot be restricted to a core group of ecclesiastical professionals; it is the _laity_ which must exercise them in the fullest measure.

## Loss and Rediscovery of Lay Involvement

Due to historical factors, the concept of the gifts of the laity was largely lost following the earliest centuries of the Christian movement. Among these factors was the institutionalism which settled upon the church in the Constantinian era. When the church made the transition from a persecuted minority to an increasingly established force within the fabric of Roman society, lay initiative in worship or any other crucial area became problematic. Liturgical functions in particular came to be concentrated in the priesthood. The demise of the Roman Empire and many of its institutions in the period of barbarian ascendancy left the church as one of the few viable structures of social organization, and the constant threat of societal disorganization further encouraged a clerical authoritarianism within the church. With the retrenchment of old institutions for the transmission of education and cultural skills, and with an emergent sacramentalism which deemphasized the service of the Word in the Christian liturgy, there was little opportunity for ordinary worshipers to equip themselves, through exposure to biblical teaching or other learning, for the exercise of their distinctive gifts.

The situation began to change with the period of the Renaissance, marked by the recovery of classical learning in non-ecclesiastical circles. The rise of humanistic scholarship, coupled with the gradual emergence from the feudal system of a class of independent "burgers" or townspeople of business and trade, began to produce a stratum of people better equipped to exercise the calling and initiative of the Christian laity. This social development, along with the rediscovery of biblical doctrine and authority, contributed to the partial recovery of the role and responsibility of lay people in the Protestant Reformation. Furthermore, the limitation of gifts of worship leadership to the ordained priesthood was challenged in the Protestant tenet of the "priesthood of all believers."

Yet even here older patterns remained largely unbroken; the persistent link between church and state inhibited the exercise of the gifts of the laity in the context of public worship. It was chiefly within the smaller communities of the Reformation, the radical Anabaptist movements, that lay involvement and leadership began to come to the forefront in community celebration. The rationalist Enlightenment, which broke down the mystique of the church/state authority structure, helped to pave the way for a more democratic thrust within the Protestant churches, as seen in the Puritan movement. The ideals of the Enlightenment and of Puritanism combined to set the tone for both political and religious life in the newly formed United States of America, where the lay leadership movement took root in several denominations, particularly on the frontier where clerical expertise was frequently unavailable. However, the growing cultural sophistication of the new nation brought a professionalism to the practice of Christian liturgy, resulting once again in the need for renewal in the exercise of lay giftings and capabilities.

On the North American scene, two factors seem to have contributed to the rediscovery of the gifts of the laity in the setting of corporate worship. The Pentecostal revival of the early 1900s, followed by the charismatic movement in the "main stream" churches beginning in the 1960s, focused attention once again on the gifts of the Holy Spirit within the body of Christ, especially the "manifest gifts." In the post–World War II period, neoorthodox theology with its stress on Reformation themes brought to the major Protestant denominations a new emphasis on the priesthood of all believers. The accompanying "biblical theology" movement further exposed the church to the recovery of the corporate nature of biblical faith, and especially to the theological force of the concept of the *laos* or people of God.

Protestantism remained largely divided between those groups open to the exercise of New Testament *charismata* and those stressing Reformation themes. Unexpectedly, it was within the Catholic community that the concept of the people of God exercising their Spiritual gifts emerged with a major impact on worship. The *aggiornamento* to which John XXIII and Vatican II gave voice saw liturgy literally break open in Roman Catholicism. One might claim that the renewal movement within the Catholic Church represented a belated acceptance of the Reformation principle of the priesthood of all

believers. The introduction of lay participation in worship came as culture shock to many of the faithful, for whom the Latin Mass, hitherto largely the province of the priest, had served as a backdrop for personal devotion. Now, with the liturgy in the vernacular and with heightened lay participation in both leadership and congregational response, worshipers were disturbed in their privacy and required to pay attention to what was happening in the corporate action. For many, the transition to the new liturgy was a disconcerting experience challenging their comfort levels. For those who caught the vision, however, the experience was one of exhilaration. In many parishes the participation of Catholic laity through the exercise of their gifts eclipsed the liturgical involvement of their Protestant counterparts. All this began to take place even before the rise of the Catholic charismatic movement.

The growing participation of Protestant laity in the leadership and conduct of public worship has been, in large measure, a response to the example set by the Catholic community. First lay participation has been written into Protestant renewal liturgies. Many of these are influenced by the shape of the liturgy which came out of Vatican II, itself an attempt to recover the pattern of early Christian worship with its sequence of entrance, service of the Word, service of the Lord's Table, and dismissal. At the same time, the Pentecostal/charismatic movement has spawned the "praise and worship" pattern, with its extended service of song; conducted properly, the praise and worship style allows for, and indeed requires, lay involvement in creative musical expression (as in the "song of the Lord" or the support of the worship team) and occasional exercise of liturgical gifts such as prophecy or the dance. Finally the emerging phenomenon of "convergence worship" brings the traditional praise and worship streams together, to create a heightened celebration of the peoplehood of the covenant community before its Lord. Worship of this type depends upon the willingness of worshipers to release themselves as channels of the manifold gifts of the Spirit.

Richard C. Leonard

## 220 • STAGES OF WORSHIP RENEWAL

*Worship renewal, like most growth in the natural or spiritual realms, takes place in stages, beginning with the awareness of the need for renewal. It culminates in a climate that encourages continued openness to the Spirit's transformation of church worship.*

In the past several decades, the research of educational specialists has made it increasingly clear that progress, development, and change occur in stages. The work of Piaget and Kohlberg in moral development, as well as that of James Fowler in religious development, have been helpful in understanding the sequence of change.

What is true in the field of moral and spiritual development appears to be true in the area of worship renewal as well: growth happens in stages. Evidence for these stages arises out of the work of pastors and church leaders who have committed themselves to a worship renewal based on biblical and historical precedent. These studies suggest seven stages of development which a local church passes through in its pursuit of growth in worship. These are:

1. The Awareness Stage
2. The Analysis Stage
3. The Knowledge Stage
4. The Resourcing Stage
5. The Experimental Stage
6. The Renewal Stage
7. *Semper reformanda*

The steps toward worship renewal are critical stages which must unfold in sequence. Obviously there is no set time frame for concluding one stage and entering another. Instead, the stages of development merge into each other, interconnecting and supporting one another. Furthermore, in any given community at any given time, people will be at different stages of development. Consequently, once a sizeable portion of the congregation has passed through these phases, leaders need to be sensitive to those who are at other stages of development in their spiritual journeys.

The process of growth takes time, whether it be the growth of a tree, a child, or a church. The process requires patience. Each stage may be enjoyed for what it offers. It is cause for celebration when renewal efforts in worship bear fruit in which meaning and joy are tied to a reenactment of God's saving acts and in which God's people are touched with his transforming power.

1. **The Awareness Stage.** The initial step toward worship renewal begins when part or all of a congregation senses there is more to worship than their present experience allows. This is the work of the Holy Spirit. Such awareness is often prompted by a visit to another church where worship is experienced in a deeper dimension, or through contact with a person, an article, or a book that challenges one's experience and concept of worship. This exposure usually results in a more intense interest in and curiosity about worship, demonstrated through noncritical questioning and a subsequent longing for a more fulfilled worship.

2. **The Analysis Stage.** The second stage of development grows out of the unfulfilled longing for the more satisfying worship that was experienced or encountered in the first stage. Initially, a person or community begins to ache for a true experience of worship. There is an unquenchable need for something more. Because a person does not know what that "something more" is, and because the church is not moving beyond a worship now regarded by some as dead, the inner self become frustrated and upset. Attendance at worship often becomes counterproductive and even damaging to the spiritual quest. At this point, when the worshiper begins to reject the worship in his or her church, two things may happen: the person may reject the style of worship but remain in silent protest, or he or she may openly criticize what is experienced as shallow and irrelevant worship. Finally, the person may explode in unresolved anger and leave the church, looking for another community where the longing for a deeper experience of worship may be fulfilled.

For this reason, it is important for a local church to implement a critical evaluation and feedback survey which examines every aspect of worship and allows for honest input from every member. This analysis will accomplish a number of things for the worshiper and for the community as a whole:

(1) The worshiper, feeling involved in the future direction of worship, will be less likely to leave the church in search of a worshiping community. (2) A diagnostic tool will bring to the surface hidden talents among worshipers which may be put to work in worship. (3) A diagnostic survey will provide the staff of the church with a sense of the congregation's disposition toward worship renewal. It may give the leadership permission to move more quickly toward worship renewal or caution them to adopt a slower,

more deliberate pace. (4) A diagnostic should pique the interest of both the leadership and the congregation toward the next stage of development, the knowledge stage.

**3. The Knowledge Stage.** The first two stages are subjective phases of development which occur in varying degrees among people and communities traveling toward worship renewal. The third stage, which is an objective period of development, is a crucial stage for several reasons. First, the field of knowledge which touches upon worship is vast and includes knowledge of the biblical, historical, and theological sources of worship; learning in the arts; some understanding of communication theory; and sensitivity to ways to introduce change. Furthermore, all of this knowledge has to be distilled and adapted to the particularities of a specific denomination or tradition. Renewed worship needs to express what is common to the church universally, but in a style acceptable to the local church in which it is being introduced. And finally, this is all made more complex by the fact that knowledge alone is not adequate for worship renewal. The church must rely on the Holy Spirit to give life to this learning as the congregation gradually begins to reshape its worship.

It is here, in the third stage, that a congregation may be most tempted to give up on the seven-step process and opt for the "quick fix." If worship renewal is seen merely as learning a few new songs or introducing more of the arts (drama, banners, dance) into worship, then a minimum amount of knowledge is demanded. The principles and practices of worship which arise out of the gospel and the biblical-historical practice of the church represent a serious discipline of study every bit as demanding as biblical studies or theology. Scholars in this field are now making this material available through books, videos, tapes, seminars, and worship clinics.

Consequently, a congregation deeply desiring renewal of worship with staying power cannot afford to bypass the stage of learning. Since there is such a voluminous amount of knowledge available on the subject, it is best for a church to have both an introductory course on worship and an ongoing study that continues to explore various facets of corporate celebration.

**4. The Resourcing Stage.** The resourcing stage—the period of gathering materials for worship renewal—begins after a certain amount of knowledge has been acquired. Like the gathering of knowledge, this resourcing will continue as the church grows. As a congregation becomes more knowledgeable about worship, the "how-to" question will naturally arise, creating the demand for a variety of resources to assist a congregation in its worship growth.

A vast amount of material is available to a church looking for such resources. In the past decade, a virtual torrent of materials prayers and confessions, eucharistic liturgies, sacramental actions, music, art, and dance has appeared. In addition, an equally impressive amount of studies and resources has been published dealing with the church year and the relation of worship to evangelism, education, and spirituality.

**5. The Experimentation Stage.** The fifth stage of development is closely related to the previous stages of knowledge and resourcing and, for best results, should follow in its turn. Nevertheless, experimentation with new forms of worship can be introduced slowly and knowledgeably, in connection with the two previous stages. Unfortunately, some churches leap to the experimentation stage with inadequate knowledge and resourcing. When this happens, a congregation may quickly revert to the style of worship they were using before they attempted worship renewal. They failed to construct an adequate foundation for making enduring changes.

**6. The Renewal Stage.** The most important hour of the week for a congregation is the hour it gathers for worship. When the people are no longer passive spectators but active worshipers, statements like "I love to worship," "I come here because of the worship," and "This worship strengthens me" will be heard again and again.

This renewed worship is worship in which God's event of salvation in Jesus Christ is genuinely celebrated and is truly experienced as a healing event by all who gather. People will go from worship not frustrated or angry, but at peace. They will know that God is there for them, that Jesus Christ is actually present in worship to touch them, to heal them, and to make them whole.

This kind of worship arises out of the gospel, the proclamation that Christ is the one who brings forgiveness and healing to our lives. It celebrates a divine action, as Christ's saving, healing, comforting, and guiding presence is made available through the Word and the Lord's Table. Finally, it issues in a genuine response to this divine action, as people worship in faith and trust, openly and receptively. This is the kind of worship in which God is glorified and with which he is pleased. It is not a lecture, yet we are educated; it is not an evangelistic service, yet we are drawn to commitment to Christ; it is not a counseling session, yet we are healed; it is not entertainment, yet we enjoy God and love to worship in his presence.

7. *Semper Reformanda*. Keeping renewal alive requires the continuing engagement of the congregation in the process which has been described. Once a congregation has passed through these various stages and entered, to whatever degree, a state of worship renewal, it is of the utmost importance for that congregation to remain diligent and watchful in its practice of worship. The Protestant reformers had a phrase for this activity: *semper reformanda,* the church must always be reforming itself.

There are several ways in which leaders may assist the church in this continuing reappraisal of worship. These include (1) teaching an ongoing course on worship, (2) establishing a worship committee whose responsibility it is to keep a vigilant eye on worship, and (3) bathing worship in constant prayer.

Robert E. Webber

# ◈ SIXTEEN ◈

# Understanding the Principles of Worship

========================================== ❧ ==========================================

*Liturgical scholars generally agree that the worship of the church arises out of the gospel and is, in this sense, event-oriented. The primary focus of worship is not an abstract deity, but the God who acts in history to redeem and restore human beings and the created order. Principles of Christian worship derive from the biblical conviction that the foundational event celebrated in worship is the dying and rising of Jesus Christ, through which evil is ultimately defeated and the creation restored and renewed. This chapter explores eight of these principles, beginning with the fundamental premise that worship celebrates Christ.*

========================================== ❧ ==========================================

### 221 • PRINCIPLE ONE: WORSHIP CELEBRATES CHRIST

*In proclaiming God's saving work through Jesus Christ in song, story, prayer, and thanksgiving, the church glorifies God and extols him for his acts of redemption. Thus it accomplishes Peter's declaration that God's people "may declare the praises of him who called [them] out of darkness into his wonderful light" (1 Pet. 2:9).*

### Worship Is Based on the History of Salvation

Christian liturgy is patterned on the history of salvation. There is the original initiative of God, who throughout the ages offers man his love. The history is carried forward by the redeeming events of Christ, the Son of God, who on the cross gives himself totally to his Father and for the salvation of mankind. He ascends to the Father and sends upon his Church the Holy Spirit, so that his *ekklēsia* may continue his redeeming work in time and space and by the power of the Holy Spirit. The Church looks toward the consummation of all things when Christ delivers the kingdom to his Father so that he may be all in all (1 Cor. 15:28).

"To the Father, through the Son, and in the Holy Spirit" is the underlying pattern of the history of salvation; so also it is the direction of the liturgy. For example, the eucharistic prayer gives praise and thanksgiving to the Father through the Son, whose redeeming acts are recalled, and in the Holy Spirit,

who is invoked on the offering (*epiklēsis*). The doxology at the end of the prayer expresses the whole truth succinctly but explicitly. Most collects begin with an ascription of praise to the Father, making petition through the Son and concluding with a mention of the Holy Spirit. This construction reminds the worshiper that the entire liturgy serves to create an entrance into communion with God, a participation in the divine life and love which constitute the Trinity.

J. D. Crichton[30]

### Worship Is Event-Oriented

In both the Old and New Testaments, God's purpose in revealing himself and in calling a people into existence, was to create a worshiping community to be a sign of his redeeming work. For example, when God entered into a covenant with the people of Israel, they met him at Mount Sinai in the first public meeting between God and his people. This meeting with God became the prototype for public worship in Israel. And it was through public worship that God's revelation, redemption, and covenant were remembered and passed down in history.

In the New Testament, the author of Hebrews takes great pains to compare Christ with the Old Testament regulations of worship. Here we see that the Old Testament forms of worship find their fulfillment in the death, resurrection, and return of Christ. We read that Christ "appeared once for all at the end of the ages to do away with sin by the sacrifice of himself" (Heb. 9:26). This means that worship in the New Testament era, even as worship in the Old Testament, hearkens back to the event at which God did a magnificent work for his people. This work is always connected with the specific event of Christ through which God revealed himself, established redemption for the world, and called into being his new people, the church. There is nothing abstract or ethereal about that.

Robert E. Webber[31]

## 222 ✦ PRINCIPLE TWO: WORSHIP TELLS AND ACTS OUT THE CHRIST EVENT

_The order of worship is designed to reveal God's action in history. Through that order, the worshiping community meets the God who has acted, and who continues to speak and act among His people._

The order of worship flows out of the principle that worship celebrates Christ. Consequently, a rule which can be followed when creating a sequence for worship is that worship tells and acts out the Christ-event. In this sense, worship is patterned after God who revealed himself and after God who became incarnate. Therefore, the twofold focus of worship becomes the Word (the Bible as the symbol of God speaking) and the Table (bread and wine as the symbol of God acting to save us). In this ancient order of worship the story of Christ is communicated in two parts: the Word of God and the Table of the Lord. In the course of time, two other parts were added: entrance for worship and dismissal to serve. Thus, the most basic and rudimentary shape of worship is fourfold.

Each of these four parts of worship contains a variety of prayers, hymns, acclamations, testimonials, and responses. The sequence of worship not only unfolds the story of God's redeeming love but also brings us through the experience of that love.

The acts of entrance form the people into a worshiping community, preparing them to hear the word of the Lord. The service of the word is the experience of hearing God speak and of responding to his words. In the service of the Table Christ becomes present to bring salvation and healing to the community gathered before him. In the dismissal God sends His people into the world to serve in his name. In each of these acts a divine work takes place, as God moves in the lives of the worshipers.

The proclamation of Christ's life, death, resurrection, and coming again are told and acted out through the service of the Word and the Table. Thus, this basic order of worship is not restricted to liturgical churches, but is appropriate for use in all expressions of the Christian faith, whether fundamentalist, evangelical, charismatic, or mainline Protestant groups.

Robert E. Webber[32]

## 223 ✦ PRINCIPLE THREE: IN WORSHIP GOD SPEAKS AND ACTS

_If worship is truly rooted in the gospel and celebrates Christ, then we can expect a divine action to occur in worship, revealed through words and signs._

### The Word as Reminder of God's Presence

There are a number of passages that accent the importance of the Word of God in worship. Very early in the biblical story we read that in the wilderness at Mount Sinai Moses "took the Book of the Covenant and read it to the people" (Exod. 24:7). The people of Israel did not have a Bible in the same sense that we do today. Yet, the Book of the Covenant served as their Scripture because it contained "all the LORD's words and laws" (Exod. 24:3). It represented the living Word of God and the agreement he had made with them.

By reading the Book of the Covenant, Israel was reminded once again that God, out of love, had chosen them and called them up out of Egypt to be a holy and unique people for himself. Apparently the reading and comments at Mount Sinai concentrated on a rehearsal of God's saving activity—bringing them up from the land of Egypt. Through the reading, the exodus-event became real and alive, and the people sensed their involvement in God's action. Consequently, the Israelites experienced the sense of having been brought out of the land of Egypt again and of entering anew into covenantal relationship with their God.

Jewish worship has always had Scripture at the center of its worship. This is seen in the development of synagogue worship, which probably had its beginnings after the exile to Babylon. By the time of Jesus synagogue worship had become a regular practice: "He went to Nazareth, where he had been brought up, and on the Sabbath day he went into the synagogue, as was his custom. And he stood up to read. The scroll of the prophet Isaiah was handed to him. Unrolling it, he found the place . . ." (Luke 4:16-17). It was perfectly natural, then, for this same practice of reading to be carried over to Christian worship. Paul makes this very clear when he says, "Devote yourself to the public reading of Scripture, to preaching and to teaching" (1 Tim. 4:13); and again, "After this letter has been read to you, see that it is also read in the church of the Laodiceans and that you in turn read the letter from Laodicea" (Col. 4:16).

When I listen to the reading of Scripture in worship, I try to remember that it is the record of God's covenant with us. It is a record of how God has initiated a relationship with me, sought me out, and brought me to himself.

Robert E. Webber[33]

### ——— Sacraments as Sign Acts ———

Ever since the New Testament, the church has found certain sign-acts essential for expressing the encounter between God and humans. These sign-acts pointed to sacred things and became ways of expressing to the senses what no physical sense could perceive, i.e., God's self-giving. The sacraments call us to "taste and see" (Ps. 34:8), to touch, to hear, even to smell "that the LORD is good." In them the physical becomes a vehicle of the spiritual as the sign-act causes us to experience what it represents.

The number of sign-acts that can be used universally in worship is limited, and there seems to be a built-in bias to conservatism in retaining those that communicate well. Those in common use today would have been familiar at any time in Christian history. Sign-acts do not change rapidly the way spoken words do. Perhaps this is one reason they seem so faithful at the solemn crises of life: birth, marriage, sickness, and death.

Only in recent years have we become fully aware of the sign value that actions have in and of themselves and have at least become willing to let them "speak" for themselves.

James F. White[34]

## 224 • PRINCIPLE FOUR: WORSHIP IS AN ACT OF COMMUNICATION

*Communication takes place in worship when the Lord speaks and acts and the people of God respond. Worship employs both the spoken word and the symbolic act so that God can touch all areas of an individual's life and communicate with people of varying personalities. By the same token, the worshiper uses both word and act to express devotion to God.*

We now know that the left hemisphere of the brain specializes in verbal skills, while the right side centers on nonverbal and inductive skills such as the spatial and poetic impulses of the person. The left side of the brain is more word-oriented and orderly, while the right side is more symbolic and creative. Although all of us function from both the left and right sides of the brain, some of us function more from one side than the other. This is why for some people the communication of words is more effective, while for others the communication of symbols is more powerful.

It is interesting that the Bible employs both forms of communication. The Scriptures range from the straightforward discourse of historical narrative and the Epistles to the highly imaginative and visual forms of communication in the prophetic and apocalyptic writings.

These new insights from neuropsychology have bearing on our current concern for the renewal of worship. As we think and plan toward new forms and approaches, we should be concerned with achieving a balance between verbal and symbolic expressions so that the whole person is inspired to worship. We must also respect the fact that some people are more comfortable with verbal communication and others with symbolic. Since all congregations include people of both types and since all people are capable of communication through both methods, we should work toward improving both the verbal and the symbolic methods of communicating Christ in our worship experience.

It is also important for us to remember that communication in words and symbols goes in two directions. While God communicates to us through words and symbols, we also respond to him through words and symbols. Worship as an act of communication contains the ingredients of speech, symbol, dialogue, interaction, and relationship.

Robert E. Webber[35]

## 225 ✦ PRINCIPLE FIVE: IN WORSHIP WE RESPOND TO GOD AND TO EACH OTHER

_More than an intellectual assent to doctrine, creed, or prayer, worship is an experience of the presence of a holy God. Response to this encounter should touch the center of the worshiper's being, creating a sense of awe and mystery. It should also result in an admission of one's unworthiness and need for repentance, and in renewed commitment to a life of obedience to the mighty and merciful God._

### ——— Response as Inner Experience ———

It is no wonder that the early Christians were struck with "awe." This is a response that goes deep into the very inner chambers of the person—a response that touches our hearts and emotions and makes us feel awe-struck. We feel the mystery and experience of the power touching us in a warm and healing manner.

This kind of response, which is motivated by the Holy Spirit, can happen in our churches today. But we have to create an atmosphere in which it can happen. We need to let go of our intellectual ideal of worship and realize there is more to worship than a sermon; we have to let go of our evangelistic notion of worship and reckon with the fact that worship is not primarily directed toward the sinners who need to be converted; we must let go of our

_The Church as Ark. A favorite symbol of the church from the very beginning of Christianity is that of the ark. A number of New Testament passages refer to the ark as a place of salvation (Matt. 24:37-39; Heb. 4:7; 1 Pet. 3:20; 2 Pet. 3:5). Perhaps these statements give rise to the symbol of the ark as a picture of the community of the church._

entertainment expectations and remind ourselves that we are not in church to watch a Christian variety show.

We have gathered together in worship to be met by God the Almighty. God, the Creator of the universe, the One who sustains our lives, our Redeemer and King, is present through proclamation and remembrance. He wants to communicate to us, to penetrate our inner selves, to take up residence with us. And, as we go through the experience of meeting with him in this mystical moment of public worship, we are to respond.

But response is not just singing a hymn, not just saying a creed, not just saying a prayer. Response, from the very beginning of worship to the end, must be a powerful inner experience of actually being in the presence of God. When we sing a hymn or say a confession or prayer, we are not merely singing or saying words, but are expressing a feeling, baring our souls, truly responding and communicating to the living and active presence of a loving and merciful God.

Robert E. Webber[36]

### ——— Worship Demands Obedience and Renewal ———

Perhaps the place in the Old Testament where we see the richest and fullest agenda of all the implications of worship is in the sixth chapter of Isaiah, the story of the prophet's vision. It begins, as all worship must, when the prophet enters into a realization of the presence, the holiness, and the glory of God. The moment of encountering the Holy is the given moment of the numinous with all the power that is latent within such a religious experience. It is a moment of vision and insight. It is a moment when the doors of perception, normally closed by man's cerebral censorship, are flung wide open. Ears which had previously seemed deaf begin at last to hear. Eyes which must have been blind in the past are opened at last. It is a definite moment in time (the year of King Uzziah's death), yet its significance breaks through the limits of time and the finite into the realms of eternity and the infinite. Although it is localized in the temple, its message not only strikes at the heart of the nation but also has spoken most eloquently to men and women of every age and every culture. The vision speaks at the same time of the glory of God and the holiness of God.

Here is no religious "kick" for its own sake, but a

demanding clarion call which originates in eternity, yet speaks directly to men and women in history, calling the nation to repentance and its citizens to service within the community. The impact, reverberating with glory from the heart of heaven, powerfully evokes a sense of sin. Worship and a sense of unworthiness come in the same breath. They invite repentance, renewal, and rededication. The ecstatic brought about a dislodging of perspective for Isaiah as real as the physical dislodging suffered by Jacob when he was lamed in his wrestling with God. The prophet finds himself seeing things now from a very different viewpoint, and a very uncomfortable viewpoint at that. There can be nothing cheap about such a gracious and given moment; it will issue in nothing less than costly commitment to the voice and purposes of God—a renewal of life and a new obedience in service.

Michael Marshall[37]

## 226 ◆ PRINCIPLE SIX: WORSHIP IS AN ACT OF THE PEOPLE

*Worship is not a service or entertainment performed for the laity, but an act that requires the participation of all members in the body of Christ. For this reason there is a need to achieve a balance between order and freedom. An overemphasis on order can lead to ritualism; an overemphasis on freedom sometimes leads to chaos. Most churches suffer from an overemphasis on order.*

Congregational participation is worship that involves the action of everyone simultaneously. But congregational action cannot occur without two very basic ingredients: the congregation must understand what they are doing, and they must intend to make the responses that are part of worship. Worship is a verb.

Worship is best understood when it carries the worshiper through a sequence of related events such as: (1) preparation for worship, (2) reading and preaching the Word, (3) Holy Communion, and (4) dismissal. In this sequence, the story of our coming to God—of hearing him speak, of entering into communion with him, and of being sent forth—is the order of worship.

These forms of traditional worship should not be discarded as useless relics of the past. Those who advocate a so-called creative worship designed to give the congregation a new spiritual high every

week soon discover that this is not only impossible but impractical. God has already established the structural ingredients needed in a meeting with him, and we cannot improve on these forms. We simply need to understand what they are and practice them in faith, believing that we really are meeting God in his Word and through his Table.

Now the question we face is this: How can we, and the church, experience a form of worship that is truly free, yet is characterized by order? This, I believe, is a question that must always be in our minds. It is an issue which lies at the heart of a lively and active worship. Order without freedom may become mere unthinking ritual. On the other hand, freedom without order may become equally unthinking and even chaotic. But the order and style of worship which we are discussing here, and which has biblical precedent, is one that re-enacts the gospel story.

The freedom I propose is that of a dynamic faith, an active and engaging commitment to what is being done, a freedom to be spontaneous within the context of order. Since order is the symbol of God's speaking and acting in the midst of his church, there can be no justification for passive worshipers who simply sit and soak it all in. Certainly, as we have seen, passive worship cannot be justified on the grounds of Scripture, theology, or history. For this reason, it is a matter of utmost urgency that the church break through the obstacle of a passive worship. And it is important that we see in worship renewal a rediscovery of a structure through which Christ is faithfully presented and rediscovered, a worship that is free and intentional.

Robert E. Webber[38]

## 227 ◆ PRINCIPLE SEVEN: WORSHIP MAKES EFFECTIVE USE OF GOD'S CREATIVE GIFTS

*The Bible envisions worship as an offering of the entire person in living sacrifice to the Lord. Creative and thoughtful use of space and art, as well as attention to the traditional church calendar, combine to make worship an experience that involves body, soul, and spirit.*

### Worship Involves the Whole Person

Worship is an activity that includes every aspect of the human awareness: heart and mind, senses and intellect. St. Paul bids us, "offer your bodies as living sacrifices, holy and pleasing to God—this is your spiritual act of worship" (Rom. 12:1). We can see how he is using the word "spiritual" here: not in contrast to the physical but rather as a quality of worship that includes the physical and ultimately transcends it. Nothing in the human experience lies outside the scope of true Christian worship. For too long, at least in the West, and perhaps especially among the Protestant churches, worship has been an activity primarily of the mind. It has been reduced to a process of edifying the mind and informing the intellect. Yet the scriptural commandments of Old and New Testaments alike are as all-embracing as they possibly can be: to love God with all our heart and soul, mind, body, passions, and strength. We need to take the concept of corporate worship even further and see our worship not only as an activity involving the whole body of Christ and all its members but also as an activity involving the whole human body—mind, heart, and spirit.

It is quite clear that we cannot and must not exclude the body with all its senses in the totally involving activity of worship. The use of the body is an outward and visible sign of the intentions of the heart and mind, as every ballet dancer and actor knows—or forgets at his or her peril. But, at a more mundane level, we also know that the use of the body for self-expression is true in the ordinary affairs of everyday life. If I am conducting an interview, the position of my body will indicate the level at which I intend to conduct that interview and will also say something of my relationship with the person I am interviewing. If I remain seated, behind a desk, and you are compelled to remain standing, I am implying that you are my inferior and you may well be on the carpet! If on the other hand you are seated and suddenly I stand up and begin to walk up and down the room, there is the chance that I shall be remonstrating and seeking to make a point or even to deliver myself of some lecture upon a topic that has become the burden of my soul. But if I come from behind the desk and pull up an armchair alongside you, the ice is broken and confidence and cordiality would be the name of the game. Truth to tell, the whole of our life is shot through with ceremonials, often unconsciously, but frequently consciously (as at dinner parties). So it would be a strange fragmentation if, when we expressed our-

selves before God, we suddenly affected a distaste for ceremonials.

Michael Marshall[39]

## Time, Art, and Space Enhance Worship

Still raging today is an age-old debate that has divided Christians throughout the centuries—just how much and to what extent the use of art forms is permissible in worship. The Orthodox position is founded on the Old Testament. These worshipers point to the elaborate artistic beauty of the tabernacle and the temple. If God permitted our senses to be involved in worship in the Old Testament, they ask, why would he forbid it in the New Testament? They also cite the example of the Incarnation. Look, they say, God became a man—a human, visible, material, sensual person. If God can communicate himself to us through a created body, why can't we respond similarly to him through color, sound, movement, smell, touch, and sight?

On the other side of the issue, Protestants draw their position from the second commandment: "You shall not make for yourself an idol in the form of anything in the heaven above or on the earth beneath or in the waters below. You shall not bow down to them or worship them; for I, the LORD your God, am a jealous God" (Exod. 20:4-5). They interpret these words as a command against the use of any icons, frescoes, or statues that depict heavenly images. Yet, many Protestants acknowledge that this verse does not specifically deny or forbid the use of such items as candles, incense, vestments, processions, musical instruments, choirs, stained glass windows, door and furniture carvings, artistically designed pulpits, tables, or baptismal fonts.

Why, then, do we Protestants have such plain settings for our worship? The issue comes down to a difference of opinion articulated during the sixteenth-century Reformation by John Calvin on the one hand and Martin Luther and the Anglicans on the other. Luther and the Anglicans believed that _whatever is not explicitly rejected by the Scripture may be used in worship._ Consequently, they were free to use the ceremonial quite liberally. But Calvin believed that _only that which is explicitly taught in the New Testament is permissible in worship._ Since the New Testament says nothing pro or con about the use of art in worship, Calvinists and their successors were not free to employ the arts as means of expressing worship to almighty God.

We cannot hope to solve an age-old controversy here. So, let it be sufficient to ask the Protestant community for a second consideration of some of the least controversial issues related to using the arts in worship—arts such as music, drama, dance, space, and color.

We are not arguing that art is *necessary* for worship. Certainly we can worship God anywhere and under any conditions. To insist that art is necessary for worship is to commit aesthetic heresy. Such insistence makes art an idol, an object of our worship. On the other hand, to insist that art is a hindrance to worship is equally dangerous. It denies that the material creation is a worthy vehicle through which God can communicate with us and we with him. Ultimately it denies the Incarnation, for it was in human, material flesh that God became present to us in Jesus Christ.

It is evident that the architecture of our church is shaped by our concept of worship; the architecture, in turn, shapes our experience of worship. It is the function of space to foster rather than hinder congregational participation. Unfortunately, the typical Protestant church employs a very closed use of space. The aisles are often narrow and the pews are situated in a style similar to that of the lecture hall. This arrangement, combined with a dominant pulpit, restricts the congregation's involvement in worship. There is very little space for musical processions, for artistic expression, for drama, or for dance. When I am in this kind of space, I always feel that my natural inhibitions are being supported and a leader-dominated worship is being affirmed.

Where space is used to enhance their interrelationship, people sustain each other. We feel more a part of the body of Christ in that kind of place. But, when all we see is the back of someone's head, when there is no eye contact with other people, our sense of the unity of the body of Christ is impaired. In a semicircle seating or a seating where two sides face each other, the sense of community is stronger. In my experience I have been edified and moved to deeper worship by observing the involvement of other people in worship. I have seen people communicate the joy of worship through their faces and gestures. For me, watching someone sing enthusiastically or prayerfully or humbly is a moving experience. Seeing others bow and kneel in prayer or watching someone reverently receiving the bread and wine increases my own participation in the community action of worship.

Robert E. Webber[40]

## 228 • PRINCIPLE EIGHT: WORSHIP IS A WAY OF LIFE

*Worship is not only an action. It is also a way of life that the church experiences in each of its members day by day. When worship is central, all of life proceeds toward it and issues from it again, in blessed rhythm.*

Worship as a way of life is summed up in the following way in the Liturgical Constitution of Vatican II: "The liturgy (worship) is the summit toward which the activity of the church is directed; at the same time it is a fount from which all the church's power flows." When I think of these words, I visualize an hourglass set on its side. At the very center, the waist of the hourglass is worship. On the left, everything that one does in life, both work and leisure, moves toward the center, worship. On the right, everything that one does in life work and leisure is empowered by worship. In this vision of life our worship stands at the center and gives shape to all that we do. Worship, then, is not only the public acts that we do as a gathered community, but our very day-to-day way of life.

What happens in worship is that our struggles with the powers of evil that disturb us and seek to dismantle our relationships and our lives are brought to Jesus, the victor over all evil. In worship we deal again and again with the ultimate truth that Jesus, who overcame the powers of evil through his death and resurrection, is able to overcome those same powers that are now at work in our own lives.

In this way worship is the "summit" toward which we always proceed. For we take to worship the issues we deal with on a day-to-day basis with an expectancy that God will bring healing into our lives. But worship is always the "fount" from which our lives flow, because worship not only brings healing to our life issues, it also empowers us to face these issues with the conviction that the last word is not the death which evil brings, but the resurrection which Jesus gives. When we are healed and empowered by worship, our day-to-day lives at home, at work and at leisure take on a new dimension. They rise to new life.

Robert E. Webber[41]

## 229 ✦ BIBLIOGRAPHY ON PRINCIPLES OF WORSHIP

### Cell Groups

Azevedo, Marcello de. _Basic Ecclesial Communities in Brazil: The Challenge of a New Way of Being Church._ Washington, D.C.: Georgetown University Press, 1987. Since Vatican II, small base communities of worship and Christian fellowship have emerged in South America and around the world. These communities break with the established structure of the church organized around power and individualism to create communities of faith rooted in servanthood and community. Out of this new configuration a new worship emerges akin to the intimate worship of the early church.

Cho, Paul Yonggi, and Harold Hostetler. _Successful Home Groups._ South Plainfield, N.J.: Bridge, 1981. Personal testimony of how the founding pastor of Christendom's largest church discovered the home cell principle.

Galloway, Dale E. _20/20 Vision,_ 2d ed. Portland, Oreg.: Scott, 1990. A nuts-and-bolts, how-to manual by the founding pastor of America's most visible cell-church congregation.

George, Carl F. _Prepare Your Church for the Future._ Tarrytown, N.Y.: Fleming Revell, 1991. The primary text, for both theory and practice, of the metachurch model based on cell groups.

Hadaway, C. Kirk, Stuart A. Wright, and Francis N. Dubose. _Homecell Groups and House Churches: Alternative for the Urban Church._ Nashville: Broadman Press, 1987. Background insights on the origins and various models of house-church cell groups.

Logan, Robert E. _Beyond Church Growth._ Tarrytown, N.Y.: Fleming Revell, 1989. A case study example of the implications of metachurch technology: vision-directed faith, celebrative worship, and development of lay cell-group leaders.

Neighbor, Ralph, Jr. _Where Do We Go From Here?_ Houston: Touch Outreach Ministries, 1990. An overview of many of the world's largest cell-group churches, along with a testimony of the author's disillusionment with the typical American "program-based" church.

### Reference Works

Davies, J. G., ed. _The New Westminster Dictionary of Liturgy & Worship._ Philadelphia: Westminster Press, 1986. The standard one-volume reference work for Protestant worship.

Fink, Peter E., S.J. _The New Dictionary of Sacramental Worship._ Bramcote, Notts., UK: Grove Books, 1990. This valuable Roman dictionary is structured as a theological and pastoral resource. The entries include theological insights, practical liturgical matters, and matters of worship that touch on pastoral and social issues.

Lang, Jovian P. _Dictionary of the Liturgy._ New York: Catholic Book Publishing, 1989. The standard one-volume reference work for Catholic worship.

Thompson, Bard. _A Bibliography of Christian Worship._ Metuchen, N.J.: Scarecrow Press, 1989. Ecumenical. Comprehensive, if not exhaustive, listing of publications on worship in print through 1981. Almost 800 pages of extremely valuable bibliography.

### Introduction to the Study of Worship

Jones, Cheslyn, Geoffrey Wainwright, and Edward Yarnold, eds. _The Study of Liturgy,_ 2d ed. New York: Oxford University Press, 1978. Ecumenical. Perhaps the most thorough introductory work to the new directions taking place in worship among all the major denominations. The book contains three parts: Part 1 is a theology of worship by J. D. Crichton. It is brief but very helpful. As important as a theology of worship is, many scholars do not address it. Crichton's work is based on excellent biblical and theological scholarship and is readable. Part 2 addresses the historical development of the liturgy, initiation, the Eucharist, ordination, the divine office, the calendar, and the setting of the liturgy in scholarly articles. Part 3 discusses liturgy in pastoral orientation. Two sections deal with the understanding of liturgy in the light of its history and worship and the pastoral office. The strength of this work is its comprehensiveness, historical orientation, and scholarly reliability.

Lebon, Jean. _How to Understand the Liturgy._ New York: Continuum, 1988. Catholic. Popular, but based on contemporary scholarship. Deals with the act of celebrating (worship as action), with matters of liturgy (signs, postures, communicating), and the liturgy itself (assembling, Word, Table, dismissal).

Webber, Robert. *Worship Old and New.* Grand Rapids: Zondervan, 1982. A standard text providing biblical, historical, and theological introduction to Christian worship. Covers all the major issues including the arts, the Christian year, and the relationship of worship to the world.

White, James F. *Introduction to Christian Worship.* Nashville: Abingdon Press, 1990. The standard introductory text to the worship of the church. Explains the connection of worship to time, space, public prayer, service of the Word, sacraments, baptism, Eucharist, and other passage rites.

## Principles of Worship

Abba, Raymond. *Principles of Christian Worship: With Special Reference to the Free Churches.* New York: Oxford University Press, 1957.

Allen, Ronald, and Gordon Borrow. *Worship: Rediscovering the Missing Jewel.* Portland, Oreg.: Multnomah Press, 1982. Protestant. Collaboration of an evangelical theologian and musician. Deals with popular issues: defining, planning, moods of worship, reading, singing, environment.

Beachy, Alvin J. *Worship as Celebration of Covenant and Incarnation.* Newton, Kans.: Faith and Life Press, 1968. The material of this book represents the collective thought of Anabaptist worship theologians and leaders. The theme of covenant represents the worship of the Old Testament, while the theme of Incarnation represents the worship of the New Testament. These scholars maintain that the exterior form of worship represented in the Old Testament is translated into an interior meaning in the New.

Clark, Neville. *Call to Worship.* London: SCM Press, 1960. A British Baptist perspective.

Coleman, Michael, and Ed Lindquist. *Come and Worship: Tap Into God's Power Through Praise and Worship.* Tarrytown, N.Y.: Fleming Revell, 1989. A popular and very helpful book describing how to achieve and experience charismatic worship.

Cornwall, Judson. *Let Us Worship: The Believers Response to God.* South Plainfield, N.J.: Bridge, 1983. A charismatic presentation of worship that deals with a number of issues such as the call to worship, holiness and worship, praise and worship and many other issues.

Empereur, James. *Worship: Exploring the Sacred.* Washington, D.C.: Pastoral Press, 1987. Catholic. Based on good scholarship. Addresses worship as the Experience process (the search for meaning in worship), the Reflection (models of worship), the Process (planning), and the Challenges (creativity).

Erickson, Craig Douglas. *Participating in Worship.* Louisville: Westminster/John Knox Press, 1989. Protestant. Based on good scholarship. Emphasis on participation. Deals with priesthood of the church, perspectives on participation, utterances of the Spirit, silence, prayer, preaching, lay-led worship, communication, participation in the mystery of Christ.

Daniels, Harold M. *What to Do with Sunday Morning.* Philadelphia: Westminster Press, 1979. Protestant. Presbyterian scholar addresses the matter of change in worship. Guidelines for the development of new forms, the centrality of the Lord's Supper, the use of art forms and creative possibilities for worship.

Gusmer, Charles. *Wholesome Worship.* Washington, D.C.: Pastoral Press, 1989. Catholic. Based on good scholarship. Deals with the many dimensions of ritual, services of Sunday and week days, reconciliation and healing, and seasons of the year.

Harakas, Stanley S. *Living the Liturgy.* Minneapolis: Life and Light Press, 1974. Orthodox. Popular; deals with both the objective and subjective side of the St. John Chrysostom liturgy. Argues for worship as a lived experience, and shows how to make the liturgy live.

Hayford, Jack W. *Worship His Majesty.* Philadelphia: Westminster Press, 1987. Protestant. Popular. Charismatic preacher and songwriter (author of "Majesty") deals with themes of renewing worship. Touches on all the themes of morning worship—Word, Table, song, structure. Also includes practical how-to information on planning and leading.

Hickman, Hoyt L. *A Primer for Church Worship.* Nashville: Abingdon Press, 1984. Protestant. Popular but based on good scholarship. This United Methodist minister explores the structure of worship, helping readers understand what is behind worship. It explains the significance of worship in Entrance, Word, Table and Christian year.

Kendrick, Graham. *Learning to Worship as a Way of Life.* Minneapolis: Bethany House, 1984. Protestant. Popular. Kendrick, leader of the charismatic movement in England and popular songwriter, addresses such matters as dethroning the powers of evil and worshiping in the Spirit. Also includes a helpful section on how to lead worship.

Kreider, Eleanor. _Enter His Gates_. Scottdale, Pa.: Herald Press, 1990. An excellent introduction to convergence worship from an Anabaptist perspective. Addresses the design of worship with chapters on form and freedom, planning worship, and songs ancient and new. Also includes a number of worship models.

Liesch, Barry. _People in the Presence of God_. Grand Rapids: Zondervan, 1988. Popular. Evangelical work explores biblical worship with strong emphasis on creativity and the arts, principles, family, small-group and large-group worship.

Marshall, Michael. _Renewal in Worship_. Wilton, Conn.: Morehouse-Barlow, 1985. Protestant. Popular but based on contemporary scholarship. Anglican writer discusses general subjects such as the nature of worship, flexibility, music, signs, symbols, ceremonies, the Word, and service to the world.

McMinn, Don. _Entering His Presence: Experiencing the Joy of True Worship_. South Plainfield, N.J.: Bridge, 1986. A popular Protestant inspirational book on worship themes.

Myers, Warren, and Ruth Myers. _Praise: A Door to God's Presence_. Colorado Springs: NavPress, 1987. This work probes the relationship between worship and praise and teaches how to praise God in all of life.

Ostdiek, Gilbert. _Catechesis for Liturgy_. Washington, D.C.: Pastoral Press, 1986. This work invites congregations to work toward a participatory worship through an integrated program of pastoral care for the liturgy consisting of catechesis, preparation, and evaluation. Through this process applied to space, action, time and speech a congregation may develop a dynamic process of involving all the people as participants in worship.

Petersen, Randy. _Giving to the Giver: Worship That Pleases God_. Wheaton: Tyndale House, 1990. A popular Protestant examination of various themes of worship.

Powers, David. _Unsearchable Riches_. New York: Pueblo, 1984. Catholic. Scholarly. Explores the importance of symbol in worship. Discusses how symbol captures personal experience and expresses it meaningfully.

Ramshaw, Gail. _Worship: Searching for Language_. Washington, D.C.: Pastoral Press, 1988. Examines how words reveal both God and the self. Writes about words we choose to explore the mystery of God, express motherhood and fatherhood of God, verbalize our belief in the trinity and other matters.

Rayburn, Robert G. _O Come, Let Us Worship_. Grand Rapids: Baker, 1980. A Reformed perspective on worship, including a very strong and helpful section on Isaac Watts.

Schaper, Robert N. _In His Presence_. Westminster, Md.: Newman Press, 1984. Protestant. Popular evangelical Anglican touches on biblical, historical, developments in worship as well as contemporary concerns for symbols and congregational participation.

Segler, Franklin M. _Christian Worship_. Nashville: Broadman Press, 1967. Protestant. Popular. A southern Baptist deals with basic issues such as the meaning of worship, a means of expressing worship, planning and conducting worship.

Skoglund, John E. _Worship in the Free Churches_. Valley Forge, Pa.: Judson Press, 1965. This out-of-print book is a major source for the study of free church worship. Asserting that free church worship is in trouble, the author points toward the future of worship that draws from the past yet retains the freedom of the free-church tradition of worship.

Underhill, Evelyn. _Worship_. New York: Continuum Books, 1989. Ecumenical. Popular but based on good scholarship. A classic. Anglican author deals with the nature of worship, ritual and symbol, sacrament and sacrifice, characters of Christian worship, principles of corporate worship, liturgical elements, Eucharist, personal worship, Jewish worship, origins of Christian worship, and Catholic, Reformed, free church, and Anglican worship.

Wardle, Terry Howard. _Exalt Him,_ 2d ed. Camp Hill, Pa.: Christian Publication, 1992. Protestant. Popular Christian and Missionary Alliance pastor writes to an evangelical audience, encouraging Christians to make worship Christ-centered, edifying for believers, and appealing to visitors. The new edition contains a section on spiritual warfare.

Webber, Robert. _Worship Is a Verb_. Philadelphia: Westminster Press, 1985. Protestant. Popular but based on scholarship. Develops four principles of worship and their implication for renewal: (1) worship celebrates Christ; (2) in worship God speaks and acts; (3) in worship we respond to God and to each other; (4) all creation joins in worship.

―――. *Worship Workshop*. Grand Rapids: Zondervan, 1990. Designed as a week-by-week study of worship in the heart, in the home, in the church, and in the world.

# SEVENTEEN

# Exploring the Psychology of Worship

*It is important that the church understand the psychology of worship. Participation in worship impacts believers emotionally and psychologically. Although worship is corporate, it is made up of individual acts. It is not only something taking place outside the self but is also something occurring within the self. The entries in this section discuss impediments to worship and look at worship as a psychological phenomenon that relates to the struggles and passions of the inner person.*

## 230 • WOUNDS THAT HINDER WORSHIP

*The person who brings a wounded spirit into the setting of worship often finds it difficult to enter into the experience of worship. Paradoxically, it is the very act of worship that offers healing for those wounds, even though the pain may hinder the hurting Christian's full participation in it.*

Worship comes alive when it becomes relational, when through it we encounter both the God with whom we are acquainted and our fellow believers with whom we are united as a body. The corporate encounters with God enrich our personal experiences with him, while our private ones invest the corporate with new life. This level of worship is not an unreachable ideal, but a vital reality to many believers. Unfortunately, there are many others for whom worship is an intellectual and behavioral routine which never rises to the level of relationship.

It is possible for sincere Christians to be limited in their worship experiences because they have, over a period of time, built emotional barriers around themselves to protect wounds they have sustained in the course of personal relationships. A person who has been hurt by a relationship will find ways to protect himself or herself from further hurt. Sometimes these protections are consciously chosen and are appropriate to the situation. But much self-protection is unconscious and serves to restrict and defeat rather than to free.

It is generally true that the height and thickness of the protective fence (i.e., the strength of the defense and its power to control relationship experi-

ence) are related to the period of life in which the wounding occurred and the severity of the damage inflicted upon the person's sense of safety and trust. Wounds that hinder worship can occur in adulthood, but usually the original and most damaging wounds are those of childhood.

Because we are made in the image of God, we are designed as children to be parented as God himself would parent us, as we see him relating to his children, Adam and Eve. No human parent can perfectly follow the model of the Father God, and every parent makes mistakes. In the life of any child, a combination of traumatic events and unhealthy and ungodly relationship dynamics can leave scars which accompany that person into adulthood.

Some of the more obvious antecedents of wounds which carry over into later life are familiar: divorce, physical or sexual abuse, alcoholism, drug addiction, abandonment, and neglect. But other, less obvious dysfunctional patterns result in woundedness as well: perfectionism, emotional neglect, conditional love based on performance, marital strife and disunity, emotional abuse, and harsh, inconsistent, or arbitrary discipline.

Early childhood relationships, particularly those with parents, are deeply formative and exert an influence in adulthood long after specific memories have faded or disappeared. Patterns of relating are established early, through modeling and experience, long before we have the ability to be aware of what we are learning. We form expectations of ourselves and others that particularly affect intimacy and authority relationships. These powerful beliefs from childhood can persist in direct opposition to the conscious thought-flow of the adult.

In a sense, the person who has been wounded has two minds: the adult or conceptual/rational mind and the childhood or experiential/emotional mind. For example, the adult mind may firmly believe that God is loving and good, but the child mind has been trained to expect judgment and rejection. The adult may fully understand the concept of grace and agree that worship is a response of joy and thanks, but to the child who has never experienced unmerited favor and radical forgiveness, the emotions of joy and thanksgiving are foreign.

If we approach Christianity exclusively through the intellect, as a compartmentalized belief system alone, we do not encounter our relational wounds and self-protections during worship. A purely cognitive faith presents no challenge to our struggles with anger, fear, and distrust. But Christianity, including worship, is grounded in relationship. If we allow it to touch us, it will touch us fully at all levels, including our pain.

### —— Expressions of Woundedness ——

A. W. Tozer reminds us in *The Pursuit of God* that "God is a Person, and in the deep of His mighty nature He thinks, wills, enjoys, feels, loves, desires, and suffers as any other person may. In making Himself known to us He stays by the familiar pattern of personality. He communicates with us through the avenues of our minds, our wills, and our emotions" ([Harrisburg, Pa.: Christian Publications, Inc., 1948], 13).

No intimate relationship can be said to be healthy unless it is so in three aspects of personality: mind, will, and emotion. Since the personalities of wounded people are shaped by their reactions to painful experiences, the results can be expressed as difficulty in any or all of these areas.

**Emotional Experience.** The fruits or evidence of the presence of the Spirit—love, joy, peace, and so on—involve processes of the mind as well as behaviors chosen by the will. But to be fully experienced as relationship, they must also involve the emotions. Believers whose emotions are numbed by pain and buried under patterns of self-protection miss the emotional component of love, joy, peace, grace, and forgiveness, and therefore miss the vitality and satisfaction of intimacy, both in relationship with God and in the experience of worship.

Some of these Christians look with secret amazement at deep, spiritual experiences in the lives of others. They are envious when people talk of being refreshed, nurtured, strengthened, and cleansed through worship. They are mystified or skeptical about worship being a love encounter—an experience of loving and being loved. Their longing for love, joy, and peace is intense, but their experience could be described as dry, empty, cold, frustrating, or boring.

Unlike the believer who flows through cycles of intimacy and distance in the course of developing a relationship with the Lord, this person knows intimacy only as a concept. No matter how hard he or she tries through discipline, study, service, participation, and any other means available, the emotional/experiential aspect of the worship relationship remains remote and unsatisfying.

There are those who experience primarily painful or negative emotions during worship. Sadness, fear, anger, frustration, and irritability seem to be stimulated by the attempt to draw near to God and to fellow believers. The evidence of woundedness is not that negative emotions occur, but that they occur with great intensity and that they persist without relief or are relieved only by periods of emptiness.

**Thoughts and Attitudes.** People wounded in childhood tend to live with an underlying, uneasy feeling that something is wrong and that someone is to blame. They often flip-flop between blaming themselves as bad or wrong and blaming someone else. As a result, they are critical and faultfinding, either toward themselves or others.

This pattern can be expressed as a habitually critical attitude; the feeling is one of chronic irritation. The focus of attention during worship becomes preoccupation with the shortcomings of fellow worshipers, frustration with those in authority, and dissatisfaction with the way things are being done. It can also occur in the form of persistent thoughts of guilt and unworthiness, a concentration on one's own failings and inadequacy, and a perception that God and fellow believers are disapproving and critical. The healing, restoring experience of being unconditionally accepted by God and by the members of his body is lost in a sea of self-doubt and anxiety.

**The Will and Behavior.** When old wounds affect behavior, it is often in the form of chronic struggles with discipline. In spite of volumes of accurate information, heartfelt surges of desire, and many pledges and recommitments, these persons cannot seem to make their wills cooperate. Efforts to bring behavior into line with Scripture, whether stopping the negative or beginning the positive, go through cycles that end in failure and frustration. The experience of worship suffers as self-image is battered and discouragement sets in.

**Reactions to Old Wounds.** Some believers, unaware that their struggles with worship are a result of woundedness, become discouraged after years of effort and disappointment. They cannot find satisfaction in a relationship with God no matter how hard they try, and they conclude that either God is not real or that he has rejected them. Ultimately, they withdraw completely from the church and the painful reminder of failure and loss. Quietly, with no fanfare, they may simply drift away. Or, in a burst of pain, they target someone or something to blame.

Other unfulfilled believers stay faithful in attendance but keep themselves safe from intimacy by remaining uninvolved and refusing to invest in the life of the community. Intimacy with fellow believers is as threatening to them as intimacy with God. They do not want to risk rejection and disappointment, even though they long to be deeply connected, loved, and accepted. Physically present, they remain in the spectator role, often going unnoticed by those who are actively involved.

Church-hopping can be a manifestation of protective withdrawal. When the challenges of relationship become too intense, wounded people may pull out and move on, searching for a different format, a different philosophy of worship, different leadership, or some other external condition to change their disappointing inner experience. Sometimes a change is helpful and productive, but if personal healing is needed, repeated changes will not solve the problem.

Probably the most tempting and frequent form of withdrawal is retreat behind a mask. Somehow church life, with its high standards and expectations, seems to promote this wearing of facades as a defense against the frightening reality of woundedness. People in leadership roles are particularly vulnerable. As their natural gifts propel them into positions of responsibility, they become increasingly reluctant to reveal their weaknesses. No one reaches in to find out who they really are or holds them accountable for genuine growth and personal healing. Burnout and dramatic plunges

into sin are sometimes the result. But an outwardly successful life of service that drags on and on, masking an inner life of spiritual emptiness, can be just as devastating.

_Attack._ Every worshiping body has had the experience of members who are continually on the attack. Nothing seems to please them, and someone else is always to blame. Often church leaders will handle these attacks by responding to the content, changing or defending policies, procedures, people, or whatever is being targeted. Sometimes, if they become frustrated because the critical person is impossible to satisfy, they will discount him or her and push the individual away. Unfortunately, the pattern of attack is not often understood, either by the church or the individual, as a self-protective defense resulting from old wounds. Because the real problem is not being addressed, no resolution occurs.

_Control._ When one's inner life (thoughts, emotions, behaviors) is out of control, it is easy to try to get a handle on things, by attempting to control others. People who have been hurt live, either consciously or unconsciously, with the expectation and dread of being hurt again. They cannot rest or relax in their relationships. They are compelled by anxiety to manage or control other people. Different personalities will choose to control with different styles: aggressive and direct, compliant and indirect, through guilt, by obligation, with kindness, by withdrawal, or through attack.

The variations are endless but have a universal result. Closeness and safety achieved by manipulation and control remain unsatisfying. Fear runs beneath the surface saying, "But what would happen if I stopped, if I let go? They would probably hurt me or leave me, and I cannot take that risk." When this fear and the patterns of control dominate a person's relationship with God, the peace of Christ is not a personal reality and worship is hindered.

## How Change Takes Place

We have described defensive reactions, attitudes, and behaviors as the protective fence surrounding wounding experiences. This fence serves to hide from others the existence of the painful reality inside. The difficulty is that the fence often hides that reality from the individual as well. The implications and significance of one's own personal history are unrecognized, and sometimes even the memories of the hurtful experiences are hidden.

As long as the individual and those around him or her are interacting only with the fence (i.e., the self-protective patterns of withdrawal, blame, attack or control) little progress will be made toward deepening the relationship dimension of worship. The beginning of significant, satisfying change is recognition of the real problem. The wounded person must be willing to look at the fence and take responsibility for what is there.

**Self-discovery.** Healing of old wounds begins by discovering that here is a link between the experiences and relationships of the past and those of the present. A common self-protective attitude in this regard is, "The past is the past; it cannot be changed, so there is no point in dwelling on it." This statement is both true and untrue. The past itself cannot be changed, but the lingering reactions (attitudes, expectations, feelings, and behavioral patterns) can, if they are looked at and understood in their original context.

The goal of self-discovery is not to dwell on the past or to assign blame. It is rather to erect instead a foundation from which real change can take place. Unhealthy relationship patterns that do not make sense in an adult framework may become clear when seen from the perspective of a child subjected to an unhealthy environment. It helps to discover how the child felt, what he or she perceived, what he or she learned, and how he or she responded.

Decisions or vows are made deep in a child's heart and remain hidden from the mind of the adult. "I will never get close enough for someone to hurt me like that again." "People will always leave me, so it won't hurt as much if I leave them first." "No one will ever love me." "You can't trust anyone." "There must be something wrong with me." These beliefs will drive a person's life until they are confronted as distortions and replaced with a new reality.

In the process of doing that, feelings associated with those early experiences will come to the surface. They are not the feelings of an adult, mediated by the rational mind; they are literally the feelings of the child, living within as if frozen in time. Simply expressing these feelings is not sufficient to bring about healing, but it seems to be an essential ingredient.

**Safe Relationships.** Self-examination at this level is rewarding, but difficult and painful as well. The decision to begin this journey is deeply personal and occurs in that private place of relationship to one-self. But walking the journey through must take place within safe, committed relationships.

An important part of the healing process is to open up and share deeply with a few people. That sometimes begins in counseling, when a person tells a painful story for the first time. But it can also take place or continue in committed friendships. Christian friendships can be the vehicle by which a wounded person risks being fully known and finally experiences unconditional acceptance. Grace becomes more than a theology—it becomes a healing interaction.

A church that takes itself seriously as a healing community will encourage the formation of committed, supportive relationships in which this kind of sharing can take place. Hurting people find it difficult to ask for help. But it becomes even more difficult, even prohibitive, if structures are not in place that encourage them to ask. Small groups, topical support groups, and discipling relationships can help, as can clergy and leadership who are alert to the need and the opportunities to bring people together.

Wounded people have often had hurtful experiences in churches, either because they initiate them or because they react more strongly to situations than do those people who are not in pain. It may be necessary for them to find a church community or format that does not remind them of either their wounding family or a previously wounding church. Finding a church in which to feel safe is good, but that is only the beginning. That safe environment must then be used to do the difficult work of healing, or the disappointment and hurt will only recur in the new context as well.

**Forgiveness and Restoration.** When a person moves toward acceptance and resolution of the past, it becomes necessary to sort out the issue of responsibility. Hurt children often assume the blame and guilt that belong to others and then grow up either blind to or confused about the implications of their own attitudes and actions. Christians committed to healing know that they are supposed to forgive those who have wronged them and seek forgiveness for their own wrongs. But they cannot do that in a meaningful way until they are clear about who bears responsibility for what.

Separating one's own wrongs from the wrongs of others is difficult work but can be greatly aided by the guidance of Scripture and the illumining witness of the Spirit. When people finally see clearly the wrong that was done to them, the world often leaves them with nothing but permission to be angry. It is the church that can take them deeper into healing with the call to forgive, in and through the Spirit of Christ, who was the ultimate victim.

And when people who have been victims finally see that they have at times followed the pattern they were given and have also wronged others, when they are able to cease to blame and to accept responsibility for their actions, then the church must offer confession, forgiveness, and restoration in and through the Spirit of Christ, the ultimate grace-giver.

**Behavior Change.** Working with the relationships of the past is important, but it is meaningful only as a _foundation_ for change in the relationships of the present. Healing the past frees a person to engage more effectively in the process of change, including some hard work in the here and now.

The goal of behavior change is to replace problem attitudes and actions with healthier ones: to break old habits, to think differently about self and others, to adopt new beliefs, to learn to trust. But for change to take place, these general goals must be broken down into step-by-step, specific, short-term goals that are connected directly to current relationships and situations. Change cannot occur in the abstract.

_Understand the old behavior._ Familiarity with the old ways of relating is an unpleasant but necessary first step toward change. Some research may be required. "What exactly happened in that messy interaction with the choir director? What role did I play that caused or contributed to the problem? Is this a pattern in me that has led to problems before?"

Unhealthy patterns of relating that begin in childhood become habitual, a series of actions and reactions that occur automatically, like falling dominoes. Habitual behavior has to be approached systematically, broken down into its component parts so that the progression can be understood. The crucial question is where and how the habit track can be interrupted to insert a new behavior that will lead to a different outcome.

_Discover the new behavior._ Healthy behavior patterns are a mystery to people who did not see them modeled as a child. They may know in general what healthy is, but they usually do not know how to make it happen. It takes time to discover and experiment with alternatives in real life situations.

In both of these steps—understanding the old

behavior and discovering the new—safe, committed relationships are valuable. Feedback about old behavior from caring and sensitive people helps the person develop an understanding of what needs to be changed. It is important to be able to go to someone and ask, "Have you ever seen me do this or react in that way? How did you feel when I did that? Help me understand how I come across and the effect I have on other people."

Learning takes place best through modeling, that is, by observing and imitating new, more desirable behavior. Close, sharing relationships provide excellent opportunities to discover new ways of interaction. The goal is not to try to become another person, but to find out how a healthier person thinks, feels, and acts in specific situations. This sort of discovery helps to develop a mental model or vision of the new behavior. Without a vision, a concrete sense of the direction of change, the process will bog down in confusion and frustration.

**Trial and Error.** Learning to change relationship patterns is not very different from learning any new skill. Anyone who has ever learned to ski knows the feeling of being overwhelmed with stimuli. Information and instructions are flying in every direction, but somehow nothing works right. If you could not see people all around you successfully skiing, you would be certain it is impossible to whiz gracefully down a mountain with two sticks strapped to your feet.

New behavior starts out messy and confusing, with many false starts and falls. Trial and error, perseverance, practice, encouragement, and support are the essential ingredients of learning. The difference between relationship change and skiing is that in relationships the stakes are higher and the feelings deeper. The old patterns of relating, though unhealthy and self-defeating, are familiar, and to that extent comfortable. In the process of change a person feels awkward and very vulnerable. Time and a lot of support are needed to enable the person to continue braving those forays into the new behavior. Ultimately, after many dashes back and forth between old and new patterns, healthier ways of relating begin to feel more familiar and natural.

## Effects of Healing on Worship

The relationships involved with worship change as healing progresses. Trust in God and fellow believers deepens, and a sense of closeness and belonging begins to grow. The level of energy for living and serving increases, but within an environment of inner calm. Familiar words of worship come alive and take on personal meaning. But the most poignant and powerful result is an overwhelming sense of gratitude to a healing God.

The Father has run with tears of love to the end of the lane to throw his arms around the estranged and broken child. He has removed the old, smelly garments of shame and alienation and has demonstrated unconditional acceptance and restoration in full. The overwhelmed child can only respond with gratitude as the loving Father continues to feed and nourish him or her with spiritual blessing from the riches of his table.

The Son, Jesus, who as a man knew what it was to be abused, and who as the Savior made healing and restoration possible, comes to life as friend. The Spirit takes shape as the ultimate counselor within, witnessing faithfully to the healing truth about Christ and his gifts: forgiveness, grace, hope, and love.

Nothing changes worship from black and white to living color, from routine to reality, and from the head to the heart, like gratitude. The worshiper whose heart is grateful sinks to his knees and pours forth praise and worship and then is grateful all over again for the privilege of doing so. The one who has experienced healing reaches out his or her hands to worship with others who also have been healed, and the unity that flows among them heals that much more in an ever widening circle of fellowship and love.

The challenges and risks of a path of healing cannot be denied. But for the believer, the rewards are beyond the level of human personality: mind, will, and emotion. When we sow to healing, which is by the Spirit, we reap the Spirit, and our rewards are eternal.

*Margaret M. Webb*

## 231 • Ten Basic Needs Met by Worship

*In worship a person gives to the Lord all of the conflicts, struggles, and disappointments that affect his or her life. Leaving them in the Father's hands, the worshiper focuses attention on the power and majesty of God. As we worship, the brokenness of our lives begins to be healed.*

People have basic needs which can be met in worship. Augustine said, "Thou hast made us for thyself, O God, and our souls are restless until they find their rest in thee." In the depths of our nature, we have certain conscious needs which must be met. There are hungers of the human heart to be satisfied. These psychological necessities have been approached in various ways. Here is one attempt to express mankind's conscious needs for worship.

1. **The Sense of Finiteness Seeks the Infinite.** In worship people seek completion—communion with "ultimate being." Sensing our limitations, we go in search for the rest of ourselves. The psalmist said,

> O Lord, our Lord,
>   how majestic is your name in all the earth!
> . . . . . . . . . . . . . . . . . . . . . . . . . . . . . . . . . .
> When I consider your heavens,
>   the work of your fingers,
> the moon and the stars,
>   which you have set in place,
> what is man that you are mindful of him,
>   the son of man that you care for him?
> You made him a little lower than the heavenly
>     beings
>   and crowned him with glory and honor.
>     (Ps. 8:1, 3-5)

2. **The Sense of Mystery Seeks Understanding.** People stand in need of knowledge. We approach God as the source of all knowledge. This act of communion may be spoken of as worshipful problem solving. Paul exclaimed, "Oh, the depth of the riches of the wisdom and knowledge of God! How unsearchable his judgments, and his paths beyond tracing out!" (Rom. 11:33). Again, he prayed that his fellow Christians might "have power, together with all the saints, to grasp how wide and long and high and deep is the love of Christ, and to know this love that surpasses knowledge—that you may be filled to the measure of all the fullness of God" (Eph. 3:18-19).

3. **The Sense of Insecurity Seeks Refuge.** In an age of uprootedness, people realize their need for refuge and stability. With the psalmist, we find ourselves saying, "God is our refuge and strength, an ever-present help in trouble" (46:1).

4. **The Sense of Loneliness Seeks Companionship**

with God. In their estrangement and lostness, people feel the need to be loved. Worship is the search for this love that alone can satisfy our loneliness. Job cried, "If only I knew where to find him; if only I could go to his dwelling!" (Job 23:3). In genuine worship, a person comes ultimately to experience personal companionship with God. "My ears had heard of you but now my eyes have seen you" (42:5).

**5. The Sense of Human Belongingness Seeks Mutual Fellowship with Other Worshipers.** The children of Israel sang a song of ascent going up to the temple, "I rejoiced with those who said to me, 'Let us go to the house of the LORD'" (Ps. 122:1). In worship the early church felt itself to be one body in Christ. Joined and knit together in Christ, each believer worked to contribute his or her part in building up the body in the love of Christ (Eph. 4:1, 4-6, 16). It is by the grace of God that a congregation is permitted to gather visibly for fellowship in worship.

**6. The Sense of Guilt Seeks Forgiveness and Absolution.** In worship the soul is laid bare before God. The worshiper acknowledges his or her guilt and pleads for cleansing. David cried out,

> Have mercy on me, O God,
>   according to your unfailing love;
> according to your great compassion
>   blot out my transgressions.
> . . . . . . . . . . . . . . . . . . . . . . . . . . . . .
> Against you, you only, have I sinned
>   and done what is evil in your sight
> . . . . . . . . . . . . . . . . . . . . . . . . . . . . .
> Create in me a pure heart, O God,
>   and renew a steadfast spirit within me.
>       (Ps. 51:1, 4, 10)

The more real a person's sense of guilt, the more necessity there is for confession and dependence upon the atoning grace of God.

**7. The Sense of Anxiety Seeks for Peace.** Anxiety is a normal experience of human beings in their finiteness. In this deep threat of nonbeing, a person seeks in worship the courage to become his or her true self. As emotional tensions build up, the individual seeks release from them in worship, the deepest of all emotional experiences. This emotional experience can reach to the depths of a person's need for rest and peace. In great distress the psalmist prayed,

> As the deer pants for streams of water,
>   so my soul pants for you, O God.
> . . . . . . . . . . . . . . . . . . . . . . . . . . . . .
> Why are you downcast, O my soul?
>   Why so disturbed within me?
> Put your hope in God,
>   for I will yet praise him,
>   my Savior and my God.
>       (Ps. 42:1, 11)

**8. The Sense of Meaninglessness Seeks Purpose and Fulfillment.** The search for meaning is perhaps the deepest quest of modern men and women. In the depth of his or her soul a person realizes that he or she was created for a purpose. In the midst of life's harassment, the believer affirms, "We know that in all things God works for the good of those who love him, who have been called according to his purpose" (Rom. 8:28). The search for meaning finds its deepest significance in the will to worship.

**9. The Sense of Brokenness Seeks Healing.** God's people cannot grapple with the enemies of righteousness in the real world without becoming broken and bruised. In a broken world, the believer seeks to be made whole. And as Tournier has said, this can happen only as God becomes incarnate in us through the Holy Spirit. Isaiah writes, "A bruised reed he will not break, and a smoldering wick he will not snuff out" (42:3).

**10. A Sense of Grief Seeks Comfort.** A person's innumerable losses leave him or her with feelings of emptiness. Human beings grieve over their losses. "'Comfort my people,' says your God" (Isa. 40:1). In the worship of the living Lord who overcame all grief and loss, the Christian hears the words, "Do not let your hearts be troubled. Trust in God; trust also in me. . . . Peace I leave with you; my peace I give you. I do not give to you as the world gives. Do not let your hearts be troubled and do not be afraid" (John 14:1, 27).

Another has summarized human psychological needs in the area of religious experience as follows: the need to find fulfillment, to make life useful, to find great moments of inspiration, to have a real encounter with another person, to know one's own identity, and to find superlative significance in a person, Jesus Christ, the ultimate meaning of life. These feelings of need are evidences of the presence of God, sure signs of his address to us.

Franklin M. Segler[42]

## 232 ◆ TOWARD A BIBLICAL PSYCHOLOGY OF WORSHIP

*The renewal of worship in our era is largely concerned with the restoration of a God-centered focus in Christian celebration. By its very nature, however, the psychology of worship tends to reverse this focus, redirecting our concern to the worshiper and his or her needs. A biblical psychology of worship places the individual within the context of corporate celebration and covenantal responsibility. Worship celebrates the victory of Christ over authorities that place people in bondage. In this setting, the gospel of Christ brings healing and liberation.*

A common approach to the psychology of worship attacks the issue from the standpoint of the benefits to the individual worshiper. These benefits may include the awareness of intimacy with God, the affirmation and healing that come through the experience of grace, the sense of identity and fulfillment which is communicated to the worshiper, or some other value which he or she perceives as a benefit resulting from the act of worship. Pathology in worship is described in terms of the failure of the worshiper to receive these benefits. If he or she remains in a state of alienation or boredom, unable to respond at any level of depth to what is being presented, and locked into destructive behavior patterns which prevent a genuine meeting with God or with other worshipers, then the experience of worship has not been successful.

While this *worshiper-centered approach* to the psychological aspects of worship yields much that is valuable in terms of understanding the emotional needs and behavioral characteristics of worshipers, it is, in our view, ultimately counterproductive in contributing to the renewal of Christian worship. Genuine Christian worship is not worshiper-centered but *God-centered*. Worship that is based on the biblical perspective must by definition be directed *away from the worshiper* and towards the proper object of worship, the God who has involved himself in the history of a people and who comes to them as Creator, Savior, and Lord.

The foundation of biblical worship is the cov-

enant graciously granted by the Lord to his servants, and worship in the biblical sense is the tribute the servants offer to the great King. When the psychology of worship is focused on whether or not the worshiper's needs are being met, the whole purpose of worship is reversed. The King becomes the servant, and the worshiper takes the place of the sovereign, expecting to receive the tribute of the servant-God and frustrated when it is not forthcoming. Such a reversal has much in common with the pagan cults of the ancient Near East—a sharp contrast to biblical faith. In the polytheistic religions, the worshiper's constant aim is to propitiate a capricious and reluctant deity, wresting from him or her the benefits associated with the seasonal fertility cycle or some other response to human need. Biblical worship, in contrast, is a response to the holiness and majesty of God and to his initiative in creating a people to declare the excellence of his redeeming work (1 Pet. 2:9-10).

Since psychology, by definition, focuses on the human *psyche* or "soul" with its perceptions and needs, can a psychology of worship be constructed in which the focus should be not on the worshiper but upon the Lord who is the true object of worship?

### Redefining Psychology in Biblical Terms

The term *psyche* is a Greek term found often in the New Testament (the Old Testament Hebrew equivalent is *nefesh*). It refers to an individual life, or what we today call a *person*. Biblically, the "soul" represents the totality of a person's being—not only his or her emotional, mental, and spiritual side but also one's physical well-being, family and property, and place and reputation in the community (see, for example, the exhaustive treatment of the Hebraic concept of the soul in Johannes Pedersen, *Israel: Its Life and Culture,* vol. 1 [London: Oxford University Press, 1946]). Both the inward and outward aspects of an individual's life are bound up with the soul. Hence psychology, understood biblically, involves more than "personality" as we conceive of it; it has to do with a person's external behavior, one's speech and actions, and how the person is perceived within the context of the community of which he or she is a part.

It is noteworthy, in this connection, that the biblical narrative seldom probes into the inward "feelings" of the people involved; where we today would describe an incident in terms of how the partici-pants felt about what was happening, the Scripture tends simply to record what they said and did. In 2 Kings 4 we find the account of a boy, taken ill, whom Elisha restores to life; whereas we would say the boy felt pain in his head and his father became alarmed, the text simply says that the boy said to his father, "My head! My head!" and the father said to the servant, "Carry him to his mother" (2 Kings 4:19). A classic example of this biblical reticence about inward emotions is the narrative of Abraham's sacrifice of Isaac (Gen. 22:1-14), in which the feel-ings of father and son are never expressed but can only be inferred from such things as Isaac's question about the lamb for the offering or the silence as "the two of them walked on together." The Gospels record the passion of Christ with a similar restraint, rarely giving us a glimpse into his personal anguish in such expressions as "My soul is overwhelmed with sorrow to the point of death" (Mark 14:34). In the context of the sweep of salvation history and the working out of God's plan of redemption, personal emotional "needs" appear to be largely irrelevant. In the Jewish culture of biblical times, they were certainly downplayed.

The biblical worshiper may testify to his or her longing or frustration, in such expressions as "My soul yearns, even faints for the courts of the LORD" (Ps. 84:2) or "My soul is downcast within me" (Ps. 42:6), but such outbursts are not the anguished cry of one for whom God has ceased to be a reality. Indeed, they are a pledge of loyalty on the part of a servant who, although surrounded by enemies, is determined to hold on to the one sure thing in his life: the Lord's faithfulness to his covenant. The worshiper's enemies are not inner hurts and dys-functional personality patterns have warped his or her response to the worship of God, but _other peo-ple,_ people unfaithful to the Lord, who are pressur-ing the worshiper in some way. Even Jeremiah's complaint, "You deceived me, and I was deceived" (Jer. 20:7) is a response to the indifference of other people to the message that is "like a fire" in the prophet's inner being (Jer. 20:9).

Set against Scripture, therefore, the psychology of worship must not remain focused subjectively on the worshiper and his or her needs. More is at stake here than our internal struggles. There is, or should be, an objectivity to what occurs in Christian wor-ship. Biblically informed worship is, in the first in-stance, an act through which God is establishing

his dominion through the praises of his people (Ps. 22:3). Enthroning God means dethroning ourselves, like the worshiping elders in the Revelation of John, who lay their own crowns before the throne of God (Rev. 4:10). The growth of the kingdom of God, in our personal lives or in our social context, can occur only when God is on the throne, receiving the honor that is due him as sovereign Lord; otherwise, what is taking shape is a rival kingdom.

Worship is an act of spiritual warfare, the procla-mation of Christ's victory on the cross over spiritual forces that would hold the people of God in bond-age to instruments of self-justification (Col. 2:14-15). Warfare requires the enlistment of soldiers, albeit wounded ones. Since the soul encompasses the whole person, not just the emotions, the psy-chology of Christian worship sees people in the totality of their being, with many strengths as well as weaknesses, with many gifts as well as defects. These gifts and strong points may still be used in the battle, even where hurts and faults persist.

Ultimately, the psychology of worship has to do not primarily with the worshiper's interaction with himself but with his or her interaction with God. The psychology of worship thus involves _how God benefits from worship_ as well as how the worshiper receives benefits and fulfillment of needs. In terms of biblical psychology, worship is the enlargement of the "soul" or life of God as his being reaches out to touch and envelop the "selves" of his worshipers. What else can be the meaning of the psalmist's invi-tation, "O magnify [_giddel,_ "make great"] the LORD with me, and let us exalt his name together" (Ps. 34:3, NASB)? In worship we "bless [_berekah_] the LORD" (Pss. 103:1; 104:1, NASB), contributing to the welfare of his being. Granted, such expressions are poetic rather than ontological; nevertheless, in bibli-cal worship we see the great King receiving the tribute of his covenant partners and benefiting therefrom.

## Recovering the Primal Worship Experience

The primal experience of worship is the sense of awe in the presence of the holy, the one who is infinitely greater than ourselves and beyond all com-prehension (see Rudolf Otto, _The Idea of the Holy,_ [New York: Oxford University Press, 1946]). The encounter with the holy comes as something which grips the worshiper at the intuitive level, filling him or her with a sense of awe and mystery before the massive presence of the sacred. (The Hebrew word *kavod,* translated "glory" or "honor," carries the basic meaning of "mass" or "weight.") There is a wonder, dread, or trepidation in the presence of a reality that cannot be comprehended within the framework of finite existence; an awareness of creaturehood and immeasurable smallness in the face of the Creator who is all. A biblical record of such an encounter with the Holy is recorded in Isaiah 6; Jacob's experience at Bethel (Gen. 28:10-22) and the appearance of the Lord on Mount Sinai (Exod. 19:16-25) are other important instances, together with the transfiguration of Christ (Mark 9:2-8 and parallels). In such an encounter we have no choice but to worship in the biblical sense of "bending the knee" (both the Hebrew and Greek words translated "worship" have this meaning), doing obeisance before the overwhelming majesty of the Creator, revealed as an absolute value.

The pathology of many contemporary worshipers is related to the loss of capacity for this intuitive response. The humanistic, technological thrust of western culture "flattens out" our world view so that it has no depth, while the relativistic philosophy of our era destroys any sense of absolute values. This lack of depth and absolutes is the cultural source of alienation and dysfunctional behavior patterns, since without a philosophical and spiritual anchor the human personality is cast adrift. Having lost all cosmic referents, a person has no choice but to become *self*-centered; the search for depth often becomes only a search within oneself—or into some allegedly transcendent realm which in reality is only a projection of the conscious or unconscious self, as in the "new age" philosophy. When self-centeredness becomes a cultural norm, and indeed a religious value (as has been well documented by writers like Paul Vitz, in *Psychology as Religion: The Cult of Self-Worship* [Grand Rapids, Mich.: Eerdmans, 1977]), it is easy to understand how the unrestrained self continually inflicts hurt upon others and receives damaging blows in return.

In such a state, the decision to turn to God for help may be futile, since (in evangelicalism especially) so much emphasis is placed on conversion as an act of *individual choice,* made in order to secure certain benefits for the self. What the alienated person needs—and all members of our culture partake of this alienation—is to be *taken captive* (to use the apostle Paul's metaphor, Eph. 4:7), caught up in the grip of the sacred. Worship that focuses on meeting human needs will never break the destructive cycle of self-centeredness. Only worship that lifts up a transcendent God, calling people to commit themselves in his service and to abandon themselves in fascination with his glory, will break this cycle and bring healing.

## Corporate Worship and Personal Identity

The prevailing psychology of worship focuses upon the aspects of worship that concern the *individual.* The main concern is the response of the individual worshiper to the worship experience itself. One issue addressed by the psychology of worship is the worshiper's *sense of identity.* Loss of identity is less of a problem in traditional cultures, where strong family or tribal bonds exist. A person always knows who he or she is, along with the proper role to assume in a given situation. In a technological and mobile culture, in contrast, the forces of social change contribute to the breakdown of these steady relationships and to a sense of alienation. The personal response is often to search for identity within the self, to "be all you can be" or to "have it your way." Another avenue of response may be seen in the contemporary stress on ethnicity— the search for identity in ethnic "roots." The psychology of worship focuses upon the pathology created when the individual worshiper is struggling with the loss or fragmentation of identity. In some persons, the struggle may be so intense that worship is weakened or blocked altogether. Also there can be a loss of identification with the other participants.

Loss of personal identity becomes an issue in worship as long as worship is viewed as an individual act. Worship in the biblical tradition, however, is never an individual act; it is always *corporate* worship, the celebration of the gathered assembly of the covenant community. The worship of Israel, the celebration of Yahweh's mighty acts, was organized around annual festivals at the sanctuary "where the tribes go up" (Ps. 122:4) as a group. When an individual speaks in worship (as in the Psalms), he does so as the representative of a group, those faithful to the Lord; the individual's offering of praise to the Lord and his testimony to answered prayer are set within the framework of the assembly (e.g., Ps. 22:25). The prophets of Israel were, even in times of rampant apostasy, representatives of a community of faithful worshipers of the Lord, epitomized by the "seven thousand in Israel—all whose knees have not bowed down to Baal" (1 Kings 19:18) of Elijah's era. The prophets took their stand not upon some esoteric revelation from the Lord but upon the traditions of the covenant, declaring the judgments against apostasy and immorality inherent within the covenant structure (see "The Concept of Covenant in Biblical Worship" in volume 1). The ability to declare these judgments with force was their prophetic gift or "inspiration."

The corporate nature of the church, the "body of Christ," is a corollary of the biblical stress on covenant and is evident in Paul's teaching concerning the Lord's Supper, the basic act of Christian worship. The bread we break, he reminds the Corinthians, is a _koinonia_ ("participation, sharing) in the body of Christ (1 Cor. 10:16-17); Christians are not to receive the Lord's Supper as an individual exercise, but are to recognize the body (1 Cor. 11:29) or worshiping community in this act.

Viewed in this perspective, concern with one's individual identity is a side issue. Introspective focus upon one's inner struggles is a diversion from the worshiper's true calling. Christian worship offers a genuine and satisfying sense of identity, but one that comes from commitment to the _corporate identity_ of the people of God, a people called into being for the purpose of clarifying not who they are as individuals, but who _he_ is and what _he_ has done: "that you may declare the praises of him who called you out of darkness into his wonderful light." In pledging themselves to the covenant, worshipers assume membership in a new family or "nation" from which their identity is derived: "Once you were not a people, but now you are the people of God" (1 Pet. 2:9-10). In short, healing comes through commitment of self to a cause greater than the self. Deliverance from sickness and agitation within the soul begins to come when the worshiper confesses that struggle itself as sin and, laying it aside, takes up the proclamation of God's greater glory in corporate celebration.

## Worship and the Organizing Principle of Self

The question of the emotional needs of worshipers can be approached from the angle of the fragmentation of personality. This is perhaps another way of looking at the issue of identity. The anonymity of contemporary society makes it possible for people to act in one area of life in a manner inconsistent with the set of values they employ in another

area. For example, a person who is a professing Christian may vote for a candidate for public office who opposes biblical principles or who may conduct himself in the home in a way he would never behave in church, at work, or in another public setting. People may go through life without being confronted with their own inconsistencies; because a person is really one _psyche,_ however, internal dissonance may build up and may result in great emotional pain.

The search for an organizing principle of self which will silence the dissonance can be an agonizing one, especially if this search is undertaken with the premise that values are relative and that the answer must come from within each individual. "Self-esteem" has been viewed as such an organizing principle, enjoying wide popularity in our technological culture precisely because it avoids the introduction of absolutes. Even Christian thinking has co-opted the concept of self-esteem; we are told we have to love ourselves, because Jesus said "Love your neighbor _as yourself_" (Mark 12:31). The issue of self-esteem is grist for the mill of the psychology of worship; lack of self-love has been seen as an impediment to worship, and the renewal of worship has been viewed in terms of how worshipers may be restored in self-esteem and released to express their "gifts."

Clearly, biblically informed worship cannot pander to the worshiper's perceived lack of self-esteem, for reasons that have been discussed above. Jesus' iteration of the "great commandment" was not a recommendation of self-love; he (and Moses before him) _assumed_ an adequate degree of "self-love," in the sense of concern for one's personal needs (cf. Eph. 5:29) and simply used it as an example of how to treat one's fellow human beings. In actuality, the "neighbor" of whom Moses and Jesus were speaking is really one's fellow member of the covenant with the Lord—a covenant which the New Testament views as expanding to embrace people of all ethnic and socioeconomic groups, people "from every tribe and language and people and nation" (Rev. 5:9). The organizing principle of "self" is _the pledge of loyalty to God,_ a commitment which brings other loyalties—including loyalty to self—into proper perspective.

## Worship and Personal Discipline

Christian worship is not the self-expression of an aggregate of individual worshipers, but the act of a redeemed people expressing honor to whom honor is due (cf. Rom. 13:7). Worship involves the subordination of individual concern to the larger concern that the name of the Lord should be lifted up. It is choreographed behavior which takes the spotlight off the worshiper and puts it on the Creator—yet, paradoxically, in so doing allows for the abundant release of individual gifts as worshipers move into the flow of praise in prophetic, musical, and artistic activity.

Participation in worship in the biblical tradition is an act of self-control; it involves the personal discipline of laying aside private concerns for the sake of the corporate witness to our sovereign Lord. Self-control, understood biblically, is submission to the will of God. As an act of self-control, worship is a vehicle for personal healing with self-control as the "bottom line" which anchors every fruit of the Spirit—joy, peace, and love itself (Gal. 5:22–23). Lack of self-control cuts us off from access to spiritual and psychological healing. To a Samaritan woman who evidently had some problems in this area, Jesus spoke of worship "in spirit and truth" (John 4:23), that is, *spirited* worship in visible manifestation of self-abandonment before the Lord, and *truthful* worship in conformity to scriptural patterns. To worship the Lord as an act of obedience, regardless of personal "feelings" of the moment, is a therapeutic, restorative act because it is an act of *sacrifice*—what Scripture calls the "sacrifice of praise" (Heb. 13:15).

A biblical psychology of worship recognizes the need to maintain worship in the Spirit, to understand worship from God's viewpoint—the tribute due him as the great King—and to view the worshiper's role as the controlled abandonment of self-concern. It would be sad indeed if in worship, as in all aspects of Christian life, having begun in the Spirit we should seek to complete it in the flesh (cf. Gal. 3:3). In the context of Paul's warning, "the flesh" means the effort to justify oneself through performance of the Mosaic law. Thus, "the flesh" is emblematic of all attempts to prove *oneself,* instead of to prove or demonstrate "what God's will is—his good, pleasing and perfect will" (Rom. 12:2). As members of the body of Christ, the corporate assembly of the Lord's worshiping people, we are not to indulge ourselves in the quest for self-pity or self-esteem; rather we are to "put on the Lord Jesus Christ, and make no provision for the flesh, to satisfy its desires" (Rom. 13:14, RSV).

## Worship and the "Performance Principle"

In the final analysis, that which lies at the root of most pathologies of personality in our culture is the replacement of unconditional familial love by the "performance principle"—the constant need to prove ourselves, to justify our right to exist. Millions live in this bondage, many perhaps outwardly self-assured, successful, and complacent but inwardly insecure and uncertain of their acceptance by others. The "self-esteem" movement largely ignores this cultural exchange. Our lives are constantly being measured by imposed or internalized standards: the values of peer groups, the pressures of economic expectations, the conventions of our various ethnic or ideological communities. To compound the problem, none of these perceived sources of value has any final arbiter who can certify that we have passed the test and validated ourselves; there is no mechanism by which we may receive the official stamp of approval. Having no definite finish line to cross, we can never know if we have won the race.

The "performance principle" of our industrial and technological age is simply the modern secular version of "the law of sin and death" (Rom. 8:2) from which Christ came to release us. However "holy, righteous and good" (Rom. 7:12), the Judeo-Christian law nevertheless pandered to "the flesh" in this respect: it set up an unattainable standard of behavior and so challenged the worshiper to commend himself or herself in relationship to its achievement. Under such a system, worship became simply one of many acts intended to make a statement about the worshiper: his or her faithfulness, righteousness, or spirituality. Within such a system there is no release from the inherent curse of judgment.

Against the background of the "performance principle," the gospel proclaims:

> So also, when we were children, we were in slavery under the basic principles of the world. But when the time had fully come, God sent his Son, born of a woman, born under law, to redeem those under law, that we might receive the full rights of sons. Because you are sons, God sent the Spirit of his Son into our hearts, the Spirit who calls out, *"Abba,* Father" (Gal. 4:3-6).

In other words, redemption is effected through a change of family loyalty and status: from being _slaves_ of the "performance principle" to being _children_ of the Father, children who no longer need to perform in order to be accepted, but who are accepted in virtue of the _relationship._ The outcome is becoming a member of Christ the Son; to be "in Christ" is to be part of a new creation (2 Cor. 5:17). Christ in his death has borne the curse of judgment (Gal. 3:14-15); by union with him in his death (Rom. 6:3-5; Col. 2:12) we have "crossed over from death to life" (John 5:24; cf. 1 John 3:14).

This is the significance of the new (or renewed) covenant in Christ. The basic condition of the covenant—absolute loyalty to God—remains in force; but Jesus, our high priest and intercessor, satisfies this condition in our behalf (Heb. 7–8), setting us free from the curse. Thus Paul could proclaim the gospel of _Christus Victor:_

> When you were dead in your sins and in the uncircumcision of your sinful nature [Greek _sarx,_ "flesh" or self-justifying behavior], God made you alive with Christ. He forgave us all our sins, having cancelled the written code, with its regulations, that was against us and that stood opposed to us; he took it away, nailing it to the cross. And having disarmed the powers and authorities, he made a public spectacle of them, triumphing over them by the cross (Col. 2:13-15).

Christian worship is the celebration of _Christus Victor,_ interpreted here as God's act of redemption liberating us from the bondage of unrelenting self-justification. Christian worship is also our response to God's act, as we bow the knee to renew our confession of covenant loyalty: "Jesus is Lord" (1 Cor. 12:3; cf. Phil. 2:10-11). In the setting of worship, our personal struggles are dwarfed by the victory of Christ over the forces of sin, death, and all that would enslave us to the constant need to prove ourselves, with all its accompanying pathology. In the setting of worship, barriers to communion with our Creator are broken down as God comes to dwell among his people, to wipe away every tear, and to make all things new (Rev. 21:3-5).

**Richard C. Leonard**

## ✍ EIGHTEEN ✍

# Challenges Facing Worship Renewalists

The renewal of worship in the local church faces major challenges. This chapter examines some of the obstacles to worship renewal. If one is to facilitate effectively such renewal, he or she should be familiar with the problems that must be isolated and resolved.

## 233 ◆ LACK OF CONCERN FOR WORSHIP RENEWAL

*For many church leaders, the renewal of worship is simply not a priority. Many churches seem content to pursue "business as usual," and pastors often yield to the tendency to elevate the sermon above corporate worship.*

We who are identified with evangelical Christianity are hard put to demonstrate any serious concern for worship in this century. As scholars we have failed to study worship or give attention to the theology of worship. Principles of biblical worship are not sought as the foundation of local church practice. Most of our evangelical seminaries have not even offered a full course in worship.

It follows that evangelical pastors have not been much concerned with worship either. In may of our circles the Sunday morning event is considered a "preaching service," in spite of the fact that the official title in the bulletin reads "Morning Worship." Viewing the preacher's singular act of proclamation as significantly more important than the entire congregation's acts of adoration, praise, confession, thanksgiving, and dedication, is espousing an expensive heresy which may well be robbing many a church of its spiritual assets. And we have been zealous to reach the world for Christ to build up the body of Christ, while at the same time being negligent in giving our first, best love to God himself—which is what worship is essentially about.

Ronald Allen and Gordon Borrow[43]

You and I may disagree on some aspects of Christian doctrine, but I am sure there is one thing on which we definitely agree: You and I personally, and the church collectively, are desperately in need of transformation. We are weary of "business as usual." We need and want a transforming experience from the Lord, the kind of spiritual visitation that will help to heal our broken homes and our split churches; that will strip away our religious veneer and get us back to reality; that will restore true spiritual values and destroy the cheap counterfeits we have been foisting on ourselves and the lost world that will, most of all, bring such glory to God that the world will sit up and take notice and confess that "God is truly among you" (1 Cor. 14:25, Phillips).

Warren Wiersbe[44]

## 234 ◆ CONTEMPT FOR PRAISE OF GOD

*The pluralism that characterizes modern Western culture threatens the activity of praising God. Those who engage in praise are made to feel as if they are out of date and out of touch with reality. However, a life of praise is the best counterattack to the pressures of a pluralistic society.*

Praise of God is continually threatened at all points. There are head-on attacks which try to eliminate it physically or to shame it into silence. There are numerous subtle ways in which it is discredited, undermined, or made to seem unfashionable or childish or ridiculously unreal. Among the threats there are some that are especially dangerous to the roots of praise. Perhaps the chief among these is the atmosphere of suspicion in which we live. Just because we live in such an open society, with free spread of all sorts of beliefs, theories and world views, we tend to be more wary of wholeheartedly adopting any of them.

At present the "conventional" wisdom of our society is certainly not that one's life should be based on the reality of God. The hypothesis that mostly operates in practice is that God is a human projection. This is omnicompetent to deal with all religious phenomena: it grants their reality but explains them in purely human terms. There is no strictly logical proof of this, but its practical acceptance has a host of important consequences. It leads to the living of a life that is in practice atheist. How can an alternative to this be posed? To argue that, on the contrary, God is Creator of man is not a very effective challenge. There is needed an alternative way of life in which this option is experienced. The activity in which this alternative is at its most drastic and explicit expression is praising God. If God is, then he is to be affirmed appropriately and appreciatively through the ecology of existence. Only then will the truth, goodness, and beauty of God have a chance of becoming clear. So our way is an attempt to evoke a life which can take many forms but whose essence is to let God be God for us, in thought, feeling and practice.

Daniel W. Hardy and David F. Ford[45]

## 235 ✦ SUBSTITUTES FOR WORSHIP

_Because church leaders have, for the most part, lost the understanding of biblical and historic worship, they have created and imposed upon their congregations a variety of worship substitutes._

For the past decade I have made it my business to sample various services of worship and to ask pastors, students, and lay people to define worship for me. Occasionally I have come across some people with extraordinary insight into the subject. But more frequently the answers are groping, tenuous, and even muddled. Recently a student who knows of my interest in worship renewal caught the frustration many of us experience by saying, "We are working against four hundred years of neglect."

Unfortunately, there is more truth than fiction in that statement. The fact is that we have not contin-

ued the interest in worship demonstrated by the Protestant Reformers. Rather, we have allowed worship to follow the curvature of culture.

I contend that there are at least four substitutes for worship in our contemporary culture, substitutes shaped more by the culture than by biblical teaching.

The first may be aptly called the lecture approach to worship. The cultural source that gave rise to the "classroom" church is the Enlightenment. The emphasis on the mind, learning, and education to the neglect of the senses and the inner spirit has resulted in a worship mentality that views the sermon as the be-all and end-all of worship. All else is lightly dismissed as "preliminaries."

A second substitute for worship is evangelism. This approach to worship resulted when evangelistic field preaching replaced worship in some quarters. It turned the church into an evangelistic tent. In churches influenced by such preaching, Sunday morning is seen as the most propitious time to get the unconverted saved. All else is made subject to this overriding theme. The climactic point of the service is the altar call.

A third replacement for worship occurs when the overriding concerns are entertainment and numbers. Television has given this approach its powerful support. It speaks in terms of the stage, the performers, the package, and the audience. It is a three-ring circus by the roadside. It gets the crowds, but what it feeds them is frequently shallow, hollow, and tasteless.

Last, but equally important, is the self-help approach to Sunday morning. It is the "me generation" dressed up in church clothes. Those who attend learn how to affirm and fulfill the possibilities of personal greatness, wealth, health, and beauty. The ministers in churches with this emphasis play into the hands of such narcissistic indulgence. "Come to Jesus, and he will make you one of the beautiful people. An expensive home, a big car, popularity, and power are yours for the asking."

Perhaps your reaction is that this analysis is too severe an indictment of church leaders. Worship, however, is one of the most important callings of the Christian church—along with evangelism, education, mission, fellowship, servanthood, and emotional healing. If some biblical, historical, and theological instruction could help us to do worship better, what have we lost?

And "do" is an appropriate word. Worship is not

something that someone does for us or to us. Rather, it is done by us. It is a verb, not a noun. It requires action. It is not passive—it is not merely watching or observing.

The doing of worship is not a new problem. False approaches to worship perturbed the Reformers. The medieval church had taken worship away from the people and located it in the work of the celebrants and choir. Everyone else watched as if they were at a play. A monumental achievement of the Reformers was to give worship back to the people. Now we have come full circle. Worship no longer belongs to the people. Again, it has become something someone does for us. Ministers lecture at us, move us into decisions, entertain us, and tell us how great we are. And we put up with it. We pay our money, go home, complain, and come back for more.

But the Bible understands worship as God-centered. In worship, God's people act out the Christ event and thereby praise, honor, and glorify God. God himself is present in the telling that occurs through Scripture and preaching. And the God who was in Christ reconciling the world to himself is savingly present as we act out his death and resurrection in the Lord's Supper. In and through the telling and acting out of the Christ story we respond to God in prayer, praise, confession, and thanksgiving. Our purpose is to give, not to get. The giving of praise and the offering of thanks are the supreme calling of the church. In those actions we minister to God and do what we were created to do—give him—Creator, Redeemer, and Judge—the glory due to his matchless name.

It is time to turn our backs on substitutes for real worship and to learn what it means to be a people who truly worship God. We are working against centuries of neglect, so we must not expect instant success. Rather, in our local congregation we must commit ourselves to honest evaluation, to study and prayer, and to new directions for Sunday morning (and evening) that will bring greater glory to God.

Robert E. Webber[46]

## 236 • MISPLACED PRIORITY IN WORSHIP

*In many liturgical congregations, the church is viewed as an organization that exists for the liturgy. This author, writing from the perspective of the Orthodox tradition, offers a reminder that worship does not exist for its own sake, but as an* expression of the reality of the church in relation to the world. His insights are useful to Christians of other traditions.

Today's liturgical crisis consists, first of all, in the mistaken concept of the function and place of worship in the church, in the profound metamorphosis in the understanding of worship in the mind of the church. Let us emphasize the fact that we are speaking here about something much more important than the misunderstanding of the texts, ceremonies, and language of divine service. We are speaking here about the whole approach to worship and its "experience."

Worship—its structure, form, and content—remain what they were before and essentially what they have always been. In this sense it is right to speak of Orthodoxy's faithfulness to its liturgy. But to understand it and to use it are two different things. A discrepancy has appeared between the basic purpose of worship and the way it is understood. The membership of the church has simply not noticed this discrepancy, and worship actually excludes the possibility of this understanding. No matter how paradoxical it may sound, what obscures the meaning of worship is that it has become

*The Alpha and Omega. This ancient symbol, based on Revelation 1:8, means that the Lord Jesus Christ is the beginning and end of all things. The letters A (Alpha) and Ω (Omega) are the first and last letter of the Greek alphabet.*

for the faithful an object of love, indeed almost the sole content of church life. Worship has ceased to be understood as a function of the church. On the contrary, the church herself has come to be understood as a function of worship.

Christian worship, by its nature, structure, and content, is the revelation and realization by the church of her own real nature. And this nature is the new life in Christ—union in Christ with God the Holy Spirit, knowledge of the Truth, unity, love, grace, peace, salvation. In this sense the church cannot be equated or merged with worship; it is not the church which exists for the liturgy, but the liturgy for the church, for her welfare, for her growth into the full measure of the "stature of Christ" (Eph. 4:13, NEB).

Christ did not establish a society for the observance of worship, but rather the church as the way of salvation, as the new life of re-created mankind. This does not mean that worship is secondary to the church. On the contrary, it is inseparable from the church and without it there is no church. But this is because its purpose is to express, form, or realize the church—to be the source of that grace which always makes the church the church, the people of God, the body of Christ, "a chosen race [and] a royal priesthood" (1 Pet. 2:9, RSV).

In fact, to the extent that the church exists not only as the living church today, but also the church handed down from the fathers, she embodies in worship her participation in God's kingdom, gives us a glimpse of the mystery of the age to come, expresses her love to the Lord who dwells within her, and her communion with the Holy Spirit. In this sense worship is the purpose of the church, but the purpose precisely of the church, as the highest and fullest expression and fulfillment of her nature: of her unity and love; of her knowledge of communion with God.

But in the contemporary approach to worship there is the characteristic absence of an understanding of it as the expression of the church, as the creation of the church, and as the fulfillment of the church. The church has been merged with worship, has come to be understood as a sacramentally hierarchical institution existing for the performance of divine worship seen as sacred, supra-temporal, immutable mystery. The church is that which guarantees the objective character of this "sacred action," its reality so to speak, and in this sense the church in her sacramentally hierarchical structure is the in-

strument of this mystery and is subordinated to it. The church cannot express, create, and fulfill herself in it, because outside the mystery itself there is no church.

There are separate believers, to a greater or lesser extent living individually by sacred contact with it, by the sanctification or nourishment received from it; there is also the "parish," i.e., an essentially lay organization, bound together by concern for the presence of this "sacred something"—for the church building and for the provision of the priesthood that it needs. But the individual believer, entering the church, does not feel he or she is a participant and celebrant of worship, does not know that in this act of worship he or she, along with the others who are constituting the church, is called to express the church as new life and to be transformed again into a member of the church. He or she has become an "object" of worship, celebrated for his or her "nourishment," so that the person may, as an individual, satisfy his or her "religious needs."

In the same way the parish does not know that worship, as an expression of the parish, transforms it into the church, gives it those "dimensions" which it does not and cannot have naturally. It remains a limited human and only human community, living not as the church but by its own necessarily limited human interests.

Having been turned into something "sacred in itself," worship has as it were "profaned" everything else in the church: her government becomes juridical and administrative in our eyes; her "material" life is strictly separated from spiritual content; and the hierarchy (having become the celebrants of the sacraments only, in which nobody sees the expression, creation, and fulfillment of the church) are naturally pushed out of the sphere of church administration, finances, and even teaching, since all these spheres have become profane and unsanctified. Now the sole content of the church's life, worship has ceased to be understood in its own real content, which is to be the expression, creation and fulfillment of the church.

The overwhelming majority of Orthodox people have no interest in the meaning of worship. It is accepted and experienced in mystical and aesthetic but never "logical" categories. It moves the soul of the believer by its sacredness, by its mysteriousness, by its "other-worldliness." And everything that happens to fall within its orbit becomes overgrown with complicated symbolic explanations. It is characteristic that in this symbolism there is no symbolism of the church.

Thus, people love to explain the divine liturgy as the depiction of the life of Christ. But who explains it as the expression of the life of the church, as the action by which she is eternally realized? Who ever sees that in this action she is not depicting the life of Christ before the congregation, but is manifesting, creating, and fulfilling herself as the body of Christ?

The believer loves the ceremonies, symbols, the whole atmosphere of the church building, this familiar and precious nourishment for the soul, but his or her love does not long for understanding, because the purpose of the liturgy is thought of precisely as the bestowal of a spiritual experience, spiritual food. For the membership of the church, worship has ceased to be the church's self-evidencing.

And finally, having become a liturgical society, existing in and for the sake of the worship experience, the membership of the church has become unable to understand that worship—as the expression, creation and fulfillment of the church—places the church before the face of the world, manifests her purpose in the world, the purpose of the people of God, set in the world with a gospel and a mission.

Having ceased to be the expression of the church, worship has also ceased to be the expression of the church in relation to the world. It is no longer seen as the leaven which raises the loaf, as the love of God directed toward the world, as a witness to the kingdom of God, as the Good News of salvation, as new life. On the contrary, worship is experienced as a departure out of the world for a little while, as a "vent" or break in earthly existence, opened up for the inlet of grace.

Alexander Schmemann[47]

## 237 • Corruption of Worship by Manipulation and Utilitarianism

*Worship is sometimes used as a tool for the manipulation of human experience. The true function of worship is not to lead people through a sequence of emotional states, to effect their behavioral change, or to promote programs or special emphases of the church or denomination. Rather, the purpose of worship is to glorify God in the world.*

A common corruption of worship is one we may call a corruption of function: the authoritarian structuring of worship to fit preconceived ideas without primary fidelity to the nature of the God revealed in the gospel. Many pastors, for example, feel led to provide guidelines for the congregation by introducing categories into the printed order (e.g., "Hymn of Consecration"). Such structuring may not be out of place when conceived with theological integrity and a certain pastoral diffidence; but it easily becomes a mechanizing of worship in order to compel the worshipers' devotion to conform to the leader's plans. Indeed, the presumptuousness of theologians in laying down liturgical structures with heavy-handed authority can easily become an idolatrous imposing of man-made structures upon the sovereign nature of the Word and a violation of the integrity of the human soul to respond to the Word in a Spirit-directed way.

The psychological rigging of worship classically illustrates this type of corruption, in which attention to people and the dynamics of personal experience is made sovereign rather than the nature and action of the Word. Commonly this corruption is a compound of more or less religious humanism and shreds of theology embodied in such frank declarations that the primary purpose of worship is "to foster the religious experience"—that worship is "to break down inhibitions" and "expand perceptions." The worshiper's feelings in particular are played upon (as well as his tactile senses in certain experimental liturgies), and the experience thus aroused, together with discussion about it, are made the content of liturgy. Such devices as "cycles" or "sequences" are employed to execute this purpose. We find "theme worship" with all parts of the service chosen to reinforce "the motif of the morning."

But clearly, to conceive worship primarily within the category of the psychology of human experience is not only to subvert its purpose as the worship of God. It is also to risk committing liturgical suicide in that an endless train of corruptions follow from this basic corruption; for worship as the contrived fostering of experience for the sake of experience opens the door to all kinds of manipulative devices, with only the leader of worship answerable for their legitimacy.

To a degree we have anticipated the next corruption to be identified—the using of worship primarily to achieve humanly chosen ends; we may call it the corruption of "utilitarianism." Forms of this corruption are legion. On a crude level they include blasphemous invitations to worship which appeal to nothing more than self-interest and practices of worship which would be amusing were they not so pernicious. Worship as a means of "character building" and of producing "socially motivated personality," worship as a means to "self-fulfillment" and "success," invitations to worship in the vein of "come to church this week, you'll feel better, do better, live better, it's the American way"—such are the more noxious expressions. The alliance of worship with political nationalism and its degeneration into modern tribalism must also be noted. Occasionally this perversion is clear-cut and thoroughgoing, at other times subtle or naive, though no less demonic.

Utilitarianism is also evident in the propagandizing with which denominational bureaucracies utilize worship for "promotion" and "cultivation." "Board of Pensions Sunday" is substituted for the First Sunday in Advent, or "Rural Church Sunday" for the feast of Pentecost; or the meaning of Worldwide Communion is measured by whether or not the amount of money collected surpasses last year's record. Perhaps the humorless hand of bureaucracy was evident at its worst in a "Crusade for Morality" launched by one denomination, in which the Sundays of the year were divided into five "emphases" with "worship and sermon" tailored to fit. Sundays in the fall were preempted for "abstinence from beverage alcohol, and personal moral regeneration," and "clean sex behavior" was laid down as the theme for Sundays in the spring!

Nevertheless, the center of gravity for liturgical reflection and decision must always remain God, the End beyond all other ends even as he is implicit in all other ends. To affirm this truth, to be sure, is not to subscribe to the theological cliché one often hears: that worship always and everywhere should be conducted _soli Deo Gloria,_ to the glory of God alone. For the God encountered in worship is never alone, and his glory always has to do with man and his life. The God of Christian devotion is always a God in relation to man and man's world, and his glory inheres in that grace which by definition has man and his moral life as its object. Indeed, in a sense God is glorified to the extent that man is ethi-

cized. Nevertheless, worship is first to be conceived as encounter with God; its reference is secondarily to man.

Paul Waitman Hoon[48]

## 238 • McEucharist: The Allure of "Fast-Food" Worship

_In their concern to reach as many people as possible with the gospel of Christ, church leaders often try to make the worship service as attractive as possible for the unchurched. When worship planning is "consumer-driven," however, serious abuses of true worship may result. The author of this entry raises some thoughtful questions about the "fast-food" approach to worship._

This is a day in which church leaders are frequently admonished to be culturally sensitive to visitors and the unchurched in their preparation and execution of worship. In a sense this appears to be wise counsel. However, an inherent danger in striving to be culturally relevant is that the church will instead become culturally driven. Indeed, in observing the push toward becoming all things to all men one might wonder whether some promoters of cultural sensitivity have not become imprisoned by the need to reach their market, regardless of how much their efforts might compromise the message of Jesus Christ.

The popular view among those who see the church as a product to be marketed is that worship is a consumer-driven service. That is to say, those areas of worship which might not appeal to visitors or non-Christians should be minimized or even eliminated in order to allow time for maximizing more appealing portions of the service. One of these persons boasted to a seminar group that his church of 2200 has become so efficient that it can take the collection in 90 seconds. As if that were not impressive enough, he went on to affirm that it can serve communion to the same number of people in just two minutes. The secret is that the plates holding bread and juice are placed under every fourth pew. At the appropriate time a designated person at the end of each pew simply reaches down to retrieve the plates and send them speeding down each row. In exactly two minutes the entire church can be served. This is a somewhat shocking example of what we might call "fast-food worship." It must be wondered to what extent this particular church might go to satisfy its customers. On the subject of McEucharist, therefore, some questions need to be asked.

**Does God Like to Be Rushed?** First of all we might ask if God enjoys being rushed or manipulated. While not every person enters a church service with pure motives, from a biblical perspective the purpose of this gathering is to recognize God and respond to him with appropriate joy and gratitude. This implies that the God who is greater than the humans who meet together in his name is the one who sets the agenda for worship, and not the reverse. Certainly God wants outsiders to be invited and made comfortable in order that they might also discover, experience, and embrace the gospel of Jesus Christ.

The question is, how much is the church willing to sacrifice and compromise for the purpose of making worship exciting and inviting? Are there limits in the areas of theology and taste which must not be violated? Or do we feel we have the right and responsibility to alter the practice of worship to such an extent that we actually mar the reflection of the nature of God in the process?

The Scriptures remind us to slow down (Ps. 46:10) and to linger in and enjoy the presence of Jesus Christ (Luke 10:38–42). They call us to wait on the Lord, not to hurry the Almighty so that his appearance can fit into our overpacked schedules (cf. Ps. 27:14; Prov. 20:22; Isa. 8:17; Hos. 12:6; etc.). It is difficult to believe that rushing at breakneck speed through certain parts of the liturgy in order to arrive at others we might deem more "appealing" is a healthy or balanced way of viewing either worship or God himself.

**Is Worship Entertainment?** Second, we should ask whether we have changed worship from that which we offer and give to God into something we receive and get for ourselves. Liturgy is supposed to be the work of the people, but it is in danger of becoming the entertainment of the people instead. In some churches it becomes a reflection of our passive society in which we are only spectators, rather than an activity into which we enter and in which we participate with God and our fellow worshipers.

Some worship professionals have advanced the idea that the primary role of the pastor is to lead the congregation and not, himself, to worship. Another maxim of the culturally sensitive philosophy is that

a congregation would rather listen to music sung to them than to actually sing music themselves. Inherent in these statements seems to be a conviction that the probability of God's presence and blessing in the service increases exponentially with the professional quality of the entertainment.

**Is "Canned" Music an Act of Worship?** A third consideration, and one related to the idea of worship as entertainment, is the change that has been taking place in church music. In recent years the advancements of technology have interacted with the taste of consumers to produce a new style of electronic music. In the church this change has manifested itself in the proliferation of accompaniment tapes and music "tracks." Initially these were used only for the purpose of guiding choirs or soloists. However, their use in providing dubbed-in voices to augment the background is becoming increasingly common. One can only wonder who is accompanying whom. While these technological advances may offer the small church a ready means of providing quality music, it can also have the result of marginalizing music. The message conveyed is that there is no need for members of a congregation to learn to play the piano, organ, or guitar. Indeed, even where there are those capable of providing live accompaniment, the difference in skill level between them and the professionals on the tape may lead the church to opt for electronic music. This minimizes participation in worship by those in the church who are gifted for this very purpose.

In addition, the use of canned music has fostered a dangerous and unhealthy concept known as "special music." This usually translates into a soloist or small ensemble who travel from church to church to minister. Since very little, in any, relationship may exist between the "special music" and the specific congregation, the selection of songs will probably neither blend with nor enhance the worship style of that church. The result is a "time out" for entertainment instead of participation in worship.

The use of outside groups to lure non-members into the church sometimes fosters competition among churches, with each one feeling pressure to keep up with others in its area and bring in a better or more widely-known traveling group to satisfy its own members and attract potential new ones. This emphasis further discourages the members of a local church in developing and offering their own gifts and musical abilities. Yet a foundational biblical principle of worship is that it is participatory.

**Is Worship a Means to Accomplishing Something Else?** In the fourth place, the consumer philosophy suggests a dangerous inversion of means and ends. According to the Bible, God's people engage in worship because it is what he enjoys. Worship is the way in which we honor and adore our covenant Lord. This implies that worship is of value in and of itself. In other words, worship is an end. It is not primarily a tool for evangelizing or attracting visitors or for recruiting teachers for Sunday school or advisors for the youth group. Neither is it intended to motivate or manipulate people into increasing contributions to the church. Nor is it a means to challenge people to become more involved in social justice or any other legitimate dimension of the church.

These approaches all view worship as a means to accomplishing something else. The problem with this distorted approach is that if worship is essentially designed to recruit, evangelize, inspire stewardship, or for any other purpose, it will rarely reach the ultimate goal of focusing on God. On the other hand, worship which begins with the assumption that God is the first priority, and which is developed in a biblical and balanced manner, will not only glorify and lead people into God's presence, but will also fulfill the secondary purposes of inspiring them to acts of devotion and service. Writing in the early part of this century, Willard Sperry observed: "Things which are ends in themselves move us far more profoundly than things which are simply means to other ends" (_Reality in Worship_ [New York: MacMillan, 1925], 249). Worship structured around gimmicks and glitter will neither glorify God nor provide people with anything of integrity. When this approach is used, it results in a desire for the gifts and blessings of God rather than a seeking after God himself. In other words, it creates another example of consumerism in which persons attending church assume that they are in charge and can "have it their way."

This is not to say that the market-driven approach to worship might not please a church initially. The pastor and other church leaders might be happy because the revamped worship style is attracting large numbers of visitors. The visitors and congregation might also be relieved that this method of wor-

ship requires less involvement and participation from them and is entertaining and therefore enjoyable.

However, on a deeper level we must ask how this philosophy of worship will shape the worshipers' image of God and their response to the needs of our broken world. Another consideration is the effect it will have on the foundation and depth of the individual's faith. Eugene Peterson examines the problem with characteristic wisdom when he writes: "The initial consequence is that leaders substitute image for substance, satisfying the customer temporarily, but only temporarily" (_Under the Unpredictable Plant: An Exploration in Vocational Holiness_ [Grand Rapids: Eerdmans, 1992], 3). Worship which is not solidly grounded in substance often leaves people with a spiritual void that they attempt to fill by seeking more exciting worship experiences, often without success. This dissatisfaction might be avoided if Christians learned from worship that God is the Creator and we are his creatures, and not the reverse.

**Are Some Parts of Worship Less Appealing Than Others?** In the fifth place, the church should examine the idea inherent in consumer-driven worship philosophy that certain parts of the liturgy are more or less appealing than others. It is common to hear the unchurched criticize the church for collecting funds, because this practice threatens or irritates them. Certainly, the solicitation of money has sometimes been abused by various religious groups. Some churches may place an excessive emphasis on money or be guilty of poor stewardship of those resources entrusted to them. However, it might also be observed that other churches might overemphasize music or preaching or some other aspect of worship.

It is well known that any portion of a worship service can be used to draw a person into the presence of God and thus transform him or her. It is not uncommon for parishioners to comment that the prayer of confession, offering, benediction, moments of silence, or the use of a banner or other symbol brought to them a fresh and enhanced experience of God's presence. Each worshiper is touched by a different aspect of the service which becomes for him or her the most significant one on that particular day. An individual's personality and background play a role in differential response to different parts of the church service. Indeed, many debates that ignite fireworks and divide congregations originate in issues of personality preferences rather than in theology.

**The Spiritual Cost of McEucharist.** An American desire for efficiency is deeply embedded in the church-marketing ideology. A church which can produce a better, more exciting, and more entertaining worship service will draw more people and thereby become a success. But the Christian community must determine the eventual cost of streamlining worship in an attempt to make it more attractive. Gerald May comments on this issue when he writes: "By worshiping efficiency, the human race has achieved the highest level of efficiency in history, but how much have we grown in love?" (*The Awakened Heart: Living Beyond Addiction* [San Francisco: Harper Collins, 1991], 10). Worship is ultimately a relationship of love in which we focus on and respond to God.

Unfortunately, the strongly pragmatic emphasis of the proponents of consumer-driven churches often obscures this relational component to worship. In fact, the persistent influence of pragmatism narrows the focus to simply what works. This so-called cost-efficient means of conducting worship tends in time to erode any sense of mystery and wonder in the presence of God. It creates instead a simplistic perception of God that categorizes life and provides easily defined answers to the issues and challenges of life which are often very complex.

Rather than concentrating on being culturally sensitive, the church should become sensitive to the formative power worship exercises over people. It should re-evaluate its idea of who constitutes the object of worship—the worshiper or God. It should abandon the attempt to rush God by skipping over what might be considered less attractive parts of the service in order to create a better performance. Let the church dedicate itself to discover anew the presence of God and to recognize that he alone is worthy of our worship.

Tom Schwanda

## 239 • CORRUPTION OF WORSHIP BY AESTHETICISM

*Because worship reveals both the terrifying power of God and his awesome mystery, it cannot always be aesthetically pleasing. Worship is a rehearsal of God's saving acts in history. Art and beauty may serve it, but must never dominate.*

The next false gospel to be identified as threatening worship today can be described as the corruption of "aestheticism." By "aestheticism" we mean the autonomy with which art insinuates its vision of reality into liturgy and takes captive the Christian substance of liturgy—the conscious or unconscious affirmation art commonly makes that the reality which Christianity names "God" is most authentically experienced as Beauty rather than as the Holy.

To reject the corruption of aestheticism in worship is not to deny the liturgical function of art. The cleft between much Protestant worship and art which prevailed until recently (and to which many congregations are still heir) was due largely to the failure to make this distinction. Rightly afraid of aestheticism, free-church Protestantism wrongly feared art. Human nature was misread, our rationality was overestimated, and our imaginative and sensuous life was underestimated. The human mind was mainly seen as a continuously working "idol factory"—in Calvin's famous phrase—and the inescapability of symbols was not understood. The relation of the divine to the natural was distorted, and spirit was opposed to matter in an unbiblical dualism. Because much Protestant worship preferred to see reality opaquely rather than honestly, the shock of the human predicament which art could teach liturgy was prudishly declined. And falsely supposing that art would corrupt rather than enhance our passion for life, much Protestant worship clung to its Puritanisms and its pieties.

Now, however, the situation has largely changed, and Protestantism has, as it were, grown up into an awkward kind of artistic age. Having learned at great cost how art when exiled from man's life at one place will reappear at another, free-church Protestantism has determined that the cleft shall be overcome. From a posture of revulsion, free churches have now moved to clasp art in such vigorous embrace that while the affinities between art and liturgy are affirmed, tensions are ignored. Driven to self-criticism by the growing sophistication of people, aware of the impact which art in its numerous forms—especially film—exerts in our mass media culture, and eager to reassert affinities which never should have been lost, free-church Protestantism has resolved that the varnished oak pulpit and bare-walled "sanctuary," the clerical sack suit and flyspecked candlesticks, the gospel hymn and the Akron architecture, must go. For good or for ill, free-church congregations have largely abandoned their Puritan legacy in a kind of cultural adolescence and, athletically overreacting as good Protestants tend to do, have undertaken to "enrich worship"—to use their favorite term—that it may be made "aesthetically exciting."

In the worship of certain free churches the fear of the Puritans has been vindicated: the god of Beauty has displaced the God of Christian revelation. The attributes of deity which Christian thought must insist upon—the personal character of God, his holiness, his active righteousness, his moral will, his judgment and mercy—are displaced by a vision of God as Beauty. The terror of God's deeds in history is made to give way to his harmony and joy. The eschatological event of Jesus Christ "shattering the backbone of history"—in Chesterton's famous phrase—is rendered into a tale of poetry and charm. "The God who acts" gives way to the God who smiles. Similarly, the person to whom such aestheticized worship is made to appeal is not the one whose soul needs redemption and whose will needs rescue; rather, it is the aesthetic individual whose sensibilities are to be titillated and whose imagination is to be intrigued. In this respect aestheticism has learned only too well from errors of the past. Persuaded that people are primarily symbolic animals, it addresses them as essentially creatures of feeling and imagination. It would engage our senses and shrive us with God's beauty rather than confront our will and search with God's holiness.

Predictably, the action of worship at its very core in turn becomes corrupted. Appreciation and impression become the proper response rather than decision. Contemplation is more fitting than commitment—"the aesthetic posture projected to cosmic ends." In a metaphor of Gerhard van der Leeuw, the right liturgical response to the thunder and lightning of Sinai is to enjoy the glow of the landscape. Further, the moral character of worship often is bleached out. Because the worshiper's aesthetic sensibilities are appealed to more than his or her conscience and will, we are not addressed in our moral predicament by a moral God. Our contrition is not evoked; our intercession on behalf of others is not claimed; and the ethical implications of worship for our life in the world are left unpronounced.

Still further, the salvational nature of worship is corrupted into a kind of liturgical hedonism. The holy agony which Christian worship authentically is becomes narcotized with aesthetic pleasure. And not seldom the song of Pan is more prominent than the *Kyrie eleison.*

To be sure, when art authentically serves liturgy instead of taking liturgy captive for its own purposes, this need not happen; let us be clear on this point. If art will subordinate its vision of reality as Beauty to the Christian vision of God as the Holy; if art will address the worshiper not with pleasure but with that judgment and mercy that beget salvation; if art will let its love of the vitalities of existence be chastened with the paschal Life of the gospel, then aestheticism is no problem. But to ask of art these renunciations is probably to ask it to yield up that autonomy which is definitive for its existence. The bald truth is that art in a sense always threatens liturgy; and liturgy rightly looks on art with an incorrigible suspicion simply because the polar enemy of liturgy is idolatry.

Given the possibilities of aesthetic corruption, therefore, it is always dangerous to think and speak of worship as an "art," of the planning and conduct of worship as the "art of worship," and of forms of worship as "works of art." Liturgical integrity is easily undermined by using the vocabulary of the aesthetic so substantively. One may perhaps speak in this fashion colloquially, but always at the risk of sacrificing theological to aesthetic canons. We do best to think and speak of art in relation to worship as an adjective, not as a noun. Let it always be remembered in this connection that historically the church has not undertaken to formulate liturgy primarily as a work of art. Its concern for liturgy has abundantly mothered artistic creation, yes; but from the primitive church to the present, the *kērygma,* the gospel, has exerted the controlling influence in the shaping of liturgy. Even in its eras of greatest artistic flowering, the church could be quite indifferent to the artistic propriety of its liturgical forms, and the outstanding contributions to the church's liturgical life were made by men and women who were not first artists but people of faith, of theological concern and pastoral integrity who placed whatever talents they possessed at the service of the gospel.

Now let it be said that the God of the gauche may be nearer the true God than the God who smiles, and the one who gnashes his teeth may be nearer the kingdom of heaven than the one who only enjoys the biblical landscape. Further, liturgy on occasion will prefer the ugly to the beautiful as a less untruthful way of rendering the encounter between God and man, in order to declare both the terrifying power and fascinating mystery of that Holy One with whom human destiny is bound up. One mark of the Holy, it must always be remembered, is that it repels as well as attracts: it daunts as well as fascinates. And worship whose forms offend may more authentically enable us to meet God than worship which only gives pleasure.

Paul Waitman Hoon[49]

## 240 • The Problem of Form and Language

*If worship is to impact the entire person, its forms and language must transcend words, engaging not only the worshiper's body but also his or her emotions and imagination. These forms should be appropriate to the majesty of God, not so familiar as to be mundane nor so unfamiliar as to be irrelevant to the worshiper.*

Worship needs to go beyond the verbal and engage the whole person in the praise of God. It is not commonly understood that we function as a multisensory and multiphasic creature, and that worship must therefore be multisensory and multiphasic—that its forms must engage the body, the imagination, and the emotions as well as the reason, and at the same time take into account something of the dynamics of the human subconscious as well as conscious life. The grip on our being which liturgical forms are entitled to exert, the evocative power they should convey, and the intensity of meaning they should embody—although always within the limits of theological purpose—are often missing. Hence the boredom which has been called the curse of free-church worship. Too often liturgical language is only prose, one-dimensional, lame, unable to get at the depths of human nature.

Secondly, the language of worship is often inartistic and downright ugly. While we must be always wary against the seduction of liturgy into art for art's sake, it must be recognized that people engage more readily in the dialogue of worship when its forms please their sensibilities while the same time remaining appropriate to the majesty of God.

A graver objection to forms employed in much Protestant worship today is not so much that they are weak or ugly as that they are unreal, and in a number of ways. For one thing, they are too strange or irrelevant to the actual life of the congregation to be real, or they are too familiar and too contemporary. Traditional forms inherited from the past, such as prayers offered in the sixteenth century language of the Tudors and Stuarts, for example, seem unreal simply because they are obsolete. We are unable to surmount their unreality simply because we do not talk or think today as the Stuarts did. Or hymn tunes cast in the semi-morbid nineteenth-century harmonies of a Lowell Mason seem inane to ears toughened to twentieth century atonality. On the other hand, forms too familiar and too modern can also fail to possess reality. Because little effort is required to grasp or be grasped by them, the worshiper is let off too cheaply and remains unengaged with any meanings other than those he or she already brings. We shall have to argue that forms which at first sight seem to offend by archaism often possess the power of the prototype to engage our deepest nature which familiar forms do not.

Paul Waitman Hoon[50]

## 241 • Areas of Challenge in Free-Church Worship

*Worship renewalists of the free-church tradition face the difficult task of changing their congregations' understanding of worship in a number of key areas. Unhealthy practices present a challenge for those who would restore a more biblical and historic perspective to the worship of these churches.*

An unreasoned and faulty understanding of the nature and purpose of worship, combined with the influence of the culture in which we live, have produced a variety of unhealthy worship practices which are found most often in churches of the free-church tradition. These forms are often result in weak, dry, or boring worship services and fail to produce a vital encounter between the worshiper and God. This discussion deals with some of the problems to be found in the worship of many such churches.

**Sermon-centeredness.** The sermon has become the most important part of the worship service. Preaching and worship are not synonymous. A worship service is much more than believers gathering to listen to the pastor preach. Unfortunately, however, in many churches the focal point of the worship service is the proclamation event. When that is so, corporate worship suffers. Anything done before the sermon becomes only a preliminary. More than a few pastors, knowingly or unknowingly, promote this by ordering their service so that the sermon is center stage—the focal point of everyone's attention.

**Pastor Domination.** Pastors do too much in the worship service. I see several reasons why this is so. First, it is the primary model that most pastors have seen. Many have grown up in small churches where the minister did everything. Second, some churches expect pastors to do all the ministry. Having little appreciation for the pastor's call to equip servants for ministry, lay people often conclude: "That's why we hired you—to minister." Third, many pastors are insecure about releasing lay people for significant ministry. In some way it is perceived as a threat to their sense of worth or importance in the church.

We must go beyond pastor-centered ministry to body ministry. Nowhere is this more important than in the worship service. Lay involvement in worship can open the door to new power and excitement. And there are countless ways to mobilize people in the worship service.

**Spectator Mentality.** Attending a worship service is similar to attending the theater or a concert—it is a spectator event. This trend grows directly from domination by the pastor. The fewer people called on to participate, the more passive worship becomes. Those in the pews sit and watch as the person up front performs. They evaluate the service based on what they receive rather than on what they put into the experience.

Watching is commonplace in our society and comes easily to most of us. We are a generation of spectators who watch television, sports events—most everything. And this has affected our understanding of the worship service. It has become another place where we watch and where we expect to be entertained.

**Predictability.** Worship services have become overly predictable. There is little question but that we need both order and consistency in the worship service. Order helps the worshiper make sense of the experience. It keeps the service balanced and holistic. Consistency enables worshipers to feel comfortable in the service. They are familiar with what is happening; anxiety is eliminated. Nothing is worse than not knowing what comes next or what to do at a certain time.

But there is a negative side to order and consistency. When the order of worship is too predictable, worshipers can quickly lose interest. The service becomes more of the same old thing. When song, Scripture, sermon, and style are identical week after week, worship loses its excitement. There is little sense of expectation. People no longer wonder what new way God will lead them to experience His presence and power. Soon, worship becomes boring.

**Traditionalism.** Form and order in worship are often dictated purely by tradition. I am not advocating change for the sake of change. What I am encouraging is flexibility and mobility in form and order. Our worship services should certainly be sensitive to tradition but not completely determined by tradition. Forms of worship should not be institutionalized. Instead, they should be carefully designed, consistent with the moving of the Spirit in this day—at this time and place in history.

**Irrelevance.** What happens in worship is not always relevant to daily living. People will not embrace Christianity simply because our message is true. They want to see that our message is relevant. Does faith work in real life? Does Christianity affect daily living in contemporary society? Is what we express and confess on Sunday relevant to life on Monday? This principle is equally true of the Christian worship service. Not only should we seek to embrace the transcendent in worship, we should also relate to the temporal. Form, order, and message in worship should be relevant to the culture, language, and experience of daily living. Otherwise, people will not easily integrate the experience of worship with day-to-day life.

**Lack of Encounter with God.** People often do not encounter God in worship. This problem is by far the most devastating. Sunday after Sunday, people leave church without sensing the presence of God in worship. The entire experience becomes an exercise in human effort. Where and when this is true, people leave the service much as they entered. They are unchanged, uninspired, and unprepared to serve Christ in the marketplace of daily living.

Why do people not encounter God in worship? Many of the reasons we have already discussed. A dryness has settled over the corporate worship service. Instead of experiencing life-giving power, churches are suffering. Form and order are there, but services lack spiritual vitality and the dynamic presence of God. They are poorly planned, lacking serious preparation and prayer. Congregations have not been taught to worship nor instructed about the power of praise. Forms are often outdated, characterized by a dead traditionalism. Worst of all, many believers have accepted the power of God in theory but have rejected it in practice. Fearing wild fire, congregations have opted for no fire at all. As a result, worship lacks its most important and powerful element, God's presence.

Terry Howard Wardle[51]

## 242 ✦ AREAS OF CHALLENGE IN LITURGICAL WORSHIP

*Renewal needs in liturgical churches include increased attention to planning and integrating all parts of the worship service, an understanding of the importance of music ministry, and greater participation by the congregation.*

If worship in the liturgical church is to be a living encounter with God that changes the hearts and lives of the congregation, it will require more prayerful, creative planning than is usually assigned to it. Specifically, the three areas which need strengthening in most liturgical worship services merit our attention.

**More Effective Preaching.** Preaching should facilitate people's prayer as a group. The use of the imagination, stories, and images are ways of bringing this about. The whole liturgy should preach or proclaim. After the environment, the music, and the other gestures of the liturgy have been planned, then the homily can be prepared. In that way it can fill in where the rest of the liturgy may fail. But how often is liturgical planning made equivalent to preparing the sermon?

**Greater Integration of Word and Music.** We must continue to look for styles of congregational singing that move the congregation away from books. The music of Taizé from France, highly repetitious but still very beautiful, is becoming increasingly popular because it can be employed with one's hands free. Fuller use of responsorial singing should grow. The integration of liturgy and music, where the

parts of the liturgy are not only sung but where the liturgy becomes a musical experience, will not succeed without music being accepted as an important ministry in the church. The restoration of the minister called cantor is, I believe, the single most necessary item for achieving a musical liturgy. A cantor is more than a song leader, a choir director, or the head of the folk group. The cantor performs a diaconal role, singing parts of the liturgy as well as leading the congregation. The cantor should be trained, commissioned, and vested. He or she should function publicly and be paid.

**Enlargement of Sacramental Experience.** The general principle that the priest should not do anything that others can do is a good working principle if it is properly understood. The priest should see himself or herself primarily as the one who motivates the others in ministry, not someone who has a special power others do not have.

In bringing about a more comprehensive sacramental life in the church, it is important to find out who is actually praying in the parish and then enlist them in forming communities. God saves people as individuals outside the church. In the church our salvation comes through community, a community which proclaims, however weakly, the value of the gospel.

James Empereur[52]

## 243 ✦ THE NEED FOR REDEFINING WORSHIP IN CHARISMATIC CHURCHES

*The charismatic movement has brought about a change in the worship in many traditional churches. Charismatics, in turn, are being influenced by traditional liturgical forms. Together, Christians of charismatic and liturgical traditions are discovering that biblical worship provides an answer to the epidemic of emptiness that plagues our generation.*

Worship is being redefined in terms of its form and focus. It isn't that valid traditions must be scorned or discarded, but that newness must refill them with meaning. It isn't that the objective adoration of God is being traded off for a shallow subjectivism on the part of the worshiper. Rather, a simple, fulfilling intimacy is being discovered by more people as they praise the Lord.

Worship is being unwrapped in the removal of sectarian prejudices which have preempted interdenominational participation in biblical practices of worship heretofore labeled and shelved by feuding parties in the body of Christ. Upraised hands are less and less a badge of the charismatic and are becoming a simple sign of Christian praise. A learned appreciation for the dignity of liturgical life is increasingly finding a place among people who otherwise would have deemed it lifeless.

Worship is being unsealed as well. A theology of worship is coming into perspective that lends a biblical dimension to the whole reformation process. The lid of traditional theology is being lifted: worship is being proposed as a dignifying, empowering act for mankind.

An awakening to the power of worship to reinstate God's divine intent for humanity can answer contemporary questions as to the human purpose. A drug-drunk, suicide-prone, binge-oriented generation lives on the ragged edge because it has become dissipated by its empty affluence of information, experience, and pleasure. In the midst of everything, so few have anything, and the questions recur again and again—"What are we here for? Why are things as they are?"

This is not an exaggeration of the problem with people today, and neither is it an exaggeration to say that worship holds the solution of their dilemma.

Jack Hayford[53]

## 244 ✦ THE NEED TO RECOVER CELEBRATION

_People of Western culture have largely lost their ability to celebrate. Festivity and celebration link people to their heritage and place in the cosmos while supplying meaning and validity to life._

Mankind, by its very nature, not only works and thinks, but sings, dances, prays, tells stories, and celebrates. We are _homo festivus_. Notice the universal character of festivity in human life. No culture is without it. African pygmies and Australian primitives frolic in honor of the equinox. Hindus revel at Holi. Moslems feast after the long fast of Ramadan. In some societies the principal festival comes at harvest or when the moon reaches a particular position. In others the anniversary of some event in the life of a cultural or religious hero supplies the cause for jubilation. There are important differences between the cultures that stress cosmic or seasonal festivals and those that emphasize historical holi-

days, but all provide an occasion for singing old songs, saluting heroes, and reaffirming new and old aspirations. When festivity disappears from a culture, something universally human in endangered.

Human beings are also _homo fantasia_, visionary dreamers and myth-makers. If no culture is without some form of celebration, there is certainly none that lacks its share of wild and improbable stories. Fairies, goblins, giants, and elves—or their equivalent—inhabit the imagination of every race. Also, in most societies, one can find legends of a golden age in the past and, in some, stories of a wondrous age to come. Students of prehistoric cultures have often said more about people's tools than about their tales. Perhaps this derives from our present obsessive interest in technology. Perhaps it is because clubs and knives remain to be found, although myths disappear. Still, both were there very early, and it was just as much their propensity to dream and fantasize as it was their augers and axes that first set people apart from the beasts.

Mankind is _homo festivus_ and _homo fantasia_. No other creature we know of relives the legends of its forefathers, blows out candles on a birthday cake, or dresses up and pretends to be someone else. But in recent centuries something has happened that has undercut our capacity for festivity and fantasy. In Western civilization we have placed an enormous emphasis on people as workers (Luther and Marx) and as thinkers (Aquinas and Descartes). Our celebrative and imaginative faculties have atrophied.

This worker-thinker emphasis, enforced by industrialization, ratified by philosophy, and sanctified by Christianity, helped to produce the monumental achievements of Western science and industrial technology. Now, however, we can begin to see that our productivity has exacted a price. Not only have we gotten it at the expense of millions of other people in the poor nations, not only have we ruined countless rivers and lakes and poisoned our atmosphere, we have also terribly damaged the inner experience of Western humanity. We have pressed ourselves so hard toward useful work and rational calculation that we have all but forgotten the joy of ecstatic celebration, antic play, and free imagination. Our shrunken psyche is just as much a victim of industrialization as were the bent bodies of those luckless children who were once confined to English factories from dawn to dusk.

Human beings are essentially festive and fanciful. To become fully human, Western industrial persons, and their non-Western colleagues insofar as they are touched by the same debilitation, must learn again to dance and to dream.

Our loss of the capacity for festivity and fantasy has profound religious significance. The religious person is one who grasps his or her own life within a larger historical and cosmic setting. One sees the self as part of a greater whole, a longer story in which one plays a part. Song, ritual, and vision link an individual to this story. They help us to place ourselves somewhere between Eden and the kingdom of God; they give us a past and a future. But without real festive occasions and without the nurture of fantasy, the human spirit as well as the human psyche shrinks. We become something less than human, a gnat with neither origin nor destiny.

This may account in part for the malaise and tedium of our time. Celebration requires a set of common memories and collective hopes. It requires, in short, what is usually thought of as a religion. For centuries, Christianity provided our civilization with both the feast days that kept its history alive and with the images of the future that sustained its expectations.

Festival occasions enlarge enormously the scope and intensity of mankind's relation to the past. They elaborate our sense of personal worth by making us a part of an epic. Fantasy offers an endless range of future permutations. It inevitably escalates our sense of our powers and possibilities. Therefore, the cultivation of celebration and imagination is crucial to religion and to humankind itself, if the biblical estimate of human status ("a little lower than the angels") has any validity. Perhaps this is why observance and revelry, ritual and myth have nearly always been central to religion, and why they seem to be making a comeback today.

Harvey Cox[54]

# Works Cited

GENERAL NOTE: All of the previously published material in this volume has been adapted.

[1] Adapted from Lizette Larson-Miller, "Introduction: Liturgy of the Hours," *Modern Liturgy* 16:12 (1989): 12–13.

[2] Adapted from Lloyd G. Patterson, "Sources, Early Liturgical," in *The New Dictionary of Sacramental Worship,* ed. by Peter E. Fink (Collegeville, Minn.: Liturgical Press, 1990): 1201–1213.

[3] Peter E. Fink, "Traditions, Liturgical, in the East," in *The New Dictionary of Sacramental Worship,* 1255–1272.

[4] John Brooks Leonard, "Traditions, Liturgical, in the West: Pre-Reformation," in *The New Dictionary of Sacramental Worship,* 1282–1293.

[5] James F. White, "Traditions, Liturgical, in the West: Post-Reformation," in *The New Dictionary of Sacramental Worship,* 1273–1274.

[6] Ibid., 1274–1275.

[7] Ibid., 1276–1277.

[8] Ibid., 1275–1276.

[9] Ibid., 1279.

[10] Ibid., 1281.

[11] Ibid., 1277–1278.

[12] German Martinez, "Reform, Liturgical, History of," in *The New Dictionary of Sacramental Worship,* 1068–1072.

[13] Stephen Bonian, "Reform, Liturgical, in Eastern Churches," in *The New Dictionary of Sacramental Worship,* 1072–1077.

[14] David R. Newman, "Reform, Liturgical, in Reformation Churches," in *The New Dictionary of Sacramental Worship,* 1077–1081.

[15] Paul Thigpen, "Ancient Altars, Pentecostal Fire," *Ministries Today* 10:6 (November/December 1992): 43–51.

[16] Robert E. Webber, "Enter His Courts with Praise," *Reformed Worship* 20 (June 1991): 9–12.

[17] Doug Adams, *From Meeting House to Camp Meeting* (Austin, Tex.: The Sharing Company, 1981), 12, 14–15, 23, 25–29, 31.

[18] Robert Taft, *The Liturgy of the Hours in East and West* (Collegeville, Minn.: Liturgical Press, 1986), 334–345.

[19] International Committee on English in the Liturgy, *Constitution on the Sacred Liturgy,* chapters 1–6; reprinted from *Documents on the Liturgy, 1963–1979: Conciliar, Papal, and Curial Texts* (Collegeville, Minn.: Liturgical Press, 1982).

[20] James F. White, "A Protestant Worship Manifesto," *The Christian Century* 99:3 (January 27, 1982): 82–86.

[21] Benjamin D. Williams and Harold B. Austall, *Orthodox Worship* (Minneapolis: Light and Life, 1990), 7–9.

[22] Excerpted from Regis A. Duffy, "Introduction," in *Alternative Futures for Worship,* Vol. 1: *General Introduction,* edited by Regis A. Duffy (Collegeville, Minn.: Liturgical Press, 1987), 13–21.

[23] Michael J. Taylor, *The Protestant Liturgical Renewal: A Catholic Viewpoint* (Westminster, Md.: Newman Press, 1963), 13–21.

[24] Robert E. Webber, "Worship: A Methodology for Evangelical Renewal," *TSF Bulletin* 7:1 (September–October 1983): 8–10.

[25] Killian McDonnell, "Introduction I," in *Presence, Power, Praise,* ed. by Killian McDonnell (Collegeville, Minn.: Liturgical Press, 1980).

[26] Kent Henry, "Worship's Current Phases and Future Trends," *The Psalmist* (April–May 1988): 4–7.

[27] Excerpted from J. D. Crichton, "A Theology of Worship," in *The Study of Liturgy,* ed. by Cheslyn Jones, Geoffrey Wainwright, and Edward Yarnold (New York: Oxford University Press, 1978), 5–29.

[28] Paul D. Hanson, *The People Called: The Growth of Community in the Bible* (New York: Harper & Row, 1986), 505–507.

[29] Marcello de C. Azevedo, *Basic Ecclesial Communities* (Washington, D.C.: Georgetown University Press, 1987), 59–60, 63–64.

30Crichton, "A Theology of Worship," 19.

31Robert E. Webber, *Worship Is a Verb,* 2d ed. (Nashville: Abbott Martyn, 1992), 29–30.

32Ibid., 45.

33Ibid., 71–73.

34James F. White, *An Introduction to Christian Worship* (Nashville: Abingdon, 1980), 146–147.

35Webber, *Worship Is a Verb,* 87–88.

36Ibid., 113–114.

37Michael Marshall, *Renewal in Worship* (Wilton, Conn.: Morehouse-Barlow, 1985), 18.

38Webber, *Worship Is a Verb,* 130–131, 135.

39Marshall, 30, 33–34.

40Webber, *Worship Is a Verb,* 183, 196–198.

41Ibid., 203–205.

42Franklin M. Segler, *Christian Worship: Its Theology and Practice* (Nashville: Broadman, 1967), 83–89.

43Ronald Allen and Gordon Borrow, *Worship: Rediscovering the Missing Jewel* (Portland, Oreg.: Multnomah Press, 1982), 9–10.

44Warren Wiersbe, *Real Worship* (Nashville: Oliver Nelson, 1986), 14.

45Daniel W. Hardy and David F. Ford, *Praising and Knowing God* (Louisville: Westminster, 1985), 11–13.

46Robert E. Webber, "Let's Put *Worship* into the Worship Service," *Christianity Today* 28:3 (February 17, 1984): 52.

47Alexander Schmemann, *An Introduction to Liturgical Theology* (Crestwood, N.Y.: St. Vladimir's Seminary Press, 1966), 22–25.

48Paul Waitman Hoon, *The Integrity of Worship* (Nashville: Abingdon, 1971), 44–55.

49Ibid., 63–71.

50Ibid., 38–44.

51Terry Howard Wardle, *Exalt Him!* (Camp Hill, Pa.: Christian Publications, 1988), 11–21.

52James Empereur, *Worship: Exploring the Sacred* (Washington, D.C.: Pastoral Press, 1987), 169–173.

53Jack Hayford, *Worship His Majesty* (Irving, Tex.: Word, 1987), 21–23.

54Harvey Cox, *The Feast of Fools: A Theological Essay on Festivity and Fantasy* (Cambridge, Mass.: Harvard University Press, 1969), 10–12, 15, 21.

# Index

*A Form for Christ's Supper*
  (Hubmaier), 216–225
Adventist Worship, 98–100,
  248–249
African Liturgical Practices and
  Worldview, 91
African-American Theology of
  Worship, 298–304
African-American Worship,
  89–95, 249–251
Alexandrian Churches, 57–59
Ambrosian Liturgy, 67–68
American Puritan Model of
  Worship, 227–228
American Revival Worship,
  88–89
Anabaptist Liturgy, 216–225
Anabaptist Theology of
  Worship, 293–295
Anabaptist Worship, 77–78
Anglican Liturgy (1662),
  204–216
Anglican Worship, 77
Anglican/Episcopal Theology
  of Worship, 291–292
Antiochian Evangelical
  Orthodox Mission, the,
  115–116
Apostolic Fathers, Worship
  Practices of, 33–34
*Apostolic Tradition*
  (Hippolytus), 36–37,
  151–152
Armenian Catholics, 114
Armenian Church, 54–56
Arts, Renaissance of, 119–121

Baptist Theology of Worshp,
  292–293
Baptist Worship, 82–83,
  231–235

Biblical Psychology of
  Worship, a, 388–393
Byzantine Churches, 51–54
Byzantine Liturgy (Ninth
  Century), 152–171

Calvin, John, 195–203
Cathedral Prayer, 8–10
Celebration, Need for
  Recovering, 407–408
Celtic Liturgy, 68–70
Chaldean Church, 45–48,
  112–113
Charismatic Churches,
  121–125, 275–281, 349–350,
  406–407
Charismatic Gifts in Early
  Christian Worship, 19–21
Charismatic Theology of
  Worship, 309–312
*Christus Victor,* and Worship,
  357–360
Church as Community,
  360–361
Congregational Worship, 83–85
*Constitution on the Sacred
  Liturgy,* the, 108–111,
  317–332
Contempt for Praise of God,
  394–395
Convergence Movement, the,
  134–140
Coptic Churches, 57–59, 114
Corruption of Worship by
  Aestheticism, 402–404
Corruption of Worship by
  Manipulation and
  Utilitarianism, 398–399
Cotton, John, 228–230

Daily Prayer, 5–11
*Didache,* 34–35, 145–148
Divine Liturgy of St. Basil,
  154–171

East Syrian Churches, 45–48
Eastern Liturgy, during Fourth
  and Fifth Centuries, 38–39
Eastern Orthodox Churches,
  44–45
Eastern Rite Catholic Churches,
  Renewal in, 111–115
Ethiopian Churches, 57–59
Evangelical Worship, Concerns
  for, 343–348

Finney, Charles G., 247–248
*First Apology* (Justin Martyr),
  148–150
*Form of Church Prayers, The*
  (Calvin), 195–203
*Formula Missae* (Luther),
  188–195
Free-Church Worship,
  272–275, 404–406

Gallican Liturgy, 63–65
Gifts of the Spirit in the
  Earliest Church, 19–21

Hippolytus, 36–37, 151–152
Holiness Worship, 97–98,
  252–254
Holiness-Pentecostal
  Movement, the, 105–108
Holiness-Pentecostal Theology
  of Worship, 307–309
Home Cell Groups, 363–364
Hubmaier, Balthasar, 216–225

Instructional and Homiletical Material, during Fourth and Fifth Centuries, 39–42
Irenaeus, 36

Justin Martyr, 35, 148–150

Lack of Concern for Worship Renewal, 394
Liturgical Diversity and Roman Influence, 61–62
Liturgical Theology, Models of, 263–266
Liturgical Worship, 266–272, 406
Liturgical-Charismatic Movement, the, 125–131
Luther, Martin, 188–195
Lutheran Theology of Worship, 286–288
Lutheran Worship, 75–76

Mainline Protestant Worship, Concerns for, 343
Malabar Church, 45–48, 113
Maronite Church, 48–51, 112
McEucharist ("Fast-Food" Worship), 399–402
Melkites, 113
Methodist Worship, 86–87, 236–245
Monastic Prayer, 10–11

Nestorian Church, 45–48
New England Congregational Model of Worship, 228–230
New Testament Worship, 32–33, 282–283
North African Liturgy, 62–63

Oral-Formal Tradition in Liturgy, 31–32
Ordination and Worship Leadership in the Early Church, 16–19
Origins of Christian Worship, the, 3–5
Orthodox Worship, Concerns for, 341

Orthodox Theology of Worship, 284–286

Pentecostal/Charismatic Manifesto of Worship, 337–340
Praise and Worship, Current Trends in, 350–351
Praise-and-Worship Renewal, 131–134
Prayers in Jewish and Early Christian Tradition, 14–15
Principles of Worship, 370–380
Problem of Form and Language in Worship, the, 404
Protestant Liturgical Renewal, 116–119
Protestant Worship Manifesto, A, 332–337
Puritan Worship, 80–82

Quaker Theology of Worship, 295–296
Quaker Worship, 85–86, 235–236

Reformed Theology of Worship, 288–291
Reformed Worship, 76–77
Restoration Model of Worship, ??–??
Restoration Theology of Worship, 304–307
Restoration Worship, 95–97, 251–252
Revival Model of Worship, 247–248
Roman Catholic Worship, Concerns for, 341–343
Roman Catholic Mass (1570), 171–186
Roman Catholic Theology of Worship, A, 282–284
Roman Catholic Worship from the Council of Trent to Vatican II, 72–73
Roman Liturgy, the, 70–72
Ruthenians, 114

Sacraments, as Sign Acts, 372
Salvation Army Worship, 87–88, 245–247
Seekers' Service/Believers' Worship Movement, the, 140–141
Small Groups, 362–364
South America, Basic Communities of, 362–363
Spanish Liturgy, 65–67
Spiritual Gifts, and the Laity, 364–366
Strassburg Liturgy (Calvin), 195–203
Substitutes for Worship, 395–396
*Sunday Service* (Wesley), 236–245
Synagogue Influence on Christian Worship, 11–14
Syrian Church, 48–51
Syro-Indian Church, 48–51

Temple Sequence, the (Praise-and-Worship Movement), 132–133
Ten Basic Needs Met by Worship, 386–387
Theologians, and the Gifts of the Spirit, 21
Theological Issues, in the Fourth and Fifth Centuries, 42
Theology of Worship, 261–263
Threefold Office Structure in the Early Church, 16–19
Tradition of Daily Prayer, the, 5–7
Trinitarian Formulary, the, 14–16
Tripartite Structure of Prayer, 14–16

Ukrainians, 114

Wesley, John, 236–245
Wesleyan Theology of Worship, 296–298

West Syrian Churches, 48–51

Western Liturgy, during the Fourth and Fifth Centuries, 39

*Westminster Directory,* the, 230–231

Worship, during the Second and Third Centuries, 33–38

Worship, during the Fourth and Fifth Centuries, 38–42

Worship, Misplaced Priority in, 396–398

Worship and Ecclesiology, 261–262

Worship and the "Performance Principle", 392–393

Worship in the Book of Revelation and the Eastern Orthodox Liturgy, 21–26

Worship Renewal, Stages of, 366–369

Wounds that Hinder Worship, 381–386